DEATH, DISSECTION AND THE DESTITUTE

Dr Ruth Richardson was born and grew up in Notting Hill, London. She was educated at Holland Park School, the City Literary Institute and the University of Sussex. After leaving school she worked as a librarian in various specialist libraries and studied art and literature at evening classes. As a mature student at university she came upon the Anatomy Act while studying Mary Shelley's *Frankenstein*. This book is the result of a decade of further research. Ruth Richardson now works at the Institute of Historical Research, University of London.

Death, Dissection and the Destitute

RUTH RICHARDSON

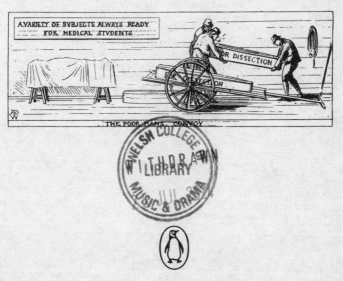

PENGUIN BOOKS

PENGUIN BOOKS

Published by the Penguin Group
27 Wrights Lane, London w8 5tz, England
Viking Penguin Inc., 40 West 23rd Street, New York, New York 10010, USA
Penguin Books Australia Ltd, Ringwood, Victoria, Australia
Penguin Books Canada Ltd, 2801 John Street, Markham, Ontario, Canada l3r 1b4
Penguin Books (NZ) Ltd, 182–190 Wairau Road, Auckland 10, New Zealand

Penguin Books Ltd, Registered Offices: Harmondsworth, Middlesex, England

First published in Great Britain by Routledge and Kegan Paul 1988
First published in the USA by Routledge and Kegan Paul, Inc.
in association with Methuen, Inc. 1988
Published in Pelican Books 1989
3 5 7 9 10 8 6 4 2

Made and printed in Great Britain by
Richard Clay Ltd, Bungay, Suffolk

For my Dear Parents
Hilda and William Richardson

CONTENTS

Acknowledgments   ix
Introduction   xiii

I   THE BODY

1 The Corpse and Popular Culture   3
2 The Corpse as an Anatomical Object   30
3 The Corpse as a Commodity   52

II   THE ACT

4 The Sanctity of the Grave Asserted   75
5 Foregone Conclusions   100
6 'Trading Assassins'   131
7 Alternative Necrology   159
8 Bringing 'Science to the Poor Man's Door'   193

III   THE AFTERMATH

9 The Act 'is Uninjurious if Unknown'   219
10 The Bureaucrat's Bad Dream   239
11 The Unpardonable Offence   261

Appendices   285
References   294
Bibliography   378
Index   408

ILLUSTRATIONS

Death in the Dissection Room by Thomas Rowlandson, c.1815 (Courtesy of the Spencer Collection, New York Public Library)   xviii–xix

PLATES

1   'The Stages of Life', broadsheet, c.1830 (St Bride's Institute)   10
2   Illustration from a late seventeenth-century book on English customs (Author's collection)   18
3   From Hogarth's *The Harlot's Progress*, c.1731 (Author's collection)   26
4   A *Memento Mori* probably dating from the 1670s (Author's collection)   28
5   Hogarth's *Fourth Stage of Cruelty*, 1751 (Author's collection)   33
6   An early nineteenth-century woodcut showing the fearful gibbet (Stephen Burke Collection)   36
7   The 'Smugglerius' cast of a man hanged at Tyburn (Courtesy of the Royal Academy Magazine)   38
8   'Modern Medical Education: Practical Results', after a cartoon by W. Heath, 1825   45
9   A 'catchpenny' spoof broadsheet, 1828 (Courtesy of the Royal College of Surgeons, London)   56
10   'The Patent Coffin', broadsheet, 1818 (St Bride's Institute)   82
11   Dead House at Crail, Fife, erected 1826 (Courtesy of Drs I.D. Innes and C. Grant)   84
12   'Modern Medical Education: Actual Practice', after a cartoon by W. Heath, 1825   96
13   Edinburgh broadsheet dated 3 November 1828 (Royal College of Surgeons, London)   134
14   A popular print showing the discovery of the murder of Mary Docherty on 1 November 1828 (Stephen Burke Collection)   136
15   Execution of William Burke, broadsheet, 1829 (Royal College of Surgeons, London)   142
16   'The Christian's Appeal against the Poor Law Amendment Act', broadsheet, c.1834 (Courtesy John Noyce)   170
17   'Burkiphoby', after a cartoon by R. Seymour, 1831   196
18   'A Few Illustrations for Mr Warberton's Bill' – a cartoon by Paul Pry, 1829 (Courtesy of the Trustees of the British Museum)   220
19   Broadsheet giving news of the excavation of the cholera ground at Paisley, 27 March 1832 (Courtesy of the Renfrew District Library Service)   225
20   The Leeds Election Banner, 1832 (Doc Rowe)   231

21   'Contrasted Residences for the Poor' – from Augustus Pugin's *Contrasts*,
      1841   269

FIGURES

1   Lives of Twelve London Resurrectionists   69
2   Economic versus Emotive definitions of 'claimed'   126
3   Anatomists' views on potential alternatives to existing sources of corpses for
    dissection, 1823   163
4, 5 Bequests/requisitions and deaths/cremations, 1900–1970   259

ACKNOWLEDGMENTS

I have dedicated this book to my dear parents, Hilda and William Richardson, who gave me a childhood rich in art, literature, music, history and discussion, and a commitment to social justice. No words can describe the magnitude of my debt to them, and no book, however good, can repay it.

I wish to thank Brian Hurwitz for help of many kinds, including patience, thought, wisdom, choice words and understanding. He has read and advised on most of what I have written.

My four sisters have in their different ways given me encouragement over the years. Other personal debts, too numerous to mention, are owed to all my friends, most particularly to Richard Clarke and his mother Freda, Melissa Benn, Betty Bostetter, Doc Rowe, Stephen Benn, Jerry White, Helen English, John Richardson, May Jones, May Reynolds, Nikki Harrison, John Heywood, John Launer, David Goldberg, Marija Anteric, Robert Thorne and Stephen Trombley.

Academic guidance and help has been given freely by Geoffrey Best, Asa Briggs, Peter Burke, Stephen Burke, Marcus Cunliffe, Anna Davin, Heather Dubrow, John Harrison, Alun Howkins, Maurice Hutt, Tom Laqueur, Peter Laslett, Peter Linebaugh, Audrey Linkman, John Lowerson, John Noyce, Roy Porter, Elizabeth Roberts, Raph Samuel, Paul Smith, Edward Thompson, Kathleen Tillotson, Charles Webster, Adrian Wilson, Jim Winter, and Eileen and Stephen Yeo.

Mike Barnet, Logie Barrow, John Belchem, Marion Bowman, Roger Cooter, Steve Cross, Mary Fissell, Peter Froggart, Peter Laslett, Ian Munro, Ivan Waddington, Paul Weindling, Joel Weiner and Bob Young have each given me useful material and information, and/or allowed me to quote from their work. Oliver MacDonagh has been a much-valued and particularly kind correspondent. My editor at Routledge, Andrew Wheatcroft, has been a great source of encouragement and advice. If ever I write another book – which at the moment feels a remote possibility – it will be the result of his enthusiasm.

The Social Science Research Council funded me for three years' postgraduate study, and for journeys which took in libraries in several British cities.

I owe a very special debt to every individual member of the staff of the British Library Reading Room, North Library, the State Paper Room, and the Department of Manuscripts at the British Museum, Bloomsbury, and at the Newspaper Library at Colindale. The security staff, especially the late Ernie Hayford, are also much valued.

Ken Hinshallwood, Local History Librarian at Paisley provided me with material on which to base my description of the 1832 riot there; Donald Anderle of New York Public Libraries gave me kind help on the Rowlandson print of *Death in the Dissection Room*; Drs I.D. Innes and Charles Grant sent me the photo of the Dead House at Crail, Fife; Tony Benn MP asked parliamentary questions on my behalf; Professor J.H. Burns, Philip Schofield and others at the Bentham Project gave important help with the Bentham material; John Buchanan Brown helped me to identify the source of the Phiz illustration used on the front cover; Jo Spence, Mike Jones and his staff, and Doc Rowe took photographs for me; and Luigi and the staff at the Primavera, Bloomsbury, made me countless cups of capuccino coffee.

I also wish to thank Mrs J. Percival and the staff at the Bentham Archive, University College, London; Barbara Williams and other staff at the John Johnson Collection at the Bodleian Library, Oxford; James Mosley and staff at the St Bride Printing Institute; Mr Lyle and the staff of the Library of the Royal College of Surgeons, London; Peter Boyden of the National Army Museum; Graham Saville and Ann Lewis at the Luddenden Foot Bookshop; Rosemary Barbour and her staff at the Scottish Records Office; Mr Nicholson and his staff of the Glasgow Public Library Service; Alan Bruford and the staff at the Edinburgh School of Scottish Studies; Father Donal O'Sullivan, and the staff of the Library of the Royal College of Surgeons at Dublin; Lady Rosamond Hanworth for her introduction to John Hopkins and the Antiquarian Society Library; Madeline Ginzburg and staff at the Victoria and Albert Museum.

The staffs of the following libraries have given me help: the Wellcome Institute Library; the Public Records Office at Kew; the Greater London Council Records Office; the Library of the Institute of Historical Research; the House of Lords Records Library; the Patent Office Library; Sussex University Library; Birkbeck College Archives; The Cremation Society of Great Britain; the Library of the Folklore Society; the Library at Senate House, University of London; the City of London Guildhall Library; Suffolk County Records Office, Ipswich; Liverpool Public Library; Manchester Central Library Local History Archives; the Manchester Studies Unit, Manchester Polytechnic; Sheffield City Library and Archives; the Borthwick Institute, York; the Cooperative Union Library, Manchester; Leeds Central Library; Bristol Central Library; Reading Public Library.

I have to thank my colleagues on the Builder Project – Professor F.M.L. Thompson, Alice Prochaska, and Robert Thorne – for allowing me time away from my work to finish the manuscript.

Despite my best efforts, there may be facts overlooked, opinions missed and errors unnoticed in this volume. For all these I offer sincere apologies.

Readers who become aware of uncanny similarities between my work and that of an Australian, John Knott, should refer to a review of his work by Roy Porter in *Medical History*, vol.31, July 1987. For me, the experience of reading Knott's efforts has been not unlike that of being bodysnatched and dismembered while yet alive.

Finally, I wish to record a deep personal debt to David Dobinson, who was the first teacher I met who didn't pretend to an omnipotence of knowledge. His admission of ignorance taught me at one stroke the integrity of an honest humility, and the possible value of my own knowledge and intuitions. His death has caused deep sadness.

Institute of Historical Research, University of London.

INTRODUCTION

> History as written by historians usually has little
> relation to the historical traditions orally preserved
> by a people.
>
> R.M. Dorson, 1976. [1]

I first became interested in the Anatomy Act by accident. I was working on a study of Mary Shelley's *Frankenstein*, and became curious to know if the fictional doctor's researches in charnel houses bore any relationship to the historical personages Burke and Hare, and the bodysnatchers. My knowledge of medical history was slim, and I had only the vaguest of ideas when that era was.

So I sought out a few standard medical histories, and found that bodysnatching was rife throughout Mary Shelley's childhood and early adult life. I found from biographies that during their courtship, she and Shelley would sometimes go and sit near the grave of her mother, Mary Wollstonecraft, in St Pancras parish churchyard. I learned from topographies and histories of London, that the ancient village of St Pancras had originally been close to the Fleet river at Battle Bridge (now King's Cross), but had been inundated so many times that its inhabitants had eventually moved further north – leaving the church and churchyard bereft of settlement. In the early nineteenth century, when Mary Shelley was in the habit of visiting her mother's grave, from its convenient location and relative isolation the churchyard was a well-known haunt of bodysnatchers.

I also learned that in 1809, when Mary was about twelve years of age, her father William Godwin had published a book bearing the title: *An Essay on Sepulchres: or, A Proposal for Erecting some Memorial of the Illustrious Dead in all Ages on the Spot where their Remains have been Interred*. The need to commemorate – to preserve, identify, and signalise – the remains of the dead clearly held some emotional resonance for Godwin. When she had died of puerperal fever after the birth of their daughter, Godwin had marked Mary Wollstonecraft's grave with a stone and planted two willows over it. The fact that the younger Mary visited the spot during her courtship brought the story full circle, and demonstrated to me that a familial preoccupation, as well as events in the social history of medicine, had contributed through some curious transmutation to her important and chilling parable for the modern world.

But the story could not end there. While following that particular trail, I had repeatedly come to a stop against the statement that grave-robbery had come to an end in 1832. Each of the medical histories I initially consulted was uninformative on quite how this had been managed, and – once again – my curiosity was aroused. How could such a practice – the very idea of which was deeply perturbing – simply be brought to a halt? The medical historians' silence itself begged questions. Eventually, out of curiosity, I discovered a volume which explained it, and set me on another trail. That was ten years ago now. This time it was events and preoccupations in my own family biography which resonated, and the volume you are reading is the result.

Unlike *Frankenstein*, my effort is not a work of fiction – so there are a great many loose ends in it, which from lack of knowledge, and faithfulness to my sources, I have been unable to tie. Inevitably, there are gaps, and it is really only now that I am about to let you read it that I myself can see its shortcomings, and very much feel the necessity of a further decade's work to do the subject justice.[2]

The work has taken me into some pretty esoteric corners of history, and I have repeatedly become aware of the unavailability of good data on many of the topics with which I have tried to come to grips. A great deal remains to be discovered, much of which will only be accomplished by detailed local studies, particularly upon surviving hospital and workhouse records.[3]

Probably the major difficulty has been that when I began this work in 1975, there was very little published work on the history of attitudes to death. I didn't really have a chronology of change inside my head – and no one else seemed to be providing one. I had no basis on which to judge the applicability to a British context of Philippe Aries' work on western attitudes to death. Although a few works had been published on the subject, I didn't know when or why gravestone designs changed from skulls and crossbones to ethereal angels, I didn't know much about the history of the huge urban cemeteries, I didn't know when the Victorian funeral gained its full personality and when it became a working-class preoccupation or attainment, I didn't know much about the folklore of death, or the psychology of grief, or of the funerary practices of our own and other cultures. David Cannadine's recent practical recommendations for a tactical onslaught upon historical ignorance of the cultural history of death,[4] had to be drawn up and worked on by myself alone. So there was a great deal of exploration to be done in many fields, most of which has been a very solitary activity.[5]

In some ways, a more difficult area with which to come to grips has been medical history. Here, where there seemed abundant material available, I had the much more difficult task of teasing out the rest of the story from the hero-worship most medical history represents. The medical gospel according to the hagiographers horrified me – one long procession of Great Men – an ever-ascending line of evolution up to the glorious and smug enlightened present, with hardly even a nod towards patients and their experiences. I hope I shall be forgiven if I have presented too violent a purgative. Others have passed this way before and have helped – in a sense given me permission – to write alternative commentary on the Great Men, and to make my focus the recipients rather than the dispensers of medical attention.[6]

I believe that my findings are important, and for this reason: the story of the Anatomy Act has never properly been told. Death studies as a discipline are in their infancy in Britain, and other social historians of death since 1800 have so far overlooked the Act entirely.[7] References by social and economic historians to the Act's existence are scanty.[8] Historians of government growth and administrative history hardly mention it.[9] I have found only one who has noticed that the 1832

Anatomy Act established the earliest centrally funded and administered Inspectorate of the Benthamite calendar of nineteenth-century administrative reform.[10] Poor Law historians often assume that popular beliefs associated with the mutilation of maltreatment of the workhouse dead have no basis in rationality or fact.[11] Historians of medicine greet the Act with little comprehension of its social meaning beyond the material interests of the medical profession.[12] They omit to address the question of what the return effects might be upon the profession's body of anatomical knowledge that it is based upon bodies obtained by coercion.[13]

Briefly, let me provide you with the bare bones of the story. In the eighteenth and early nineteenth centuries, all medical education was transacted on a private basis. Since Henry VIII's time, the sole legal source for corpses for dissection had been the gallows – bodies of murderers handed over to the anatomists as a *post-mortem* punishment. Over the course of the eighteenth century, increased interest in human anatomy and physiology, alongside a growing demand for good doctoring, promoted a black market in corpses. Anatomists offered money for them and were supplied: dismembered, they sold to students at a profit. Every buried corpse in the country was vulnerable to the predations of the bodysnatchers – most particularly in the metropolis and the larger towns and cities – leading to immense popular opposition. For long the bodysnatchers alone bore the brunt of popular execration, but eventually in 1827–8, a change in case law led to the conviction of an anatomist.

The profession had long been demanding reform, and this development was the cue for the establishment of a Select Committee to investigate. I produce material to suggest the Committee was in the hands of a group of people who had already made up their minds as to what the recommendations would be. The Committee's *Report* was published several months before the Burke and Hare murders for dissection came to light in Edinburgh. The first Anatomy Bill was assisted by the discovery of their crimes, and passed the Commons. However, with the country in the midst of political turmoil over parliamentary reform, the Lords in their wisdom advised it should be withdrawn for reconsideration.

There the matter rested for a couple of years longer, until late in 1831 a new case of burking was discovered in London. Almost immediately a new bill was introduced to Parliament, passed with little opposition, and remains the basis of modern law on the subject. It recommended that instead of giving hanged murderers, the government should confiscate the bodies of paupers dying in workhouses and hospitals, too poor to pay for their own funerals. What had for generations been a feared and hated punishment for murder became one for poverty.

This book discusses why and how such an Act came to be part of British Law. It examines the background, formulation, meaning, impact and effects of the Anatomy Act. It falls into three major parts whose central pivot is the Reform era and the Act's passage, placed between a view backwards over the previous century for roots and causes, and another forwards to within living memory for effects.

Section *I: The Body* is essentially introductory, and contextualises the corpse itself socially, medically and commercially, by dealing with three parallel views of the body which coexisted over the century prior to the Act's passage in 1832 – popular sentiment and superstition,

– clinical detachment, and
– commercialisation.

Section *II: The Act* is the central core of the book, and focuses down upon the 1820s and early 1830s. It examines the factors promoting a change in the law, the framing of the bills, public and parliamentary debate on the subject, and the Act's passage.

Finally, Section *III: The Aftermath* offers an impression of the Act's impact and long-term effects.

A dialogue between two historians helps place my work in the context of recent debate on nineteenth-century popular culture. R.D. Storch quotes a passage from a paper by H.D. Moorhouse on the quiescence of the British working class:

> The initiatives and responses of the powerful helped suppress possible alternatives. Some groups have power to define the terms in which struggle occurs and through which they are experienced, and they do use this power. To concentrate on working class response and resolution is like trying to understand a punch by looking at the bruise, not at the fist. [14]

Storch then comments:

> Much popular cultural change in the nineteenth century was in the way of rolling with the punch. And necessarily so. [15]

Now in my own work, the Anatomy Act can be understood as the fist. The bruise is the terrible fear of death on the parish which permeated the culture of my own and my parents' childhoods, and of their parents before them.

As a child in the mid-1950s in London's Notting Hill, I can clearly remember the local belief that the chimney of a nearby hospital (an old workhouse infirmary) belched the smoke of human fuel. In my school playground small children nodded knowingly, and told each other that those who went in there never came out. I cannot recall having heard adults discuss the chimney, or the hospital mortality rate. Nor did I understand about workhouses and the politics behind them until I was much older. Of course hundreds of local people entered the hospital sick and came out better – I myself eventually survived the experience unscathed. But in the mid-1950s, less than a decade had passed since the National Health Service had transformed the place into a benign institution. People associated hopelessness, coercion, death, and unspeakable *post-mortem* treatment with the bleak exterior of the old workhouse.

These childhood experiences have given me a lasting interest in the transmission of popular culture and the ground of truth which can underlie it, and in the terrible stories about what was done to the poor before the days of the Welfare State. The fear that the hospital served also as a crematorium held a peculiar fascination for me. It was this memory which resonated when I discovered what the Anatomy Act actually did.

It should be clear from what has already been said, that I use the word 'poor' in its widest sense. It signifies those who – whatever their occupation or present fortune – could never be, or never feel to be, fully sure of their own distance from the workhouse. It therefore includes all working people, particularly the elderly, and much of the lower middle class, whose financial security was often only fragile. It signifies as much a state of mind as an economic reality – the pauper's funeral was an object of fear and loathing outside as well as inside workhouse walls. 'Popular' is defined by the Oxford English Dictionary as pertaining to the common people. In his *Keywords*, Raymond Williams describes its operation '. . . from the point of view of the people rather than from those seeking favour or power from them'. 'Popular culture' he defines as that 'actually made by people for themselves'. Although one would wish to be more precise, this loose meaning conveys the sort of constituency in which I am interested.

The era of the Anatomy Act is like a gift for anyone interested in attitudes towards the body, the dead, death, grief, and beliefs in the afterlife. Over the period 1828–32, the controversy threw up debate on all these subjects – topics which generally remain submerged at a non-verbal level. We are living at a time when the debate is again in the melting pot, and with equally broad moral and social dimensions. Definitions of life and death, and the morality and safety of commercial values in tissue and organ transplantation, blood donation and surrogate parenthood, are in the news daily. It is perhaps timely that older roots of the subject should be re-examined.

Frankenstein was published in 1818 – only a decade before the Select Committee on Anatomy was appointed by Parliament. Mary Wollstonecraft's daughter warned in her book of the dangers of subordinating life to 'science'. The real monster of the book is the doctor scientist who loses touch with his own humanity. Frankenstein is emblematic of the fears of our day, as much as of his own.

'Death in the Dissection Room' by Thomas Rowlandson, c.1815.

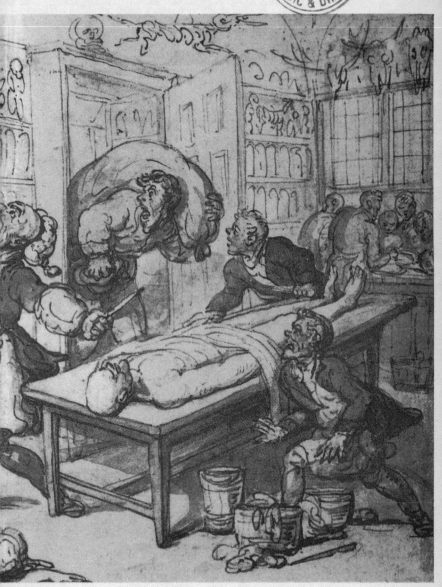

Courtesy of the Spencer Collection, New York Public Library.

I

THE BODY

The body is a source of great
anxiety, derived above all from
the fear of death.

Stephen Kern, 1975

THE CORPSE
AND POPULAR CULTURE

We have but to scratch the rustic to find the barbarian underneath.

E. Clodd, 1893[1]

There was a clamour against the anatomists, emanating, it is true, from a frothy, democratic class, blind to their own interests, and ungrateful for the many benefits they had received from the medical profession.

H. Lonsdale, 1870[2]

It is to be lamented that ceremonies so innocent and interesting should fall even into partial disuse, and though fully sensible of the improvements made both in men and manners, yet I must still regret many good customs now forgotten and neglected . . . which . . . have antiquity for their authority and affectionate remembrance for their aim.

S.I. Law, 1817[3]

The current obsession with keeping everything tidy, not accepting long grass and leaning tombs, and treating a funeral as a refuse disposal problem, reflects a deep malaise in society . . . Death was never a tidy thing: it is foolish to try and make it so, and to compartment it away from life and the living.

James Stevens Curl, 1972[4]

Without a broad understanding of its cultural context, the social meaning and importance of the 1832 Anatomy Act cannot fully be grasped. The violent popular antipathy experienced by grave-robbers and anatomists is comprehensible only when informed by some understanding of traditional attitudes towards death and the corpse. These would be hard indeed to reach, were it not for the fortunate existence of an extensive body of work on death customs and beliefs, collected by the eighteenth and nineteenth centuries' equivalents of today's social anthropologists – antiquaries and folklorists.

Over the century before the Anatomy Act's passage, industrialisation, rapid urban growth and great social change were in process. During the same period in which most folklore collecting was begun, professional undertakers were establishing their trade in urban areas, and the 'respectable' funeral – defined primarily by its cash value – became an article of middle-class aspiration.[5] The full histories of the funeral and of the undertaking business in Britain have yet to be written[6] – and this is not the place to elaborate. However, it is important to notice that the development of undertaking presaged a fundamental shift of meaning from the funerals the antiquaries witnessed and recorded. It represented an invasion of commerce into the rite of passage; the substitution of cash for affective and older, more traditional social relations. By the 1830s – though the butt of ridicule and scorn in some quarters – the undertaking business was well-established, and poised for expansion in promoting and providing the Victorian celebration of death. I return to this subject in my final chapter.

An important point to make here is the extent to which secular death ritual survived alongside the commercial variety. Probably from a lack of profitability, undertakers were less intrusive in lower social strata. Other than for the provision of the coffin, and possibly transport, in the early part of the nineteenth century the working class had little need of their services. In the middle classes, where social fluidity, aspiration and insecurity would provide a ready market for a plethora of manuals on funerary and other etiquette, the undertaker had it more his own way. Even into our own century, whereas wealthier people would purchase the undertaker's services complete – often guided by *his* ideas of what would be seemly – the urban working class often provided their own shrouds and usually laid each other out.[7]

In *Religion and the Decline of Magic*, Keith Thomas has discussed on the one hand parallels between beliefs and practices in extant 'primitive' societies and those of our own forbears in the mediaeval period; on the other, he draws attention to the long-term survival of such beliefs – in some cases up to the present day.[8] The Anatomy Act period falls between these two eras, and shares important characteristics with each. It was a period of profound contrasts and conflicts, none more so than in 'scientific' and 'superstitious' views of death.

A good illustration of the simultaneous existence of different levels of belief, sophistication and scepticism[9] is to be found in the columns of the *Morning Herald* newspaper of 14 February 1829.[10] One report tells the story of a woman who had recently died and been buried in a village near Mansfield. Before her death she had entrusted to a close woman friend some letters from her dead son, with the injunction that they were to be laid with her in her coffin. The friend forgot, and was very distressed until – soon afterwards – the village postman died. The woman arranged to have the letters put into *his* coffin, as she firmly believed that he would be as diligent a postman in the other world as he had been in this. Two inches below the report, there appeared an advert for the *Lancet*, offering hospital case-reports, and the text of a lecture on the materiality of the mind.

———————

The upsurge of interest in popular culture which occurred over the century preceding the Anatomy Act was a pan-european event which deserves much more interest than it has so far received.[11]

Unlike today's anthropologists, the antiquaries and folklorists – upon whose evidence we mainly have to depend – were largely unaware of their own cultural preconceptions. Their motivations are unclear, but it seems likely that they were aware on some level that they were living through a period of unprecedented change, in which customs and beliefs they themselves found anachronistic and quaintly interesting might entirely disappear. From a wide reading of their material, one gains the impression that most British folklore collectors were urbane gentlefolk with leisure-time to spare, observing – as sympathetic outsiders – customs and practices in which they had probably never taken part themselves, and which reflected beliefs they found alien or only distantly familiar.[12]

Although few of the antiquaries seem explicitly to have drawn moral lessons on the lines of Pugin's *Contrasts* (1836–41),[13] in their awareness of the need to chronicle these 'vulgar errors' there is an element of nostalgia for a golden past – and hence an implicit criticism of a less-than-golden present. The word 'folklore' is itself a coinage of 1846 – and reveals both the movement's condescension and nostalgia. The desire for an understanding of 'origins' can be seen on one level as a local application of early anthropological interest, and on another as a groping towards an understanding of individual and collective psychology before the development of appropriate discourse.[14]

The shortcomings and limitations of folklore materials are well known.[15] Cultural traditions and beliefs recorded as 'antiquities' or 'vulgar errors' were neither recorded nor understood at the time in terms of actual social contexts,[16] and the extent to which this material can be interrogated in the light of present-day preoccupations is limited. Nevertheless, the use of folklore material in the work of leading historians has shown its value in an understanding of popular culture.[17]

Folklore beliefs resemble a language or patchwork, built up of assorted materials over a long period of time. Though the dynamics of popular memory merit more scholarly attention, all indications are that folk memory can be extremely long. While lending itself to local variation, collective mythification and individual accretion, it can often also be surprisingly accurate. The Opies found that 'at least a quarter and very likely over half' of children's rhymes they recorded in the 1940s and 1950s were over 200 years old.[18] A song collected in the field by Cecil Sharp in the early years of this century, was almost identical to a seventeenth-century black letter version.[19]

Oral traditions can preserve beliefs as effectively as nursery rhymes and fairy stories: tales of the bodysnatchers still circulate even today in the Edinburgh region.[20] A present-day researcher of death customs working in cultural 'backwater' areas of Cumberland County, Pennsylvania, has recorded death beliefs, omens and customs surviving into within living memory which are remarkably similar or even identical to nineteenth- and twentieth-century British ones. Beliefs that a bird entering the house or a cock crowing at midnight portended a death, and customs like orienting the body towards the east, and watching and waking the corpse probably arrived in Pennsylvania with British colonists in the mid-eighteenth century.[21] The comparatively small variations they exhibit from surviving British customs – despite long separate development – suggest a robust resilience and, by implication, very long roots.

A few customs can be dated with some certainty a very long way indeed. It is well known that when Christianity arrived in Britain it adopted, as a matter of policy, indigenous feasts and festivals as its own.[22] The custom of orienting the dead with their feet towards the rising sun, for example, is known to pre-date Christianity.[23] In folklore, the custom is associated with the belief that the last trump will sound from the east: Christianity effectively overlaid an older custom with its own gloss.[24] Many old country churchyards – whose graves go back to the eighteenth century and earlier – embody the past popularity of the oriented grave. Despite Puritan opposition in the seventeenth century,[25] its significance seems to have been lost sight of only with the advent of huge urban cemeteries during the nineteenth century, which were planned on picturesque, utilitarian and socially stratified lines, rather than upon those of tradition.[26]

So although we cannot be sure how far back any of the death omens, superstitions and rituals discussed here actually go, many have been recorded at least since the early eighteenth century, and a proportion of them survive in some form today. Despite prolonged search, however, it is not known if anyone in the 1820s and 1830s consistently sought out material which would have been specifically useful to this study.[27] Although Edwin Chadwick's work on urban interments provides important corroborative material for the early 1840s,[28] he had no sympathy with the subject. Being primarily interested in burial practices for administrative rather than cultural reasons, he probably missed a great deal.

Our best guides to the subject remain Pennant, Brand and the Victorian folklorists.[29] Many of the beliefs and practices they recorded are corroborated by other documentary sources, and have resurfaced in material recorded by field researchers, including the present writer, in the 1970s and 1980s.[30] Where multiple references to such customs and beliefs have been found, and other forms of corroboration have arisen, I have adopted Charles Phythian Adams' view, that 'to reject the possibility of historical continuity . . . is often likely to be a less scholarly decision than visa versa.'[31]

To appreciate the meaning of this material, we must come to terms with our own hostility to superstition,[32] for it is discernible from the surviving material that there existed in the eighteenth and early nineteenth centuries indications of a popular theology. Strong elements of both animism and fatalism, and a belief in a dynamic interrelationship of the individual and the numinous in nature are aspects of popular culture which seemed even at the time to have more to do with witchcraft and magic, than with the March of Intellect.[33]

The significance of the human corpse in popular death culture at the time of the Anatomy Act seems to have been coloured by a prevailing belief in the existence of a strong tie between body and personality/soul for an undefined period of time after death. This belief underpinned the central role of the corpse in popular funerary ritual, and gained added power from confusion and ambiguity concerning both the definition of death and the spiritual status of the corpse. The result was an uncertain balance between solicitude towards the corpse and fear of it.

The religious ethos of the folklore of death is a curious and varied amalgam of orthodox, obsolete and ersatz Christianity and what can only be called quasi-pagan beliefs.[34] The word 'pagan' has connotations of impiety, yet nothing could be further from impiety than the profoundly religious – not to say devout – character of popular belief. To assess the full significance of popular – as opposed to orthodox – religion is problematic, and our language does not assist the attempt. Christianity has had a totalitarian effect upon the language, whereby the word 'religious' is virtually synonymous with adherence to an organised religion, most commonly Christianity itself. Anything without the pale has been regarded as pagan or profane.[35]

Yet any serious attempt to evaluate attitudes to death expressed in folklore must sooner or later use the word 'religious' in its widest – not necessarily Christian – sense; and use it in connection with an essentially unorganised heterogeneous laity, whose ritual and liturgy were transmitted orally and by example, varying from locality to locality, and across time.[36] David Clark's recent book *Between Pulpit and Pew* analyses the gap between orthodox and popular belief today, a gap which has seemingly existed since at least the Reformation.[37] Clark defines the two belief structures as 'official' and 'folk' theology, and concludes that they exist in a state of simultaneous conflict and symbiosis. His conclusions parallel those of the Victorian folklorist G.L. Gomme, who saw a 'principle of antagonism' and a 'practice of toleration' in the relations of Christianity towards folklore.[38]

The discrepancy between church and laity is occasionally evident in the survival of beliefs or practices which may at one time have been accepted and promulgated – but subsequently jettisoned – by theologians. Possibly because it is one of the most stressful rites of passage, this is particularly the case in folklore associated with death.[39] The forms of such survivals can be curious. Several traditional observances seem to embody the belief that *post-mortem* customs enacted or arranged by survivors could affect the fate of the dead person's soul. These observances would seem to have depended on a vague belief in a form of intermediate purgatory or limbo between death and judgment – officially expunged from the rubric of the established church since the Reformation.[40]

The nineteenth-century poor's 'occasional conformity' – observing church rituals when it suited them to do so,[41] and most particularly at rites of passage – perhaps served as a form of spiritual insurance policy. The assumption by survivors of an ability to affect the fate of a departed soul seems to have depended, just as selectively, upon a popular memory of purgatory, and the ideas which lay behind pre-Reformation indulgences and requiem masses. It seems likely that contemporary catholicism contributed to these beliefs. Although customs like these could probably have been seen as heretical by the established Church at the time they were recorded, they depended upon two essentially Christian concepts: the vicarious location of sin, and the sacramental nature of an edible communion.

A widespread custom of this sort was the final refreshment customarily taken at eighteenth- and nineteenth-century funerals before the corpse left the house. This type of communion in the corpse's presence has been recorded all over mainland Britain north of an imaginary line from Bristol to the Wash, and particularly in Yorkshire.[42] The refection seems to have been served buffet-style – standing up, guests helping themselves or being helped informally to food and drink, often as they entered the house in which the corpse lay. The foods given tended to be sweet, usually wafers or finger biscuits (but sometimes cake) and wine – often spice or mulled – or spirits. Some references to the custom mention the use of special ceremonial vessels: a loving cup or communal tankard, and a willow basket for the funeral cakes.[43]

Discussion of death practices and beliefs involves discussion of symbolic as well as practical meanings. Almost all death customs appear to have been capable of operating on more than one level – to serve more than one need.[44] In the case of ritual eating in the corpse's presence, it is hard not to infer some confused relationship with the Sacrament; indeed, it seems likely that there was a vague association with the celebration of Holy Communion at funerals prior to 1552.[45] If this is the case, the lay ritual bespeaks popular misapprehension of the Sacrament's orthodox theological meaning. Addy, one of the more reliable field collectors, recorded in the 1890s what appears to have been a transcription of a Yorkshire belief:

> When you drink wine at a funeral every drop that you drink is a sin
> which the dead person has committed. You thereby take away the
> dead [person's] sins, and bear them yourself.[46]

Another folklorist recorded the following in the 1900s in Herefordshire. A man

> . . . was invited to the funeral of a farmer's sister, and on arrival was taken upstairs to the room where the corpse lay. At the foot of the bed was a box on which a clean white cloth and a bottle of wine, with glasses, had been placed. He was asked to drink, but refused on the ground that he never took wine, whereupon the farmer said 'But you must drink, sir. It's like the Sacrament. It's to kill the sins of my sister'.[47]

It is not difficult to see in such a belief a kinship with 'sin-eating'. This custom was recorded in the seventeenth and eighteenth centuries particularly in Wales and its border-areas, but also in Scotland. One well-documented case survives from early nineteenth-century Fenland,[48] which suggests the custom may have been more widespread than available documentation might initially indicate. The practice of designating a scapegoat to bear the sins of the dead was a curious one – indeed, most of the writers who have discussed it have done so with undisguised incredulity, and occasionally repulsion.[49] It involved the ritual consumption of food and drink which had been in direct contact with the corpse or coffin, by a person who undertook to take upon him or herself the sins of the deceased. Recorders of the custom seem frankly astonished that anyone would willingly risk their eternal soul for the small fee the ritual yielded – usually only a few pence. The food given to the sin-eater was usually reported to have been bread and ale or milk, although salt was sometimes substituted for the drink.[50] Like the pre-funeral refection, sin-eating was believed to provide for the vicarious assumption of the sins of the dead. Alongside other death customs of the period, it can be seen as an example of what Ernest Jones calls 'omnipotence of thoughts' in folklore, which would seem on one level to conflict with Christianity:

> every custom or ritual or formula designed to bring about results in the outer world . . . is based ultimately on the idea that the human mind possesses the power to influence the course of nature in the outer world, a power which religion attributes to the deity, and achieves by the more indirect technique of prayer.[51]

It is impossible to know how such an apparent heresy could have arisen, and how it became popularly acceptable. It seems possible that the old funerary custom of the nobility – giving food doles to large numbers of the poor in return for prayers for the deceased's soul – had some sort of residual influence.[52] Doles had continued to be given as a form of charity by traditionally minded wealthy families well after prayers for the dead were declared theologically invalid.[53] Fusion with the idea of bearing others' sins would seem to be a popular innovation of uncertain date.

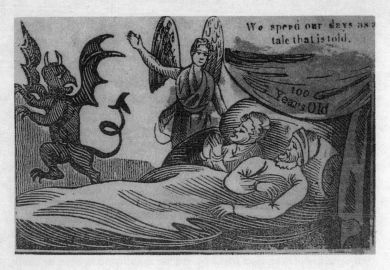

1   'The Stages of Life', broadsheet, c.1830, detail

Indications of confused Christianity in early nineteenth-century popular belief can also be found in the ballads and woodcuts on cheap penny broadsheets, printed and sold widely among the poor before newspapers became cheaply available. One, published in London by Catnach, probably in the late 1820s or early 30s is entitled: *The Stages of Life . . . the various Ages and Degrees of Human Life explained by Twelve different stages from our Birth to our Graves*.[54] The top of the sheet portrays an arc of steps, on each of which stand two figures, female and male. Each step represents a decade of human life, ascending to fifty years old, and descending again to ninety. The sheet is a conglomeration of visual and verbal imagery: blocks of typography in the lower part (mainly hymns and devotional verse) contrast and balance the large number of woodcuts in the upper part of the sheet. Other sheets of this type often work on the basis of direct comparison, as for example a similar Catnach sheet entitled *The Stages of Man's Life, compared to the Twelve Months of the Year*, which ends with a snowy December and the verse:

> So now I must this world forsake
> Another man my place must take.

The Stages of Life provides an epitome of this sort of iconography, featuring among its woodcuts scenes from the life-cycle – 'Christening', 'Marrying', 'Dying', 'the Burial' – and biblical scenes such as Christ in the Storm. Its impressive central cut features the Last Day of Judgment, and shows the sea in the process of giving up its dead, and imp-like demons driving people into the jaws of hell with pitchforks. Other judgment sheets of similar vintage show the earth opening up into dark oblong holes from which the dead are in process of rising.[55] *The Stages of Life* also contains a nineteenth-century version of the *Ars Moriendi*. An ancient couple '100 years old' are seen lying together on their deathbed, while an angel and a demon hover over them. Pictorial representations of this subject date back to the second quarter of the fifteenth century, when there was a pan-european interest in 'the Art of Dying Well'.[56] The struggle between good and evil which took place in the dying person's mind as they looked back over their life was believed to affect their soul's destiny. The angel and demon fought it out over the deathbed, and the winner carried away the soul.

The iconography on this nineteenth-century broadsheet is mediaeval. It is to be found in illuminated manuscripts, Gothic cathedral windows, and church wall-paintings long whitewashed over. Scenes of demons driving people into the open jaws of hell were enacted in miracle plays. Belief in physical resurrection – of the sea actually giving up its dead – dates from the earliest days of Christianity, and formed the basis of the logic of the mediaeval charnel house. Although the Methodist revival dealt in threats of hellfire, the appearance of the old visual imagery on these sheets suggests the influence of other, older, mental roots.[57] Owen Chadwick, speaking of popular belief in the Victorian period has said:

> though the belief in real demons faded before the century began
> [people] were still conscious of the powers of darkness, replacing the
> demons of legend with the demons of the subconscious or the
> demonic processes of society . . .[58]

The folklore and iconography discussed here suggest that Chadwick's reasoned view is perhaps a little sanguine. We shall see below that some death customs were said to be intended to protect the newly departed soul from the depradations of evil spirits. The concept is largely alien to us today, but the iconography of the Catnach broadsheet exemplifies the presence of such confusion in popular belief in the 1820s. That images of physical resurrection and of demons pushing souls into the jaws of hell should make their appearance on nineteenth-century broadsheets is mysterious, and may testify to the persistence of folk memory, the power of popular tradition, and the resilience of popular iconography. They are a powerful reminder of disregard or ignorance on a popular level of the details of contemporary theological debate.[59]

Though elements in folklore beliefs and practices do seem to exhibit a remarkable degree of internal consistency – or at the very minimum, self-reference – the surviving material neither embodies a coherent theology of its own (beyond a ready acceptance of the supra-human) nor a consistent philosophy of life. Nor should we expect at this late date to unearth – from the assorted material left by folklore recorders operating in different periods and places – a discrete popular theology or philosophy to which these beliefs can be ascribed. Although there are totemic elements in the recorded material,[60] they do not warrant the confident assertion that they represent a distinct system of belief.[61]

The character of the material left to us may in fact have less to do with the earlier existence of a distinct 'integrated system' of popular belief, than with the interests and culture of those involved in the recording. A great deal of the material we have to work with suffers from moral bias, and often a puritanical distrust of superstition or of vulgar enjoyment – as John Burrow has observed: 'superstitions are the heresies of an enlightened age'.[62] A case in point is Henry Bourne's 1725 description of contemporary corpse-watching in different social classes. Bourne was writing for an educated audience, and used the occasion of a description of classical observance to moralise on contemporary practice.

> How unlike to this ancient Custom of Watching is the modern one of locking up the Corps in a room, and leaving it there alone? How unlike to this decent Manner of Watching is the Watching of the Vulgar, which is a scene of Sport and Drinking and Lewdness? Watching at that time with a dear friend is the last Kindness and Respect we can shew him; and how unfriendly is it, to change it into Negligence and too great Resignation? How unchristian, instead of a becoming Sorrow and decent Gravity, to put on an unbecoming Joy and undecent Pastime . . .[63]

It seems clear that the educated Bourne neither shared nor sympathised with popular custom, though he knew of it. As we shall see below, the 'Vulgar' would probably have been horrified at the disrespect and possible danger involved in leaving a corpse alone.[64] Bourne's homily suggestively reveals the existence of a social gulf in the meaning and practice of this ritual as early as 1725, and suggests that the folklorists are at their least reliable recording notions of decency and indency, for example, which were socially mediated.

It seems more likely that popular beliefs about death coexisted with varying degrees of belief, ignorance or disbelief in orthodox religion. Stress upon the avoidance of an evil principle, protection from (diabolical) pollution, and the possibility of future resurrection reveals that such beliefs were by no means clearly distinct from Christianity.

Possibly because they understood and shared its meanings, the antiquaries seem to have largely overlooked the discernible Christianity in much of what they found. Although historians are undecided about the extent to which elite and popular cultures overlapped,[65] a culture of death based upon exposure to Christian teaching and practice was certainly shared over traditional social boundaries. In many cases folklore collectors seem to have ignored this shared material, and to have concentrated instead upon customs and beliefs lacking in their own traditions. What they often appear to have recorded, and which at least one late Victorian folklorist recognised, was a templated image of their own ignorance: 'The Folk', said Joseph Jacobs in 1893,' is simply a name for our ignorance.'[66]

The popular beliefs the antiquaries and folklorists chronicled offer no alternative to Christianity in either the long-term fate of the soul, or the existence of heaven and hell. Heaven and hell are alluded to as termini whose derivation was recognisably Christian – hell has flames – yet whose character, topography and location are subject neither to dispute nor conjecture.[67] Yet there appears to be no significant presence one can easily identify as the Christian God.[68] The nearest approximation seems to be a fatalistic and inscrutable power which was believed to operate in an apparently arbitrary manner, giving warning through omens and signs, conveyed by other-than-human means, like the Death-Watch Beetle.

The numinous presence in folklore seems neither to share the benign characteristics ascribed to the deity in neo-platonism, nor the judgmental paternalism of Cheap Repository Tracts or the nineteenth-century hymnal. Nor is it confined to received 'traditional' pagan images of folk-custom – the maypole, fertility rites, or celebration of the solstices. The nearest approximation to it in the 'great tradition' would be the brooding presence found in the works of Thomas Hardy. George Eliot perceived with her customary accuracy of insight that:

> . . . strange lingering echoes of the old demon-worship might perhaps even now be caught by the diligent listener among the grey-haired peasantry: for the rude mind with difficulty associates the ideas of power and benignity. A shadowy conception of power that by much persuasion can be induced to refrain from inflicting harm, is the shape most easily taken by the sense of the Invisible in the minds of men who have always been pressed close by primitive wants.[69]

This power, which '*by much persuasion can be induced to refrain from inflicting harm*', seems to have been felt as immanent, liable to be active at any time, most especially at important moments of human life. It was believed and feared that the dead could return. The pathetic fallacy – that nature shows involvement in human concerns – seems to have prevailed.[70] Belief seems to have been operating in the law of signatures and in sympathetic magic. If a candle burned in such a way as to form a hood around the flame, this was known as a 'winding-sheet', and forewarned a death. Coffin-shaped folds in linen, or coffin-shaped cinders thrown out of a fire carried the same message.[71] The earth was believed to possess magical qualities, as might everyday substances like salt or iron, and both animate and inanimate objects might behave strangely when a death was imminent. A spontaneous and disturbing household event – like a picture or a flitch of bacon falling from its hook – could presage a death, as could a door opening by itself, or otherwise unaccountable animal or bird behaviour.[72]

The individual could have a dynamic relationship with this power. One could receive from it cures for sickness – sometimes from the corpses of hanged felons – warnings of death, assurances of blissful afterlife. It also had to be offered due respect – propitiatory offerings could be made, and actions believed to precipitate bad luck or death – like shutting a door upon a corpse, or bringing lilac into a house – were to be carefully avoided.[73] The dying or dead could be cared for by the living in such a way as to ensure the speedy release and future wellbeing of the departed spirit.[74]

The great bulk of the recorded death omens, beliefs and customs do not concern large questions of theological discourse – being primarily concerned with the safe navigation of everyday life, and in particular with the fraught period immediately after death and before burial. As Donald McKelvie has recently observed, for informants 'the broad division is into those things resulting in bad luck, and those things resulting in good luck'.[75] One of the fundamental differences between this popular belief structure and Christianity seems to have been that the individual *per se* was not always held to account personally for what he/she had done, or failed to do. If yew was accidentally brought into a house with other evergreens at Christmas, for example, a death was believed to follow. But the death would not necessarily be that of the person picking the yew, or bringing it into the house, it might be any kin or friend.[76] Similarly – as in the case of the pre-funeral refreshment mentioned above – it was believed that the actions of kindred or friends could affect the individual, even after death. This reciprocal relationship of responsibility is a particularly important element in folklore customs associated with death: the object of many *post-mortem* rituals by survivors, as we shall see in a moment, seems to have been the protection of both body and soul of the dead from evil or danger.[77]

Modern funerary practices and language often obscure the role of the corpse in the proceedings by euphemism, affected delicacy, and outright evasion. In the seventeenth and early eighteenth centuries, the corpse's position was very different. It had an importance in the proceedings which is exemplified with arresting clarity in surviving funeral invitations. These often featured an illustrated border showing funeral processions, open graves, emblems of mortality such as heaps of bones, figures of Death in the form of a skeleton, skulls and cross-bones, and mourners surrounding the shrouded or coffined corpse. The text printed in the centre of these invitations invariably asked the mourner to *accompany the corpse* of the dead person, rather than merely to attend the funeral.[78] It can be inferred that those who could afford such invitations were probably members of middle and higher social strata, and that the illustrations reflect customary observance at that time. Although among the financially fortunate changes in attitudes may have begun to occur, over the century before the

Anatomy Act became law the corpse continued to occupy a similar central role further down the social scale. The centrality of the corpse was popularly crucial.

The physicality of a human corpse is undeniable. It is a carcass, with a predisposition to decay, to become noisome, obnoxious to the senses, and harrowing to the emotions. Disposal of such perishable remains is imperative. Today, preparation of the dead for disposal is regarded as a sanitary problem, dealt with professionally by hospitals and undertakers; and deodorised procedures may be found in manuals for nurses, morticians and crematoria officials. But in folklore, this process, with its intimate physical knowledge of the pathology of putrefaction, was counterpoised by a profound conception of the corpse's metaphysical attributes. This is reflected in a number of beliefs and rituals.

Several beliefs which attribute sentience to the dead body seem to lead towards the conclusion that there existed a conception (said by anthropologists also to operate in primitive societies)[79] of a period between death and burial in which the human being was regarded as 'neither alive nor fully dead'.[80] Indications of belief in this transitional state may be found in omens which presaged further deaths if a corpse's eyes refused to close, or if *rigor mortis* failed to set in.[81] It is shown in the East Riding custom of placing food and wine beside the corpse in case it woke,[82] and in the erroneous belief that a signature or mark taken while the corpse was still warm had the same stature before the law as one made in life.[83] Other beliefs of this sort hinged upon the corpse's ability to indicate displeasure if the will read in its presence was false, or – in the case of a murder – if the murderer came into its vicinity.[84] Such beliefs suggest a widely held conviction that the human corpse possessed both sentience and some sort of spiritual power.[85] Whether this power was believed to have been a legacy of the live self, a prefigurement of the future state of the soul, or to emanate from some other source, is unclear.

Uncertainty surrounding the corpse's spiritual status may have borne some relationship to the difficulty and uncertainty involved in defining when death had actually taken place. This was usually only ascertained by listening for a heartbeat, or testing for breath on a piece of mirror or glass – both notoriously unreliable methods.[86] *Rigor mortis* and the signs of putrefaction take time to manifest themselves, and in the meantime, there might legitimately be doubt. A 'limber' corpse – one which failed to show signs of stiffness – was an object of particular fear.[87]

Confusion in church teaching may well have contributed to the uncertainty. Since the demise of purgatory, even in official eschatology there had existed debate as to the soul's fate: whether it was judged at death and passed direct to a final home, being re-united with the body and judged again at the last trump; *or*, whether it slept in the grave until Judgment Day, when body and soul would rise together from the tomb.[88] Not surprisingly, the difficulty was reflected at a popular level. The grave goods recorded as having been buried with the dead in their period seem to reflect wishes to assist the soul in four possible ways: on the *post-mortem* journey; in gaining entrance to heaven or purgatory; during the life thereafter; or in the life after physical resurrection. The intention seems often to have been combined or confused between these four possibilities.[89] Ample documentary evidence that this confusion was operating during the half-century before the Anatomy Act may be had from epitaphs. A few examples will suffice – *first*, sleep:

> A loving husband, a father dear,
> A faithful friend lies buried here.
> He in his prime was snatch'd away,
> To sleep in this cold bed of clay.   (1794)[90]

> Within this bed of dust I lay
> No more to see the light of day,
> To my long home I now am gone,
> And all my work on earth is done.   (1811)[91]

> Beneath wide Ocean's distant wave he sleeps,
> While Widow's love in silent anguish weeps,
> Till that dread day when from his waking bed,
> The raging sea shall render up its dead.   (1827)[92]

. . . and *second*, immediate translation:

> Pain and trouble did I endure
> 'Till God was pleased to send a cure.
> He call'd me from this earthly clay
> To dwell in realms of endless day.   (1809)[93]

> Four children here within their graves are laid,
> The love of life to God they quickly paid.
> Although no shining virtues they can boast,
> They're yet received to join the Angelic host.
> Their innocence secures a blest retreat,
> They are more favour'd than the rich and great.   (1803–4)[94]

If the soul left the body at death and migrated to its heavenly resting place, there would exist the danger that, disembodied, it could remain hovering around the haunts of the living. If on the other hand, it slept in the grave, then it would somehow be present in or near the body after death. In either case, awareness of the corpse's uncertain metaphysical nature could relate to a belief that an individual's 'nonmaterial component'[95] could retain its attachment to the body for an unspecified period after death.

A corpse has a presence of its own. It resembles the dead person, yet it is not that person. Death transforms the body of a known individual into something else – removing them from the realm of the ordinary in which survivors continue to have their being. It impresses survivors with the power of death, of its arbitrary effects; it is a menace to the living, a reminder of their own mortality, a threat of further death. In the popular culture of the British Isles, as in that of many other peoples, death was believed to work some paradoxical magic – for after death the body possessed powers the living person never had, and commanded awe, even fear, when the living individual never may have done so.[96]

A related area of ambiguity in popular belief is the uneasy relationship between fear and solicitude, discernible in customs associated with the care of the dead body. In general, and in contrast to many primitive death customs discussed by anthropologists, British death customs seem remarkably tolerant of the departed spirit, inclined to solicitude and sentimentality, rather than to fear and dread. However, a profound latent dread is evident in the breadth of popular ghostlore, and in particular in the connection of haunting and disturbed or incomplete remains.[97] This ambiguity seems to indicate contemporary unease as to whether the departed spirit was friendly or hostile to survivors. Taken as a whole, the material collected by folklorists suggests that what appears as solicitude and tolerance resulted not from any *lack* of fear and dread; but rather, from an understanding and knowledge of the correct forms of funerary ritual, and a tenacious belief that if due respect be given to the dead, both the future repose of the soul and the comfort of the mourners would be assured.[98]

What was popularly thought of as a 'decent' funeral was a composite ritual. Other than the coffin and religious service, most of its components were provided within a community – without recourse to undertaker or churchman. Apart from the burial service, it was composed of secular rituals – which included physical attentions to the corpse, watching, waking and viewing the corpse, some form of refreshment, and lay ceremonial surrounding the transport of coffin to church and grave. Folklorists barely address the importance of the religious service itself, seemingly taking its form and effect for granted. Nonconformity, however, certainly affected the form of the service, and whether or not adherents were buried in consecrated ground could be a source of contention.[99] Poor funerals observed in the Lake District by Dorothy Wordsworth in the 1800s suggest that simple religious belief could provide common comfort.[100]

The preparation of the corpse for the grave was generally referred to as 'laying-out', 'streeking' or rendering the 'last offices'. This corporate ritual was regarded both as a physical and a social necessity, and was imbued with spiritual overtones. The task is reported to have been done traditionally by women.[101] It involved washing the corpse, plugging its orifices, closing the eyes and mouth, straightening the limbs, and dressing it in

2   Illustration from a late seventeenth-century book on English customs, showing the viewing of the dead, and the distribution of rosemary and wine customary among the wealthy

winding sheet or shroud. In cases of suicide, these observances were sometimes neglected, but their importance in the vast majority of deaths in the community cannot be overestimated.

Washing the corpse and the reasons for it are not subjects widely discussed by folklorists. The practice seems to have been so familiar as to provoke no need for explanations. The difficulties of giving blanket baths to the infirm and dying are well known even today, so that a person sick for some time may at death be less than spotless. *Post-mortem* relaxation of bladder and rectal sphincter adds physiological imperative. Moreover, there is ample evidence of the widespread observance at this period of the custom of viewing the bodies of the dead by kindred and neighbours. It would of course have been considered disrespectful, and would reflect badly upon immediate kin, if a corpse was not clean, presentable, and as far as practicable, odourless.[102]

A cluster of symbolic associations also adheres to the ritual. It has biblical (and classical) precedent. Furthermore, the Old Testament designates the corpse and all who handle or approach it unclean.[103] Ritual washing may possibly have represented a popular mode of removing the taint. Seen in this way, corpse-washing may be understood as a protective ritual for mourners and corpse alike.

Several customs suggest that the treatment and attributes of the corpse –

particularly in the period shortly after death – were believed in some important way to affect the future fate of the soul. A similar idea emerges in anthropological material.[104] A belief in some sort of sympathetic magic was perhaps responsible: the belief – extant in the highest scientific circles in the seventeenth century – that a wound could be healed at a distance by treatment to the *weapon*,[105] seems to find an echo in the belief that corpse care could affect the soul's fate. Customs like orientation, burial in consecrated ground and the provision of grave-goods retain emotional resonance whether taken at face value as a social imperative, or on a symbolic, or sympathetic-magical level. Part of the power and popularity of such practices no doubt derived from their ability to be understood at multiple levels of meaning, and at various levels of intellectual sophistication.

So also with the washing of the dead. The ritual ablution of the corpse may have signified a lay absolution, a baptism for the next life. Until the seventeenth century the baptism of weak infants was allowed by the Church to be carried out by midwives.[106] It is not unlikely that a ritual purification at death might popularly have been regarded as having similar spiritual significance – particularly as laying-out and midwifery were often undertaken by the same women.[107] Moreover, ordinary water was believed capable of acting as a barrier to evil spirits,[108] and of cleansing departing souls.[109] The ritual ablution of the corpse might also have been held to attain spiritual value – providing either a purification for immediate entry to heaven, or serving as a figurative insurance that the corpse would rise up clean and fresh at the last trump. A woman still engaged in the laying-out of the dead in a small Suffolk village told me in 1980: 'the washing is so that you're spotless to meet the Lamb of God.'[110] Resonant with meaning, the washing of the corpse involved not only the sweat of death, but the sins of the earthly life.

The eyelids are generally the first parts of a body to set in *rigor mortis*, just before the jaw, about three or four hours after death. After about ten hours, stiffening of the body will usually be complete. *Rigor mortis* does not pass off for another 36 hours – sometimes longer. So to avoid the omen in which a corpse whose eyes refuse to close represents a threat to its kin, this part of the laying-out would have to be done quite soon after death. Proverbially pennies were used to hold the eyes closed until set. There seems to be a parallel with the pennies sewn in linen bound upon the navels of new-born babies – each serves a physical purpose, and the resemblance goes beyond the coin used to the personnel involved. I have myself spoken with a woman who followed both practices in her work as midwife and layer-out, and interviewed another whose mother did the same, in both cases since the Great War.[111]

After the eyes, the mouth would be closed. The wide chin band of the shroud cap would hold the chin up, or a bandage passing under the chin and tied at the top of the head. Sometimes a Bible propped against the chin is said to have served the same purpose.[112] Adjustment of the body after death would be completed with the straightening of the limbs. Brand, writing in the 1770s, referred to the laying-out as 'streeking', and said it was done upon a special board.[113] David Clark records the survival of such a board at Staithes near Whitby, and its use there within living memory.[114]

Mention of any mode of holding the arms straight is lacking, so it seem likely that as today, the arms were customarily placed cross-wise over the breast, or over the stomach.[115] To aid the straightening of the legs, the ankles were tied together during laying out with bandages called footbands. In some areas, these were said to be left on to prevent the spirit from walking, but in others they were cut or loosened (like all knots on or near the body) just prior to burial, to facilitate speedy resurrection at the last trumpet.[116]

Clothing for the dead is referred to in the literature simply as a shroud or winding sheet. The two are not synonymous. The winding sheet was, as its name suggests, a sheet in which the corpse was wrapped or wound in such a way as to allow the face still to be seen until burial. Illustrations of the dead wrapped in this way appear on seventeenth- and eighteenth-century funeral invitations. The sheet seems to have been tied or sewn above the head and below the feet, so that the figure wrapped in it resembles a double-ended sack, or a somewhat rotund Christmas cracker.[117] The curious parallel with birth persists in references to the winding sheet as 'swaddling clothes'.[118]

Until the seventeenth century, the poor were often buried without a coffin, with only the winding sheet between their flesh and the soil, so it is possible that the shroud as an article of clothing developed coterminously with the use of the coffin, and this primarily among the affluent.[119] Certainly the shroud in some instances appears to have served as an indicator of status – though not always of economic status.[120]

The type of shroud usually mentioned in the folklore – like that perhaps familiar today from our own grandmothers – bore a resemblance to old-fashioned nightclothes but was often a distinct garment. It seems always to have been white, with long sleeves, often with some ornamentation (smocking and/or embroidery) around the neck opening, and long enough to envelop the feet. Sometimes a cap and white stockings appear in descriptions of the traditional shroud, and occasionally gloves and a muffler.[121]

The phraseology of the Acts for Burial in Woollen[122] shows that in earlier periods ordinary clothing could be used instead of either winding sheet or shroud. Passed from 1666 onwards, these Acts were not repealed until 1814, by which time they had fallen into disuse. They were designed to provide a boost for the home wool industry by enforcing the use of woollen shrouds and grave-clothes. Eighteenth-century official affidavits interdicted 'any Shirt, Shift, or Shroud' unless made solely from wool.[123] Many folklorists refer to this legislation, and some record the belief that it

was lucky to be buried in linen – a belief which represents a clear
assimilation into folklore of contemporary working-class attitudes. Since
only the affluent could afford to pay the £5 fine the Acts demanded in cases
of contravention, they were the only ones buried in linen. Christ was
buried in linen, so this unpopular legislation may have caused distress to
the devout, particularly among the poor.[124]

Considerable importance was often attached to the provision of the
shroud. In the north of England in the last century, shrouds were
customarily prepared many years in advance, and were sometimes included in the wedding trousseau.[125] More recent evidence suggests that the
importance of the shroud was by no means confined to the north, and
survives elsewhere even today among the very elderly.[126]

The preparation of a corpse for burial cannot be an easy job, and it
behoves us to think for a moment of the skills involved. Not only would
physical strength be needed to lift and roll a heavy body, but awe and fear
of the dead must be controlled, particularly while performing the most
intimate services. Moreover, manual dexterity would be required at the
time we are considering, for sewing and pinning the grave-clothes, so that
the body would appear presentable. The winding of the sheet had to be
done in a particular way, so as to leave enough to tie or sew head and foot,
and leave the face exposed to view, and to cover it before burial. Beyond
these skills, the layer-out or handywoman also often possessed a store of
knowledge concerning *post-mortem* ritual. The importance of her role has
been discussed elsewhere.[127]

Since much of the ritual surrounding the corpse was of a domestic
nature, with matters of life and death resting on a pinhead,[128] it can be
imagined that a later generation of male practitioners of the art (undertakers) might desire to shake off the eschatological implications of these
attentions. Present-day urban experience testifies that this has largely
been achieved, a success which cannot have occurred without important
shifts in popular attitudes.[129] Historical changes of this nature should not
lead us, however, to ignore the metaphysical (or 'superstitious') dimension
in these old-fashioned beliefs and practices; nor should their domesticity
lead us to misprize or disparage their importance in the popular culture of
their time.

This is not to say that customs may not have been followed many
hundreds of times, even over generations, without a thought of meaning –
needing no further justification than the existence of a tradition. The
custom of corpse-dressing with rosemary – one which goes back at *least* to
the Elizabethan period[130] – offers a case in point. Sticking the winding
sheet with emblems of emotion – rosemary for fidelity in love and
remembrance, yew for sorrow, rue for pity and regret, box as a symbol for
the life everlasting – was a customary way of permitting mourners to
express a reaction to a death.[131] For some it may have served an analogous
function to the Victorian memorial card or present-day memorial column

insert, both of which are often addressed as if directly to the dead person.[132] The mourner in both cases – like a poet sighing to an absent love – might be content that the emotion had been expressed, perhaps supposing on a symbolic or telepathic level that the message would be received.

A case recorded in Lincolnshire in the 1870s provides evidence both of the observance and the meaninglessness of the custom. An old man was considered 'a very ill-conditioned husband' when he said of his late wife, that he 'never liked her looks since he married her half so well as when he saw her with rosemary under her chin'.[133]

<hr>

Watching the dead can be dated with certainty at least back to the fourteenth century. Brand records it in 1777, and Malkin gives a good description of it as he found it observed in South Wales in 1803:

> . . . it is an invariable practice, both by day and night, to watch a corpse; and so firm a hold has this supposed duty gained on their imaginations, that probably there is no instance upon record of a family so unfeeling and abandoned as to leave a dead body in the room by itself, for a single minute, in the interval between death and burial. Such a violation of decency would be remembered for generations.[134]

Watching took place over the entire duration of the period between death and burial. It could be accomplished by a lone person, and is known to have been observed in higher social strata at least until the mid-seventeenth century. Henry Bourne's comment of 1725 given above suggests that attitudes were changing at that time.[135] A London police officer who appeared before the Select Committee on Anatomy in 1828 said that he had been responsible for recovering over fifty bodies burgled from private houses. Unfortunately, he gave no details of the circumstances under which they were stolen – whether the bodies were being watched, waked, or left alone.[136]

In urban areas where entire poor families lived in one room, the ceremonial importance of watching could possibly have been less crucial, as the body would hardly have been left alone in any case. Nevertheless, great importance has usually been placed on the observance of the custom wherever it has been recorded – in some places up to our own time.[137]

Waking took place on the eve of the funeral, and was more of a social occasion.[138] Funeral wakes were observed among the poor in Wales and Scotland throughout the nineteenth century, and among urban poor immigrant communities originating from these areas, and from Ireland.[139] By the nineteenth century in those not of Irish/Welsh/Scottish descent the social function of the wake was absorbed by the pre-funeral refection, and by the funeral feast *after* the funeral.[140]

There can be little doubt that if carried out fully, watching and waking would go some way towards ensuring that death had actually taken place, and that the corpse was not merely in deep coma. It is said more frequently, that the noise made by those involved, as well as the lighting of the death chamber, served as a protection for the body from evil spirits.[141] Catrin Stevens, in her recent work on the funeral wake in eighteenth- and nineteenth-century Wales, described the wake custom of 'trouncing' as it was observed in about 1800: 'the coffin would be carried back and fore through the room 'midst unearthly clamour of feet'.[142] Here, the creation of noise was deliberately undertaken in the belief that the body/soul would be protected from evil spirits. During the bodysnatching era, watching and waking would have been justified on the more practical ground of defending the body, though at least one case is on record in which waking failed to prevent a corpse-theft.[143]

According to Hazlitt, both the boisterous 'abuse' of wakes, and religious opposition to it, were of 'pretty old standing'.[144] Both Bourne (1725) and Brand (1777) recorded revelries, while Pennant hinted openly at sexual immorality at Highland wakes in the 1760s: 'such gambols and frolics among the younger part of the company that the loss which occasioned them is often more than supplied by the consequences of that night'.[145] In both Wales and Scotland during the course of the nineteenth century, however, religious opposition to the customary funeral wake was broadly effective in curtailing festivity, and in translating boisterousness into religious fervour, whose later subsidence also virtually spelt the demise of the custom. Both Crombie, a folklorist recording in Aberdeenshire in the 1890s, and more recently Catrin Stevens testify to this process.[146] A similar process probably took place in England at an earlier period.[147]

Most commentators on watching and waking agree that the older versions provided an opportunity for the expression of heightened emotion – whether obvious grief, religious intensity, fear or good-natured fun. There was lay discussion of mortality and spirituality very different from the religious orthodoxy of the later wakes – taking the form of an exchange of tales of 'spectre funerals, ghosts, hobgoblins. . . .'[148] Practical joking – imitating the voice of the dead person, or animating the corpse by subterfuge – was also recorded.[149] The gamut of human reactions to death – ranging from black humour to the dark night of the soul – seems to have had legitimate expression on these occasions. By providing an atmosphere in which heightened emotion could freely find cathartic expression, the wake may have aided necessary adjustment to loss, and provided a healthy basis for the social acceptance of bereavement.[150]

Viewing the corpse, or the 'last look', a custom still extant today, can be dated back with certainty at least three centuries. It was observed in all social classes until the Great War.[151] Viewing was a 'more or less ceremonial visit of condolence which always included one to the room in which the dead person lay'.[152] Like waking, it served a double function – part visit of condolence to close mourners and part a last respectful visit to the dead. Perhaps because of its high incidence and general acceptability, folklorists tended not to collect or solicit reasons for its observance.

The acceptability of the custom even in higher social strata is shown by the fact that English etiquette writers hardly referred to it until the period between the two World Wars, when they began to do so with antipathy. One, writing in 1936 recommended the dead 'should be protected from unnecessary display', and provided a pretext for the refusal of access: 'a refusal can always be mollified by remarking that the deceased would prefer to be remembered as he [or she] was in life'. The author admitted his views were not shared by all, and in doing so, provides an insight into the motives of those adhering to the custom at the time: 'some may feel that the dead person is, in some way, slighted if the most intimate friends and relations have not paid . . . a last farewell'.[153]

It is clear from folklorists recording the custom in the nineteenth century that viewing was not popularly confined to the 'most intimate friends and relations', but was – on the contrary – open to all. Florence Peacock's sentiments of unease and distaste (expressed in 1895) colour her account, but also serve to characterise the openness with which the custom was observed:

> it is a common and most reprehensible practice to make a kind of show of the dead. Not only are the relations and those who love the departed suffered once more, and for the last time, for ever in this world to gaze upon all that is mortal of him who has assumed immortality, but anyone that likes may come and stare out of vulgar curiosity.[154]

Both these writers were frowning upon a custom which was current throughout the Anatomy Act era. It appears that the custom was long observed in all social classes, but fell out of favour among the higher strata of society around the turn of the twentieth century. The two writers quoted reflect the attitudes which caused the decline. At first, the custom began to be confined to close relatives and friends – both children and the vulgar curious being excluded. This denial of access has since become general, and a previously widespread custom became first circumscribed to the private family realm, then to adults, and – more recently still – comparatively rarely observed.[155]

Among lower social strata the importance of viewing the dead in the early nineteenth century is illustrated by a chapbook ballad entitled *The Unfortunate Fair; or, The Sad Disaster*, dating from about 1800.[156] We take up the ballad halfway through. A sea captain returns from a long voyage to find his true love, Maria, ill in a workhouse:

> In haste to the workhouse he straight did repair;
> O, shocking disaster! this news he did hear,
> He enquir'd for Maria, his joy and delight,
> When for answer was giv'n, She dy'd, sir, last night.
>
> Then raving distracted, let me see her, did cry,
> On the corps of his true love he wept bitterly;
> He said, take this purse; let her coffin be lead;
> Farewel, dear Maria, then turned his head.
>
> Then straight from his side his sword out he drew,
> And then his own body he plung'd thro' and thro',
> Saying, dearest Maria, since you can't be my bride,
> I still am determined to ly by your side.
>
> Farewel to all pleasure, my joy and delight;
> O the tears that were shed at this shocking sight;
> And to see this sad sight thousands did repair,
> In one grave were laid this most beautiful pair.

The ballad's last stanza indicates the normality of public viewing, and a pride in the numbers of people doing so which is akin to that found in nineteenth-century reports of attendance at grand funerals.[157]

Though closely related to viewing, *touching* the corpse was more frequently 'explained' by folklorists, probably because it was more easily associated with superstition, and with the poor. It was, like viewing, recorded widely throughout the nineteenth century, and is said to have been extant in most districts of England as late as the 1940s. The custom usually involved touching the corpse's brow during viewing; in some cases the touch took the form of a kiss.[158]

Explanations of the custom collected by folklorists are many, among them that it acted as a preventative of bad dreams; it removed the fear of death; otherwise the mourner would be haunted by the dead person, or dogged by ill-luck; that it was an act of sympathy with the mourners; it signified that the toucher bore the deceased no grudge; and, in Cornwall, that by the act of touching, the toucher gained the dead person's strength.[159] Several folklorists record agreement that it would have constituted a singular discourtesy to refuse to view and touch the dead if invited to do so.[160]

The number of reasons given for the observance of the custom is unmatched by any other, and suggests a vigorous popular culture associated with it. Folklorists have suggested that at the back of these explanations lies a common root – the belief that a murdered corpse will bleed if approached or touched by the murderer. Clare Gittings cites a Hertford trial in 1629 at which such an event was used in the prosecution's evidence.[161] Nevertheless, the reasons offered for the custom's observance should be taken at face value for what they tell us about its perpetuation.[162]

3   From Hogarth's *The Harlot's Progress*, c.1731 – showing the viewing of the dead,
rosemary and wine customary among the poor

Rather than aiming to affect the future life of the soul, both viewing and
touching seem to have addressed themselves mainly to the state of mind of
those left behind, and seem to represent a deliberate breach of the pollution
barrier surrounding the corpse. Conflated, the reasons given above invest
the double ritual with a triple value – as a ritual farewell, as a gesture of
condolence to other mourners, and as a mode of helping the individual
survivor to come to terms both with a particular death and with death in
general. Viewing and touching were thought to help heal grief.[163]

It is perhaps understandable that the majority of *post-mortem* customs
should have been associated with the corpse left behind, rather than the
intangible atmospheric milieu of the spirit itself. The physicality of the
corpse demands attention – it is the ultimate evidence that a death has
taken place. Besides, the spirit/soul's insubstantiality and the immateri-
ality of the dangers believed to beset it, would render assistance from the
physical world difficult.

Nevertheless, some customs did address this incorporeality directly – as
we've seen, noisy wakes were said to be designed to ward off evil spirits,
and some of the physical attentions offered to the corpse were believed to
possess an eschatological dimension – simple and apparently trivial
domestic attentions seem to have possessed an importance beyond the
obvious. So also with observances associated with the corpse's environ-

ment; for example, the ringing of bells was believed by some to disturb the atmosphere and confuse evil spirits, possibly thwarting their designs on the escaping soul.[164] The tolling of the church bell was among the first provisions in pauper funerals to be the subject of expenditure cuts by the Poor Law reformers. It was nevertheless highly valued by the poor, especially so in rural areas, even into the late-Victorian period.[165]

Other customs of this kind include the opening of windows and doors to allow the spirit/soul free egress,[166] the covering of reflective surfaces – particularly mirrors – either to prevent omens or haunting.[167] Fires were extinguished and clocks stopped as significators of death, or to prevent an omen.[168] Although some folklorists suggest that blinds, mourning hangings and clothing were intended to provide a measure of protection from evil spirits, these also served as indicators to outsiders of the new status of the dead person and his or her kin.[169]

The fact that clocks and mirrors are recorded as objects of significance at death raises a point which so far has been only hinted at, which concerns the age and social distribution of these customs and beliefs.[170] Mirrors had long been morally ambivalent objects – on the one hand they appeared in Renaissance emblem books signifying the vanity of life, while on the other they were used by moralists to 'reflect' painful truths – consider for instance the title of Bateman's 'Christall Glasse of Christian Reformation' of 1569. Manifestly, clocks mark worldly temporal existence – yet they seem also to have attracted meaning beyond their simple function. The favourite Victorian song 'My Grandfather's Clock' tells of a clock which stops dead at its owner's death – as if the machine was somehow identified with the allotted span of a particular human life. The covering of mirrors and the stopping of clocks when a death occurred reveals a wish to counter (or restate?) their eschatological implications. Yet clocks and mirrors were to be found in comparatively affluent homes, and importantly, only became easily available to the richer peasantry in the course of the eighteenth century. Ambivalence towards these articles may have been of long standing, but their association with death observances probably became customary as clocks and mirrors became usual household articles.

The existence of these customs should alert us that 'superstition' was by no means confined to the poor. Nor was an attachment to the integrity of the body. The financially fortunate would not have spent good money on multiple coffins, patent cast-iron coffins and other contraptions to protect their dead had they, too, not shared a similar disgust at the thought of being anatomised after death.[171] A lawyer's indictment against a body-snatcher perhaps expressed what the great majority of people felt about grave-robbery and dissection in 1822:

> . . . for the sake of wicked lucre and gain, [the accused] did take and carry away the said body, and did sell and dispose of the same for the purpose of being dissected, cut in pieces, mangled and destroyed, to the great scandal and disgrace of religion, decency and morality.[172]

4   'Watch and pray because you know not the houre' – a *Memento Mori* probably dating from the 1670s, and featuring a mirror

A recurring characteristic of popular death customs is a janus-like ability to be understood *either* as a friendly gesture of protection and help to the soul on its journey, *or* as an expression of dread – revealing a desire to hasten it thither, and prevent as far as possible its remigration.[173] To highlight this ambivalence is by no means to trivialise the emotional turmoil of grief, nor to cast doubt upon the real grief mourners historically experienced. The intention is rather to draw attention to that raw nerve of the psyche which finds great difficulty in adjusting to loss, in contemplating death, and in achieving the transition from grief to equilibrium which treads a faltering path between love and mortal fear. It is precisely this raw nerve which underpins the meanings invested in traditional death and mourning customs *across social barriers*. The same raw nerve also underlies the judicial adoption of punishments inflicting damage or destruction upon the corpse. The infliction of damage upon the corpses of executed criminals – the quartering of traitors, and the use of dissection upon murderers – historically constituted a deliberate judicial breach of society-wide norms and values. Had Britain lacked a consensus attaching deep importance to the *post-mortem* care and integral burial of the corpse, such punishments could have held no cultural meaning. The very fact that such methods were enlisted and maintained in the armoury of judicial terror – and against the worst of transgressors – reveals the cultural importance of the taboos such punishments violated.[174] Meanings and values attached to the customary treatment of the dead meant that in the early nineteenth century, dissection represented not only the exposure of nakedness, the possibility of assault upon and disrespect towards the dead – but also the deliberate mutilation or destruction of identity, perhaps for eternity.

Of course ideas about the eschatological effects of dismemberment were spurned by contemporary rationalists. The *London Medical Gazette* carried an editorial in May 1828 ridiculing the 'vague idea that the identity of the individual is hazarded by the dissection of his remains'. The *Gazette* asserted that the belief that the 'immaterial spirit still clings to the mouldering body, and can be affected by what it suffers' was 'a notion for the times of ignorance and darkness . . . which we presume no person is so weak as to believe at the present day'.[175]

In spite of itself, this critique acknowledged the reality of popular culture as a palpable resistance to 'scientific' medicine. The trenchant tone suggests that in the recesses even of the rational mind, there lurked the fear – which had to be sternly repressed – that mutilation of the corpse might have eschatological implications. An early nineteenth-century cartoon of the interior of a London anatomy museum on the Last Day of Judgment shows a group of revivified headless and legless corpses, bewilderedly seeking their lost parts.[176]

———◆———

The cultural and intellectual tumult of the reform era is epitomised in its popular iconography, which features symbols of both past and future: the comets and old emblem-book images of blindfolded Justice – *vox populi vox dei* – stand beside the incandescent printing press and its caption 'knowledge is power'.

The theory that by the reform era 'old' popular culture was losing its hold among its 'erstwhile patrons'[177] both in the upper classes and among working-class radicals at this time, is of value in an understanding of the divided radical opposition to the Anatomy Bill. Nevertheless, popular death culture was much more robust than was perhaps the case for other aspects of 'old' popular culture. The huge nineteenth-century funerals staged by the friendly societies, trades unions and Chartists[178] – not to mention those of such personages as the Duke of Wellington – probably had more to do with a conceptual undertow deriving from the culture I have described here than to changing attitudes characterised at the time as the 'March of Intellect'.

———◆———

THE CORPSE
AS AN ANATOMICAL OBJECT

At the gallows standing at the conjunction of the Tyburn and
Edgware roads, we find that the history of the London poor and the
history of English science intersect.

Peter Linebaugh, 1977.[1]

Unquestionably hospitals are the best schools of medical instruction;
for in them we have the patient's conduct under control, and can
regulate and closely trace the progress of disease . . . the medical men
have by degrees converted the hospitals of this country into schools of
medical instruction . . . the practical knowledge of our profession is
much more readily obtained in hospitals than it can be anywhere
else.

John Abernethy, surgeon, 1827.[2]

Away, then, with the humbug, the cant, the love of science, the
disinterestedness, and the pretended liberality of hospital teachers.
Away with the hypocritical cry of their sacrifices, and the welfare of
the community. These heads of the profession convert the science of
which they are ever chattering, into a mean and sordid trade, and
those institutions which were founded in the purest spirit of
benevolence and philanthropy, are transformed into warehouses of
human wretchedness.

Lancet editorial, 1829.[3]

The hospitals are their warehouses, and the sufferings of the patients
and the rights of the pupils . . . are the commodities in which they
deal – cruelty to the former, and insult to the latter, being
occasionally thrown into the scale as make weights. . . .

Lancet editorial, 1833.[4]

The study of anatomy by dissection requires in its practitioners the
effective suspension or suppression of many normal physical and emotional responses to the wilful mutilation of the body of another human being. It
requires working 'beyond the range of ordinary emotions'. 'Anatomy is the
Basis of Surgery', said William Hunter in an introductory lecture to

students, 'it informs the Head, guides the hand, and familiarizes the heart to a kind of necessary Inhumanity'.[5] This 'necessary Inhumanity' we would now call 'clinical detachment'. It represents a defensive barrier, which permits the anatomist to execute tasks which would, in normal circumstances, be taboo or emotionally repugnant. The term 'clinical detachment' carries with it both the positive connotation of objectivity, and the negative one of emotionlessness. Historically, bearing in mind all that has been said in the previous chapter, the ability to regard the human corpse as an object of close physical study represents a cultural detachment of no small dimension.

The acquisition of clinical detachment can be seen as a historical process both in the lives of individual clinicians and, over a much longer period, in the history of medicine itself. William Harvey, whose *De moto cordis et sanguinis* – proving the circulation of the blood – was published in 1628, had reached his findings 'by autopsy on the live and dead, by reason [and] by experiment'.[6] Harvey dissected his own father and sister *post-mortem*,[7] which suggests the considerable extent to which he had become able to divorce himself from traditional attitudes to the human corpse.

In degree, Harvey's clinical detachment was probably quite untypical of anatomists of his own or of later generations. An examination of the development of anatomical iconography from the Renaissance to our own day, reveals a progressive denial of symbolic and humanist meanings of human anatomy, which seems to have taken several generations to complete. In 1672, twenty years after Harvey's death, Alexander Flint, an unknown young anatomy student in Edinburgh, adorned his notebook with a sketch of a skeleton in the role of Death – messenger of mortality – indicating that he had not yet significantly distanced himself from contemporary popular death imagery.[8] Flint was at a crucial early stage in his career, when the influence upon him of traditional images and values was probably doing battle with those he would have to adopt in order to succeed in his future profession.

Tales of the bodysnatching era occasionally feature anatomists suffering shock and horror when the corpse they are about to dissect turns out to be that of a relative or friend.[9] Although the prominent theme in these tales is the infliction of a fictive retribution upon the anatomist, they also reveal some popular recognition of the difficulties involved in acquiring clinical detachment, and the location of the clinician's Achilles heel. This chapter seeks to discuss some of the implications of acquiring the 'necessary Inhumanity' of clinical detachment through dissection of the human corpse; and of the extent to which, by the turn of the nineteenth century, both the dead and the living body had alike become objectified, or 'reified', within the anatomical and surgical fraternity.

During the bodysnatching era, in the later eighteenth and early nineteenth centuries, British anatomy as a discipline was very much the product of its own history. Anatomy tuition was primarily a foundation course for its twin discipline, surgery – a relationship which dated from classical times. Until the Renaissance, medical texts had relied heavily on anatomical knowledge set down by Galen in the secondary century AD – which was 'meagre, distorted, and bore little relationship to the dissected body'.[10] But during the Renaissance, in 'enlightened' circles, a change in attitude had taken place towards the study of anatomy by dissection. In Italy this change of attitude manifested itself in influential patronage, and the establishment of anatomy schools in centres of academic medicine like Padua, which became pre-eminent as a European centre of anatomical and medical learning. The same change fostered the work of Andreas Vesalius and of Leonardo da Vinci. Each of these men's work represents a unique fusion of anatomical knowledge and artistic genius. Leonardo's work was hidden from public view until the late eighteenth century, and was not therefore influential in the history of the study of anatomy in the way in which Vesalius' *De Humani Corporis Fabrica* became after its publication in 1543. *De Fabrica* revolutionised Western perceptions of human anatomy, replacing the inaccurate mediaeval rote descriptions with careful observations from real dissections of the body. The beautiful, large and carefully executed woodcuts from *De Fabrica*, showing the human body in various stages of dissection, were reproduced in reprints, in plagiarisms, and in other people's works for centuries.

In the sixteenth and seventeenth centuries, Italy led Europe in anatomical teaching, technique, and in patronage. British anatomists often travelled there to study – Harvey, for instance, had studied at Padua.[11] In Scotland, dissection received royal recognition and patronage in 1506, when James IV granted the Edinburgh Guild of Surgeons and Barbers the bodies of certain executed criminals for dissection. England followed this lead only slowly. Three years before *De Fabrica* appeared (and eighty years before Harvey's work brought British anatomy international recognition) in 1540 the companies of Barbers & Surgeons were united by Royal Charter, and Henry VIII granted them the annual right to the bodies of four hanged felons.[12]

These royal grants represent the inception in Britain of a relationship between the medical profession, the ruling elite and the judiciary on the one hand, and between dissection and exemplary punishment on the other, which are crucial to the history of anatomy in these islands. Both relationships survived without intermission until the 1832 Anatomy Act, and each was in some sense reinforced by it. By these sixteenth-century royal enactments, dissection became recognised in law as a punishment, an aggravation to execution, a fate worse than death.

The dissections so enacted were nominated public dissections. Part of the punishment, indeed, was the very publicity involved in the delivery from hangman to surgeons at the gallows, and later in the public exhibition of the opened body itself.[13] Dissection was added to the array of punishments available to the bench, and rendered public by royal desire, so that

Behold the Villain's dire Disgrace!
Not Death itself can end.
He finds no peaceful Burial-Place
His breathless Corse, no Friend.

Torn from the Root, that wicked Tongue
Which daily swore and curst!
Those Eyeballs, from their Sockets wrung
That glow'd with lawless Lust!

His Heart, exposed to prying Eyes
To Pity has no claim:
But dreadful! from his Bones shall rise
His Monument of shame.

5 Hogarth's *Fourth Stage of Cruelty*, 1751 – an official dissection at the Company of Surgeons.
Notice the dog in the foreground

the punishment inflicted upon the body of the murderer should publicly be seen to transcend that already inflicted on the scaffold.

The principle involved in the spectacle was akin to that in the uglier punishment of hanging, drawing and quartering, whereby parts of the criminal's body would be set on spikes in various parts of the city. However, dissection differed in two important respects – its executors were medical men; and besides accomplishing the dismemberment of the wrongdoer, their work aspired to benefit the study of medicine. The surgeon-anatomist thereby became an executioner of the law.

The Company of Barbers and Surgeons was not unwilling to assume this role. The task represented not simply a means whereby anatomical material legally became their own monopoly – it also represented royal indulgence and encouragement of their 'scyence and faculty of surgery'.[14] That this was no small consideration will be understood if we bear in mind the comparatively low status of surgery at this period.

In Britain, as in other parts of Europe, medicine had long been divided into physic and surgery. This historical split did not represent any real division in the therapeutic principles on which treatment might be based, but was the result of an ecclesiastical ruling dating from 1163, when the Council of Tours issued an edict to the effect that the church abhorred the spilling of blood.[15] Ecclesiastical personnel hitherto involved in curative procedures involving the shedding of blood were prevented from so doing. Their function was taken up by all sorts of empirics, many of whom were barbers.[16] In the course of time, the more theoretical and scholarly remainder of medicine, known as physic, also became the province of lay practitioners. Of a higher social status than the barber-surgeons, they looked down upon the manual and bloody tasks of blood-letting, tooth-drawing and so on, with disdain.

This division, with its rather unsavoury social implications, was still operating at the time of the Anatomy Act, though increasingly events had supervened, and voices were raised against it.[17] In evidence before a Select Committee appointed to discuss medical education in 1834, the President of the Royal College of Physicians, Sir Henry Halford, was questioned as to why the College did not admit any person engaging in the practice of midwifery. At this time, many elite surgeons were operating in this area, having largely displaced female midwives in the care of the wealthy.[18] Sir Henry's reply is indicative of the social superiority assumed by old-fashioned physicians at this time:

> I think it is considered rather as a manual operation, and we should
> be very sorry to throw anything like a discredit upon the men who
> have been educated at the Universities, who had taken time to
> acquire the improvement of their minds in literary and scientific
> acquirements by mixing it up with this manual labour. I think it
> would rather disparage the highest grade of the profession.[19]

For over a century prior to Sir Henry's statement, surgeons had been involved in an endeavour to improve the status of their calling in the eyes of 'Society'. They had succeeded in severing their connection with the barbers in 1745, and their history since that date had been one of upward social mobility, achieved in the face of such views as Halford's. It was a long and uphill struggle, and was being undertaken with vigour throughout the period in which the Anatomy Act was in gestation and passage.[20]

In France, a similar situation had long existed, but in the late seventeenth century, surgery underwent an upsurge in prestige as a result of a much-publicised operation on Louis XIV for an anal fistula in 1687. The operation was successful, which is less surprising when it is appreciated that the surgeons involved had spent a year practising on less prestigious mortals with the same complaint.[21] Paris was endowed with five chairs of surgery by Louis XV in 1724, and despite the protests of the physicians (who until then held a monopoly in the tuition of the theory of surgery), surgeons occupying these chairs were allowed to teach both surgery and anatomy. Their Académie Royale de Chirugerie was founded in 1731. By the second half of the eighteenth century, Paris had acquired much international prestige as one of the most important European centres for anatomy and surgery.

Britain's surgeons fared less fortunately in their quest for royal favour. Viewing the improved status of surgery in France and the pre-eminence of Paris with some envy, many hoped as did Gooch in his *Practical Treatise on Wounds* (1767) that the King of Great Britain might be pleased to give encouragement and sanction to a Royal College of Surgery here.[22] These hopes were to remain unfulfilled for another thirty years, however: not until 1800 did the Company become the Royal College of Surgeons.

During the seventeenth and eighteenth centuries, the impact of philosophical debates concerning the existence of soul in animals meant that among those exposed to this discourse, some sort of biological continuity between humans and brute creation came to be more widely accepted. R.M. Young has observed that human beings were accepted by some to differ 'only in degree from the nearest sub-human species', and that the implications of this discourse were reflected in 'a heightened interest in apes and savages'.[23] It is likely that a similar impetus served to prompt recognition of the animality of the human species, opening the way to legitimation of comparative anatomy and the dissection of the human body on a wider scale than had hitherto been known.

The mid-eighteenth century seems to have been a key period in the official recognition of the need for the study of human anatomy in Britain. In 1752, an Act of Parliament for 'better Preventing the horrid Crime of Murder' gave judges discretion in death sentences for murder, to substitute dissection for gibbeting in chains. Hanging in chains was consciously designed as a grim fate. The corpse of the victim was treated with tar, enclosed in an iron framework, and suspended from a gibbet – either at the

6 An early nineteenth century woodcut showing the fearful gibbet

scene of the crime, or at some prominent site in the vicinity. The body would of course decay over time; birds would tear the flesh, pieces would fall to the ground. The gibbet with its creaking human-scarecrow corpse occupied an important place in popular imaginative apprehension of 'justice' and judicial retribution. As an exemplary punishment it was exceeded in power only by dissection. The intention of both punishments was to deny the wrongdoer a grave.[24]

Until the 1752 Act was passed, only six criminals' bodies a year had been available to the surgeons, after the addition of a further two by Charles II to the original grant by Henry VIII.[25] By the 1750s, the death penalty was being invoked for the most paltry of crimes against property, so it was a judicious move to single out the punishment for murder by this additional refinement.[26]

From its wording, those who framed the Act appear to have been concerned to a much greater extent with the infliction of punishment, than with incidental benefit to science. The Act directed that a murderer should be sentenced immediately upon conviction, execution should follow within a maximum of two days and that the body should immediately be conveyed to the surgeons' premises for dissection. Dissection was described as a 'further Terror and peculiar Mark of Infamy', and it was explicitly stated that 'in no Case whatsoever the Body of any Murderer shall be suffered to be buried'. The Act also decreed that rescue, or attempted rescue, of a corpse from surgeons' custody would be thenceforward punishable with transportation 'to some of His Majesty's Colonies or Plantations in America, for the term of Seven Years', and that if those so sentenced were to return in that period, they, too, would suffer death. The surgeons were regarded by law as agents of the Crown, and protected as such.

Despite the peripherality of concern with the pursuit of anatomical knowledge, the 1752 Act's ordinances did in fact benefit both anatomists and artists. After its foundation on the authority of George III in 1768, the Royal Academy of Arts appointed the anatomist William Hunter as Professor of Anatomy. In 1775[27] the College of Surgeons acquired the bodies of eight men at once from Tyburn. Hunter thought that the physical development of one of them would benefit the artists, and it was conveyed back to their premises while still warm, before *rigor mortis* had set in. An observer recorded that Hunter was seized with idea that 'the body might first be put into an attitude and allowed to stifen in it, which was done and when he became stif we all set to work and by the next morning we had the external muscles all well exposed ready for making a mold from him'.[28] The Royal Academy houses to this day a cast of this flayed hanged man from Tyburn Tree.[29]

Hunter himself was an influential figure in the study of human anatomy in the eighteenth century. He had lectured to the artists on the very topical subject of Nature's superiority to Art.[30] He also ran his own private anatomy school in London, where he taught anatomy in the 'Parisian' manner, which involved each student having access to an individual corpse – instead of watching a demonstrator dissect or lecture on models, anatomical preparations, or diagrams, which was the general practice elsewhere. Hunter was responsible for the tuition and training of his more famous brother John, ten years his junior, in anatomy and comparative anatomy and in the art of making anatomical preparations, in all of which John Hunter came to excel.

In 1765, William Hunter had submitted for government patronage a scheme for a central school and museum of anatomy, 'for the improvement of anatomy, physic and surgery'. He offered £7000 of his own money, and the endowment of a chair in anatomy. The poor reception of his far-sighted ideas (despite influential support)[31] provides a good indication of the limits of official interest in anatomy at the time. Disappointed, thereafter his energies were directed towards his large practice as an 'accoucheur' (man-midwife) and to a new anatomy school he built in Great Windmill Street, which also housed his museum of anatomical specimens. At his death in 1783, his collection was donated to Glasgow, where it remains.

After a long period of apprenticeship with William and other eminent

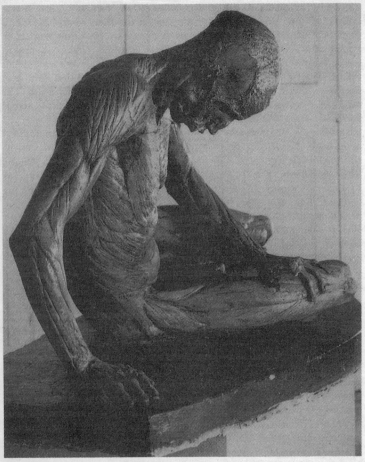

7   The 'Smugglerius' cast of a man hanged at Tyburn, and flayed at the Royal Academy of
Arts

surgeon-anatomists, and a term as an army surgeon in the Seven Years'
War, John Hunter set up on his own in 1763.[32] Returning on half-pay to
London, he established himself in practice; but his real interest was in
comparative anatomy and experimental surgery. His teaching was influential upon the generation of surgeons who had reached positions of
power during the era just prior to the Anatomy Act – particularly Jenner,
Cline, Abernethy and Astley Cooper. Hunter survived his brother by ten
years, during which time the official climate of opinion had become more
aware of the importance of anatomical and surgical exploration. On his

death in 1793, after some lengthy negotiations, his own museum – unique, and highly important in the history of comparative anatomy – was purchased for the nation, and eventually housed in a building erected for the Royal College of Surgeons, in Lincoln's Inn Fields, where it may be found today.

The importance of the Hunters in British anatomy rests not only upon their anatomical discoveries,[33] but on their teaching methods, which in their time were comparatively original and very influential. They fostered in students an intimate knowledge of structure and function, through constant work on the bodies of both animals and human beings, and the acquisition of acute observation and manual dexterity. Most importantly, they stressed a high degree of physiological and pathological knowledge[34] leading towards diagnostic accuracy and to the ability to devise new surgical techniques.[35] Pupils absorbing these lessons also observed the lucrative results of William Hunter's entrepreneurial skills, and John Hunter's perception of the future importance of the teaching hospitals.[36] The brothers jointly stood for a curious amalgam of medical patronage and nepotism. Their quest for financial and social success had a meritocratic impulse which depended upon genuine expertise and committed hard work. They were the most influential figures of their generation, forming the transition between the early eighteenth-century anatomy school proprietors and the great teaching hospital entrepreneurs of the early nineteenth century.

Despite their connections with the Company of Surgeons, it would have been impossible for the Hunters or their contemporaries to have pursued their own work or teaching without a source other than the gallows for their human 'subjects'. By law, the Company technically held a monopoly on human dissection which it did not mean to lose – in 1714 the surgeon-anatomist Cheselden had been disciplined for undertaking dissections privately.[37] However, the regulations became a dead letter as the eighteenth century progressed. Schools of anatomy had existed privately in London from the turn of the eighteenth century, but the evidence for their activity is scanty. Peachey lists twenty-four lecturers in anatomy – Cheselden among the earliest – based in London between 1701 and 1744.[38] William Hunter had attended a school run by Dr Nicholls in the early 1740s, and Hunter had purchased his own Covent Garden school as a going concern in 1764 from a surgeon-anatomist by the name of Sharpe.[39] At this period, the Company of Surgeons had only just severed its connections with the barbers, and had no hall of its own in which to give public dissections. The private schools seem to have taken advantage of this state of affairs and began to offer 'hands on' dissection, advertise their activities, and to compete publicly for pupils.[40]

The Company was a City livery company, and for long seems to have been more concerned with company dinners than with experimental

surgery. It was generally held to be intellectually stagnant.[41] The establishment was known to be avaricious, nepotistic, self-perpetuating,
exclusive and corrupt. Nevertheless, it was also by Royal authority an
examining body, without whose certificates no reputable surgeon could
operate. A rising generation of general practitioners – qualified as physicians and/or apothecaries as well as surgeons – felt themselves to be
entirely unrepresented by it. Calls for reform were many and vocal
throughout the half-century before Victoria's accession.[42]

The private anatomy schools existed on sufferance then, officially
having no 'right' to teach anatomy by dissection, and no legal source of
'material' upon which to teach. We shall see in the next chapter how they
obtained bodies illegally. The main function of the private schools seems to
have been the supplementary tuition of anatomy to students studying
surgery at the hospital schools, as well as those who had already trained as
apothecaries but could not afford the hospital tuition fees. Both categories of student attended – particularly during summer when the hospital
schools were closed – in order to pass surgical examinations.

That the Company's examinations lacked rigour was an important basis
of calls for reform. Their scientific inferiority to continental qualifications
was common knowledge. Voices of complaint asserted that the examinations tested very little, as they were solely verbal, involving no dissection or
surgery, and could often be passed by paying the fee, and learning answers
by rote.[43] Objectively, the lack of rigour on the part of the examining
authority was noticeable in the level of incompetence among those who
had qualified and were in practice. Many lives were lost as a result of poor
surgical expertise.[44] Surgical mortality was *expected* to be high. Many
patients died on the operating table, or shortly after leaving it, from pain,
shock, loss of blood and exhaustion. Many more died afterwards, having
survived the surgery, but not the ensuing infection.

Most of the operations being undertaken were essentially the same as
those which had occupied surgeons for centuries; the majority being
amputations.[45] Improvements had been made, but in general they were
minor variations on old themes – involving the use of new instruments, or
improved timing on the part of an individual surgeon. One exception to
this generally bleak picture in the early eighteenth century was due to the
introduction by William Cheselden of a new technique of operating for the
removal of stones in the bladder.[46] The operation, known as *lithotomy*,[47]
had previously resulted in an average mortality of 50 per cent, but
Cheselden achieved a marked reduction to 10 per cent, mainly from the
swiftness of his operating technique. While previously lithotomy could
take up to an hour, Cheselden was known to have undertaken it successfully in 54 seconds, and rarely took more than a minute. The main saving of
life was a direct result of the speed of the new operation, as many patients
had previously died from exhaustion and blood loss in the slower procedure, and survivors had suffered a greatly increased risk of potentially

mortal infection from protracted exposure to the foetid atmosphere of the operating theatre.

Cheselden's technique had evolved as a result of his knowledge of anatomy, gained on the dissection table. Half a century later, the Hunters successfully developed the practice of arterial ligature from knowledge gained in the same way, and from researches in comparative anatomy. After observation of *post-mortem* appearances of ruptured and damaged blood vessels, and experimentation with ligatures on live animals, they developed a safer treatment for otherwise fatal aneurysms.[48]

Despite these advances, it would be true to say that surgery at the time of the Anatomy Act bore a greater resemblance to that of the seventeenth century than to surgery today.[49] The predominant reasons for the resemblance reside in ignorance of the causes of sepsis and other surgeon- or hospital-spread infections, and the inability of surgeons to anaesthetise their patients.

Descriptions of hospital operating theatres, and the procedures used in them, leave no doubt as to why the surgery of this period was known as 'heroic'. Surgery was accomplished on the conscious, screaming patient, by surgeons with dirty overalls, dirty instruments and dirty hands. The operating table was a slab of wood, channelled to allow the blood to drip down into buckets of sawdust. The patient (referred to by John Hunter as the 'victim') was tied down, and held still when necessary. Charles Darwin intended in early life to become a surgeon, and actually enrolled at Edinburgh, in 1825–6. He attended only two operations, but

> rushed away before they were completed. Nor did I ever attend
> again, for hardly any inducement would have been strong enough to
> make me do so; this being long before the blessed days of chloroform.
> The two cases fairly haunted me for many a long year.[50]

If the operation was conducted in a teaching hospital, the patient's agonies would be observed by dozens of students, all exhaling into the atmosphere of the operating theatre, and jostling each other for a view.[51]

Wounds were dressed using methods known almost from the beginning of recorded history, with no regard for cleanliness. Pus was inevitable.[52] Robert Liston, an accomplished surgeon active in the 1820s and 1830s, attempted to reform techniques of wound dressing: 'the hot dressings, filthy unguents, greasy poultices, stimulating plasters, and complicated bandages, must give place,' he said, to simpler methods.[53] Liston had strong words to say about his contemporaries and the surgical instruments then in common use: 'our armamentaria' he said,

> should contain simple and efficient instruments only; the springs,
> grooves, notches and sliding blades, in many instruments seeming to
> be chiefly intended to compensate for want of tact and manual
> dexterity – to enable those, who have not made the art of surgery a

study, to bungle through those operations that chance or official situation may throw in their way, or put within their grasp.[54]

Liston's condemnation of bungling surgeons in official situations was a direct critique of the methods by which many surgeons – particularly in London – were appointed to their posts in the early nineteenth century: jobbery and nepotism. Like many of his professional colleagues – for example Thomas Wakley, founder of the *Lancet* – Liston was a convinced meritocrat, very much in favour of reform throughout the entire profession of surgery, holding that practical surgical ability should be the only basis on which such appointments ought to be made.[55]

That this was far from the case emerged in the evidence of James Wardrop to the Select Committee on Medical Education, in 1834, itself an important result of pressure from within the profession for medical reform. Asked if nepotism prevailed to any great extent in the major London hospitals, Wardrop replied:

It has been very notorious in one of them; and this, perhaps makes us forget those of less importance. I should think you would find, if you go over the list of surgeons of the hospitals of London, that a considerable proportion of them are either immediately or more distantly, related to someone or other of the medical officers who have preceded them.[56]

The 'notorious' case to which Wardrop referred became so by means of Wakley's journal, which was a consistent and most effective forum for calls for medical reform after its foundation in 1823. Wakley himself was a fiery, provocative and passionate surgeon, reformer, and later MP – whose life reads as a catalogue of struggles on many fronts to reform (particularly medical) abuses.[57] In 1828 Wakley had published the fact that Astley Cooper had no less than five relatives working in key positions in the United Hospitals (St Thomas' and Guy's) and revealed that their joint annual income – extracted from students – was £3000. Wakley was banned from entering St Thomas' Hospital for his pains.[58]

In the early years of the *Lancet*'s publication, Wakley was involved in several court cases. He had founded the journal in a direct attempt to break the monopoly on current medical knowledge held by what he referred to as the 'gang of hospital surgeons'.[59] One of his techniques in this campaign was to publish the lectures given in the hospitals by major figures such as Astley Cooper and John Abernethy. All sorts of expedients were used to prevent him from obtaining and using lecture texts,[60] but after a prolonged exchange in the courts, Wakley established the right in 1825 to publish Abernethy's lectures on the principle that hospital lectures given in a public capacity were public property.[61]

Astley Cooper, more astute than Abernethy, had reached an accommodation with Wakley whereby he would be free to publish Cooper's lectures, provided that Cooper's name did not appear beside them. Although the agreement was carefully observed, Wakley was in no way bound to Cooper, and continued to print criticism of the nepotism at the United Hospitals.

Even among insiders of the profession, scepticism was openly aired – though sometimes apparently unintentionally – as to the motives of many men involved in 'charitable' medical work. A contemporary medical observer unwittingly revealed his own scale of priorities when he said that the function of medicine was in 'improving the health of the people and thereby enhancing the respectability of the profession in the eyes of the public'.[62] Wakley frequently impugned the 'getters up and. . . pretended charitable supporters' of the charity hospitals:

> there is more of downright hypocrisy, humbug and intrigue practised in them than can possibly be imagined. . . . At least half the money which is now subscribed for the benefit of the afflicted in our hospitals and dispensaries, never reaches, in any form, the persons of the poor.[63]

Wakley was by no means alone in these views. The author of a work on medical etiquette dating from 1839 listed many ways in which practitioners were known to draw attention to themselves, their piety, and their charitable generosity, in order to ingratiate themselves with local social elites, and thereby boost their income from private practice:

> A petition for charity forms an excellent plea for calling on the wealthy and putting in a good word for number One – the more so, if nobody else will do it.[64]

Moreover, as Abel-Smith has shown, 'it became known by private patients that the hospital staffs possessed the most advanced knowledge. Charitable work became the key to fame and fortune.'[65]

So the medical and social status quo operated in such a way as to skew the direction of medical benefit in favour of the financially fortunate: they were primary beneficiaries of medical knowledge and expertise gained from practice upon the bodies of the poor.[66] Although standards of doctoring were by no means uniformly good,[67] and even royalty could suffer death at the hands of very eminent medical figures,[68] every doctor had a vested interest in the survival of a paying patient, which was not the case with every poor one. Doctors would avoid 'bold' surgery or untried treatments upon their private patients.[69] When treatments were proven, on the other hand, monied patients benefited soonest.[70] With conservative medical treatment, and their own existing advantages of better diet, housing, care and attendance, private patients' chances of survival were, simply, 'much greater' than those of the poor,[71] who had the dubious freedom to choose either the cheaper treatments of the druggist or empiric, parish or charitable help, or to do without.

That poor people sought hospital treatment at all is a measure of the desperation generated by serious illness or injury. To many, to enter hospital was synonymous with death. Surgery was widely believed to be little more than live butchery,[72] and much of the therapeutics, as well as the surgery, practised upon the poor was known to be experimental.[73] Medical ethics at this period was more concerned with solving territorial disputes between practitioners than with the morality of patient mortality.[74]

Amongst those who had survived the attentions of physicians and surgeons in hospitals, the scale of mortality from hospital-spread infection (sepsis, pyaemia, gangrene and erysipelas)[75] was proverbial. In 1828, 13-year-old Mary Williamson embroidered a sampler illustrating the façade of Manchester Infirmary. It was accompanied by the following verse:

> Here too the sick their final doom receive
> Here brought amid the scenes of grief to grieve
> Where the loud groans from some sad chambers flow
> Mix'd with the clamours of the crowd below.[76]

Similar sentiments about hospital mortality emerge in a satirical cartoon of the 1830s entitled 'An Essay on Modern Medical Education: Practical Results', which features an ill-ventilated hospital ward furnished with heavy bed hangings enshrouding the patients, and a chair constructed from human bones. The entire medical staff – doctor, nurse and apothecary – are shown as skeletons. While the apothecary uses the *memento mori* chair to support a large mortar to mix a potion, the nurse proffers a steaming bowl to a patient whose limp arm may just be seen hanging from the bed. The doctor in the foreground is fashionably dressed, and grimaces towards the viewer, apparently unaware or unconcerned that a patient at his side (whose bed-clothes resemble shroud and cap) has fallen head-first to the floor in a dying paroxysm.[77] The cartoon was probably intended to portray a voluntary (charity) hospital rather than a public workhouse infirmary. Even though these provided better facilities and staffing ratios,[78] they were nevertheless hopeless places for the sick poor.

In March 1828, Wakley published details of an operation undertaken by Bransby Cooper, Sir Astley's nephew, and a surgeon at Guy's. The operation involved the removal of a bladder stone from Stephen Pollard, a 53-year-old labouring man, married and with six children, from near Lewes in Sussex. The case is discussed here at some length, as it exemplifies several points which concern our subject: the social relations of medicine, the status of the patient's body, the treatment meted out in charitable institutions, and the assertion on the part of an outspoken minority of practitioners of the need for urgent reappraisal of medico-surgical attitudes towards the bodies and the persons of the poor.[79]

8 'Modern Medical Education: Practical Results', after W. Heath, 1825

Lithotomy is a surgical operation of some antiquity, recorded from at least 200 BC.[80] More recently, it is known that Harvey undertook it,[81] and that Pepys underwent it in the seventeenth century.[82] As we have seen, Cheselden could perform it in less than a minute in the early eighteenth century. In 1828, Bransby Cooper took nearly an hour to remove a small stone, and his exhausted patient died the following day.

The description of the operation which appeared in the *Lancet* was taken from a medical eyewitness's report. A scathing indictment of surgical incompetence, it described at some length the protracted course of the operation; the operator's inability to locate the stone after the first incision; the use of several different instruments in the search; probing the cavity with his fingers; his exclamations of ignorance of what was going on; more attempts with other instruments; and so on. Pollard was bound on his back in a crouching position, with his hands tied to the soles of his feet, and his knees to his shoulders. He cried out many times that he had rather the stone stay in. Eventually, it was located.

'Never shall we forget', said the *Lancet* report,

the triumphant manner in which [Bransby Cooper] raised his arm and flourished the forceps over his head, with the stone in their grasp. The operator turned to the students and said, 'I really can't conceive the cause of the difficulty', the patient being upon the table, bound, while the operator was *explaining*.[83]

After further treatment by bleeding and with leeches, Stephen Pollard survived the operation by only twenty-nine hours, all of them in great pain.

The *post-mortem* examination was also published in the *Lancet*, showing that the stone was neither large nor encrusted, that the bladder was within the normal range, that the perineum was not deep (as Cooper had maintained during the operation), and that there was a cavity 'to a great depth' between the bladder and the rectum. On the basis of these two reports, Wakley felt justified in publishing both, and after commenting that the average maximum time in which the operation was usually performed was six minutes, proceeded to suggest that

the unfortunate patient lost his life, not because his case was one of extraordinary difficulty, but because it was the turn of a surgeon to operate, who is indebted for his elevation to the influence of a corrupt system, and who, whatever may be his private virtues, would never have been placed in a situation of such deep responsibility as that which he now occupies, had he not been the nephew of Sir Astley Cooper.[84]

Wakley offered to substantiate his allegations in a court of law – throwing down the gauntlet to Cooper to sue him for libel. Cooper did so, claiming £2000 damages. The ensuing court case was a milestone in the history of medical accountability. Wakley conducted his own case, advised by the future Lord Chancellor Henry Brougham, and used this chance to expose and to attack both bad surgery and nepotism in public hospitals. His opponent was represented by Sir James Scarlett, a top barrister of the day, and an implacable adversary of press freedom.[85] Although Bransby Cooper won the case, the damages awarded by the jury were a derisory £100. Since Scarlett had asked for exemplary damages, the jury's decision was tantamount to an acceptance of the truth of Wakley's allegations. Wakley's costs were defrayed by public subscription, the surplus being sent to Pollard's widow.

Accounts of the trial reveal a great deal about the social relations of medicine at this time. Wakley served the Treasurer of Guy's with a subpoena and induced him to admit in court, very much against his will, that Mr Callaway – Cooper's assistant in the operation – was probably the better surgeon of the two; yet had not been considered for the post to which Bransby Cooper had been appointed.

Not a few professional pretensions were deflated in court. Cooper's counsel made the mistake of referring to the *Lancet* medical correspondent on the case, James Lambert, as a 'hireling'. Wakley turned the social snobbery expressed in this term upon its author: Sir James, he said, 'had forgotten that he himself was acting for hire at the very moment he was speaking', an observation which was greeted with laughter in court. However these events seem to have had little effect on the social perceptions of Wakley's more conservative colleagues. Commenting on the case in the course of a lecture at the Westminster Hospital, Sir Anthony Carlisle said that the *Lancet* reporter was 'unworthy to associate with gentlemen'.[86]

The social relations of hospital surgery are seen perhaps most clearly when we look at the position of the patient. Pollard had come to town to be operated on by the 'nevey of the great Sir Arstley'.[87] The voluntary hospitals at this period were charitable enterprises, receiving patients of 'low social class and status'.[88] At St Thomas's for example, patients applying for admission had to petition the 'Worshipful . . . President, Treasurer and Governors' . . . that they would be pleased to admit them since they were in 'low circumstances, and destitute of friends'. Fees were, for a 'clean' patient, three shillings and sixpence, for a 'foul' one, ten shillings and sixpence.[89]

We shall have reason to refer to this petition below. Its importance for us here lies in the clarity with which it defines the social status of the patient. One like Stephen Pollard, a working man, married with six children, would come cap in hand, to beg relief from the pain of his affliction; and finding this great institution willing to open its doors, would be expected to be duly grateful. The situation of a patient like Pollard *vis-à-vis* the doctors in a hospital was therefore markedly different from that between doctor and patient in private practice, where an operating surgeon could be chosen by a client free to assess various practitioners' reputations, and to dismiss a doctor or refuse to pay for unsatisfactory treatment. These alternative doctor-patient relationships have recently been characterised as 'doctor-controlled' and 'client-controlled'.[90]

In the doctor-controlled environment of the charitable hospital, the patients 'would constitute a relatively passive clientele, which would be powerless in the face of, and unable to challenge, medical aims and demands', thereby providing 'an ample source of clinical material'.[91] In teaching hospitals such as Guy's or St Thomas's, this *clinical* material was also cast in the role of human *teaching* material. Stephen Pollard's lithotomy was more than a surgical operation undertaken to relieve a working man of bladder stone: it was – like all operations performed in the operating theatres of the major London teaching hospitals – a means whereby (sometimes over a hundred) paying students could observe surgical technique.[92]

Medical authorities were loth publicly to admit that patients treated in charitable institutions were generally regarded as experimental material, upon which practitioners would gain experience which would subsequently be turned to their own social and pecuniary advantage in private practice. No salaries were paid to the surgical staff of the charitable hospitals but, as F.N.L. Poynter has shown,[93] such posts were eagerly sought after, bringing as they did not only patients but pupils. Within these institutions, the top permanent medical personnel were medical entrepreneurs, whose reputations were heightened by their hospital status. Pupils paid high fees for tuition, and patients provided the material on which they were taught.

The charitable institutions also found their uses for the students, as they acted as unpaid medical auxiliaries, and when trained, unpaid medical staff, easing the hospital responsibilities of the honorary post-holders. Affluent parents paid out good money to send their sons to study under influential hospital consultants, as these men were powerful patrons possessed of large private practices built upon reputation and expertise gained within the hospital. Thus the intimate relationship between charitable hospital treatment and training, medical patronage, and the lucrative market of private practice was predicated upon the availability of a relatively passive pool of humanity upon which surgeons could learn and develop their craft. This the charitable institution provided.

The element of theatricality implicit in the naming of operating theatres signifies their potential to provide the locus for an action to be performed, a spectacle displayed.[94] A charitable operation provided the means whereby this potential could be realised. The *Lancet* report of Cooper's behaviour in the course of the operation on Stephen Pollard makes clear that the interest of the operator and his audience was not upon the human being, but on the operator's battle with abnormal pathology. A stone was to be extracted, and extracted it was. This was despite the known risks of prolonged bladder surgery,[95] and despite the existence of the technique of lithotomy 'a deux temps', whereby in difficult cases the patient would be given bed rest between incision and extraction of the stone.[96] The technique was known to save lives, and yet it was not used on Stephen Pollard. His life was not important. What was important was his stone. When it was ultimately extracted, Cooper displayed it and discussed it with his audience. His role was that of the central protagonist – the patient was peripheral to the action. Stephen Pollard remained exhausted, bound on the slab.

Evidence given in court by Sir Astley Cooper in support of his nephew was seen by Wakley to epitomise the attitudes of old corruption towards the lives of poor patients.[97] Sir Astley more or less admitted that his nephew was neither fully skilled nor experienced when he took up his post at Guy's: 'give him time, let him work his way, and I have no doubt he will be a most excellent, a most thriving surgeon, a most brilliant operator.' Wakley asked indignantly ' . . . is *this* to be the way our hospitals are to be conducted?' and asserted that the charitable basis of such hospitals meant that poor patients had a moral right to 'the best and most scientific practice of surgery as any nobleman in the land'.[98] His was a blow both for meritocracy in medicine and for patients' rights.

There are several indications that the Pollard case was not an isolated one. Liston, in the introduction to his *Practical Surgery*,[99] argued for an increased knowledge of anatomy:

Many poor creatures have been sacrificed in consequence of the ignorance, carelessness, and self-sufficiency even of scientific professors, who have either despised or neglected the study of surgical anatomy, the consideration of the casualties which may arise during the various operations, and the due education of their fingers. The infliction of unnecessary pain, through want of adroitness in the use of instruments, and consequent protraction of the operative procedure – the hazarding in the slightest degree the safety of any one who puts confidence in us, and entrusts to us his life, or of any one who, as in public practice, is, by chance, and without the means of appeal, thrown upon our care – cannot by any means be palliated or defended – and is, in point of fact – highly criminal.

Liston's reference to 'many poor creatures' suggests that his long experience of hospital medicine had given him the opportunity to observe many such deaths.

It could truthfully be said that high hospital mortality was the price paid by the poor both for the advancement of scientific surgery,[100] and the advancing social status of surgeons. That this had been so in the case of eighteenth-century obstetrics and the charitable provision of lying-in hospitals has been shown by the historian Margaret Connor Versluysen.[101] That Astley Cooper ran a free clinic for the poor from his own home to trawl for 'interesting' cases is recorded by his biographer Brock.[102] That surgeons were not unaware of the direction of benefit is explicit in the following excerpt from the dedicatory epistle to Gooch's *Practical Treatise on Wounds*:

In the last half-century . . . hospitals have been founded . . . by voluntary contributions, which not only afford the best relief to the greatest and most deplorable objects of charity, but have a direct tendency to promote and perfect the knowledge of this art, making the benefit extend to all ranks of people.[103]

Had not the *Lancet* been in existence in 1828, there can be little doubt that Stephen Pollard would never have become known other than as an added statistic to the fatality list at Guy's. We may never know how much of the life lost in charitable institutions – like his – was lost as a result of slipshod surgery. The incision made in Pollard's perineum was so ragged[104] from the repeated insertion of various unclean instruments and digits, that in the unlikely event of his surviving the protracted operation, there was almost no chance of his also surviving the sepsis thus introduced.

Many like him may have appeared in lists as having died of hospital fever, whose deaths modern historians of medicine might attribute to poor hygiene, and ignorance of anti- or a-sepsis,[105] while in fact deaths such as Pollard's were often a direct result of the lack of due respect towards the person under the knife; respect which arguably was lacking in part because of the social relations of the operator and recipient of the treatment.[106]

As a result of the Pollard case, Wakley and his correspondent were ostracised by an outraged sector of their profession, and the *Lancet* referred to with execration by various reputable medical authorities and societies.[107] Their reaction provides an indication of the extent to which it was considered bad form for fellow surgeons to break ranks, and to expose to the public gaze the nature of treatment available to charity patients at this period.[108]

———————◄▒▒▒►———————

The use of the corpse as teaching and experimental material bears a close relationship to the use of the live body. For the study of anatomy and of surgery, it is necessary for the practitioner to develop – even to cultivate – clinical detachment while work is in progress. In the case of the dead body, this may be accomplished with comparative ease, in so far as once dead, the human body – whatever the popular culture of the era – may be much more readily objectified than the screaming writhing body of a living patient. This ease of objectification provides an underlying reason why in the 1830s anatomy, and particularly dissection, was promoted as constituting the basis for all scientific knowledge of the human body;[109] and why even today, for many students a corpse is the initial object of study.[110]

But when this necessary objectification is carried over from the dead to the living, there exists the real danger that the individuality of the live patient is placed in some risk. The Pollard case strongly suggests that the danger was heightened in operations conducted upon charity patients, to the extent that the very existence of the person under the knife was put at risk. Clinical detachment was an important component part of this danger. At the period of this study this could be compounded with a disregard of the individual as a person – a result of social alienation on the part of some surgeons, not unlike that of those contemporary employers to whom workers became no more than 'hands'.[111] In the hands of some hospital surgeons, poor patients became no more than clinical material.

This is not to deny that some poor people in this era benefited from the surgery they underwent, but simply to suggest that the benefit often took rather the form of that accruing to the criminals who in the 1720s had been used in the medical experimentation of inoculation.[112] That is to say, the benefit was often incidental to the experiment, and the outcome potentially doubtful.

In 1828, Sir Astley Cooper, Bart. was the President of the RCS, Teacher of Anatomy and Surgery, and Surgeon at Guy's Hospital. In that year in a court of law, he defended his nephew's surgical ineptitude, the cause of Stephen Pollard's death. In the same year, he stood before the Select Committee on Anatomy to argue for parliamentary assent to the enforced use as dissection material of the corpses of people too poor to pay for their own funerals.

Before the Act's passage Wakley wrote: 'The patients in our hospitals, from whom practical knowledge is to be derived, are . . . just as much within the surgeons' power, as dead bodies are at the disposal of Parliament or the public.'[113]

We shall see in a moment the extent to which many surgeons had already assumed control over the corpses of the poor, and how the influence of medical entrepreneurship extended beyond the anatomy school, effecting a transformation in the status of the human corpse. Clinical detachment had transmuted the object of veneration and supernatural power which the corpse was in popular culture, into an object of scientific study; entrepreneurial medicine eventually transformed it into an object of commercial exchange: a commodity.

THE CORPSE AS A COMMODITY

If the horrid traffic in human flesh be not, by some means or other, prevented, the churchyards will not be secure against the shovel of the midnight plunderer, nor the public against the dagger of the midnight assassin.

Lancet editorial, 1829.[1]

The husband, the wife, the offspring, toothless age or toothless infancy, are marketable. Such is the march of intellect, such is the rage of science.

Anon: *An Address to the Public*, 1829.[2]

The process by which the corpse became a commodity is shrouded in secrecy, and can be mapped and analysed only with difficulty. Surviving scraps of evidence suggest that corpses began to acquire money-value during the late seventeenth or early eighteenth century. The primary cause of this development was the paucity of legal supply – for despite the enactments of 1540, 1565 and 1663, the number of murderers' bodies legally available to the anatomists was only six per annum. During the course of the century which elapsed before the next decree on the subject in 1752, the surgeons took it upon themselves – by means outside that already granted them – to obtain dead bodies for dissection. Harvey's discovery of a safe source of extra-legal dissection material within his own family does not seem to have established a trend – later anatomists resorted to gallows and graves.

Agents representing early eighteenth-century surgeons would invite condemned Newgate prisoners not already under sentence of dissection to barter their own corpses for money. Occasionally, prisoners yielded to the temptation: to pay prison expenses, or to purchase the customary decent apparel for their launch into eternity.[3] This source of corpses, however, was fraught with danger and uncertainty for the anatomists. Riots at gallows often sought to deny surgeons dissection rights over the dead, regardless of whether currency had changed hands. So even after what surgeons may have regarded as a *bona-fide* transaction, they may neverthe-less have found themselves empty-handed, with no recourse to law for their loss, and violently unpopular into the bargain.

The surgeons were neither passive nor innocent parties to what went on at the gallows. To gain their quarry, they (often corruptly) obtained the apparent support of the panoply of law from executioner and others involved in public executions.[4] The situation at the gallows was exacerbated by competition among the surgeon/anatomists themselves, for increasingly, they would vie with each other and with official representatives of the College of Surgeons – itself seeking vainly to maintain a monopoly on dissection. In time, acceptance of a bribe by sheriff or executioner developed into the demand for one. Often the bodies of the dead taken by the anatomists were neither from the legally sanctioned number of murderers, nor of those who had sold their own bodies. They were, quite simply, snatched.

Just as the surgeons disregarded legal restraints upon the corpses they could take from the gallows, the crowd disregarded legal permission for some to be taken, and (but for the cases of really unpopular murderers) contested the right of the surgeons to *any* felon's body. Dissection was a violently unpopular punishment, and besides, the crowd's hostility was fuelled by the superstitions and beliefs which continued to adhere to gallows corpses. Cures for skin complaints, scrofula, goitres, wens, ulcers, bleeding tumours, cancers and even withered limbs were said to be effected by the touch of a recently hanged person.[5] From what is known of popular beliefs surrounding the corpse in normal circumstances, together with the curative role of the gallows corpse, it is not surprising to find that popular revulsion towards dissection itself and its use as a punishment should have found vent at the gallows – particularly as many of the crimes for which people were hanged during this period were trifling. In such cases, the historian of the riots at Tyburn, Peter Linebaugh, observes, 'the added humiliation of the surgeon's scalpel to the hangman's noose rendered the injustice of the law all the more loathsome'.[6]

The surgeons' alacritous involvement in the execution of unpopular sentences, and with a penalty which struck at the very heart of popular taboo, was a material aggravation of popular hostility towards anatomy and dissection, and promoted distrust of the medical professions. Popular abhorrence was expressed most assertively and effectively in violent riots at Tyburn gallows. To prevent a dangerous riot there in 1749, the Sheriff of London withdrew civic support for the surgeons by taking the gallows bodies into his own custody, and handing them over to their friends for burial. Thereafter, only murderers whose sentence explicitly included dissection were given over to the surgeons.

No reliable figures exist of the number of bodies which were obtained by Georgian anatomists, and no objective measure can be made of the number they actually required. Estimates of need were based upon opinions concerning the level of expertise a student might gain per corpse dissected. When the debate emerged in public in the 1820s and early 1830s, some anatomists were arguing that it was imperative for every

student to dissect at least three corpses, while others were stating that parts
adding up to one entire corpse would be perfectly adequate.[7] The best
figures on which any sort of estimate can be based date from returns of
students and corpses made by twelve London anatomy schools for the 1828
Select Committee on Anatomy, covering the year 1826, which show that
592 bodies were dissected by 701 students.[8] We have no way of ascertain-
ing equivalent figures for the eighteenth century, but two things are clear:
first, that increased interest and competition in the study and tuition of
anatomy meant that at the turn of the nineteenth century only a small
proportion of students could be accommodated by the hangman; and
second, that even before the Tyburn sheriff's intervention in 1749, other
sources were being exploited. It had become public knowledge before this
date that the judicially granted source of corpses for dissection was
inadequate, and that the shortfall was made up by exhumation.

Grave-robbery – exhumation for dissection – dates back at least to the
seventeenth century in Britain. Shakespeare's own epitaph, dating from
1616, is often used as evidence for this:

> Good frend, for Iesus sake forbeare
> To digge the dust enclosed heare.
> Bleste be ye man [that] spares these stones,
> And curste be he [that] moves my bones.[9]

More certain evidence that bodies were actively being stolen in Edinburgh
in the late seventeenth century may be found in contemporary comments
on the disappearance of an executed gipsy's body, in 1678. Some observers
thought that the gipsy may have revived after an incomplete hanging,
'which, if true, he deserves his life, tho the magistrates deserved a
reprimand' but others thought 'his body was stolen away by some
chirugeon, to make an anatomical dissection on'. The fact that those
discussing the missing body should suspect surgeons as a plausible second
to revivification suggests that the practice was not unknown.[10]

Historically, it would seem that the earliest grave-robbers were surgeon/
anatomists themselves, or their pupils. As early as 1721, apprentices'
indentures issued by the Edinburgh College of Surgeons included a clause
binding trainee surgeons not to become involved in exhumation, which
suggests that they had been doing so. The clause was known to be
honoured more in the breach than the observance.[11] Later, students were
known to have accompanied professional bodysnatchers as observers[12]
and to have obtained bodies themselves.[13] It is said that in Scotland
anatomy students could pay for their tuition with corpses rather than coin,
which suggests their tutors' complicity.[14]

Records kept by the Company of Surgeons in London probably provide
the earliest known association of monetary cost and corpses. The Com-

pany accounts list the costs of obtaining corpses on hanging days in the early eighteenth century: the greater the difficulty involved – the higher the cost.[15] For the London entrepreneurial anatomists, grave-robbery provided a useful fall-back when gallows costs were high, and was certainly being resorted to by the early decades of the eighteenth century. By the 1720s, the stealing of bodies from London graveyards was almost a commonplace, and it is clear that even at this early date the task was already being undertaken by a new strata of entrepreneurs. In an anonymous work, entitled *A View of London and Westminster*, which appeared in 1728, the author noted wryly:

> The Corporation of Corpse Stealers, I am told, support themselves and Families very comfortably; and that no-one should be surprised at the Nature of Such a Society, the late Resurrections in St Saviours, St Giles's and St Pancras' Churchyards, are memorable Instances of this laudable Profession.[16]

Because transactions between grave-robbers and surgeons were necessarily covert, it is not possible to date the inception of corpse commodification with absolute precision. Yet the above comment suggests that the social relations underpinning the material basis of anatomical study underwent an important change during the half-century spanning the period 1675–1725. It was probably during this period that the human body began to be bought and sold like any other commodity, smuggled or otherwise.

Anatomists and surgeons had begun to establish schools, and probably sold dismembered parts of bodies to pupils. In this period, too, the foundations of the great collections of medical specimens were established, and it is more than likely that – just as was the case with natural history specimens – private auctions began to serve as a means of promoting exchange.[17] By the 1740s anatomists were advertising their activities in print, and using special offers of extra tuition in the competition for students. By 1800, in medical circles, market terminology was being applied to human corpses apparently without embarrassment.[18]

———— ◁▰▰▷ ————

Heightened public awareness of what was going on meant that the danger involved in exhumation became, as we shall see, considerable.[19] Anatomists, fearful of punishment, riot, prosecution, and damage to their reputations, offered money for corpses rather than snatch them themselves. A surgeon's or a student's motives for exhuming the dead could be construed variously as due to a commitment to objective anatomical enquiry, a thirst for knowledge, a desire to succeed professionally, to make money or to cut a figure in the medical and/or social worlds of the day. A person not involved in surgery or the study of anatomy who would undertake to resurrect

More DEAD BODIES
Discovered!!

**Being an account of the apprehension
of a Carter with three cart-loads of
Dead Bodies on their road to Edinr.
by the inhabitants of PEEBLES, on Monday last,
and such a dreadful scene of bodies, limbs, and
heads displayed before the eyes of the astonished
multitude, as is beyond description : with the
singular manner in which the Carter made his
escape from the fury of the villagers,**

PEEBLES, Febr. 2d, 1824...On monday 7th current, three
carts loaded with dead bodies were intercepted at the New
toll-bar, near the 'village of PEEBLES. This dreadful discovery and seizure was affected in the following manner :... A
labourer coming up with the carts, on the new road,
about two miles south of PEEBLES, was struck with the
nauseous smell that saluted his nostrils on passing. Strongly
suspecting that "all was not right," he made bold to interro-
gate the carter as to the nature and description of the luggage
and the cause of the effluvia. The fellow at first appeared
not a little disconcerted, and as if anxious to evade the question,
but being eagerly importuned, and threatened with the constables, he at length was constrained to admit that he had a
few dead bodies in his carts, but that none of them belonged
to this part of the country, all of them having been collected
from the yards in the neighbourhood of Dumfries. The half
petrified and indignant countryman with a degree of caution and
conduct highly creditable to him. concealed for the present,
the true state of his feelings, and under pretence of curiosity,
and the promise of inviolable secrecy, requested. and was reluctantly permitted to put his hand into a sack; and touch one
of the naked bodies. Having thus obtained by his courage and
address all that he wanted (a complete confirmation of his suspicions) he quickly took leave of his companion, and hying to
the village told all that he had heard and felt. Nothing could
exceed their consternation and resentment of the inhabitants
upon the receipt of this intelligence, if it was not the alacrity
which they displayed on the occasion. With that good sense
and decision for which they are remarkable, instead of wasting
their time in minute investigations and useless vituperation, they
instantly preceeded in one grand promiscuous body, with the
constables at their head, to the toll-bar, blocked up the
gateway, seized the horses, and had the carter and his goods in
safe custody long before a people less wise and energetic could
have concerted the measure.

After the discussion of certain preliminaries anent the production of a warrant, (which the chief Constable in his hurry
had neglected to procure, but with the formality of which the
prisoner, on the consideration of a dram of whisky, agreed for
the present to dispense,) the carts were laid open, and such a
scene displayed before the eyes of the astonished multitude as
beggars description. Whole carcases, limbs, heads, &c. were
promiscuously huddled into bags and boxes. Some of the
bodies appeared to have been dreadfully mangled about the
throat with knives, and others to have been strangled. In
short, the scene was such as the pen of a Smollet could only
describe...for the dead bodies, O reader, were not the dead
bodies of men and of women, but of plucked geese, and hens,
and of lawfully murdered swine, on their hebdomadal pilgri-
mage from the Dumfries to the Edinburgh mharket.

It is needless to add, that the naked body which the honest labourer felt was that of a denuded goose, and that the
yards from which the sly carter pretended they were taken,
were not the yards of the Grave-digger. but of the Farmer.

9   A 'catchpenny' spoof broadsheet, designed to cash in on a bodysnatching scare in the
Peebles area, 1828

bodies from the 'dormitories of the defunct'[20] probably had only one motive – money.

The development of bodysnatching as a trade in itself was probably uneven and piecemeal, and until the later establishment of summer dissection, seasonally dependent. John Hunter would seem to represent the surgeon-anatomist in an intermediary phase between being supplier of his own raw material, and consumer only – delegating supply to others. In the 1750s he was responsible for procuring corpses for his brother William's London school – both liaising with resurrectionists, and serving as one himself.[21]

Within a generation, in London at least, anatomists look to have delegated the job almost entirely. In 1795, a professional gang of fifteen bodysnatchers was exposed as the result of the discovery of exhumation in a Lambeth burial ground. They worked seasonally – winter only – serving 'eight surgeons of public repute, and a man who calls himself an Articulator' by resurrecting corpses from at least thirty different burial grounds in the vicinity.[22]

It is not known what sort of fees were paid to resurrectionists in the early eighteenth century, although as is clear from the passage above concerning the 'Corporation of Corpse-Stealers' a comfortable living could probably be made from this calling in London as early as the 1720s.[23] By the 1790s, the Lambeth gang was said to have been selling adult corpses for 'two guineas and a crown' while children's sold for 'six shillings for the first foot, and nine [pence] per inch for all it measures more in length'.[24] These prices tally with Sir Astley Cooper's evidence before the Select Committee in 1828.[25] He had been apprenticed to an uncle in London in 1784, and in his evidence said that the cost of corpses during the period he had been involved in procuring them had risen from two guineas apiece to, at times, fourteen guineas.

At the time Cooper was speaking, he said he thought the price was fairly stable, at eight guineas. Joshua Brookes ran a private anatomy school in Blenheim Street (near Oxford Circus), and on occasion, had very unsatisfactory relationships with the resurrectionists. He told the Committee that he had paid as much as sixteen guineas for a body.[26] Others said prices could go as high as twenty guineas.[27]

The prices quoted are for unremarkable corpses. These would be used for the tuition of basic anatomy to students, or by a surgeon either for examination and practice prior to a difficult or unfamiliar operation, or for experimentation of surgical procedures.[28] The costs involved in obtaining physiological freaks for museums could be much higher.

An exceptional example will illustrate the point. In the 1780s, a man named O'Brien known as 'The Irish Giant' was exhibited in London. He was well over seven feet tall.[29] He died in London in June 1783, causing (according to the papers of the day)[30] a flurry of activity among the many anatomists who would have liked his body for their collections. Eventually

– despite O'Brien's careful funeral arrangements and his expressed wish to
be buried at sea to avoid being dissected by surgeons – John Hunter
obtained his body, by bribing the undertaker to remove it from the coffin
prior to the funeral ceremony. The body cost him in the region of £500.[31]
Not surprisingly, the skeleton was highly prized by Hunter – it stands
today in a glass case facing visitors as they enter the portal of his famous
collection in the Royal College of Surgeons in London's Lincoln's Inn
Fields.

But such cases as this were extremely rare – no bodysnatcher could
depend on physiological phenomena for regular income: run-of-the-mill
corpses provided that. According to one bodysnatcher examined by the
Select Committee, 'a man may make a good living at it, if he is a sober man,
and acts with judgement, and supplies the schools'.[32]

The qualifications this man made to his statement are instructive, in so
far as he indicated three ways in which a bodysnatcher might ruin his own
chances of a good living from resurrecting corpses: drink, poor judgment
and supplying other outlets than the anatomy schools. Commercial pressures on the anatomy schools made their proprietors anxious to treat
suppliers well and to pay on the nail – attributes which naturally added to
their attractions for the bodysnatchers. The other outlets to which the man
was referring could have been individual surgeons, physicians, dentists,
artists, sculptors, and/or students. To supply them may have been more
risky for two reasons: potentially poor financial reliability, and their
comparative inability to arrange either official indulgence of corpse-traffic
or financial protection to imprisoned resurrectionists.[33]

Drink, certainly, seems to have been a major preoccupation with some of
the resurrectionists. One London gang is known to have met regularly in
public houses, and to have spent considerable periods of time drinking
together. When not out on reconnaissance, snatching or disposing of
bodies, members of the gang were invariably out drinking, or 'intoxsi-
cated' at home. According to some sources, the most successful bodysnatchers owed their success in grave-robbing sorties, in business arrangements with the anatomists, and in relations with their fellows, to their
ability to remain sober.[34]

———————

Although the only legal source for bodies for dissection was hanged
murderers, exhumation was not technically a crime of theft; for although
dead human bodies were in fact bought and sold, in the eyes of the law a
dead body did not constitute real property, and therefore could neither be
owned nor stolen.[35] William Cobbett made much of the anomaly of this
situation, when in 1822 he pointedly observed:

> to steal the body of a sheep, or pig, or calf, or ox, or fowl of any sort, is
> a capital felony, punished with DEATH; and . . . to receive any such

body, or to have it in your possession, knowing it to be stolen, is also a felony, punished with TRANSPORTATION.[36]

Cobbett's anger was rooted in the long and bitter battle surrounding poaching, and the manifold unjustices inflicted against working-class country folk by their 'betters'.[37] Although cases are recorded in which grave-robbers received public whippings – much to the gratification of the crowd – the legal basis of their punishment seems unclear.[38] *The Times* expressed the hope in 1794 that the Archbishop of Canterbury would move Parliament to change the law 'making it *death* to rob a churchyard', but this penalty never materialised.[39] Bodysnatchers were occasionally sent down with light sentences for the misdemeanour of an offence against public mores, but until the 1820s, only if clothing or other 'property' was removed from a grave was a felony believed to have been committed. Until the late 1820s no medical practitioner was convicted for conspiracy or possession. So from the point of view of judicial punishment, exhuming the dead was for a very long period a relatively safe occupation. We shall see at a later stage, however, that those involved in bodysnatching had much to fear from discovery by the public, so their work always involved circumspection.

Probably the best extant description of grave-robbers' technique is to be found in the memoirs of a Victorian President of the BMA, Sir Robert Christison, which contain detail so precise as to suggest the author had been an eyewitness/accomplice in his youth.[40] The bulk of the work was done at night, using wooden shovels where noiselessness was crucial, and a 'dark lanthorn' – a device commonly used by burglars: designed to shed light where necessary, but not to attract attention.

Bodysnatchers invariably worked in small gangs, to allow at least one person to be on the look-out for potential danger. Freshly-filled graves meant that in general the digging was easy, as the earth was still loose, and not yet compacted by settling. Canvas would sometimes be laid by the grave to receive the displaced earth, so as to leave none on surrounding turf. A hole would be dug at the head of the grave, down to the coffin, and hooks or a crow-bar inserted under the lid. The weight of earth on the rest of the lid acted as a counter-weight, so that when pressure was exerted the lid invariably snapped across, and the body could be hoisted out of the grave with ropes. Sacking would be heaped over the lid beforehand to deaden the sound of cracking wood. At this stage in the proceedings, the corpse should in principle have been stripped and the grave-clothes thrown back, before the earth was shoved back into place, and the body trussed up neck and heels in a sack.

So the bodysnatchers' tools were simple ones. Often the barest essentials would suffice. The riot at Paisley discussed below was caused by the discovery by some boys of 'two shovels and a hook at the end of a cord hidden near a burial ground'.[41] Presumably, suspicions were aroused simply by the association of these articles with their location.

Most accessible of all to the predations of the resurrectionists (as the bodysnatchers were also known) were the mass graves in which the urban poor were buried. 'When I go to work,' said one of the resurrectionists (identified only by the initials 'AB') examined before the Select Committee on Anatomy in 1828,

> I like to get those of poor people buried from the workhouses,
> because, instead of working for one subject, you may get three or four;
> I do not think, during the time I have been in the habit of working for
> the schools, I got half a dozen of wealthier people.[42]

Poor graves were probably vulnerable from the earliest days of grave-robbery. In 1768 Laurence Sterne's body was buried in the additional burial ground of St George's Hanover Square in the Bayswater Road. It is said to have been stolen, and to have turned up on a slab in Cambridge two days later; where it was recognised, and re-interred.[43] The story is lent some credence by the fact that Sterne died 'insolvent', and was in all likelihood, interred in a pauper's grave.[44] Whether or not the tale is true, it illustrates two things about the resurrectionists: first, that the London trade served anatomists elsewhere; and second, that they were extremely swift and efficient. It is the sort of twist to his life that the author of *Tristram Shandy* might have appreciated.

In the 1790s, the antiquarian Thomas Pennant fondly hoped that a published appeal by him would cause the poor to be buried with some dignity and concern for public health. He was profoundly disappointed by a subsequent visit to the churchyard of St Giles-in-the-Fields, a long-term favourite with the bodysnatchers:[45]

> In the church-yard I have observed with horror a great square pit,
> with many rows of coffins piled one upon the other, all exposed to
> sight and smell. Some of the piles were incomplete, expecting the
> mortality of the night. I turned away disgusted at the view, and
> scandalized at the want of police, which so little regards the health of
> the living as to permit so many putrid corpses, tacked between some
> slight boards, dispersing their effluvia over the capital.
> Notwithstanding a compliment paid to me in one of the public
> papers, of my having occasioned the abolition of this horrible
> practice, it still remains uncorrected in this great parish.[46]

Pit burial of the poor was common practice all over London, and in inner-city areas of provincial cities throughout Britain. Depth of pits varied, depending on land available, soil type, and the pecuniary interests of those involved in graveyard 'management'. In St Botolph's, Aldgate, only a few years after the passing of the Anatomy Act, two men (one a gravedigger, the other his would-be rescuer) died together at the bottom of a grave about twenty feet deep. They had probably died from asphyxiation, from an excess of methane and other gases in the grave, emanating from the decomposing bodies which saturated the surrounding soil. These men, commented G.A. Walker, a London surgeon who campaigned for burial reform in the early years of Victoria's reign:

> met with a premature death in what is called a pauper's grave. Such graves are dug by order of parish officers and others [and] are frequently kept open for many weeks, until charged nearly to the surface with dead bodies.[47]

Stealing bodies from such graves cannot have been difficult.

The state of urban burial grounds in the early nineteenth century[48] and the pit burial of the poor are two major reasons why the bodysnatcher quoted above said he preferred to work on poor graves. They were probably the easiest and most obvious source of dead bodies for dissection, after the gallows. The bodysnatchers' mode of work on these graves was to scrape off the top layer of earth (usually only a few inches thick) and lift the coffins in succession. After the removal of their contents, the empty coffins and displaced soil were replaced, so that the disappearance of bodies was not suspected.[49]

A private manuscript diary now in the Library of the Royal College of Surgeons is the only known surviving written source left by a working resurrectionist. It was probably kept by Joshua Naples, one of the London fraternity of bodysnatchers, and covers the period from late November 1811 to December 1812.[50] Naples is said to have been a civil and well-conducted man, but weak, and for this reason unreliable. However, he was liked by the surgeons because of his respectful manner. He was an active bodysnatcher from at least 1811 (when he started the *Diary*) to 1832, when he was made redundant by the Anatomy Act, and was taken on as a 'servant' in the dissecting room at St Thomas' Hospital.[51] Naples's *Diary* is of great importance as a document, for the insight it provides into the practicalities of the resurrecting business during the early years of last century. Although by no means expansive, its abbreviated entries tell more about life as a resurrectionist than any number of surgeons' memoirs.

In the course of the year the *Diary* covers, Naples's gang supplied all the major schools of anatomy in London[52] as well as sending bodies to Edinburgh, and 'to the country'. In one entry, for 13 January 1812, which must have represented the peak of the winter season, Naples records the delivery of bodies to Brookes, Bell, Carpue, Frampton and Cline[53] – all proprietors of private London anatomy schools – and of two further corpses to St Thomas' Hospital. On other occasions, entries show that sometimes the bodysnatchers worked for nothing – wrong information leading them to dig for a putrid body.

The risks of the job seem to have been various. On a few occasions, the *Diary* records meeting the 'patrols' – once a member of the gang was arrested and he and the gang's cart was impounded.[54] One evening of particularly bad luck (26 August 1812) in the first burial ground the snatchers visited, 'dogs flew at us' and in the next (the St Pancras old ground) they unexpectedly found a watch set there to guard, and so went home. Other hazards could result in wasted effort, as for example once when the gang unearthed a body which was 'bad with the small pox' which they left in the ground. On another occasion, they travelled some distance to a burial ground but found the 'private door' locked. Clearly there had hitherto been some arrangement with the sexton of this ground to allow the gang access.[55] On several occasions, Naples mentions that the party could not go out at all, as the moon was too bright. On one page he had copied out for his own use a table showing the phases of the moon.

The *Diary* also gives a few indications of inter-gang rivalry in this period, for instance, when on 7 August 1812 after daytime reconnaissance, the men went to a ground referred to as 'St John's'[56] and found that the body they sought had already been removed: 'the other party had got the adult'. On the way home, a member of the gang was 'taken into the watchouse with the ladder'. J.B. Bailey, a Victorian historian of bodysnatching, comments that this piece of bad luck may have been the result of 'the other party' informing on Naples's gang.[57] Fortunately, the arrested man 'got clear' the following day. The ladder was presumably needed to scale the burial-ground wall, and gives some indication of the risks undertaken by the resurrectionists – a man carrying a ladder (even a rope one) around in the middle of the night can only have aroused suspicion. It is the only evidence found that ladders were in fact used by resurrectionists.

Another reference to inter-gang rivalry appears in a reference to a 'Jew' – probably a man called Israel Chapman[58] – also in the trade. On the 24 August 1812, Naples mentioned that returning from a reconnaissance expedition, the gang met this man's 'drag' near Charing Cross, and followed it until dark, when they 'lost scent' and went home. Bailey comments that this was probably intended to prevent Chapman from doing any business; but the next day it turned out he had already sold a body at St Bartholomew's anatomy school. Naples records that the gang had a row with the school over this, but must have been pacified as they supplied an adult woman's body there the following day.

It is not known whether Chapman dealt only in Jewish bodies, but these were certainly highly sought after by the schools, for reasons which were clear at the time: 'as the Jews bury early, their cemetery [yields] the best and freshest subjects, equal in freshness to the body sent to the venal undertaker, who having interred sand, inwardly chuckles at the solemn words, "dust to dust".'[59]

After the passage of the Anatomy Act, Bransby Cooper (the same man involved in the death of Stephen Pollard), conducted an investigation into the bodysnatchers' methods of work in the course of researching his uncle's biography, which was published in 1843. According to Bransby, whose informants were apparently *bona-fide* resurrectionists, these people had some pride in their work, which manifested itself in leaving the graves they had robbed looking as closely as possible as they had been before the exhumation. Bransby says the appearance of a grave after a resurrection was 'the chief point of distinction between what was termed a good or slovenly workman'.[60]

Later, we shall look at the many forms popular opposition to body-snatching took, and what efforts were made to thwart the resurrectionists. One technique was to place, in specific places on a grave, small and otherwise inconsequential objects – like a stick, stone, shell or flower – so that disturbance would be detectable. Bransby records that the most experienced bodysnatchers had an eye for such indicators, and would reserve and replace them to prevent detection.[61] There is no doubt that given the number of bodies that must have been snatched during this period, there were comparatively few cases of riot or of prosecution. So it would seem that in many cases such precautions were closely observed, and that many resurrectionists owed their continued livelihood to their observation.

It is not clear from Bransby's description whether the shell or stick technique was utilised by the very poor only. A passage in his book about pit burial immediately precedes one on the care the resurrectionists took to replace these indicators. In fact, it would have been a mode of detection which would commend itself to people of all social classes who buried their relations in graveyards and burial grounds – which would have included all but the very wealthy.

Even where they were buried in graves rather than pits, the poorer classes remained the most vulnerable to the predations of the bodysnatch-ers, as their coffins were so cheap and flimsy. Those who were financially more fortunate could afford stouter coffins, which would offer greater resistance against the resurrectionists' usual techniques. The solid wooden coffins of the moderately affluent would sometimes have to be sawn across.[62]

From what is known of mass graves and cheap coffins, and from the bodysnatcher's testimony before the Select Committee, it seems certain that the great majority of resurrected corpses were those of the poor. However, wealth did not ensure complete immunity: Sir Astley Cooper, appearing before the Select Committee, may have chilled the hearts of many present when he stated:

> The law does not prevent our obtaining the body of an individual if we think proper; for there is no person, let his situation in life be what it may, whom, if I were disposed to dissect, I could not obtain.[63]

Being questioned a little more closely on this statement, he went on:

> the law only enhances the price, and does not prevent the exhumation; nobody is secured by the law, it only adds to the price of the subject.[64]

Sir Astley's words prompt the inference that in many cases, the bodies of wealthy, intellectual, eccentric, insane, aristocratic or otherwise medically 'interesting' people from the middle and upper classes were obtained by various means.[65] The period during which the bodysnatchers were most active coincides with the inception of the great museum collections of anatomy and comparative anatomy, collections which depended very often on the bizarre and the monstrous, or simply upon the illustrious. In the Hunterian Collection at the Royal College of Surgeons in London, for example, amassed by John Hunter in the second half of the eighteenth century, may be found monstrous births (animal and human) in bottles, the skeletons of physical freaks, a cast of the brain cavity of Dean Swift's skull, death masks, murderers' skeletons and relics, and all sorts and conditions of medical prodigies – feet, heads, internal organs – pickled or dyed to show their peculiarities to better effect.

The collection also houses a number of preparations purchased after Hunter's death from Sir Astley Cooper's personal museum. Among them are dried examples of ligatured aneurysmal blood vessels, tied during surgery many years before the death of the person whose body provided the 'subject'. One such preparation was obtained by Cooper in the 1820s, after he was alerted by a surgeon from Beccles in Suffolk, of the death of a 'case' upon whom Cooper had operated over twenty years previously.[66] Sir Astley paid Hollis and Vaughan, two of his London resurrectionists, seven guineas for the 'subject' and nearly the same in expenses, for obtaining the body. All that is recorded about how the corpse was secured is that 'the surgeon gave them every facility to obtain it'.[67]

No evidence has been found as to whether this body was in fact exhumed, or if Hollis and Vaughan obtained it by other means: for there were other ways besides exhumation by which the resurrectionists could obtain 'subjects'. In this instance, for example, there is no information forthcoming either of a willingness on the part of the person concerned to be dissected, nor any familial opposition to it. The local surgeon was alive to Sir Astley's interests, for he 'had watched the case for years' and when death occurred, swiftly informed the baronet.[68] It is not known if the information had been solicited. Nevertheless, the fact that Hollis and Vaughan were paid to go and fetch the body suggests that some obstacle existed, while at the same time, the relatively small fee suggests that the obstacle could not have been very great. Quite possibly, it was a routine exhumation, but it may have involved bribing the sexton (something the local surgeon may have been unwilling to undertake), or, if the body had not yet been buried, other strategies may have been required.

For example, bodysnatchers were said have hired women to pose as broken-hearted relatives at workhouses, so as to claim the bodies of dead paupers.[69] In some parishes little was done in such cases to check the validity of claims, as giving up a body represented one fewer funeral on the local rates. With less official connivance but partly from the disorganised state of local government at this period, public mortuaries seldom existed, and bodies awaiting inquest were often stored in a locked room in a public house, or in a barn. An attempted case of snatching in such circumstances was reported from the Gaythorn Tavern in Manchester in 1831, where the body of a drowned woman was lying.[70]

Even where a public dead-house did exist, the same method was sometimes used. Sir Astley's steward was forced to return three bodies obtained in this way by Page – a bodysnatcher about whom very little else is known – who had stolen them from the Newington parish dead-house. Sir Astley had paid him £34.2s 6d for them, which he presumably lost.[71]

Again, in other circumstances, bodies could be obtained by liaison with servants.[72] Bodysnatchers are said to have obtained access (usually by bribery) to the coffin of a dead master or mistress lying in state, and to have replaced the body with a suitable weight. In many cases, the substitution of weights could be more easily effected by the undertaker,[73] and for this reason bribes were said to have been paid to them by resurrectionists. However, the widespread observance of the custom of viewing the corpse discussed earlier meant that this type of enterprise would not have been generally feasible, except perhaps among the wealthy, where leaden coffins – which were usually sealed by soldering in advance of the funeral – were in use. The recovery of bodies snatched in this manner could, however, be more easily effected, as the financially fortunate could offer rewards, which might outweigh the power of the bribe.[74]

In a country area, some way from the nearest school of anatomy, exhumation would probably have been the easiest and least suspicious mode of obtaining the body of an interesting 'subject'. Certainly, the body which Hollis and Vaughan obtained together from Beccles was not an expensive one from Sir Astley's point of view.[75]

However low his opinion of their characters,[76] Sir Astley had a very high opinion of the efficiency of the men in his pay. According to his nephew, Sir Astley boasted on one occasion that he could procure 'within three days, the body of a dignified official personage, who had been buried in a place apparently of inpenetrable security'.[77] All available evidence concurs that Astley Cooper had a remarkable way of getting what he wanted. While other surgeons found themselves the dupes and victims of the bodysnatchers,[78] Sir Astley 'so managed' according to his nephew,

> as to secure a better supply than most of the other teachers . . . there was not a burial place in London from which he could not . . . obtain any particular subject he might wish to be exhumed.[79]

Bransby's view gains credence from the fact that when asked by the Select Committee about prices paid for corpses, of those questioned, Sir Astley gave the lowest estimate.[80]

Astley Cooper was himself a curious mixture of the astute and able meritocrat, the brilliant and hardworking anatomist/surgeon, and the nepotistic patron of 'old corruption'. Physically attractive, and personally charming, he was able to consolidate in his own career the upwardly mobile track revealed to him by the Hunters.[81] He navigated his negotiations with bodysnatchers with quite as much ease as his consultations with wealthy clients. In the same year in which he gave public evidence of his collaboration with the resurrectionists, he was appointed surgeon to the King.[82] The irony of this contrast is compounded by Sir Astley's contempt for the bodysnatchers with whom he had dealings. Before the Select Committee, he gave it as his considered opinion that they were 'the lowest dregs of degradation'.

Let us consider, for a moment, the evidence for Sir Astley's assertion.

It is unfortunate that but for Naples's *Diary*, none of the material available to the historian of this subject was left by the resurrectionists themselves. All of it appears by the grace of and through the mediation of people like Bransby Cooper, whose evidence is both interested and partial – biased by class and professional loyalties (and in Bransby Cooper's case, compounded with family loyalty) – against the bodysnatchers. Virtually nothing positive is said about them. Yet they were of crucial importance to the history of the study of anatomy in Britain, and no examination of the subject would be complete without some discussion of them.

Sir Richard Owen, the nineteenth-century comparative anatomist and naturalist, left among his papers some manuscript notes which were probably made in the 1840s in response to a request for information for Bransby Cooper's work on his uncle's life.[83] The notes list and describe resurrectionists of whom Owen had personal knowledge. They contain information on the physical appearance and personal characteristics of ten men, and give details Owen had learned of their previous lives, their mode of operation, and what became of them after the Anatomy Act was passed.

According to Owen, Naples was in the original gang who were the 'regular' resurrection men for the London schools in 1814. The others in the gang at this time were Butler, Ben Crouch, Jack and Bill Harnett, and Hollis. It seems that this group eventually broke after bitter argument into two rival gangs, largely because Ben Crouch felt that higher prices were called for, while others (notably Bill Harnett and Naples) were willing to continue at the old rates.

The situation was complicated by the amateur involvement of Spitalfields weavers, whose activities threatened the 'regulars' livelihood, and who therefore risked physical violence or denunciation to the police when members of the original gang caught them in the act. The latter method of removing rivals – giving information to the police – seems to have been a favourite with Crouch, who appears from all accounts to have been, in his heyday, a tyrant, both towards his fellows and to the surgeons. Richard Owen described him as a heavy hulking tallish man, with coarse features marked with the smallpox . . . His manners were always rude, coarse and offensive, even when attempting to be civil.

Owen continued:

He was the counsellor, director, controller and treasurer of the whole party, and in dividing the spoils took especial care to cheat the rest of the party, who usually were not very clear-headed by the time their general accounts were gone through.[84]

According to Owen, both Crouch and Jack Harnett (an inseparable pair) had at various times worked in France and Spain, ostensibly as sutlers – selling provisions to the soldiers in the French and Peninsular campaigns – but in fact traversing the battlefields extracting teeth from the mouths of the dead. This in itself could be a highly lucrative occupation, as dentists paid well for what was then the basic material for dentures. Resurrectionists in Britain often found teeth a valuable sideline, removing them as a matter of routine before delivering corpses to the anatomists. 'It is the constant practice to take the teeth out first,' said one, 'because if the body be lost, the teeth are saved'.[85] A great deal of money could be earned in this way. Bransby Cooper cites an instance in which Murphy (a man who in the 1820s assumed a similar role to that held in the 1810s by Crouch) gained access to a burial vault attached to a nonconformist meeting house. In a few hours' work he extracted enough teeth to earn himself £60.[86] The prospect of profits of this magnitude must have gone a long way in the suppression of scruples concerning the repulsive nature and morality of the work.

Rural earnings for men during the first thirty years of the nineteenth century could be as low as nine shillings a week, and even skilled male urban workers seldom realised more than thirty shillings.[87] The attraction of large sums of money was, no doubt, the major reason why working people became bodysnatchers. However, not all those involved were as enterprising or as avaricious as Murphy. The prices given for bodies at the time Naples was writing his *Diary* (1811–1812) were about half of what they were in the 1820s when Murphy was at his most active, and were more or less fixed at four guineas for an adult body – but less if the body had undergone a *post-mortem*.[88] The *Diary* mentions the sale of teeth, extremities, and on one occasion, a head, to the anatomy schools, as well as foetuses, and the bodies of children.

Despite all these possible sources of income, it would seem that after expenses had been deducted,[89] and the remainder shared out among the gang, individual earnings as recorded in the *Diary* are not very impressive. Settling up seems to have taken place every week or so, and for those weeks Naples recorded figures, his share appears to average at about eleven guineas weekly. This might represent daily reconnaissance, delivery of bodies in London, and packaging and dispatch to Edinburgh or other destinations, as well as several nights' resurrecting. Although in comparison to the wages of working people in ordinary occupations, these body-snatchers were earning a very good living indeed, in comparison to the yield from Murphy's escapade, their income was modest.

The unpopularity and danger of the task of obtaining bodies from graves had fallen to the resurrectionists because the anatomists and surgeons were unwilling to expose themselves to the risks involved. Fees for human corpses reflected some component of compensation for the risk undertaken by resurrectionists, and it was for this reason that they probably had some justification in asking for higher fees, particularly in the 1820s, when strenuous popular opposition to grave-robbery made their task even more dangerous than before.

Bransby Cooper, not usually noted for his understanding of the lives of working people, nevertheless understood that the comparative wealth resurrectionists could achieve was the attraction – and could be the downfall – of those who became involved in robbing graves. Discussing various unsuccessful attempts some bodysnatchers made to consolidate their small fortunes in property, Cooper commented:

> The inconsiderate expenditure of money which distinguished these people is easily accounted for, when we consider the comparatively large sums of money which they sometimes suddenly received; never before, perhaps, having had more than a few shillings at a time in their possession.[90]

Evidence given before the Select Committee in 1828 concerning the character of those involved in the exhumation of the dead for dissection makes no such allowances. References to the bodysnatchers, both in evidence and in questions from the chair, are heavy with distaste. Cumulatively, the evidence as to their character is that they were thieves, felons, villains of the blackest dye. The Committee's *Report* went so far as to say: 'If, with a view to favour Anatomy, exhumation should be allowed to continue, it appears almost a necessary consequence that thieves should also be tolerated'.[91] Yet a comparison of the testimony given before the Committee with the later writings of Sir Richard Owen and Bransby Cooper serves to question the accuracy of this assertion.

Given the state of the law at the time – the dead human body did not constitute property, so taking a corpse from its grave was offensive, but not theft – the bodysnatchers could not fairly be called thieves on the ground that they 'stole' dead bodies. Taking this as a basic premise, from the material left by Sir Richard Owen and Bransby Cooper a table has been constructed showing the names, previous occupations and later lives (where these are known) of twelve men, who represent the most well-known and regular London resurrectionists in the period c.1810–1832 (Figure 1).

Previous life		Later life
Porter in a dissecting room	BUTLER	Articulator and dealer in bones; sentenced to death for mail-coach robbery, but reprieved
Sailor, then corn porter	'Patrick' CONNOLLY	In business in London with 'an excellent character'
Son of Guy's Hospital carpenter. Introduced into bodysnatching by Sir Astley Cooper	Ben CROUCH	Bought a hotel at Margate but failed when his source of capital became known. Became 'deeply connected with thieves'. Died in poverty
Younger brother of Ben	Jem CROUCH	Killed in action abroad, while serving with the British Legion
?	Bill HARNETT	Died of TB in St Thomas' Hospital, with a violent fear of dissection
?	Jack HARNETT	Invested money from bodysnatching. Died leaving c.£6000 to his family, c.1840
Gravedigger: lost his job through conniving with bodysnatchers	Bill HOLLIS	Hackney coach business; through disloyalty, became destitute
Gentleman's servant discharged for stealing glass from carriage windows. Served time in hulks	'L' (?Tom LIGHT) (?LLEWELLYN)	Horsekeeper and carrier/con-man?
Superintendent of St Thomas' Hospital dissecting room	William MILLARD	Failed as a restaurateur and died in prison after being caught bodysnatching
?	MURPHY	Invested money from bodysnatching in property, became 'respectable'
Son of 'respectable' stationer and book binder. Navy, then gravedigger – enticed into bodysnatching via sale of teeth	Joshua NAPLES	Given a job at St Thomas' Hospital dissecting room
Stone-mason's labourer	VAUGHAN	Transported for theft of grave-clothes

Figure 1 Lives of Twelve London Resurrectionists
Sources: See chapter 3, note 51.

The table shows that according to available information, only one of these men was associated with crime before his involvement with the surgeons. It seems likely that if any further information of this nature had been available to Sir Richard Owen or to Bransby Cooper, they would not have refrained from repeating it. The crime involved the stealing of plate glass from the carriage windows of the man's wealthy employers – only a petty criminal activity.

The men's different fates are also instructive. Two died during or shortly after their involvement in the trade. Two more disappear from view as a result of their calling – one died in prison under sentence for attempted bodysnatching, the other, with his wife (who had also been involved) was transported for the theft of grave-clothes. Only two appear to have been involved in crime; one directly – being convicted for highway robbery, and the other, by association – allegedly 'deeply connected with thieves',[92] while two more, both involved in cabbing or carrying, seem to have operated on the fringes of the law. The remaining four men managed in varying degrees to assume a normal, even 'respectable', lifestyle. It would appear that the connection between bodysnatching and crime was somewhat overstressed before the Select Committee.

Apart from the information contained in the table given here, the evidence for an association between bodysnatching and crime seems largely to have been based on hearsay, and is not specific as to whether those involved were already criminals, or became so as a result of their calling. The three unnamed bodysnatchers questioned by the Select Committee were not asked how they became involved in their grisly business, or if they had any other trade. In the opinion of Benjamin Brodie, the resurrectionists were

> the outcasts of society, who, being pointed out as resurrection men, [are] unable to maintain themselves by any honest employment and are driven to become thieves and housebreakers. . .[93]

It would seem from the table that the first association with resurrecting the dead was invariably an occupational one, rather than the result of supposed criminal propensities. Previous occupations are known for nine of the twelve men appearing in the table. Excluding the one who had been involved in petty crime, all remaining eight had some occupational association with handling or dealing with the dead: two had worked in dissecting rooms, two had been gravediggers, one was a stone-mason's labourer, probably accustomed to erecting and re-erecting tombstones. Another was a corn porter, persuaded into the business by a seasoned bodysnatcher, who had probably employed him and his cart in the transport of dead bodies around London.

The most convincing evidence of the corrupting influence of the 'profession' is to be found in the life of Ben Crouch. His connection with bodysnatching came by way of his father's occupation – carpenter at Guy's

Hospital. He probably taught his son the art of making cheap coffins for the poor people dying there, and needing burial in the hospital 'crib' or poor ground. From an early stage in his training, Crouch junior must have learned that as often as not, the coffins his father made were emptied of their contents by the resurrectionists – if, indeed, they ever had any contents.

Ann Millard, herself the wife of a resurrectionist, refers to a case in which a man with a medically interesting enlargement of the head died at Guy's. A mock funeral was conducted for the benefit of the dead man's family, but his skeleton was said in 1825 to be 'one of the greatest curiosities in the museum at Guy's Hospital'.[94] Whether Sir Astley Cooper (who was teaching anatomy and surgery at Guy's at the time) had any knowledge of this case is not known, though this seems more than likely. Naples's *Diary* mentions many visits to lift bodies from Guy's 'crib'. The young Crouch probably learned to make his coffins with a measure of cynicism.

The spatial element present in the language Sir Astley used to describe the bodysnatchers ('the lowest dregs of degradation') indicates that his most strongly felt reaction to them was one of *social* disgust, which he conveyed to his (approximate) social peers on the Select Committee.[95] It is difficult to believe that this disgust had not also communicated itself to the resurrectionists themselves. This may go some way towards explaining the hostility which appears to have characterised much of the dealing between surgeons and resurrectionists – particularly with Crouch, who seems to have lacked the deference[96] and fidelity of Naples or Harnett.

From Bransby Cooper's *Life* of his uncle, it would seem that Sir Astley cordially hated Crouch. This dislike was most probably mutual, fortified by the powerful position each held with regard to the other, and the grudging interdependence of their relationship. Sir Astley's evidence to the Select Committee was aimed, in the long term, at denying Crouch and his ilk their livelihood. It is a fine irony if Sir Astley was thinking of Crouch when he called the resurrectionists the 'lowest dregs' and adverted to their criminal propensities, since according to Sir Richard Owen it was in fact Sir Astley who was personally responsible for Crouch's introduction to the 'profession'.[97] If this calling corrupted Crouch, responsibility rests partly with the baronet.

Despite the peculiar status of the human corpse in the eyes of the law in the early nineteenth century, being legally defined as 'non-property' did not prevent the corpse from being regarded otherwise in the world outside the courts. Outside of, and in opposition to, the law, a small but important sector of the population – anatomists, artists, physicians, surgeons, articulators, dentists, and their suppliers – depended in varying degrees for their economic survival upon the ease with which the human corpse could be treated as a commodity.

Corpses were bought and sold, they were touted, priced, haggled over, negotiated for, discussed in terms of supply and demand, delivered, imported, exported, transported. Human bodies were compressed into boxes, packed in sawdust, packed in hay, trussed up in sacks, roped up like hams, sewn in canvas, packed in cases, casks, barrels, crates and hampers; salted, pickled or injected with preservative. They were carried in carts and waggons, in barrows and steam-boats; manhandled, damaged in transit, and hidden under loads of vegetables. They were stored in cellars and on quays. Human bodies were dismembered and sold in pieces, or measured and sold by the inch.[98]

That part of Charlotte Atkins, of James Burwell, Eliza Brightman and her infant son, of Mark Rivett or of Jane Burdell which had been washed and laid out, watched and waked, buried and wept over by bereaved families, was nominated by the anatomists a 'subject' and by the resurrectionists, a 'thing'. No longer an object worthy of respect, the body of each of these people[99] became a token of exchange, subject to commercial dealing, and then to the final objectification of the dissection room.

The apotheosis of this process is to be found in the cases in which living human beings were deprived of life for the sake of the fee anatomists paid for their cadavers. Burke and Hare, and the 'London Burkers' Bishop and Williams, are discussed later. The point here has been to draw attention to the process of reification and commodification which occasioned their crimes.

II

THE ACT

A necessity for doing something cannot be admitted to be identical with a necessity for doing mischief.

Michael Sadler, 1842

THE SANCTITY OF THE GRAVE ASSERTED

Whatever the possessors of the practical insensibility, acquired in the dissecting room, may assert to the contrary, we hold it, with the greater part of the community, to be at once a formidable and lamentable evil, that a parent cannot commit its offspring, nor the offspring its parent, to the earth, without the distressing suspicion intruding itself upon the mind, that in a few hours one or the other may be torn from its last resting place, and made an object of traffic among a band of ruffians.

Lancet editorial, 1829.[1]

We covet a lengthened if not a permanent residence in the grave . . . It seems, indeed, to be a prevalent notion that the body must be preserved in some way or other, that it must be suffered to rest in peace, quietly to await the general resurrection.

London Medical Gazette, 1828.[2]

Popular tumults at gallows – vocal, violent, and often successful in denying surgeons their prey – were a contributory factor in the decision in 1783 to transfer London executions from Tyburn to Newgate itself. Since both prison and surgeons' hall were contiguous to the scaffold, would-be rescuers were put at a decided disadvantage. The move was part of a general change, which over the following century resulted in the gradual withdrawal of execution from the public realm of the gallows, to the privacy of the prison.[3] This process ensured among other things that the criminal was more surely in the power of the punishing authority; less liable to escape or to rescue prior to execution, and wholly at its disposal afterwards. So, in the half-century preceding the Anatomy Act, those whose death-sentence included dissection were increasingly certain to undergo it.

Tightening official grip on the body of the offender, however, rendered dissection no less abhorrent. On the contrary: friends of a man hanged and dissected at Carlisle in the 1820s undertook to revenge him, and inflicted severe personal injuries on all medical men involved. One was killed, and another shot in the face.[4] Although this was of course an extreme reaction, it was certainly the case that hanging the corpse in chains on a gibbet was popularly regarded as preferable to dissection.[5] What later incredulous commentators seem to have missed or misunderstood was that in eighteenth- and early nineteenth-century popular belief, not only were the anatomists the agents of the law, but they could be the agents of death. Genuine cases were known of incomplete hangings, in which the 'dead' were brought back to life,[6] and plans for celebrated corpse-rescues centred on the possibility that the noose had not fully done its work. Folk-tales circulated about famous criminals revived by friends, and these ideas were fostered by the publicity Humane Society resuscitations attracted after apparent drownings.[7] Increased control over the body of the condemned rendered rescue and revival virtually impossible.

It was popularly understood that the surgeons' official function and interest in a murderer's corpse was not to revive, but rather to destroy it. Dissection was a very *final* process. It denied hope of survival – even the survival of identity after death. Above all, it threw into relief the collaborative role of the medical profession in the actual execution of death. The Carlisle surgeons bore the brunt of the resentment and frustration felt by the dead man's friends, for in their eyes the doctors had murdered him more surely than the hangman's rope.[8]

Popular hostility to dissection derived from sources older and deeper than its use in public execution – it would not have been introduced in the Tudor era as a punishment for 'the most heinous kind of criminal homicide'[9] had government not appreciated its power in infringing popular taboos. Its continuing success as a punishment is evidenced both by its bitter unpopularity and its regular use right up until 1832. This success resulted from its flagrant trespass upon popular belief, and the insolence of its denial of customary observances. Dissection represented a gross assault upon the integrity and identity of the body *and* upon the repose of the soul, each of which – in other circumstances – would have been carefully fostered.

Whatever the theological position on the spiritual status of the buried corpse, Christian sentiment endorsed the need for permitting the natural decay of the integral body, and for its protection during the process. An extract from a newspaper appeal for subscriptions towards the building of a cholera monument in Sheffield in 1835 will illustrate:

> . . . the Committee ventured to commence the work, with the
> reasonable expectation that they would be enabled so to secure and
> signalise the spot, that it may remain, for generations to come, an
> unviolated sanctuary of the relics of our unfortunate townspeople
> and neighbours, who were thus awfully removed by a malady so little
> understood, and so much dreaded that they were not allowed to be

laid in the graves of their fathers, but even in death, by a decree of the legislature, were required to be buried 'without the camp'. In the lonely spot provided for their interment, the bodies of three hundred and thirty-nine of these, our kindred, our neighbours, or our friends, were day after day deposited, with Christian rites; and there they await – as yet without a stone to tell where they lie – the summons of the last trumpet.[10]

The subject of physical resurrection was a controversial one in the years preceding the Anatomy Act, brought to the public eye largely as a result of the bodysnatchers' activities. A prosecuting lawyer at Norwich Assizes in 1828 seems to have expressed a general sentiment when he said that:

every decent man would expect, that when he had followed the body of his wife or daughter to the silent tomb, 'where the wicked cease from troubling, and the weary are at rest,' their cold clay should there remain till the last trump shall sound, and the graves give up their dead.[11]

To its critics, the lawyer's view may have been irrational and logically indefensible, but they recognised its force. Both the *Examiner* and the *Lancet* responded swiftly – vilifying him with pandering to 'the vilest prejudices'.[12] Wakley sought to subvert the lawyer's self-appointment as spokesman for Christian values, by undermining his argument:

it rarely happens that religion is dragged into the service of forensic argument, without suffering degradation. . . . What an idea of omnipotence is conveyed in [the] supposition, that the miracle of the resurrection could be frustrated, or affected by the misdemeanour of a body-snatcher!

Yet even Wakley admitted that 'ties of kindred or friendship' were grounds for a 'natural horror' of dissection.[13]

As in the search for genuine evidence of the bodysnatchers themselves, it has proved difficult to find first-hand evidence of the emotional responses of people whose relatives and friends were found to have been stolen from their graves. Nevertheless, the evidence available permits an intuition of the stress inflicted by such a discovery upon those whose minds were already riven with grief.

Much has been written in the present day on the subject of grief and its therapy, and of the dangers to the psyche of unresolved grief. It is recognised that cherishing the memory of a dead person can have an important therapeutic effect on the grieving survivor, and that even today visiting/tending a grave can aid the process of coming to terms with loss.[14] The conflict of interest between bereaved and bodysnatchers was necessarily at its sharpest when mourners were at their most vulnerable. Corpses were most valuable when freshest – at precisely the same period during which most funerary customs were focused, and in the earliest stages of post-funerary grief.

To a grieving spouse or parent of the early nineteenth century, the trauma of finding stolen the body of that person near whom one had intended to lie after one's own death, for example, cannot have failed to have had a deeply distressing effect; compounding the loss of the live person by death, with an existential ache for the dead physicality of the person lost again, and irrevocably, by theft. Colin Murray Parkes' work on bereavement in our own time discusses some mourners' strong imaginative perception of their dead relatives' sensations in the grave – suffering in inclement weather, for example.[15] To such a mourner, the conception of their spouse or child dragged out of the coffin, shoved into a sack, manhandled in transit, stretched out on a slab, decapitated or dismembered, and cut about by (possibly irreverent)[16] training anatomists, may in many cases have resulted in profound psychological disturbance.[17]

Although it was not articulated in these terms at the time, it was nevertheless recognised by contemporaries that the discovery of body-snatching could cause mourners deep emotional distress. Newspaper reports occasionally shared this recognition with their readers, as for example, in a report from *The Times* in 1832, concerning the theft of a poor man's body from the dead-house at Cripplegate Workhouse.

The dead man's daughter, whose elderly mother was at that time lying bedridden in the workhouse, applied to Sir Peter Laurie, sitting at the Guildhall, for assistance. Her father's body, which she had gone to view, had been sacked up, humped over the workhouse wall, dragged through a lumber yard, and loaded into a cart. A young boy who had witnessed the gang of four resurrectionists in their activities was intimidated by one of them until the cart was out of sight. The woman hoped that Sir Peter would assist her to recover the body, 'for she was much hurt at the circumstance'.[18]

Another report provides an indication of the effects of such emotional disturbance on a mass scale. In February 1795, three men were discovered leaving Lambeth burial ground carrying five human bodies in sacks. The Vestry records continue:

> . . . in consequence of such a discovery, people of all descriptions,
> whose relatives had been buried in that Ground, resorted thereto,
> and demanded to dig for them . . . being refused, they in great
> numbers forced their way in, and in spight of every effort the parish
> Officers could use, began like mad people to tear up the ground.
> [Many empty coffins were found.] Great distress and agitation of
> mind was manifest in every one, and some, in a kind of phrensy, ran
> away with the coffins of their deceased relations.[19]

Such demonstrations of public anguish occasionally found expression in riot and violence against bodysnatchers, or anatomists. More often, the conflict between constructs of the human corpse as 'sacred', 'scientific' or 'saleable' was fought in the graveyards: the commodification of the corpse provoked a spirited public assertion of the sanctity of the grave.

In the century before the Anatomy Act was passed, the general state of urban churchyards left much to be desired. In the *Commons Journal* for 1746–7 for example, may be found the text of a petition from the parishioners of St Andrew's, Holborn, praying for Parliamentary assistance in their sorry plight. The two parish churchyards, the petition said,

> are so full of Corps, that it is difficult to dig a Grave without digging up some parts of a Corps before decayed; which makes it very offensive to the Inhabitants & the Reason many Corps are carried out of the Parish to be buried.[20]

Over the course of the eighteenth century, urban churchyards which had originally served small parishes for centuries became inadequate for their population, as the growing hamlets they served became surrounded and absorbed into larger towns. This was the case all over London, and in the vicinity of burgeoning provincial metropolises, over the entire period bodysnatchers were active. The situation did not improve until the mid-nineteenth century, after much activity in favour of burial reform both in and outside Parliament. Change was eventually effected by a series of Orders-in-Council enforcing the closure of inner-city graveyards; and by a parallel series of Acts of Parliament, authorising the purchase of land and the sale of shares by private cemetery companies.[21]

There is little doubt that the poor state of urban burial grounds had long worked to the bodysnatchers' benefit. Nor was this unknown at the time. Those who could afford to avoid burying their relatives in such grounds, did so. But many people could not find the money for a vault in a church or chapel, and had little option but to risk burial in an urban burial-ground, or to try one a little further out of town. Even these, however, had a high incidence of disturbance.

In the 1780s, a little book entitled *A View of Society and Manners in High and Low Life*[22] mentioned under the heading 'Resurrection Rig' that this was a slang term for earning one's living by listening for passing-bells, frequenting ale-houses to learn who had died, and colluding with undertaker or sexton to obtain bodies for a 'Resurrection Doctor', usually for the sum of five guineas apiece.

> This Resurrection Rig is carried on in little country churchyards within a few miles of London, where it is particularly necessary to survey the churchyards weekly. . . to inspect and enquire very minutely [into the causes of any disturbance to graves.]

It is clear from this passage that it was common knowledge that the connivance of undertakers, and particularly of burial-ground employees was important in the success of the enterprise. In central London, the co-operation of sextons was essential, and in many cases, these people were themselves closely involved in the business of exhumation. One observer described in some detail a technique used by gravediggers, even in quite deep graves, by which the coffin was buried, but the body which should have been in it was left in the loose earth just below the surface, for ease of snatching.[23] Figure 1, which lists the previous occupations of several known bodysnatchers, shows that at least one had previously been a gravedigger who had lost his job as a result of connivance with resurrectionists, turning to bodysnatching as a means of livelihood. Burial reformers suspected that sextons were merely carrying out orders, and that responsibility for graveyard malpractices rested above them.[24] A witness of the appalling state of poor graves at Preston was driven to the conclusion that the clergy actively encouraged bodysnatching by the practice of pit burial.[25]

There can be little doubt that the majority of corpses sold to the anatomists were those of the poor. The social imparity in the source material for anatomy was largely due to the advantages of which the financially fortunate were able to avail themselves by virtue of their affluence. Gradations of social class were very evident in the burial practices of this era; the aristocracy and other very wealthy people had their vaults and private chapels, triple coffins (wood, lead, wood) and retinues of servants to guard their remains. The cost of a funeral for the aristocracy in the early 1840s could go to £1500[26] – beside which the funeral bill from the Lower Grosvenor Street undertakers of Miss Martha Harley's funeral in 1824 looks modest at £803.11s.[27] A considerable part of the cost in such funerals often covered transport out of the metropolis to (safer) vaults near country seats. The financially comfortable – like the Right Honourable Lady Elizabeth Colville in 1839 (£48.19s.6d)[28] often also had double or triple coffins, but were less secure in a church or chapel, or even less so if the vault was in a churchyard.

Respectable tradespeople could spend between £20 and £50 on stout coffins, often double, and a deep grave situated in a private burial ground whose management offered better protection than a church or parochial burial ground. Henry Angelo's funeral cost £18.13s.6d in Marylebone in 1834, and included double rows of best nails on his coffin, while Joseph Tillett's funeral cost £7.14s.6d and included a half-oak coffin, and truncheon-bearers in the procession.[29] Between this level of affluence and the pit burial that the very poor endured came a spectrum of poor-ish coffins and graves, all of them easily vulnerable to the predations of the resurrectionists.

The sense of vulnerability to which Wakley referred in the epigraph to this chapter affected all social classes. It was sometimes justified, too: in 1829 Wakley knew of at least one London graveyard catering for substantial citizens which was actually owned by an anatomist.

> From this place he had obtained a famous supply . . . as it was a
> secure and 'comfortable resting place'. . . and he could charge pretty
> handsomely for burying a body there, and afterwards get from his
> pupils from eight to twelve guineas for taking it up again! Such is the
> profitable traffic of the human carcass butcher: a traffic which has
> led, in some schools, to the dissection of thrice as many bodies as were
> required for the purposes of science.[30]

As it became evident that despite stout coffins and deep graves, even the
affluent were liable to do service on the anatomist's slab, various entrepreneurs began to market security devices for graves. Metal coffins were
patented as early as 1781,[31] but it was not until 1818 that a coffin was
registered with the expressed purpose of frustrating the resurrectionists.

The Patent Coffin, as it popularly came to be known, caused a public
sensation when it was introduced.[32] Patented by Edward Bridgman, a
London tallow chandler, the coffin was designed to be made in cast or
wrought iron, with concealed spring catches on the inner side of the lid to
prevent levering, and joined in such a way as to thwart any attempt to force
the sides of the coffin apart. In the same patent application, Bridgman
described designs for a way of connecting head and foot stones by secure
iron bars, and for a cast iron vault-tomb built upon similar principles to the
patent coffin, but extending some distance below ground, to serve as a
resurrectionist-proof receptacle for more than one wooden coffin.[33]

Others followed Bridgman in this enterprise, patenting their ideas for
securing corpses inside coffins with iron straps,[34] or for reinforcing wooden
coffins with metal bands fastened with an 'original screw', which once in
place could not be withdrawn.[35] In Scotland, the most usual method used
by those who could afford it, was the 'mortsafe', an iron grid or cage, either
wholly encasing the coffin and buried with it, or set in mortar above
ground, covering the whole extent of the gravespace.[36] Several of the last
design may still be seen *in situ*, in Greyfriars churchyard – in the centre of
Edinburgh – which was continually vulnerable to resurrectionist
activity.[37]

The wealthy could also afford, on an individual basis, to pay people to
guard their graves,[38] sometimes with guns at the ready,[39] or they are said
to have utilised their gamekeepers' spring guns, to catch any unwary
bodysnatcher who had failed to observe the trip-wires during daylight
reconnaissance.[40]

The poor, of course, could not avail themselves of sophisticated coffins
and protective devices, but nevertheless did their best with what was to
hand; mixing sticks and straw with the earth returned to the grave, so that
the loose earth over their dead would not be so easy to remove, the fibres
choking the bodysnatchers' wooden shovels.[41]

Unable to afford the more effective forms of deterrence to which the

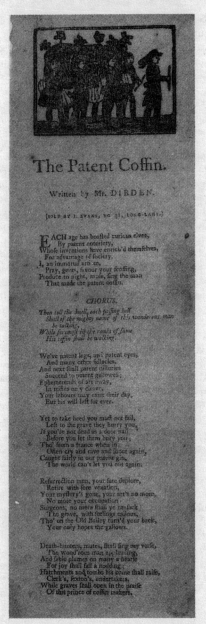

10 'The Patent Coffin', a popular song, broadsheet, 1818

wealthy had access, the poor were induced to act communally. Whole parishes would unite against the resurrectionists, erecting watch-houses in parish churchyards,[42] or lamps to light the ground at night.[43] Some parishes had communal mortsafes or 'jankers' – huge coffin-shaped pieces of stone or metal put on new graves.[44] One, described by a historian of Aberdeenshire, was seven feet three inches in length, two and a half feet wide at the shoulders, and was one and a half feet in depth. 'The weight of it was great, and it could only be lifted with a block and tackle. Its use effectually prevented "lifting".'[45] In Scotland, several parishes erected dead-houses, where for a certain fee, coffins were stored securely for weeks, so that bodies would be useless from putrefaction before burial. One such dead-house might serve a relatively large number of villages,[46] although fees could be high. One may still be seen today at Crail, in Fife.

In other places, the poor instead clubbed together to provide mutual protection in the event of a death. Alexander Somerville relates how in 1819 his brother, a cooper at Innerwick, a small village near Dunbar, organised 'a parish watch for the churchyard, to prevent resurrectionists from disturbing the repose of the dead . . .'[47] Cobbett, speaking to a Manchester audience in 1831, referred to the protection the game laws provided for the 'property of the rich' and contrasted the position of the poor, endeavouring to protect their dead relatives. He told the story of one of his own workers who had asked 'with tears in his eyes' for an advance of twelve shillings on his wages, to pay towards the cost of having a watch on the grave of his daughter, who was about to be buried.

> Judge you, gentlemen, of the feelings of country people on the
> subject, when I tell you there are clubs in the country parishes of
> Sussex, Kent, Surrey, Hampshire, and I suppose in all the northern
> counties . . . for the purpose of forming a fund for defraying the
> expense of watching the graves of relations . . . [or] of the members
> themselves . . .[48]

From the presence of an anatomy school in the vicinity, many areas of Britain were under constant threat. All burial grounds in London, Edinburgh, Glasgow, Dublin, the University and county towns, Aberdeen, Manchester, Liverpool, Birmingham, Bristol and Exeter, were vulnerable to grave-robbery for this reason, as well as grounds within easy riding distance of these. With swift steam navigation, ports which may previously have been ignored became the source of traffic for other towns. Very often, however, precautions might not be observed unless some indication of likely attention from bodysnatchers was present, and inhabitants of many areas did not feel it necessary to be on constant alert. Often this meant that bodysnatchers could work in relative safety out of the vicinity of the schools, sometimes for long periods of time, their activity being unsuspected. A case of this kind occurred in Great Yarmouth in 1827. A party of bodysnatchers hired a house near the churchyard and

11   Dead House at Crail, Fife, erected 1826 and still extant

operated from there – in league with the local grave-digger – for two
months. Bodies were tightly packed in cases shorter and narrower than
coffins to avoid suspicion, and sent by stage-coach via Norwich, to
London.

Eventually, the suspicions of the local police were roused, and they
determined to catch the gang in the act. But, through 'misplaced confidence' in the grave-digger, the bodysnatchers escaped, and were only later
caught by the active efforts of a police officer, Peter Coble. Three men, one
of them the London resurrectionist Vaughan operating under an assumed
name, were tried for the offence.

Between discovery and apprehension of the gang, news got out around
the town. According to a manuscript description written after the event by
J.F. Cooper,[49] Mr George Beck – a local baker whose wife had recently
died, determined to examine her grave. If was found to be empty:

> A great sensation followed; and the Church-yard became thronged
> with People who employed themselves in opening the different
> Graves of their deceased friends or relations. This extraordinary
> scene continued during three or four days, the result of which was,
> the discovery of the exhumation of a number of bodies. . . .

The similarity of this description to that reproduced above concerning the
Lambeth case in the 1790s[50] is striking. The mixture of grief and anger felt
by the bereaved inhabitants is evident from Cooper's notes. Upon capture,
it was lucky for Vaughan that he was not recognised by the crowd, 'who
were . . . awaiting his arrival, until [he] had nearly reached the Town Hall,

or his life would have been in imminent danger . . .'.

It has proved difficult to trace any further cases of bodysnatching in Great Yarmouth for some time after this date, so it would seem that the trauma of discovery served both to alert the local population, and to warn off prospective resurrectionists. Mary Gidney died soon after these events at the age of 74. Her tombstone perhaps expresses the hopes of all those subsequently buried in Great Yarmouth churchyard:

> May spotless spirits of the just
> Watch o'er her Tomb and Guard her Dust;
> Preserve it safe in soft repose,
> Till the Arch Angel's Trumpet blows,
> And then immortal may it rise
> And mount in glory to the skies![51]

Despite the legal position that the human corpse did not constitute property, by the early nineteenth century there existed a sizeable sector of the community whose economic existence and survival depended in varying degrees upon the investment of property in the human corpse. Similarly, although the law generally failed to regard the removal of a corpse from its grave as a theft, or as a crime meriting severe punishment, the popular consensus of opinion demanded redress for the wrong which had been done to the dead, to their mourners, and to the community.

As a result of these paradoxes, guardians of the law found themselves in a difficult position, both with regard to the medical profession, and to public opinion. The disjunction between statutory and popular conceptions of justice for bodysnatchers is particularly evident in descriptions of an 1832 case, in which two medical students were caught at Inveresk, a village near Edinburgh, attempting to snatch a body from the churchyard. They were 'confined in a private house' until morning, when *at their own request, they were committed to gaol* as ' a place of greater security from the threatened vengeance of the outraged citizens'. The following afternoon,

> . . . a crowd of several hundreds assembled round the gaol, provided with axes and other implements to break it open, and do execution upon the offenders, who . . . had been previously remitted to the sheriff. We understand they have since been liberated on Bail.[52]

It was not unknown for anatomists to have the ear of public officials of quite high status, and to command the sympathies of the bench. Magistrates and judges were closer socially to top physicians and surgeons than were the generality of their 'subjects'. Some may indeed have had a genuinely enlightened interest in science, or more self-interestedly, may have recognised the benefits accruing to their own social strata from the use of snatched bodies. Nevertheless, such personages were not uniformly sympathetic to grave-robbery, and were very much aware that if sentences were too lenient, the public would not be slow to take the administration of justice into its own hands, and lynch law might prevail.[53]

The position of the police was even more problematic, in that because of the social origins of most officers, there was likely to be sympathy among them with the experience and feelings of mourners in cases of bodysnatching. Glennon, a Southwark police officer interviewed before the Select Committee, had been responsible for the recovery of between fifty and a hundred bodies stolen before burial from local houses. His commitment to this activity was personal, and so highly regarded was he for this, that neighbours presented him with a silver staff in appreciation.[54] However, orders could be passed down to officers like Glennon to turn a blind eye to the theft of bodies from poor grounds – not to be over-zealous in seeking out either who was responsible, or the whereabouts of stolen bodies.[55] Officers could be sacked for failing to observe such orders,[56] so an individual's commitment to law and order – which was often synonymous with keeping his job – was liable to conflict with more private beliefs and loyalties.

In the Yarmouth case, in an area unaccustomed to resurrectionist activities, both the police and the local magistrates were active in the apprehension of the grave-robbers. Nevertheless, when the case came to court, two members of the gang were discharged, and the other, Vaughan, was sent to London for trial, where he received a sentence of only six months' imprisonment. To put the lenience of this sentence into some perspective, it should be remembered that contemporary poachers were regularly transported for the theft of wild fowl.[57] Whether Vaughan's luck was due to the leniency of the local bench, its interest in fostering the study of anatomy, or to instructions received from above, is unclear. The London school to which Vaughan had been supplying Yarmouth corpses was Sir Astley Cooper's, and it is known that the baronet had sent an assistant to the hearing with funds to bail Vaughan out. Cooper paid Vaughan an allowance of ten shillings per week for the duration of his imprisonment.[58]

Relations between the surgeon-anatomists and their suppliers are difficult to ascertain, since of necessity their negotiations were held in secret. Occasionally, however, indications arise of their peculiarly interdependent relationship. For example, if a bodysnatcher had been working exclusively for a single anatomist or school, as in this case, the anatomist might feel obliged to assist with character references for the court or with funds – for living expenses in prison, fines, and perhaps to provide bail sureties.[59] These attentions were based upon notions of responsibility mutually agreed upon, but for which documentary evidence survives only for the part played by the surgeon-anatomists. The resurrectionists' part in this bargain can only be ascertained negatively – by observing how little trouble actually arose at the schools themselves, and how rarely prosecutions involved their employers.

From this negative evidence, we can infer that the resurrectionists' part in the bargain was to take most of the risk involved in obtaining bodies, to supply them at agreed prices and to deliver them with the utmost circumspection, so as to draw no unnecessary public attention to the anatomists or their premises.[60] For, despite all that is said here concerning popular opposition to the activities of bodysnatchers and their employers, if we consider the scale of grave-robbery which must have proceeded to supply all the schools, individual surgeons, physicians, dentists, artists, and students in Britain – probably involving several thousand bodies annually – it will be clear that discovery, although it emerges sporadically in the press, was comparatively rare.

The nature of their bargain with the anatomists meant that the resurrectionists took the brunt of popular feeling against grave-robbery. In addition, the graves they opened were often at a distance from the schools they supplied.

It is not surprising that to the kin or neighbours of those whom the bodysnatchers unearthed the surgeon/anatomists were only of distant and secondary importance as targets of abuse and blame.

Many instances might be cited – like those at Lambeth, at Great Yarmouth, and at Inveresk – in which the public response to the discovery of a grave-robbery was one of violence and near-riot. At Hereford, in January 1832, two men were apprehended for stealing the body of William Hardman, an army veteran, whose naked body had been delivered to the local coach-office in a hamper. The men appeared before the Mayor, and throughout their three-hour examination, 'a large mass of persons' waited angrily outside. The resurrectionists were ordered to be transferred to the country gaol: 'On their way thither, they were followed by an immense crowd, and assailed with the most vociferous expressions of disgust and contempt . . .'.[61]

A similar scene occurred at Greenwich that April when, after 'a determined resistance', three known resurrectionists were apprehended by police, with a cart in which were found the bodies of two elderly men. *The Times* reported that those arrested were members of 'a desperate gang of resurrectionists, who have for this long time past been a terror to the inhabitants of Deptford, Greenwich, Camberwell, Peckham, Woolwich, and the whole of the west of Kent.'[62] A rumour that the men in the cart had been 'burked' (murdered for dissection)

> . . . instantly spread like wildfire. A crowd of several thousand persons soon assembled . . . and in the most menacing and outrageous manner called upon the police to let the Burkites out, saying that it would soon be revenged upon them. At one period . . . it was thought that the station-house would be completely pulled down by the infuriated and incensed assemblage.

When brought out to be transferred before the magistrates, the resurrectionists were escorted by about forty policemen, but

. . . the mob commenced an attack upon them with stones, bricks and
missiles of every description, several of which struck them and the
police in diverse places; and the hootings, execrations, and yellings of
the mob, might have been heard nearly half a mile off.

On arrival at Deptford,

. . . the police had the utmost difficulty to prevent their prisoners
being sacrificed to the indignant multitude, which was most anxious
to inflict such punishment upon them as it thought they deserved.

The social composition of such vociferous crowds is difficult to ascertain.
Other than in comparatively rare cases of destruction of property – which,
as will appear at a later stage, were by and large urban affairs directed
against anatomists – no arrests were reported to have been made and
records have not been found which discuss the identity of individuals
involved. Nevertheless, some indication can be inferred in such cases of
broad social support for the crowd's actions.

At Great Yarmouth, those whose bodies were found to have been stolen
had recognisable grave-spaces, and relatives living locally who dug for
them over a period of days. Only one had a gravestone.[63] Elizabeth Beck
was 21 when she died giving birth to her daughter. They were buried
together in a grave which already held Elizabeth's mother, who herself had
died at 23 years of age in 1809 when her own daughter was only 3.
Elizabeth's name was added to her mother's stone. Her husband George
recorded the barest essential information on the gravestone, perhaps
reflecting a desire for simplicity, lack of space remaining, or alternatively a
lack of money – inscriptions on gravestones, then as now, were charged for
by the letter. Although he was a baker, George Beck may not have been
able to afford more at the time.

Elizabeth's husband was the first person in Great Yarmouth who,
hearing rumour of bodysnatchers, insisted upon digging in St Nicholas's
churchyard; and was the first to verify their handiwork. The charge on
which the bodysnatchers were committed for trial was based upon George
Beck's oath, and that of others whose relatives were found missing from
their graves.

Even if George Beck was not among the crowd which assembled outside
the Town Hall, and which gave vent to violent feelings towards the
prisoners, it is unlikely that he disapproved of these sentiments. In this he
would have been in the good company of many local worthies. The police
had been energetic in their pursuit of the resurrectionists; and had done
little to prevent the mass excavation of the parish churchyard over a period
of days; nor did they try to arrest any of those threatening violence outside
the Town Hall. In the absence of the Mayor, his deputy was described as
being 'indefatigable' in the investigation of the 'distressing business' as

were the local magistrates, who had met until a 'late hour' on several occasions.

The local church was responsible for the sacking of the gravedigger, Jacob Guyton, who had colluded with the grave-robbers. The person who left record of these events in an elegant hand, and who was probably an eyewitness of the near-riot outside the Town Hall, shared the crowd's low opinion of the bodysnatchers, referring to them as 'wretches', and Vaughan as 'the master fiend'. So although we cannot name or otherwise identify 'faces in the crowd',[64] we have evidence to suppose that the local elite inside the Town Hall, shared – albeit more discreetly – the sentiments expressed in the street.

Despite the social breadth of the revulsion from bodysnatching, we must nevertheless bear in mind that only a proportion of the public gave street expression to the violence of their antipathy. The extent of this proportion may perhaps be gauged from reports of the size of the crowd protesting at Greenwich in 1832, when the West Kent gang was taken. Although Greenwich at that period had a population of only twenty-five thousand people,[65] the crowd which took to the street, at short notice, was estimated at 'several thousands' strong.[66] That public wrath of this magnitude should have been so swiftly mobilised suggests not only the existence of vigorous routes of oral communication but also that public feeling in defence of the dead was broadly based, strongly held, and easily roused.

Although we have no direct means of knowing the exact social composition of the crowds at Greenwich, Deptford or Great Yarmouth, from what is already known of crowd composition in other contexts in this era it can be inferred that the riots and protests against resurrectionists were the work of a fair cross-section of the working population in any given locality. The concerns of the crowd reflect the concerns of that part of the population to whom this form of expression was one of traditional usage.[67]

The overt intention of crowds upon occasions such as these was to inflict injury or destruction upon those responsible for the exhumation and sale of the buried dead. This provides a strong contrast to the way in which other dealers in dead flesh – poachers – were protected by their communities.[68] That the violence evinced toward bodysnatchers was more than 'theatre'[69] is shown by cases in which crowds did inflict considerable violence – even death – upon resurrectionists when the chance had availed itself. Charles Darwin witnessed a riot in Cambridge in about 1830, and described it in his diary:

> Two bodysnatchers had been arrested, and whilst being taken to prison had been torn from the constable by a crowd of the roughest men, who dragged them by their legs along the muddy and stony road. They were covered from head to foot with mud, and their faces were bleeding either from having been kicked or from the stones; they

> looked like corpses, but the crowd was so dense that I got only a few
> momentary glimpses of the wretched creatures . . . I forget the issue,
> except that the two men were got into the prison without being
> killed.[70]

The retributive violence offered by these crowds to the bodysnatchers
suggests that the nature of their occupation incited more than simple
anger. Other historians have shown[71] that riots and protests against
transgressions of *economic* morality – like inordinate price rises on food, or
causing unemployment by the introduction of new technology – were
generally directed at property, not at life or limb. Transgressors against
the crowd's *social* morality were ridiculed with rough music, or shamed by
being burned in effigy. The bodysnatchers had neither property to lose,
nor were they settled in the communities which ostracised them, and so
were not amenable to either of these regulatory forms of traditional crowd
protest.

The poor were by no means unaware that their own dead were the most
vulnerable to theft by such entrepreneurs.[72] They were paid by the wealthy
to guard their roomy graves, they delivered to rich people's homes the
triple coffins money could buy, they soldered their lead coffins for them,
sealed their secure vaults, and dug their deep graves. They watched their
sumptuous funerals pass, and they sang songs about patent coffins they
could never hope to buy.[73]

The crowd's expression of violence towards the bodysnatchers, then,
was an amalgam of an inability to express anger in more traditional and
less violent ways, an active defence of traditional funerary custom, and a
bitter sense of class betrayal. Those who robbed the graves of the dead
were the agents of a social injustice, and their trade in corpses made a
mockery of the meanings and values popularly invested in customary
death practices. The bodysnatchers were the living exemplars of innova-
tive market logic – they had betrayed the deepest sentiments of their own
class by their ruthless trade in human flesh. The bitter verbal and physical
assaults on these people constituted in part an expression of a deep
frustration with the order of things in a society which permitted the
triumph of such a pitiless example of free trade.[74]

Popular notions of the respect due to the dead are particularly evident in
accounts of a full-scale riot at an anatomy school in Aberdeen, in early
January 1832. Contemporary reports[75] did not disclose the identities of the
dead bodies involved, and it is not likely that they were ever ascertained.
Yet ignorance of the names, local origins or social backgrounds of these
'subjects' does not seem in any way to have diminished popular reaction to
their dissection.

The disturbance began when some young boys saw a dog digging in the earth behind a recently built anatomy school in St Andrew's Street. The school had been viewed with suspicion ever since its foundation was laid – a suspicion which had evidently been sustained by the fetor of the school's back yard. The children raised the alarm when they found the dog had unearthed human remains.

A crowd gathered swiftly, and before long the school was invaded, and the lecturer in surgery, Mr Moir, chased out. Three mangled corpses were found on the premises and local police who had appeared on the scene ordered them to be taken away. Though this was probably intended to remove the focus of attention from the school itself it was, as events transpired, a tactical error. It did not put an end to the destruction and looting which had begun before the arrival of the police; and served instead to increase the anger of the crowd outside. Members of the crowd covered the bodies with fragments of clothing, and carried them off around the town, while those who remained began to burn the school down. The crowd shouted encouragement to those inside in their effort to set the building alight, while at the back some enterprising rioters began an attack on the rear wall, simultaneously undermining its foundations and battering its fabric. In a short time the entire wall collapsed, while the fire inside the building took hold. 'The crowd', reported the *Aberdeen Journal*, 'did not appear to rest satisfied until the place was razed', and the same procedure was begun on the front wall.

At this point the Lord Provost of Aberdeen, magistrates and a body of special constables arrived on the scene, to the cheers of the crowd. He addressed the rioters, promising that 'if the feelings of the public had been hurt . . . every enquiry would be made, and every satisfaction afforded'. A party of soldiers was in reserve, but 'it was deemed advisable' not to bring them too near the riot, and they were stationed down the road until it was all over. An abortive attempt was made to bring a fire-engine to the scene, but the crowd denied it access to water. Eventually the front wall also fell, 'leaving only the two gables and the roof standing, which formed a grand burning arch'. These too were attacked, and fell together 'amid the loud and continued cheers of not less than 20,000 individuals'. The school was fully demolished by eight o'clock, and the town was quiet by ten in the evening.

Nearly five months later, three men appeared at the local assizes charged with wilful fire-raising and assault. Alex Murray, flesher, Alexander Allan, private soldier, and George Sharp, blacksmith, each pleaded guilty to mobbing and rioting, but not to fire-raising or assault. The judge said 'that as the prisoners could not be proved to have been the ring leaders . . . and as there appeared to have been gross negligence on the part of the medical gentleman . . . he would receive the prisoners' plea and depart from the more serious charges.'[76] They were each sentenced to twelve months in Aberdeen gaol.

These events exemplify certain elements which are found to recur in anatomy riots and demonstrations elsewhere,[77] some of which may also be familiar from accounts of eighteenth-century food riots. First, there existed a long-standing warning[78] – of which all anatomists and resurrectionists could hardly have been unaware – of a very brittle tolerance on the part of the crowd towards bodysnatching and anatomical premises. It registered in press reports that the building of this school had been viewed locally with suspicion and covert hostility. Nevertheless, many other such establishments were not destroyed, nor were they subject to demonstrations. The Aberdeen school, like these, may well have survived local disfavour had its personnel respected decency, and disposed of dissected remains with circumspection. Burial of remains without funeral or rite in the earth of the school's back yard constituted a cavalier disregard of publicly recognised norms; and in the light of known popular sentiment was not only a negligent but a provocative act.

The remains cannot have been buried well, as their odour had aroused attention and suspicion prior to their accidental discovery. Children recognised immediately that an infringement of common decency had taken place, an awareness which was soon shared, and confirmed by adults. Events seem to have reached a critical stage at this point. The formation of an 'informed crowd-nucleus', with strong grounds for grievance and a knowledge of public sympathy with its 'nascent demand for redress', seems to have been a crucial development of many other riots. In most cases, redress could be offered.[79] Not so at Aberdeen, however. None could be offered to the dead, stolen from their graves, dissected against their will, and buried in a heap in a back yard; nor could it be offered to their families. Things had gone too far for any form of redress except revenge to be meaningful.

Although the bodies in the yard, and those half-dissected inside the school were not identifiable, the crowd seems to have felt that their treatment represented a crime against the whole community, demanding public retribution. It is indicative of the crowd's code of decency that the bodies were covered in 'fragments of clothing' before being taken round the town to drum up support.[80]

At what stage in the proceedings it became agreed strategy to damage the school itself is unclear, but it would seem that events moved rapidly. Being traditional practice, the crowd did as precedent allowed. Destruction was confined to that building only, and it was complete. The 'law-giving mob'[81] had executed sentence. It is worth noticing that the role of the authorities also followed precedent. Recognising at any early stage that 'the feelings of the public' may have been hurt, the prudent elite[82] – cheered by the crowd – permitted the destruction of the school. The building was sacrificed to maintain public order. Had the available troops been sent in, a riot with a legitimate and limited objective might have developed into a general riot or a bloodbath. Events justified the Provost's trust in the traditionalism of the crowd.[83] Once the building was destroyed, the twenty thousand observers and participants in its demolition went home, justice done.

———◆———

Over the half-century preceding the Anatomy Act, alongside events such as those described in this chapter, a vigorous pamphlet and periodical literature contributed to a public debate on anatomy. The need to obtain an alternative source of corpses for dissection, other than by 'violating the dormitories of the defunct', was widely recognised.[84] A recurring theme in this debate was the effect of grave-robbing and dissection upon physical resurrection. Yet the fear that dissection denied the 'subject' life in the world beyond the grave was less often seriously asserted in print by lay critics of bodysnatching[85] than it was ridiculed by members of the medical profession.[86] Their ridicule has all the characteristics of defensiveness about it, and suggests that the anatomists were acutely aware of public disquiet on this score.

The situation was not an easy one. Theology, philosophy, and popular religion had differing perspectives on the existence and nature of the soul. A state of confusion seems to have operated in which the 'psychological concept of mind was conflated with the theological concept of soul',[87] and considerable doubt existed among a majority even of the medical profession, as to whether mind was dependent or independent of the physical body.

An acrimonious debate had erupted within the profession on the materiality of mind in 1816, when the surgeon/anatomist William Lawrence put forward in a lecture his belief – derived from French philosophy – that mind was a function of the brain, dependent upon physical processes for its existence. The logical corollary of this view was that the mind/soul could not survive physical death, and Lawrence's theory was immediately vilified as representing an argument for atheism. Lawrence's name was associated with Tom Paine and Lord Byron, as a supporter of revolution.[88]

This debate, however, seems to have been conducted entirely separately from that concerning the need for greater anatomical knowledge. The present writer has sought in vain for any serious contemporary medical discussion of the soul's physical location, and the effect of dissection upon its fate. The medical debate Lawrence initiated confined itself to *mind*, and it was generally only in the works of pamphleteers that a conflation with *soul* seems to have arisen. Even in this literature, mention of the potential spiritual implications of dissection was rare.[89] A letter to the *Lancet* in December 1828 implied, however, that dissection might be destructive, or at least disturbing, to the soul. A lecture by the London anatomist Dermott on the materiality of the mind had just appeared in the journal, in which he had suggested that the soul might be a latency in life, a function dormant until after death. In reply, a clergyman wrote to ask:

. . . scientific men, as well as divines, will surely be curious to hear if Mr Dermott has, in the course of his physiological researches, found out this dormitory – has detected the sleeper napping in its cell, like a toad in a block of marble, and caught it while just beginning to exercise its new found powers, and to shake off the slumbers of some threescore years; or if it make its escape from the body ere his knife can reach its abode, has he found, at least, the place where it has recently been, just as at Chillingham Castle in my neighbourhood, they show in one of their marble chimney-pieces, not the toad but the cavity where the toad lay [?][90]

Soon afterwards, the atheist Richard Carlile published a comment on the debate in his paper the *Lion*. The radical deist Robert Taylor wrote in, fresh from a lecture on the structure and function of the brain, where discussion had focused on neurological specimens. The lecturer, Mr Mayo, had mentioned that nerves 'receive the impressions of that immaterial substance from which their functions are derived'. Afterwards, Taylor had gone up to look more closely at the specimens, and enquired after the 'immaterial substance':

Mr Surgeon Guthrie took the gist of my enquiry, with exquisite good humour, and said 'he feared that I should find some difficulty in getting a sight of that' and the learned lecturer joined in the ruse, with an excellent evitation that 'it might very easily be shewn to any person who had a mind to look for it'.

Taylor finished by asking 'How angry would a priest have been at such a question?'[91]

Although some observers contended that the medical profession as a whole was irreligious,[92] this was not in fact the case. Many of those who actively advocated greater facilities for anatomical exploration were sincerely religious, justifying dissection on the ground that it made manifest the hand of the Deity in the design of the human body.[93] Yet although they saw in materialism a 'pernicious tendency'[94] towards atheism and subversion and viewed overt professions of disbelief with suspicion, they nevertheless agreed with defenders of Lawrence in the futility 'of any attempt to connect the dogmas of Religion with the demonstrations of Anatomy'.[95]

The main medical defence of the legitimacy of dissection seems to have been simply in terms of its ultimate medical benefits.[96] Although this justification was argued assertively and persuasively by many medical authorities, its limited nature leads to the suspicion that some sort of taboo was operating upon this public discourse, associated with an active disquiet as to the moral and social acceptability of the mutilation of the dead. It is as if these authorities could say almost nothing constructive about the destructive nature of dissection; as if their justification applied only to the ends, not the means, of their work.

The literature of the anatomy debate rarely provides direct evidence of medical unease concerning what actually took place inside dissecting rooms. What indications exist are invariably oblique, as if the subject was really too indecent to discuss, unless by euphemism, suggestion, innuendo, inference. Even literature specifically aimed towards medical students seems to suffer: no warnings were offered the novice of the carnage an early nineteenth-century dissecting room would reveal – no indication of the need mentally to prepare for a first experience of the practice of dissection, nor of the need to control repugnance, fear, nausea. Manuals of dissection seem studiously to have avoided reference to the potentially unpleasant nature of the activity they describe, and its moral or philosophical implications. The language used epitomises 'detachment' and emotionless 'objectivity'. Reference seems entirely lacking as to the means by which bodies were obtained, to the identity or personality of the dead person upon whom the student might spend many hours toil. Indeed, any notion of the individuality, even the *humanity* of the body was lacking, as also was reference to the theological or teleological significance of its destruction.[97]

Nevertheless, many members of the medical profession seem to have agreed with William Lawrence that the dissection room was 'a dirty source of knowledge';[98] and, while recognising the medical value of dissection, nevertheless held a profound distaste for it. G.J. Guthrie, Professor of Anatomy and Surgery at the Royal College of Surgeons, devoted over a third of his 1832 pamphlet on the Anatomy Bill to a discussion of the hypocrisy of doctors who recommended dissection for the poor, yet who went to considerable pains to ensure that their own bodies did not undergo even *post-mortem* examination. Though offering no analysis of the basis of this medical prejudice, Guthrie was able to recognise it in himself, and spoke honestly to its justification.[99]

From scattered references elsewhere to the disrespect and maltreatment of the dead in the process of dissection, we can gain some impression of the grounds for this medical distaste, as well as the materials from which rumour and popular hostility to dissection were probably woven.[100] 'Who', asked one writer,

> even among the practitioners of medicine, does not shudder at the mere contemplation that the remains of all which was dear to him, of a beloved parent, wife, sister, or daughter, may be exposed to the rude gaze and perhaps to the INDECENT JESTS of unfeeling men, and afterwards be mutilated and dismembered in the presence of hundreds of spectators.[101]

That some of the indecency of the dissection room was sexual – as this passage suggests – there can be little doubt. An eighteenth-century anatomical model represented a parturient woman 'chained down upon a table, as if opened alive'.[102] When Knox was assumed to have collaborated with Burke and Hare in the murder of several poor inhabitants of

12 'Modern Medical Education: Actual Practice', after a cartoon by W. Heath, 1825

Edinburgh, it emerged that he had shown no circumspection in displaying the body of Mary Paterson (a young woman whom Burke and Hare had smothered) to all and sundry in his school, that men had come to draw her body, comments had been made upon her physical attributes and that Knox had even had her body preserved in spirits so that he could continue to indulge in necrophiliac voyeurism.[103] Although in this case there is no specific mention of physical indency, at least one documented reference survives of corpse profanation in a London anatomy school.[104] A cartoon showing the Day of Resurrection in a London anatomy school featured a woman demanding the return of her virginity, apparently lost since her arrival there.[105]

Nor was sexual indecency the only indignity perpetrated upon the bodies of the dead. References to the maltreatment of corpses in transit to the schools emerge frequently – as in a report in the *York Chronicle* of the discovery of the body of a young woman and her baby packed tightly into a box 'about two feet square, and nailed close on every side'.[106] Even if these dimensions were understated, it is clear from the tone of the description that contemporaries were shocked at the force inflicted upon these bodies in packaging them in so small a space.

Findings by Professor Macartney of Dublin on the pathology of fever were called into doubt in 1818 by an observer who knew of the manner in which medical students exhumed the bodies on which Macartney had based his observations:

> The bodies, tied up in a sack, neck and heels, are subject to great violence during their transport from the Burying ground – as, for example, they are dropt from a high wall, by which it is well known

fractures of the cervical vertebra not unfrequently occur . . . the
cadaver is roughly handled in the dissection room, being often left
with the head hanging over the table, by which means the blood
gravitates, and congestion of the brain is the consequence.[107]

Nor was this violence inflicted upon the bodies of the dead solely by
medical students and resurrectionists. The distinguished anatomist
Joshua Brookes let fall in relating an anecdote to Bransby Cooper that he
had kicked a sack containing a newly delivered corpse down a flight of
stairs at his anatomy school, as if this was his customary practice.[108] 'If
surgeons', wrote one observer,

continue to violate the rules of decency by their conduct at the
dissecting table, if the bodies, instead of being decently interred, are
to be cast away as mere filth, or given as food to . . . animals, they
may wait long before they can obtain bodies from any
unexceptionable source.[109]

The belief that anatomists allowed human remains to be treated as offal
was widespread during the late eighteenth and early nineteenth centuries.
The famous print by Hogarth, 'The reward of cruelty', which has as its
subject a public dissection at the Company of Surgeons, shows in the
immediate foreground a dog about to devour the corpse's heart. Francis
Grose, writing in the later eighteenth century, said that 'keepers of wild
beasts' were widely supposed to 'save the surgeons the disagreeable labour
of reinterring the many dead bodies after they have done with them. By
this means', Grose mused,

an Alderman who was never out of the sound of Bow Bells, equally
runs the risk of finding his tomb in the bowels of tigers, lions and
crocodiles, with a man who enlists to serve the East India or Royal
African Companies.[110]

An investigation following upon the discovery of bodysnatching in Lambeth in 1795 was told: 'human flesh has been converted into a substance
like Spermacetti, and Candles made of it, and . . . Soap has also been made
of the same material'[111] – a statement which may perhaps assist the
modern reader, with memory of Nazi practices, to appreciate the more
sinister and fearful aspects of the anatomy question.

In the 1820s and 1830s, the medical expression of reservations about
anatomists' attitudes and behaviour towards their subject matter tended
to be extremely circumspect. In general, there seem to have been a
self-imposed medical silence upon the subject. It may be found in operation in the published defence that Robert Knox composed to justify his
own failure to prosecute for libel those accusing him of complicity in the
Burke and Hare murders – a failure which had appeared tantamount to an
admission of guilt. Knox said he had been advised by several eminent

medical figures that 'there was one ground on which it was my duty to resist the temptation of going into a court of law' which was, 'that the disclosures of the most innocent proceedings even of the best-conducted dissecting-room must always shock the public and be injurious to science'.[112] Whether or not Knox was using this advice as an excuse to conceal his own guilt, he was referring to the existence of a 'professional' silence which had been passed on from teacher to pupil in dissection rooms for at least fifty years.[113]

No doubt many rumours which fuelled popular prejudice against the anatomists were based upon exaggeration and surmise. Nevertheless, it is clear that a cultural gulf stood between the dissectors and those who felt themselves their potential victims, which in their more honest moments, doctors themselves would admit to crossing. Sir Robert Christison, in memoirs which remained unpublished until the 1880s, substantiates a factual basis for popular fears that anatomists cared more for them dead than alive. Speaking of his time at St Bartholomew's Hospital in the 1820s, Christison wrote:

> there was . . . usually a race between the relatives and the students – the former to carry off the body intact, the latter to dissect it. Thus dissection was apt to be performed with indecent, sometimes with dangerous haste. It was no uncommon occurrence that, when the operator proceeded with his work, the body was sensibly warm, the limbs not yet rigid, the blood in the great vessels fluid and coagulable. I remember an occasion when Cullen commenced the dissection of a man who had died one hour before, and when fluid blood gushed in abundance from the first incision through the skin . . . Instantly I seized his wrist in great alarm, and arrested his progress; nor was I easily persuaded to let him go on, when I saw the blood coagulate on the table exactly like living blood.[114]

I have argued that fear of dissection, and belief in the sanctity of the grave, were by no means confined to the poor. The wealthy spent good money on strong vaults and patent coffins, and the 'middling classes' obtained the benefit of stout coffins and deep graves. Doctors assured the integrity of their own (and their relatives') bodies after death,[115] though few publicly admitted their own repugnance to dissection. City gentlemen petitioned Parliament for an end to the 'appalling and afflicting' practice of 'robbing and profaning the sacred sanctuary of the dead',[116] while others felt so strongly they urged that the punishment for every resurrectionist should be one from classical antiquity – coupled to a corpse and paraded through the streets until both live and dead bodies 'were amalgamated in putrefaction'.[117]

Although the poor were most vulnerable to grave-robbery, as Wakley observed, their social superiors were by no means immune:

> The security inspired by rank and wealth against these irreverent intrusions on the sanctuary of the dead, is, we all know, a mistaken confidence, since neither marble nor heraldry is a protection against such practices; for what the audacious atrocity of the resurrection-man cannot, the venality of the sexton certainly, will accomplish.[118]

The social breadth of the revulsion from grave-robbery and dissection can neither be explained nor understood unless we appreciate the currency of a *shared* conception of respect for the dead and of a *shared* sense of vulnerability to grave-robbery, crossing class barriers. Until the Anatomy Act, both currents contributed to an apprehensive public consciousness of the anatomy question. Reactions varied throughout society, but it was the fact of this shared consciousness which led to a surprising degree of indulgence from above in cases of riot against resurrectionists and surgeons, an indulgence which was lacking to a marked degree in official dealings with poachers, or with contemporary rioters with more manifest economic or political motivations.[119] This same shared consciousness accounts in part for the reticence of government to grapple with the anatomy problem.

FOREGONE CONCLUSIONS

I would recommend, in the first place that the bodies of all our kings be dissected, instead of expending seven or eight hundred thousand pounds of the public money for their interment. Next, I would dissect all our hereditary legislators. After that, the bishops, with a host of those priests and vicars who feed themselves, and not their flocks. . . . Were there a law passed to this effect, I would willingly consent that my body should be given 'for the promotion of science'.

Henry Hunt, 1832.[1]

Tis obvious, pardon me, Sir, that by far too much importance has been attached to the testimony of Sir Astley Cooper and Mr Abernethy, who are teachers of anatomy, and not physic, in London. I mean no disrespect nor disparagement towards these gentlemen; but why this stress upon their testimony?

William Horsley, open letter to Henry
Warburton, December 1828.[2]

It is curious that the WHIG REFORMERS *are for this bill*, and that the TORIES *are against it*! What *sort* of a reform *the Whigs* have in view we may guess from this circumstance. For my part, I [find it] very hard to believe that those who are for this bill *mean the people any good* by the Reform Bill. . . . If *reform* be to bring us laws like this; if it be to bring us rulers who think it a good thing to make the *trade in human bodies free*; if this be the '*free trade*' they meant to give us; if this be a specimen of their *political economy*; if '*cheap*' human bodies be their sign of national prosperity, in short, if measures like this be the result of *Parliamentary reform*, better, far better, remain as we were, poor and oppressed, but not put *upon a level with the beasts that perish* . . .

Cobbett's Weekly Political Register, 1832.[3]

In the spring of 1828, on the suggestion of Henry Warburton, MP for Bridport, the House of Commons appointed a Select Committee,

> to inquire into the manner of obtaining Subjects for Dissection in the Schools of Anatomy, and into the state of the Law affecting the Persons employed in obtaining or dissecting bodies.[4]

Bransby Cooper, as well as more recent authorities on the history of medicine, has ascribed this development to the discovery of 'the horrible crimes' of Burke and Hare. In fact, Burke and Hare were busily engaged in murdering poor street folk for dissection, and enjoying the proceeds thereof, whilst the Committee was sitting. The Select Committee's *Report* was published several months before the murders were discovered.[5] There were quite other reasons for the Commons' investigation.

A growing atmosphere of crisis afflicted the anatomy business during the mid-1820s. Edinburgh's reputation as a centre of medical excellence was said to be at risk because a consistently high pitch of public vigilance against grave-robbery had caused a chronic shortage of bodies.[6] Wakley believed an important cause of increased stress on graveyards in London and its environs in these years was directly due to an artifically produced increase in demand, engineered by the Royal College of Surgeons.[7] In his evidence to the Select Committee, Wakley drew attention to the enactment of two College bye-laws, restricting recognition of students' anatomical certificates to those awarded by RCS 'recognised' schools and universities, and only during the winter dissecting season. These bye-laws, passed in 1823 and 1824, had resulted in an influx of students to the hospital schools of the metropolis in the decade's mid-years.[8] Wakley said this had ruinous consequences upon private and provincial anatomy schools, and,

> had the direct tendency of throwing all the fees which could arise from teaching of Anatomy in this country, into the pockets of the London hospital surgeons, and their immediate dependents and relatives. . . . It is not a little singular, that the members of the [College's] Court of Examiners by whom these bye-laws were enacted, were themselves, at least seven of them, London hospital surgeons.[9]

The College's manoeuvre was due at least in part to a decline in the number of students registering for anatomical tuition in England. Since anatomy teaching at this period was run on strictly business lines, for the profit of teachers, it meant that high costs involved in the procurement of bodies were passed on to the students.[10] This in turn caused wealthier students to choose to study at Paris or elsewhere on the continent,[11] where they might combine their studies with a Grand Tour.

Lizars described the situation succinctly in his *System of Anatomical Plates of the Human Body*, published in Edinburgh in 1825:

> Subjects have now risen to the enormous sum of twenty guineas, – a sum sufficient to enable a student to go to Paris, study his profession, and return home.   . . . In such a state of things it is hoped that these Plates will form some substitute for the subject. The original design was to aid the sudent in dissection.[12,13]

After the revolution in France, bodies of the very poor had been made available to anatomists in a similar manner to that eventually enacted in Britain by the Anatomy Act.[14] The second Treaty of Paris in 1815 had made the prospect of travel in Europe safer, and students deserted at a high rate. Despite the College's regulations, the number of medical students in London dropped in the five years 1823 to 1828 from around a thousand to about eight hundred.[15] It took little stretch of the imagination to calculate prospective losses of income, and prestige, if such an exodus were to continue.

Worse still for the anatomy tutors, students who remained in the metropolis were deeply discontented and restive. They held meetings, sent deputations, threatened to migrate *en masse* for the continent, and publicly accused their teachers of parsimony.[16]

The intensification of public vigilance in graveyards, and the physical dangers involved in grave-robbery, induced bodysnatchers to exploit other avenues of supply. They tried to obtain more workhouse dead, made private arrangements with servants and undertakers, rifled graveyards further out of town – and there was also the expedient of importing from Ireland or the continent. However, despite sometimes ingenious packaging of bodies, and their camouflage as goods or game, detection involved considerable danger.[17]

Since prices reflected risk, it was natural that resurrectionists should demand higher fees from the anatomists. Higher prices made their risks worthwhile, and this led to quite audacious cases of snatching, even from private houses – like the case of Mrs Davis of Jamaica Street, Edinburgh, stolen from her coffin while awaiting burial[18] or an instance from Dublin in 1831 reported in *The Times*:

> On Friday evening last, about six o'clock, a party of resurrectionists rushed suddenly into a house in Bow-lane, where the corpse of an aged female, named Carrol, was being 'waked' by her friends and neighbours, in an upper apartment, and succeeded in possessing themselves of the body, which they bore off, before the persons present could offer any effectual resistance. The ruffians acted with the most revolting indecency, dragging the corpse in its death-clothes

after them through the mud in the street, and unfortunately baffled all pursuit. Information was shortly after given at College Street police office of the transaction, and an officer with some constables immediately visited the College of Surgeons. They were informed that the body had not been brought there, but were not permitted to search. Several of the fellows engaged in this outrage are well-known resurrectionists, but though the police are acquainted with their haunts, strange to say that none of them have been apprehended yet.[19]

Several observers noted with disgust resurrectionists' manipulation of the 'market' for dead bodies, to their own financial benefit. The Royal College of Surgeons at Edinburgh complained bitterly of this 'degraded and ungovernable class of men', and the way in which they made capital out of localised gluts and shortages.[20] In fact, they were doing no more than other business people would do with other merchandise in a free market; moving goods from one part of the country in which there was a glut, to one in which there was a shortage – and making money from the transaction.[21]

Opinions among surgeons seem to have been contradictory: some said the resurrectionists were fiercely competitive,[22] while others thought they worked in concert to raise prices. One surgeon, in evidence before the Select Committee, ascribed high prices to 'combinations' among resurrection men.[23] 'Combination' was a word fraught with political and subversive overtones at this period. It was applied to any attempt on the part of working people to raise wages, and had signified working people's own organisations in recently repealed anti-union legislation. To the Select Committee, the world effectively meant 'conspiracy'.[24] Naturally, no derogatory mention was made of the anatomists' own combination – the 'Anatomy Club' – which had the expressed intention of fixing prices paid to bodysnatchers at a low level, and for some time succeeded in this aim.[25]

The respective social aspirations of anatomists and resurrectionists permeated their relationships with tension. We saw earlier that more successful resurrectionists endeavoured to purchase respectability with investments in property and business.[26] For them, social success consisted in financial and property status – though in at least two known cases this foundered when past reputations became known. Surgeon-anatomists, like other members of the medical profession of their day, were often readily successful in making money, but aspired beyond respectability, via professional prestige, to gentility.

But although their upward social mobility in this era was impressive,[27] the surgeon-anatomists were dogged by the unholy association with bodysnatching, and the taint of 'trade'. These were associations which tarnished the image, and about which they were particularly sensitive.[28] The

resurrectionists' behaviour aggravated this sensitivity. Throughout his
account of them, Bransby Cooper deprecates the bodysnatchers'
'independence'.[29] Plainly, their lack of deference and their ability to
partake of the profits accruing from anatomy tuition, [30] were thoroughly
irksome to those whom they supplied.

———————◆◆◆◆◆———————

Shortages could be caused by other eventualities than manipulation of the
'market' by resurrectionists. For example, an increase in public vigilance,
a low rate of mortality in a given area or for a given season, or an increase in
demand, could each have an important effect. From 1828 onwards,
existing tensions were materially exacerbated on a national level by
parliamentary discussion of the subject of a new source of supply, and from
popular opposition to the expedient being considered. Several of the worst
dissection riots occurred after Warburton's reintroduction of the Select
Committee's recommendations during the Reform crisis.[31]

The bodysnatchers were not alone in their search for alternatives to
grave-robbery. Although it was virtually undisputed[32] that there existed
no adequate substitute for dissection of the human corpse in anatomy
tuition, anatomists, anxious to dissociate themselves both from the odium
of exhumation and the high prices demanded by resurrectionists, tried
other alternatives. Models, casts, preparations, plates, animals, even
artificial corpses were used.[33] Methods of preserving human flesh – ice,
spirits, salt, nitre – were tried in an attempt to reduce wastage of available
resources by putrefaction.[34] Although these rather old-fashioned expedients had their uses, it was generally agreed that they were inadequate.[35]
Nevertheless, anatomy schools in the 1820s were obliged to depend upon
them to a greater extent than their proprietors wished, or their students
desired.

Tutors of anatomy whose schools were not attached to major hospitals
were at a disadvantage[36] in the search for alternatives to the employment
of resurrectionists. Although all tuition of anatomy in this era was undertaken for private profit, anatomists teaching within the framework of
major hospitals were cushioned against the worst excesses of competition
by the availability both of charitable funds and resources,[37] and of hospital
mortuaries. While their colleagues in 'independent' anatomy schools
depended almost wholly upon resurrectionists for their supplies, hospital
anatomists benefited directly from the high mortality inside their institutions.

Available evidence suggests that an illicit process of appropriation of the
dead hospital poor was widely adopted, with or without the knowledge and
connivance of hospital authorities and their appointed chaplains.[38] Coffins buried in the graveyards of the major London charitable hospitals
were often empty, or subsequently became so.[39]

The generous assertion of the charitable foundation of St Thomas' Hospital was that

> those patients who are buried at the request of their friends, under the direction of the charity, are decently interred by the clerk, in the hospital burial ground, in the immediate vicinity of the charity.[40]

In fact, three well-worn routes existed whereby the bodies of such unfortunate patients found their way to the slab. Many were in fact buried, but did not long remain so. Naples and his colleagues used St Thomas', Guy's and St Bartholomew's burial grounds frequently. Other bodies disappeared before burial. At the London Hospital, a chaplain 'at last . . . said he would not read the service over coffins full of stones any longer'. His stand was probably rooted in self-interest, however. The chaplain was probably the Rev. Valentine, of whom Ann Millard observed:

> . . . he is a strenuous advocate for the rights of the Church, and the strict observance of decency, seldom permitting a deceased patient to be dissected before burial, as such a practice would obviously tend to diminish the fees for interment.[41]

Some patients failed even to undergo the honour of a mock funeral. The admission procedure at St Thomas' Hospital lent itself to this, for it was such that poor patients begged for admission by means of a process in which they were – perhaps designedly – caught in a double-bind situation; admitting their 'low circumstances' and that they were 'destitute of friends', yet having to provide admission fees, and the sum of one guinea – a 'respectable guarantee' – as security for their 'removal, when cured, or their burial if they die in hospital'.[42]

Ann Millard commented upon the potentially damaging effect such a petition might have upon the spirits of already sick people, faced with the prospect of death in a hospital to which they had applied for a cure. She also pointed out the innate discrepancy between a requirement that applicants be 'in low circumstances and destitute of friends' while asking them to provide fees and securities against their own death.[43] Their apprehensions were apparently routinely soothed by a kindly porter, who would offer to stand surety for the guinea fee. If they survived treatment, the porter would be thanked for his kindness; if not, he would take charge of the body, and sell it to the dissecting room for four guineas.[44]

Patients who died in the hospital without having consigned their bodies to the porter might nevertheless find themselves on the anatomists' slab through another arrangement, this time through the steward's office. In 1825 a fee of three and a half guineas was said to have been paid by the teachers of anatomy 'for many years . . . for every subject transferred from the dead house to the dissecting room'.[45]

We have no means of knowing what proportion of the bodies used for dissection in hospital schools were obtained using these methods. No records were kept of such transactions. Of the hospitals in the metropolis, only the London Hospital, with a poorer class of patients and no entrance fees or securities, is known to have been able to supply its own anatomy school adequately, on occasion even offering surplus bodies to other hospitals' schools, for a fee.[46] These were of course keenly accepted, since all the other anatomy schools suffered from – sometimes severe – shortages, and the London's fees probably undercut 'market' prices.[47]

Surgeon-anatomists attached to other hospitals constantly found their own mortuaries insufficient. For example, both Benjamin Brodie of St George's Hospital and Astley Cooper at the United Hospitals frequently dealt with resurrectionists,[48] and liaised directly with senior members of government to obtain official indulgence of their traffic. This latter point was shrouded in secrecy, but – as we shall see in a moment – these eminent surgeons had considerable influence upon individual members of government in arranging merciful treatment for captured or convicted body-snatchers, in aiding importation of bodies from abroad, and in obtaining official protection for corpses in transit.[49]

There was even an admission that in the 1820s the Home Secretary, without any legal instrument to justify his so doing, had made available for dissection bodies of the dead from His Majesty's prisons, and from naval and military hospitals.[50] Such practices illustrate the extent to which anatomists were able to regard the bodies of the socially disadvantaged as their own perquisites prior to the Anatomy Act, and the extent to which this view was endorsed by government.

Nor was this attitude confined to London. In 1819, the Humane Society of St John offered to fund a watch for the Hospital Fields burial ground in Dublin. The ground held the largest concentration of paupers' graves in the city, including those buried from the hospitals, and was well-known as a favourite resort of bodysnatchers. However, the Society's genuinely charitable gesture met with a sharp rebuke from Macartney, Professor of Anatomy at Trinity College. He protested that the watch would damage the medical school, which brought business worth £70,000 a year to Dublin, and went on:

> I do not think the upper and middle classes have understood the
> effects of their own conduct when they take part in impeding the
> process of dissection . . . very many of the upper ranks carry in their
> mouths teeth which have been buried in the hospital fields.[51]

The professor may be thought to have been somewhat tactless when he made this rather crass appeal to the self-interest of the 'upper and middle class' supporters of the charity. Yet he did no more than enunciate the tacit assumptions held by an influential proportion of his profession, assumptions which would colour the Select Committee's *Evidence* and *Report*.

As if to provide a perfect illustration of 'structural and ideological diversity'[52] in government, a case reached its conclusion at Lancaster Spring Assizes in early March 1828 which entirely changed the anatomists' legal position.[53] Ironically, the prosecutor was the Crown. Five defendants were charged with conspiracy, and with unlawfully procuring and receiving the dead body of Jane Fairclough, a young woman buried in Warrington Baptist burial ground the previous September, and disinterred within a few days. One of the accused was a medical student, and another a surgeon-apothecary; none was a professional resurrectionist. The conspiracy charges failed, and three of the defendants were acquitted. Two were found guilty of possession, however. In his directions to the jury, the presiding judge, Baron Hullock, observed:

> the only bodies legally liable to dissection in this country, were those of persons executed for murder. However necessary it might be, for the purposes of humanity and science, that these things [exhumation and dissection] should be done, yet, as long as the law remained as it was at present, the disinterment of bodies for dissection was an offence liable to punishment.[54]

The judgment rendered surgeon-anatomists vulnerable to the same taint of criminality as the resurrectionists who for so long had borne the brunt of prosecution alone.[55] The writing had been on the wall for anatomists since reports had appeared only a month earlier of a case at Liverpool, in which a 'respectable teacher of Anatomy'[56] had been convicted of causing a body to be disinterred. On this basis, virtually every anatomy school proprietor in the country would be vulnerable to prosecution. Within two months, in the spring of 1828, a dramatic change had taken place in the legal status of the study of anatomy, one which all practising anatomists found deeply alarming.[57]

It was undoubtedly this change in case law which prompted Parliamentary activity. So much is evident both from the Select Committee's brief, and from the chronology of events. For at least a century the inadequacy of the sole legal source of bodies for anatomy had been regarded as a major obstruction to medical knowledge, and had constituted a perpetual threat to public order at gallows and in churchyards – yet nothing had been done. Baron Hullock's judgment was made on 14 March 1828. Within forty days, Parliament, which had always thought it 'too hazardous a risk' to do anything about the problem, had established a Committee to investigate. Before sentences in the Lancaster case had even been handed down, the Select Committee had all but completed hearing evidence.[58]

Jeremy Bentham – the great exponent of Utilitarianism and of the philosophical principle 'the greatest happiness of the greatest number' – was known to have an interest in the problem of anatomy. It was public knowledge that the grand old man intended to bequeath his own body for dissection. Bentham was, according to John Stuart Mill, a thinker who 'failed in deriving light from other minds', and who 'when he had solved [a] problem himself, or thought he had done so, . . . declared all other solutions to be erroneous'.[59]

His followers appear to have absorbed his modes of thought in this respect, but with additional vigour. Though they attempted to make the Select Committee on Anatomy appear a value-free investigation – the Committee saw more witnesses on more occasions, and submitted a longer report with more pages of evidence than did the average Select Committee of 1828[60] – their assiduity was more apparent than real. Unwelcome views were simply not heard. The Select Committee was a means to an end.

All the Committee's administrative papers were lost in a catastrophic fire at the Houses of Parliament in 1834, and no record survives of its members' attendance, of the nature of their discussions, or even of when they met – other than for the taking of evidence. However, it is known that Henry Warburton, the 'avowed Benthamite'[61] MP for Bridport, who had persuaded the Commons of the need for a Select Committee on Anatomy, wrote the Committee's *Report* himself.[62] A close examination of the published *Evidence* leads to the conclusion that, like some other Parliamentary reports, 'it was based on speculative, anecdotal, and ultimately political judgments . . . on prejudices . . . [and] bias'.[63]

This is a serious contention. Yet similar allegations have been made by other historians concerning other measures of the same era, notably the 1833 Factory Inquiry, the 1834 Poor Law Report, the 1844–5 Commission on the Health of Towns, and the Report of the 1834–5 Commission on Municipal Corporations. The Webbs called the latter 'a bad case of a violent political pamphlet being, to serve Party ends, issued as a judicial report'.[64] All these enquiries were manipulated by Benthamites.[65] Evidence of Benthamite influence on the drafting and passage of the Anatomy Act suggests that the Select Committee on Anatomy was another such.

This influence is all the more significant because the Anatomy Act established the first centrally financed and administered national Inspectorate of the nineteenth-century 'revolution in government',[66] predating the Factory Inspectorate – which even historians of inspection date as the first – by a year.[67]

There certainly existed voices which are *not* identifiably Benthamite, in favour of anatomy reform on similar lines. For example, in his *Hunterian Oration* of 1819 the surgeon John Abernethy had raised the idea of using paupers' bodies – seemingly the earliest occasion on which this expedient was mooted seriously in this country.[68] Other ideas for potentially feasible alternative sources had been circulating within the profession for some time – evidence of which survives in a secret correspondence between

London anatomists and Robert Peel in 1824, via Peel's personal consultant, Astley Cooper.[69] Thomas Wakley's running public commentary in the *Lancet* brought the issue to public scrutiny. But although potentially feasible alternatives to the dissection of the very poor were put forward by opponents of Warburton's Bill, none of their voices was heard officially by the Committee.

The process of gaining the Anatomy Act's passage provides a fine illustration of the workings of Parliamentary Benthamism, as revealed in the work of the historians Lucy Brown and Samuel Finer.[70] Finer has pointed to the role of sympathetic MPs who would move for a Select Committee, and thereby gain the right to nominate a majority of its members. That Warburton used his position in this way is evident from the weight of Benthamite representation on his Committee.[71] The names of Hume, Baring, Graham, Spring Rice, Poulett Thompson and Hyde Villiers appear as 'first degree Benthamites' in Finer's analysis – all were on the Committee. A passage reproduced below from an important correspondence between Bentham and Peel reveals that another member, John Smith, belongs in the same category. Others, like Hobhouse, were keenly sympathetic (what Finer calls 'irradiated Benthamites') and in some cases yet other connections may also have been operating – for example in 1833, Littleton, another member of the Committee, was nominated for the post of Speaker by Hume. Peel himself was also a member of the Select Committee, and although not a 'disciple' of Bentham, was by 1828 sympathetic to the expedient in mind. Yet another Committee member, Dawson, was Peel's brother-in-law, and Mr Bransby Cooper, also on the Committee, was Astley Cooper's older brother. Astley Cooper himself proved a key witness during the Committee's hearings.[72]

The Select Committee on Anatomy conforms in characteristics besides its 'packed' membership to Finer's analysis of other public enquiries manipulated by the Benthamites, for example, the 'pre-selection' of witnesses, and skilful use of the parliamentary recess to get on with the work while other MPs were absent and to stimulate favourable public opinion. The Committee represents a prime example of the manipulated public enquiry which was a favourite instrument for achieving official status for Benthamite views. It epitomises what Finer calls 'the use of the Select Committee as an offensive weapon'.[73]

And the association with Bentham himself could hardly be closer. Manuscripts survive in the Bentham Archive at University College, London, which include letterbook copies of correspondence between Bentham and Peel on the subject two years before the establishment of the Select Committee, of autograph draft letters; and – most significantly – Bentham's handwritten draft, dated November 1826, of a parliamentary bill on the subject. Despite Bentham's bequest of his own corpse for dissection and curious preservation (which has remained one of the most enduring facts of his biography)[74] these manuscripts have not previously been published, and no discussion of their importance has so far been found.[75]

The correspondence with Peel consists of a single exchange of letters, initiated by Bentham on the 1 April 1826.[76] Denying that he was asking Peel to act 'in contempt of Public Opinion and its tribunal', Bentham solicited Peel's attention to the 'distressed state of medical science', and offered 'an effectual cure . . . without wound to individual feelings'. His key recommendation was that by the act of applying for treatment, all hospital patients should be deemed to have given consent to the dissection of their bodies in the event of death. Bentham suggested the Christian burial of dissected remains, the use of hospital administrators in keeping dissection records (with copy certificates to survivors), as well as newspaper publication of the names of the deceased. Importantly, with reference 'to the feelings of relatives', Bentham drew a distinction between dissection and *post-mortem*, suggesting that dissection should perhaps be limited to corpses for whom no application for burial had been made. He did not find it necessary to define whom his suggestions would affect. All hospital patients at this date were by definition unable to pay for other medical treatment – so Bentham's chosen constituency for dissection material would be all those who died in poverty with no relatives to bury them, and those whose relatives were too poor to do so.

Bentham went on to say that in 1825 he had seen similar regulations in operation in a Paris hospital, St Louis, and that English physicians there had told him that France was ahead of England in the 'art-and-science' of anatomy as a result. The influence of the French precedent may have come by way of Bentham's medical friend Thomas Southwood Smith, whose influential article 'The Use of the Dead to the Living' had been published in the Benthamite *Westminster Review* in 1824. Bentham went on humbly to mention the bequest of his own body.

> so that my last moments have for their comfort the assurance that how little service soever it may have been in my power to render to mankind during my life time, I shall at least be not altogether useless after my death.

He ended with an indication that more research would be necessary before a final draft of a bill could be written up. Bentham added as a postscript that he would 'with pleasure, do whatever is most agreeable to [Peel] in relation to this business, except the giving it up', adding:

> If the design meets your approbation, the simplest course is for you to take it up as of yourself without my appearing in it. But if in that case you had rather it should appear called for *ab extra*, and that the call should appear in some Newspaper, so shall it be. . . . If I do not receive any commands from you within a week from the date of this letter, I shall conclude that you are not disposed to take up the matter

yourself, and I shall in that case also send the letter to some
Newspaper, for the chance of seeing it taken up by some one else.

The letter was marked '*Private*'. Peel's reply[77] from Whitehall on 4 April
1826, was marked '*Private and confidential*'. It read:

I have given much attention to the subject on which you have
addressed me, and have had personal communication upon it with
many eminent anatomists.

I think I may say with truth – that in consequence of the measures
adopted by me – the difficulty of procuring Bodies for dissection in
the Schools of the Metropolis, has been of late very materially
diminished. I very much doubt however whether this be a fit subject
for legislation, or even for public discussion – and whether there is not
great danger that the attempt to legislate would throw new
impediments in the way of anatomical Science.

Among those with whom I have conversed on this matter, are
many Governors of Hospitals – and I am confident that an active
opposition would be made by them to such a legislative enactment as
that which you propose.

Perhaps on rigid inquiry it might be found – that without the
existence of any legislative authority for it, a pretty free use is made of
the bodies of those Patients who die in public Hospitals. I should be
sorry by any public Act to provoke too much inquiry into present
practice.

There are other sources of supply open at present – not in
contravention of Law – which I apprehend public discussion would
effectually close.

I have entered into this detail in the hope of satisfying you – that if I
do not adopt your suggestions – it is not because I am insensible to
the importance of the subject – but because I fear the consequences to
Science of too open an interference in a matter, in regard of which
public feeling is naturally so easily excited.

I am, Sir,
Your obedient Servant,
Robert Peel.

Peel was usually parsimonious with his words, so the length of his reply to
Bentham suggests that he took the correspondence very seriously.[78] His
respectful rejection prompted two draft replies from Bentham – one dated
12 April 1826, and the other twelve days later. There is no evidence that
either were ever sent – Bentham coded all his letters, and both drafts lack
the code.[79] The first referred to Bentham's conviction of the need for
medical reform.[80] Recognising Peel's 'personal apprehension' of incurring
'odium', Bentham promised to observe his desire for secrecy. If he did not
hear from Peel within a week, he would regard himself as having Peel's

permission to show the correspondence to Mr John Smith, MP, 'of the coincidence of whose sentiments with mine', Bentham wrote, 'I am sufficiently assured'.

The subject was still on Bentham's mind, however, for the second draft reply again expressed his support for medical reform, and a promise of secrecy; but reveals that Bentham seems to have felt that by sharing his proposal with Peel, he had ceded the initiative.[81] Much of this draft was concerned with reasserting control: arguing against Peel's contention that the subject would not benefit from legislation, Bentham expressed the fear that murder might occur unless change was effected, and offered a title for the projected bill: '*A Bill for the more effectual prevention of the violation of Burial Places*'. Bentham offered to take responsibility for the engagement of 'some other MP to take it upon himself' to introduce the bill to Parliament. If he did not hear to the contrary within a week, he would conclude that Peel had 'no objection to the seeing the matter brought before the public in Parliament by some other hand.'

The letterbooks are quiet on the subject until 6 November that year – just before the start of the new Parliamentary session – when a draft bill, now headed: '*Body Providing Bill*' appeared in Bentham's hand.[82] It contained all the elements Bentham had listed in his first letter to Peel – primarily the plan for legal recognition of an unspoken contract between patient and charity/hospital: in return for free medical care, in the event of death the patient's corpse would be at the disposal of the hospital's dissectors. Should surviving relatives swear to their relationship within 24 hours of the death, the body would be given up to them for burial without dissection, but in cases of 'extraordinary symptoms', the medical practitioner would have the right to make an 'aperture' to determine cause of death. A forfeit of £100 would become payable to the relatives if the body was not then returned. The proposed bill went on to direct Christian burial for dissected remains at the anatomist's cost and, importantly, repeal of the Act under which murderers were dissected.

Bentham's proposed bill almost certainly provided the basis of the first Anatomy Bill. The prevention of disinterment was primary in the first bill's text and title ('A Bill for preventing the Unlawful Disinterment of Human Bodies and for Regulating Schools of Anatomy'), and the supposed unspoken contract (charitable treatment while alive in return for dissection after death) between patient and anatomist was implicit in its clauses. The two texts accord so closely in spirit that it seems more than likely that Bentham did as he had suggested to Peel, and delegated his project to Mr John Smith, MP. The only John Smith to whom Bentham could have been referring, was John Smith of Dale Park – brother to Lord Carrington – MP for Midhurst since 1812, and one of the many Benthamites nominated to the Select Committee.[83] In fact, only three voices were recorded as having spoken during what seems to have been a cosy Commons debate in April 1828 when assent was granted for the establishment of a Select Committee: those of Warburton as proposer, Smith as seconder, and Peel, accepting their proposal on behalf of the government.[84]

The choreography of relationships and views which resulted in the appointment of the Select Committee is not fully known. Yet contact ascertainably took place beforehand on the subject between Bentham and Peel, and probably between Bentham and Smith. Warburton was a rather opaque young MP closely aligned with the Bentham/James Mill axis.[85]

Between Bentham's draft and the submission of the first bill to Parliament in 1829, a great deal of research and added drafting had indeed been done – much of it apparently undertaken independently of the Select Committee's sessions. Warburton and Smith probably appreciated that some other less interested form of control than hospital administrators would be necessary to oversee the Act's provisions. It had probably also become evident to them that public notification of deaths in workhouses would have given undue publicity to high workhouse mortality, and could prove counter-productive. Bentham is in part exonerated from the results of their handiwork in this respect by his wish to give relatives and friends the chance to know of their kin's passing by publishing the names of the dead. The Paris morgue served an equivalent purpose. The Select Committee recommended no imperative, and no mechanism for informing family or friends when someone died in an institution.

Bentham's draft bill had included a clause repealing the judicial dissection of murderers. For reasons unknown, this was mysteriously dropped from Warburton's first Anatomy Bill. It is beyond doubt that such a significant clause would only have been omitted for tactical reasons: an explanation of which, it seems to me, must be sought in the relationships and loyalties of those most prominently involved. My reading of the interests and *dramatis personae* leads me to suggest that the basis of an explanation is provided by a possible scenario in which Warburton and Smith had already been working together on the draft bill – as a result of Bentham's previous abortive correspondence with Peel – when the crucial change in case law criminalising anatomists occurred.

From what is known of Peel's close personal relationship with Sir Astley Cooper it seems more than likely that the import of Bentham's letter – and later, Baron Hullock's perturbing 1828 judgment – formed the basis of conversation between the two men. With Peel's earlier objections to legislation undermined by the crucial change in case law, he, Cooper and the Benthamites were in accord – except for the murderers' clause.

The Royal College, of which Cooper was President in 1828, wanted to preserve its privileged right to corpses, even to the extent of assuming control of the entire administration of distribution under the planned Act. For good Benthamite reasons Warburton and Smith were opposed to ceding this power to the Royal College, and probably thought that the omission of Bentham's clause repealing the dissection of murderers a small price to pay to pacify the College. After all, the supply from that source was little more than token. Moreover, by omitting it, and leaving the College with its own independent supply, Warburton and Smith would gain for their own scheme the important support of both Peel and Sir Astley Cooper, and thereby of the College itself. Cooper and the College may have been satisfied to bide their time – should the Act have proved a failure, the claim to rights over control of distribution could be reasserted.

In the event, Warburton ran into implacable opposition – most particularly from Wakley – for the omission, and was forced to repeal the dissection of murderers in his second Bill. As his first bill stood, the poor were classed alongside 'the worst of criminals', as potential subjects for dissection.[86]

Interestingly, Bentham did not himself address the need for an inspectorate of anatomy. Nor does he seem to have appreciated the potential for conflict between the 'independent' private schools of anatomy, and the schools attached to hospitals which yielded income to top surgeons. His followers did. The first bill spent a considerable amount of its bulk on the institution of seven 'Commissioners', specifying the frequency and content of their meetings, their staff, their power to issue licences, to issue regulations for anatomy schools and to receive reports from paid peripatetic Visitors, the penalties available to them for infringement of their powers, and other forms of administrative detail.[87] The fact that none of these innovations had been discussed in the course of the Select Committee's hearings reinforces the impression that the Committee served the function of what we would now call a public relations exercise. As the Bentham-Peel correspondence reveals, a great deal of the real work behind the *Report* had probably already been done.

———◆———

The 1834 fire means that we have no records as to how the witnesses called to give evidence were chosen or approached by the Committee. The forty men whose opinions constitute the evidence on which the *Report* was based, look to have been hand-picked. They included twenty-five members of the medical profession, several of whom represented the College and metropolitan hospital hierarchy, and seventeen of whom were surgeon-anatomists.[88] Five of these medical witnesses were called before the Committee for the sole purpose of describing their experience of anatomical tuition abroad. Discounting these, of the remaining thirty-five witnesses, only one was based anywhere other than London.[89]

Twelve of the witnesses were public servants of various kinds; four of these were involved in medical administration, and a further four were central London magistrates; two of them were police officers, and two were parochial office holders from the parish of St James, in London. The remaining three witnesses were said to have been resurrectionists, whose identities were kept – and remain – secret.[90] It is difficult to believe that any resurrectionist alive to his own interest would have participated willingly in a scheme to render himself redundant, without having some prospect of protection or preferment from one or other of the gentleman-surgeon witnesses. Without the expertise of such an intermediary, indeed, it is unlikely that a committee of parliamentarians could even have located three bodysnatchers, or – even more importantly – persuaded them to speak.

One of these possible mediators may have been Dr James Somerville, who himself gave evidence and who was later to become the first Inspector of Anatomy. He must have had recent dealings with bodysnatchers, as he worked as an assistant to Benjamin Brodie (member of the council of the College of Surgeons, and Surgeon to the King) in his private anatomy school. It will be shown in a moment that Somerville had acted as an intermediary between anatomists and government before.

The identity of another of these intermediaries can be inferred from the fact that one of the resurrectionists referred to a book in order to verify his evidence. It is probable that this witness, 'CD', was Naples, the author of the *Diary*. Since Naples was given a job in the dissecting room at St Thomas' Hospital after the Act was passed, the intermediary facilitating his appearance before the Committee could have been the St Thomas's surgeon, J.H. Green, who also gave evidence. The fact that a job was found for him suggests that Naples's evidence was considered satisfactory.

Evidence is also lacking as to who posed the questions put to those giving evidence, how it was decided which questions should be put to whom, and which topics avoided.[91] For example, none of the resurrectionists were asked their personal histories, or for their opinions of the anatomists they supplied. Their employers, however, were invited on several occasions to comment adversely on the bodysnatchers, often with leading questions, like the following:

> You are of the opinion, therefore, that by tolerating exhumation, you are in fact tolerating the existence of a set of the most depraved men in society?[92]

or,

> Is it not the duty of the magistrates, inasmuch as the exhumators are principally thieves, to endeavour as much as possible to put them down?[93]

Not surprisingly, replies to both questions were affirmative. Only one anatomist, John Abernethy, when asked:

> Is it not the case that [the resurrectionists] sometimes give information against the very persons they undertake to supply?

refused to respond as his questioner had expected, saying

> I cannot accuse them of any breach of faith with myself.[94]

The assumption of a connection between bodysnatching and other crime was given added weight by the evidence of one of the resurrectionsists, 'AB', who, when asked.

> What are the employments for which you think the raising of bodies is sometimes made a cover?

replied:

> I think for thieving, by the greatest part of the men that have lately got into the business; they are nothing but petty common thieves.[95]

It should be borne in mind, however, that this man's reply fell almost directly after his evidence had been interrupted by the chair, and Dr Somerville asked in the man's hearing for a verbal testimonial of his character.[96] Dr Somerville's reply was succinct:

> The witness is not one of those who live by other means but what he professes.

The chair was not satisfied, and probed Dr Somerville:

> Is he one of those who inform against the dissectors, after supplying them?

Despite Dr Somerville's negative reply, it need not surprise us if we detect something in the bodysnatcher's subsequent testimony to suggest that he felt himself to be on trial before a bench of parliamentary men,[97] that he overstated the sins of others from a defensive desire to exonerate himself – even to assert his own professional status for the benefit of the gentlemen on the Committee: 'they get a subject or two, and call themselves resurrection-men'. Some of this man's replies give the uneasy impression of his having been groomed.[98] In fact his evidence did little more than show that by the late 1820s, bodysnatching was being used as a cover for burglary, not by the regular resurrectionists, but by thieves who by reason of official leniency towards anatomy, adopted resurrecting as a guise.[99] The Select Committee's *Report* made much of the man's evidence when it was published in the summer of 1828.

Much of what was offered as *fact* in the *Report* concerning an association of bodysnatching and crime, was in reality based on the expressed *opinions* of gentlemen surgeons and anatomists – opinions often expressed in emotive terms of disgust and revulsion. It is difficult to say, given the available sources, what proportion of the surgeons' expressed disgust of the resurrectionists was in fact social disgust, affected delicacy, resentment at the bodysnatchers' lack of deference and success in maintaining a cut of the profits, and a conscious or unconscious desire to disassociate themselves from the distasteful and unpopular mode in which the bodysnatchers obtained corpses for dissection. Surviving memoirs and biographies, however, lead to the conclusion that all these elements combined into a powerful amalgam. Sir Astley Cooper – as we have seen – referred to the bodysnatchers before the Committee as 'the lowest dregs of degradation'. He continued:

> I do not know that I can describe them better; there is no crime that they would not commit . . . if they would imagine that I should make a good subject, they really would not have the smallest scruple, if they could do the thing undiscovered, to make a subject of me.[100]

Sir Astley appears to have shared the widespread sentiment against dissection himself – in fact he underwent a *post-mortem*, but from the size of his stone sarcophagus it would seem that he made quite sure that he would not personally undergo dissection.[101] His fear of dissection is as discernible in the passage just quoted as his mistrust of the men in his pay. Moreover, he reveals elements of the defensive tactic the bodysnatcher had employed when asserting his own difference from 'petty common thieves'. Sir Astley painted the resurrectionists in the darkest colours. He disassociated himself from their activities through expressions of distaste, and by posing as a potential victim. Much of his desire to effect this object seems to have stemmed from his own wish to be seen by the Committee as a man possessing delicacy of feeling and a gentility which – despite his baronetcy – he seems to have felt the need to demonstrate. Quite why this should have been necessary to a man pre-eminent in his profession, Surgeon to the King, and President of the Royal College, is only apparent if we consider whom he was addressing.

Prior to the passage of the Reform Act in 1832, virtually all Members of Parliament shared privileged social status, 'tinged with aristocracy and family pride', and shared a homogeneous social heritage and a common political tradition.[102] A recent historian of the old regime, G.P. Judd, has shown that a number of forces combined to render MPs 'into a cohesive and therefore effective elite corps'. These included shared social backgrounds and status, cultural values and traditions, wealth, community of professional interests, and the fact that 'they had served long enough together to acquire that habit of co-operation which is born only of long continued association'.[103]

Although by the 1820s there were signs of change, the ability of the eighteenth-century ruling elite to self-perpetuate by the absorption of mercantile and industrial elements should not be underestimated; nor should the extent to which this ruling elite survived the reforms of 1832. Only three of the twenty-four MPs on the Select Committee failed to obtain re-election in 1832.[104] Most members of the Committee had aristocratic connections, over half of them were or subsequently became titled, and most of the remainder were landed gentry.[105] The position of a self-made surgeon-baronet in this social context was not really one of equality, even though his elder brother was a Committee member. Judd has shown that in the entire century preceding the passage of the Anatomy

Act, although many MPs had connections with the Church or the Bar, only eleven MPs had professional connections with medicine: concluding from this negligible total that 'in the old regime medicine did not enjoy the prestige accorded to the other professions'.[106]

It should be borne in mind then, that the evidence was given in a bastion of social prestige, to a tribunal of socially privileged men; and that the medical evidence was given by an upwardly mobile and socially aspiring group of doctors, who were very much aware that to many of the MPs they addressed, medicine – and particularly surgery – was 'a pursuit not quite fit for a gentleman'.[107]

The politics behind the Select Committee were yet more complex than a simple statement of class relations, however. Power relations between the members of the Committee and its medical witnesses were more complicated than, probably, shall ever be known. We do know that both Home Secretary Robert Peel and Spring Rice – members of the Committee – had already had private dealings with witnesses Benjamin Brodie and James Somerville, in facilitating the supply of dead bodies from abroad.[108] On this more shall be said in a moment. It is not known how many of the MPs on the Committee saw their own medical practitioners give evidence, but much can be surmised from the knowledge that in 1826, Astley Cooper's clientele included the King, the Prime Minister, the Duke of Wellington, Peel himself and many other leading politicians.[109] He and Brodie would be appointed to embalm the body of George IV at his death in 1830.

The Royal College was an exceptionally powerful body in this era. Of this Henry Warburton, instigator and chairman of the Select Committee was very much aware. Two years earlier, he had been responsible for a failed parliamentary move to reform the College's corrupt hierarchy.[110] In 1834, two years after his Anatomy Act was eventually passed, Warburton chaired another Select Committee investigating medical education, with a view to reform.[111] Once again, and despite the passage of the Reform Act, the College remained unscathed. It should not be thought surprising that such influence existed. It has already been mentioned that the College's President, Astley Cooper, had gained his baronetcy from the successful removal of a sebaceous cyst from the royal scalp, and had become wealthy ministering to his select clientele.[112] Other members of the College's hierarchy were similarly well placed.

As Peel's letter to Bentham shows, government indulgence of the profession's need for corpses prior to the Anatomy Act was effected through direct liaison between these men and government ministers. Manuscript evidence of concerted action of some sort between Peel and Sir Astley survives in the British Library collection of *Peel Papers*. A letter dated 16 December 1826 discusses a man called Phillips who seems to have been involved in the importation of bodies from abroad. Peel wrote to Sir Astley 'I hope he is a fit person to be entrusted with the use of our names in so delicate a business'.[113]

Both Cooper and Brodie gave evidence on this subject to the Select Committee, but Sir Astley's responses to questions were confined to rather obsequious praises of Peel and the Marquis of Lansdowne, apparently in an attempt to divert interest from the details of their co-operation. Cooper was probed, but finding three consecutive answers evasive, his questioners let the matter rest.[114] Benjamin Brodie was a little less guarded, and disclosed: 'Mr Peel gave the subject much consideration, and did a great deal by removing impediments to the importation from abroad of dead bodies,' and that when on one occasion 'the Thames police did interpose some difficulty . . . it was removed by a stronger hand.'[115]

The younger Somerville was even more informative. He had been employed personally to oversee an abortive attempt to establish a regular system of corpse importation from Paris and Dublin. The Parisian bodies were putrid on arrival, and the proprietors of the Dublin steam-boat had threatened to impose a fine of fifty pounds for every corpse found on board. The first consignment was discovered, and the Thames police seized it and waited to arrest whoever should arrive to claim it. The Home Office intervened to extricate Somerville.[116]

We shall see in a later chapter that importation was one among several potentially viable alternatives to the use of paupers' bodies available for the Committee's consideration in 1828; but most of these alternatives either failed to emerge in evidence, or were accorded no importance by the Committee and the majority of their parliamentary colleagues. The published *Report* featured witnesses' replies only when in harmony with the project of using paupers' corpses. Dissenting opinion, having barely a peripheral place in the *Evidence*, scarcely registered in the *Report*.

Bransby Cooper says that discussions upon 'some plan' for an alternative source of dead bodies 'without offending the feelings of the community' went on over a considerable period, between Lord Liverpool (Tory Prime Minister in the early 1820s) and members of the College council. Lord Liverpool, 'from the friendship and strict confidence which existed between himself and Sir Astley Cooper, took a lively interest in the subject'.[117]

Bransby Cooper implies that these discussions culminated in the appointment of the Select Committee, which ratified a plan already agreed between Brodie, Cooper and the Home Secretary.[118] There may well be elements of truth in this. After all, the Committee's first three witnesses were College men: Cooper, Brodie and Abernethy. Nevertheless, the College did not have everything its own way – it very much wanted sole control over the Act's administration, and was denied it, despite the likelihood that the future Inspector James Somerville was probably their nominee. Benthamite weight on the Committee, together with Wakley's evidence, was probably crucial in ensuring the College was given the back seat in the Act's administration. Nevertheless, the pre-determined appearance of the Committee's findings, and the ease with which a consensus of opinion was apparently created in the process of eliciting evidence, suggest that important parts of the *Evidence* were not entirely spontaneous. As one reads the *Evidence*, the possible scenario I outlined above looks increasingly close to the likely reality.

The following exchange between Sir Astley Cooper and his questioner on the Committee – most probably Warburton himself[119] – illustrates the consensus in process. To the sympathetic question:

> Is it not distressing to men of character and education, as the teachers in the schools of anatomy are, to be obliged to have recourse to a violation of the law, in order to obtain a supply of bodies and perform their duty towards their students?

Sir Astley replied:

> the great difficulty teachers have to contend with, is the management of those persons, and it is distressing to our feelings that we are obliged to employ very faulty agents to obtain a desirable end.[120]

His reply deftly deflected the charge of criminality away from himself and towards the resurrectionists, and the Committee's attention away from his duty to his students, to greater and more abstract matters. From this sort of exchange, which took place in the very earliest stages of the evidence,[121] it would seem that despite the social and professional tensions present, witness and questioner had a great deal in common, and ultimately, shared the same goal.

———

The Select Committee collected evidence on a number of topics. These included the overwhelming necessity for anatomical knowledge and enquiry, the difficulties involved in obtaining a regular supply of bodies for dissection, and the 'distress' experienced by anatomists in having to deal with resurrectionists. Particular interest was expressed in anatomists' legal position since the important changes in case law, and in anatomy tuition abroad. The potential failure of alternatives to exhumation (especially importation from Ireland or abroad) was raised, but, as noted above, none of the more feasible or imaginative alternatives was raised for discussion.

An extensive reading of a wide range of material – books, pamphlets, reports and editorials in the popular and medical press, petitions and letters from members of the public, and other such sources addressing this subject-area – would suggest that on some of these topics there was public, as well as medical consensus. The primary area of agreement seems to have been the need for anatomical knowledge and enquiry. There was widespread public appreciation of the need for dexterity in surgical technique, and an understanding that this was best gained upon the bodies of the dead, rather than on those of the living.

Almost no voice was raised throughout this period which questioned this perceived need.[122] An epigraph to this chapter suggests that some medical practitioners, particularly physicians, felt that too great an emphasis was being placed upon the curative value of knowledge gained from dissection, and too little upon other areas of medical discovery and knowledge.[123] Wakley in particular was scathing about the waste of *post-mortem* facilities, and asserted that far more could be learned from observing the course of a fatal illness, and from a subsequent examination of the morbid pathology, than a simple study of structure would ever yield.[124]

The Select Committee reported that there existed a paramount need for the study of anatomy by dissection. Sympathy was expressed for the anatomists in their difficulties in obtaining bodies for dissection, and their distress at having to deal with 'ruffians'. Deep concern was registered at the turn of events in the courts. The Committee's main recommendation was a foregone conclusion: appropriation of the corpses of the poor.[125]

The alacrity with which the Select Committee's proposal was taken up in certain sections of the parliamentary elite[126] is indicative of its profoundly political nature. One of the most revealing aspects of both *Evidence* and *Report*, and one to which attention will be drawn in the process of a discussion of the text, is the emergence and repeated use of a number of key words, whose definitions and implications seem to have been studiously avoided, or left intentionally obscure. It is only by careful examination of the verbal and topical contexts[127] of these words that the modern reader can appreciate the implications of what was being said during the hearings, and in the finished *Report*. Since the key recommendation and the justification offered for its adoption occupy a comparatively small part of the *Report*, and since they amply repay close and critical reading, it will be useful to give them here. Emphasis has been added to highlight pivotal words and phrases discussed below:

1   It is the opinion of almost all the witnesses . . . that the bodies of
     those who during life have been *maintained at the public charge*, and
     who die in workhouses, hospitals, and other charitable
     institutions, should, if not *claimed* by next of kin within a certain
     time after death, be given up, under proper regulations, to the
     Anatomist; and some of the witnesses would extend the same rule
     to the *unclaimed* bodies of those who die in prison, penitentiaries,
     and other places of confinement . . .

2   The plan proposed has this essential circumstance to recommend
     it – that provided it were carried into effect, it would yield a
     supply of subjects that, in London at least, would be adequate to
     the wants of the Anatomist. [Figures were then given of the

number of persons allegedly dying 'unclaimed' in London
workhouses in 1827.]

. . . it may be inferred from those returns which have been
procured, that the supply to be obtained, from this source alone,
would be *many times greater* than that now obtained by
disinterment; that when added to the supply to be derived from
those other sources which have been pointed out, it would be
more than commensurate to the wants of the student, and
consequently, that the plan if adopted, as meeting the exigencies
of the case, would eventually be the means of suppressing the
practice of exhumation.

3   If it be an object deeply interesting to the *feelings* of the
community that the remains of friends and relations should rest
undisturbed, that object can only be effected by giving up for
dissection a certain portion of the whole, in order to preserve the
remainder from disturbance. Exhumation is condemned as
seizing its objects indiscriminately, as, in consequence, exciting
apprehensions in the minds of the whole community, and as
outraging in the highest degree, when discovered, the *feelings* of
relations. If selection then be necessary, what bodies ought to be
selected but the bodies of those, who have either no known
relations whose *feelings* would be outraged, or such only as, by not
claiming the body, would evince indifference on the subject of
dissection.

4   It may be argued, perhaps, that the principle of selection,
according to the plan proposed, is not just, as it would not affect
equally all classes of the public; since the bodies to be chosen
would, necessarily, be those of the poor only. To this it may be
replied; 1st, – that even were the force of this objection to a certain
degree admitted, yet that, to judge fairly of the plan, its
inconveniences must be compared with those of the existing
system; which system, according to the evidence adduced, is
liable in a great measure to the same objection; since the bodies
exhumated are principally those of the poor; 2dly, – that the evils
of this, or of any other plan to be proposed on this subject, must be
judged of by the *distress* which it would occasion to the *feelings* of
surviving relations; and the unfairness to one or another class of
the community, – by the *degree of distress* inflicted on one class
rather than another; but where there are no relations to suffer
distress, there can be no inequality of suffering, and consequently
no unfairness shown to one class more than another.[128]

The extract has been divided into four numbered sections to facilitate
analysis. The first section contains the crucial recommendation that
'unclaimed' paupers' bodies should be given over 'to the Anatomist'.

Section two makes the point that this plan would effectually remove the need for exhumation by providing a source 'many times greater' than the present supply. The third expresses the Select Committee's view that, to prevent the whole community from suffering the effects of exhumation, a part of it must be sacrificed; and goes on to argue that relatives' feelings should be the sole criterion upon which the choice of 'selection' should be made. The last section postulates a possible objection to the plan on the ground of class injustice. This is at first admitted, and a defence is made with the assertion that the proposed change in the law will represent no material change in the social origin of subjects. The final passage urges once more that relatives' distress rather than class injustice (which is now denied) be the measure of the usefulness of the proposal.

This summary does not, of course, do justice to the nuances of meaning and of attitude which may be discerned in the full text; but it does allow a view of the structure of the proposal and its justification. I shall comment briefly on each section before going on to discuss other aspects of the *Report*.

It is worth noticing at the outset, that the first paragraph contains the imputation that the recommendation is put forward on the advice of witnesses. In fact, it was the Chairman who first mentioned this sector of the population for the consideration of a witness – as it so happened, Sir Astley Cooper.[129]

The main import of this section, which contains the key proposal upon which the remainder depends, rests upon the meaning of the verb 'to claim'. It is significant – both in itself, and with regard to the later history of the Committee's recommendations – that neither witnesses, *Report*, nor public or parliamentary debate established a clear and unequivocal definition of the word 'unclaimed'. The use of the word in the *Report* was not discussed at any length – precisely who would be affected was never specified.

It is not discernible whether the word 'claim' was intended to mean simply to profess oneself a relative, and to accompany the parish funeral; or, to appropriate the body and finance burial oneself. Both possible meanings can be understood from witnesses' evidence,[130] and the text of the *Report* could be taken to support either interpretation.

The difference between these meanings may appear unimportant, unless it is remembered that those whose bodies were henceforth to be appropriated for dissection would be the very poorest members of society. It is manifest throughout both *Evidence* and *Report*, that the Select Committee intended workhouses to be the major source of 'unclaimed' bodies. Despite later semantic alterations to the texts of the Bills which sought to implement the Committee's findings, members of both Houses of Parliament understood this to be the case.[131]

Since parochial authorities were not responsible for the provision of public rooms for waking, watching, or funerary social gatherings, for poor people to honour a relative or friend who had died in a workhouse by any of

the customary funerary observances discussed in Chapter 1, it would have
been necessary for the body to be removed from the workhouse, for these
activities to be enjoined elsewhere. To remove the body would mean
assuming responsibility for funeral costs – something many people in the
poorest realm of life self-evidently could not afford to do.

To the relatives of a person dying in a workhouse the possible meanings
of 'to claim' – attending a parish funeral, or alternatively, having to
underwrite the costs of a private interment – would have held vastly
different implications. But the financially fortunate men on the Select
Committee seem not to have conceived – or not to have wanted to do so –
that such a difficulty existed. They chose to ascribe all failure to claim to
'indifference'. This was in spite of a witness's evidence of late claiming on
the grounds of poverty:

> Poor people wish to avoid the expense of the funeral, and therefore
> they do not apply till some time after the funeral has taken place
> at the expense of the parish; they then generally apply for the
> clothes . . .[132]

– and in spite of the fact that on at least two occasions, questions were put
to other witnesses which show that the Chair and other members of the
Select Committee *could not have been unaware* of the contingencies of poverty,
and their bearing upon eligibility for the designation 'unclaimed'. John
Webster MD was asked to recollect from experience of anatomy schools
abroad, if he was 'aware of the practice, that a supply was . . . obtained
from the bodies of those whose friends could not afford to bury them?'.[133]
Thomas Rose, a surgeon working at the workhouse infirmary of the Parish
of St James was asked to supply the Committee with an idea of the annual
number of parish deaths, and an estimate of the proportion of 'unclaimed'
bodies which might be made available for dissection. A series of questions
were asked and a series of answers given, but from confusion in terminology it is not easy to see what Rose's replies actually meant.[134] From the drift
of questioning it seems clear that the economic basis of 'claiming' was the
key point at issue.

A further area of equivocation is to be found in the specification 'next of
kin' which appears in the first section. This limitation on 'claiming' denied
the true nature of many poor people's mutuality within a network of
friends and acquaintances. This seems inexplicable in the light of the fact
that four of the *Report*'s appendices carried headings which referred to
'friends' rather than 'relations' undertaking the payment of funeral
expenses.[135] Events in the early years of the Anatomy Act's implementation suggest that claimants' relationships would be narrowly defined, and
that friends of the deceased (like those of Polly Chapman, whose story is
told later) – who though not next of kin were likely to experience distress,
and were clearly representing the dead person's wishes – were refused the
right to prevent dissection from taking place.[136]

It is also worth noticing that in this section the phrase 'those who during life have been maintained at the public charge' appears as a qualification for dissection. To the members of the Select Committee and the great majority of their parliamentary colleagues, this phrase could only have one meaning: paupers. As we shall see later, opponents took up the phrase, and inverted it to apply to the other end of the social scale, to the numerous government nominees in receipt of state pensions and sinecures, whose names and incomes appeared in Reform literature and broadsheet revelations of state corruption, such as Wade's *Black Book*.[137]

The central point of the second section of the extract is that the Committee's proposal would yield 'many times' the number of bodies for dissection than was currently provided by grave-robbery. Reference was made to an appendix of the *Report* for support of this assertion, but an examination of the figures provided there reveals that the Committee's point can only be substantiated if the word 'claim' was to be understood in narrowly financial rather than emotive terms.

Figure 2 has been constructed from the figures provided, which show deaths in the workhouses of 131 London parishes in 1827.[138] The crucial category is the number of people (2161) who died in the workhouse, and whose relatives accompanied the parish funeral. If the word 'claim' was intended to be understood as an *emotive* category – taking into account the distress of friends and relations – this group would be counted as 'claimed', and only 1159 bodies would have been made available for dissection in 1827. The figure of 1159 represents people who died alone, and whom no one came forward to bury or accompany to the grave. It includes an unknown proportion of bodies *apparently* 'unclaimed' by reason of ignorance on the part of survivors of the event of death, or fear of enforced contributions to funeral costs.

If, however, 'claim' was intended to be understood as an *economic* category – counting only those who died in the workhouse fortunate enough to have surviving relatives or friends able to find the money to pay for the funeral – 3320 corpses would have been available to the anatomists in 1826. This figure takes no account of the 'distress' of relatives who accompanied the parish funerals of their kin.

The figures and the *Report*'s assertions concerning them are put into some perspective by another of the *Report*'s appendices, which provided information on the number of corpses actually dissected in the London anatomy schools in 1826.[139] It shows that nearly 600 bodies were obtained that year by illicit means.

The Committee's assertion that 'many times' this number could be obtained from the workhouse dead reveals that their use of the word 'unclaimed' inferred solely financial criteria. Had survivors' emotional attachments been recognised, only *twice* as many corpses (1159) would have been available – hardly the 'many times' of the Committee's sanguine assertion. Defined solely on financial grounds – ignoring the distress of

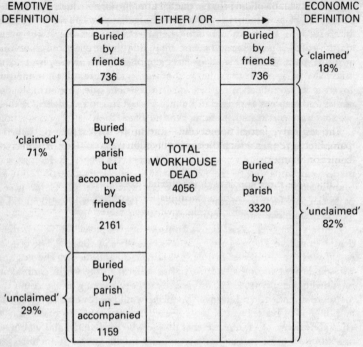

Figure 2   Economic versus Emotive definitions of 'claimed'

Sources: See chapter 3, note 51.

relatives and friends who happened to be very poor – over *five* times as many corpses were left 'unclaimed' (3320).

This examination of the figures on which the recommendation was based reveals that the *Report's* emphasis on relatives' distress was entirely spurious, for it ignored the feelings of those too poor to bury their own dead.

The opening sentence of the extract's third section discloses the sacrificial nature of the transaction involved in the Committee's proposal, and is tantamount to an admission that not only was the rest of society liable to grave-robbery, but that they loathed and feared it. The 'unclaimed' dead were henceforth to be sacrificed to save the rest of society from liability to exhumation, by means of an assumption of power on the part of the Select Committee to select and consign them. This assumption of power itself reveals the limitations of the Committee's view of the whole question, for it is indicative of an inability – or unwillingness – to think in any terms other than the use of compulsion upon the powerless, as had been precisely the case in the appropriation of executed murderers.

The last section of the passage quoted attempts to demolish a postulated charge of class injustice in two contradictory ways. This in itself is interesting, for it reveals a certain defensiveness towards such a criticism on the part of its author. The first reply admits the discrimination, but justifies it on the ground that the recommendation would lead to no super-added injustice, as it merely codified, legalised and institutionalized existing arrangements. In other words, there was no injustice in the fact that the poor were economically unable to obtain secure burial, so there would be none in a law which enforced the use of their dead for dissection.

Interestingly, James Somerville – the future Inspector – published a pamphlet in 1832 in which the same objection was countered in a precisely contrary manner:

> Objections more specious than solid have been raised against this source of supply . . . such as the injustice of consigning the bodies of the poor to be dissected; but those who have started such objections with the best intentions, are, perhaps, not aware that the traffic now extensively carried on in dead bodies, is not exclusively derived from the graves of the poor. . . . It is to be observed that there is often greater facility in stealing a dead body from a vault than from a grave. The subjects on the anatomist's table too often bear unequivocal marks of having come from some other than the pauper's grave; the appearance of hands, face, and skin, and the marks of rings on the fingers, plainly demonstrate that the person has not belonged to the working class.[140]

Wakley attributed the *Report*'s 'fallacious' argument to Peel. 'It is notorious', he said, 'that the resurrectionists have no respect for classes.'[141]

Warburton's second reply in the *Report* attempted to annul the burden of his first. The wording adeptly drew upon the old tradition of Death being the Great Leveller – '. . . where there are no relations to suffer distress, there can be no inequality of suffering, and consequently no unfairness shown to one class more than another.' The absence of effect upon surviving relations must therefore mean a parallel lack of class injustice.

Warburton's casuistry fails on two counts. First, it relies upon the identity of the terms 'unclaimed' and 'no relatives'. It has already been shown that these terms were by no means synonymous. Second, and most importantly, it leaves the individual out of the question entirely. Behind this disregard lay a fallacious parallel with exhumation, whereby during life the dead person had not known – though may well have feared – the future fate of their own corpse.[142] The author invited readers of the *Report* to assume that those consigned by poverty to dissection would be similarly ignorant, when the legislative nature of the appropriation meant this would patently not have been the case.

The absurdity of this disregard of the individual is manifest if a comparison is made with the law as it stood in 1828, while Warburton was penning the *Report*. The legal use of the terror of dissection at that time was not intended, and did not operate, primarily on the basis of the infliction of 'distress' upon a murderer's relatives. The primary intention of the law as it then stood was to prevent murder by striking fear into the potential murderer prior to the commitment of the crime; failing which, the sentence upon conviction was intended to 'impress a just Horror in the mind of the Offender', and only subsequently, upon 'the Minds of such as shall be present'.[143] By ignoring the individual whose body the *Report* intended to consign for dissection, and stressing instead the 'distress' of relations, its author attempted to deny in a poor person dying alone in a workhouse the existence of those very feelings of horror and torment which the law had for generations intended the murderer should undergo before death. When news of the Committee's recommendations broke, people already in workhouses reacted with terror to the prospect of being dissected.[144]

The postulation and disposal of an argument concerning the social injustice of the *Report*'s main recommendation – the force of which the author evidently felt impelled to deflect – reveals rather than conceals his awareness that the argument had some force. Had the real criterion for eligibility for the slab been defined by the absence of 'distress', and if only the relatives of the dead were permitted to feel it, then the law could simply have directed that all those dying in Britain without relatives would henceforth be eligible for dissection. By sequestering only those dying without relatives to 'claim' their bodies from workhouses and hospitals, the Committee designated poverty the sole basis for selection. So long as the criterion for eligibility was economic, no argument based upon 'distress' could justify it, except by deceit.

<hr />

Uses of the words 'unclaimed' and 'feelings/distress' in the *Report* have been discussed with a view to gaining insight into points at issue in the parliamentary and public debate surrounding the future Act. 'Examination' is another of these important words. Criticising the Committee's proposals for legislation, the surgeon/anatomist G.J. Guthrie highlighted its meaning: 'I personally,' he wrote, 'have no objection to be opened and *examined* as to the cause of death, but I do not intend to be *dissected*, if I can avoid it . . . '[145] Guthrie's prose makes plain the existence of two distinct processes; a distinction emphasised both by his use of precise terminology, and in his contrasting emotive response to each. To the Professor of Anatomy at the Royal College of Surgeons, to be 'examined' was to undergo what we would now term autopsy, or *post-mortem*. 'Dissection' on the other hand – the slow methodical process of sundering flesh and sinew, cartilage and bone – was something quite different. Guthrie nowhere made explicit the basis of his dislike of dissection. But it can be surmised from this passage that he could not shake off 'unscientific' or irrational beliefs and fears; that like very many of his contemporaries he held a deep repugnance towards dismemberment.

There seems to have existed some ignorance among the members of the Select Committee on Anatomy concerning the difference between these two operations. At an early point in the taking of evidence, Sir Astley Cooper was asked to explain.[146] Later exchanges with other witnesses would suggest that the distinction had been understood, and that while 'dissection' held its time-honoured meaning, 'examination' was the more generally medically favoured term for autopsy or *post-mortem*.[147] Clear and repeated evidence emerged as to the public tolerance of the one and antipathy towards the other.[148]

In the context of later events, it is interesting to note that the word 'dissection' – familiar to everyone as the murderer's fate – first began to be avoided in the *Report*, where the phrase 'the Anatomist' emerges as an alternative destination for paupers' bodies. 'Dissection' was in fact utilised correctly in the first Bill, but in the second Bill a new phrase – 'anatomical examination' – emerged, which served to cloud the qualitative difference between the two procedures; as if renaming the process would somehow strip it of its punitive meaning. I argue in a later chapter that semantic massage in Parliament and the resulting anatomy legislation – which possibly had roots in the *Report*'s unease – was not unintentional.

Certain key motifs, which run through the debate from its early stages to the successful passage of the Anatomy Act, emerge together in public for the first time in the evidence Sir Astley Cooper – the Committee's first witness.

Crucially, the phrase 'anatomical examination'[149] as a euphemism for dissection appears as Sir Astley's. So too is the equivocal meaning of 'unclaimed',[150] and the emphasis upon survivors' distress: 'I conceive the great principle on this question is this, that dissection should never outrage the feelings of the living'.[151] The extent to which these ideas were strictly those of Astley Cooper himself is unclear. Bentham had drawn a strict differentiation between dissection and *post-mortem* which Cooper's phrase 'anatomical examination' served to fuse; but the stress on survivors' feelings and the preference for using the undefined 'unclaimed' would appear to have been Bentham's. Although Bentham did not devise the term 'unclaimed' for those who would be taken for dissection under the future Act, his definition – 'those for whom no application has been made' – was equally equivocal.[152]

To contemporaries such as Horsley, author of an epigraph to this chapter – who lacked inside knowledge of Bentham's role in the proceedings – it appeared that Sir Astley was wielding undue influence. Doubtless, Sir Astley *was* important, but the coincidence of his views with Bentham's – probably the primary influence – seems too near to be accidental.

Bransby Cooper was under the clear impression that his uncle had had some crucial role, even that the Committee owed its existence to his conversations with government ministers. Perhaps given the evidence to hand, it is feasible to suggest that Sir Astley's evidence had been orchestrated in advance, and it was for tactical reasons that he was called first to the witness box. The manner in which the dialogue with his questioner was conducted seems indicative of a mutual foreknowledge. Questioner and witness seem so often in accord, and question and answer so frequently complement one another, that the suspicion arises that both had stage-managed in advance what topics would be covered, in what order, and with what results. A feeling of bland good manners pervades this encounter, which gives no indication of development over the course of questioning, and every indication of having existed before the hearing began.

It is this atmosphere, as much as anything else known about the Select Committee and its *Report*, which leads to fundamental doubts of the validity of its findings.

Guthrie's verdict on the Committee's handiwork was that it 'said everything it did not mean, and meant everything it did not say'. No part of the bill lacked a double meaning.[153] Others, too, thought it purposefully disguised its real meaning.[154] The Committee's reasoning seems to have fooled nobody but those who wished to share the assumption that the poor somehow experienced emotion differently from the rest of society. The *Report*, and those who endorsed its recommendation, coolly ignored the fear, apprehension and terror the poor would suffer in expectation and fantasy of dying in the workhouse.

'TRADING ASSASSINS'[1]

Burke and Hare . . . it is said, are the real authors of the measure, and that which would never have been sanctioned by the deliberate wisdom of parliament, is about to be extorted from its fears. . . . It would have been well if this fear had been manifested and acted upon before sixteen human beings had fallen victims to the supineness of the Government and the Legislature. It required no extraordinary sagacity to foresee, that the worst consequences must inevitably result from the system of traffic between resurrectionists and anatomists, which the executive government has so long suffered to exist. Government is already in a great degree, responsible for the crime which it has fostered by its negligence, and even encouraged by a system of forbearance.

Lancet editorial, 1829.[2]

But woe to the riches and skill thus obtained,
Woe to the wretch that would injure the dead,
And woe to his portion whose fingers are stained
With the red drops of life that he cruelly shed.

Ballad on William Burke, c.1829.[3]

It is disgusting to talk of anatomy as a science, whilst it is cultivated by means of practices which would disgrace a nation of cannibals.

Lancet editorial, 1832.[4]

The Select Committee on Anatomy submitted its *Report* and *Evidence* to the House of Commons on 22 July 1828, three months after it had been appointed, and just before the summer recess. At that time, no one present could have known that at least ten people had already been murdered for sale to an Edinburgh anatomy school.[5] Before the opening of the next parliamentary session six more murders would have followed, and one of the men responsible would already have been executed.[6]

The Burke and Hare murders are critically significant to the history of anatomy in Britain. They are dealt with here at some length because they locate the intersection of the three major themes outlined in my first section – the importance of the corpse and its integrity in popular culture, the emotional detachment of the clinical 'scientific' view, and the process whereby the corpse attained the status of an article of trade. By 1827–8 (if not before) the position had been reached at which the bodies of the poor had become worth more dead than alive. Free trade in medical tuition had reached a fitting apogee.

After the murders were discovered, many were quick to remark that such crimes had privately long been foreseen – which is confirmed by Bentham's reference to the possibility in his 1826 letter to Peel. Arguing against the continued existence of resurrectionists during his evidence to the Select Committee in early May 1828, Sir Henry Halford had remarked:

> . . . they ought not to be tolerated at all if possible, and for the reason
> I will now present to your minds: when there is a difficulty in
> obtaining bodies, and their value is so great, you absolutely throw a
> temptation in the way of these men to commit murder for the purpose
> of selling the bodies of their victims.[7]

In fact, there is no evidence to suggest that either Burke or Hare had ever gained a livelihood by bodysnatching.[8] All available information indicates that the men hit upon the idea of supplying the anatomists by accident. An old man died owing money in Mrs Hare's cheap lodging house, and the two men decided to sell his body to cover the debt. Burke's confession shows that Dr Knox became implicated by chance, when a student whom Burke and Hare asked for directions in Surgeons' Square advised them to take the body to his anatomy school rather than to Monro's.[9] The need to request directions suggests that both men were novices in the disposal of dead bodies. They were paid £7.10s for the body, which must have seemed a huge amount to such men, who usually earned a thin living by labouring and cobbling old shoes. It amply covered the old man's debt. Burke later confessed: 'that was the only subject they sold that they did not murder, and getting that high price made them try the murdering of subjects'.[10]

Later, when another lodger fell very ill, Burke and Hare eased him into coma with whisky, and smothered him. The transition from innocence to murder was facilitated by the easy money and lack of suspicion they had met at Knox's school. This time they received £10. Fifteen more people – twelve women, two handicapped youths, and an old man – were murdered in the same way before the killers' source of income was discovered. All were very poor vagrants or street folk, lured to their deaths by promises of drink and hospitality.

The sordid story eventually came to light not as a result of suspicion at the anatomy school of the aetiology of death, but from the discovery of an old woman's body in the straw of Burke's bed. Mary Docherty had come to

Edinburgh from Donegal, in search of a long-lost son. Hungry, and without money, on the 31 October 1828 she had chanced to beg in a gin-shop, where Burke had noticed her and invited her home to eat. She was murdered the same night – after the guests at a Hallowe'en party at Burke's had retired for the night – was stripped and hidden in the bed-straw until a convenient moment should arise to package the body and deliver it to Surgeons' Square. Foolishly, Burke behaved oddly when the previous evening's guests returned the following day, and aroused their suspicion by directing that no one should go near the bed. Concerned about the old lady who had been so merry the night before, at an opportune moment the visitors were drawn to make their discovery. To save his own neck Hare subsequently turned King's evidence, convicting his confederate, who was hanged and publicly dissected.

Sir Walter Scott attended the execution, on 28 January 1829:

> The mob, which was immense, demanded Knox and Hare, but,
> though greedy for more victims, received with shouts the solitary
> wretch who found his way to the gallows out of the five or six who
> seem not less guilty than he.[11]

Scott understood and sympathised with the popular opinion that the wives of both men had probably acted as accomplices, and that Knox and members of his staff were accessories to the crime of murder.

That a vocation which professed 'no object but that of conferring benefit on others'[12] in healing the sick and the saving of human life should have been responsible for the commission of so many premeditated murders, was seen as an unspeakable paradox. 'Shall it be said', asked one practitioner, aghast, 'that we owe it to that science which professes to alleviate human suffering [that] her votaries be encouraged to encourage ... Murder?'[13]

Knox's culpability in the Burke and Hare murders was fiercely discussed in public and medical circles; but throughout the criminal investigations and the judicial disposal of Burke, the anatomist kept silence. He was not called upon to give evidence at Burke's trial, and appeared to feel no obligation to defend his failure to discern that sixteen of the seventeen bodies he had purchased from Burke and Hare had undergone violent death, and had been neither laid out nor buried.[14]

His own role in the destruction of evidence was crucial – it was because of a lack of evidence[15] upon which to convict both couples that the prosecuting authorities offered Hare immunity from prosecution, and on his testimony charged Burke with the deaths of three of the sixteen victims. Eventually Burke and his wife Nelly stood trial for the death of the last victim, Mary Docherty, only. Her body had been recovered from Knox's school, whither Burke and Hare had hurriedly removed it when their guests went to inform police of their discovery.[16] Nelly Burke's case was found not proven.[17]

Extraordinary Occurrence,
and Supposed Murder, &c.

An Account of a most Extraordinary cir-
cumstance that took place on Friday
night, the 31st October 1828, in a
House in the West Port, Edinburgh,
where an old Woman of the name of
Campbell is supposed to have been
Murdered, and her Body Sold to a
Medical Doctor.

WE have various accounts of the above melancholy occurrence, which, of course, we
cannot vouch for. There is no doubt, however, of
the circumstance, of the body of an old woman
being seen on the floor of the house of Burt or
Burke, in the West Port, and of the same body
being taken from a Lecture Room to the Police
Office yesterday morning, under very suspicious
circumstances of having been murdered. We copy
the following paragraph from this day's Evening
Courant on the subject, which is the only account
yet published of this affair :—

" An old woman of the name of Campbell, from
Ireland, came to Edinburgh some days ago, in
search of a son, whom she found, and who afterwards went out of town, in search of work. She
took up her lodgings on Friday, in the house of
a man named Burt or Burke, in the West Port. It
appears that there was a merry making in Burke's
that night ; at least the noise of music and dancing
was heard, and it is believed the glass circulated
pretty freely among the party. The old woman, it
is said, with reluctance joined in the mirth, and
also partook of the liquor, and was to sleep on
straw alongside of Burke's bed. During the night
shrieks were heard ; but the neighbours paid no
attention, as such sounds were not unusual in the
house. In the morning, however, a female, on
going into Burke's, observed the old woman lying
as if dead, some of the straw being above her. She
did not say any thing, or raise any alarm ; but, in
the evening, circumstances transpired which led to
a belief that all was not right, for, by this time the
body had been removed out of the house, and, it
was suspected, had been sold to a public lecturer.
Information was conveyed to the police, and the
whole party taken into custody. After a search,
the body was found yesterday morning in the lecture room of a respectable practitioner, who, the
instant he was informed of the circumstance, not
only gave it up, but afforded every information in
his power. The body is now in the police-office,
and will be examined by medical gentlemen in the
course of the day. There are some very strong
and singular circumstances connected with the
case, which have given rise to the suspicions."

Edinburgh, 3d November, 1828.

PRICE ONE PENNY.

13   Edinburgh broadsheet giving news of the discovery of the last Burke and Hare murder, dated
3 November 1828. First reports mis-named the victim.

It was not until a week after Burke's execution, and until Hare had been freed from custody – after a prolonged legal wrangle as to the status of his immunity with regard to the other murders – that Burke's confessions were published. Until then, the public did not know except by rumour the number of murders involved, victims' identities, the technique used to deprive them of life, or the possible extent of Knox's involvement.

There were two confessions, published simultaneously on 7 February 1829.[18] One was the officially recognised statement of guilt which Burke had verified in the presence of a Roman Catholic priest, the Edinburgh Sheriff and the Procurator-Fiscal. The other confession was obtained as a scoop by the Edinburgh newspaper, the *Evening Courant*. This was authenticated both by Burke's signature, and by its content, which was more expansive and detailed than the official version of events. It contained the gruesome information that one victim, Mary Paterson,

> was only four hours dead till she was in Knox's dissecting rooms; but she was not dissected at that time, for she was three months in whiskey before she was dissected. She was warm when Burke cut the hair off her head: and Knox brought a Mr--- a painter, to look at her, she was so handsome a figure, and well shaped in body and limbs. One of the students said she was like a girl he had seen in the Canongate as one pea is like to another. They desired Burke to cut off her hair; one of the students gave a pair of scissors for that purpose.[19]

The *Courant* confession went on to say that Burke and Hare

> entered into a contract with Dr Knox and his assistants that they were to get £10 in winter and £8 in summer for as many subjects as they could bring to them.

It also recorded Burke's belief that he thought it providential that they had been detected in their 'murdering career', or he did not know

> how far they might have gone with it, even to attack people on the streets, as they were so successful, and always met with a ready market: that when they delivered a body they were always told to get more.

A detail which appeared only in the official confession was that Knox was present on two occasions when Burke and Hare delivered murdered bodies, and that in one case he had approved of a corpse's freshness, but asked no questions.[20]

At about the same time as Burke's confessions were published, a sixpenny pamphlet appeared under the pseudonym *Echo of Surgeons' Square*, purporting to expose the 'Secrets, Accomplices, and other Facts, relative to the late Murders'.[21] The pamphlet has since been attributed to David Paterson, who had worked as doorkeeper at Knox's school. Paterson had been sacked from his post after divulging at Burke's trial that he had tried

14   A popular print showing the discovery of the murder of Mary Docherty on 1 November
1828

to profit from the sale to another anatomist of a body he had purchased on
his employer's behalf.

Doubtless the pamphlet was intended to settle old scores, and exonerate
Paterson himself from blame; but nevertheless, much of it has a ring of
veracity. The pamphlet affords a great deal of inside information about the
running of a dissecting establishment at this period, and provides some
priceless vignettes: of the Edinburgh anatomy lecturers massed to cast lots
for a share of a cargo of Irish corpses;[22] or of the humour involved in a
mis-delivery of a fine ham and other edibles which arrived as many other
hampers had done, without an address. The body in a hamper in the same
consignment never appeared.[23]

The *Echo*'s apparent veracity in these particulars lends credence to other
parts of the text – in particular to those which accord with Burke's
confession, like the interest of Knox and his students in Mary Paterson's
naked body, and the earnestness with which Burke and Hare were urged to
supply the school with more bodies.[24]

The pamphlet made two major disclosures, both of which added to
suspicions of Knox. The first was that more than one of the bodies supplied
by Burke and Hare had blood at the mouth, nose or ears;[25] and the second,
that the head and distinctive feet were severed from the body of Daft Jamie
– a well-known Edinburgh character – and his dissection hastened, when it
became known that he was missing from the streets.[26]

The *Echo* recommended that the Lord Advocate, to whom the pamphlet was addressed as an open letter, prosecute a judicial enquiry into Knox's role in the murders. It is significant that the title-page and adverts for the work carried the epigraph: 'What? Shall wealth screen thee from justice?'[27] openly articulating the widely shared suspicion that Knox was receiving preferential treatment at the hands of the law, and that there was some kind of a cover-up in progress.

Although stories had circulated orally and in the press concerning details of the murders, the publication of Burke's confessions, Paterson's allegations and Hare's release from custody, caused a furore in Edinburgh. Crowds had collected at Knox's school before, and they did so again. Burke was dead; Hare and the two women had been hounded out of the city, reviled wherever they were recognised, risking death whenever they ventured out of police custody. Knox remained, teaching and dissecting, his silence seemingly expressive both of contempt for popular opinion, and his belief that he held no form of accountability to the public.

But Knox seemed virtually alone in this belief. Even his social peers felt the need for some form of enquiry, if only to protect the international medical reputation of Edinburgh. When even the anger aroused by Burke's confessions went unanswered by Knox, a self-appointed committee announced it would do the job. However, the announcement met with the general suspicion that Knox's social and medical position in Edinburgh was such that he would receive privileged treatment as of right, which would ensure that the enquiry would gloss over past sins and exculpate from blame, rather than censure or expose unpalatable truths. Sir Walter Scott, invited to sit on the committee, would have none of it. Once again, his sympathies seem to have coincided with popular opinion, when he characterised the committee as a 'whitewash' of a 'much to be suspected individual'.[28]

Failure of the law to investigate Knox's role in the multiple murders had provoked widespread resentment and disbelief; but the self-appointment of a lay committee whom no one believed objective was no substitute for the official enquiry many had hoped for and expected. At this period, poor people were routinely imprisoned, transported and even hanged for the smallest of crimes against property. This seemed a clear case of one law for the rich and another for the poor.[29] All the murder victims had been very poor, and the law had offered them neither protection nor redress against the man who commissioned their deaths. Justice had not visibly been done. Nor was this feeling confined to the poor. Wakley, writing in the *Lancet*, said that had

> the receiver of these sixteen strangled bodies been punishable as well
> as the murderer, the crimes which have cast a stain on the character
> of the nation and of human nature, would not have been
> committed.[30]

On 12 February, the day after the committee of enquiry announced itself, thousands of Edinburgh people mobilised to give Knox a thorough public shaming.[31] An effigy, bearing a 'tolerable resemblance' to the doctor, rendered unmistakable by the words 'Knox, the associate of the infamous Hare' fixed to its back, was borne noisily through the city streets by a large and rapidly expanding crowd.[32] When the demonstration reached Newington, the effigy was ceremonially throttled,[33] and publicly hanged from a tree facing Knox's house. It was then cut down, and after an abortive attempt to set it alight, it was torn to pieces, 'amidst the huzzas of thousands'.[34]

A 'skimmington' – or 'stang-riding' – was a traditional mode of expressing public disquiet, and of obtaining popular justice.[35] It would usually be mounted publicly to shame transgressors of implicit social codes – in cases of wifebeating, flagrant marital infidelity, or of over-speedy remarriage by widows or widowers. In his *Mayor of Casterbridge*, Thomas Hardy describes in some detail a West Country skimmington denouncing a marital infidelity. The skimmington was a composite custom, generally featuring one or more of the following elements: it was a vibrant popular ritual associated with noise, known as 'rough music' – a cacophony of sound which Violet Alford has described as an 'overture on pots and pans, whistles and bells';[36] it often focused upon some sort of processional progress, and could feature a symbolic figure at its focus – an effigy – the burning of which was usually the climax of the event. These processions might also feature some sort of re-enactment, and were often closely associated with a specific locality. A key component in the custom's perpetuation was its ability to serve as a vehicle for the expression of collective popular disapproval – a sentiment which could range from scurrilous hilarity and ridicule, through vilification, to a much more serious and potentially threatening expression of collective malediction.

The Edinburgh skimmington conforms to this general description in almost every particular, but there is one important difference – effigies were usually burnt: Knox in effigy had a different treatment. It is worth noting the crowd's understanding of the limits of its own proper sphere of activity – Knox himself could have been lynched without much difficulty – but the crowd was satisified in a traditional way to act out, rather than to enforce, its views. The effigy stood for Knox – carried in procession through the town, and ritually executed opposite his house, amid rough music and general turmoil. The symbolic punishment expressed not only popular disgust towards Knox and a desire for retribution, but also a thorough distrust of the legal process which not only permitted Hare to go free, but appeared to condone Knox's silence.[37] The event was also an expression of popular disbelief in the committee of enquiry's impartiality.

Though their appearance and shouts were threatening, the demonstrators offered nothing beyond symbolic violence until they were attacked by police, who made a charge from Knox's front door, having received access from the rear of the house. The destruction of Knox's effigy may have vented and assuaged public anger, but by this ill-advised action – apparently acting in defence of Knox – the police aggravated the situation. The retreating crowd threw missiles, causing police injuries and broken windows. However, although the skimmington crowd subsequently dispersed 'quietly',[38] demonstrators regrouped in various parts of the city later that afternoon, and the police were hard put to cope as smaller crowds assembled in different districts, with discreet intentions. One group paraded along Princes Street, the main road of the elegant new part of town, and was dispersed in the High Street. Another collected in the West Port area, the poverty-stricken neighbourhood in which the murders were committed, and marched to the College of Surgeons, where windows were broken. The Cowgate was the scene of another gathering, though its intentions are unknown as it was dispersed by police, who arrested several of the most active demonstrators. After dark Knox's house was attacked a second time and suffered damage, while a further abortive attempt was made upon Surgeons' Square.

About twenty people[39] appeared afterwards in court, and were dealt with with comparatively leniently. Most were dismissed from lack of evidence, and those convicted were only bound over and fined.[40] Their fines were paid from a collective fund, said to have been collected even before the demonstration.[41] Adjacent householders whose windows were broken in the attack on Knox's house were reported to have had their windows replaced gratis the following day. Although there was no indication who was responsible, it was assumed that the demonstrators had not intended the innocent to suffer, and that some affluent sympathiser had footed the bill.[42]

There can be no doubt that this day of demonstrations was a manifestation of a very wide public concern that Knox's silence was a guilty rather than a dignified one.[43] The leniency with which demonstrators were treated in court, and the sympathetic tone of much of the newspaper coverage[44] suggest that this view was by no means confined to the Edinburgh crowd. A wide consensus of opinion existed – one which included many to whom crowd activity was not a traditional mode of expression – that Knox had a public responsibility to make his position known, and that the public deserved to know more than his silence would yield. One newspaper spoke for many when it declared

> the agitation of public feeling will never subside till the city be
> released of this man's presence, or until his innocence be manifested.
> In justice to himself, if he is innocent, in justice to the public if he is
> guilty, he ought to be put upon trial.[45]

The committee of enquiry met and took evidence – none of which was made public. Contemporary sceptics as to its objectivity would have cited in self-justification the fact that when its report eventually appeared, it was submitted to the press by Knox himself. It appeared in the *Caledonian Mercury* on 21 March 1829. In the committee's view, Knox had been 'incautious' in accepting Burke and Hare's story that the bodies had been purchased from the relatives of the deceased, when this was known to be a highly unusual source of supply. The anatomist should have been more vigilant when purchasing freshly dead bodies from people of the 'notorious' character of resurrectionists, and he should not have delegated this responsibility to his assistants or doorkeeper. Nor should these receivers have been directed by Knox to refrain from making enquiries concerning the source of supply in such cases. In the belief that neither Knox nor his staff entertained any suspicion of the murders, the committee's one censure was that Knox had 'unintentionally' given a 'degree of facility to the disposal of the victims . . . which under better regulations would have not existed'.

An interesting point in the committee's report was that long before the murders, Knox had advocated a source of corpses potentially adequate to the needs of anatomists: direct purchase from relatives of the bodies of 'deceased persons in the lowest ranks of society'. His mistaken belief that this source was a feasible one may have meant that when Burke and Hare offered their first freshly dead body and named this source of supply, they were more than readily believed. In the first instance they were telling the truth, but subsequent cases should have roused suspicion.

The report caused Knox to break his long silence, for he accompanied its submission by a letter making clear his disagreement even with the committee's one rebuke. In his view the receipt of murdered bodies was a 'mere misfortune' which 'would almost certainly have occurred to anybody else' in his situation. He expressed neither sorrow nor regret that sixteen people had met their deaths, and no contrition for his own part in their demise. Knox represented himself as the blameless object of popular prejudice, misrepresentation and calumny. He ended by stating that he would never seek to vindicate himself further.

The tone and content of this letter reveal Knox to have been an obstinate, proud and unyielding man. Much of the anger expressed against him was doubtless provoked by his own behaviour, for had he admitted to shock and shame at the outset, or taken an active public part in the prosecution of the murderers, it is unlikely that he would have become the object of popular vilification. His failure to take either course and his persistent repudiation of responsibility for what had happened, gave the impression of guilt or of guilty knowledge. Knox was not made the object of popular vilification in haste: more than three months had elapsed between the discovery of the murders and the rough music, in which time he had been free to give his version of events. Knox rode out the storm, but his failure to disassociate himself from Burke and Hare blighted his life and career thereafter.[46]

These murders throw into relief the collective values of the poor. One of

Burke and Hare's victims clutched tightly in death to twopence-halfpenny. Her corpse raised £8 from Knox.[47] The distance between these two sums is an indication of the incentive which existed to the very poor to sell their own dead to the doctors. Yet despite the unremitting poverty of their lives, and the magnitude of the incentive held out to them, such sale was virtually unknown. Sir Robert Christison recollected:

> In a conversation I had with [Knox] before the information obtained from Hare and his wife had been communicated to me, I observed that the body taken by the police from his rooms must have been delivered there while warm and flexible, and consequently never had been buried. He made very light of this suggestion, and told me that he had ten or eleven bodies brought the previous winter to his rooms in as recent a state; and that they were got by his providers watching the low lodging houses in the Cowgate, Grassmarket, and West Port, and, when a death occurred, purchasing the body from the tenant before anyone could claim it for interment. But Dr Knox could scarcely have been so little aware of the habits of the low populace who frequent these dens, as not to know that a death in one of them brought a constant succession of visitors to look at the corpse, and keep up a series of orgies till they saw it carried off for burial; and consequently, that no such arrangement with the lodging-house-keeper as he described was practicable.[48]

Christison's lack of sympathy with the poor is evident from his derogatory description of their funeral observances – yet his estimation of the refusal to sell their own dead is patently rooted in the real world, and belies his own and Knox's estimate of their bestiality.[49] Christison's knowledge of the Edinburgh poor goes deep enough for us to ascertain a deep popular antipathy to market innovation in the realm of personal relations, by the frank refusal to co-operate in regarding the commodity value of a corpse above its affective meaning.

In his discussion of the eighteenth-century French judicial code, Michel Foucault has drawn attention to the importance in the ritual of judicial punishment of the symbolism of poetic justice.[50] There can be no doubt from descriptions of the Edinburgh skimmington and the treatment of Knox in effigy, that this concept was well understood by the Edinburgh crowd of the 1820s. As we have seen, some sort of enactment of the transgression/accusation traditionally played a role in a skimmington. Knox's symbolic body was throttled, then hanged, and finally dismembered. The throttling was probably an enactment of the manner in which Burke and Hare's victims were believed to have met their deaths – a symbolic burking. The hanging of the effigy was the punishment the crowd evidently believed appropriate in this case. At this point some reports

EXECUTION.

A Full and Particular account of the Execution of W. BURKE, who was hanged at Edinburgh on Wednesday the 28th January, 1829; also, an account of his conduct and behaviour since his condemnation, and on the Scaffold.

Early on Wednesday morning, the Town of Edinburgh was filled with an immense croud of spectators, from all places of the surrounding country, to witness the execution of a Monster, whose crime stands unparalleled in the annals of Scotland: viz.—for cruelly murdering Margery M'Conegal, and afterwards selling her body to the Doctors in October last.

Whilst this unhappy man was under sentence, he made the following Confession:—that he had been engaged in this murderous traffic from Christmas, 1827, until the murder of the woman Docherty, or M'Conegal, in October last; during which period, he had butchered Sixteen of his fellow-creatures, and that he had no accomplice but Hare,—that they perpetrated these fearful atrocities by suffocation. When they succeeded in making their victims drunk, the one held the mouth and nostrils, whilst the other went upon the body, and in this manner was the woman Docherty killed; they then sold her body to Doctor ——— in his rooms, and received payment at his house: and that they were never Resurrectionests; all the bodies they sold being murdered, except one, who died a natural death in Hare's house.

At an early hour on Tuesday, he was taken in a coach from the jail on the Calton-hill to the Lock-up, a prison immediately adjacent to the place of execution. He spent the day in silence, reading, and devotion, and on Tuesday night he slept soundly for several hours. About seven o'clock, the two Catholic clergymen arrived, and were admitted into the cell, and they were soon after followed by the Rev. Mr Marshall. The religious ceremonies being performed, he talked firmly, declared that death had no terrors, and expressed a hope of pardon and happiness. During the night, Burke stated that he was happy, that he had at last been arrested in his career of crime, and brought to justice. Though he had been a great offender, yet he rested on the atonement of the Saviour for salvation. When the irons were knocked off, he exclaimed, "Thank God these are off, and all will be off shortly." Shortly after eight o'clock, the procession set out for the place of execution. Bailies Crichton and Small, with a party of town officers, first ascended the scaffold, and they were followed by Burke, supported by the two Catholic Clergymen. He was dressed in decent black clothes, and was perfectly firm and composed. The moment he appeared, the crowd set up an appalling shout, which continued for several minutes. The murderer and the Catholic clergymen then knelt down and spent a few minutes in devotion, and the religious exercises were concluded by a prayer from the Rev. Mr Marshall. As soon as the executioner proceeded to do his duty, the cries of "Burke him, Burke him, give him no rope," and many others of a similar complexion, were vociferated in voices loud with indignation. Burke, in the mean time, stood perfectly unmoved, and gazed around till the cap was drawn over his face, and shut the world for ever from his view.

The executioner having completed his preparations and placed the signal in Burke's hand, the magistrates, ministers, and attendants left the scaffold. The crowd again set up another long and loud shout, which was followed by cries for "Hare, Hare!". "Where is Hare?" "Hang Hare!" and so on. Burke lifted his hands and ejaculated a prayer of a few sentences—then dropt the napkin, and momently the drop fell. The struggle was neither long nor apparently severe; but at every convulsive motion, a loud huzza arose from the multitude, which was several times repeated even after the last agonies of humanity were past. During the time of the wretched man's suspension, not a single indication of pity was observable among the vast crowd—on the contrary, every countenance wore the lively aspect of a gala day, while puns and jokes on the occasion were freely bandied about, and produced bursts of laughter and merriment, which were not confined to the juvenile spectators alone—"*Burke* Hare too!" "Wash blood from the land!" "One cheer more!" and similar exclamations, were repeated in different directions, until the culprit was cut down, about nine o'clock, when one general and tremendous huzza closed the awful exhibition—and the multitude immediately thereafter began to disperse.

Burke's body is to be dissected, and his Skeleton to be preserved, in order that posterity may keep in remembrance his atrocious crimes.

PRICE ONE PENNY.

mention an abortive attempt to set fire to the effigy – again a traditional feature, as in Guy Fawkes celebrations today. The Edinburgh crowd seems to have thought better of this, and instead tore the effigy to bits. It cannot now be known whether this was intended to be understood as a symbolic dissection, but this would seem likely. If so, we have some clue as to popular views of what dissection entailed. If this active dismemberment was intended as a dissection, it implied that Knox should be regarded as, and deserved to be treated as, on a level with Burke.

Let us return for a moment to the punishment judicially inflicted upon Burke. In broadsheet and newspaper accounts of Burke's execution, it is evident that the crowd wanted even more poetic justice than his sentence had directed. Cries of '*Burke him*' and '*Burke Hare too*' mark the coinage of a new verb in the language.[51] Though Burke reportedly held no fear of it, the subsequent dissection of his body was an intentional irony, rendered even more spectacular by the presiding judge's expressed desire that Burke's skeleton should be preserved in memory of his crimes.[52]

The 'public' dissection of Burke's body was witnessed only by a select number of ticket-holders. Afterwards, two thousand students who had been involved in a near-riot at their exclusion from the occasion, were permitted to file past.[53] On the following day, Burke's partly dissected body was exhibited on its slab to between thirty and forty thousand members of the general public.[54]

Burke's dissection represented the apotheosis of a punishment to fit a crime. But it also represented a medical, judicial and political paradox, whereby the punishment worked ultimately to prompt further crimes of the same type. After the later execution of Bishop and Williams the 'London Burkers', in 1831, Edward Gibbon Wakefield observed:

> The inducement to this species of murder is the value of a dead body. The value of dead bodies arises from the scarcity of them in proportion to the demand for them. The scarcity of dead bodies for the purposes of dissection arises from a violent prejudice against dissection, in the vulgar mind. The thought of being dissected after death, or of having the body of a relative dissected, is quite horrible to the great majority of people of all conditions. This prejudice, against the conversion of inanimate flesh to the only useful purpose of which it is susceptible, has been fostered in various ways; and in particular by the law, which directs that the bodies of murderers shall be 'anatomised'. Sentence of dissection was passed on Bishop and Williams, for the express purpose, one might almost think, of strengthening the vulgar prejudice against dissection.[55]

The law directed people 'to cultivate their prejudice against dissection',

15   (*Opposite*) Execution of William Burke, broadsheet, 1829

and, thought Wakefield, provided 'a motive for the crime which the same law punishes to the uttermost'. My next chapter shows that Wakefield was at the forefront in formulating methods whereby popular feelings against dissection could be moderated.

Wakley, too, was sickened by the association of his own healing profession and the execution of the death sentence, using every possible argument to persuade his more recalcitrant fellows to an understanding of his views. His arguments in a *Lancet* editorial of March 1830[56] mix moral indignation concerning the 'impropriety of medical men coming in to the assistance of the hangman, and completing the final injunction of the law' with arguments about professionalism. The use of dissection in the context of execution tended 'to lower the character of the profession in the public mind', the association of anatomist and hangman was 'a degrading coalition'. Many of Wakley's contemporaries became concerned to separate dissection and execution mainly because they believed such a divorce would have a beneficial effect upon the social status of surgery.

An indication of broader medical opinion may be gained from a debate by members of the Westminster Medical Society. In early 1832, a member submitted for the Society's consideration a petition which ascribed popular hostility towards dissection to its association with the punishment of murder, and prayed that the legislature would abolish the practice.[57] The proposer suggested in debate that murderers' bodies should be declared 'dishonoured' and unworthy of beneficial use to society. Instead, paupers' bodies should be used, and dissection regarded as an honour. The suggestion was derided by another doctor who

> questioned the propriety of making at once so long a stride – that that which had long been looked upon as a badge of disgrace, should all on a sudden be ordained a mark of honour. This would, surely 'astonish the natives'.

His point was greeted with hilarity.

Two doctors disagreed with the petition, ascribing prejudice against dissection to 'a natural repugnance'. One thought that even if the punishment were to be abolished immediately, 'it would not abate one jot the prejudices now in existence, which were, in his opinion, coexistent with human nature itself.' Nevertheless, the petition was adopted, probably for the reasons another member gave; he agreed with 'the spirit which dictated the resolution', namely, 'that medical men should not be "*the finishers of the law*" '.[58]

The surgeon-anatomist, G.J. Guthrie, heartily disagreed with such arguments, and expressed himself perfectly willing to execute dissection upon hanged murderers. He believed dissection a gross indignity, a dishonour fit only for those who had put themselves outside society's mores by committing capital crimes. Guthrie was a prominent member of the Royal College hierarchy (indeed, he would later be President), and he had the College's interests as well as the poor's at heart when he wrote an open letter to the Home Secretary in 1829, asking;

> where is the justice in taking the body of a poor person . . . whilst the remains of those who die under criminal sentence, or are deprived of life, as criminals unfit to live, are to be treated with respect? If such a measure be adopted, it will be a monstrous act of injustice to the poor of this country.[59]

Admitting that he loathed the idea of being dissected himself, Guthrie accused other members of his profession of hypocrisy:

> if a medical man maintains the opinion that dissection is an unobjectionable process which people ought to submit the dead bodies of their friends to for the sake of science and the benefit of the living, I in my turn maintain, that they are bound to set the example.

Citing several instances of medical men who had recently died, and who by ensuring their own burial had clearly shown that they shared the popular abhorrence of dissection, Guthrie ridiculed the idea that these or any contemporary members of his profession would attribute their own prejudice against dissection to the connection with punishment. Guthrie hinted that dissection often involved indecency and disrespect, and that those who had experience of it knew better than to allow their own bodies to be so treated. He described as laughable the fashionable medical and media opinion that the stigma would disappear if the punishment were to be abolished.

Guthrie seems to have had a sharp awareness of the pervasiveness in the Parliamentary committee and its medical witnesses of the contradiction evident in wider public opinion concerning anatomy. Everyone recognised the validity and need for anatomical knowledge; but few were willing personally to constitute the supply.

Why so prominent an anatomist as Guthrie was not called to give evidence before the Select Committee is unknown.[60] In admitting his own loathing of dissection, Guthrie expressed a personal affinity to the wider public hostility, which is more than can be found to have been expressed openly by any of the witnesses appearing before the Select Committee, or indeed, by the author of the *Report*. Nevertheless, Guthrie's sincere belief that dissection would retain its stigma, and his insistence that it should therefore remain a punishment, were – in a sense – adopted by the Committee, though not at all in the way in which he had intended: dissection retained its stigma and remained a punishment – but for transgressors of the social rather than the criminal code. Recommending the dissection of paupers, the *Report* effectively recommended a redefinition of poverty – from being seen as a state of pitiable misfortune to one of criminal responsibility.[61]

Parliament, re-convened after the recess, was invited to endorse this redefinition when Warburton submitted his *Bill for preventing the Unlawful Disinterment of Human Bodies, and for Regulating Schools of Anatomy* on 12 March 1829.[62] The Burke and Hare scandal was still very much current news, as the Edinburgh skimmington had taken place only a month previously, and the enquiry's report on Knox had not yet been published. Applying for leave to bring in his bill, Warburton asserted that if the bodies of the dead from public institutions were denied, 'the science of anatomy would rapidly sink into decay'. Affecting a figurative wringing of hands, he said that great difficulty had surrounded the choice of future 'subjects', but he challenged any objector to provide him with an alternative where none existed, other than the continuance of grave-robbery and murder. Warburton said:

> he was happy in contemplating that if his project was adopted, it would be the means of exonerating hereafter a beneficent and humane profession from the possibility of being implicated, in the charge of being confederates with either resurrection-men, or a class of villains whose atrocities had so very recently been brought to light.

Warburton was seconded in an emotional speech from an elderly member of the Select Committee, Mr Ralph Leycester, who called anatomy 'the lamp of science which illumined the path to skill', and reiterated that the only alternative to exhumation and concomitant villainies had happily been found set forth in his honourable friend's proposals. Mr Leycester added:

> it would, indeed, be a melancholy satisfaction to those whose last moments received consolation from the public charities, to know that they would be able after death . . . to repay the debt they owed to those who administered comfort to them during the last stage of their existence.[63]

Mr Hyde Villiers represented the bill as 'a measure of charity: for it was the poor who would always reap the great benefit of it'. No one in the House objected. The Select Committee's premises and findings seem to have been accepted without reserve. The Lord Advocate stood to add his voice; no measure appeared to him to be 'so unobjectionable', for 'no feelings could be outraged'. The poor, he said, as if from first-hand knowledge, 'went into the hospitals with the hope of being cured, and were regardless of the fate of their bodies after death'. The Home Secretary, Peel, deplored the fact that teachers of anatomy were compelled to associate with those who committed the 'most egregious violations of decency', and said 'it could not . . . be charged as an objection to this bill, that it would render the poor who died more liable to be dissected than the rich.'

Warburton was granted leave to bring in his bill.

Warburton's parliamentary success thus far was due not simply to public pressure for a change in the law on grave-robbery, or to the national trauma of the Burke and Hare murders. The Benthamite expedient of consigning paupers' bodies to the slab coincided with several current strands of opinion concerning poverty and the poor, most of which were strongly rooted in self-interest.

It sometimes happens that an artist creates – consciously or not – an artefact which epitomises some aspect of the spirit of the age. A key passage in *Oliver Twist*, which Dickens seems intentionally to have imbued with significance, may be seen in this way. The book was Dickens's first novel after *Pickwick*, and was published in parts over the first year of Victoria's accession – 1837–8 – at the height of the Anti-Poor Law movement. The writing of it was a political act of no small importance.[64] Its value here resides not in any influence upon the Anatomy question, but in that it crystallises contemporary attitudes towards poverty.

By the time the book was published, the social impact of Benthamite/Malthusian policies – of which the Anatomy Act was an early success – was manifest. The book was Dickens's call to the ruling elite to restore social equilibrium by a return to benevolent paternalistic values. His appeal was one of many in the 1830s – Cobbett, Oastler, Sadler and many others viewed the repudiation of traditional responsibilities towards the poor as a revolutionary step. Observing that poverty was being re-cast as a crime, and that the poor were being treated as if they had neither 'natural, social, nor domestic feelings', Oastler had said that the New Poor Law would 'lay the axe to the root of the social compact: it must break up society, and make England a wilderness'.[65]

This Tory-Radical sentiment had a strongly deteriorationist and arcadian streak which was not without popular support. In a broadsheet petition, poor women in the West Hampnett workhouse chided the Duke of Richmond:

> Formerly noblemen fed all the poor!
> And none from their halls were sent hungry away,
> Your ancestors would in gone-by times of yore
> Have scorned a poor boy's suet pudding to weigh.[66]

Augustus Pugin used the image of the poor workhouse inmate being taken away for dissection as a focus of attention in his *Contrasts*, in which he compared provision made for the poor in the new workhouses with that of an idealised mediaeval monastery. *Oliver Twist* drew attention to a similar contrast: between the open-hearted kindness of ideal private charity and the tight-fisted cruelty of the workhouse.[68]

The book was subtitled *The Parish Boy's Progress* – highlighting allegorical overtones of Bunyan's Christian in the ironic parallel of two journeys to a Celestial City. Oliver's journey began with a blessing, and ended in betrayal. His celestial city was a travesty, 'a dirtier or more wretched place he had never seen'. No angels welcomed him there, the only people to take

him in were London thieves. On the way, exhausted with walking and
fainting with hunger, he was driven to beg from some passengers on a stage
coach:

> but there were very few who took any notice of him; and even those
> told him to wait till they got to the top of the hill, and then let them see
> how far he could run for a halfpenny. Poor Oliver tried to keep up
> with the coach a little way, but was unable to do it, by reason of his
> fatigue and sore feet. When the [travellers] saw this, they put their
> halfpence back into their pockets again, declaring that he was an idle
> young dog, and didn't deserve anything; and the coach rattled away
> and left only a cloud of dust behind.[69]

Poverty could either be ignored altogether, or the demand could be made
that the poor should earn by impossible labours the charitable help which
Christianity teaches should be given freely. Even then, they would receive
disparagement, insult, and even injury. Throughout his journey, Oliver
was spurned and rejected; he was suspected of criminality, threatened with
dogs, abused, and intimidated with threats of both jail and the workhouse.

The passage is additionally valuable in its indication of a shift in the
grounds for assistance for those in need, which marks a divide between the
era of the Anatomy Act and our own. Today, though under threat for
similar reasons, the criterion for relief from poverty rightly rests upon
necessity. During the period the Anatomy Act was being formulated and
Dickens was writing, an older, more paternalistic view of charitable help to
the needy was compounded and in some quarters almost eclipsed by the
morally loaded qualification of '*desert*'. Helping only the 'deserving poor'
involved the imposition of social and political value-judgments on the
distribution of poor relief. Because Oliver could not perform the feat they
chose and expected of him, the travellers abused him, and mutually agreed
that he was beneath their consideration, despite the child's evident need.

The view that the poor were morally reprehensible, that their poverty
somehow reflected moral shortcomings, was of course a comfortable one
for the financially fortunate. Yet the embodiment of industry as a primary
social virtue for the poor was understood to be less simple than St Paul's
pronouncement that if a man do not work, neither shall he eat. Philo-
sophers and economists a generation before Dickens was born had understood that poverty was a necessity in a society based upon capital:
'Everyone but an idiot knows', wrote Arthur Young in 1771, 'that the
lower class must be kept poor, or they will not be industrious.'[70] According
to Patrick Colquhoun in 1806, poverty 'is the source of all wealth, since
without poverty, there could be no labour . . . no riches, no refinement, no
comfort, and no benefit to those who may be possessed of weath.'[71]

Half a century before the Anatomy Act, then, the perpetuation of social
inequality was recognised as crucial for both the production and the
preservation of wealth. Nevertheless, this society, aware that poverty was a

necessary part of its fabric, developed a system in which those suffering it were treated as if the fault was entirely their own, a state of affairs which was given an apparently sound academic basis by the work of the Reverend Thomas Malthus. Malthus believed poverty inevitable: 'the pressure of distress on this part of a community is an evil so deeply seated that no human ingenuity can reach it'.[72] Malthus pronounced the two great 'checks' on population growth to be 'misery and vice', and all but absolved society from attempts at alleviation by warning that population had increased rapidly 'whenever these causes have been in any considerable degree removed'.[73] Malthus was convinced that financial assistance to the poor caused pauperism. He recommended that all such assistance be withdrawn, and that deterrent workhouses be instituted to ensure that only the abjectly destitute and desperate applied for relief.

Malthus's ideas were greeted with wide approval in the higher walks of life, particularly among the new rich. Samuel Whitbread, speaking in the House of Commons in 1807 pronounced:

> . . . many persons agreeing in this position, have wished the whole system [of poor laws] was well expunged from our statute book; and perhaps I would not go too far in saying, that such is the prevailing sentiment.[74]

Bentham's own view is manifest in his correspondence with Peel and his proposed 'Panopticon', an architectural design – vilified by Pugin – which he intended would provide an authoritarian system of constant surveillance for adoption in the construction of prisons and, significantly, of hospitals and workhouses. Bentham's utilitarian followers – such as Warburton, Smith, Hume and others on the Select Committee – had adopted Malthusian ideas to the extent that E.P. Thompson has commented:

> it is scarcely possible to think of middle class utilitarianism without thinking also of Malthus and of orthodox political economy: the doctrine of utility could only be interpreted in the light of the 'laws' of population and those of supply and demand.[75]

They promoted the need for a uniform system of Poor Laws under central administration, with 'machinery to eradicate mendicancy & idleness'.[76]

No unbiased research was undertaken at the time to ascertain if these assumptions were correct; but recent historical enquiry has shown that Malthus's contention that the allowance system (similar to today's unemployment and social security benefits) caused exponential population growth, was 'fundamentally erroneous'.[77] One historian has observed that 'the notion of gradually snowballing relief costs is purely imaginary'.[78] Nevertheless, at the time, the high cost of poor rates was utilised to support arguments for reform of the old Poor Law. In the opinion of Sir Francis Head, one of the early Commissioners in the New Poor Law administration, 'the poor rates of any country is the symbol of its improvidence'.[79]

James Dawson Burn, a contemporary of Dickens, commented bitterly that the wealthy in this era knew

> little or nothing about the real condition of the labouring community, and from both the conduct and expressed opinions of some of them one would conclude that they did not consider themselves of the same flesh and blood.[80]

The travellers on the coach, though not themselves wealthy, seemed to personify this view – almost as if the poor were another species; they even called Oliver a dog.

To reveal in fiction the effect of environment upon the character seems to have been one of Dickens's aims in the book. He details the process by which the naked babe of his first chapter became the shabby beggar-boy, whom the travellers regard as bestial. The process is seen to operate contrariwise to that of William Godwin's notion of perfectibility. Contemporary social anthropologists were also concerned with the effects of the environment upon character. Some thought the human race a single species, with gradations of colour to parallel those of civilisation – the more civilised, the whiter the skin.[81] Others believed industrialisation had had a degenerative effect upon the race, and justified the argument by comparing the poor to savages and animals.[82]

The extent to which this view was a commonplace in the early 1830s will be evident if we recall the laughter at the Westminster Medical Society, when one of the medical gentlemen commented that to designate dissection an honour would astonish 'the natives'. The language used by commentators on crowd activity frequently stressed the brutishness and bestiality of those involved.[83] The corollary of this is of course the stress upon the civilised gentility of the financially fortunate we have noted during the meetings of the Select Committee.

The ability to assume that the poor were so very different from themselves legitimated the neglect and denial of poor people's feelings by the Select Committee and supporters of its findings; and permitted the Lord Advocate to assert before Parliament – with no voice raised in objection – that the poor were 'regardless of the fate of their bodies after death'.[84] Such strenuous parliamentary denials of intended injury to the poor of course reveal rather than conceal motives and preoccupations.

Yet despite the differences – real and imagined – between rich and poor, there was a fundamental similarity between them: the fear of dissection, which was shared across class boundaries. Though implicit in the *Report*, the admission that this was the case surfaced only rarely. Professor Guthrie was highly unusual as a public figure who openly admitted his kinship with the poor in this respect. Among Warburton's supporters the silence on this repugnance as a sentiment personally held is deafening. During the course of the Anatomy debate, this defensive position seems to have become consolidated. Fear of dissection was spoken of as a *vulgar prejudice*, not as something close to the hearts of such enlightened supporters of science as these men wished to be seen to be.[85]

However, at one moment early on in the debate, Sir Robert Peel fortuitously articulated the contradiction in this stance. Speaking before Parliament at the time of the nomination of the Select Committee, Peel derided Warburton's praise of popular education in the removal of repugnance towards dissection amongst 'mechanics':

> . . . the only point . . . in which that honourable member's anecdote
> respecting the victory obtained over prejudice in the Mechanics'
> Institute failed, was, not that a few weak stomachs grew qualmish,
> but that none of those eager disciples of information had, in order to
> show their disdain of vulgar prejudices, justified the eulogium the
> honourable member had pronounced on them by offering their own
> dead bodies to be dissected; for this vulgar prejudice was not against
> seeing bodies dissected, but against being ourselves dissected.[86]

Repugnance to dissection was a 'vulgar prejudice' held by 'mechanics'; but the use of the word 'ourselves' very tellingly embraced Peel and his parliamentary colleagues. The comment is highly significant, for the assertion that education cannot dispel the prejudice discloses the tacit admission that Peel and his fellows – despite the best available education – feared dissection themselves.

———————

This parliamentary exchange of views between Warburton and Peel concerned a series of lectures on human anatomy delivered by George Birkbeck at the London Mechanics' Institution in the summer of 1827.[87] Several of the lectures, by general demand, had been given on a real human corpse.[88] Observers were struck by the number of 'mechanics' who regularly attended the lectures, and attested to their 'deep interest' and 'profound attention'.[89]

Birkbeck's courage in the public use of such potentially shocking teaching material, to a non-medical gathering at such a venue, was deeply appreciated by his audience. A report in the *New London Mechanics' Register* makes clear that at least part of this appreciation stemmed from the fact that Birkbeck had openly disregarded the belief that people of this social background 'neither possessed the disposition to receive scientific instruction, nor the ability to profit by its communication'.[90] The positions taken by Warburton and Peel with regard to these lectures were perhaps predictable. Henry Warburton was himself a reformer, and a Benthamite. His praise in Parliament of the impulse towards the conscious shedding of superstition and fear of dissection – of which the rapt audience at Birkbeck's lectures provided clear evidence – was expressive of his political sympathy with the campaign for a broader franchise. That Warburton nevertheless sponsored the Bill which visited dissection upon the workhouse poor is a useful indication of the limits of his reforming sympathies.

Peel's lack of regard for the effect of the lectures, on the other hand, was consistent with his Tory view of political radicalism and reform, of which the self-education he so witheringly dismissed was an important manifestation. In spite of their apparently profound political differences Warburton and Peel nevertheless co-operated closely both on the Select Committee, and during the Act's passage through Parliament.

Despite Peel's scepticism, there did exist a significant body of opinion at this time enlightened enough, often through self-education, to hold repugnance to dissection unreasonable. This cluster of opinion was by no means homogeneous, but tended to be comprised of working people and intellectuals who, through experience of political radicalism, rationalism, secularism and/or utilitarianism, had arrived at a position of aversion to superstition, and an equally strong belief in the power of reason and the pre-eminent value of education. The atmosphere of this rational and radical culture of the 1820s and 1830s has been well described by Edward Thompson, who has demonstrated the almost 'evangelistic zeal' for knowledge shared by many at the time.[91]

The superstitious and sentimental attachment to the corpse discussed in my first chapter formed an unspoken backdrop to the world view of each individual in Birkbeck's audience – which renders the respectful response to his lectures all the more remarkable, and explains in part both Warburton's appreciation of its significance, and Peel's scepticism as to how deep popular education could reach.

As we shall see, the lack of uniformity in this radical culture is amply illustrated in its variety of response to Warburton's Bill. In simple terms, the scientific endeavour involved in anatomy divided the radical community, and rendered it ineffective as a body of opposition.

The reasons behind the divisive role of 'science' in the radical culture of this period are not far to seek. To simplify, on one hand there were those who believed 'the march of intellect' inherently socially progressive, and whose awareness of issues of social class was subsumed in this belief. To them, superstition or sentiment was emblematic of ignorance, and was to be shunned. As Thompson has observed: 'the "march of intellect" and the repression of the heart' went along together.[92] On the other hand, many radicals who both saw the need for anatomy and recognised the necessity of seeking alternative sources for its supply, were nevertheless sufficiently cognisant of the social relations of medicine in this period and awake to the class issues involved in Warburton's proposal, to campaign against it. In the final analysis, the former grouping acted effectively in support of the ruling elite in the successful redefinition of poverty as crime, and the use of dissection to terrorise the poor.

A passage by Roger Cooter is remarkably apposite to this contradiction in the culture of radicalism, and is worth quoting here in full:

. . . the radicals' faith in science as a levelling resource directed against aristocracy and clergy was an effective source for their cultural exploitation by the radical bourgeois promoters of science. The willingly accepted rhetoric surrounding physiology heightened the sense of a 'barbaric' past in which men were kept in ignorance of the beneficial laws of nature at a time when it would have been more pertinent for working people to have focussed their attention on their economic situation as a class. Risking oversimplification of a tremendously complex and subtle transformation, one can summarise that artisans who accepted physiology as a further manifestation of reason and rationality with which to hammer the old order, to leaven the social milieu, and to improve social relations . . . unwittingly became the defenders of the irrational social arrangements being advanced through the new economics. Their materialism was expropriated and co-opted by positivists who, relying on the same anti-authoritarian assumptions that had once unified what at times had been a fiercely independent artisan-led Jacobin movement against constituted authority, now rendered those assumptions protective of the new progressive industrial order. Failing to perceive the ideological power that Reason had assumed, artisans became its victims . . . destined to promote and safeguard the Reasonable bourgeois world.[93]

Cooter's insights apply with painful precision to the Anatomy Act debate. His reference to awareness of a *barbaric past* applies precisely to the vilification of superstition and prejudice, which some radical supporters of the Bill – along with more affluent supporters, like Peel – used to asperse the credibility of their opponents. Warburton, Hume, Birkbeck, Bentham, Astley Cooper, and even Wakley were what Cooter terms *bourgeois promoters of science*, while the enthusiastic audience at Birkbeck's lectures were indeed *artisans* – working people eager to partake of the forbidden knowledge that rich and poor alike were anatomically composed of flesh and blood.

But so blinded were many by this old knowledge offered afresh in the mantle of science,[94] that they failed to discern that far from promoting social equality, this consanguinity was about to be turned to the service of their masters. They were thus misled into supporting and even advocating a measure by which the rich were safeguarded from the possibility of dissection, by means of a legalised coercion of the very class to which – despite their present intellectual divergence – they could through economic circumstances so easily return.[95]

Probably the most influential embodiment of this anomalous role is to be found in the 'milk and water radical',[96] Francis Place. A tailor by trade, Place's importance in English radicalism at this period, particularly in its parliamentary impact, is without parallel in anyone of his social status. He was not a public figure, preferring to work with others quietly and effectively behind the scenes, a successful strategist in the Westminster elections of Burdett in 1807, Hobhouse in 1818, and – with Hume – in the repeal of the hated Combination Acts in 1824.[97]

Place's position in the anatomy debate was coloured to a very great extent by his relationship with middle-class utilitarianism. By the 1820s Place was intellectually 'captive' to Benthamism,[98] and was in close alliance with Hume – Benthamite, free-trader and Warburton's close parliamentary ally.[99] The precise influences affecting Place's adoption and championship of the idea of dissecting the dead poor are unknown, but it would seem likely that they came from Hume's direction. Place's attitude toward poverty was hardly one of respect or pity. A self-made master-tailor, who had 'improved' himself by dint of hard work and self-education, Place championed only the 'respectable' portions of the working class. Although on the one hand he regarded himself as respected by working people and possessing ready access to their opinions, Place also held a measure of contempt for those who had failed to follow his own example, or those who regarded his alliance with middle-class utilitarians as a spurious mode of benefitting the working classes.[100]

Place's personal papers together with the *Proceedings* of the National Political Union – which organisation he hoped would provide an effective opposition/alternative attraction to the more radical National Union of the Working Classes[101] – provide a valuable indication of the management, not to say manipulation, of opinion of which Place was capable. In this instance, it resulted in 1832 in a petition to Parliament from the NPU Council in favour of Warburton's Bill. This was something of a *coup* for the Bill's supporters, as the NPU was believed to represent radical members of the working classes, and had also expressed itself actively in support of parliamentary reform. The NPU was not a democratic body, indeed, the historian Maccoby has referred to it as a propaganda agency.[102] Place so arranged matters that debate on the adoption of the petition, which he drew up himself, took place during meetings of the Council, an even less democratic assembly than a general meeting.

Initially Place had written to Thomas Bowyer, another member of the Council, 'a working man, much acquainted with numbers of other working men, and well respected by them',[103] for his views on the propriety of soliciting support for Warburton's Bill from working people by means of petitions to Parliament. The reply was unequivocal:

> Dear Sir,
> You ask whether petitions should be got up in favour of Mr
> Warburton's Anatomy Bill. My answer is, that if a man wished to
> have his head broken, and to go a short way to get it done, he would
> pursue a very direct and certain course to such an end, by collecting
> together a large number of persons and advising them to petition in

favour of that measure. Depend upon it, that out of the circle of those
who think deeply, there is much greater disposition to make subjects
of the hospital surgeons, than to become their subjects.[104]

Bowyer went on to ascribe all the difficulties besetting anatomy to 'great
prejudice', and recommended tackling it by a public debate. One was
accordingly arranged to take place at the end of February 1832. The hostile
audience had previously been admonished by the chairman, who told
them that, as they were attending a Council meeting, they had neither the
right to be present nor any right of participation, and that any disruption
would lead to the meeting being continued in private.[105] Place made his
address, speaking at great length in favour of the Bill. He read out
Bowyer's letter, and went on to vilify 'Ignorance' – by which he plainly
meant all those who opposed the petition. He quoted Sir Astley Cooper
with warm approval, said that the Bill should be approved by all 'reasonable men', and assured everyone present that 'those most forward to
induce the legislature to consider the best mode of obtaining bodies, are
undoubted active sincere friends of the working people.'

Place was answered by a man called Thomas Murphy, whom Place held
in some contempt for his lack of education.[106] Murphy, however, spoke
well; and demonstrated that it would be not only the very poor who might
be liable to be dissected; old age, financial difficulties, or sickness might
cause any of those present to make their end in a workhouse or a hospital,
and so fall under the provisions of the Bill. He could see nothing in the Bill
to remove 'what its supporters were pleased to call the prejudice of the
people', and was about to bring forth a copy of the Bill for discussion when
he was interrupted by Place, who stopped him abruptly saying the text had
been altered since the last printing. Place's assertion may or may not have
been correct,[107] but it would seem that he was suspiciously eager to prevent
any discussion of the actual text of the Bill. Murphy was plainly disconcerted by the sudden interruption and Place's public imputation of his
ignorance. His flow of oratory was disrupted, and the end of his speech was
an anticlimax, though he rallied to say 'alter it how anyone pleased, it was
an inhuman Bill'.

Thomas Wakley of the *Lancet* spoke next.[108] Turning the altercation to
advantage, he said he thought it 'absurd to petition in favour of a Bill
which was undergoing continual alterations'. He offered it as his experience that the rich were much more prejudiced than the poor against
post-mortems, and said that his fear was that the Bill held out inducements to
workhouse and hospital personnel to neglect their patients, or even to
accelerate their deaths. At one point in his speech, Wakley displayed the
oratory for which he was famous in print, when – no longer pretending to
address the Council – he turned full on the audience and warned that the
Bill 'was aimed at *them*',[109] and that they would be the ones to be dissected,
not the rich.

One suspects that Wakley said much more, but since Place took the minutes, or at least wrote them up,[110] we have only his version of events. The next speaker attacked Wakley and Murphy on the grounds that they were arguing on the basis of emotion, not of justice and reason;[111] while another said though the working people were ignorant, he was sure that when the facts were laid before them, they would part with all prejudice. The Bill, he assured them, promised many beneficial results.[112]

After an adjournment of a month – during which time Place had his own address published separately and distributed widely under the NPU's auspices[113] – the debate resumed. An attempt to add some resolutions to the proposed petition was quashed by the Council; and the audience was told unequivocally that the Bill was

> a step in civilisation, useful to all, but most particularly to the
> working people who would show their good sense and the decrease of
> absurd notions and superstitions by signing the petition in its
> favour.[114]

Place then rose again to address the assembly. He began by saying that the 'passion and prejudice' – which characterised the opposition – must give way to 'judgment'.[115] He told his listeners that the Bill would benefit the poor, and that this opinion was held by other eminent men (such as Astley Cooper, Abernethy and three other anatomists), whose judgment he thought would 'scarcely . . . be disputed'. Warming to his theme, Place waxed indignant in defence of the social status of his audience, accusing his opponents of 'boldly and indiscreetly' assuming that the Bill could affect members present. 'The members of this Union', he declared, 'are not "the poor", pride and ignorance may call them "the lower classes" but I say they are not "the poor". Whose bodies . . . are to be given up?' he asked rhetorically, and, answering his own question, replied:

> None but such as no-one will claim, none but such as no-one will
> bury, and is this the case with the members of the union? Certainly
> not. Is there a member who does not belong to a benefit club, which
> will pay for a decent funeral, for him or his wife; have not most of
> them the ready means either through the club or from his own
> savings, to provide the means, and is there a near relative of such a
> man for whom a decent funeral would not be provided? Surely not.
> The Bill has then no reference to the members of the Union in this
> respect much more than it has to the rich.[116]

Having flattered the social aspirations of all present, lulled them into a sense of security, and invited them to join him in forgetting about the real poor (who in any case had hitherto been 'buried in a way, truly disgusting'), Place changed his tack, and trivialised the proceedings by describing how as a tailor he took the measurements of female clients without any hint of 'indelicacy'. Drawing a parallel with dissection, Place assured his audience that dissection likewise showed no indelicacy, even to the bodies of 'the most delicate females'. The sexist wit with which Place both emphasised his kinship with the world of toil, and his support of the Bill, was decisive.[117] His humorous comments about female anatomy provided light relief to a grim discussion, and were greeted with laughter and cheers. The upshot was a petition to Parliament from the Council of the NPU in support of Warburton's Bill.[118]

Besides his propulsion of the NPU Council, Place may have been instrumental elsewhere in support of Warburton's proposal. It is not difficult to discern a parallel between the 'packed' Select Committee, prepared witnesses, and secretive passage of the (much more laudable) repeal of the Combination Acts in 1824,[119] with the parliamentary progress of Warburton's Bills on anatomy. Place and Hume were the joint acknowledged architects of the former,[120] and were staunch supporters of the latter measure,[121] so it would not be stretching the evidence unduly to suggest that the continuity of personnel and strategy involved in these measures may well have assisted in Warburton's eventual success.

The first Anatomy Bill was dubbed 'The Midnight Bill' by the writer of a letter in the *Lancet*, who complained with shame and indignation at the secretive manner in which that Bill made its progress through Parliament.[122] A later chapter will show that this process continued to an even greater extent with the successful second Bill, for which Place's efforts at the National Political Union were also designed.

Warburton's first Bill failed as a result of *aristocratic* pressure in the Lords on 5 June 1829,[123] following a concerted defence of the poor from such old paternalists as the Archbishop of Canterbury, the Earls of Malmesbury and Harewood, and the Lord Chief Justice, Lord Tenterden. This defence took the form of an assertion of the right of the poor to decent burial[124] and criticism of pursuing people 'beyond the limits of the grave'.[125] The Lords found objectionable the 'principle of interfering with the bodies of persons who had not offended against the laws',[126] and concluded that they should respect the 'unconquerable objection' to dissection held by many poor people.[127] The Duke of Wellington lent his support to the Archbishop of Canterbury's advice that the Bill be withdrawn. He did so not on the grounds of respect for the dignity of the poor, but because:

> He was aware of the opposition that would be raised to it, and of the quarter from which that opposition was to come; and knowing too how much influence that opposition was likely to have upon the country, he could not help feeling that it was extremely desirable that such effects should not accompany the measure as it passed into a law.[128]

Wellington was acutely aware of the huge and mounting pressure for parliamentary reform, and feared that the passage of such an Act at such a time was politically hazardous. The Bill was withdrawn on the understanding that the government itself would submit a measure on the subject in the following session of Parliament. In the event this did not materialise, and it was not until the height of the political turmoil of the Reform crisis that Warburton again attempted to change the law.[129]

ALTERNATIVE NECROLOGY

... the slightest examination of the Bill will prove, that instead of inflicting any grievance upon the poor, it will prove their deliverance from great pain, anguish, apprehension and misery.

Lord Calthorpe, 1829.[1]

For hearts as feeling with affection pure
Dwell in the breasts of the neglected poor,
As ever warm'd the sons of wealth and pride,
Who in their splendid palaces reside!
Statesmen of Britain, tell us, is it true?
Laws so oppressive eminate from you;
Laws that pass harmless by the tyrant's door,
But fall with terrors on the friendless poor!
If carving bodies be a harmless thing,
Like Cromwell, set the example by your——![2]

From a broadsheet entitled *The Christian's Appeal Against the Poor Law Amendment Act*,
reprinted by H. Talbot of Cambridge, c.1834.[3]

Jeremy Bentham died on 6 June 1832. He left elaborate directions for the distribution of mourning rings containing locks of his own hair, and for other funerary paraphernalia. He also left precise directions about the preparation of his body for its long home, which was not to be a grave, but a display cabinet. His body was bequeathed to Dr Southwood Smith, who had known the old man well, and who had agreed to perform a public dissection upon his remains. Printed invitations were hastily distributed, intimating Bentham's 'earnest desire ... that his Body should be appropriated to an illustration of the Structures and Functions of the Human Frame', and that Dr Southwood Smith – author of the influential 'Uses of the Dead to the Living', just reprinted[4] – would deliver a lecture over the body 'on the Usefulness of Knowledge of this kind to the Community'. The lecture was given on 9 June at the anatomy school Smith shared with Richard Grainger at Webb Street, Southwark.[5]

Afterwards, Bentham's severed head was dessicated to preserve it entire, his skeleton was articulated in a seated position, and was surmounted by a wax portrait head of the great man as he had appeared in life. Dressed in his accustomed clothes (stuffed and padded out to appear life-like) Bentham's 'Auto-Icon' or self-image was housed in a glass-fronted showcase. After various vicissitudes, this now resides in the cloisters of University College, London, where it may be seen daily. It was Bentham's wish that this process would save his admirers the necessity of commissioning stone sculptures of him.[6]

Aside from the evident egocentricity of Bentham's posthumous requests concerning his anatomy, it should be recognised that it took courage for a man born in the mid-eighteenth century – Bentham was born in 1748 – to leave his aged body for public dissection at a time when much public anguish and fear surrounded the operation on all but the worst criminals.[7] That said, it is also incumbent upon us to recognise that there was perhaps more going on in this episode than Bentham or his admirers would have cared to admit. There are too many sub-texts to the detailed directions for his posthumous physical existence to deal with fully here, but two in particular are worth mentioning. First, by ensuring that, though dissected, his body would remain as if entire, Bentham endeavoured to endow the popular conception of dissection with altered meaning. But the perpetuation of physical identity after dissection which was available to a great philosopher like Bentham could never become real for people who were about to be pressed into the anatomists' service by recommendations of Bentham's own making; and achieved by his own acolytes.[8]

Second, there appears to have been some conflict in Bentham's intentions. For though he recognised that dissection would become stigma-free only by the elimination of popular prejudice, this in turn depended upon the removal of the stigma. Bentham's own dissection was intended to allay public prejudice. However, a coercive Anatomy Bill would counter its impact, perpetuating the appearance of punishment. Perhaps Bentham's hope was that his own dissection might persuade the poor to submit willingly to their fate, and thus provide immeasurable happiness to their social superiors.

Although he had been among the earliest to campaign in favour of the idea, Southwood Smith seems by 1832 to have had some reservations about the wholesale appropriation of the 'unclaimed' poor. In an article he had written for the *Westminster Review* in 1829, Smith had expressed an understanding of the feelings of the poor towards bodysnatching. The poor, he said:

> often feel deeply and in the bitterness of wounded spirit, execrate the
> hardness of their lot: they imagine, it must be owned with some
> colour of reason, that they live only for the rich; this detestable
> practice [bodysnatching] leads them to suppose that they must still

serve their masters even after death has set them free from toil, and that when the early dawn can no longer rouse them from the pallet of straw to work, they must be dragged from what should be their last bed, to show in common with the murderer, how the knife of the surgeon may best avoid the rich man's artery, and least afflict the rich man's nerve.[9]

Curiously, despite this awareness of the social issues involved, in 1829 the author could see no parallel with the social bias of the proposed first Bill. By 1832, perhaps Southwood Smith had become aware of the smugness with which his peers were advocating the expedient, or – in the midst of the Reform crisis – he had developed misgivings about the larger political uses of the proposed Bill. He gave the oration over Bentham's body as he was bid, paying respect to the dead man's courage, and attesting to Bentham's abhorrence of the prejudice against dissection. While he was speaking, a thunderstorm broke, shaking the building. Smith proceeded 'with a clear unfaltering voice', referring with particular emphasis to Bentham's wish to set an example to others to rise above their prejudice. As lightning flashed outside, his face 'as white as that of the dead philosopher before him', Smith braced himself to deliver a powerful broadside at the invited guests – medical men and intellectuals alike – and at those whom he knew would subsequently read his oration in print.[10] 'How is it to be expected', he asked,

> that the uninstructed and ignorant – that those whose minds are full of prejudice and error, and whose habit of yielding to every impulse renders them the victims of violence – how is it to be expected that this unfortunate class of our fellow-men, hitherto in all ages and communities too large a class, will sacrifice their own feelings for the public good, when the best regulated shrink from the obligation? We foster the prejudices of the ignorant; we sympathise with the feelings that have their origin in this prejudice and ignorance; we ourselves act from impulse . . . It is our duty, not by legislative enactments to force others to submit to that which we are unwilling should be done to ourselves, but to set the example of making a voluntary sacrifice for the sake of a good which we profess to understand and appreciate.[11]

His references to the ignorance, prejudice, violence and populousness of the working classes are evidence enough that Smith had little sympathy with them. But by this scathing indictment of the hypocrisy of his peers in both medical and political elites – Brougham, Mill and Grote were all present in the room – Smith placed himself alongside militant radicals in the demand for a bill which would lessen rather than augment public feeling against dissection.

───────◆───────

Medical history has been written largely in ignorance of the corralling of

opinion on anatomy between 1828 and 1832.[12] The Select Committee's
endorsement of the project meant that after publication of its *Report*, the
appropriation of paupers' bodies gained potency as if it was the only
answer to the problem. Official sponsorship of the idea had the effect of
eclipsing all others. Voices like Southwood Smith's were cries in the
wilderness. During parliamentary discussion, the possibility barely registered that alternatives so much as existed. Legitimation of the idea – by
whatever dubious means – has since had long-term, wide-ranging, and
even international repercussions.[13]

The fact is, that room for manoeuvre *did* exist whereby the injustice
which was subsequently enshrined in law might have been avoided. This
chapter seeks to examine options – ignored in their own time and ever since
– which were put forward by contemporaries. Though we know these ideas
were unsuccessful in deflecting the momentum of the Benthamite project,
their nature and feasibility deserves examination and reappraisal.

Broadly speaking, opinion fell into four camps. Bodies for dissection
could be obtained by stealth, by coercion, by voluntary donation or by
inducement.

Of course there were those who, like Peel, believed that with the
connivance of the authorities, a supply of dead bodies ample to the
anatomists' requirements could continue to be obtained by authorised
stealth from poor graves, hospitals and workhouses.[14] It would seem that
until at least the mid-1820s, such a policy of stealth was favoured by the
anatomists themselves, who wished above all to avoid publicity. Peel's
letter to Bentham discussed above shows that in 1826 the Home Secretary
himself was very much in favour of authorised stealth, and was unwilling
to entertain the necessity of legislating on the matter at all.

Francis Place claimed later that the subsequent desire for legislative
action on the part of the medical profession was almost entirely due to
himself. Four years after the Anatomy Act's passage, in 1836, Place wrote
up his version of events, noting his own importance in suggesting and
drawing up a petition for the medical publisher, Highley, in the winter of
1827–8.[15] According to Place, Highley solicited signatures from his clients,
the petition was eventually presented to the Lords, and it was this which
prompted the legislation. Whether or not Place's egocentricity represents
objective truth in this instance (and from what we already know this seems
more than doubtful), it would appear that in parallel with the growing
demand for parliamentary reform – which utilised the right of petition to a
grand extent – anatomists became increasingly willing to agitate publicly
for the right to dissect without fear of prosecution or riot, and without
abuse from their suppliers.

This shift in tactics is most clearly marked if we compare two documents: one, a volume in the Peel papers containing a series of confidential
letters on the subject from anatomists, dating from 1823;[16] and the other, a
published open letter to the Home Secretary from the Council of the Royal

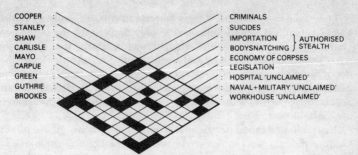

Figure 3 Anatomists' views on potential alternatives to existing sources of corpses for dissection, 1823

Source: *Peel Papers*, BM. Add. Mss 40371.

College of Surgeons, published in December 1831.[17] These two modes of communication with the Home Secretary are themselves characteristic of the increasingly public nature of the anatomists' stance over these years.

In 1823, probably as a result of the failure of the Anatomical Society to control corpse prices,[18] Astley Cooper solicited from several fellow anatomists ideas about what could be done to break the power of the bodysnatchers. The replies were handed over to Peel, and are preserved among his papers. It is not clear from this correspondence whether Cooper's initial approach mentioned legislative intervention; but it is remarkable that most of the replies seem to favour covert official connivance at existing supply routes.

One of the most significant aspects of the correspondence is the diversity of sources suggested. Crucially, there was no consensus favouring the use of unclaimed bodies from workhouses. In fact, most of the anatomists stressed the possibility of extending the use of dissection not necessarily as a public punishment, but as a matter of course, to *all* criminals: executed, dying in custody, or unclaimed after natural death in custody. Some suggested importation from abroad, if only as a means of breaking the bodysnatchers' monopoly and forcing them to accept lower rates of pay. Others recommended authorised grave-robbery of 'certain bodies' – by which was presumably meant bodies from open pit-burials. The diversity of opinion these letters display is indicated in the table given here. In view of the later change in the law, the most noticeable division of opinion concerned the use of the bodies of the poor from workhouses and hospitals. Less than half of the correspondents classed these institutions as suitable sources, together with prisons. Two anatomists recognised that to proceed along these lines would invite hostility; one suggested that prisoners should initially be the chosen source. The remaining majority either omitted to utilise poverty as a criterion for dissection or limited its application to those dying in prisons or in naval and military hospitals.

Two of the most eminent of these correspondents, Sir Anthony Carlisle and G.J. Guthrie, voiced fundamental objections to the use of the poor. Carlisle objected on moral and ethical grounds, fearing that the 'forlorn wretches driven within [hospital] walls' might 'attempt to escape their doom by crawling away in the agonies of death, or to beseech a rescue from pending horor through the interference of relatives'.[19] He felt the same argument applied to those dying in workhouses 'with the appearance of uncharitableness, if not cruelty'.

Although a decade later he would have changed his views, in 1823 Guthrie thought workhouses could provide 'the greatest resource', but viewed with disfavour any enactment availing anatomists of dead bodies from such a source, as 'great clamour' would ensue. He advised the exploitation of this source by stealth. He also thought it would be a tactical error to publicise or legalise the existing practice of taking the dead from hospital mortuaries, for he believed that many poor people might spurn hospital treatment if they feared they would be dissected in the event of death. In his discussion of this point, Guthrie privately admitted to Sir Astley and through him to Peel, that hospital patients were in fact being used for experimental surgery, something the poor already understood:

> the poor frequently object to enter [hospitals] because they think
> they may be experimented upon. & it be admitted to men of
> education that when an operation is to be tried for the first time it is
> generally done in an Hospital.[20]

One of Sir Anthony Carlisle's points was that a programme of economy in the use of corpses would allow the chosen supply to be utilised more fully. In this, Guthrie concurred. He considered the numbers of corpses required for anatomy seriously overestimated, and believed 'when subjects are cheap and plentiful, the manner of dissecting is slovenly, and great waste ensues'. Both men recommended the use of criminals' bodies. Guthrie shrewdly observed that if criminals' and suicides' corpses were used, they would be

> given up by the public almost without comment, or rather with
> satisfaction, & once the law is established, no-one will think it a
> hardship. The idea that it prevents their own friends from being
> taken up [ie: resurrected] will soon silence everyone.

Guthrie's argument with regard to the tactical benefits of silencing public opinion by the appropriation of social outcasts was eventually found to be useful, though it was the poor who were so designated.

The spirit of stealth which characterises these letters seems to have all but evaporated in the seven years which elapsed before the publication of the Royal College of Surgeons' open letter to the Home Secretary late in 1831. The atmosphere had changed. During that period, most importantly, attitudes towards the poor had begun to harden as a result of the growing battle for Reform. In addition case law had changed, incriminating anatomists. First Burke and Hare and then the London Burkers (of which more in my next chapter) were discovered to have committed murder for the anatomists' premium. It was undoubtedly the last discovery which provided the opportunity for Warburton's renewed intention to submit a second Anatomy Bill to Parliament, and which prompted the College's letter.[21]

The tone of the letter was respectful but firm. It drew attention to the fact that by its charter, the College was required to examine the proficiency of future surgeons, from whom a knowledge of anatomy was required 'as the most important part of surgical education'. Thus bodies 'have necessarily been procured by illegal means . . . disgusting to society at large'. The regulations, the letter continued,

> have therefore had a tendency to encourage . . . a direct violation of
> the law, and to establish, in the procurers of dead bodies, a set of men
> living by practices which are revolting to the feelings of society . . .
> and likely . . . to become trained and gradually habituated to the
> commission of still greater crimes.

The letter went on to say that models and preserved parts of bodies could provide no substitute for the anatomical knowledged gained in dissection; and that surgeons were caught in a contradiction of law which could punish both the acquisition of this knowledge and the lack of it. The College, however, regarded all these problems as insignificant beside the advent of burking, whereby fees paid for corpses had 'operated as a premium for murder'. This was a serious admission of culpability, which was to be further compounded by an expression of fear that if the College continued to require anatomical proficiency from candidates to its examination, more such murders might occur:

> It is vain to imagine it always possible to distinguish the body of a
> person who has been murdered from that of one who has died a
> natural death. The very individuals [Bishop and Williams] who have
> lately suffered on the scaffold would probably have escaped detection
> if they had been more circumspect and wary in their conduct.

Towards its end, the letter reveals one factor behind the College's decision to address the government in so candid and self-incriminating a manner:

> who can venture to say that crimes similar to those which have just
> now filled the public with dismay will not again be committed? More
> criminals will undoubtedly arise; new victims will be added to the
> list; and the medical profession will be necessarily degraded from the
> high station which it ought to hold as having in its relations to society
> no object but that of conferring benefit on others.

Ingenuous though this avowal of altruism may appear, it is worthy of

notice first, that the College expressed no pity towards the burkers' actual
or potential victims; and second, that its prime concern seems to have been
the deleterious effects of burking upon the profession's status. The College
offered no suggestions for alternatives to the use of murderers' bodies, but
was clearly making a bid for a say in the matter – promoting itself as the
body best qualified as body-broker in any new legislation. Wakley dis-
trusted the entire document – his verdict was that its authors were
'cunning rogues'.[22]

The increased stridency of tone in medical voices on this subject in the
1820s seems to have reached a peak after the failure of the first Anatomy
Bill in 1829, when an unofficial but active cluster of practitioners began
openly to assert that there existed 'only one remedy' to the problem of
anatomy. Predictably enough, this was the use of the 'unclaimed'. According to this view, only three possibilities for government action existed: ban
dissection,[23] permit bodysnatching and burking, or use the 'unclaimed'.
These limited options received wide public attention as a result of a
persuasively argued article in the *Quarterly Review* in the spring of 1830, by
the eminent gynaecologist Robert Gooch, then dying of consumption.[24]
Thereafter many reports echoed similar sentiments:

> to the framers of the bill, aided by competent advisors, we leave the
> details of its provisions, begging them to carry this at least in their
> minds – that there are only three plans from which to select: one, to
> prohibit the study of anatomy altogether, and cause surgery to
> relapse into the infancy of the art; another, to support the breed of
> resurrection-men, plunder graves, and after all, supply the nation
> with half-informed anatomists and unskilful surgeons; the last is to
> give up unclaimed bodies to the schools of anatomy, by which
> resurrection-men would be abolished, the buried lie quietly in their
> graves, and the nation be supplied with an ample stock of expert
> anatomists and dexterous surgeons.[25]

It is not possible to suppose that the effective limitation of options this
analysis propounded was accidental. It had been a tactical element in
Warburton's campaign from the outset. The exclusion of options had been
a feature of the evidence provided to the Select Committee – something the
Committee itself was unlikely to challenge – and its *Report* had been written
up by Warburton himself. The manner of the Committee's appointment,
the way in which it had conducted its enquiry, found its findings and made
its recommendations, was viewed by both its ultra-Tory and ultra-radical
opponents as 'shamefully partial'.[26] When the subject was raised again by
the introduction of the second Bill late in 1831, Guthrie went on record as
saying that he regarded the Committee's proceedings as so biased as to
merit the appointment of a new Select Committee. As Professor of
Anatomy and Surgery at the Royal College of Surgeons, he was an
establishment man, and certainly had the College's interests at heart – but

this renders his analysis of the Committee's proceedings no less valid. His radical suggestion was hedged around with public disclaimers of intending offence to no one, least of all to Warburton:

> . . . although the Committees which took this subject into consideration were Committees on public measures, still their proceedings appeared to me to be conducted in the same manner as Committees on private Bills. That is, there were gentlemen attending where opinions were taken privately as well as publicly, on various points. These persons were mostly gentlemen in private life, who approved of the various clauses proposed in that Bill, and who had their own objects in view. There were none present in opposition to them. The questions put to the witnesses . . . did not elicit the whole of the opinion of the different individuals who were called before it; not that there was any dishonesty in the proceeding on the part of the Members of the Committee, such a supposition cannot be entertained for a moment; but these gentlemen did not understand the subject fully, and there was only one party present to assist in elucidating it.[27] Few people knew that a Committee on Anatomy was sitting, fewer knew its objects. From these observations I think it will appear more reasonable and fair, that on any future Committee, there shall be an equal chance for all parties, and all opinions. The public will be the gainer.[28]

By making such charges in so polite, yet public, a manner, speaking so reasonably of the need for a new committee, Guthrie intended to circumvent Warburton and his supporters. Having been overlooked by the Select Committee perhaps he, more than most, understood the contempt with which they regarded opposition. Nothing came of Guthrie's remonstration, but it is nevertheless important that a contemporary observer of such prominence should have commented so disparagingly on Warburton's parliamentary tactics.

The certainty of tone and conviction with which the Bills' supporters addressed the subject, and the dire consequences they warned could transpire from the choice of any source other than the 'unclaimed' may well have proved convincing to readers of the quality press. But if so, they were convinced by sleight of hand. The restricted options offered by their limited analysis served to divert attention from potential sources of corpses for anatomy which did not depend upon coercion for their provenance.

Bentham's dissection took place less than two months before Warburton's bill became law. During the preceding decade or so, a small but steady stream of bequests and offers of bequests of bodies had appeared in the press. The most spectacular of these concerned a mass pledge, begun on the initiative of Professor Macartney of Dublin. First reports appeared in early 1828, and put the number of signatories at over fifty, and by November 1831 these had risen to four hundred, many of whom were said to have been involved in medicine.[29] However, no report has yet been found[30] of any case in which a bequest promised in this document actually took place. Nor did this silence escape comment from London medical observers, who not only failed to follow Dublin's example, but rather ungraciously criticised it.[31]

Why did Parliament and the medical profession as a whole fail to take up the possibility of voluntary donation of bodies via bequest, as a preferable alternative to bodysnatching and burking on the one hand and to the appropriation of the poor on the other?[32] Many, like the surgeon Benjamin Travers, may have concealed their own ambivalence towards dissection by sneering at the 'spurious liberalism' of those who had the courage to leave their bodies for anatomy.[33] Possibly, too, the willingness to bequeath was regarded askance as symptomatic of an unfashionable – even dangerous – religious unbelief, just as the willingness to protest against the dissection of the poor was comfortably dismissed as indicative of superstition.

Certainly, this period had witnessed an unprecedented upsurge of active and articulate atheism. We have already seen the furore over Lawrence and the debate on the materiality of mind. On a popular level, the most public manifestation of 'open and combative' atheism was the 'General Farce', a major London demonstration organised by the National Union of the Working Classes in March 1832.[34] It was staged by 100,000 people in flagrant opposition to the government's General Fast – which had been intended as a collective national supplication to the Almighty to spare the nation further mortality from the cholera epidemic then raging.[35] Undoubtedly, government prosecution of the leaders of the Farce (and simultaneously of publishers of Paine's *Rights of Man*) reveal that the ruling elite associated republicanism and atheism, and these jointly with subversion – despite the fact that even parliamentarians recognised the absurdity and irrelevance of the Fast.[36]

The willingness to bequeath one's own body for dissection was indeed associated in some cases with undisguised infidelity. An extreme example compounded with sentiments of crass utilitarianism appeared in 1829 in Richard Carlile's paper *The Lion* as the text of a speech delivered by 'Our French Scholar', at the hotbed of infidelity, the British Forum.[37]

After referring to Warburton's first bill as a 'scientific and most wise and humane proposition', the 'scholar' attacked the wastage of materials to 'detrimental putrefaction' in the burial of coffins and grave-clothes, and ridiculed the 'Romantism of the Grave'. He[38] then proceeded to give details of his own will, in which it was directed that his body should be dissected, his skin tanned and used to cover an armchair for (among others) Henry Warburton, that his skeleton should be given to an anatomy class, failing which it should be dismembered, the skull going to the London Phrenological Society, and his bones to a turner to be made into 'knife-handles, pin-cases, small boxes, buttons, etc.' The softer mass of his flesh after dissection was to be collected in a vase inscribed with ornamentation expressive of Truth and Liberty, quick-limed, ('in order to prevent for ever any bad smell') covered in earth and planted with a rose; the whole to be set in the gardens of the 'intended University'.[39]

This remarkable document concluded with a miscellany of ideas and recommendations, among them a project for teaching midwives anatomy, a recommendation that men should not marry superstitious women or those without knowledge of human anatomy, and another directing mothers to insist upon *post-mortem* examinations upon their dead children. Some features of the Frenchman's discourse are familiar from other literature in favour of Warburton's bill: the attitude expressed towards the poor is a mixture of contempt ('the mob') and distant benevolent sympathy – those who supported the bill should bequeath their own bodies for dissection as a proof of their 'sympathy towards the poor'.

The whole speech and its recommendations were reprinted as a penny pamphlet. In a later edition of the *Lion*[40] the Frenchman wrote in to say that in the intervening period, he had learned 'it is not very easy to promulgate anti-superstitious principles, and that the ignorance and the prejudice of the mass is yet too powerful'. After 'abundant' sales at the outset, publishers had refused to handle the work, and street sales 'stopped suddenly' after the vendors were followed in the streets by people who took it upon themselves loudly to inform crowds of potential buyers about the tract's vile contents.

The speech seems to represent a sincere – if misguided – attempt to combat opposition to dissection by a bold attack upon the traditional superstitious attachment to the corpse. In directing that his own bones should be turned into knife-handles, the scholar offered a conspicuous denial of any belief in the numinous properties with which the corpse was popularly invested. It must have taken either courage or foolhardiness to publish such iconoclasm in the 1820s. Had it appeared with an attack on the proposed Anatomy Bill, the pamphlet might conceivably have found a market; but to couple it with a profession of support for Warburton would suggest that the 'scholar' was naive to an extreme to expect any other reception to the street sale of such a work.

Although he published the speech, Carlile himself does not seem to have wholeheartedly endorsed the scholar's views. In an editorial on human dissection, Carlile affirmed its primary importance to surgery, and went on to offer his own reasons for preferring dissection to decomposition. He said he would quarrel with no form of supply other than burking, but he did not favour Warburton with uncritical support:

> I do not like any idea of supply that makes a distinction in society. I
> would not have the distinction thrown particularly upon the poor,
> nor on the diseased, who die in hospitals, though such subjects as the

THE CHRISTIAN'S APPEAL

AGAINST THE

POOR LAW AMENDMENT ACT.

BY A WORKING MAN.

For the time will come when they will not endure
sound doctrine ! but after their own lust shall they heap to
themselves teachers, and they shall turn away their ears
from the truth."—PAUL.

" Therefore, thus saith the Lord, concerning the Prophets
that speak my Name, and I have not sent them, yet they
say, sword and famine shall not be in the land—by sword
and famine shall those prophets be consumed."—JEREMIAH.

PRIESTS of the living God ! awake, arise,
And be no longer heedless of the cries
Of those, that sink beneath the lawless sway
Of English Juggernaut—that onward rolls its way—
Of bloody triumph in its horrid car,
Whilst dying victims' groans are heard afar ;
And splendid show, and heathen revelry,
Despoiling all that's beauteous fair and free,
The Gospel of our Jesus whispers peace,
Dries every tear—bids every sorrow cease,
Its essence, love, heals all her earthly woes,
And makes the desert blossom as the rose ;
But Priests and statesmen, have gone far astray
Far from their God ! walking in their own way ;
A heathen crew, bowing at Mammon's shrine,
Stupid and blinded by the fumes of wine,
But sure amid the vast and mighty host
Of law church glory—or dissenters' boast,
Some may be found to advocate the cause
Of suffering man ! and heaven's offended laws !
Ye messengers of God ! ye who profess
To be as fathers to the fatherless,
To help the widow and defend the poor,
To chase despair and sorrow from their door.
Can ye, unmoved, in Jesu's temple stand !
While foul oppression desolates the land ?
And countless wretches cry for lack of bread,
While bloated tyrants on their victims tread ;
Madly blaspheming God's most holy law—
And you ! refuse the sword of truth to draw !
Behold yon aged hoary-headed sire,
Bow'd to the earth, by the low brutal ire
Of poor-house jailor, and his helpless mate
Pine in a sep'rate dungeon o'er their fate ;
Two sons he had—their father's chokest care,
One crossed the seas, for planting mischare,
Which on his father's little farm had stray'd,
The other griev'd at such usual chasm made,
In lawless hour join'd a Christino band,
And fell a victim in a distant land,
In his old age the father so bereft,
Had still a sweet and lovely daughter left
Prop of his age and sweetner of his life,
A kind assistant to his feeble wife :
But this last prop—this beauteous smiling flower—
Fell in the snare of a base villain's power—
A fiend who held the villagers enchain'd
And all the profits of their labour drain'd
This purse-proud ruffian, with insidious wile,
His only hope—his daughter did beguile ;
From the sweet rural cot he lur'd away
The lovely girl to ruin and betray—
This last foul stroke the father could not bear,

It fix'd upon his brow a dark despair ;
And e'er three moon's had fill'd their silver horn,
His goods and chattels from his cot were torn,
And ruin like a whirlwind swept away
The stock collected in a happier day ;
Driven before the wind and pelting storm
Of Bastile fury—lo ! the bending form
Of the old man, his anxious care-worn brow,
He smites in anguish, solitary now ;
No rural cot, no lovely daughter's smile,
No sons, to soothe him in the dread Bastile—
No tender partner of his sorrows near,
To cool his bosom with a falling tear ;
At thoughts of by-gone days he inly mourns,
And vainly on his wretched pallet turns :
No help is nigh, a dread and fearful gloom
Surrounds him with the horrows of his doom.
A worse than felon's doom ! for when his life
Returns to God ! then, then, the bloody knife
Must do its work—the body that was starved,
By puppy doctors must be cut and carved :
Priests of my country ! ye whose Living Head,
Wept when he saw that Lazarus was dead !
Can ye unmov'd with hearts as hard as Burke ;
Behold the scalping knife thus do its work ;
See guiltless labourers doom'd by tyrant rule
To be the may-sport of the wealthy fool ;
With hand's unhallow'd severing the thread,
That binds the heart to the lamented dead.
For hearts as feeling with affection pure
Dwell in the breasts of the neglected poor,
As ever warm'd the sons of wealth and pride,
Who in their splendid palaces reside !
Statesmen of Britain ! tell us, is it true ?
Laws so oppressive eminate from you ;
Laws that pass harmless by the tyrant's door,
But fall with terrors on the friendless poor !
If carving bodies be a harmless thing,
Like Cromwell, set the example by your — !
Or take your Premier, or your Premier's ——
And cut them up to benefit the poor ;
Let splendid paupers have an equal share
Of your humane, and senatorial care !
Sons of my country ! rise, in manhood stand !
Wipe this foul blot from our once happy land !
God of my Fathers ! Israel's Lord of Hosts !
Sweep the vile heathen from our christian coasts ;
Raise up a LEADER ! who in thee shall trust,
And hordes of tyrants then shall bite the dust :
Inspire the people with a godly zeal
To fight the battles of the public weal,
Resistance, in a just and holy cause,
Is sanctioned by divine and human laws !

Reprinted by H. TALBOT, Cambridge

latter, from the peculiarities of their cases, will be the most desirable to the surgeon; but I would have some rich and influential people set the example to the poor, and remove the dread that now arises from the distinction. Our Royal Family, for instance, are, in part dissected, as soon as dead, for the purpose of embalming. . . . Suppose, then, the king were first to leave his body to the surgeons, and make it fashionable to do so, the odium or degradation of the thing would instantly vanish, and the surgeons would have work enough, if they dissected all that were presented.[41]

In this suggestion Carlile was not alone.[42] Nor was he straying too far from feasibility. Though it was primarily intended to effect the preservation of the corpse, royal embalming involved considerable damage to the body, including the entire removal of the viscera. Embalming was in the news at the time – public memory was still fresh of the King's order to embalm the body of Princess Charlotte after her tragic death in 1817, and George III himself was destined to be embalmed within a year of Carlile's suggestion.[43] Nor did Carlile overstate the influence of Court and Crown, as may be understood from the experience of the distressed Birmingham button-makers, who benefited directly from a fashion in 1830 for gilt buttons they themselves had prompted by the gift of some to the new King.[44]

Nevertheless, because dissection had for so long been regarded as a fate worse than death, Carlile's comment was obviously highly contentious, and was certainly intended to be so. Yet it is worth noticing that while both he and his 'French scholar' might have appeared subversive in their atheism and republicanism, in fact neither of them opposed the Anatomy Bill: the Frenchman approved Warburton's proposal, and Carlile asked that the King set the example *to the poor*. There is every reason to accept the genuine commitment of both men – Carlile left his own body for dissection on his death in 1843, and although no reference has yet been found to the French scholar's own disposal, it is known that he carried out his sister's wishes in this respect after the passage of the Anatomy Act.[45] Ultimately, however, neither of their schemes was likely to aid those who stood to suffer from the Act, for they were too distant from any likelihood of becoming real.[46]

The association of a willingness to undergo dissection and a lack of religious faith is not uniformly discernible in other cases of bequest. The Dublin mass-pledge, for example, was said to have numbered among its signatories several members of the clergy, although no instance of this kind on the mainland has yet been found.[47] One man, who offered his body for sale to a Salisbury surgeon, did so with the comment that he would as easily find it 'at the general resurrection' in the anatomist's laboratory as in a tomb.[48]

The motives behind many of the bequests reported in the press are unclear. Some are attributable to enlightened self-interest, as in the case of the medical signatories of the Dublin pledge. Some donors, like Bentham, appear to have been individuals with some axe to grind, or with some trait of eccentricity which rendered their gesture newsworthy.[49] Dr Sims of Bath, for example, drew public attention to his disgust of funeral pomp, Dr Courtney of Broadstairs left his body to the projected London College of Medicine as a political gesture against the monopoly of the Royal College of Surgeons, and Captain St George Lyster announced his bequest in *The Times* (referring to an 'interesting' war wound) in order to shame Sir Henry Hardinge, whom Lyster alleged had denied him a war pension. Five radical newsvendors – G. Trotter, J. and T. Willis, J. Prince, and J. Murray – imprisoned for selling unstamped newspapers, wrote to the *Cosmopolite* newspaper to bequeath the money raised on the sale of their bodies for the support of others in their pitiful condition. Others, like Major Cartwright, reached the press by virtue of their fame, and intended in this way to influence public opinion.[50]

And there are indications that the anatomy debate caused quite ordin- ary people to leave their bodies for dissection. Further instances may continue to emerge as a result of local studies, but for the moment we have no way of knowing how representative the following cases were.[51] The fact that they too also reached the press – through no intention of the people involved – perhaps indicates that they were unusual, and that they may have heralded rather than represented a more general change in public opinion in favour of dissection. In January 1828, a woman dying in St Thomas' Hospital, London, called another patient to her side and told her that she wished to be dissected. She repeated her assertion for several medical students. An officer in the hospital bureaucracy refused to observe her wish, although since the woman had already had her legs amputated, and since on *post-mortem* her pelvis was removed for the benefit of the hospital's museum, there seems little justification for this position. The woman's case was reported because of interest in the bequest and the intransigence of the officer concerned.[52]

Another case was that of a patient in the Bristol Infirmary whose bequest of his own body for dissection in May 1828 was transcribed in full for the benefit of the readers of the *London Medical Gazette* by the house apothecary, William Morgan:

> The last Will and Testament of me, Patrick – – –, of the City of Cork, kingdom of Ireland.
> I, Patrick – – –, though weak in body, am of sound mind and memory, do make this as my last will and testament; that is to say – I give my body to the surgeons and apothecary of the Bristol Infirmary, to be by them, or the young students, anatomised, and disposed of otherwise, as their wisdom may think fit, as soon as it please God to call me, which I hope will not be long; and I do earnestly request that Mr Morgan, the apothecary to the house, may take upon him the superintendence of the dissection of my body.[53]

Morgan assured the *Gazette* that Patrick's act was 'entirely voluntary and disinterested' to stress that no money was involved. The journal commented upon the 'remarkable' facts that the man was 'an individual of humbler rank' and that he was Irish.

A further case occurred in which a woman bequeathed her own body and that of her newly born child to the anatomy school of the new London University.[54] Because this bequest took place after the passage of the Anatomy Act, and because it raises some important issues pertinent to my later discussion of the Act's early impact, it is dealt with in more detail in Chapter 9.

Cumulatively, all these reports of bequests for dissection suggest that in some circles, the superstitious fear of dissection had begun to lose its force. In these circles there existed not only an awareness and an understanding of the need for dissection and for a new source with which to supply it – but a willingness personally to constitute that supply. It is almost impossible for us now to discern the social origins of this minority, but it is possible to say that they were neither aristocractic nor uniform.

These bequests indicate that Warburton and his supporters underestimated or ignored the extent to which in their own time voluntary donation might have provided a viable alternative to the coercion of the poor.

———————

Nor was spontaneous bequest the only alternative source of bodies available to those anxious to change the law. The anatomists' correspondence of 1823, for example, reveals that during the course of the anatomy debate many suggestions were put forward as alternatives to bodysnatching (and later, burking) which were often also alternatives to the use of the workhouse poor. Not all of these suggestions were feasible; but taken together they do indicate that had Warburton and his colleagues been interested, the corpses of workhouse inmates perhaps need not have been sequestered to this service.

One suggestion centred upon the authorised solicitation and importation of bodies from abroad: to export the problem. The feasibility of this source was doubted on two grounds; first that dead bodies constituted an 'abominable' cargo and that the notoriously superstitious fears of ship's crews might operate 'even to mutiny', particularly during storms.[55] The second doubt was more germane to practicality, as it questioned what would befall this source in time of war.[56] The value of well-trained surgeons had been forced on the attention of the military hierarchy during the Napoleonic Wars, still very much within living memory, so a doubt of this nature over a source was enough to put paid to its chances of becoming official policy. That the idea was nevertheless feasible, despite Somerville's failure, is suggested by the fact that in 1828, at least one man is known to have been making a living from the export of corpses from Ireland.[57]

Further ideas to which objections were raised were the purchase of bodies either while the donor was still alive, or from relatives after death had taken place.[58] To the first idea it was objected that since the body did not constitute real property, the law could neither enforce nor protect such a bargain. Moreover, there was nothing to prevent a donor from selling his or her body several times over.

It was this possibility which prompted Thomas Hood to write his poem Jack Hall (punning on *jackall*) which first appeared in 1827.[59] It concerns a bodysnatcher who meets Death in St Pancras parish burial ground. Taken to Death's door, he is so angrily received by the inmates – on account of his erstwhile occupation – that he flees back home. On his death-bed, Jack is attended *gratis* by a 'swarm' of doctors, whom Hood likened to vultures and ravens. His scepticism about the altruism of the doctors' concern for the dying man is explicit.[60] At last Jack breaks his silence as to the fate of his remains:

> 'Alas!' he sighed, 'I'm sore afraid,
> A dozen pangs my heart invade;
> But when I drove a certain trade
>   In flesh and bone,
> There was a little bargain made
>   About my own.'

> Twelve suits of black began to close,
> Twelve pairs of sleek and sable hose,
> Twelve flowing cambric frills in rows,
>   At once drew round;
> Twelve noses turn'd against his nose,
>   Twelve snubs profound.

> 'Ten guineas did not quite suffice,
> And so I sold my body twice;
> Twice would not do – I sold it thrice,
>   Forgive my crimes!
> In short I have received its price
>   A dozen times!

> Twelve brows got very grim and black,
> Twelve wishes stretch'd him on the rack
> Twelve pairs of hands for fierce attack
>   Took up position,
> Ready to share the dying pack
>   By long division

. . .but when they return from long deliberation upon how to divide the spoil, the doctors find Jack's body already stolen away by someone else.[61]

It is not inconceivable that some such case had indeed occurred, which would go some way towards explaining Sir Astley Cooper's sharp reply to a caller who offered the baronet the benefit of such a transaction. Alternatively, since the notes are undated, it may be the case that Cooper was fearful of dealing with a potential burker. The exchange appears on a slip of paper in the collection of Cooper papers at the Royal College of Surgeons:

> Sir, I have been informed you are in the habit of purchasing bodys
> and allowing the person a sum weekly knowing a poor woman that is
> desirous of doing so I have taken the liberty of calling to know the truth
> I remain your humble servant

Although Cooper was not entirely averse to this practice,[62] he wrote his reply on the reverse: 'The truth is that you deserve to be hanged for making such an unfeeling offer'.[63]

Purchase of bodies from relatives of the deceased was suggested as a cheaper alternative to purchase from resurrectionists. If treated with decency, one observer suggested, and the bodies returned to their families after dissection, 'the mere defrayment of burial expenses would often be a sufficient consideration'.[64] Wakley campaigned vociferously against the idea of buying corpses, as he felt that any fee whatsoever given for a corpse would perpetuate the material motive for burking.[65] To critics of the suggestion that relatives should receive the fee, the same objection prevailed:

> Will not an unprincipled executor or relative be as likely to kill a
> helpless and forlorn wretch, dying perhaps in an obscure garret, and
> attended only by his heir, as a resurrection man will be to 'burk a lost
> traveller, or a stray apprentice in the dark', – while the respectable
> part of the poor will be shocked at the imagined outrage on
> Christianity committed by the bill.[66]

By far the most frequently proffered suggestion for a new source of supply was to extend the punitive use of dissection hitherto inflicted only upon murderers, to those guilty of other crimes. A broad spectrum of opinion favoured this source, favour which was predicated upon the belief that dissection constituted a degradation, only justly to be inflicted upon criminals.[67]

Some supporters of this suggestion added pauper dead to those from prisons – just as some of the anatomists had done in their confidential letters to the Home Secretary – a suggestion which of course reveals a particular attitude towards poverty. Traditionalist critics of Warburton's proposals, however, made a strong distinction between the honest workhouse poor and inmates of prisons.[68] Guthrie, who as we have seen was not totally opposed to the dissection of the 'unclaimed', thought that criminals' bodies should be taken in preference. He argued on the broad principle

> that every man who dies under a criminal sentence should be
> delivered over for dissection; and that every suicide who destroys

himself in gaol, to avoid, in all probability, a criminal sentence,
should equally be delivered up. There is, I acknowledge, some
trouble attending this and there cannot be a doubt of its being much
more convenient to send to a poor-house and take the bodies of the
poor as they are wanted; but is it the justice which every man has a
right to expect will be the foundation of an Act of Parliament? I
answer distinctly that it is not; that it is a . . . most wicked
degradation of the poor man to take him for the sole purpose of
convenience, as long as there is a convicted criminal who might be
taken in his place. It is a question between justice and convenience.[69]

Petitions to Parliament from less prestigious figures probably represent
popular opinion more closely than Guthrie, yet in these too we find a
similar distinction, and – among others – recommendations for the use of
the bodies of convicted felons, suicides and duellists in preference to the
'unclaimed'.[70] The poor people of the workhouse of the parish of St Ann,
Blackfriars, were shocked that the 'unfortunate and destitute, though not
criminal poor' were about to be subjected to 'the same public Ignominy
after death as the felonious murderer and assassin', and petitioned parliament in 1829 to prevent it.[71]

As we have seen, an important sector of the medical profession wished to
expunge the use of dissection as a punishment for murder from the statute
book. To sever their association with the hangman, they believed, would
improve the public image of both the profession and its anatomical
pursuits. In the period between the failure of the first Bill in 1829 and the
passage of the second in 1832, the conviction that the profession should
unilaterally cease co-operation with government in the administration of
punishment emerged several times, most particularly in Gooch's influential article in the *Quarterly*. Gooch suggested that a programme of polite
non-cooperation would register publicly the profession's own dignity, and
its desire to dissociate itself from the taint of the scaffold:

. . . though our legislators have the power of course of maintaining
this law, we apprehend they have no power to compel medical men to
execute it, and we venture to suggest that all those who value their
characters as gentlemen, and members of a scientific and honourable
profession, that it rests with themselves to decline a task which
requires them to become post mortem executioners, and actually
places them on a level with the hangman.[72]

Others besides Gooch protested that the use of dissection as a punishment
was a degradation of the profession; they recommended that criminals'
bodies should be left untouched, and that only the bodies of the 'unclaimed' be used.[73] But this view was itself contradictory, for it implicitly
and sometimes openly rested upon the belief that those dying in need of a

parish burial were nothing other than petty criminals themselves: 'It must not be forgotten', said one observer,[74]

> that the unclaimed poor in our hospitals and almshouses are mostly those whose lives have been vicious and characters abandoned – the prostitute, the vagrant, and the sot. If any are to suffer after death for the community, it should surely be those who have contributed evil rather than good to it when living.

Guthrie dismissed this sort of argument with the contempt it deserved by saying that such a policy visited *post-mortem* punishment upon small rogues instead of large ones. He ridiculed the line of reasoning whereby to dissect murderers, forgers, robbers, rapists and arsonists represented a disgrace to the art, but to do the same to 'small rogues' was 'no disgrace at all, either to the art or the individual'.[75]

Other medical observers feared that by dissecting paupers, the profession would incur dishonour of equivalent magnitude to that resulting from its existing association with the gallows. In an open letter to Warburton which appeared in *Cobbett's Weekly Political Register* in 1832, William Horsley, a doctor from North Shields, said that he thought the use of the 'unclaimed'. . .

> may be politic enough in the way of trade; but, for the honour of science, the credit of the profession, and the peace of society, I conjure you to pause ere your Committee sanction with their honoured names, so degrading, and at the same time so uncalled-for an expedient.[76]

Horsley's fear was not that dishonour would accrue to the profession from the extension of punitive dissection to semi-criminal paupers. Rather it was that the profession would disgrace itself by becoming the agent of injustice.

Cobbett vilified Warburton and his supporters in the columns of his *Political Register*, steadfastly denying the validity of arguments which imputed criminality to the poor *en masse*:

> the unfortunate persons who die in poor houses and hospitals have, in numerous cases seen better days, and have, during many years, contributed in direct payments towards the maintenance of the poor and the sick . . . those of them who have not so contributed, have all been, so long as able to work, compelled to pay heavy taxes out of the fruits of their hard labour . . . every working man . . . pays full one-half of his wages in taxes; and that, therefore, when he becomes so poor, helpless and destitute, as to die in a poor house or in a hospital, it is unjust, cruel, barbarous to the last degree, to dispose of his body to be cut up like that of a murderer![77]

Cobbett's view of the mischances of paupers' lives would appear to have been borne out in the case of the writer of a letter protesting against Warburton's proposal, which appeared in the *Lancet* in 1829, signed 'One of the "Unclaimed" '. It was from a Worcester man who said he had previously possessed property to the value of £20,000, but was rendered a debtor by the foreclosing of a mortgage. As a result, his wife had died of grief, and he believed this had been a contributory factor in the deaths of his two daughters from consumption. He said that he was now 'the poverty-stricken and emaciated inmate of a workhouse, without a single relation to notice me'. He expressed horror that an Act of Parliament was about to consign him to dissection because he was poor. 'Gracious heavens', he went on, 'and can this take place in England [?] In the abstract, dissection I should disregard, but I look with horror upon being classed with and treated like a murderer'.[78]

Those in opposition to Warburton's proposal made frequent reference to the similarity of treatment intended for the poor and that undergone by the murderer. It is not difficult to understand why this was the case, even though under pressure Warburton eventually added a clause to his second Bill which would repeal the enactment under which murderers were dissected. Everyone – whether in or out of a workhouse – had lived an entire life in the knowledge that dissection was a stipulated sequence to a murderer's execution. Anyone of middle age or older may have met witnesses or heard tales of the gallows riots resulting from the surgeons' attempts to obtain executed malefactors.

Most people within workhouse walls were elderly, sick, physically disabled, or mentally handicapped, and in times of dearth, younger families – all those for whom the old Poor Laws provided a safety net from death by starvation or cold. Few were there from choice, and many felt a deep repugnance to the attempts to change the law to render them liable to dissection after death. Among indoor and outdoor paupers in the neighbourhood of Whitechapel, Bethnal Green and Spitalfields in 1829 the alarm was said to have been 'particularly strong' at the prospect of the change in the law, and elderly women in receipt of Poor Law assistance 'appeared quite horror-struck'.[79] We have seen that the poor inmates of the workhouse of St Ann, Blackfriars, petitioned Parliament against the Bill in horror and amazement.[80]

For these poor people it was not only unfair and demeaning to be made the future objects of dissection, but for them, the legislation would act retrospectively; denying them the funeral they had been allowed to expect. Even if this was to be only a pit-burial between deal boards, it was to them preferable to being taken for dissection, like so many murderers they had heard of, often during long lives. The length of popular memory helps explain why the repeal of murderers' dissection was little more than a cosmetic exercise; and why it was less than honest of Warburton and his supporters to assert that if passed, the stigma of the gallows would cease to operate. Inhabitants of Tenterden, in Kent, petitioned Parliament from 'feelings of deep regret', that such a Bill had been introduced. They regarded the Bill as a 'gross violation of the feelings of our poorer brethren', and one which encouraged 'a heartless system of infidelity, which would have us repudiate the blessed hope of immortality, and place ourselves on a level with the beasts that perish'.[81]

Those who opposed the Anatomy Bills from sympathy with the poor did so with the understanding that the effect of Warburton's proposals, far from removing the stigma of dissection, would effectively augment the humiliation which already attached to poverty. Mechanics from Lambeth petitioned Parliament because they felt they could not

> quietly and conscientiously acquiesce in subjecting the honest and
> persecuted poor to that last species of degradation, which has
> hitherto only been legally enforced, by way of stigma, on the bodies of
> murderers.[82]

Edward Gibbon Wakefield argued that when dissection was part of the state armoury of punishment for murder it represented the '*ne plus ultra of punishment*', while the application of it to the 'unclaimed' would not only act to confirm popular feeling against it, but would redefine it as the '*ne plus ultra of misfortune*'.[83]

It was from those opposing Warburton's Bills that the most interesting and – apart from the use of criminals – the most feasible suggestions came. Basically, they addressed three aspects of the problem: economy of resources, modes of tackling public feeling against dissection, and definitions of pauperism and respectability.

The suggestion that more economical use might be made of corpses in dissection did not constitute an alternative source of corpses in the same sense as other proposed alternatives. But it nevertheless constituted a critique of the management methods operating in anatomical tuition, and of the estimates of need upon which the Select Committee had based its findings. As such, it questioned the need for legislation to requisition the bodies of the 'unclaimed'.

A minority of medical practitioners did mount such a critique, but at the time, their ideas were disregarded in the face of a deluge of medical opinion – both in the press, and in petitions to Parliament – in favour of Warburton's proposals. It was not until after the Anatomy Act was passed and the use of the 'unclaimed' was found not to be the panacea its supporters had canvassed, that greater attention was paid to the amount of wastage customarily involved in dissection,[84] and to the value of morbid anatomy in the understanding and tuition of pathology. It was much later still that medical authorities began to question the primacy of dissection in the medical curriculum.[85] To express these opinions in medical circles in the 1820s and 1830s was to risk being regarded as heretical. Nevertheless, some took the risk.

Some of this criticism was no doubt generated by professional rivalry between physicians and surgeons. Physicians during this period were often backward-looking, and favoured conservative treatment; but nevertheless, their arguments against excessive emphasis on dissection had some justification. Most importantly, they drew a distinction between anatomy and dissection, which had often been overlooked in the public and parliamentary debates.[86] The terms were not synonymous: as well as the study of structure involved in dissection, 'anatomy' was a more extensive discipline in this period, and embraced the study of physiology and pathology.[87]

The physician-critics fully recognised the importance of physiology.[88] What they criticised was what they saw as too great an emphasis upon dissection in the creation of ordinary practitioners – arguing against excessive tuition in dissection except for those who would ultimately specialise in surgery or in the tuition of anatomy. 'The present supply of bodies', said one, 'is adequate for the formation of experts'.[89] Another pleaded: 'Be it not said . . . that we need many operative surgeons . . . and let these be select, so that matured by much experience, they may be fully competent'.[90]

The Bransby Cooper lithotomy scandal had become public only as a result of the status of the personalities involved, and the medical nepotism to which it attracted attention. Such bungling operations were commonplace in this period among the inept, the newly and badly trained, the inexperienced, or those called upon only rarely to use skills acquired many years before – so the plea for surgical competence and expertise had considerable objective justification.[91]

Understandably, physicians' opinions on medical education placed greater stress upon diagnostics, physiology, pathology, pharmacology and therapeutics in general, than did the surgeons.[92] An anonymous writer praised 'Chemistry' – by which was meant therapeutics and pharmacology – saying it would 'diminish surgery, and should be cultivated to lessen the affliction of the knife'.[93]

Hunter's view that surgery often represented a failure of medicine, was repeated by these physicians;

> the true doctrines of physic . . . are eminently calculated to avert
> pending calamity . . . to supercede the necessity for operations,
> which, at best, are painful and calamitous to the afflicted.[94]

Besides economy in the use of corpses for dissection, physicians recommended the value of models, plates, drawings and preparations, as well as the tuition of surface anatomy on live models, rather than dead.[95] Above all, they stressed the paramount importance of long clinical experience.[96] The physicians were aware of Wakley's points about the College's creation of an inordinate demand for corpses in the metropolis. One observed that 'it were as manifest as "the sun at noon-day" that bodies became needful in support of the college law and the rage for dissections'.[97]

An important element in the critique of contemporary anatomy did not, however, emanate from physic. The *Lancet* – whose editor was himself a surgeon – was the forum for an ongoing critique of the College of Surgeons' deleterious influence on the tuition of anatomy. As we have seen, Wakley believed responsibility for the acute shortage and high cost of corpses in the London area since the mid-1820s could be traced to the College's restrictive practices. The failure of the first Anatomy Bill hardly caused Wakley to fall silent: in an editorial in October 1829 he criticised the manipulation of parliamentary and public opinion by those in favour of the failed Bill:

> Our ears are pretty familiar with the declamations of hospital surgeons and lecturers, about materials for the cultivation of the science of anatomy. In the present year, these gentlemen have loaded the tables of both houses of Parliament with petitions, remonstrances, and tomes of evidence, on the scarcity of subjects, and the expense of obtaining them. The journals, too, in the interests of this contemptible oligarchy, have been assailing all who opposed them, with every contumelious epithet which the vocabulary of abuse could supply. Anatomy was put forward as the 'all in all' in medical science. . . . For not ministering to its diffusion, both Parliament and the public were denounced as enemies of science and of humanity, and . . . many centuries in the rear of the proprietors of the hospital schools, in the 'march of intellect'. We admit, and have always admitted, the . . . vast utility of the science of anatomy . . . but is PATHOLOGY nothing, because anatomy is so vastly important?'[98]

In the last part of this passage, Wakley expressed something of the physicians' argument that dissection could never be the sole basis of a successful medical or surgical practice. Although Wakley did not articulate the whole of their argument, it is clear that he too was aware that the existing emphasis upon dissection was out of proportion to the needs of the profession. Wakley went on to discuss the extraction of fees from students at the hospitals – for which he asserted there was no justification in the charitable foundations of hospitals such as Guy's – and the extent to which these fees purchased knowledge or experience. He attacked the hospital teachers for taking no pains to instruct students in clinical medicine, whilst pocketing their fees – knowing that the students must pay up or risk being ineligible for the membership examinations at the College of Surgeons – of which the lecturers themselves were often councillors/examiners. In disgust, Wakley declared all the apparent medical altruism of the hospital surgeons 'cant', and asserted,

> it is the objects of the surgical reformers to drive the base money-changers from our temple, and to dissolve for ever the disgraceful connexion which exists between the College and the hospitals.[99]

The *Lancet*'s public stance on this and related subjects of course attracted correspondence expressing dissatisfaction with the administration of medical education and practice, and demanding medical and surgical reform. A letter from a country anatomist, signed 'A Lover of Justice', complained in January 1832 that no new Bill 'for legalising the sale of dead bodies of the poor' was necessary. The College Council had only to recognise certificates from provincial anatomy schools:

> . . . let them prove their disinterested virtue by consenting to enlarge
> the field of available anatomy by opening schools at the country
> hospitals and breaking up the monopoly of a few hospital lecturers,
> who would seem almost willing to buy the revered bodies of the
> indigent, rather than give up one iota of an unjustly assumed
> prerogative.[100]

Correspondence of this nature often inspired fiery editorial comment critical of those whom Wakley believed guilty of the misuse of power and authority. One such exchange appeared in December 1831, just after the introduction to Parliament of the second Anatomy Bill. A medical student at St Bartholomew's Hospital wrote to reveal the wastage – in terms of use as a teaching resource – of the hospital's ample *post-mortem* facilities. Students who had paid fees for a regular class in 'morbid inspections' found *post-mortems* proceeding without notification at all hours, and by men 'either incapable or unwilling to impart the information therefrom'. Wakley used the letter in an editorial, commenting: 'the *post-mortem* dissections in the other [London] hospitals are conducted with equal carelessness, or . . . altogether neglected'. He went on:

> If we compare the value of the dissection of a dead body, casually
> taken into the dissection-room, with a careful examination of a dead
> body which has died from a disease whose progress and symptoms
> were carefully marked throughout, what are we to think of those
> surgeons, who, while they vociferate complaints against the
> legislature for not providing subjects of the former description for the
> 'instruction of students', constantly neglect the advantages presented
> by the latter, although it is a species of instruction for which each
> surgical pupil pays twenty-six guineas.[101]

Wakley went on to name the surgeons responsible, and to identify them as members of the RCS Council. 'In point of fact', he went on, 'the lecturers on anatomy wish to cover the frauds which they practise upon students, by uttering volumes of cant respecting the 'welfare of the community' and 'the security of the public health'.

Scepticism about professional motives was by no means confined to the pages of the *Lancet*. At a public meeting at Blackburn in the spring of 1832 one speaker observed that: 'Dissection like most other good things is abused, and made a trade of, more for the sake of money than for the good of science'.[102]

Many of Warburton's opponents were anxious that a coercive *post-mortem* punishment specific to murder should not become one specific to poverty. The fear was not only that the poor would thus be victimised in preference to murderers; but that in the long term, dissection would continue to suffer public opprobium, since the association with punishment would persist. To this sector of opinion, it was paramount to tackle the interrelated problems of obtaining a just source of corpses and disconnecting the association with punishment. To do both would entail measures designed actively to combat public feeling against dissection.

Some suggested that Parliament had a special responsibility to promote public generosity towards dissection, in so far as 'ignorance and prejudice' had been 'engendered and fostered by bad legislation'.[103] But the hope that Parliament would willingly attempt to alter public opinion was known to be vain. It was common currency – in these circles as it was in the vociferous lobby in favour of the Bills – that feelings against dissection spanned class barriers, and that many of those who would discuss and vote for the Bills in Parliament, felt horror at the thought of being forced themselves to undergo dissection.[104]

It was this knowledge which underlay accusations of hypocrisy which assailed the ruling elite as a result of the parliamentary consideration of Warburton's proposals. A petition from the Paisley Reform Society which begged the House of Commons to 'pause and reflect before they pass into Law a measure fraught with present injustice, and the seeds of future crime', addressed this hypocrisy directly:

> should the House arrive at the conclusion that a legal provision for the dissection-table must be made, the Petitioners respectfully suggest, that those whose education and habits have got the better of their prejudices may be called upon to make the sacrifice; if to come under the knife be of no consequence, why do medical men take such pains to be sheltered from its incisions? Surely it cannot be expected that the poor will be jeered out of their feelings of abhorrence for a system, which the rich, the wise, and the powerful take such extraordinary care to guard against.[105]

G.W. Dermott, a surgeon – who, as we shall see in a moment, devised plans to encourage voluntary bequest – did not believe that the same prejudice existed among the 'higher classes' or among 'professional men'. He reasoned that these people ought therefore to lead the way in making exemplary bequests.[106] In this way, he believed, public prejudice would be overcome. Many others shared the view that exemplary bequests would help remove public antipathy to dissection. A few, like Bentham, made their views known in life, and undertook to embody them after death. Others, like Carlile, discussed the value and effect of such bequests, and hesitated not to suggest who would provide the most encouraging models for public emulation.[107]

The following passages originate from a petition which the butchers and salesmen of Leadenhall market submitted to the Lord Mayor of London in 1829, in an abortive attempt to obtain his agreement to present their opinions to Parliament.[108] The amalgam of formal humility and deference with frank class insurbordination, ideality with practicality, didacticism and wry humour, renders the tone of this document as near to an authentic working-class voice on the subject as we are likely to find.

The petition 'Humbly showeth' (as was the wont of most petitions) that the petitioners observed that superstitious attachment to the 'perishable remains of humanity' had, under circumstances peculiar to this country, become 'the enemy of science'. They believed a change in public opinion would result from exemplary dissections, but wished to observe:

> That the very nature of example would seem to imply that it should be conspicuous, that it should proceed from above and not from below . . . especially when it is . . . to combat long-cherished and widely extended prejudices among the mass of the population,

but that the Bill before Parliament

> rejects the principle of example . . . or employs it in a manner which must render it perfectly useless, by calling upon the humble and ignorant to instruct the exalted and the wise. . . .
>
> That in the spirit of this conviction your petitioners would humbly recommend to your Honourable House that all the High Dignitaries of the Church, and all the Judges of the land, and all Generals and Colonels commanding regiments, all Admirals and Captains in commission, men whose duty, and ambition, and profit it is to serve their country in life, should dedicate their bodies after death to promote the advancement of knowledge in one of the most useful branches of practical science.

The petitioners wished to free from this obligation: 'married men, or . . . men leaving daughters or unmarried sisters to lament their loss', but recommended:

> that in all other cases the bodies should be given up, beginning with those of the Ecclesiastic bench, and proceeding according to the scale of rank through all the divisions of those public servants of the highest class.
>
> That your petitioners would also recommend that the remains of such great personages as should undergo anatomical dissection, should be interred with extraordinary honours, so that the lower classes might be taught to see distinction and not disgrace in the operation to which they are so adverse at present.

That by the adoption of this simple plan, or of some plan founded upon the same principle, your Honourable House will better consult the object which all enlightened men have in view, than by proceeding to legislate at once against the prejudices of the ignorant, without taking any other step to subdue them than the abrupt dictum of a compulsory Act of Parliament.

The Lord Mayor was shaken by some of the suggestions, and gave his reason for declining to present the petition to Parliament his objection to 'a compulsory measure on so tender a point'. 'He really thought', he said,

that the lower orders ought not, on such occasions, to be exclusively selected. That prejudice should exist was quite natural; and, no doubt, the poor must be as strongly influenced as the rich by that antipathy . . . He had already expressed his disapprobation of a compulsory act, as regarded the poor; and he could not think of recommending a measure of a similar tendency, as regarded the other ranks of society.

Despite the Lord Mayor's decision, his discussion with the sponsors of the petition was friendly, and a great deal of laughter is recorded in the report we have of the event. With regard to judges, and the remainder of the legal profession, for example, Mr Michael Scales of Aldgate High Street said he did not expect much.

It was an old proverb that a lawyer would sell his soul to Old Nick for a trifle, but it was not certain that he would be willing to dispose of his mortal remains upon such cheap terms.

Humorous comments about bishops and aristocrats were also greeted with laughter. It should be noticed that this petition was intended to affect the fate of Warburton's first Bill in 1829; humour is by no means a conspicuous element in petitions against the second Bill. Political events led opponents to take altogether a more serious view of Warburton's revival of his proposals during the Reform crisis.

The unwillingness to become exemplars imputed to lawyers in this encounter also seemed – despite the Dublin mass bequest, and the three medical bequests mentioned above – to have some truth on the greater part of the medical profession. Guthrie publicised the fact that the late Dr Gooch – author of the influential pro-Warburton article in the *Quarterly Review* – far from leaving his own body for dissection, 'took care to have himself buried in the usual manner'.[109] The suggestion that doctors – and particularly surgeons – bore a unique responsibility to make this gesture resurfaced many times,[110] while responses to it indicate that there existed a profound unwillingness on the part of many practitioners to do so. An editorial in the *London Medical Gazette* – a conservative rival to the *Lancet* which frequently expressed hostility towards the Bills' opponents – called the suggestion that doctors should leave their own bodies for dissection an 'absurd proposal', because it did not adhere to the 'principle' of 'employing for anatomical purposes none but the unclaimed', and was 'totally regardless of the feelings of [doctors'] surviving friends'.[111]

The elevation of Warburton's *proposal* to a *principle* shows how tenaciously some held to the Select Committee's recommendations, and how closely the arguments used in the *Report* were repeated – particularly in respect of survivors' 'feelings'.[112] This passage, and many like it, obscured the fact that there was no definition of 'unclaimed'. It serves to show how the Committee's endorsement of the proposal effectively foreclosed discussion of, and limited support for, any alternative.

A further attack from an anonymous pen upon the suggestion that doctors should donate their own bodies, provides an indication of the deep unease many medical men felt at the thought; and perhaps why it was that Warburton's proposal, and the arguments in its favour which appeared in the *Report*, were so easily accepted by the profession, and so assiduously promulgated:

> It has been recommended to the profession to give themselves and families to dissection. I am confident that very few would have the heart to resign their families; and I trust their general good conduct would prevent their families from giving up the beings that cherished them.[113]

To this observer, dissection remained a punishment. That anyone might willingly undergo it was incomprehensible. The importance of this view lies in its pervasiveness – it was the basis of a great deal of the public 'prejudice' against dissection. The failure even to comprehend the possibility that options to coercion existed, provides one reason why so many people (medical and otherwise) actively or passively supported the Bills.[114]

The 'feelings' argument was fallacious. I have shown that had survivors' feelings genuinely been the sole criterion for the choice of dissection material, all those dying without relatives should have been designated; instead, the designation 'unclaimed' meant the effect of the proposal fell only upon those dying without money enough to cover funeral expenses: it was an *economic* designation. The emphasis placed by Warburton's supporters upon survivors' 'feelings' as the only genuine criterion for consideration was therefore a deliberate obfuscation of both the personal and the economic issues involved in their campaign.

The duplicity of this position was not lost upon the opposition; indeed, it was intentionally thrown into relief by the outspoken assertion that medical treatment was not charitable which demanded such a fee, and that definitions of pauperism were incomplete which failed to include 'state paupers'.[115] An 1832 petition from Blackburn elucidates this view:

should the House think it proper that the dead bodies of those only who, whilst living, have been burdensome to the public, should be made instrumental in alleviating human suffering, the Petitioners recommend to the notice of the House all pensioners and sinecurists, who are receiving large sums of money from the Public without doing one act of service for the same . . .[116]

This recommendation had a certain popular appeal: the failed 1829 Leadenhall Butchers' petition quoted above was said to have been suggested by local paupers, to 'improve' the Anatomy Bill 'by substituting individuals of rank in society in place of those to whom Fortune has been a niggard of her favours'.[117] Similar sentiments emerged in Henry Hunt's speeches, Cobbett's *Political Register* and in other petitions, for example, that of the Lambeth Mechanics:

if nevertheless the House deem it necessary to keep the anatomical schools open, and to provide proper and deserving subjects for the same, the Petitioners in all humility recommend to their especial notice all such persons, male or female, who are in the receipt of unmerited pensions, the surgical practitioners themselves, suicides, duellists, convicted felons, and the Members of the late Parliament who voted for Mr Warburton's Bill.[118]

Although these opinions were described as 'abominable babble' by those who disagreed with them,[119] a feasible precedent existed abroad in Finland, where all Crown appointees were obliged to leave their bodies for dissection.[120]

It might be argued that the two positions (dissect the poor/dissect the rich) had much in common – particularly in the appeal to coercion. The distinction between them, however, is absolute. The suggestion that 'rich paupers' should serve on the slab was both defensive and impossible of realisation. Although the first Bill had failed in Parliament as a result of a Tory/radical alliance, it is inconceivable that such an alliance might ever have entertained support for a Bill which nominated Crown pensioners and sinecurists to the status of dissection material: witness the failure of Henry Hunt even to so much as propose it in Parliament – probably from the lack of a seconder – and the Lord Mayor of London's refusal to carry the suggestion even through the doors of Parliament.

Of course, the suggestion that such an alternative should be adopted in Britain served several functions; it was an articulation of outrage on the part of those whose sympathies lay with the workhouse poor; it drew attention to the injustice of Warburton's proposal by calling for poetic justice upon those who wanted *only* the poor to be dissected; it pointed out the profound social and economic inequalities of the society of the day and the old corruption by which these were sustained; and it represented the hope that this verbal turning-of-the-tables might touch the conscience of the rich. Presumably the intention was to prompt the ruling elite to jettison Warburton's proposal, through an insight into how it might feel to be so coerced.

The revival of the Select Committee's proposal after the failure of the first attempt, and during a very sensitive period in the battle for the Reform Bill, was greeted with warnings that this would 'tend to inflame the whole body of work-people against those privileged classes who make the laws',[121] and would 'embitter the minds of the poorer classes against the Legislature and the higher ranks of society'.[122] That disaffection was indeed the result of the canvass for Warburton's second Bill may be shown by the petition from the inhabitants of Blackburn. The petition expressed the signatories' 'feelings of indignation and abhorrence' towards the new Anatomy Bill:

> Should the said Bill unfortunately pass through Parliament . . . it will at once convince the working people of this Country that there is one Law for the rich and another for the poor, and that the poor are looked upon as beasts of burden, or as a species of beings inferior to their Rulers, and that their only business in life is to sweat and toil for others to enjoy in extravagance and luxury the produce of their honest industry, and that after death their bodies must be cut up and mangled for the benefit of their lords and masters . . .[123]

The breathless prose catalogues insult, maltreatment and betrayal, and a sad and bitter reproach of the treachery of the Bill's supporters. The petitioners of Blackburn thought

> it would be monstrously cruel, and a flagrant abuse of power, to pass into Law such a Bill. . . assuming a right to dispose of the bodies of those whose only crime is in becoming burdensome to some of those institutions which they have laboured hard for many years to support.

Indeed, the question of whether or not Parliament had the right to dispose of paupers' corpses in the same way as it had over murderers, was never adequately addressed or answered. The right was assumed.[124]

Petitioners tried repeatedly to remind parliamentarians of their duties towards the poor, and of the right of the poor to justice. Members of the Worcester Political Union said they rejoiced 'at every means which is calculated to ameliorate the condition of society, and to detract from that sum of human misery, pain, and affliction to which mankind are necessarily or accidentally subject', but, they believed 'feelings of humanity and the voice of mercy alike dictate that such benefits should only be sought to be promoted by proper and benevolent means'.[125]

Words and phrases redolent of biblical prose in passages such as this were also reminders of the Christian duties of mercy and charity. Many wealthy people whose tombs and memorials were still comparatively new had adorned them with personifications of these virtues; so such reminders may have had some hope of effect. Yet there is a note of real exasperation in the Paisley Reform Society's answer to the 'feelings' argument, and the consignment to dissection of the 'unclaimed':

> to talk of the absence of the relatives of the pauper as a reason why his remains should not be respected, is to insult the humanity of a Nation professing a creed which teaches that all are brethren.[126]

The reminders of religion, entreaties for mercy and equity, accusations of treachery, invocations of retributive poetic justice, and suggestions of alternatives, fell upon deaf ears. This is all the more regrettable since it was in the literature of dissent that the most imaginative, feasible, and forward-looking suggestions for alternative sources of corpses were to be found.

Two opponents of the use of the 'unclaimed' – one of whom was himself an anatomist – proposed plans which did not require the coercion of either criminals or the poor, whereby a source of corpses free from the stigma of punishment could potentially have become available to the anatomists. Neither plan was perfect, but each provided an alternative way of thinking about the problem, each trusted to public awareness of the need for corpses for anatomy, and each was libertarian enough to allow everyone the freedom to choose whether or not they would be dissected after death.

In 1829 the surgeon-anatomist G.W. Dermott submitted a plan to the *Lancet* which floated the idea of the creation of a fund, whose interest would be available for the purchase of the bodies of willing 'subjects' during their lifetime.[127] Aware of the existing objections to purchase during life, Dermott suggested a central register of those who had promised their bodies, and direct liaison with parish authorities to assure *bona-fide* provenance and death certification. Registration, liaison, and correct administration would, he believed, remove both the necessity for grave-robbery, and the incentive to murder. Dermott allowed for the redemption of the promise by means of the return of the premium, which was not to exceed £7.

Both the fund and distribution of corpses were to be entrusted to a committee of 'opulent and respectable men, not more than one-third of whom shall be of the medical profession'. By this means, Dermott hoped to prevent the favouritism and nepotism which infected the contemporary surgical hierarchy from affecting the management of his scheme. Recognising that to launch such a plan successfully some great example would be necessary, Dermott suggested a mass bequest on the lines of the Dublin example:

> I know many medical men who are willing to give their bodies over for dissection, to promote the interest of science; I, for one, would be willing to set the example. With this conviction, I suggest that the profession, *en masse*, (for the purpose of giving a primary impulse to

the plan) voluntarily make over their bodies for dissection to the committee, upon the condition that they are reclaimable, by paying to the funds of the committee the standard value of a subject.

Although Dermott suggested the calling of a public meeting, and approaches to Parliament to effect this or a similar plan, no further reference to his idea has so far been found in the medical press,[128] so it would seem to have died a natural death from a failure of professional interest. If this is indeed what happened, it did not seem to deter Dermott from floating a similar plan late in 1832, when it became evident that the Anatomy Act proved not to be all that its promoters had promised.[129] This too, seems to have been ignored. A Mr Stephen tried to promote a 'mortuary fund' on similar lines, through the Royal College of Surgeons in 1831, but nothing further is known of him or his scheme.[130]

Another interesting and potentially productive plan appeared in a pamphlet by Edward Gibbon Wakefield, which was published while the second Bill was in the process of its passage through Parliament.[131] Wakefield feared that dire political and social unrest would ensue if the Bill was passed, and offered his scheme with this fear in mind. It appeared at a more rudimentary stage of development than Dermott's scheme, and its drift can best be conveyed by direct quotation:

At present, those classes which affect superior sense and liberality of opinion, are, with some few honourable exceptions, quite as much prejudiced on this point as the most ignorant and stupid of the populace. In vain does the wise, benevolent, and illustrious Bentham talk with the utmost cheerfulness of having left his body for dissection; in vain do a few generous men direct that their remains shall be made of service to the public; in vain do we preach to the poor of the unreasonableness of caring for mere flesh, which the worms will dissect at all events; in vain it is to strive against this prejudice amongst the poor, so long as the prejudice shall be cherished by the rich. Wealth always was, and always will be, respected. Let the rich set an example of rational conduct to the poor, and in the course of a very short time the murderous value of dead bodies will be at an end. But the wealthy, who run little or no risk of being 'burked', are without the motive for setting such an example. Let a law, then, create the motive. This might be done in various ways; such as, for example, by directing that the bodies of all who receive above a certain amount of public money, shall be liable to be claimed for the public good; and, (what would clash less with our system of government), by excusing from payment of legacy duty, the representatives of those persons, who had bequeathed their bodies for dissection, and whose bodies had actually been dissected. Considering the immense value which is, in this country, attached to money, even by the dying, the adoption of this last suggestion, might soon diminish the revenue. But by then the object in view would have been accomplished . . .[132]

Neither Wakefield nor Dermott made extravagant claims about the number of corpses the adoption of their plans would yield. At the time, and particularly to those who feared dissection, such schemes might not have seemed likely to produce as many corpses as the requisition of the poor was said to promise.[133]

Nevertheless, had Warburton and his supporters genuinely sought a new source of stigma-free corpses, and been open-minded as to its provenance, there could have been public discussion of the options suggested by their opponents. Indeed, there need not have been adversaries. A less inflexible attitude might have induced not only consideration of such alternatives, but perhaps even attempts to test their viability. Both discussion and investigation were lacking.

The reasons for this rigidity are ascertainably political and economic. All available evidence indicates that even before the Select Committee was appointed, Warburton and his colleagues were bent on assuming the same power over the dead poor as the law had hitherto offered only over murderers. This had been Bentham's plan, and it would be adhered to. Doubtless part of their intention represented a socially laudable intention to assist medical knowledge. This aspect of their work these men were at pains to advertise, and medical history has so for been written largely as they would have wished. Yet such a view of their handiwork is limited. The Bill's opponents viewed as bogus the assumption on the part of its proponents of a pose of social benefaction. They understood the Bill's political and social aims, and saw that its medical implications were only of secondary importance.

Had the socially beneficial provision of an adequate supply of corpses been their sole intention, Warburton and his colleagues would have had nothing to fear from open discussion of the merits of all potential sources put forward by contemporaries – even if only for the purpose of eliminating them from public consideration. Their unwillingness even to discuss the possibility of alternative sources is suggestive. Debate would have given credibility to their opponents' arguments. Publicly to entertain the existence of alternatives to requisitioning the poor would have denied credibility to their own argument that no further options existed beyond the continuance of murder, or the abandonment of anatomical tuition.

Moreover, such discussion would have threatened the achievement of other, more important, Benthamite aims: *first*, the Anatomy Act offered a unique chance to establish a nationally organised and centrally funded inspectorate – an institution of central importance in the Benthamite programme of government reform. In such an emotive and self-evidently necessary field of reform as the prevention of grave-robbery and murder, traditional opponents of government intervention and centralisation could be depended upon to offer little opposition. Once agreed, its establishment would provide an important precedent. *Second*, Warburton and his supporters recognised that the powerful popular aversion to dissection would assist in the achievement of their long-term aim of 'reforming' the Poor Laws on Malthusian lines. Popular fears of dissection would be harnessed by the Anatomy Act and channelled towards future use in the enforcement of the New Poor Law. The concept of the deterrent workhouse, so punishing that only desperation would induce the poor to apply to the parish, was only two years away from being enshrined as the key institution and image of the New Poor Law.[134] Dissection would augment its potential intimidation value.

In all probability, the expressions of righteous anger, horror, and humane indignation which greeted Warburton's Bills were a source of gratification, rather than concern, to the Benthamites. They had begun to appreciate the inestimable publicity-value of outcry in the achievement of their aim of cutting public expenditure on poverty by curtailing demand for poor relief, in the cause of what Edward Thompson has described as 'perhaps the most sustained attempt to impose an ideological dogma, in defiance of human need, in English history'.[135]

Of course not everyone who supported the Bills was a committed Benthamite. Other factors had served to change opinions among the ruling elite between the Bill's failure in 1829 and its passage in 1832, particularly the growing pressure for Reform. The very creatures many parliamentarians despised were mobilising on an unprecedented scale to demand political power. The watershed probably came with the Reform Riots in Nottingham and Bristol in October 1831, and the rekindling of old fears of the revolution in France.

Together, contempt and fear are apt to create a powerfully vindictive amalgam – and this is indeed what is to be found in the language, attitudes and legislation of much of the ruling elite in the 1830s. The criminalisation of poverty – which would find parliamentary endorsement in both the Anatomy Act and the New Poor Law – is one of the most important indicators of the intensity of social tension in the Reform era.

BRINGING 'SCIENCE TO THE POOR MAN'S DOOR'[1]

'For' (he observed), 'if every one were warm and well-fed, we should lose the satisfaction of admiring the fortitude with which certain conditions of men bear cold and hunger. And if we were no better off than anybody else, what would become of our sense of gratitude; which,' said Mr Pecksniff with tears in his eyes, as he shook his fist at a beggar . . . 'is one of the holiest feelings of our common nature.'

Charles Dickens: *Martin Chuzzlewit*, 1844.[2]

the bill exposes to the odious sale none but the bodies of the poor; and this the labouring poor very clearly perceive. They well know that the bodies of the rich will never be sold . . . that the rich do not go to poor houses and hospitals . . . that the rich are not unclaimed when they die. . . . Injustice consists much more in the partiality of a law, or of a judgement, than in the severity of either.

Cobbett's Weekly Political Register, 1832.[3]

'Medical knowledge is at a low ebb among us,' said Mr Bulstrode, who spoke in a subdued tone, and had a rather sickly air. 'I, for my part, hail the advent of Mr Lydgate. I hope to find good reason for confiding the new hospital to his management.'
'That is all very fine,' replied Mr Standish, who was not fond of Mr Bulstrode; 'if you like him to try experiments on your hospital patients, and kill a few people for charity, I have no objection. But I am not going to hand money out of my purse to have experiments tried on me. I like treatment that has been tested a little.'

George Eliot: *Middlemarch*, 1871.[4]

Burking was confirmed in London in early November 1831, only a few days after the Bristol Reform riots. Three years almost to the day had passed since the discovery of the Burke and Hare murders, and in the intervening period a great deal had happened. The Swing riots had upset the illusion of rural calm – and had been viciously repressed – nineteen rioters had since been executed, and nearly five hundred transported to Van Dieman's Land. In France, Louis Philippe had gained power in the July Revolution of 1830, while the popular 'sailor' King, William IV, had acceded to the British throne. London's streets had acquired the Metropolitan Police and Shillibeer's horse-drawn omnibuses. Several confusing changes of government had recently been the result of growing national pressure for parliamentary reform. A month before the 'London Burkers' were discovered, Nottingham Castle had been burned in reform riots when the House of Lords had thrown out the second Reform Bill. Ominously, the first case of asiatic cholera was confirmed in Sunderland in mid-October. The country was in a high pitch of political excitement. The first Anatomy Bill's failure seemed a distant memory, and despite the setbacks, the achievement of Reform seemed irresistible.

Warburton moved swiftly to take advantage of the furore surrounding the discovery of the London Burkers to introduce his second Bill. The third Reform Bill had been introduced by Lord John Russell only three days earlier – conveniently overshadowing the new Anatomy Bill.

<hr />

Murder for dissection had been foretold in urban legend. Before the discovery of real events, tales had been circulating that children were being stolen for dissection.[5] Stories like this may indeed have had older roots[6] but they also had a ring of modernity about them – some said the new steamships, then being adopted on the main British sea routes, were transporting victims' corpses to their destinations[7] – and all of the stories related to a very topical preoccupation. Even before the Burke and Hare murders had been exposed, these tales were so widely believed that one anatomy school in Dublin was forced to work under police protection, and at least two bodysnatchers were said to have died from the results of popular violence.[8]

In the two-month-long period of limbo between the discovery of the Edinburgh murders and the publication of Burke's confessions, the myth seems to have arisen that he and Hare had disposed of their victims by suffocating them with large medical pitch plasters clapped over mouth and nose, and various stories centred upon such attempts.[9] Both series of murders provoked a powerful public reaction of anguish and fear which became known variously as 'Burking Mania',[10] 'Burkiphoby'[11] or 'Burkophobia'.[12] So pervasive was the fear of murder for dissection that the newspapers were peppered with cases of attempted burking,[13] suspected burking,[14] threatened burking,[15] burking in jest[16] and even in children's play.[17]

<hr />

Almost contemporaneously with the discovery of the London Burkers, a young man's body was found in a box on a coach at Leeds, in transit to Edinburgh. His case illustrates the impact burkophobia could have on the ordinary bodysnatching business, for burking was immediately suspected when it was discovered that the man had died a violent death.[18] Thousands of local people came forward to view the body, but at the opening of the inquest, it remained unidentified. It was shown that the man had been 'strangled by pressure on the throat', and that his body had never been laid out. Public excitement increased; particularly as those held in connection with the suspected crime included such apparently respectable figures as a Leeds seminary proprietor and an attorney's clerk, besides a butcher, a packer, and a joiner.

Eventually, the body was identified as that of a young collier, Robert Hudson. He had hanged himself, and although permitted burial in the village churchyard at East Ardsley near Wakefield, being a suicide, he had not received traditional burial care. His corpse had been stolen the following day, only three days after death.[19]

Freed from suspicion of burking, the men in custody were charged at York Assizes with conspiracy to disinter bodies. The gang's operations, and the extent to which they were protected from detection by the respectable status of some of those involved, were revealed when a defendant turned King's evidence.[20] Detailed press coverage sustained public interest over the winter and into the early spring of 1832, when all but the schoolmaster were given prison sentences. The case caused almost as much disturbance in the north of England as did the discovery of burking in London. There can be little doubt the gang were genuine resurrectionists, and that the experience of being taken for murderers was one which many bodysnatchers risked in these years.

Whereas a few years earlier a writer could almost praise the resurrectionists for serving to prevent the stagnation of medicine,[21] after the discovery of burking it was generally assumed – as it had been in the Leeds case – that all bodysnatchers were potential murderers: that the commission of murder was merely a further stage of development on from the robbing of graves. Although neither Burke nor Hare had worked as a resurrectionist, the progression from one job to another was nevertheless generally believed to have taken place in their individual lives. Historically, it is undoubtedly true that burking developed from grave-robbery as a means of realising the corpse's commercial potential. Yet even modern medical authorities repeat the contemporary assumption that the original burkers' involvement in murder had developed from exposure to the corrupting business of dealing in exhumed bodies. The lay perception that Burke and Hare were bodysnatchers remains.[22] The assumption is instructive: it marks an appreciation that the inevitable consequence of commerce in corpses was murder.

Bishop and Williams, on the other hand, seem to epitomise the process. They had existed on the fringes of the London underworld[23] and were

17 'Burkiphoby', after a cartoon by R. Seymour, 1831

seasoned suppliers of the schools. In his confession Bishop said he had
supplied between 500 and 1000 disinterred corpses to the London anatomy
schools.[24] Apart from this important difference, their case was a London
version of Burke and Hare.[25] All three victims to whose deaths they
eventually confessed were very poor street folk to whom Bishop or
Williams had offered hospitality. The murderers disabled their victims
with laudanum administered surreptitiously in rum, and when they were
insensible, suspended them headlong in a well in Bishop's garden.

This form of murder left no marks, and little other evidence of the cause
of death, and had the men been a little more circumspect, they might have
evaded detection altogether. For despite their knowledge of the pathology
of exhumed bodies the body of their last victim – the 'Italian Boy' – was
offered for sale in an extremely fresh state, still in *rigor mortis*. They may not
have known that in some cases of violent death the natural coagulation of
the blood can be delayed: the boy's teeth had been removed with a bradawl
after death by a colleague, May, leaving blood in the mouth. The blood,
the stiffness of the body and the fact that it had never been laid out,
together raised the suspicions of staff at King's College when the body was
examined with a view to purchase. 'It was the blood that sold us', Bishop

was said to have confided in May.[26]

The acclamation of the crowd outside the court when the guilty verdict was returned was so great that the judge could no longer be heard inside the courtroom. Rumour had it that on the eve of his execution Williams had made another confession, never made public, to the effect that he and Bishop had together murdered about sixty people for sale to the anatomists.[27] On the following morning, 5 December 1831, the streets leading to the Old Bailey scaffold were 'thronged with people – chiefly of the working classes', who greeted the London Burkers' launch into eternity with cheering and exultation.[28]

At the revelation of burking in London, the 'burkophobia' had broken out afresh. Suspected and attempted burkings continued to be reported in the press throughout the trial, leading one newspaper to comment:

> The Burkophobia seems to be at its height in the metropolis at the present time; and scarcely a day passes but reports are circulated of the supposed sacrifice of fresh victims to the 'interests of science'. We suppose in future, this epidemic will as regularly make its appearance in winter as the hydrophobia does in the summer.[29]

The entire case, from discovery to execution, was over within a month,[30] but public anxiety remained at a high pitch. Fuelled no doubt by the ordinary incidence of serious murder attempts, the fear of pitch plasters[31] and of going out after dark 'in any but the most frequented places'[32] perhaps had some justification. Although it is always possible to deride the exaggerations of rumour, and to dismiss such reports as mob hysteria, there is good reason to suppose that some may have had a basis in 'copy-cat' crimes. At least two well-placed observers – Wakley and James Somerville – independently committed to print their opinion that the detection/conviction rate for burking was entirely unrepresentative of the incidence of the crime. Somerville plausibly argued that there were 'many others' in addition to Burke and Bishop, 'whose greater caution in the selection of their subjects, greater skill in the various arts of destroying life, and more circumspection in their dealings, have screened from the hand of justice'.[33] Wakley himself believed the number of probable victims ran into three figures.[34]

Although there were others who believed such fears completely groundless,[35] Warburton's second Bill – introduced only ten days after the London Burkers' execution – was undoubtedly hastened through its early parliamentary stages on a wave of burkophobia. Various members of both Houses expressed shock and horror at the re-emergence of burking, and voiced their belief that something should be done to prevent further bloodshed.

Although this horror was probably quite genuine, it was co-opted for their own purposes by Warburton and his parliamentary colleagues. At several crucial moments in the parliamentary progress of the Bill, when the opposition had argued persuasively, or when general discussion threatened to delay its passage, the Bill's supporters did not scruple to remind all present of the late 'enormities'.[36] The reminder served as a way of curtailing debate by the introduction of a note of urgency, and decoyed parliamentary attention from important issues arising from the Bill itself, to the fact of a crime deplored by all present.

Had such a tactic emerged only once, the modern reader of the debates might be inclined to overlook its result; but since it occurred on no less than four important occasions,[37] and since so much else regarding the Bill's promotion and passage seems to have been similarly contrived, it is not difficult – as in the case of the Select Committee – to discern strategy in this and other manoeuvres.

⸺◆⸺

In the period between the submission of his two Bills, Warburton seems to have undergone a sea change in his ability to navigate Parliament. A comparison of the texts and progress of both Bills shows him to have been much more sophisticated in 1831. The first Bill had been lengthy, explicit and detailed almost to pedantry. The second was deceptively simple, and half the size. Even the titles reflect the change; the 1829 attempt had been entitled: *A Bill for preventing the Unlawful Disinterment of Human Bodies, and for Regulating Schools of Anatomy*, while the second Bill made no reference to the emotive subject of grave-robbery, and called itself simply: *A Bill for Regulating Schools of Anatomy*.

The excision of emotionally charged subject-matter and phraseology was a feature of the later Bill, the most concise illustration of which may be found in the clause-summaries printed in the margins of the official texts. Whereas the 1829 version summarised the key clauses: 'The bodies of persons unclaimed dying in any Hospital or Workhouse may be delivered for dissection,' the later rendering was: 'Persons having lawful custody of Bodies may permit them to undergo Anatomical Examination.' The important thing to notice is that all specific mention of workhouses, hospitals – and hence the precise social status of the proposed subjects of dissection – had been deleted, while the intentions of the Bill remained precisely as before.

This superficial simplification of style and content is paralleled in Warburton's own manner; for whereas the *Hansard* transcripts show him to have been almost loquacious in the championship of his first Bill, he guided the second through debates sparing his words, with circumspection, and in a 'low tone'[38] of voice. At the opening of the Commons debate on the second reading, for example, Warburton said merely that he did not 'feel it necessary to detain the House at this stage upon a Bill, the principle of which had been recognised and acted upon by a former House of

Commons', before he sat down.[39]

Once again, it is perhaps possible to discern Bentham's influence here. In the Bentham collection of manuscripts at University College, London, is preserved an undated sheet of autograph draft notes addressed to Brougham, offering advice on how to avoid parliamentary discussion on law reform measures.[40] It advised him to speak principally of the imperfections he sought to reform; to avoid speaking of the remedies contemplated (to avoid provoking 'prejudices which will be played off against you'); and to defer by pleading 'that you think it will be too much for you to take upon yourself the task of developing and defending them on the present occasion', or that not enough information was available at the time, and so on. This is not to imply that Warburton saw these notes – but that it seems beyond doubt such coaching was a feature of parliamentary Benthamism.

Warburton's newly acquired parliamentary dexterity utilised such techniques successfully at various stages of the second Bill's passage – though on at least one occasion, when pressed, he reverted to his former style.[41] In general, however, he studiously cultivated a low profile, both for himself and his Bill. At times, this operated to the avoidance of debate, to equivocation and even to dishonesty.

In one important instance, two of Warburton's supporters made misleading statements to the House of Commons, asserting that both the inhabitants of Blackburn and Henry Hunt, the MP presenting their hostile petition, had mistaken the meaning of the Bill's crucial custody clause.[42] The petitioners had correctly taken the clause to mean that workhouse keepers would thenceforth be free to sell for dissection the bodies of people who died in their institutions. The denial of this understanding by two of his colleagues, and their imputation that both Hunt and the Blackburn petitioners were deluded, was an outright deceit which Warburton allowed to pass uncorrected.[43]

The timing of debates – most of which took place late at night, or in the early hours of the morning when few members were present – assisted the avoidance of discussion. The radical MP 'Orator' Henry Hunt, veteran of Spa Fields and Peterloo, and the 'solitary champion of the working class reform movement in the unreformed House of Commons',[44] described the position to his Preston constitutents:

> I stand alone against the principle of that Bill, you can have no idea how they harrass me, and what I have to contend with. Warburton gives notice for his Bill to go into Committee, at least three times a week. This stands on the orders of the day, which never come on till after one o'clock [am.], on each of the days, or rather nights. I am obliged to wait in attendance till it is called on; then he puts it off for two or three days more, in the hopes of my being absent, and in that case it would pass through the Committee *pro-forma* without opposition. As long as I remain, 50 or 60 members remain, fearing

that I should divide the House. But as soon as I am gone, 8 or 10
members pass all the Bills upon the notice book without hearing or
reading one word of them.[45]

The *Commons Journal* for this period supports Hunt's description of events.
Warburton's Bill was in fact deferred no less than eighteen times, and most
of these deferrals took place after midnight.[46] When the Bill *was* debated, a
variety of deft devices was used to defer discussion to a later date, or to
deny debate on the grounds that a point had already received attention
and need not do so twice.[47] On another occasion, discussion was refused
outright.[48] Warburton contrived to arrange that parliamentary assent was
obtained for the public funding of salaries and expenses for the inspectors
his Bill proposed, even before their appointment had been debated.[49] A
significant amount of detail concerning the Bill's administration was left to
the Home Secretary's discretion, which had the dual effect of keeping the
Bill short, and curtailing the attention it demanded.[50] Repeated complaints were made by members of both Houses that the Bill was being
hurried through without proper discussion; but such protests proved
fruitless.[51] An attempt even seems to have been made to inhibit public
discussion of the Bill, by the closure of the press gallery during debate.[52]

Hunt was not in fact the Bill's sole parliamentary critic, though he was
certainly the most committed and consistent.[53] The impression he gave his
constitutents of a clear imbalance of forces in favour of the Bill, and of a
body of MPs who said little but who always voted with Warburton, bears
close comparison with the picture in the surviving records. In every debate
in which a division was called, speakers against the use of the workhouse
dead seem to have represented the bulk of the opposition vote, whereas
those speaking in support bore little numerical relation to the size of the
vote – always a clear majority – in favour of the Bill.[54]

Divisions lists for these debates perished in the fire of 1834, so the
identities of those who constituted Warburton's silent majority may never
be known. Hunt, however, described the nature of the alliances thus:

A pretty situation we, the people, are in; the only chance of support
that I have, is from a few of the Tories. . . . The Whigs hate the people
more, much more, than the Tories, if possible.[55]

Analysis of the political affiliations of speakers for and against the Bill
supports this view, and shows parallels with the parliamentary reception
of the New Poor Law in 1834: two loose alliances – one of traditionalist
ultra-Tories with ultra-radicals, the other of Benthamites with free trade
Whigs and Tories – opposed each other on the floor of the House. In both
instances, predictably, the most consistent group of speakers overtly in
favour was the Benthamites and their allies – in the case of the Anatomy
Bill, Warburton, Hume, Spring Rice, Lord Althorp, and Macaulay.[56]

In the Commons, these speakers were circumspect in discussion of the Bill's class implications – even, as we have seen, going so far as to deny their existence – which suggests that at least some Members present were not entirely of their persuasion and required mollification. In the Lords discussion was much less guarded, since Lord Minto (who had introduced the Bill) behaved rather ineptly as if the Bill's class bias was known and inevitable, though regrettable. He admitted,

> that it would be an improvement, if the provisions of the Bill could be so framed as not to point out so distinctly as it did, that its operation had reference to a particular class.[57]

In reality, the clause had been very carefully worded to obscure its class target – only those who had grasped its implications recognised its crucial importance.

Available indications suggest that members of both Houses who remained silent in debate, but supported the Bill in divisions, may have done so for a variety of reasons. There may have been some who could not see beyond the superficial appearances of equity in the Bill to its real purpose; and others who – like Fife – believed something must be done and that Warburton's Bill would do.[58] Others still must have fully grasped its implications and positively approved, recognising that Warburton's strategy was '*taisez-vous*', the silent system Hume had used so successfully in the repeal of the Combination Acts, in which 'even its staunchest supporters were warned not to speak'.[59]

The small parliamentary opposition was no less diverse in character. There were a few extremists who thought the Bill did not go far enough, and that none *but* the workhouse poor should be dissected. They argued that sick hospital patients should be permitted to die without the suspicion that they were being disposed of by their doctors[60] – though according to such reasoning inmates of workhouse infirmaries would surely have had a right to the same assurance.[61] After quite impassioned speeches in support of their position, these MPs probably either abstained or voted with Warburton at the final Commons vote on the Bill.[62]

What genuine opposition was made came mainly from Henry Hunt, and a handful of ultra-Tories. Hunt was the Bill's most persistent opponent in all its stages through the Commons. He spoke at least once in every debate, vowing repeatedly to do all in his power to prevent its passage, and tabling amendments to every clause. He argued strongly in favour of the reform of the medical hierarchy, and of rendering medical education less exploitative of students, as well as of the dead poor. He argued that surgeons should bequeath their own bodies for dissection, and derided the sham equity of the Bill's pivotal clause. Hunt rightly saw that the wording of the clause would permit the sale of corpses, and feared the effects upon the poor of what he regarded as a legal incentive to institutional burking, or neglect. His much-vaunted threat to table an amendment whereby the 'rich paupers' on the *Civil List* would become eligible for dissection never materialised – possibly because he alone supported it.[63]

Apart from Hunt, only a handful of traditionalists took it upon themselves to defend the poor. One was Colonel Sibthorp, who warmly advocated that instead of the poor, all horse-stealers should be hanged and dissected.[64] Another was the champion of benign factory legislation, Sadler, who believed: 'even if the Bill should do any good, it would be at the expense of the morality, the decency, and the proper feelings of the living'.[65] Though they frankly recognised the impossibility of preventing the Bill's passage,[66] its opponents continued to question the designation of poverty as the sole criterion for dissection, and to express their horror that a punishment for murder would henceforth be visited solely upon indigence. The ultra-Tories were aware of the infringement of tradition, funerary custom and mores which was in active contemplation, and attempted to touch Parliament's conscience by the evocation of sympathy and pity.[67]

They failed. Paucity of opposition rendered the enterprise hopeless. At the third reading in the Commons, only four votes were cast against the Bill, and in divisions on some of his amendments, Hunt's vote stood alone against forty-nine of Warburton's supporters.[68]

Outside Parliament, a series of anatomy riots and disturbances erupted as the second Anatomy Bill was receiving parliamentary attention. The serious disturbances at Aberdeen, Inveresk, Hereford, Greenwich, Deptford – and other places which will be discussed more fully later – all took place in this period. It is impossible now to tease out the relative importance of the several strands of influence which may have been operating to provoke such disturbances. Excitement surrounding the Great Reform Bill, fear of the cholera, and of course burkophobia, may each have fed into a general level of anxiety. In addition, the fact of the Anatomy Bill's reintroduction after more than two years in abeyance may have provoked a sense of imminent victimisation on the part of the poor. Parishioners of Lambeth who petitioned Parliament in January said that they had

> a great horror of burking, but they entertained a still greater horror at
> the provisions of the Anatomy Bill which would in their opinion be
> the means of opening the door for a new and refined species of
> Burking.[69]

There was a feeling of fear in the air that Parliament and the doctors were hatching something extremely sinister.

It was perhaps to be expected that arch-traditionalists like Sadler should warn: 'the great mass of the British public was alive to this subject, and they contemplated with extraordinary disgust any advancement in science which was to be made at their expense'.[70] Yet Warburton and his colleagues could hardly have been ignorant of the emotive impact of their proposal, or unaware of the extent of the Bill's unpopularity, for they were informed even by their own supporters in Parliament. Though unrepentant, even Macaulay recognised the Bill's unpopularity, and the Attorney General, another staunch supporter, deplored the personal 'opprobrium which has been so lavishly heaped upon Warburton for his part in the Bill's progress'.[71]

The Bill's supporters were by no means ignorant of popular opinion, but they believed it of no importance. As Edwin Chadwick was later to reveal when the inhumanity of the New Poor Law was assailed from many sides, committed Benthamites were profoundly negligent of popular feeling, however justified.[72] Nevertheless, at times in the debates – despite their knowledge of the safety of their parliamentary majority – Warburton and his colleagues often convey the impression of having felt beleaguered and on the defensive. In support of Parliamentary Reform Warburton and his colleagues had popular support and were using it for all it was worth; however, on anatomy, popular support was with their opponents.

Their defensiveness was manifested occasionally in an arrogance and belligerence of manner,[73] and more frequently in accusations and aspersions cast upon those who spoke up against the Bill. They accused their opponents of ignorance and misunderstanding, prejudice, misinterpretation, of unfairness, of 'false humanity and sickly sensibility', hypocrisy, unreasonableness, and a desire to shackle or prevent the study of anatomy in Britain.[74] By way of contrast, they portrayed *themselves* as patrons of science and medicine, enlightened victims of prejudice and ignorance, champions of social equity, protectors of the dead and the living, and even benefactors of the poor.[75]

———————

It can be appreciated that dialogue between such adversaries would be problematic. In a very real sense, throughout the parliamentary debate, there was no genuine engagement between the two sides. In all the key areas of debate, it was as if the Bill's sponsors and supporters had appropriated the entire terrain – denying their opponents even conceptual space in which to operate.

Three examples of this appropriation are to be found in the confusion of terminology designating dissection and *post-mortem*; the denial of alternatives to the coercion of the poor; and the assertion of the Bill's equity. Each example had undergone a process of misrepresentation in the Select Committee's *Report*, and codification in the Bill took the process a step further. It is noticeable that each depended to some extent upon verbal ambiguity or sleight of hand. For this reason, it will be useful to note what

Bentham himself had to say about the language of the law, whose two-fold objective was, he thought:

> partly to prevent information from being conveyed to certain descriptions of person; partly to cause such information to be conveyed to them as shall be false, or at any rate fallacious; to secure habitual ignorance, or produce occasional misconception'.[76]

This passage could be viewed either as a powerful critique of jargon and mystification in the law, or as a sermon on how to govern by misrepresentation. Bentham's recommendation that prospective legislation should be circulated to those whom it would primarily affect[77] suggests he intended it to be understood in the first sense. Although in one instance his disciples on the anatomy question are known to have sent a copy of the Bill to the petitioners of Blackburn, this was done not in order to illuminate, but rather to mystify; both the text of the Bill and the comments of its advocates were intentionally deceptive.[78] Together, they constituted a direct invalidation of Bentham's legal reform ideals, while simultaneously propounding a law of which he approved.

The confusion between dissection and *post-mortem* – which has been noticed in the syntax of the Select Committee *Report* – was perpetuated in the second Bill. Warburton had retained the word 'dissection' throughout his first failed Bill. In the second, it was entirely replaced by the euphemism, 'anatomical examination'. The significance of the alteration lies in the general usage of the word 'dissection' in the vocabulary of the day. Most commonly, it was associated with the punishment of murder. Newspapers, broadsheets and ballads from the gallows literature of this period often featured the formal death sentence with phrases such as: 'he was launched into eternity, and after hanging the usual time, he was cut down, and his body given to the surgeons for dissection' or, 'his body was conveyed to Surgeons' Hall for dissection; and his children placed in Cripplegate Workhouse'.[79]

In the public mind, the word 'dissection' could not fail to have been associated not only with the death sentence, but with the punitive destruction of the body. In substituting the term 'anatomical examination', the authors of the second Bill intended to attenuate its meaning by a verbal trick, which misleadingly stressed durability rather than destruction. This did not go unnoticed, but the minority in parliamentary opposition was powerless to prevent the use of the new phrase in the drafting of the Act. The effect of Warburton's tactic was attenuated by the studied deliberation with which the phrase was avoided by the opposition, and their blatant reference to the Bill as the 'Dissecting Bill'.[80]

Denial of the existence of alternatives to the coercion of the poor was accomplished more by silence than by refutation. In the course of the debates, several alternatives referred to in the previous chapter were raised in Parliament, as possible options to the use of the poor. But almost no argument was mounted by the Bill's supporters to refute or disprove their feasibility. The low level of engagement will perhaps best be shown by a comment made by the Attorney General, in the debate on the Bill's third Commons reading:

> If the honourable member for Bridport [Warburton] had seen any better remedy he would have been ready to adopt it; and it was only because he saw none better than this that, after the lapse of three years, he had brought forward the present measure.[81]

Warburton was pictured as a profoundly reasonable man, amenable to suasion, who had attained a level of expertise and wisdom in medical matters which admitted of no question; and hence, likewise his policy. This elevation effectively meant that any alternative suggested at the parliamentary debate stage did not merit discussion. The manipulation of the Select Committee had paid off – the opposition's suggestions were ignored.

This tactical silence was facilitated, and even appeared justified by the supporters' assertion that the clause permitting donation of corpses for dissection made no indication of the class origin or financial status of future subjects, and hence apparently applied equally to all social classes. The idea had originally been propounded by Abernethy in 1819,[82] but Warburton had overlooked its value in drafting the first Bill. His second attempt incorporated the suggestion in all its subtlety. It was an outright and intentional deception which gained currency by repetition. And superficially, it seemed plausible – the clause indeed did not specify the social origin of its victims, except by inference:

> And be it enacted, That it shall be lawful for any Executor or other Party having lawful Possession of the Body of any deceased Person, and not being an Undertaker or other Party intrusted with the body for the Purpose of Interment, to permit the Body of such deceased Person to undergo Anatomical Examination, unless, to the Knowledge of such Executor or other Party, such Person shall have expressed his Desire, either in Writing at any Time during his Life, or verbally in the Presence of Two or more Witnesses during the Illness whereof he died, that his Body after Death might not undergo such Examination, or unless the surviving Husband or Wife, or any known Relative of the deceased Person, shall require the Body to be interred without such Examination.[83]

A direct comparison with the suggestion as it was conceived by Sir Benjamin Brodie before the Select Committee in 1829 sheds light upon a possible derivation of the clause, and – importantly – its intended application:

> It might . . . be enacted, that it is not lawful knowingly to dissect the bodies of any persons without the consent of their relations or friends,

or executors, or legal representatives; and this clause might be so
worded as to include the overseers and churchwardens of parishes
under the latter denomination, if cases of persons dying without
friends in poor-houses; and it might be further enacted that, even
with their consent, no body shall be dissected if the individual had by
his last will and testament expressed his wish to the contrary. Now if
some such declaration and enactments as these were made by the
legislature, I have no doubt that a supply of subjects . . . would be
immediately obtained by . . . purchase [from poorhouse masters].[84]

The Bill's authors had adopted Brodie's suggestion almost entire, with the
important difference that friends of the deceased were removed from its
consideration. They had been included in Abernethy's original proposal,
so this was a significant deletion.[85] Viewing workhouse masters and Poor
Law Guardians as the executors of the 'unclaimed' dead would serve the
same purpose as naming workhouses in the Bill.

It is worth noting that neither of these two passages specified that
donation should be gratuitous. The implications of this are explored
below. In addition, the clause was entirely permissive, and provided the
inspectors appointed under its auspices no powers with which to compel
recalcitrant parish authorities to donate their unclaimed dead. The Act's
administration therefore came to depend upon persuasion of various
kinds, which – as the following chapter shows – gave the inspectors a great
deal of difficulty, rendered distribution variable, and corruption likely. It
gave the public a greater measure of control over the administration of the
Act, at a parish level, than its authors are ever likely to have intended.

Both Brodie and the Bill's promoters envisaged a comprehensive donation subject to objection, rather than one subject to the consent of the
deceased. As a point of principle, the distinction at stake remains the most
important in the entire text of the Bill, and one which did not become law
without strenuous opposition.[86] Hume's assertion before Parliament that
'none without consent' would be dissected[87] was a direct misrepresentation of the effect of this clause. As the Earl of Eldon pointed out, none
without consent is very different from all without dissent.[88] Even an MP in
agreement with the broad principles of the Bill[89] thought this too much to
enact:

The protection this clause pretended to give to those who wished not
to have their bodies dissected was perfectly nugatory. How was it to
be proved that they expressed this negative wish? Persons moving in
the class of life of the honourable member for Bridport, would take
care to leave some testimony of their wishes in this respect by will or
otherwise; but the poor and ignorant, even if they knew of the
provision, would not have the same facilities for expressing such a
wish. Instead of requiring a negative to prevent dissection, an
affirmative should be required to permit it.[90]

The issue was made more poignant by the knowledge that the clause had as its object people dying in workhouses and hospitals; in the first place, because at that time many were likely to be illiterate or barely literate and hence unable to leave written directions; and in the second because any witnesses to such a death would either be other inmates powerless to see the dead person's wish observed, or institutional personnel who might benefit financially by disregarding it.[91]

By definition, paupers had no property, and hence no one outside the institution to prove their wills. Moreover, no facility whatever was envisaged in the Bill by which the wishes of those affected by it could be registered, nor – once expressed – any safeguard to make a wish binding upon institutional personnel. Nor did the Bill envisage an obligation to inform survivors when a death had occurred – and since it permitted corpses to be taken when only forty-eight hours had elapsed after death, there was a likelihood that relatives' absence could be construed as 'indifference'. The clause was a mandate for official disregard both of mourned and mourners' feelings.[92]

———————— ◆◆◆ ————————

The final text of the Act contained twenty-one clauses. Of these, sixteen were concerned with administration and interpretation, and a further three served to clarify the law concerning the legality of bequest and dissection. Of the two remaining, one was the custody clause reproduced and discussed above, while the remaining one abolished the use of dissection as a punishment for murder – the clause whose omission from the first Bill had provoked such opposition from Wakley and others.[93] Apart from the linguistic changes which had appeared in this Bill, the addition of the murderers' clause was the one major alteration which had been promoted by extra-parliamentary criticism. Although this was undoubtedly an achievement, there cannot have been much comfort to a pauper in the knowledge that he or she would be dissected on the slab *instead* of a murderer, rather than *alongside* one.

We shall see below that the number of Anatomy Inspectors appointed and the powers with which they were invested proved to be woefully inadequate. But there were other crucial omissions which had other fundamental effects upon the administration of the Act. For example, the clause ensuring Christian burial of dissected remains left no provision whereby skeletons for medical education might legally be obtained, other than by importation. The same clause also posed a question-mark over the legality of removing specimens or creating preparations from the tissue and bone of appropriated bodies, and did nothing to specify or clarify their legal or property status.[94] Furthermore, nothing in the Act prohibited grave-robbery, or provided for any further deterrent against it than was available to the courts from pre-existing case-law.

More seriously, there was no reiteration of the negative property status of the human corpse, nothing to ensure that the transfer of bodies from 'executor' to anatomist should be gratuitous, and no embargo upon the sale of corpses, entire or dismembered. This effectively meant that the known motive for both bodysnatching and burking was permitted to persist.

Although some of these omissions and inadequacies might have been due to oversight, there is no evidence to suggest that this was the case in each instance. For example, it is unlikely that references in the first Bill to the prevention and punishment of grave-robbery can have been *accidentally* left out of the second version. A much more convincing explanation is that the Bill's silence represented an understanding on the part of its backers that, if through popular opposition the legislation failed to provide an adequate supply of corpses, anatomists could safely revert to their old sources of supply. In omitting to enact any further penalty for grave-robbing than was already available, and protecting anatomists by rendering the dissection of corpses legal, the Bill more or less provided for this eventuality.

The silence concerning specimens and skeletons was probably due to a fear that authorisation of their extraction would have jeopardised the credibility of the Bill's burial clause. Supporters had stressed the importance of this provision, as it signified that the treatment offered to bodies dissected under the Act was superior to that previously meted out to murderers. The burial clause was of crucial importance to the sustenance of such arguments, and to the maintenance of parliamentary support.[95] The Bill's authors may have thought omission, in these instances preferable to clarification.

Publicity surrounding the commercial value of corpses had been too great for it to have been unintentionally disregarded. Why then, should the subject have been omitted from the Bill? The need for positive legislation to outlaw commerce in human remains had long been one of Wakley's central disagreements with Warburton. Wakley viewed the reduction of the human corpse to a mere article of commerce and the existence of a trade in this article between resurrectionists, murderers and anatomists, as wholly dishonourable to the profession of medicine.[96] He believed the assignment of *any* financial value to a dead human body constituted an incitement to crime; and he argued that its prohibition should form the basis of any new enactment on the subject. Nor was this argument to be found solely in the columns of his two journals, the *Lancet* and the *Ballot*.[97] In a letter criticising the Bill which appeared in the more conservative *London Medical Gazette*, Benjamin Travers, a surgeon at St Thomas's Hospital, laid out the argument forcefully:

> how is the profession exonerated, by this Bill, from the unmerited degradation of being compelled to carry on this odious traffic? There are gentlemen, now living ornaments of their profession, who have been in former times obliged to act as their own purveyors, and to join

in the perilous and ungrateful service of robbing graves for the means of education.

This necessity, painful and disgusting as it was, was honourable in comparison with that to which we have been reduced by the systematic employment of resurrection-men; whose daring monopoly of their craft, sharpened by its risks and the severity of its penalties, became so gainful as to plunge them into a reckless sensuality; the next step to which was midnight murder. How long the infamous practices of these men have been perpetrating, to meet the increasing demands and secure the enormous prices paid by rival schools, we have no means of knowing: that the discovery is recent affords no proof that the crime is so. . . .

Whatever other provisions may be thought advisable, the profession owe it to themselves to stand out for this – that the trade in bodies shall henceforward cease, and be declared a violation of the law of the land.[98]

James Somerville, who was soon to adjust his views while working as Inspector of Anatomy, was even more explicit in the recommendation of a conscious policy of *de*commodification: 'By rendering the dead body no longer a marketable article – by depriving it of value, the temptation to become possessed of it by murder would immediately be removed.'[99] Like many others, Wakley, Travers and Somerville each advocated this policy from an appreciation that allowing unbridled market forces to operate in this area of medicine constituted a direct danger to society. It had promoted crime, had posed a long-term threat to the maintenance of civil order, and had resulted in multiple murder.

A further disagreement between Wakley and Warburton lay in their views of how best to prevent bodysnatching and burking, while nevertheless providing material and encouragement for the study of anatomy. Wakley argued for a policy which would effectively remove impediments to a system of free voluntary bequest, on the lines of the system used widely today.[100] As we saw in Chapter 7, others of this persuasion were slightly less sanguine than Wakley, and advocated positive legislation to stimulate bequests, at least in the initial stages of the change. As a group they believed that the establishment of a system in which bequest was encouraged would generate a further supply by conquering public feeling against dissection. The sector of opinion they represented urged legislative enforcement of decommodification, by outlawing the commercial exchange of corpses, in the hope that an alternative supply would emerge as the gift of those willing so to foster knowledge of human anatomy.

Warburton's policy left less either to trust or chance. It depended upon the provision of means whereby the bodysnatchers' and burkers' prices would be undercut by the immediate substitution of an appropriated alternative supply. But this policy was more complicated than simply flooding the market with cheap goods: the corpse would remain saleable, dissection would remain coercive and retributive, and furthermore, its administration would entail the establishment of a centralised government agency whose role was to oversee both the activities of local officials, and the provision of a supply of corpses to consumers.

There is an element of irony to be found in the position of Warburton and his colleagues. In economic policy they were stout advocates of non-interference in trade,[101] and of cuts in government expenditure. They believed in the operation of market forces. Yet they formulated and championed a 'collectivist' Anatomy Act which ensured major state intervention in the market-place of medical education. The evil and dangerous results of *laissez-faire* – from grave-robbery to murder – which had been permitted to operate in the field of anatomy tuition for so long, were therefore directly responsible for a situation in which confirmed non-interventionists effectively combined the Elizabethan concept of 'provision'[102] with Victorian 'collectivist' government intervention – and committed themselves to the establishment of a centrally based and funded bureaucracy.

The Act provides an early and exceptionally fine instance of the recognition in nineteenth-century legislation of the direct contradiction between the dogma of *laissez-faire* and the protection of public well-being.[103] Yet the nature of this contradiction, and the conflict it caused (and would continue to cause) was not openly aired during the entire parliamentary passage of Warburton's Bill. It would be more than a decade before the Bill's ardent supporter, Macaulay, would concede before the Commons that

> the principle of non-interference is one that cannot be applied
> without great restriction where the public health or the public
> morality is concerned.[104]

The text of the Act itself typifies the mutually moderating force of what the historian A.J. Taylor has called 'the prescriptions of the economists pointing towards *laissez-faire*' and 'the pressures of the humanitarians invoking state intervention'.[105] This is perhaps because the Bill's advocates were themselves unsurely balanced between these two positions,[106] an ambiguity discernible in their handiwork. The Act's centralism, collectivism and intervention were tempered with deference to anti-centralism, and to the creation of private profit from human remains.

The Anatomy Act represents an early instance, and a prime one, of the transformation of economic individualists into collectivists when social rather than crass economic issues were raised,[107] and of what Karl Figlio has perceptively described as 'socialising the costs of capital's pathogenicity'.[108]

———— ◄▦▦► ————

The Act's relationship to private profitability is complex, and largely covert. Parliamentary supporters asserted that the Bill would benefit the poor by providing 'cheap' anatomical tuition. But this argument by no means represented a recognition that medicine should be a social service, rather than a profitable business. Rather, it was used to counter their critics' argument that the Bill would benefit mainly the rich and dissect only the poor. The argument that the Bill benefited the *poor* gained currency by repetition. Warburton, for example, utilised it during the committee stage when forced to defend his Bill against a spirited attack on its class bias, by Sir Charles Wetherell. His object, Warburton said, was:

> not merely to promote the ends of science, but to bring that science to the poor man's door, that the practitioner who attended the poorest man might be equally qualified with the practitioner who attended the rich.[109]

Warburton's argument can be seen to have developed strategically from the frank denial of the Bill's class injustice, used only a month earlier by his parliamentary colleagues, in response to petitioners from Blackburn. The petitioners had naively solicited support from MPs John Wood and Joseph Hume against the Bill. The replies returned by both men promoted the Benthamite view that the Bill was 'equally applicable' to rich and poor.[110] Their letters were published in the radical Preston paper *3730* alongside one from Warburton, which fudged the very class issues the petitioners had carefully addressed. Patronisingly, he assumed them ignorant and ill-informed:

> I am inclined to think . . . from a perusal of the Blackburn petition . . . that the Meeting, which agreed to that Petition have formed a judgement on the Bill without having its clauses distinctly under their consideration. . . . Anxiously desirous that the people should at this period, when I hope increased power is about to be given to them, should prove by all their acts, that they are not, as their detractors represent them to be, incapable of reflection and the creatures of impulse and passion; but that they can take a just view of the consquences of public measures as well as their representatives themselves . . .

Warburton enclosed a copy of the Bill for their edification. Alongside these letters, from Hume, Wood and Warburton, *3730* also printed two from Henry Hunt, who was MP for Preston, in which he expressed his own incredulity:

> How you could write to the parties you have named, in hopes that they of all men would support your Petition, I cannot conceive. Not one of them but will support Warburton . . . if you were in earnest in sending to these men . . . you were in a state of delusion. . . . The Whigs hate the people more, much more, than the Tories, if

> possible. . . . . I will take the [text] with me to the House this day, to
> shew them that you understand the nature of Warburton's Bill as
> well as they do.

Hunt rightly saw that all opposition to the Bill would be successfully
dismissed as 'ignorant vulgar prejudice'. He recognised the argument.
Just as Feargus O'Connor had observed on the Reform Bill, the people
were accused of being 'yet too ignorant', while the real meaning of this dismissal was 'that they had too much knowledge'.[111] The issue operating
since before the inception of the Select Committee had been *whose* knowledge and *whose* morality would receive public endorsement in the act
of legistlating.[112]

Warburton's assertion that his Bill would be the means of achieving
better surgical attention for the poor was misleading on several counts.
The Bill made no attempt to ensure that anatomical tuition would become
cheaper.[113] There was nothing in its text to ensure or enforce a standard
pricing structure between supplying institutions and the tutors of anatomy. Nor was there anything to prevent the use of bribery or 'influence' to
obtain supplies and advantages over other anatomists. No recommendations were made, or powers conferred, pertaining to the equitable distribution of the bodies the Act would make available.

Furthermore, the Bill contained nothing to indicate the desirability of
passing on to the student any financial benefit accruing to tutors as a result
of its enactment; this was left to the discretion of the tutors, and to the
action of market forces. In his arguments for decommodification, Wakley
had pointed out that market forces had already been shown to operate by
pushing corpse prices upwards; and that the Bill contained no safeguards
against a recurrence of the effect. He warned that if it became law,
anatomy tutors attached to the great metropolitan hospitals would have
undue advantages over the smaller independent tutors, from the free use of
their own hospital mortuaries. Wakley was borne out by events: despite
their excellence, most of the independent schools of anatomy in the
metropolis became defunct within a comparatively short period after the
passage of the Anatomy Act.[114] Other longer-term factors certainly influenced this result, but the Anatomy Act certainly did nothing to assist the
survival of these schools, and probably contributed to hasten their
demise.[115]

The Bill therefore failed to legislate for cheaper or fairer medical
education. Even had this resulted, however, Warburton's Bill could no
more have ensured that the direction of benefit would have been towards
the poor, than it could have established a national health service. Warburton's involvement with medical reform meant that he could not have been
unaware[116] that whatever potential his Bill might have possessed to
produce a shift towards greater equity in the distribution of medical
attention, would have been actively inhibited by other factors.[117] It was

disingenuous to assert before Parliament that such a change could result without the enactment of other, more fundamental, changes in the social basis of health care which, of course, the Bill did not attempt.

Indeed, in one vital respect Warburton's Bill actually militated against all said he stood for. One of the Bill's clauses limited the categories of medical practitioner who could legally qualify for a licence to dissect. Apothecaries were excluded.[118] Apothecaries represented the lowest status of medical practitioners, and the cheapest. It is inconceivable that Warburton could have overlooked their need for a knowledge of human anatomy. They were in all likelihood denied for strategic reasons: probably as a result of a trade-off for support from the Colleges of Physic and Surgery – whose members were, of course, permitted licences.

Warburton's Bill did indeed bring 'science' to the homes of the poor; but in a sense very different from that which its promoter intended would be understood by his speech. His argument was an attempt to persuade recalcitrant parliamentary humanitarians into compliance with the Bill, by assuaging their consciences with wishful thoughts of bringing benefit – rather than anguish – to workhouse inmates. Henry Hunt answered Warburton's comment in the same debate by saying that 'if a bungler existed, that bungler would gain the attendance on the poor'. He said that Warburton had 'wished an impossibility' in his expressed hope that the Bill would benefit the poor.[119]

The shortcomings of hospital and workhouse medicine in Warburton's day have already been described. Things improved very little throughout much of the next half-century. Except in areas in which the rigours of the measure were attenuated by local opposition, Guardians appointing staff to parish medical posts under the New Poor Law were invariably more interested in the lowest tender on offer than in the best qualifications. A knowledge of dissection was of peripheral concern.[120] Working-class lives were cheap, and expendable. Throughout the nineteenth century and beyond, workhouse inmates' health needs were being neglected: 'Scores and scores of distinctly preventable deaths'[121] took place in Victorian workhouse infirmaries.

Even in cases of honourable exception to a generally bleak picture, when a good doctor with a social conscience was appointed to a workhouse post, there was little indeed – despite a knowledge of anatomy – which could be done to alleviate the suffering within such walls. Grossly overworked,[122] and poorly paid,[123] with practically no support from any other source,[124] the workhouse doctor could find facilities appalling.[125] Until the 1870s and 1880s many workhouses had no separate buildings for the sick.[126] In others, infirmary buildings were old and makeshift, inadequate in size, airless, and – well into the second half of the century – without sanitation.[127] Nurses were often unpaid and usually unqualified[128] – Florence Nightingale's onslaught upon standards of hospital nursing after the Crimea had little impact on the workhouse variety, even into the

1890s.[129] The sharing and overcrowding of available beds[130] was common, as was persistent undernourishment. Patients were often mixed indiscriminately,[131] the insane with the convalescent, the infectious and the frail, the dying and the giving birth.

Dr Joseph Rogers, a founder of the Poor Law Medical Officers' Association, described in his autobiography the conditions in the wards of the Strand Union Workhouse on his appointment as parish medical officer in the 1840s.[132] His book makes harrowing reading. Rogers's efforts to effect change, and to lower the dreadful mortality and workhouse-induced morbidity – in the face of penny-pinching opposition from Poor Law Guardians – were truly heroic. With other such doctors, Rogers's agitation for change was eventually influential in the findings of the *Lancet Sanitary Commission* which enquired into the state of workhouse infirmaries in 1865. By this time, Wakley himself was dead, and the task had fallen to his sons. Their report was an indictment of the care available to the workhouse poor. Pointing out that the much-vaunted voluntary hospitals accommodated only a fraction of the hospitalised sick poor,[133] the investigators described the workhouse wards in which the rest were to be found:

> They are closed against observation; they pay no heed to public opinion; they pay no toll to science. They contravene the rules of hygiene; they are under the government of men [Guardians] profoundly ignorant of hospital rules. They are separate from the world of medical observation, and from the sphere of benevolent and voluntary visitation and aid. The doctor and patient alike are the object of the pinching parsimony.[134]

The investigators' description of the lives of the people in one workhouse stood for many: 'they lead a life which would be like that of a vegetable were it not that they preserve the doubtful privilege of sensibility to pain and mental misery'.[135]

As far as medicine outside the hospitals was concerned, a growing population – and particularly a growing middle class – meant an increase in demand for good doctoring, for which an increasing number of people above the poverty line were able to pay.[136] Although more doctors were also being qualified, it would be a long time indeed before a surplus of well-trained doctors would become accessible to the very poor.

Henry Hunt's view was borne out by events. In mid-Victorian society, Ivan Waddington has shown, the poor were the primary users of apothecaries for medical advice, and 'the great majority of unqualified practitioners' were practising among them.[137]

This 'inverse care law'[138] – whereby areas of greatest medical need received the worst available care – was the direct result of the operation of *laissez-faire* in medicine, and could hardly be corrected simply by government intervention in the provision of corpses for dissection. Its continued operation ensured that the benefits Warburton said he expected from the

Anatomy Act would in fact work to the advantage of the financially fortunate on two counts: they would be primary beneficiaries from any increase in availability or improvement in medical care, *and* they would no longer be required to do unwilling service on the anatomist's slab. Asserting that the poor would be the Bill's primary beneficiaries, Warburton knowingly denied they would be its primary victims.

The parliamentary passage of the second Anatomy Bill reveals that although everyone present was aware of the Bill's intention to single out the very poor for dissection, assertions of its social equity won the day. Invited by the Benthamites' casuistry to participate in a collective fiction, Parliament knowingly complied. The Bill's opponents, whose compassion and social indignation had been met with the imputation of ignorance and misinformation, were aware of the deception being practised, but had no political power to prevent its becoming law, which it did on 1 August 1832.

III

THE AFTERMATH

'If you've got nothing,
you can't do nothing about it.'

London Undertaker, 1978

'THE ACT IS UNINJURIOUS IF UNKNOWN'.[1]

If the rich treat the poor with inhumanity they must take the consequence, and as the poor have not the privilege to avail themselves of the 'vengeance of the law', their enemies ought not to complain when they sometimes exercise the vengeance of their passions.

Richard Carlile, c.1818.[2]

Far be it from us to obstruct the means whereby medical and surgical knowledge is best obtained. If the law were impartial, we should not object to it, but when it is called in to add to the terrors and penalties of helpless and friendless poverty, we hold it to be an abomination, and denounce it accordingly.

Leeds Intelligencer, 1832.[3]

The people . . . are not blind, stupid or mad, and they prefer a bungling operator to a skilful 'Burker'.

Lancet editorial, 1831.[4]

Almost nothing is known of existing workhouse inmates' reactions to the Act's passage. Examination of surviving workhouse records in different parts of the country has so far yielded an insight merely into how very little has been permitted to survive beyond the establishment of the welfare state.[5]

However, what evidence is available – including the wider reaction of potential inmates outside the workhouse – is perhaps predictably, hostile. Given all that has so far been said about popular feelings and attitudes to dissection, it would not be altogether unexpected to find that further research would yield more of the same.[6]

What reaction has been found from inside workhouses, dates mainly

from the first wave of shock, when paupers first heard what was being planned. In March 1829, a letter appeared in the *Morning Herald* newspaper, from someone who had been an official Visitor for eleven years at the Swansea House of Industry.[7] The writer, H. Sockett, described events in the workhouse in 1817, when

> a few cases were considered as proper to be examined by the surgeons at the infirmary. . . . A rumour soon spread through the house, and among the poor people, that they were to be dissected, and it is impossible to describe the anguish and distress it occasioned; and I verily believe that, if they had not been assured that it should not be repeated, there was not a poor creature in the house who would not have preferred dying for want in the streets, to the enjoyment of relief upon terms so repugnant to their feelings.[8]

Similar disturbances may well have occurred in other workhouses when news of Warburton's first Bill became public in 1828–9. Early 1829 seems to have been a key period: the petition to Parliament from inhabitants of the workhouse of St Ann's parish, Blackfriars, was sent in March, and a letter signed 'One of the "Unclaimed" ' from a Worcestershire workhouse, appeared in a May issue of the *Lancet*. Taken together with reports of a commotion in Shadwell Workhouse in the same month, these cases[9] suggest that this period may prove a more fruitful source of evidence on the subject than 1832. By the time of the Reform crisis – if the Swansea and Shadwell cases are anything to go by – Warburton's intentions would have been old news.

In May 1829, terror was unleashed among the workhouse poor of St Paul's, Shadwell, when a man newly admitted into the House read out to fellow inmates details of discussion of the first Anatomy Bill in Parliament, from a newspaper he had smuggled in. The news caused a great disturbance, as the inmates viewed dissection with such abhorrence they were horror-struck at the thought that they might be forced to undergo it by law. At mealtime, the man complained about the food, and expressed a suspicion that it contained human as well as animal remains – an allegation which landed him before the local magistrate, to whom he was described as 'one of the most turbulent paupers in existence'. So anxious was the workhouse master to disprove the allegation that the workhouse dietary included 'Nattomy Soup' that he actually brought along a bowl of workhouse broth to the court, and produced details of its recipe. The poor man who had caused the rumpus was admonished for making unfounded allegations, and sentenced to twenty-one days in a House of Correction.

This incident permits a glimpse inside the workhouse to the reaction of existing inmates, and allows us to perceive the process whereby protesters or dissidents inside such institutions could be marginalised, and their

18 (*opposite*)'A Few Illustrations for Mr Warberton's Bill' – a cartoon by Paul Pry, 1829

complaints denied. This case reached court, and was reported in the press. There may have been others which received no such publicity, and so are not known to us.[10] It is worth bearing in mind that despite the removal of the trouble-maker in this case, the information had already been broadcast, and would be buzzed around the wards long afterwards.

According to the *Morning Chronicle*'s report of the court case, the prisoner was not accused with causing a disturbance against the Anatomy Bill, but of making unfounded allegations about the workhouse broth. No reference was made to the accuracy or otherwise of his allegations about the prospective dissection of his workhouse audience. The court's focus was upon the fact that 'many of the paupers became so frightened at the pauper's assertions, that they refused to partake of their food'; and the disturbance which ensued from the newspaper reading was officially conflated with reactions to the man's suspicions about the broth.

The suspicion itself is eloquent testimony to the poor's understanding that they were regarded as bestial by their social superiors: both in the sense that they readily believed their own remains might be used for food (along with kittens and donkeys), and also in the sense that had the story been true, the workhouse authorities would have been guilty of bestialising inmates by making them unwitting cannibals.

Both the seriousness with which the Shadwell inmates took their fellow's allegations, and the master's evident anxiety publicly to disprove it, indicate the profound distrust with which workhouse personnel could be regarded when the topic of dissection arose. The remarkable multiple cartoon by Paul Pry entitled 'A Few Illustrations for Mr Warberton's Bill'[11] (see p.220) also dating from 1829, features in its three central vignettes the involvement of workhouse, hospital and prison personnel in the procurement and sale of the carcasses of the poor. One image represents butchered parts of human bodies hanging up outside a shop – just as butcher's meat was then customarily displayed for sale. The legislative temptation offered to employees in institutions to evade or ignore the poor's wishes about dissection had been raised by the Act's opponents during parliamentary debates.[12] Pry's cartoon and the 'Nattomy Soup' episode show that the suspicion was popularly shared, and that the darker fear of institutionalised burking also lingered. The idea that workhouse food contained human remains persisted for decades, and well beyond Shadwell: 'The Poor Workhouse Boy', a late-Victorian street ballad, which featured the burking of a young inmate by the workhouse master, has this disagreeable subject as its central theme.[13]

The disturbance at Shadwell coincided with the first wave of 'burkophobia', following upon the Edinburgh murders. Only a couple of weeks before burkophobia was reactivated once again with the arrest of Bishop and Williams in London, the long-awaited arrival of epidemic cholera was confirmed in Sunderland. The Central Board of Health's stream of warnings and regulations to combat cholera – pasted up on walls all over the country – had already raised apprehensions of the disease.[14] All over Britain an increase in the investigation, by medical professionals and concerned members of the social elite, of the slums and poverty in which the poor lived, also raised profound suspicions among those being investigated.[15] Over the winter and spring of 1831–2, choleraphobia and burkophobia coexisted.[16] They proved a dangerous admixture when regulations were enforced to remove poor cholera victims to special hospitals, and to bury their dead swiftly in isolated cholera burial grounds.

During the coldest part of the winter, the cholera had progressed only slowly, but it broke out with ferocity with the arrival of the spring. It was this difficult time that Warburton chose to introduce his second Bill for parliamentary approval; in the midst also of a high pitch of political excitement aroused by the government's reluctance to pass the Reform Bill. And along with the huge demonstrations in favour of Reform went others of a different sort: only a few days after Warburton's generous offer to bring 'science to the poor man's door' during the committee stage on 11 April, the poorer inhabitants of Paisley took to the streets to demonstrate their view of the 'science' on offer.

<hr />

In 1832, a severe trade depression was affecting Paisley. So bad were conditions in the town that they formed the subject of a memorial for assistance from the local Police Commissioners to the then Home Secretary Lord Melbourne.[17] The commissioners' own 'respectable' visitors, sent to verify the situation, witnessed 'misery, destitution and suffering' exceeding all their expectations. 'Vast numbers' of poor people 'had the greater part of their bed and body clothes lying in pawn', and whole families were sleeping on straw or bare floors with only half a blanket between them. The commissioners warned of the likelihood of high mortality from diseases of malnutrition, exposure, and cholera.

In January, as we have seen above, the anatomy school at Aberdeen had been entirely destroyed after the discovery of foetid human remains buried in the back yard.[18] During the course of February and early March, news arrived from London, Glasgow and elsewhere of disturbances associated with the undignified burials enforced upon poor cholera victims.[19] Just along the Clyde, in an incident concerning the 'treatment' of an old woman in the Gorbals, a crowd pelted doctors with mud and hooted 'medical murderer', 'cholera humbug' and 'burkers'.[20] From Edinburgh came news of an attack upon the cholera hospital van, after a woman whom the crowd believed was only drunk was about to be taken forcibly to the cholera hospital. The van was stoned, and then thrown into a canal basin. Women in the crowd demanded that the hospital itself should be razed to the ground, but only its windows were broken before police intervened. The general feeling amongst the crowd was that 'the doctors took cholera patients under their care merely to try experiments upon them'.[21]

In early February, the Paisley Reform Society's petition against the Anatomy Bill had been presented in the Commons, expressing the Society's abhorrence of 'sacrificing the feelings of one class of the community to those of another', and suggesting that 'those whose education and habits have got the better of their prejudices' should be called upon to bequeath their bodies instead.[22] Details of the Bill's provisions would have been discussed in Paisley's radical coffee houses, and on street corners. Later the same month, the long awaited first cases of cholera appeared in the town, and the magistrates distributed a handbill announcing the designation of a boggy field over a mile out of town as the burial ground for victims of the disease too poor to purchase their own grave-spaces.[23] Although the town's authorities had sense enough to think better of a suggestion that a field near the town slaughterhouse should have been so used,[24] they did little to render the new burial ground attractive to the poor. The remote place to which their dead were to be banished was not recorded as having been consecrated,[25] and no arrangements were made to have it watched.[26] It was enclosed only with a wooden fence.[27]

On 25 March, a Sunday, some people walking near the new ground discovered two shovels and a hook attached to a rope.[28] Under the suspicion bodysnatchers had been at work, the implements were brought back to town, and exhibited next day in a shop in Blacklaw Lone[29] – a street which was the locus of an early case of cholera, and which also housed the home of an officer of the Paisley Society for Protecting the Dead.[30] A crowd soon gathered, and – determined to uncover the truth – made its way to the cholera burial ground. One of the first coffins raised was empty, and was carried shoulder-high back to town. Rumour had preceded it, and as the crowd approached the town centre, it rapidly increased in size. There followed a demonstration of profound popular dissatisfaction with the town's doctors. Bearing the empty coffin as the emblem of collective grievance, the crowd proceeded in a systematic and disciplined way to attack the shops or houses of at least ten doctors (seven of whom were surgeons), the cholera hospital – destroying the van sent to remove the sick poor to its confines – and the house of a prominent member of the Paisley Board of Health.[31]

Despite a hurried proclamation by the magistrates of a reward of £50 for information leading to the capture of the resurrectionists, 420 panes of glass were broken in the space of a few hours.[32] Troops arrived when the riot was virtually over, and were not used. The town was calm by early evening, by which time 'official' exhumations had begun at the burial ground to ascertain the extent of the traffic in bodies. These continued the following day and – too late – a watch was mounted on the ground. Handbills were printed to announce that only three bodies had been found missing out of a total of eighty people buried in the ground. None was identified by name. By that time the information was in any case of little moment. The cholera hearse was pelted with stones in the west end of the

REPORT
TO THE
MAGISTRACY,
AND
BOARD OF HEALTH,
CONCERNING
The INVESTIGATION
IN THE
New Burying Ground
At the Moss Lands.

We, the Subscribers, appointed Yesterday by the People assembled upon the New Burying Ground, in the Moss Lands of Paisley, to see the Coffins inspected, which had not already been examined, Report, that we employed Labourers and superintended the examination of Seventy-one Coffins, being all that remained uninspected, and we found a Body in each of these Coffins, with the exception of two which were empty. We began our examination yesterday afternoon about five o'clock, and finished it at half-past five o'clock this afternoon, and the Labourers employed by us were, Hugh Murray, William Develin, James Jones, William Gallocher, Arthur M'Luskie, James M'Garvie, Robert Gilmour, William M'Cuat, Thomas Docherty, John Knox, Edward Kaine, James Orr, John Barr, John Broadly, John Kelso, Thomas Robertson, William Morrison.

We understand that nine Coffins had been examined before we began our Labours, and one body only was awanting of these.

Signed by us at Paisley, this 27th day of March, 1832.

Alexander M·Alpine, Weaver, George Street.
James Crawford.
Allan Mann, Weaver, Queen Street.
John Henderson, Weaver, Barclay Street.
John Andrews, Weaver, North Croft.
William Dixon, Weaver, George Street.
William Craig, Weaver, Moss.
James Burns.

ALEX. GARDNER, PRINTER.

19   Broadsheet giving news of the excavation of the cholera ground at Paisley, 27 March 1832

town that evening,[33] but the disturbance was all but over.

The crowd's attack upon the doctors' property met with a howl of shock and horror from 'respectable' elements in Paisley, alarmed both by the riot and by the likelihood of a catastrophic epidemic of cholera in its wake. The crowd was described as 'unprincipled', 'lawless', 'ignorant' and 'prejudiced'; and the 'rational and unprejudiced part of the community' hastened repeatedly to express in public its collective admiration of the doctors ('our best benefactors') and to disassociate itself from the crowd.[34] News of the riot, measures to combat the cholera, respectable opinion of the 'brutal and savage passions' of the 'lawless mob', and of the terrible destitution, wretchedness and suffering of the town's poor jostled for space in the following Saturday's *Paisley Advertiser*.[35]

Commentators on the disturbance were unanimous in their vilification of the crowd, and made no effort to recognise or understand the genuine grievance it had expressed. Nevertheless, embedded in these hostile contemporary reports may be found evidence of the crowd's restraint. Although many of its members had been armed with posts taken from the cholera ground fence, no personal injury was done to the doctors. Only one theft was recorded during the entire disturbance – a small sum was taken from a shop at the height of the uproar. Two chimney sweeps who broke into the cholera hospital were later taken into custody, in the company of the hospital porter, all of whom were found drunk after illicitly imbibing some 'medicinal' whisky.

Two days after the riot, the medical men of Paisley collectively resigned from all public duties. At the same time, the poor were refused parish coffins or the use of the parish hearse for their dead.[36] This led to unprecedented scenes of tragedy in the town, such as when a labouring man named Hamilton pushed a wheelbarrow through the centre of town, bearing his daughter Martha's coffin, with a shovel beside. Hamilton's pitiable courage shamed a kind-hearted 'gentleman' into procuring a burying place for the body in the Abbey ground – the traditional burying ground in the centre of Paisley, in which the better-off citizens were still permitted to bury their cholera dead.[37] Bodies for which no charitable aid could be obtained decomposed in fetor in poor homes.[38] The entire poor of Paisley – not just the 'young men of unprincipled habits and lawless boys, aided and assisted by ignorant and prejudiced women'[39] who were said to have been responsible for £104.17s.3½d's worth of damage[40] – were made to feel the vulnerability of their poverty, and the mighty power of civic and medical retribution.

There were riots and disturbances associated with cholera in many major towns and cities throughout the spring and summer of 1832.[41] In the early riots, poor people doubted the existence of the disease at all,[42] believing it to be a figment of the authorities' imagination – designed to permit coercion of the poor into hospitals for use in vivisection experiments, for dissection after death, or to keep down the population. In the

Paisley riot, for example, one doctor whom the crowd believed had cast doubt upon the existence of cholera was said to have been cheered in the street.[43]

Even when the existence of the disease became accepted, the authorities often behaved towards the poor with such insensitivity that disturbances could be triggered off at a moment's notice. In official street notices, for example, issued by the Oxford Board of Health,[44] cholera was hardly regarded as a biological entity but a means of retribution upon the morally suspect:

> all Drunkards, Revellers, and to the thoughtless and imprudent of both sexes . . . You are now told for the third time, that Death and Drunkenness go hand in hand . . . Death smites with its surest and swiftest arrows the licentious and intemperate . . . [45]

After exposure to sentiments such as these, contemporaries might be forgiven for distrusting the assertion that the staff of the cholera hospital would receive 'with kindness' and treat 'with care' any poor sufferer. As a result, only 16 per cent of cholera victims entered the portals of the Oxford cholera hospital: most preferred to stay at home, where they did in fact have a better chance of survival.[46]

The disease was a swift killer, and highly infectious. A victim could be dead within hours, after violent purgings and vomiting had caused rapid dehydration and loss of body salts, causing visible physical shrinking and rigid muscular cramps. These cramps, or spasms, often relaxed only after death, causing sudden convulsions which could be mistaken for signs of life. Signs of death could be equally deceptive, as in many cases the body was blue ('as if dip't in a solution of indigo'), stiff from muscular spasm, 'cold as marble' and with heart and breathing rates so low as to be imperceptible.[47] Cases were reported of people who survived a medical diagnosis of death,[48] and when we consider that the medical test for death was merely the holding of a mirror near the mouth to seek signs of breath, we need not disbelieve such reports, nor discredit as unreasonable the widespread fear of premature burial or of dissection taking place before life was extinct.[49]

Many disturbances were prompted by the popular desire to defend traditional death observances. This was especially the case where customs were threatened by official policies – like the order for burial within twenty-four hours of death,[50] which would of course have denied families the opportunity of viewing, watching and waking their dead. Burial in quicklime was regarded as unseemly, and faced strong opposition.[51] This can be understood when we remember that when dissection was removed from the *post-mortem* punishment of murderers, burial in quicklime within prison precincts was substituted. Given what was known about working-class death customs, treating the cholera dead as nothing but a hygiene problem, and hastening both disposal and decomposition by dictat, was insensitive to say the least – and bound to provoke trouble. Equally hurtful could be the decision to bury the poor cholera dead without church services,[52] or in unconsecrated ground.[53] The worst disturbances, however, were usually associated with distrust of doctors, and with fears of burking or dissection.[54]

People involved in these disturbances – as was the case at Paisley – were accused of ignorance and prejudice. They can certainly be viewed in such a light today. Yet they were surely no less knowledgeable than their betters in this respect. The fact was that nobody knew either the cause or cure for cholera. In Paisley, the wealthier classes had subscribed to a 'Fumigating Committee' which funded torchlit processions bearing fuming mixtures of sulphuric acid and chloride of lime to pass through the streets, in a ritual attempt to purify the town's air.[55] Such experiments as this – reminiscent of civic responses to the Black Death, and even earlier plagues[56] – were a deluded attempt to fill the gap in medical knowledge.[57]

One of the worst riots in 1832 took place at the Swan Street cholera hospital in Manchester, only a few weeks after the Anatomy Act became law. The *Manchester Guardian* called the riot 'one of the those ebullitions of prejudiced feeling on the part of the lower classes against the medical officers of a cholera hospital, from which we had hoped that this town would have continued free', and went on to describe the riot which had resulted from a man's discovery that his 3-year-old grandchild who had died in the hospital had been beheaded, its head replaced in the coffin by a brick.[58] Despite his suspicions, the old man had allowed the funeral to proceed, but had gone back afterwards to confirm his worst fears. A crowd soon formed, and distraught, the man led an attack on the cholera hospital. Some people in the crowd took the headless body round the town to drum up support, and a rumour spread that the child had been murdered.[59] About two thousand people rushed the hospital gates, broke all the front windows and made a bonfire of all the movable furniture they could lay hands upon. No windows were broken in the wards, and from 'consideration of the safety of the patients', the hospital itself was spared, although the cholera van was destroyed. Women went through the cholera wards, seeking to rescue their friends.

At this stage the police made a determined raid and took two people into custody, diverting attention to an attack on the local police station. After some chaos, a local Catholic priest had the courage to stand on a barrel before the hospital gates, and address the crowd. He explained that the hospital's doctor, Dr Lynch, knew nothing of the child's mutilation, and that it had been done illicitly by an apothecary, who had since fled. The information pacified the crowd, who listened 'with patient attention', and the arrival of troops from a nearby barracks caused a hasty dispersal.

The child's head was subsequently found in a search of the apothecary's lodgings and sewn back to the body, which had been taken into custody in Piccadilly by the city's Beadle. A warrant was issued for the apothecary's arrest, but he was never seen again. The child was reinterred the following day, attended by a concourse of several hundred people, 'of whom three-fourths were females'.

Once again, press comment upon the riot was predictably hostile. Even the *Republican and Radical Reformer* commented:

> The lamentable ignorance displayed by the rioters of Manchester . . . affords a convenient handle to the opponents of Universal Suffrage. See, they say, would you trust such men with the elective right? No, we should say, not yet; but, at least, allow us to prepare them for the exercise of their rights. Instead of inviting them to cheap gin, invite them to cheap political publications.[60]

The argument was for a reduction in the 'taxes on knowledge', but succeeded at the same time in casting the aspersion that the Swan Street riot had been caused by gin, as well as by ignorance. The *Poor Man's Advocate*,[61] however, took the disturbance more seriously:

> Much censure has been cast upon the working people of Manchester, on account of the late riot at the Swan Street cholera hospital. The 'liberal' newspapers are unanimous in considering the affair as a most melancholy proof of 'brutal ignorance', and all that we have heard speak of it, seem to condemn it as an unpardonable offence.
>
> With all due deference to such high authorities as sevenpenny newspapers, we take the liberty of thinking otherwise. We contend that it is no proof of 'brutal ignorance' in the people, insisting on having the bodies of their friends and relatives buried entire and unmutilated. . . . It is, indeed a decided proof that they suspected that all was not right at the Swan Street Hospital, and from the published report of the 'Board of Health', it is clear that their suspicions were not unfounded. . . . The relations and others who witnessed this shocking and suspicious discovery very naturally became enraged at somebody. They could only suspect the officers and others at the hospital from which the body came.

To the argument that the law was open to those with a grievance of this sort, the *Advocate* replied:

> . . . and there are the bakers and the butchers' shops open to the starving multitude if they choose to purchase the bread and beef. So that all who die of hunger have only themselves to blame.

The paper went on:

> . . . The law is not open to the people who may have their relatives carried away and cut up by the surgeons. The 'anatomy bill' has passed the legislature, and is now the law of the land.

The *Advocate* asserted that those excluded by poverty from the possibility of prosecuting legal proceedings, and against whom the law was so evidently biased, had *only* riot as a means of expressing a just sense of grievance, or of gaining redress.

The political powerlessness of the poor was perhaps shown nowhere more clearly than at Leeds in December 1832, during the first General Election contest after the passage of the Reform Act.[62] The Anatomy Act had become a fierce political issue in the town during October, when the workhouse trustees had passed by a majority of one a series of resolutions deploring grave-robbery, warmly acknowledging the passage of the Act, and appointing a committee to oversee the distribution of workhouse corpses to Leeds anatomists. Two days later, by means of 'a manoeuvre',[63] a further resolution was added directing that a notice to this effect be printed and posted up on the wall of every ward in the workhouse:

> it being highly essential that the friendless poor should be made
> acquainted with their condition, owing to the new act of Parliament,
> so that they may be informed how to prevent their bodies being given
> to the schools of anatomy for dissection . . . [64]

The resulting publicity caused a public furore. The resolutions were printed in the local papers, and reprinted nationally by Cobbett.[65] Urgent letters passed between Leeds anatomists and the Inspector in London concerning a complete lack of 'subjects'.[66] On 1 November, the annual vestry meeting to elect trustees for the forthcoming year was stormy, and a new resolution was carried disqualifying from reselection all who had voted in favour of dissecting the workhouse poor.[67] New trustees hostile to the Act were elected, despite efforts on the part of supporters to appear disinterested benefactors of the poor, and to persuade the noisy gathering to favour the merits of the study of anatomy. The meeting was less disposed to discuss this abstract issue than the Act's class bias:

> let them act under a measure which dispenses equal justice to all – the
> rich as well as the poor – the fat sinecurist as well as the worn-out
> labourer, and then, when all are dealt equally with, they might talk as
> much as they pleased about the necessities of science . . . (Loud
> cheers).[68]

Derek Fraser has shown that, because until 1832 Leeds was unrepresented in Parliament, civic politics had assumed great importance, and the national conflicts of Tory/Liberal/Radical interests were reproduced there in vibrant microcosm.[69] The Anatomy Act was an emotive issue, the more so as one of the Liberal candidates for the two new seats created by the Reform Act was Macaulay – scholar, Benthamite, and parliamentary sponsor of the Anatomy Act. The other was Marshall – a rich and highly influential local manufacturer. In direct and implacable opposition to

20   The Leeds Election Banner, 1832

these stood Michael Sadler, leader of a Tory-Radical alliance, parliamentary champion of the Ten Hours Movement and the factory children, vocally opposed to the exploitation of the poor – live or dead – which the Liberals already represented to many at that time.[70]

Nomination day, 10 December, was the occasion of huge excitement in the town as rival processions formed in support of the candidates. The *Leeds Intelligencer*'s description dwells particularly upon three major banners carried by 'operatives' in Sadler's procession; one bore the signatures of 40,000 working people from Manchester urging the Leeds electors to vote for Sadler; another showed a view of Marshall's mill, with half-clad shivering factory children hurrying to work in a snow storm; the third – which caused consternation at the Home Office and anger in the conservative medical press,

> represented a skeleton, on a black ground with a yellow border, holding in its right hand a scroll inscribed 'Anatomy Bill to better the condition of the helpless poor'. Underneath, the words 'Macaulay and the Anatomy Bill'.[71]

Yellow was the Liberal colour, and the significance of carrying it in a procession which showed a sea of blue (Tory) and white (radical) favours could hardly have been lost upon contemporary observers. The skeletal portrait served the role of a retributive skimmington effigy with a difference – a figurative dissection, as well as a political jibe. Resonances from the imagery of street literature of this period reveal the full and bitter implication of the image. The visual irony was multiple: the skeleton not only represented Macaulay without his fine clothes, naked beneath his skin as useful a 'subject' as any pauper, but it represented him as the very personification of Death. Death often still appeared on penny broadsheets as in the mediaeval Dance of Death – a skeleton taking 'all sorts and conditions' of people to the grave, and accepting no denial. Not only did the banner metaphorically dissect Macaulay, just as he had been responsible for inflicting dissection upon the bodies of the poor. It suggested his Bill would be the means of visiting death upon the helpless poor. It all but accused him of burking. The enormity of the accusation and the insolent ridicule of the image were brilliantly matched by the simplicity of the banner's conception. It was a provocative riposte to an Act which provoked and taunted poverty. The banner represents a clear and powerful articulation of working-class opinion of the Act in Leeds.

There was turmoil at the hustings. Some Liberal supporters made violent attempts to capture and destroy the banners – which were obviously seen as deeply insulting.[72] But they were well defended, and the attackers were driven off. Marshall and Macaulay, perhaps defensively at the sight of Sadler's immense popular support, made efforts to coerce Marshall's millworkers into showing support for their employer. Sadler lost the poll. His support, broad and active though it had been, was mainly from the voteless working class. They returned to more traditional modes of expression, and burned effigies of Marshall and Macaulay in the streets.[73]

Doctors who had marched in Sadler's procession were subsequently vilified in the *London Medical Gazette* as a disgrace to their profession.[74] The newly appointed Inspector of Anatomy, Somerville, wrote twice to Teale, a Leeds anatomist, for information concerning the banner, as he wanted 'the opportunity of contradicting some statements to the effect that some of the surgeons at Leeds had followed that Banner which was so much calculated to excite vulgar prejudices'.[75]

No replies to these requests survive in Anatomy Office files, nor in Somerville's surviving letterbooks. Teale may have kept silent from an inability to gratify the Inspector's preconceptions, for in a later edition of the *London Medical Gazette*,[76] W.A. Jackson MRCS wrote to explain that he and other 'medical men ... attached to conservative principles' had indeed marched in Sadler's procession – but under another banner – and that this did not necessarily imply endorsement of the sentiments of the 'operatives' who had carried the anatomy banner: 'Mr Sadler being supported by several totally independent parties, it could not reasonably be expected that one should dictate to the other what banners should be carried in the procession'. Ridiculing the *Gazette*'s exaggerated horror,

Jackson candidly subscribed himself as 'one of those degraders of their profession who followed in the wake of the Leeds anti-anatomical banner'.

It can be assumed that the Inspector of Anatomy already knew the identities of the medical men concerned, as he had written on 2 January to Baines – owner and editor of the Liberal *Leeds Mercury*, and a powerful figure in Leeds politics – to ask for newscuttings, and further information concerning the banner.[77] Baines was a staunch supporter of the Anatomy Act,[78] and it would seem that his collaboration with Somerville subsequently had the desired effect: on 16 January 1833 – only four weeks after the election – the Inspector informed a Sheffield anatomist who was having his own difficulties in obtaining 'subjects':

> even in Leeds where this question has unfortunately been mixed up
> with the keenest political feeling and the suspicions of the multitude
> excited by the display of Anatomical Banners, there I am happy to
> say the School [of anatomy] has succeeded in obtaining a Body
> during the last week, with every prospect of a greater supply. . . [79]

Richard Oastler's epitaph of the defeat, that ' "the People" don't live in £10 houses'[80] was truly spoken: in Leeds, Sadler's Tory-Radical alliance had lost the poll, and the victory at the vestry was circumvented. The Leeds anatomists' dissection of a local person's body illustrates not only the poor's powerlessness at the polls, but also their inability to counter the patronage and influence which the incoming government was active in wielding.

Four separate events – a theft, an inquest, an allegation and a bequest – all of which occurred in the immediate aftermath of the Anatomy Act's passage, provide a flavour of its early character and application.

In September 1832, the sexton of the poor burial-ground at Cripplegate was apprehended with two assistants in the act of hurriedly conveying a shrouded and coffined body to St Bartholomew's Hospital. It emerged that the body was that of Henry Tovey, who had died in the workhouse on 20 September of 'diseased lungs'.[81] There seems to have been some confusion as to whether the sexton's action had been approved by the workhouse master and was a genuine case of donation under the Act, or whether it was a case of bodysnatching. One suspects that many such bodies had passed over the same terrain before; and though it is plausible that the hurry was induced by fear of hostility to the Act, it seems much more likely to have arisen from a guilty desire to hush up a dis- or a non-interment.

At the hearing, the constable, Mr Postan, drew attention to the omission in the accompanying documents of several important details required by law. The magistrate, Sir Chapman Marshall, concluded the hearing by saying he was sure 'nothing wrong was intended' but 'the Act had not been put into operation with all the caution and strictness which the delicacy of the matter required'. He ruled that the prisoners be discharged, and the body buried without 'examination'.

The opportunities the Act provided for nefarious peculative dealings between anatomists and the employees of institutions in which the poor died had long been forewarned by its opponents. This case shows how what was probably a shabby private understanding between corrupt parties could so easily appear to be nothing more than a minor and accidental deviation from the Act's ordinances. The later history of the Act is littered with such clerical errors, and administrative oversights.

In this instance, the strict observation of the law worked to the poor's benefit, which – according to the *True Sun*'s reporter on the spot – gave 'great satisfaction to a crowd of paupers who had assembled about the office'. Not so in the case of Polly Chapman, reported in the same paper on 1 December 1832. The passage is worth quoting here in full:

> On Monday evening an inquest was held on Mary Ann Chapman, otherwise 'handsome Poll', aged about twenty-two, an unfortunate prostitute, who drowned herself on Wednesday night in a fit of mental derangement in the London Dock. It appeared that the deceased, who had described herself to her unfortunate associates as related to a coach proprietor named Chaplin at Rochester, was of sober and harmless disposition. Through inability to pay her rent she had been turned out of her lodgings on the morning of her suicide. A verdict of 'mental derangement' was returned; and Mr Holiday, the Churchwarden, asked Mr Baker the Coroner, if he could legally give up the body to the London Hospital, as it was not claimed by any relatives. Mr Baker strongly advised him to do so, as an example to prevent suicide amongst unfortunate women.
>
> Several of the latter class of females, who had conducted themselves with great decorum during the proceedings, here begged with tears and the greatest earnestness, to be allowed to pay a mark of respect to their unfortunate companion, by burying her in consecrated ground, for which purpose they had already raised £3 by subscription, and given to an undertaker. They described her as of the best and most inoffensive disposition, and incapable of injuring anyone.
>
> The Coroner, however, replied that it was necessary to make an example. The spirit of the Anatomy Bill would not be acted up to if the body was not given up. Any resurrectionist might claim the body as a friend, and afterwards sell it. A Juror said he thought the London Hospital had bodies enough from the poor-houses; and that the poor creatures present had shewn much good feeling, and ought to have the corpse. Mr Wilson, the Overseer, wished to take the sense of the Jury on the subject. After such discussion it was decided that the body should be sent to the hospital. The announcement of this

decision was received with the most bitter lamentations by the
females, who appeared much attached to the deceased.

Polly Chapman's inquest throws up several key points. It illustrates the
mutual understanding of coroner, jury and claimants, that dissection
retained the retributive and castigatory qualities it had always been held to
possess when it had been used against murderers, and which the Act's
supporters had said would dissolve away with its repeal. The coroners'
own diction highlights the exemplary and deterrent value of dissection,
much as the women's attempt to deflect the punishment by their stress
upon Polly's inoffensive and harmless nature. The 'spirit' of the Act, which
confined 'claiming' to nearest known relatives was grasped and promulgated even though the women attending the inquest were *bona-fide*
claimants in any ordinary sense. Polly Chapman was not 'unclaimed'. The
Anatomy Act alone made her so.

The earnestness and feeling of the women was focused upon the need to
show respect to the dead woman; a respect which would find expression in
the traditional form of funeral and burial. To this end they had already
collected money. They could not have been much more affluent than Polly
Chapman herself – driven to suicide by the inability to pay her rent – so £3
must have represented some sacrifice. Although we have no way of
knowing what customs these women would have observed, and with what
precise meanings these would have been invested, it is clear both from their
earnestness and grief that the integrity of the body, the decent observance
of death ritual, and burial in consecrated ground meant a great deal to
them.

Last, we cannot fail to notice that Polly Chapman and her friends were
'unfortunate women'. The coroner, churchwarden, overseer, and jurors
were all men. Although one juror expressed pity for the women, the
remainder did not. A sub-text to this incident is that Polly Chapman's
dissection was ordered less to benefit medicine than to punish 'unfortunate
women'. The coroner's wish that his order would deter such women from
suicide was a direct judgment upon female sinners of her ilk who might also
seek escape from their often desperate lives.

As the law had stood before the Act, the penalty of dissection was
proclaimed in open court to impress all present with the heinousness of the
crime of murder. As it stood in this inquest, it impressed each woman with
a sense of her own transgression and of her powerlessness in the face of
respectable manhood. Each lament had in it a wail for the self, for the
women saw in Polly Chapman's fate a prefiguration of their own.

A couple of days after this inquest was reported in the press, a free fight
took place between anatomy students in the metropolis, as the result of
allegations of maldistribution of corpses. On 3 December 1832, a meeting
of medical students at the Albion public house in Great Russell Street
broke up in violent disarray after disquiet had been expressed concerning

the uneven distribution of corpses under the Act.[82] Students from other schools voted to take immediate measures to correct what they saw as a partiality by the new Inspector towards St Bartholomew's, King's College, and the London University medical school (now University College Hospital). Although in 'the interests of science' the *Times* correspondent at the scene drew a veil over the worst of the proceedings, 'outrageous scenes' and 'language of the most violent character' were mentioned, as well as 'cards exchanging hands in all quarters, and the whole meeting . . . all but engaged in a general conflict'.

The next morning's edition of the *True Sun* newspaper featured on its front page a letter from G.W. Dermott (the anatomist who had promoted a scheme for the encouragement of bequests) making the same complaint, and arguing both for medical reform and for more bequests.[83] Surviving Anatomy Office records confirm that allegations of maldistribution and suspicions of corruption were endemic in the early years of the Act's application. Equitable distribution – discussed at a later stage – was to prove one of the most intractable problems the Act created.

The publication of Dermott's letter may have had an effect upon Charlotte Baume, whose bequest of her own body and that of her dead baby resulted in her brother's arrest[84] on suspicion of murder. He was already on Home Office police files,[85] for it was he who in 1829 had produced the pamphlet described earlier, in which were published details of his will, bequeathing his bones for knife handles. Charlotte was the sister of Peter Baume, the 'French scholar' whose 'vile' tract had been ridiculed and vilified in the streets. She had distinct ideas of her own. Her disposal is singular in that no record of a similar bequest has yet been found in this period. She was a woman of 'extraordinary opinions', who seems to have lived and died by her feminist/republican principles – birthing her child outside conventional marriage, and making a rational and benevolent decision about their joint disposal in the event of death.[86] Her desire was to be dissected in the anatomy theatre of the new London University, and then cremated. Any money obtained for her corpse was to be devoted to charity.

Her brother was arrested on suspicion of murder, as both Charlotte and her child had been delivered promptly to the anatomy school, without either the usual funerary observances, or having been examined by the parish searchers. Charlotte Baume had died on the 16th, and her child on the 18th of December 1832, but suspicion did not result in arrest until Boxing Day, when her brother appeared before the magistrate of Hatton Garden Police Office. He seems to have been very agitated, and justly upset by the imputation of foul play. Eventually, the accoucheur – a surgeon named Cole from Charlotte Street – confirmed the causes of death, and verified that her brother's actions had been dictated by Charlotte's own wishes.

The case caused a flurry at the Home Office. The Inspector of Anatomy was asked for information concerning a report of the case in *The Times* newspaper.[87] His hurried reply to Viscount Melbourne gave the impression that he was in command of the situation, and that the bequest had been genuine. However, later correspondence[88] shows that Somerville was driven to demand the requisite paperwork from the University's Professor of Anatomy, and that dealing with a bequest was altogether a new occurrence, for which there was no administrative machinery or precedent. It seems not to have occurred to the authorities that the Anatomy Act could spawn such an event, despite the important custody clause which expressly permitted it. More than any other single piece of evidence, this unpreparedness indicates that the Act was hardly credited even by those who administered it with the likelihood of voluntary application.

Somerville seems to have missed or ignored the opportunity the Charlotte Baume case afforded him of stimulating further bequests by publicising correct procedures for their administration. This oversight may have arisen from embarrassment at the suspicion of murder and arrest of next-of-kin in the case. However, no record has been found of an apology to Peter Baume for his unfair arrest, nor any sign of approbation that he was the agent whereby two fresh corpses were made available for dissection.[89]

These four incidents give an indication of the character of the Act's application in the early years of its administration. Bequests were scarce and unexpected, and, as far as can be ascertained, originated in a small constituency. It was said that in the first ten years of the Act's existence, only six bodies had been bequeathed to dissection.[90] No record of the identity of the other donors has yet been found in the surviving records. Other than in radical humanitarian circles,[91] public interest in voluntary donation seems to have subsided with the passage of the Act.

Henry Tovey, on the other hand, probably represents a much larger sector of the population – recorded in workhouse records as having been buried, but in fact sent illicitly for dissection. The ease with which such transactions had been accomplished before the Act perhaps suggests their potential extent afterwards, with this difference only – a middle layer of entrepreneurs, the bodysnatchers – had been eliminated from the question. Cases which came to light after the Act were usually, like Tovey's, direct deals between parish employees and anatomists, to mutual profit. They liaised directly under the Act in any case, and this legitimate relationship could be used as a cover in less licit activity, just as at Cripplegate workhouse.

Though students seem to have become less restive, allegations of corpse maldistribution and favouritism like those which caused the disturbance at the Albion public house did not subside, but went on to cause much ill-feeling within the profession, and eventually contributed to Somerville's dismissal. The marketplace competition which governed the anatomy business at this period was antipathetic to the co-operation Somerville perhaps hoped for in his term of office. The secrecy with which his work was conducted may have exacerbated the situation, in so far as the tutors were not sufficiently in his confidence to appreciate his position. As we shall see, Somerville's own probity was questioned on more than one occasion, and whether he was in fact above suspicion of complicity in breaches of the Act may never be known.

Of these incidents, the inquest on Polly Chapman is perhaps the most painful, and illustrates most nearly the emotional effects of the Act upon the poor. We have no way of knowing in how many cases bereaved friends' and lovers' grief may have been exacerbated by enforcement of the 'nearest known relatives' rule. The lamentations of Polly Chapman's friends shall have to stand as testimony for them all.

THE BUREAUCRAT'S BAD DREAM

The fact is, the Anatomy Act is a tissue of blunders, and
consequently, works wretchedly.

John Birtwhistle, Surgeon, 1833.[1]

The plea is, that the law is for the benefit of the poor. The poor
demur, and allege that they neither want such a law, nor desire its
advantages. Still, the law is forced upon them. The poor, thus pressed
by the generosity of the anatomists, earnestly entreat that they may
not continue to be the objects of such a bounteous charity. . . . As
they do not understand the value of the gift, they appear inclined to
question the motives of the donors. Who can marvel at such a result?

Lancet editorial, 1841.[2]

From an administrative point of view, the Anatomy Act turned out to be a
bureaucrat's bad dream. To write its full administrative history would
require another book, so I have confined myself here to an outline of its first
decade or so, and a more general overview of its application since.

As Inspector of Anatomy for England and Wales, Somerville was solely
responsible for the implementation of the Act south of the border. When
Craigie, the Inspector for Scotland, was relieved of his post for 'want of
proper care and attention' in 1836.[3] Somerville was given responsibility
north of the border as well. Some viewed this concentration of responsibility askance,[4] but nevertheless, for the Act's first ten years, Somerville was
almost alone in the task. It seems almost unbelievable that a transition on a
national scale from criminality and murder to a more law-abiding system
was entrusted to so small a staff. What was expected of Somerville can best
be gauged by the fact that after he, too, was removed from post in 1842,[5] his
job was filled by three people – one for London, another for the provinces,
and yet another for Scotland.[6]

The post was hardly intended as a sinecure. Parliament had agreed
upon an annual salary of £100,[7] on the assumption that each inspector
would sustain a private medical practice. No doubt the low figure served to
soften parliamentary distrust towards the idea of funding an inspectorate

at all. Doubtless, the amount of work involved in getting the Act into operation adversely affected Somerville's practice, and by 1842 he was being paid £500 for his services in England and Wales, and £400 for Scotland[8] – which large sums included expenses, and presumably some compensation for loss of private earnings. Somerville's life was made easier at the outset, however, by the support of S.M. Phillipps, Permanent Under-Secretary at the Home Office, and more distantly, of the Home Secretary, Lord Melbourne. He was also eventually given the services of a clerk and a messenger.[9]

Not least of Somerville's problems was the Act's profound inadequacy. In one of his curiously worded quarterly reports, Somerville put it thus:

> the Anatomy Bill when it first came into operation in October 1832 soon convinced its warmest supporters that however judiciously framed, to meet this peculiarly delicate and difficult question would be if left wholly to the discretion of those primarily interested in it, a constant source of contention, probably an ultimate failure, but immediately destructive to the usefulness of the private schools, or those not connected with Hospitals.[10]

The two major difficulties with which the Inspector's task was fraught were entirely predictable, because they were of long standing. First, popular hostility to dissection; and second, the competitive business basis of anatomy tuition. The first would entail the careful persuasion of recalcitrant parish authorities, the rigorous maintenance of secrecy, the enforcement upon anatomy tutors of rules concerning 'decency' and correct and timely burial. The second meant the assumption on the part of government – through the Inspector – of the right to interfere with market forces by overseeing the distribution of corpses between schools. The Act provided no machinery whatever to cope with either difficulty. It could neither force recalcitrant parishes to give up their dead, nor prevent the more powerful schools from monopolising what bodies were available.

Some parochial authorities had strong objections to the dissection of their dead poor, and either failed or refused to co-operate. At Whitechapel workhouse in November 1832, an approach by anatomists was snubbed by the master who feared that 'the whole parish would be up in arms' if he was to comply.[11] Somerville attempted to circumvent such opposition as this by issuing invitations to the Boards of Guardians of 'all the principal parishes in London' to send deputations to the Home Office, for a briefing by Phillipps. The result was, according to Somerville: 'at the Termination of the Anatomical Session in May 1833, every School had enjoyed an ample supply, at an expense so reasonable . . . that the success of the Bill was placed beyond a doubt'.[12] There can be little doubt that assurances of secrecy and public ignorance of the enterprise – as well as potential savings to parish funds – recommended the scheme to some parochial officers; but it is likely that there were also other motivations at work. A broad reading of Somerville's correspondence with parish officers and anatomists, yields a wide use of name-dropping, influence, and manipulation of power which was quite frequently based on bluff. In the provinces, local worthies were pulled in to exert muscle.[13] Many individual members of vestries and workhouse boards may have been impressed or overawed by such manoeuvres.

Much of Somerville's manipulation is not accessible to us, as he arranged in difficult cases to visit personally, and kept no official record of what passed.[14] His tactics seem to have failed with the Reverend Gregory of the London parish of Spitalfields. He had attended a Home Office briefing and his deputation had agreed to adopt the Act, but the parish subsequently failed to supply any bodies. One of Somerville's letters reveals both why this was the case, and the manner in which the Inspector and other parishes dealt with the wishes of the poor:

> It is . . . a source of much uneasiness that your parish while they
> adopt the Bill have accompanied its operation with such provisions
> as effectually to render it nugatory – For while in other Parishes the
> inmates of the Workhouses are left to be guided by their own feelings
> the plan adopted by yours of recording their wishes effectually
> defeats your intentions.[15]

The vicar was apparently providing some sort of a register in which the inmates of the workhouse could record their wishes; and given the choice, they evidently opted for burial. The letter provides important evidence that H.M. Inspector of Anatomy actively promoted a policy which denied the poor the right to express their wishes on the matter. Whether Gregory accepted Somerville's suggestion of a personal visit we have no record, but it appears from returns made by the Inspector to his superiors, that Spitalfields – along with several other London parishes – continued to withhold its dead.[16]

Somerville had hoped that the Home Office briefings would serve the dual function of prompting the appropriation of parish corpses, and furthering the plan of a 'General Distribution'.[17] Since the Act had failed to supply any mechanism whereby a fair distribution of available 'subjects' could be enforced, the Inspector was placed in the position of witnessing the development of a series of monopolies which threatened the very existence of some of the smaller schools. Those worst affected by this manifestation of the competitive spirit – or what Wakley called 'the fighting system'[18] – naturally entreated that something be done for them.[19] Somerville seems to have recognised the justice of their claim, as well as the danger of ignoring it – appreciating that dexterity in dealing with resurrectionists had ensured their survival prior to the Act, and that such again might be the case. Some suspected that his sympathy masked a desire to control the supply for his own reasons, but Somerville later protested that the distribution of corpses had been foist upon him against his will.[20]

Many parishes favoured the monopolising schools for good reason. Guy's Hospital was one of the main offenders. The hospital seems to have extended the offer of preferential hospital admission to the sick poor of parishes agreeing to grant the hospital exclusive use of parish dead.[21] Smaller anatomy schools independent of the hospitals could offer no such incentives to parish authorities, and were unwilling to adopt the system by which Mr Stanley, anatomist at St Bartholomew's Hospital, obtained exclusive use of the dead from one large parish – by the payment of high 'fees' to the parish undertaker.[22] Inspector Craigie experienced similar obstruction from Monro and Mackenzie in Edinburgh.[23] Nothing in the Act prevented the successful deployment of private inducements such as these.

Somerville recognised the urgency of creating some other distribution network, without which a situation could develop in which the old market could reassert itself.[24] Pressure from the private teachers favoured the foundation of a 'fair' system, but they were adamant that its administration should be independent of the corrupt Royal College of Surgeons,[25] which would have favoured the very same anatomists as already benefited from the monopoly system. Stanley, for example, later became President of the College – though Somerville's letters and reports are peppered with exasperation towards him.[26] Evidently, Stanley's position was that of an entrepreneur in any other walk of life – combining the desire to make money and be successful with the simultaneous desire to frustrate the same aim in his competitors.[27] The Inspector was caught between market forces and the cry of the other anatomists for 'equality in the conditions of competition',[28] while at the same time endeavouring from self-interest and loyalty to the Act to save it from failure.

Somerville first suggested a distribution on the basis of a *per capita* calculation based upon student numbers, but repeatedly encountered the tutors' ruse of fabricating students. In 1834, after two years' frustration, he suggested a new system of student registration, to be supervised by himself,[29] but was instructed by superiors to await the planned bill on medical registration. This was the first major check to his bureaucratic momentum that Somerville had suffered. It certainly did nothing to assist his control and distribution of corpse supply, as it meant that the Inspector lacked objective data on which distribution could fairly be made. Somerville was driven to use the best register available at the time, at the Society of Apothecaries – a 'manifestly defective source' for the information he required.[30]

The profession as a whole was probably keen enough to disassociate from the past traumas of burking, bodysnatching and serving at the gallows, to grasp with both hands the opportunity for a fresh start within the law. But a significant proportion of anatomists appear to have seen the Act merely as a source of cheap corpses and a means of rendering the bodysnatchers redundant, and no more. The impression gained from a wide reading of Somerville's letterbooks is that many anatomists failed to appreciate the responsibilities of their new position. Somerville was faced with widespread non-compliance – particularly concerning the decent burial of dissected remains – and an administrative load with which a part-time Inspector could not hope to cope alone. Somerville had tried to maximise what little power the Act invested in him by developing a rather complicated system of certificates, warrants and receipts, by which every stage in a corpse's travels between death and burial should ideally have been logged.[31] A great deal of the surviving correspondence is concerned with inadequate paperwork.

The problems facing the Inspector were not, however, merely clerical. There are numerous instances of active circumnavigation and non-observance of the Act's and/or the Inspector's demands. Most frequently, anatomists kept bodies beyond the stipulated time of six weeks after death.

In many cases the Inspector's repeated entreaties for the submission of certificates of interment suggest that remains were simply not being buried. In other cases, burial certificates were falsified; and in others still, unspecified indecencies occurred.[32] Somerville was personally committed to the Act's success, and did not entertain inviting adverse publicity by prosecuting through the courts such transgressions as revealed themselves. In most cases he seems to have managed by appealing to the anatomist's honour, his duty to the profession or to a higher authority, with a verbal reprimand, or with the occasional last resort threat to withdraw a licence.[33]

The 'serious alarm' which Somerville said he felt at the thought of public exposure[34] of such transgressions was rooted in an appreciation of the fragility of popular tolerance towards his proceedings. He understood that his work was often viewed askance by members of parochial authorities and individual workhouse personnel, as well as by the poor folk under their administration.

Several cases occurred in the first few years of the Act's operation in which the discovery of untoward behaviour associated with the procurement, distribution or treatment of corpses resulted in suspension of supply. One of these was at Whitechapel workhouse – where, as we have seen, the master had refused to co-operate with the anatomists. It would seem that the parish beadle subsequently made a corrupt arrangement with anatomists at the London Hospital, and delivered corpses there without the knowledge of the parish authorities – corpses for which he had also been paid for burying. When news of this 'arrangement' emerged, an enquiry was held in an open vestry meeting in the presence of ratepayers, which of course spread news of the scandal round the parish. The supply stopped altogether. A similar form of corruption was exposed at Shoreditch, with a similar result.[35]

Both cases took place before Somerville had established a 'general distribution', but the tables he compiled of the sources from which corpses were obtained in the London area show that supplies terminated in other parishes at later dates and for varying periods.[36] Stoppage occurred in spite of direct liaison with the Poor Law Commissioners, who had promised Somerville to do 'everything in their power' to prevail upon Guardians to provide corpses under the Anatomy Act.[37] Although it is unlikely that every case in which supply was suspended was the result of some public scandal, Somerville was beset by a constant fear of public exposure, and a persistent desire to remove 'from Public observation and discussion every circumstance relative to the transaction of Schools of Anatomy'.[38]

In this desire for secrecy, Somerville was supported by his superiors.[39] He gave instructions to anatomists experiencing difficulties in obtaining supplies, as to ruses they could adopt which would lessen opposition:

> I beg to suggest the propriety of your following a plan, which has been in many cases very successful, as an opening for ulterior proceedings, that of removing the body to your premises for a few days only say 3 or 4, by which you will be enabled to demonstrate the viscera, and return the body without disfigurement, so as not to disgust or shock the feelings of any person. The expense of the interment defrayed by you, decency in the Removal and other considerations, will I have no doubt powerfully promote your views.[40]

Hoping that no circumstance would occur 'to excite the feelings of the poor against the operation of this enactment',[41] to others he recommended 'great discretion', that corpses should always be removed 'by undertakers in Coffins as if for the purpose of interment', and that 'the utmost precaution' should be taken in the 'observance of the usual rites with this difference only, that the appearances are made more respectable than those of paupers'.[42] After further exposures in the late 1830s and early 1840s,[43] he endeavoured to lay down rules to exclude members of the public from dissection rooms.

One of the most serious loopholes in the Act was that it did not render illegal the removal of parts from bodies. That anatomists were involved in such activity is clear from cases in which dismemberment was discovered – such as the decapitation which had sparked off the Swan Street riot at Manchester.[44] A Salisbury anatomist, Mr George Sampson, no doubt proceeded to purchase dismembered parts of bodies or to remove parts from bodies which were not 'unclaimed', after he received Somerville's reply to an enquiry as to the legal status of such activity. Somerville covered himself by saying that the practice was 'not contemplated by the Act', that it was inadvisable, and that it risked providing murderers with a safe means of disposal of dismembered corpses. He nevertheless informed Sampson that returns were not required for parts of bodies, and ended:

> I do therefore most sincerely hope that in availing yourself of any such opportunity you will employ your utmost discretion in

preventing any discovery by which much prejudice could not fail to be excited.[45]

Despite the Inspector's assiduous secrecy, diplomacy and administrative innovation, the supply of corpses fell short of demand from the moment of his appointment. Somerville himself was deeply dissatisfied with the supply from the outset, and seemed to think things would improve.[46] However, in London, after initial success, the number of corpses available for dissection dropped, rose, and dropped again; so that in Somerville's last full season in office (1841-2) the supply was 36 per cent lower than it had been in his first.[47] Nor did this figure improve under the inspector replacing him: Somerville's first five-season total of 2965 corpses delivered to the London schools has only since been bettered once – between the 1887 and 1892 seasons, when 3032 bodies were consigned for dissection.[48] In the provinces,[49] things got off to a poor start, and got worse, only improving after mid-century. As a result of shortages, bodysnatching remained a feasible alternative for enough provincial anatomists for it to represent a serious problem throughout the Act's first decade, and beyond.[50]

To be fair to Somerville, he did about as well as the resurrectionists had done. Over his ten-year period in office, the annual average of bodies dissected under the Anatomy Act was 538 in the London area;[51] while the Select Committee Report gave annual averages of 534 for 1826 and 1827, obtained by bodysnatching before the Act's passage.[52] Such figures suggest that the anatomy tutors' persistent complaint of shortage was in part based on their subjective disappointment in the Act. The expedient of commandeering the bodies of the dead poor had been held out as potentially much more fruitful than grave-robbery. So although the new supply was certainly cheaper, and less fraught with danger, the tutors rarely exhibited much appreciation of these advantages when they found no increase in supply.[53] Somerville's efforts were repeatedly met with a demand for more corpses. As time went by, these demands merged with doubts concerning the Inspector's probity, as he was now responsible for a system in which maldistribution apparently persisted, and moreover exhibited himself hostile to scrutiny of his records.[54]

Somerville's removal from office in 1842 seems to have resulted from his lack or loss of control over the rather weak and haphazard system he had been forced to develop and get along with. He was increasingly beset by difficulties,[55] probably the most important of which was that he had made few useful allies. He suffered the hostility of the powerful hospital anatomists, who deeply resented his intervention in their business affairs, and who believed his 'general distribution' was weighted in favour of London University, to the other hospitals' detriment. The Royal College of Surgeons, dominated by the hospital men, still nurtured designs upon the control of the distribution itself. On the other hand, the smaller anatomy school proprietors seem to have felt a grievance that the 'general distribution' benefited the hospitals. Parish authorities which failed to supply were in any case largely unsympathetic to Somerville, while even in parishes which donated corpses regularly, staff may have resented the existence of a responsible bureaucrat potentially able to detect or thwart corrupt trans- actions. In short, being an Inspector of Anatomy was a fairly thankless task.

No doubt the inadequacy of the Act's drafting deserved much of the blame for this professional hostility, but Somerville was so closely identi- fied with the Act that he attracted personal blame which should perhaps have been directed elsewhere. Somerville said as much himself.[56] Added to this, a change of government in 1841 brought a new Home Secretary – Sir James Graham – who, possibly from expediency, was less supportive of Somerville than previous incumbents of the post had been. Phillipps – ever the professional civil servant – trimmed his sails to the prevailing wind,[57] and because the Act itself was so weak, this loss of support from his superiors seriously affected Somerville's position. Finally, there was the long campaign against the Act, Warburton, and the Inspector himself, which was prosecuted with great energy by a London surgeon, William Roberts, and his supporters.[58]

Very little is known of Roberts beyond what we can glean from the pamphlets he published.[59] He was the inventor of an antiseptic process to preserve human tissue, extending the period over which a corpse could be useful for dissection. Roberts had intended to take out a patent on the process, but in the interests of science had agreed to hand over the formula to Henry Warburton, on the promise of a government gratuity. During the same period, Roberts also made public his disagreements with the Ana- tomy Act. The promised gratuity never materialised. Whatever the merits of his process – at the outset Somerville, Astley Cooper, Benjamin Brodie and other important figures had praised it in written testimonials – it does seem that Roberts was shabbily treated, and apparently for political reasons.[60]

Over a period of nearly twenty years Roberts addressed public meet- ings, published pamphlets and broadsheets, and caused chagrin at the Home Office, by circulating information about the Act both in and outside workhouses.[61] As a result of his activities many poor people may have evaded the knife by signing declarations stating a desire not to be dissected. Probably many more were buried entire as a result of parochial authorities' fear of public exposure.[62] The marked drop in corpses avail- able for dissection from workhouses in the London area after 1838 can be ascribed to Roberts's influence.[63] By 1840, Somerville – despite mobilising the Poor Law Commission in his support to prevent the circulation of Roberts's material to workhouse inmates – was driven to employ someone (paid from his own pocket) to visit workhouses and keep 'a vigilant watch for unclaimed bodies'.[64]

An entirely different picture of Somerville's administration emerges from Roberts's pamphlets than is found in the records the Inspectorate has left to posterity. Roberts's energetic critique hardly provides unequivocal evidence of the simple opportunism which was ascribed to him by Somerville and Warburton.[65] Nor does it give an adequate explanation of his popular support, or of the help he was given by other of the Act's opponents – local politicians, anatomists, and Members of Parliament.[66]

The available evidence suggests that Roberts's search for a means of preserving corpses was initially motivated by opposition to the Act. He seems to have been active since the 1820s in the local politics of St Marylebone, a district known for its radicalism, and where the Anatomy Act was a contentious issue from its inception.[67] In the 1832 general election, a parliamentary candidate was quizzed on his view of the Act, and reassured his questioner – whose identity, unfortunately, is unknown – with the undertaking that:

> although a friend to dissection . . . he respected the prejudices of others on the subject, and would use his utmost to obtain a revision of the present Bill, because it made the inmates of hospitals and workhouses the subject of it. . . [68]

Marylebone had consistently failed to provide corpses at the rate Somerville expected. A comparison with St Giles's workhouse – in which there was also an average of over 200 deaths a year – manifests Marylebone's non-cooperation, for in the first ten seasons (1832–42) St Giles's delivered 709 of its 'unclaimed' poor for dissection, while in the same period, St Marylebone gave up only 58. St Pancras, a neighbouring parish affected by Roberts's campaign, gave only 82 corpses in the same period.[69]

Roberts's criticism of the Act was cogent, socially informed and highly effective. Arguing from the premise that rich and poor alike loathed and feared the idea of being dissected, he asserted that bodysnatching had been a fairer system than the one enacted by Parliament:

> It is a point not to be lost sight of, that all classes of the community had their share of the annoyance; all were liable to be reached by it. By the Bill of 1832, the upper and middle classes were protected, while the poor alone were left exposed.[70]

He drew attention to the fact that advantage had been taken of burko-phobia to gain the Bill's passage; and to the deceptive language in which the Bill had been framed. He declared that it had been accomplished

> with consummate art. One of its main objects was to victimise a certain class, and it accomplishes its purpose without naming that class.[71]

Roberts defined the social origin of the Bill's victims as:

> the poor and destitute, and all that immensely numerous class just

above the poor and destitute, who, by honest industry, and in the
sweat of their brow, earn their bread, and subsist upon . . . wages.
The Bill of 1832 is directed against them, covertly, but none the less
specifically, and exclusively.[72]

He argued that the term 'anatomical examination' was a misnomer,
designed to deceive the public, and that its use was intended to lend
credibility to the burial clause.[73] Speaking from an inside knowledge of
dissection rooms, Roberts revealed that after dissection, there was no
'body' to bury, as customarily, 'three fourths or two thirds of the body
[has] been wasted, or consigned to troughs, pits and night-carts'.[74] It was
this pitiful wastage, this treatment of poor bodies as nothing better than
detritus,[75] which Roberts hoped his preserving process would obviate. He
seems to have been motivated by the genuine belief that its adoption would
facilitate the conservation of corpses to an extent which would mean that a
much smaller supply would be adequate to the profession's needs. This
smaller supply, he argued, could – and morally should – be provided by
criminals dying in custody rather than by the honest poor. Figures he
provided of deaths in custody at this period do seem to support his
argument.[76]

Moreover, criminals' bodies were more 'interesting' than those of the
workhouse poor, for reasons which were best explained by the Inspector
himself:

the Bodies from the Hulks . . . are most prized at the Schools on
account of their being for the most part young subjects and better
adapted for the display of human structure than the aged inmates of
the workhouses. . . [77]

. . . a private comment which goes a long way to define who constituted the
usual subjects for dissection.

Roberts ultimately concluded that his 'process' would never be welcomed by those who were in the business of making profits out of selling
dismembered parts of bodies to anatomy students. In a pamphlet he
published in 1855, Roberts referred to a list of prices charged to students at
London University anatomy school, which if correct, shows that sizeable
profits were to be made on the volume of turnover of human raw material,
sold in parts – head and neck, right and left upper extremities, and so on.[78]
According to Roberts, Henry Warburton himself was a shareholder in the
school, and it was a matter of public notoriety, 'that he has applied the Act
to advance the pecuniary interests of himself and friends . . . by a traffic in
the bodies of the destitute poor'.[79]

Roberts believed this had been achieved through Somerville's agency.
The Inspector, he alleged, had given his patron's school preferential
treatment in terms of corpse distribution, to the detriment of other schools.
It has proved impossible at this late date to prove or disprove the accuracy

of this accusation. Warburton was indeed a shareholder of the new medical school at London University, which at this period was a joint stock association. Other shareholders included his Benthamite parliamentary colleagues who had promoted the Anatomy Act, for example Hume, Brougham, Macaulay and John Smith. No records seem to have survived to throw light on the financial implications of this information. Somerville's own figures of corpses delivered to the other London schools do show a disparity of distribution in favour of the University medical school, which could be taken to support Roberts's charges – but since no figures for student attendance seem to have survived for the duration of Somerville's period of office, the suspicion cannot be proven either way.[80]

The hospital schools of anatomy were still able to appropriate bodies from their own mortuaries, which helped – as before the Act – to buffer their proprietors from severe shortage. By the mid-1840s, most of the private anatomy schools not attached to hospitals, and lacking this built-in supply, had either been absorbed by the hospital medical schools, or had gone out of business.[81] The strain imposed on the smaller establishments by difficulties in the distribution system perhaps explains the active support Roberts received from Dermott, Tatum and Foster – anatomist-proprietors of small schools which subsequently ceased independent trading.[82]

If Roberts's allegations were correct, or partly so, they would go some way towards explaining why Warburton's Act had omitted to render the sale of corpses or their parts illegal, when both practices were known to lend themselves to corruption and murder. Wakley had publicly argued long and hard in the *Lancet* in favour of a prohibition upon commerce in corpses, so the omission of such a prohibition must have been a conscious decision on Warburton's part. Roberts's allegations would seem to imply that this omission masked an intention that the Act should leave a loophole by default, and thus preserve the potential of the human corpse to retain commodity value in anatomy tuition. Despite the seriousness of his allegations, neither Somerville nor Warburton sued Roberts for libel.

Somerville secretly admitted, moreover, that Roberts's campaign was based upon 'pretty correct information'.[83] One charge the Inspector virtually admitted. It concerned the undertaker whom Somerville officially employed to transport corpses between workhouses and anatomy schools, and from schools to burial.[84] The undertaker, whose name and fees crop up with some frequency in Somerville's correspondence, had previously been Master of Holborn workhouse, and was said to have made an extra income at that time by selling the bodies of poor people whom he recorded as having been claimed by relatives.[85] Roberts accused him of corruptly profiteering from the burial of dissected remains while working for Somerville:

decking out a journeyman undertaker in canonicals, to represent a clergyman of the Established Church of England, to read the burial service over several hundred shells [thin coffins] interred in a place of unconsecrated ground, called Globe Fields.[86]

Somerville pleaded ignorance before a board of enquiry, which eventually investigated these and other allegations, but he failed to convince, and was censured by the Home Secretary.[87] He may indeed have been ignorant of the Globe Fields burial charade, but, as Roberts succinctly observed: 'the Inspector, who is paid out of the public purse has either neglected his duty, or connived at the contravention of the Act.'[88]

The fact that Henry Warburton was a Member of Parliament, a medical reformer and a disciple of Bentham and James Mill, does not necessarily cast doubt upon Roberts's allegations. For all his respectable credentials Warburton was not, it seems, above graft. He was forced to resign his parliamentary seat in 1841, as a result of a scandal surrounding complicity in bribery at his own election in Bridport the same year. Benthamites were expected to eschew the methods of 'Old Corruption', and Warburton's involvement was a great disappointment to his friends.[89]

In his absence from Parliament, Warburton's attempt to put a lid on criticisms of the Act – and Somerville – finally came to grief. He had taken responsibility in 1840 for the establishment of a Parliamentary commission of enquiry which then persistently failed to report, despite repeated Home Office requests.[90] With Warburton out of the House, the Home Secretary appointed another official enquiry, which failed to exonerate Somerville from complicity in contraventions of the Act when it reported in early 1842.[91] A further enquiry with wider terms of reference was conducted shortly afterwards by the Royal College, and was granted access to Somerville's records – much against his will.[92] Its report was completed in August 1842, and Somerville was sacked almost immediately, being given £100 in lieu of notice.[93] Roberts would surely have added Henry Warburton's absence from Parliament to the factors contributing to Somerville's demise.

<hr/>

Although Somerville's speedy removal from office indicates an acceptance on the part of his superiors of the force of some of the accusations against him, his importance in the difficult years of the Anatomy Act's inception cannot be overlooked. The Act's unpopularity, its poor drafting, and the professional non-cooperation it faced meant that the establishment of its provisions was potentially at risk throughout the decade of his office.

Warburton's Bill, by delegating responsibility for crucially important details to the Home Secretary, had left the new Inspectorate's status, powers, staff, and administrative machinery imperfectly defined. Somerville was placed in the awkward position of asserting his own status, defining his own powers, employing his own staff, and devising the machinery the Act's administration demanded, but which Parliament had been unwilling to give. In some respects he managed to obtain Home Office backing, but in others there existed discrepancies of opinion between himself and his superiors as to where the limits of his power lay. One of Somerville's major problems was that there was almost no precedent to assist in defining his status or role. Moreover, Somerville found himself no longer regarded as an independent authority on anatomy – as he had been when giving evidence to the Select Committee – but as an employee. He can perhaps be forgiven if his initial enthusiasm was dampened by disappointment, and if his commitment to the Act became less of a personal conviction than a means of earning a living.[94]

Whether or not in the interests of an easier life Somerville delegated too much responsibility to minions, or whether his past history – of exploiting patronage, and executing with official connivance devious arrangements for the procurement and transport of corpses – led him to go into deals on his own behalf, may never be known. Temperamentally, he lacked both the cheerless ruthlessness of a Chadwick, and the upright and compassionate humanity of a Fitzpatrick.[95] The Inspectorship was a job he had dearly wanted and manoeuvred for,[96] and for which he had appeared well qualified. Another person in the same post, operating within the Act's shortcomings, may well have found other answers to the problems he faced – but for Somerville they had meant using manipulation and influence where possible, overlooking transgression when necessary, subordinating the investigative and regulatory function of his post to the administrative and bureaucratic. Even if its roots were in self-interest, his regime established the practicality of the Act's principle by the time of his dismissal, and set the pattern for its next eighty years.

<hr />

William Roberts and the Royal College – though both involved in the campaign against Somerville and the Act he administered – were by no means allies. Each had entirely different aims and motives: the College sought to reassert its ancient monopoly over corpse-provision, while Roberts's motive, and that of his supporters, was to subvert the Act's social inequity. Doubtless the sacking gratified both parties. But Somerville's removal proved a hollow victory for both. The campaign had been couched in terms too personal for it to affect the genuine faults or shortcomings of the legislation itself. In effect, Somerville's departure limited the damage, proving a check rather than a boost to the achievement of further concessions. The basis of the Act's failings remained intact, and moreover, firmly in Home Office hands.

The next two years saw opposition on both fronts sustained, and influential enough by 1844 to gain a parliamentary debate on a demand for a Select Committee to enquire into the Act's operation – but to no effect. Protected by parliamentary immunity, Warburton – who had by that time returned to the Commons for a different constituency – diverted discussion of the Act's ethics or demerits by a waspish attack upon Roberts. Ignoring the pressure for an enquiry from the direction of the College, Warburton focused almost entirely on Roberts and his populist agitation against the Act inside workhouses and public houses. At this time, to address a meeting in a public house was considered socially demeaning[97] and Warburton's aspersions upon Roberts deliberately struck a note of parliamentary disgust. As Douglas Hay has observed, 'a gentleman who trifled with the mob or called into question the ultimate justice of the law was execrated by his fellows as a knave and a fool'.[98] Despite a spirited appeal by Duncombe that the House should not 'Burke' all enquiry on the subject, Lord John Russell carried the day after issuing the chilling warning that if the 'clamour' for an investigation should be heeded, repeal might follow, and with it a revival of the horrible spectre of burking. The reappearance here of the spectre of burking evokes a strong sensation of *déjà-vu* – and serves to reinforce suspicions of its tactical use in the 1832 debates. Only ten MPs voted in favour of an enquiry.

In 1841, only a year before his dismissal, Somerville had expressed his own anxiety that the untoward exposure to public knowledge of a single instance of corruption or indecency could spell the Act's demise.[99] Probably the most interesting comment to emerge from the Commons debate was made by Sir James Graham, to the effect that 'the silence with which the Act had been carried into execution was the best proof of its success'. The fear of publicity these sentiments belie was rooted in a desire to keep opposition and non-cooperation to a minimum by fostering public ignorance. Fostering public ignorance, and thereby public silence, had been an integral characteristic of the Act's administration from its earliest days – even back to the Select Committee.[100] Of course the fact that 'unclaimed' paupers were sent for dissection was common knowledge. But the routine daily (or nightly)[101] operations which effected the transfer of corpses from workhouse to dissection room were assiduously kept covert. Successive Inspectors did all they could to keep from public knowledge details of the Act's routine administration.

In this respect, the first ten years of the Act's existence provides a microcosm of its operation over the remainder of the nineteenth century. Reading through the surviving correspondence of the Anatomy Inspectors and their Home Office (and later Ministry of Health) colleagues, one is struck by the repeated recurrence of the old problems – opposition, riot, shortage, maldistribution, speculation, disinterment and non-internment of corpses, indecency, misconduct, collusion, corruption.

Running like a dark thread through this correspondence is the avidity on the part of successive Inspectors for secrecy, manifested primarily in what seems to be a genuine fear of the press. A perturbing case occurred at Sheffield in the 1880s, in which the wrong corpse was sent for dissection, and relatives were given instead the body of an unidentified old man. The then Inspector, Mr Birkett, wrote to the proprietor of the Sheffield Anatomy School – appositely named Mr Skinner – who had failed to notice the mistake:

> every act of indiscretion on the part of any of the authorities
> concerned with the supply of subjects for dissection allows an
> opportunity for the editors of newspapers to indulge their
> propensity of pandering to the prejudices of the unlearned which
> invariably arrests or diminishes the supply of subjects.[102]

In terms of structural faults in the Act and of incidents in its daily running by which these were exposed, the paramount desire for secrecy operated not only counter to democracy – for Parliament, too, was often kept in the dark[103] – but both fostered and concealed outright injustice. A case in point is that of Henry Gillard.[104] He was born, with a stillborn twin, in September 1839. Three weeks later, both he and his mother died in the Queen Adelaide's Lying-In Hospital, near London's Golden Square. The following day, Henry's older brother Robert and their uncle came to visit, and were told the sad news. They said they would arrange for the bodies to be collected for burial, but were informed by the hospital's matron and secretary that the child had already been buried.

Henry's father, William Gillard, was a working man, and could get no time off until the following weekend to investigate what had happened. He visited the local Registrar's office, where he found that neither his wife's death nor that of the child had been registered by the hospital, so he promptly registered them himself. Mr Gillard already suspected that something was amiss, so he went back to the hospital and demanded to know where Henry's body had been laid. Both matron and secretary were surprised by his return, and – perhaps intimidated by his anguish – reluctantly wrote out a note addressed to the porter of the anatomy school in Little Windmill Street,[105] directing him to deliver up the body to the bearer.

When Mr Gillard got to the school, being Saturday, it was closed. So once again he returned to the hospital. This time, the secretary was a little more accommodating and – probably anxious lest Mr Gillard should make public the way in which he had been treated – offered to go himself to confer with the hospital's Physician-Accoucheur. The two gentlemen decided to direct Mr Gillard to return again to the hospital on the following morning. When he did so – bringing an undertaker with him – the little body was ready for collection, with marks upon it to show where it had been.

No news of the case ever reached the press. The entire transaction would have remained unknown to us, had not Mr Gillard the confidence and wherewithal to pen a letter of complaint to the Home Secretary. An investigation ensued which revealed that *all* the proceedings had been illegal. The body had been removed before the legally stipulated interval had elapsed, nor was it 'unclaimed'. The Inspector had received no information of any part of the transaction, and none of the required paperwork had been submitted to him. A web of lies and deceit surrounded the relationship of the school and the hospital. Yet the investigation went no further. Despite multiple contraventions of the Anatomy Act and the existence of penalties for punishment, nothing was done.

For over two months Mr Gillard awaited a reply to his letter. None came. So in February 1840 he wrote again. This time he received a reply to the effect that an enquiry revealed what he already knew. Eventually, after another letter from him, he was informed that it was 'not a case in which prosecution would be necessary or advisable'. The Inspector had in fact recognised the wrongdoing, and had reported the salient events to his superiors, indicating which clauses of the Act had been violated. The decision to take the matter no further had been made at the highest level.

Mr Gillard was a law-abiding man. He didn't incite a riot, but he lacked the money to institute a private prosecution. The Act's much-vaunted concern for the 'feelings' of surviving relations is shown by this case to have been calibrated with their wealth and social status. Only social non-entities used such a facility as a lying-in hospital. Gillard was socially inconsequential, and was treated as such. No apology was ever made to him.

Gillard was probably unusual in that he, or someone closely interested in his case, was literate, and had the temerity to write direct to the Home Secretary. How many more such cases never reached the notice of anyone outside the institutions involved we shall never know. Enough cases emerged of corrupt dealings between workhouses or hospitals and anatomists for us seriously to infer that cases like Henry Gillard's were only the tip of a very large iceberg. Official silence and inaction in such instances as came to light cannot fail to raise the suspicion of collusion, or at the very least indulgence.[106]

The case of Benjamin Alcock,[107] Professor of Anatomy at Queen's College, Cork, provides an unexpectedly intimate glimpse of the extent of official connivance in illegal proceedings under the Act during the 1850s. Alcock was a distinguished anatomist, after whom a canal which envelops nerves and vessels deep in the pelvis is still named. He was related to Rutherford Alcock, who had served as Inspector of Anatomy for the London area for two years after Somerville's dismissal.

It seems that the Anatomy department at Cork 'suffered repeated interruptions in the supply of subjects' and that Alcock objected, believing that since its statutes rendered the College responsible for procuring teaching materials, he should not personally be called upon to commit a misdemeanour to do so. This course had actually been suggested to him by the Inspector of Anatomy for Ireland, Professor O'Connor, and urged by Sir John Long, the highest authority under the Anatomy Act in Ireland. The suggestion was that Alcock, like tutors elsewhere suffering shortages, 'should obtain subjects from the poorhouse by claiming bodies in the capacity of a friend of the deceased; upon the impropriety of which', said Alcock, 'it is unnecessary to dwell'.

Probably as a result of spurning the suggestion, the Professor was asked to resign, and when he submitted a petition of grievance to Queen Victoria it was promptly returned to the Lord Lieutenant of Ireland to deal with, and Alcock was sacked. Among the grounds for this decision were that he possessed 'little appreciation of the responsibilities of his position, or regard for the peace and harmony of the institution'. Alcock responded by publishing a pamphlet in his own defence. In particular, he complained bitterly that:

> an arrangement for obtaining subjects, which was admitted by the
> author to be illegal, and which involved the commission of a
> misdemeanour, received sanction from the Earl of St Germans, and
> the non-adoption of it was made a ground for my condemnation.

After a few years living on in Dublin, Alcock threw in the sponge, and emigrated to America. He had broken ranks with his profession, and with the English ruling elite in Ireland, and was never forgiven. He would probably never again have obtained an academic post in his subject in British dominions. Like Roberts, Alcock could never have expected official interest or indulgence after having denounced officially countenanced skulduggery.

There seems little reason to suspect Alcock's veracity. Tacit permission for unsavoury practices was certainly given by successive Anatomy Inspectors, weighting the enforcement of the Act against the exercise of free choice by the poor, and in favour of the anatomists. The extent of the Inspector's geographical responsibility meant that his investigative role was all but in abeyance unless an informer spilled beans, or a newspaper carried a story. Difficulties involved in the detection of malpractice, and the permissive stance of the administration, suggest that the incidence of illegality and indecency by anatomists after the passage of the Anatomy Act was much higher than the available records show. Even when on rare occasions gross malpractice *was* unearthed by an Inspector, retribution was notional.[108]

The indications are that throughout the nineteenth century, the surgical and administrative elites of Britain were prepared to turn a blind eye to (sometimes gross) breaches of decency and of the Act's regulations, so long as the public was kept in ignorance and the dissecting tables supplied. The profession itself had long roots in illegality and negligence towards popular feeling, and as a profession went along with the letter of the Act only as far as it suited itself to do so. The only Victorian change to the Act was made in 1871, and was the result of persistent non-compliance of anatomists with the burial clause. It simply permitted a longer period in which to dissect.[109]

Although personnel changed, both at the Home Office and in the Anatomy
Inspectorate – and in small but discernible ways, policies changed with
them – the endeavour to preserve secrecy continued into our own century.
Back in the dark days when Somerville had been fighting for his survival,
he had composed a report on his own achievements in the post, in which he
declared that he had laboured to 'divest the question of Anatomy of party
bias of every kind'. He trusted that 'no mistaken view will now tempt any
well-intentioned persons to direct popular attention to the subject'.[110]

Eighty years later, just after the Great War, Dr Alexander Macphail was
appointed the new Inspector – first for the provinces and then also for
London – and did precisely what Somerville had warned against. He, too,
probably believed his role a-political. But he reckoned without the canny
class-consciousness of the representatives of the young Labour Party on
local Boards of Guardians.

The two previous Inspectors – Charles Hawkins (who had held the post
1858–92) and W.H. Bennett (later Sir William, Inspector 1892–1921) –
had each imposed their personalities upon the office.[111] After initial
difficulties, Hawkins had increased the number of corpses available for
dissection; comparatively quietly, cultivating institutional goodwill and
sustaining secrecy. His successor had let things go along much as Hawkins
had left them, and though distribution was relatively trouble-free, numbers inevitably dropped – most noticeably after the introduction of old age
pensions in 1908 and health insurance in 1911.[112]

In 1921, the Anatomy Inspectorate had just been transferred from the
Home Office to the newly created Ministry of Health, and Macphail was
the first Inspector to be appointed under the new regime. He inherited a
situation in which there were 'deplorable shortages'[113] in anatomy schools
all over Britain. With ministerial consent, a circular explaining the dearth
and touting for bodies, was sent to all county and borough lunatic asylums,
which institutions now provided an increasing proportion of appropriated
bodies.[114] Macphail advised his superiors that a fee should be offered to
officials who made 'unclaimed' corpses available, 'too small to be a bribe
and just enough to keep the officers keen . . . five shillings or so, is thought
by most to be certain to secure increased supplies'.[115]

If he had possessed none before, Macphail's provincial experiences
with socialist Guardians might perhaps have led him to arrive at some
awareness of the social and political issues involved in his work. Reporting to his superiors a scene in 1920 with the Board of Guardians at
Ipswich, he had described the 'vehement' and 'insistent' expressions of
the Labour members upon the need for an appeal to the rich for bequests,
rather than one to Guardians for the bodies of 'the poorest of the poor'.
Macphail reported a widespread wish that the 'well-to-do' should con-
tribute to the study of anatomy, hinting that an adjustment in the law
might be advisable.[116]

Despite this important evidence of his sense of fair play, when Macphail became full Inspector he nevertheless attempted to hush up and suppress opposition to his campaign to get more pauper corpses. In Kingston-upon-Thames in 1924 (no change in the law having materialised) he seems to have tried to win over the opposition by deception. During a noisy meeting of the Kingston Board of Guardians one speaker demanded to know: 'why rich men living in Park Lane should not give up their bodies in the interests of science' . . . and was answered by a Poor Law Guardian who had been assured that they did so 'in hundreds of cases' and that the 'representative of the Ministry' had informed him that 'it was the source which was now chiefly relied upon'.[117]

Fortunately, we can ascertain the truth of what the 'representative of the Ministry' had told the Kingston Guardians. Although no official figures seem to have survived specifically for 1924, the number of bequests in that year is unlikely to have been much above that of ten years earlier – none at all; or ten years later – less than 4 per cent of the total dissected. In the London area in the winter season of 1934–5, the total amounted to 9 bequests out of 261 corpses dissected. Provincial figures were even lower. At the time of Macphail's visit to Kingston, we may safely conclude that over 95 per cent of all 'dissection material' was composed of appropriated bodies.[118]

The same meeting was told by a local clergyman that the local poor would suffer great harm if the Act was to be adopted in Kingston. Another speaker failed to see why people from surburban villas should not also be liable for dissection. The Kingston Guardians refused to adopt the Act. The local paper carried a sympathetic report of the proceedings, with the editorial comment that 'the friendless poor have quite enough to go on with without having this gruesome shadow to face'.[119]

It was just this sort of publicity Somerville had most feared. Macphail himself had attempted to prevent it when in 1920 he had instituted talks with a Mr Manning of the *Daily Mail* preliminary to discussions with Lord Riddell, President of the Newspaper Proprietors' Association, with a view to 'exercising a general control over ill-advised newspaper reports' on the sources of materials for dissection, '. . . to secure that such reports will not appear in future'.[120]

These discussions cannot have been wholly successful, since several newspaper stories describing similar opposition as had occurred at Kingston emerged over the next few years. For example, at Hammersmith the Guardians had actually agreed – on Macphail's prompting – to donate the 'unclaimed' for dissection. But at a meeting in 1923, a furore arose which reached the pages of the local paper,[121] when revelations were made concerning the burial of dissected remains. Coffins were said to have been boxes unfit even for the carcass of a dog.[122] A member of the board, Mr H.E. Granger, subsequently wrote Macphail an aggrieved letter, in which he explained his views.[123] He had been one of the Hammersmith Guar-

dians who had originally voted for the donation of pauper corpses.
Afterwards, he had decided to check up on the administration of the Act in
his district and had found to his horror that some bodies were never sent
back for burial. Those that were returned had been in coffins made of
unplaned wood, riddled with knot-holes, without handles, and with only a
slip of paper glued to the lid to identify the remains within. He estimated
that each coffin would have cost less than half-a-crown.[124] Mr Granger felt
cheated and disillusioned, and said that many other members of the board
felt the same.

In another case, the *Essex Times* and the *Romford Times* reported in full the
scandal of an 'unclaimed' pauper donated for dissection after a decision by
the Tory majority group on the Romford Board of Guardians.[125] John
Crosby was a veteran of the Indian Mutiny. He had died in 1921 an old
man without relatives, and too poor to pay for his own funeral. When the
news of his dissection broke, his body was reclaimed after local protests. A
military funeral was arranged, and John Crosby was buried with full
honours. His funeral procession was followed by Labour members of the
Board, who had opposed the dissection of the Romford poor. Speeches
were made at the graveside, and one councillor informed all present (and
incidentally, readers of the local press) that it was possible for poor people
to avoid dissection by making a declaration to that effect. The transmission
of this information evoked considerable interest elsewhere – the extract is
marked heavily at this point in Anatomy Office files.[126]

Another socialist, Mr Lambert, followed with a moving funeral oration
in which he expressed implacable opposition towards the Act's social
injustice:

> As Labour members who recognised the rights of all they held that if
> it was good for John Crosby to have his body put on the dissecting
> table it was good for anybody else. There should be no distinction. If
> it was necessary at all, let them be ballotted for, but they did protest
> against this man's body being taken to the dissection table without
> his sanction beforehand, while Lord Tom Noddy was allowed to go
> quite free because he could make a pomp and show of it.

The Act's implications, therefore, called forth almost identical social
analysis from Mr Lambert of Romford in the 1920s as from its opponents
almost a hundred years earlier, of which he almost certainly had no
knowledge.[127]

It says a great deal for Inspector Macphail that upon his death in 1938 he
left his own body for dissection: the only Inspector ever to have done so.[128]
In this gesture, Macphail not only demonstrated a personal lack of
hypocrisy, but stands as an emblem of a more general change in attitude
towards the dissection of the dead. His period in office, covering the

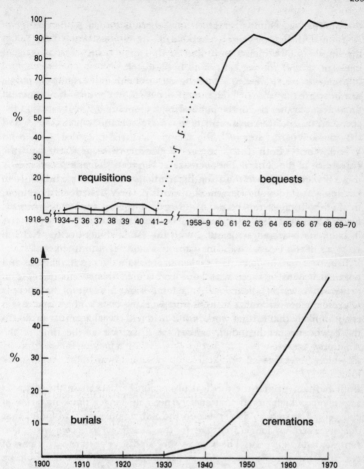

Figures 4 and 5 Bequests/requisitions and deaths/cremations, 1900–1970
Sources: See Chapter 10 text, and note 130; Cremation Society of Great Britain

inter-war period, witnessed the first rise in the number of bequeathed bodies for a century.

This rise marked the inception of an important trend. Available figures are approximate and incomplete.[129] Yet they point to a change which began on a small scale after the Great War, perhaps even partly prompted by Macphail's less-than-circumspect approach. It would seem that from the period up to and including the 1914–18 War the total number of bodies dissected can be accounted for by pauper bodies taken under the Act from workhouses, hospitals, asylums, and prisons. Between the wars, although the number of bequests remained low, there is evidence of a change of attitude. This becomes more marked after the Second World War, when the numbers of bequests rose, and in the 1960s seem to have reached between 70 and 100 per cent of all bodies used.[130]

More research is needed before the reasons behind this change in public attitudes are fully clear.[131] That there occurs over a closely similar period an almost parallel rise in the popularity of cremation[132] suggests that the social meaning of the corpse and its spiritual associations has changed, and that the key period in which this change occurred preceded the Second World War.[133] Both trends bespeak a growing disbelief in the spiritual coherence of the corpse. The increase in bequests suggests in addition a more benign public view of scientific medicine. The possible influence of changing attitudes of government towards poverty – particularly evident in the abolition of the Poor Law Board in 1929 – cannot be ignored. Further work will need to be done to see whether the meteoric post-war rise in bequests bears an association with the establishment of the NHS in 1948, or of the Death Grant in 1949, as would seem to be likely.[134]

Research remains to be undertaken to ascertain the social, religious and political origins of those who have constituted this recent increase in generosity towards 'science'.[135] Anecdotal evidence suggests that there is at present a not insignificant input from working-class sources, and that it is not unlikely that further work in this field will reveal a similar profile to those who bequeathed their bodies for dissection at the time of the Anatomy Act.[136]

———— ❧ ————

Both Parliament and the medical profession had access in the 1830s to arguments which urged that society need no longer think in terms of compelling anyone to do service on the slab against their will, and that doctors need no longer partake in the anathema coercive dissection represented to the poor. The hope was for a positive gesture on the part of government to create a new climate of opinion in which people would be encouraged freely to donate their bodies, much as they do today. In the event, the decision was taken to assume the power of compulsion towards the poorest and most deprived sector of society; and the medical profession accepted the role assigned. In addition to the trauma inflicted upon the poor as a class, the decision probably contributed to delay an increase in bequests for dissection by at least a century.

———— ❧ ————

THE UNPARDONABLE OFFENCE

O Poverty! thou art the unpardonable offence. . . . Thou hast neither rights, charters, immunities nor liberties!

G. Beaumont, 1808.[1]

No working man will ever again expect justice, morals or mercy at the hands of a profit-mongering legislature.

Bronterre O'Brien, 1836.[2]

The cause of the difficulty . . . is little under our control . . . the weather is extremely mild and seasonable . . . the inmates of the Workhouses are few beyond any precedent, while the scarcity of deaths is even more remarkable . . . Our only enemy is the extraordinary mild season.

James Somerville, H.M. Inspector of Anatomy, to Benjamin Harrison, Treasurer at Guy's Hospital, December 1833.[3]

. . . suppose me to fall sick or lame, I'd rather die than see her begging a morsel of bread from the flint-hearted hired overseer, and see her shut up in one den while I was shut up in another, and hear of her dying perhaps, and of her body being cut to pieces like the carcass of a dead horse at the dog kennel. Oh, no, master: hell shall have me rather than expose her to this.

Dick Hazle to Farmer Stiles in William Cobbett's play
Surplus Population and the Poor Law Bill, 1834.[4]

Perhaps the best tribute to the success of the Act, is the very small alterations which have been made in it between 1832 and the present day.

James B. Bailey, 1896.[5]

Why was it that visitors to Victorian slums were so incredulous of the inhabitants' care of their dead? How do we make sense of Victorian health reformers' need to define working-class corpses as 'nuisances', and the enactment of regulations enforcing removal? Again, what was the basis of their patronising view of death insurance, which was considered by the Victorian poor to be more important than health insurance, and which bulked disproportionately large in their meagre budgets? And why were later commentators so very dismissive of the working-class love of showy funerals?

The apparent inability of Victorian social observers to comprehend the meaning of death for members of another social class suggests the existence of distinct class-bound death cultures in Victorian Britain – an important aspect of the cultural gulf which divided the 'two nations' of rich and poor. This final chapter argues that the inception of this culture-gap can be traced to the early 1830s; that this period of social and political watershed profoundly influenced working-class death culture, a culture so potent as to survive into our own century, and even into our own time. Covering a similar time-scale to the previous chapter – from the Act's passage to the Welfare State – I seek here to discuss the Act's symbolic and instrumental meanings, and its long-term social implications.[6]

Although survey methods were in their infancy in the 1830s, government ministers drew heavily on the results of a survey conducted by Baines at Leeds in 1831 when they came to draft the Reform Bill. It had shown that a £10 property qualification would demarcate and exclude the working classes from the vote. Edward Thompson has observed that the £10 qualification offered 'a definition of class of almost arithmetical exactitude. In 1832 the line was drawn in social consciousness by the franchise qualification with the crudity of an indelible pencil'.[7] It required no such survey to discern that the Anatomy Act drew a similar line in a similar place, demarcating and isolating the propertyless as its victims.

The parliamentary chronologies of the Reform Bill and the Anatomy Bill were intimately intertwined. It is almost as if Parliament, sick with resentment at having to extend the franchise, found solace in taking revenge on the poor for their temerity in demanding a say in government.[8] A close relationship between the two Bills was perceived at the time – a rash of cartoons appeared during the Reform Crisis showing politicians 'burking' Old Mrs Constitution, 'burking' the Reform Bill, as 'burkers' exulting over their victim, or as anatomists dismembering the Reform Bill in the Tory Charnel House.[9] It was surely not merely a coincidence that a cleverly doctored version of the Anatomy Bill which had failed in 1829 succeeded in passing through Parliament in 1832, neck-and-neck with the Reform Bill. In the interval, attitudes towards the lower orders had hardened, and neither appeals to paternalist sentimentality nor fears of mob rule – which had thwarted the first Anatomy Bill before – could muster sufficient parliamentary voice to prevent its passage, only a few weeks after the Reform Act. A few MPs may perhaps have been guiltily aware of their broken bargain with the working classes,[10] but the new brutality which would be responsible for the New Poor Law two years later was in the ascendant even before the Reform Act had altered parliamentary personnel.

The distribution of political power in the reformed electorate closely resembled the redistribution of risk decreed by the Anatomy Act. Just as the Reform Act was designed to 'associate the middle with the higher orders of society', strengthening 'both the State and property rights against the working class threat',[11] so the Anatomy Act bought off the allegiance of the propertied classes with legal apparatus to protect their defunct remains.

———————————

Ignorance of the Anatomy Act in our own day should not lead to an underestimate of its impact upon popular consciousness at the time of its passage. We have seen something of the popular hostility to the measure – ranging from workhouse unrest and riot to political demonstration and civil disobedience. Sporadic popular unrest against the Act, though often associated with more sedate political activity, revealed kinship to the agitations against bodysnatchers, burkers and anatomists before the Act's passage.

Indeed, unrest could still be triggered by similar events – as in Sheffield in 1835, when the anatomy school was entirely demolished after the caretaker's wife, being violently beaten by her husband, shrieked 'murder!' and set off a long-brewing riot.[12] The demolition expressed in traditional form a hostility which was also found in political meetings concerning the Act's repeal, held in the town that year.[13] We can see the interaction of politics and popular unrest again in Cambridge in 1833, when a dispute over the legality of consigning a poor man's body to dissection led to a noisy public meeting, which in turn developed into an attack on the anatomy school to liberate the body.[14] The overseers' decision to call an open meeting on the matter was described by Somerville as 'most culpably imprudent'.[15] The man had not died in the workhouse, but was poor enough to qualify for a parish coffin. The upset in the town caused such severe shortage that even three years later it was necessary to transport bodies to Cambridge from the Woolwich hulks.[16]

Contraventions of the Act also met violent hostility. In 1834, a major riot was narrowly avoided at Hull when Somerville was speedily despatched to investigate reports which had reached London that the anatomy school had been daubed with graffiti accusing the owner of burking and graverobbery. Despite assurances from the anatomists concerned that the accusations revealed nothing but the prejudices of the ignorant mob, the Inspector did in fact find disinterred remains on the premises. The matter was hushed up.[17] In the London parish of St Giles, 'considerable excitement' was caused when in 1841 it was discovered that the workhouse mortuary keeper had – for a bribe – decapitated a smallpox victim's body.[18]

Fear of anatomy legislation often prompted or exacerbated riots and other disturbances against cholera regulations,[19] and it seems likely that further research will bring to light other cases like Henry Gillard's, which could so easily have developed into something more than an exchange of letters.[20] There were later cases like that of Rosanna Rox, who called the Mayor of Newcastle to her aid in 1841 when her mother's corpse was taken forcibly away by men working for the local anatomists.[21] Despite considerable provocation – her mother's body had been hastily immersed in near-boiling water at the Surgeon's Hall, in preparation for flaying, which would have removed all trace of identity – Rosanna Rox didn't cause a riot. Hers was a case in which inability to defray the costs of a funeral had led to a denial of kinship. The anatomists' justification for the force and deceit used to obtain the body was that – despite the presence of mourners – they had taken it to be unclaimed. Like Mr Gillard, Rosanna Rox didn't cause a public disturbance, in spite of ample justification. The law-abiding poor endured the experience of powerlessness and swallowed feelings of hurt and injustice, though they did not forget. Such stories were in all likelihood told many times over around fires and in public houses, assimilated into local lore, augmenting fears of the pauper's doom.

The various forms of opposition the Act encountered, however, seem comparatively subdued, and not at all as violent as some commentators had feared. That this was the case is in part due to the nature of the Act and its implementation – which was piecemeal, covert, and intentionally low-key, designed to minimise public impact. Moreover, it primarily affected isolated individuals incarcerated in institutions, who had already suffered social death, and whose experience of facing physical death went unrecorded and unknown in the outside world, other than in general terms. In about 1834, a Cambridge printer – no doubt hoping to cash in on local hostility to dissection after the 1833 riot – reprinted a broadsheet which featured the following poetic description of such a death. . .

> . . . lo! the bending form
> Of the old man, his anxious care-worn brow,
> He smites in anguish, solitary now:
> No rural cot, no lovely daughter's smile,
> No sons, to soothe him in the dread Bastile –
> No tender partner of his sorrows near,
> To cool his bosom with a falling tear;
> At thoughts of by-gone days he inly mourns,
> And vainly on his wretched pallet turns:
> No help is nigh, a dread and fearful gloom
> Surrounds him with the horrors of his doom.
> A worse than felon's doom! for when his life

> Returns to God! then, then the bloody knife
> Must to its work – the body that was starved,
> By puppy doctors must be cut and carved:
> Priests of my country! ye whose Living Head,
> Wept when he saw that Lazarus was dead!
> Can ye unmov'd with hearts as hard as Burke;
> Behold the scalping knife thus do its work;
> See guiltless labourers doom'd by tyrant rule
> To be the may-sport of the wealthy fool;
> With hands unhallow'd severing the thread
> That binds the heart to the lamented dead.[22]

But how ever much the poem's author might have sought to evoke sympathy towards the workhouse pauper by the passionate re-creation of such an end, and however many times this sort of demise in fact occurred, the encounter with Death and the prospect of dissection was always faced by the individual – alone in an austere institution, too poor to merit either moral indignation or notice other than from those who were equally powerless.

On a political level, the reasons behind the quiet – even quiescent – reception to the Anatomy Act's passage are not far to seek. They can be partially ascribed to the political climate in which the Act was passed, for its synchronicity with the Reform Act meant that it sank almost without trace in the press of the day.[23] Jubilation and comment surrounding the passage of the long-awaited and much fought-over Reform Act absorbed so many column inches of newsprint in the mid- and late summer of 1832 that the Anatomy Act's passage and early implementation went by almost without notice.

Other factors served also to minimise public hostility, not least the relief felt in many quarters that the dead would henceforth lie peaceful in their graves. There seems little doubt that in places free from the shadow of poverty, the plight of the poor was receiving diminishing sympathy at this time. The ethical position of those absolved by the Act from suffering unnecessary fear of the slab could not have been wholly comfortable. Limited sympathy for the poor may have been tinged with a measure of guilt for personal salvation from the anatomists. To many, the derivation of corpses was – as it remains today – unpleasant to ponder. The Act's definition of the pauper as social outcast was embraced by many with guilt, embarrassment, or alacrity, but at any rate with silent acquiescence.

It is a byword that Britain's colonial rule was sustained in many cases by the doctrine of divide and rule. The Anatomy Act – like the Reform Act – illustrates its utility in the government of the home territory. Divide and rule ensured not only that the voteless poor would be designated society's scapegoats, but also that the 'sharpened quest for respectability'[24] – so evident in the 1830s[25] – would mute sympathetic protest. For, however likely it was in a socially mobile society that individual members of the propertied classes possessed the potential to expire within workhouse walls, it was a feature of aspiration rather than economic reality[26] that as a class they did not identify with the improvident poor. This limited sympathy for the very poor – as Francis Place's success at the National Political Union shows – extended even to members of the labour aristocracy.[27]

Even in quarters in which the expression of resentment and political outrage could have been expected, the response was not as vocal as might have been predicted. There was no immediate howl of anger. The reasons behind this are, once again, not difficult to discern. Among those with an understanding of the real implications of the Reform Act, the mid- and late summer of 1832 and beyond was a period of profound despair. If it had not done so before, political disillusion set in more generally after the 1832 election, when it became clear that the main beneficiaries of the immense mobilisation for reform had been the very people who had dishonoured their bargain with the working class – who had created the Anatomy Act, and who promised yet worse.[28]

Almost immediately debate focused on the proposed 'reform' of the Poor Laws, and radical sights were set on a defence of the live poor, as well as the dead. That summer had seen a decisive shift in political power. In a parliamentary sense the result was perhaps predictable. In a national political sense, although things would never again return to the position before the huge campaign for Reform, the new self-confidence the working class had gained in the mobilisation for Reform received a decisive blow in the Reform Act, and another – smaller, weaker, but no less significant – in the Anatomy Act. The *coup de grâce* would come in the New Poor Law.[29] The full enormity of the betrayal may have taken some time to sink in, but no later record has been found of such triumphant and spirited ridicule of the Anatomy Act as had been exhibited at the Leeds election.[30]

<hr />

The Anatomy Act was in reality an advance clause to the New Poor Law. Its easy passage was an important political moment, permitting the recognition that – using the right strategies – legislation which openly turned its back on the old paternalism, and antagonised the poor as a class, could be passed with little opposition. It paved the way for the systematic dismantling of older and more humanitarian methods of perceiving and dealing with poverty. It was an invitation to self-interest rather than to charity. It was simultaneously an act of deference to the cash nexus, and an instrumental and symbolic degradation of poverty. It conferred respect and approval upon the Benthamite dictum of utility in a most tender area of human consciousness. Only incidentally did it endorse the respectability of scientific medicine. Above all, it served as a class reprisal against the poor.[31]

The Reform crisis and its resolution had engendered a consciousness among the ruling elite that the middle classes represented no real threat to the established order, and on the contrary, might provide the means and policies whereby it was reinforced. Edward Thompson has described the alliance as one in which 'blood compromised with gold to keep out the claims of *egalité*.[32] The Anatomy Act at once symbolised this consciousness, cemented the alliance, and demonstrated its power. The parliamentary insignificance of the ultra-radicals was known, but what the Anatomy Act's passage satisfactorily proved beyond doubt was the rout of benevolent paternalism.

The fluid geography of social alliances resolved into the vindictive regime elected late in 1832; a regime which was repeatedly to be responsible for the deliberate exacerbation of social inequity. Gwyn Williams has observed that this was accomplished with the

> perceived humiliation of measure after measure, the new Poor Law,
> the restriction of the right of petition, the punishment of the Dorset
> labourers and Glasgow spinners, even the Anatomy Act and the
> pursuit of the propertyless beyond the grave . . . [33]

One of the few recent historians even to notice the Anatomy Act, Williams has seemingly made an association here with its passage and the new regime, although it was in fact passed by the *old* one, the same that – under threat – had eventually assented to the Reform Act. The association, however, is entirely understandable – for the alliances and lines of battle which had emerged in the Anatomy debate, both in and outside Parliament, were reinforced by the 1832 election, and became clearer still over the next two years as political conflict focused on the Poor Law.

Together, these three important pieces of legislation – the Reform Act, the Anatomy Act and the New Poor Law – formed a wedge which sundered the 'two nations' of rich and poor. For all its gradations – witness the Leeds survey[34] – the middle class fell on the more fortunate side of the divide. And the boundary would be marked with the stern edifice of the workhouse – an institution so 'severe and repulsive' as to make it 'a terror to the poor and prevent them from entering' – a regime consciously designed to be as harsh as possible, and fraught with indignity.[35] Entrance into the workhouse entailed the breaking up of families, the sale or destruction of personal belongings, the rigid curtailment of personal freedoms, meagre rations, uniform clothing, and a host of punishments for minor infractions of discipline. The dissection of the dead was an inspired addition – one whose potential had been overlooked even by Malthus.

The poor were by no means unaware of the influence of Malthus upon their social superiors, and its implications for themselves.[36] Almost as soon as the establishment of deterrent workhouses was mooted, they were popularly dubbed 'bastiles'.[37] The threat of insurrection the name implies was perhaps secondary to the tyranny the workhouse would represent, and to a popular understanding of the imputed equation of poverty and crime.

Ann Digby reproduces a broadsheet dating from 1836 entitled 'The
Glorious Working of the Whigs', which features the following lines:

> Why should the Whigs raise up their Prisons high
> With gloomy fronts, and walls that reach the sky;
> Are such dark Dungeons to immure a band
> Of Rogues and Swindlers that infest the land?
> 'No!' some cry, – 'They are for one crime more
> The crime of being old, infirm, and poor!'[38]

With the publication of the pamphlet by 'Marcus' in 1838, things took on
an even darker aspect. The pamphlet propounded a 'theory of painless
extinction' and recommended control of the poor's 'surplus' population by
wholesale infanticide using 'the surreptitious invasion of a gas which
contains not the element of life'.[39] It was believed in radical circles that the
pamphlet – which was by no means a spoof on Swiftian lines, and was
taken with deadly seriousness – had been written either by Brougham or
by one of the Poor Law Commissioners, though both attributions were
strenuously denied.[40] The principle on which the 'diabolical work' was
based seemed to be all of a piece with the New Poor Law and the Anatomy
Act, evoking a sinister constellation of associations: a shocking and fearful
amalgam of indignity and appalling official heartlessness towards the
poor, comprising population control by starvation or burking, gassing of
babies, separation of families; and vivisection upon the live bodies of the
poor besides dissection after death. The pamphlet and the New Poor Law
both came, said an angry critic, 'from the same place, and they are both
directed toward the same end – the crushing, starving, murdering of the
poor'.[41]

The ominous undertones hindsight may detect are chillingly sustained
by the fact that opponents actually called the New Poor Law apparatus the
'concentration' system.[42] Nor are these echoes to be lightly shrugged off.
A *Blackwood's* lampoon of 1838 suggested the use of paupers' skin for
leather, and 'Marcus' likened the poor to lepers. George Godwin said that
in the 1850s he had seen poor people 'used as though they were not of
the same species as those who crowded them into passages, and pushed
and drove them like so many sheep and oxen'.[43] On a political level the
affinities between Malthusian and eugenicist ideas are known. The
New Poor Law 'bastiles' seem to have prefigured some of the functions
ascribed to the Nazi camps, such as breaking individuals into docility;
spreading terror through the rest of society, and the destruction of individuality – for example in the way in which families were broken up and
people were referred to by numbers instead of names.[44] The attitude of
those enforcing the bleak fate of the pauper's corpse in the English
workhouse bears an affinity to that of those others who built gas ovens for
Jews, gipsies and political opponents. Each is the product of an attitude of

21   (*opposite*) 'Contrasted Residences for the Poor' – from Augustus Pugin's *Contrasts*, 1841

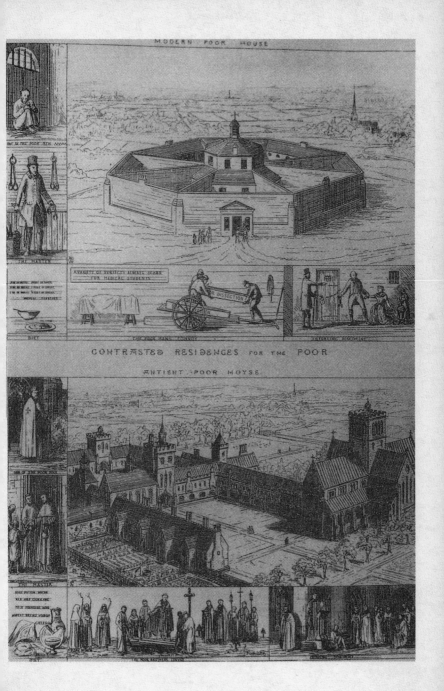

CONTRASTED RESIDENCES FOR THE POOR

mind in which other human beings can smugly and routinely be written off as non- or sub-human.

James Bray observed in 1839 that those in power were 'experimenting as to the length which human endurance of oppression can go'.[45] People alive at the time of the New Poor Law *feared* what was to be done to them in hospitals and workhouses. It takes a strenuous leap of historical sympathy[46] to attempt to comprehend their fears. A nameless apprehension can constitute a deeper source of disquiet than hindsight can easily recreate.[47] From our position in history, we have seen these things, we know they are possible, that they have been done. We cannot perceive their continuity in history without some recognition, and some disquiet.

Moreover, contemporary apprehensions had a factual basis. Some Poor Law historians would have us believe that much of the terror was the result of a public relations exercise on the part of the Poor Law's protagonists, magnified by the apprehensions of the poor.[48] None the less, mortality in the workhouses was so high that William Farr estimated in 1837 that cholera mortality was probably raised 50 per cent 'by confinement within their walls'[49] and in 1841 Wakley was to call them, with barely controlled anger, 'ANTE-CHAMBERS OF THE GRAVE'.[50] Mortality is amenable to statistical analysis of the sort Farr was adept at, but no one sought to measure the mental anguish of workhouse inmates or of those who shivered with fear outside. The deliberate creation of the myth of the cruel workhouse should not blind us to the actual cruelty and misery a 50 per cent rise in mortality represents.[51]

⸺◆⸺

Although its distinct identity was appreciated in some radical political circles for a considerable period of time,[52] in general, the Anatomy Act seems to have been assimilated in radical political consciousness virtually as an appendage of the New Poor Law. As early as September 1832 – only a few weeks after the Anatomy Act's passage, the association between the two hated pieces of legislation – the one enacted, the other planned – was made in the radical Preston paper *3730*. Thereafter the association was a commonplace.[53]

In a popular sense, the two enactments were seen as conjoint. The broadsheet from which the verse description of a pauper's death was reproduced above was entitled 'The Christian's Appeal against the Poor Law Amendment Act – By a Working Man', and was popular enough to merit reprinting. Written entirely in verse, it tells the tale of the old man's life and death, and ends:

> Resistance in a just and holy cause
> Is sanctioned by divine and human laws![54]

Nothing in the entire broadsheet would have led the contemporary reader or listener to understand that the dissection of the poor was ordained by anything other than the New Poor Law. The same conflation was often a feature of public speeches by celebrated anti-Poor Law campaigners.[55] Because it was perceived at the time as an advance clause of the New Poor Law, the Anatomy Act did not call forth a protest movement distinct from the Anti-Poor Law Movement. In Sheffield, Samuel Roberts's campaign against the Anatomy Act – whose climax was the demolition of the anatomy school in 1835 – was associated with local activity against the New Poor Law.[56] Marylebone, where William Roberts was active, was also a focus of Anti-Poor Law activity.[57]

There can be little doubt that the resentment and fear the Anatomy Act engendered contributed to the bitter opposition mounted against the New Poor Law, and this in turn was transformed again into a renewed demand for political rights when the Anti-Poor Law Movement flowed into Chartism, in the late 1830s.[58] The workhouse poor, and all who recognised their own potential to become victims of the 'class legislation' of the period (the phrase is contemporary),[59] received a bitter blow with the defeat of Chartism in 1848. With the hope of the Charter went all hope of an alteration or repeal of vindictive legislation against the poor, for a generation.

Objectors to the Anatomy Act – like those opposing the New Poor Law – have been vindicated by posterity. One historian of health and ill-health in nineteenth-century Britain, Barry Smith, has observed that Anti-Poor Law campaigners' predictions about the New Poor Law bore more relation to reality than did those of its advocates.[60] The same can be said of the Anatomy Act. Despite Benthamite avowals of the Act's social equity, only two years after its passage, in 1834, Inspector Somerville stood before the Select Committee on Medical Education, with Henry Warburton in the chair, and testified that many bodies went 'unclaimed' solely through poverty.[61]

In the course of the first century of the Anatomy Act's application, almost 57,000 bodies were dissected in the London anatomy schools alone. Less than *half a percent* came from anywhere other than institutions which housed the poor.[62] The close relationship this statistic reveals between the Anatomy Act and the New Poor Law was administrative because it was political. The Poor Law gained deterrent value as a result of the association, while the Anatomy Act depended upon the administrative machinery of the Poor Law for its implementation.[63]

At the time the Act was passed, the medical profession was evidently eager to gain respectability by severing its association with the hangman. Throughout the Act's first century of operation, the profession remained willing to benefit materially from the social control inherent in the law, while simultaneously providing a means whereby that social control was itself reinforced. Such are the ways in which the ruling elite 'organises ideological consent to its dominance'.[64]

It may be an accident of history that during roughly the same era in which the human corpse became an article of commerce, so also did the 'respectable' funeral.[65] The three views of the human corpse discussed in Section I – popular solicitude, clinical detachment, and commercialisation – were operating over the century preceding the Anatomy Act, coevally with the development of the respectable funeral on the one hand and its diametric opposite, the pauper funeral, on the other.

The commercial development and economic viability of the undertaker's trade may in fact have been more closely related to that of the bodysnatcher than has hitherto been recognised. From at least the 1720s the two professions developed as it were in tandem. There can be little doubt that undertakers benefited from public fears of *post-mortem* insecurity. In the celebrated case of the Irish Giant discussed in chapter 3, a symbiosis between the two professions is particularly apparent: the undertaker was paid well on the one hand by the Giant, for a burial secure from the anatomists; and on the other by the anatomist Hunter for handing over the corpse. The history of the funeral industry cannot be charted here,[66] and its relationship with the resurrection-business can only be inferred, but two elements in its appeal are nevertheless worthy of notice – the endeavour to preserve the body's identity and integrity, and the close relationship of these to the commercialised – and conspicuously 'respectable' – funeral. It seems likely that raised public awareness of what rapidly became a codified social gradient in coffin strength and burial plot security – and the relative degrees of safety these offered from predation – enhanced death's potential to serve as a locus for the expression of social status and aspiration.[67]

Of course, death had always served as a rite for the statement of social place. What was new was the growth and consolidation of undertaking as a profession which 'sold' death to a market below the aristocracy. Over the century preceding the Anatomy Act, undertakers had begun to set up shop in urban areas and to purvey their services in the creation of funerals to suit the pockets and aspirations of the expanding middle classes. Over a similar period, the 'respectable' funeral developed, depending less upon rank and birth than cash. In the undertakers' hands, the funeral came to possess flexible potential in the assertion of financial status: various levels of expenditure could purchase equally various permutations of coffin strength and durability, grave or vault size, security, commemoration, and funerary display.[68] Manifest in the increasingly commercialised trappings of death, the funeral came to be the rite of passage *par excellence* by which to assert financial and social position – a secular last judgment which had as its goal the exhibition of worldly respectability. The process came to full flower in the Victorian funeral.

Many of the constituent elements of the Georgian and Victorian bourgeois funeral were derived from the heraldic funerals of earlier generations, originally the preserve of the nobility. The parallels were summarised by Edwin Chadwick in 1843:

> the two men who stand at the doors being supposed to be the two
> porters of the castle, with their staves, in black; the man who heads
> the procession, wearing a scarf, being a representative of a herald-at-
> arms; the man who carries a plume of feathers on his head being an
> esquire, who bears the shield and casque, with its plume of feathers;
> the pall-bearers, with batons, being representatives of knights-
> companions-at-arms . . .[69]

Respectable funerary display was a powerful articulation of social aspiration and attainment. It demonstrated at one and the same time wealth
and – in stark contrast to the pauper's funeral – distance from the
workhouse. Other elements were more closely related to the ideal of
security of tenure in the grave. Those who could afford to do so purchased
double or triple coffins – one of which would usually be lead, a metal
known as a preserver of corpses.[70] Coffins were invariably described as
'stout', and rows of coffin nails were a status symbol for a considerable
period. Deep graves, secure vaults, patent coffins and the many other
expedients available to the financially fortunate were purchased in the
hope of acquiring what Lord Radnor desired for his own body – a tomb
more secure than his own home. Sir Astley Cooper probably had three
coffins inside his stone sarcophagus – the Duke of Wellington outdid even
this, and had four.[71]

The early nineteenth-century undertaker provided those with adequate
funds the prospect of rotting entire within a secure coffin, hermetically
sealed from both the soil and the dust of less eminent corpses. The
appalling state of urban churchyards and burial grounds in this period
hardly provided the ideal setting for such a polite form of decay, and those
that could, saw to it that they would be buried elsewhere. The speculative
development of extra-mural cemeteries from the 1820s rendered the rural
ideal attainable to a much wider market, and allowed more room for the
erection of impressive monuments, and clearer stratification along class
lines.[72] Cemetery monuments made claim on the future in the *physical*
world: staking out a larger space than required; sited over the body itself –
protected by railings, stonework, or other forms of territorial marking; and
surmounted by an impressive and identifiable monument. The
nineteenth-century tomb was intended as a permanent statement of
worldly achievement and stature.

Although there are other sub-texts to the purchase of privacy and
wholeness in the tomb, the importance of the hope of the soul's survival, or
future resurrection, cannot be overlooked. The *London Medical Gazette*'s
publication in 1832[73] of a strenuous denial that the mode of disposal could
in any way affect the soul's fate, suggests that such a belief was potent at
the time and was felt by some to require invalidation. Contemporary
tombs abound with reference to sleep, rest, resurrection, and the hope (or

assurance) of future meeting. As recently as 1962 a Commission established by the Archbishop of Canterbury stated: 'We ought to reject quite frankly the literalistic belief in a future resurrection of the actual physical frame which is laid in the tomb.'[74] Long after the Victorian crisis of faith, and despite the growth of cremation and the widespread religious scepticism and inactivity of our own period, the hope would seem to spring eternal.

The commercial protection of the identity and integrity of the corpse – like many of the folk observances from which it in part derived – can be understood as a form of insurance. Whether or not physical resurrection would actually take place, it served as a metaphor for the possibility of providing a secure future for the soul, if such could possibly be attained. The double metaphor by which even the afterlife figuratively became a marketable commodity was assessible to all but those lacking adequate means.

Prior to the triumph of Malthusian values, poor people were generally accorded some dignity in parish burials.[75] The calculated indignity of the pauper's funeral dates from the industrial period. Ruling elites in various parts of the country had begun in the later eighteenth century in a piecemeal way to cut public expenditure on poverty. A key aspect of this process was the creation of a new death ritual which both propagated and reinforced the notion that to die in poverty was an unpardonable social offence. The pauper funeral was an object of popular dislike before the Anatomy Act, and the provision of dignified burial an important feature in the early appeal of working-class organisations.[76] But the Anatomy Act's crucial endorsement and exacerbation of the social meaning of the new rite, transformed dislike into desperation. The Anatomy Act initiated a standardised nationwide applicability ... all deaths in parish control, a characteristic taken up with relish by the New Poor Law's centralised administration, which issued directives concerning the saving of costs on shrouds, coffins and graves, and banning the use of palls or bellringers.[77,78]

In the Victorian period, shrouds were often lacking altogether, and the poor person buried naked, wrapped only in paper, or with a strip of calico stretched over the body. Coffins were of the cheapest possible materials and standards of workmanship, made of the thinnest wood, often unplaned, and with a layer of sawdust instead of a lining. Relatives were offered no last look, and no say in when or where burial should take place. The journey to the burial ground was hasty and careless. Pauper graves were dug in land attached to the workhouse itself, or in the most neglected parts of local grounds. The graves themselves could go twenty or more coffins deep, all generously treated with quicklime to hasten speedy re-use. No monument marked a pauper's grave, a number would invariably be the sole indication of the space in which generations of workhouse and parish poor would be laid.[79]

The calculated shabbiness and indignity of the pauper funeral served to enhance the attraction and meaning of the pomp and display undertakers provided for their more fortunate clients. A carefully constructed negative image of the respectable funeral, it provided a simultaneous fillip for economic concepts of respectability, and of social failure. The religion of parsimony[80] deconsecrated the bodies of the poor, and disinherited them from that potential future the leaden coffin and impressive monument so comfortingly assured. Dissection added a penumbra of fear to death on the parish – casting fundamental doubt upon the likelihood that any pauper would reach even the flimsy coffin and the unmarked grave.

Although stress upon upward social mobility had long roots in popular culture,[81] assent to a purely economic notion of respectability was by no means culture-wide. The word 'respectable' was scarcely uttered in radical political circles in the 1830s without a smirk – for it represented the deification of property for which their political opponents stood.[82] Speaking at an Anti-Poor Law meeting in 1837, the great radical orator Richard Oastler ridiculed a description of one of the Poor Law Commissioners as 'a very civil respectable gentleman'. 'I am sure,' he said, 'you have not a pauper in Huddersfield who would not be "very civil" for £800 a year – and you know, that the sum would, at once, make the pauper as "respectable" as the Commissioner'.[83]

Although the prevailing view of what should be deemed worthy of respect was the object of their ridicule, radicals and Chartists – like everyone else – invested death and disposal with immense significance.[84] Though they aimed to glorify and commemorate other values, their funerals shared with the commercial variety the notion of the public exhibition of respect through spectacle, display and magnitude of numbers.[85] This is also true of the funerals provided for friendly society and trade union members.[86] But spectacular funerals were for the working-class the exception rather than the rule. Throughout the nineteenth century – despite the sneers of social superiors – working-class funerals were generally very simple affairs, sufficient rather to mark avoidance of death on the parish than the emulation of social superiors.[87]

These modest funerals were nevertheless a considerable achievement in the face of near impossible odds, and their provision was the source of tremendous anxiety. And this is just as the authorities had intended. Although the available figures are incomplete, they are suggestive. The Anatomy Act appears to have been an important stimulus to the very rapid growth of friendly and burial societies in the decade after 1832.[88] In that year, for example, the Manchester Unity of Oddfellows had 561 Lodges, and 31,000 members; ten years later this had multiplied more than sixfold to 3500 Lodges and 220,000 members.[89]

The promotion of prudential habits among the working classes had been the object of legislation in 1829, and was also the avowed intention of the

New Poor Law administration, so the Anatomy Act cannot have been solely responsible for this effect.[90] Nevertheless, it seems equally unlikely that the growth was uniquely promoted by the New Poor Law, as was asserted with self-satisfaction by the Poor Law Commissioners in their first annual report in 1835.[91] Somerville's complaint of dire corpse shortage, which forms an epigraph to this chapter, shows that in the one full year which fell between the passage of the Anatomy Act and that of the Poor Law (Amendment) Act, the homeless poor – aided by a clement winter – voted with their feet, and found somewhere other than the workhouse to lodge or die.

The mass adoption by the nineteenth-century poor of expedients to avoid death on the parish articulates a defence of decent burial as spirited as the anti-resurrectionist riot, or the fight at the gallows. The variety of strategies involved attests to the diversity of social circumstances of those who feared such an end. 'The desire to secure respectful interment of themselves and their relations, is,' observed Edwin Chadwick in 1843,

> perhaps the strongest and most widely diffused feeling among the labouring classes of the population. Subscriptions may be obtained from large classes of them for their burial when it can be obtained neither for their own relief in sickness, nor for the education of their children, nor for any other object.[92]

Chadwick noted that the anxiety was for 'respectful interment', but refrained from naming or defining the *dis*respect which was so widely feared. The larger and more reliable friendly societies and insurance organisations, which provided sick pay as well as burial insurance, catered mainly for those in regular and better-paid employment. But a large proportion of the poor were excluded from their provisions by seasonality of work and low wages. A variety of burial clubs and societies – of varying reliability – emerged to cater for them. Many were small, local efforts, based on the enterprise of an individual publican or undertaker; while some grew much larger – to have tens or even hundreds of thousands of members. Most of these clubs and societies were sustained by small weekly contributions from a farthing or halfpenny to twopence or threepence, and paid out burial allowances ranging from £2 to £10. The actuarial basis of many of them was so unsound that they eventually ceased business, taking with them the carefully saved deposits of their members.[93]

In his report on urban burial, Chadwick reproduced the text of a typical placard advertising one of these small societies, displayed in a London public house.[94] Such notices were apparently frequently headed 'In the midst of life we are in death'. This one extolled the virtues of the 'United Brothers' and Sisters' Burial Society' which was run jointly by the publican and a local undertaker. The placard suggested that membership would provide alleviation from the unexpected sufferings and anxieties which, in the 'labouring class' might 'crowd about . . . advancing years'.

The notice listed uncertainty of employment, long illness, and want of friends as sources of anxiety when the contemplation of 'that awful change which we must one time or another undergo' arose, as a result of the fear of 'pecuniary burthen' and 'anxiety respecting our mortal remains'. Later observers have suggested that these public house burial clubs – of which there were many – represented an intermediary stage of development between the common practice of passing round a hat in a public house to raise the cost of a cheap funeral, and the bigger societies which often lost sight of their local roots and sociable function.[95]

The precariousness of working-class life in the nineteenth century meant that a spell of illness or unemployment might result in the loss of the entire amount desposited in a friendly or burial society, as a result of lapsed payment of premiums.[96] Lapse rates were high, and many societies depended for their profit upon them remaining so. In some flagrant cases – exposed by a Royal Commission on the subject in the 1870s – societies caused lapses deliberately by withdrawing their collectors from entire districts.[97] More fortunate members of the working class avoided the catastrophe that an accidental or enforced lapse of payment entailed, by saving up a lump sum in good times. The advantage of this form of saving was, as one observer stated to Chadwick, that it ensured 'under any change of circumstance, a decent burial'. Cases in his own experience had occurred in which

> upon the happening of the death, the party has been found to have
> died at last an inmate of a poorhouse, and destitute of every kind of
> property, save only the little fund appropriated for the purpose I have
> stated.[98]

The intensity of working-class feeling on the subject of decent burial was such that even in cases in which no nest-egg had been accumulated, or through unforeseen vicissitudes burial society deposits had been lost, there were still safety nets of communal action to prevent application to the parish. Probably the best known of these expedients was the 'friendly lead', or 'select harmonic meeting', which by the 1900s – in London at least – seems to have been a speciality of certain trades, particularly costers and cabbies.[99] The 'friendly lead' was an evening of entertainment provided by a person's friends or workmates, usually at a public house, at which everyone present would do a 'turn' – sing, tell a story or a joke – and everyone would pay an entrance fee and/or a donation. Eulogies of the dead would boost the takings. These gatherings could be very large affairs, so the cost of burial would be spread widely, and money left over would go to the family.[100]

A similar sort of gathering was the funeral raffle, which also generally took place in a public house, and involved eulogy and remembrance as well as 'the pleasure of a gamble' for a 'good cause'.[101] An 1890s ballad interspersed with monologue, 'Broken up!' tells the story of an Irish building worker, killed falling from a high scaffold with his hod of bricks. His broken body is reassembled complete – lacking a collar-bone, which another worker is sent back to seek – and his workmates arrange to cover the cost of his funeral, by combining his wake with a raffle:

> But they tell me next Saturday evenin',
> They're arranging a raffle for me,
> When Patsy Malone will be chairman,
> And the vice will be Micky Magee.

> Spoken: It'll be a sort of farewell benefit just to pay my funeral expenses like, and buy a new hod, and then I shan't be able to be there myself. You'll see me there standing with the plate just by the door, there'll be plenty of good songs, one or two good fights, and there'll be an undertaker there waiting for orders. It'll be better than a wake . . .[102]

Disasters of this sort often called forth the printing of a ballad or a commemorative sheet of some sort to sell in order to raise money for surviving family.[103]

The simple logic of lessening the burden of burial costs by spreading them over a large constituency lay behind the most commonly used expedient apart from insurance – neighbourhood, work or pub collections.[104] The women who collected between themselves in a vain attempt to save Polly Chapman from the dissector's knife provide an early example of the adoption of this expedient as a means of avoiding the Act's operation.[105] Indeed, women were often traditional figures in taking round 'the basin' in working-class districts, to within living memory.[106]

Collections such as these depended upon the likelihood that the deceased or their family was well known in a given context – a locality, a trade, or a pub. People who fell through even these large nets were in the worst predicament of all, and the expedients they used bespeak their own desperation. The most frequently mentioned is the keeping of dead bodies for long periods, so that although a pauper funeral was inevitable, the body would be useless to the dissectors. This had been a well-known tactic used to thwart the bodysnatchers in Scotland where communal corpse-safes had been constructed on this very principle before the Anatomy Act.[107]

Public health reformers like Chadwick seem to have been ignorant and careless of the logic which lay behind the storage of corpses for days in overcrowded living accommodation, and revealed their ignorance when they inveighed against it in their many diatribes against the bestiality and moral depravity of the poor.[108] Other observers recognised that poverty, and not depravity, was the reason an uncoffined child might be found 'decently disposed' inside a cupboard in a slum house in London's Gray's Inn Lane, with its little mug marked 'Mary Ann' beside.[109] It is hardly likely that any family would aim to induce decomposition by keeping a body for any time in this way. In most such cases it is likely that collections and other attempts to raise funeral money had failed, and that a desperate position had arisen before the arrival of public health officers with orders to forcibly remove the 'nuisance'. Nevertheless, such families do not appear to have solicited a pauper's funeral until the body was already well dead.[110]

A similar delaying tactic was probably at the back of the increased number of working-class people demanding investigations into the causes of death of workhouse inmates, which in the 1860s resulted in a dire shortage of corpses for anatomy. This may have been a joint result of Wakley's long campaign to expose workhouse mortality to coroners' scrutiny, the *Lancet* Sanitary Commission's enquiry of 1866 into the state of workhouse infirmaries, and the subsequent Royal Sanitary Commission of 1868–9.[111] By this period, middle-class fears could perhaps be more openly expressed, and the *Free Lance* newspaper in 1869 struck an uneasy balance between levity and real disquiet at the prospect of a resurgence of grave-robbery or burking:

> Now this is all very well for 'unclaimed' destitute vagrants, but it won't do for you or me, you know.

> 'Rattle his bones over the stones,
> He's only a pauper whom nobody owns,'

> are lines which were written . . . when 'subjects' were not scarce. To do anything of the kind now would be a mere waste of useful material, and 'wilful waste makes woeful want' as much in 'subjects' as in bread and butter. Moreover it increases our risk, you know. . . . Let the masters of our workhouses and the managers of our prisons do what they can to preserve us from this examination *post-mortem*. They can effect the object by taking care that the 'unclaimed' reach their proper and legitimate destination.[112]

The political strategy of the Anatomy Act forced the poor to provide for themselves or face the consequences. Dissection after death became one of the darker elements in the terrible stigma of the pauper's funeral, and one of the props with which the fear of the workhouse was supported. So potent was the fear of 'the House' that people were induced to starve,[113] to emigrate,[114] to turn to prostitution,[115] even to commit suicide,[116] rather than enter workhouse portals. Advising an uncle to join him in America, emigrant J.F. Bray wrote: 'ANYTHING before an English workhouse'.[117] Desperate fear of death on the parish infected and afflicted the entire working class in the Victorian era. Women faced with the prospect of having to find the price of a funeral became sick with anxiety.[118] Funerals, and even graves, were acquired by hire purchase.[119] Any and every means by which the poor could raise money was pressed into service in the defence of decent burial. The Anatomy Act exacerbated 'the insecurity of lives already precarious'.[120] It rendered agonising the bereavements of the poor.[121]

The strength and breadth of cultural hostility to parish burial, and the extent to which indignity in death proved so powerfully effective an element in the hard-headed enterprise to disgrace death in poverty, are perhaps best evidenced by the persistence of the fear of pauper burial beyond the turn of the nineteenth century. Just before the Great War, burial insurance was considered so essential by the women of Lambeth that the budgets they recorded for the Fabian Women's Group survey *Round About a Pound a Week* show that in the region of *10 per cent* of pitifully meagre incomes were regularly set aside for this purpose.[122] Between the wars, investigators of 'industrial assurance' (as this lucrative branch of the insurance business was known) found:

> the present effect of the pauper funeral is of much greater significance [than social emulation], for its avoidance is considered as a dire necessity, and constitutes the stimulus which drives people to enter life policy agreements however ill they can afford it.[123]

And the fear has survived even the advent of the Welfare State: in 1978 the author interviewed an elderly man from London's Notting Hill, who had recently contributed to a pub collection which succeeded in saving another 'regular' from having a pauper funeral. Asked what he thought was involved, *why* a parish burial should be such an object of avoidance, the man did not know. All he knew, and had contributed towards, was that pauper burials were to be shunned at any cost.[124] After giving a lecture on the subject in the East End of London in the spring of 1986, I was approached by a working-class woman, perhaps in her early forties. She told me that her old mother had recently called all her children together to announce the fact that she had saved up enough money for her own funeral, and went on to tell them all what she wanted done when her time came. Her daughter told me that none of her siblings could make any sense of the announcement, and thought their old mum was dementing. She now understood why her mother had been so insistent about it all: it suddenly made sense.

Pervasive present-day ignorance of the Anatomy Act is the result of a historical silence. It seems to me that this silence has been generated by a threefold effect of the Act itself. One silence is the silence of complicity – assiduously cultivated by the Inspectorate and adhered to by the profession. A further silence is that of acquiescence – of those in wider society who benefited, perhaps guiltily, from the scapegoating of the poor. The final silence goes deeper still.

'What is felt', says George Steiner in *Language and Silence*, 'may occur at some level anterior to language, or outside it'.[125] Working-class people reared since the Great War can recall the strenous imprecations of their own parents never to allow them to undergo disposal as a pauper,[126] and can readily repeat the same contemptuous phrases loaded upon those who failed to move heaven and earth to protect a relative from such a fate.[127] But, when pressed to say why this mode of disposal has been held such an object of fear, they cannot say.

'You didn't want a pauper's funeral . . . it was a kind of failure of your life'.[128]

The full meaning of the pauper funeral has entered the sphere of myth. Though it has a sound grounding in objective truth, the fact of dissection which stands behind its fearsome reputation has become cloaked in silence. Over the course of Victoria's reign, the fact that the misfortune of poverty could qualify a person for dismemberment after death became too intensely painful for contemplation; became taboo. The memory went underground of a fate literally unspeakable.

Bequests of bodies now ensure that the social injustice the Anatomy Act represented before the Welfare State no longer operates. Should any reader wish to bequeath their body to anatomy, information can be obtained from:

HM Inspector of Anatomy,
DHSS,
Hannibal House,
London SE1

APPENDICES

1 Anatomy schools in London, 1826 and 1871
2 Definition of 'claimed'
3 Corpses per student, London area, 1843–1970
4 Parliamentary chronology of Reform and Anatomy Bills
5 Bodies taken under the Anatomy Act: the first ten years' sources

APPENDIX I

ANATOMY SCHOOLS IN LONDON, 1826 and 1871

INDEPENDENT ANATOMY SCHOOLS

1826	*1871*
Great Windmill St	
Little Windmill St	
Webb St	
Dean St	none
Little Dean St	
Chapel St	
Howland St	
Aldersgate St	

HOSPITAL ANATOMY SCHOOLS

1826	*1871*
	Charing Cross
Guy's	Guy's
	King's College
London	London
	Middlesex
St Bartholomew's	St Bartholomew's
	St George's
	St Mary's
St Thomas'	St Thomas'
	University College
	Westminster

Sources: *Report* Appx 14, and MH74/16: 19.7.1871: Letter from Charles Hawkins, Inspector of Anatomy, to all practising schools, to inform them concerning the Amendment to the Act

Note: MH74/12: pp.140–141 lists sixteen schools operating in 1834 omitting Dean Street and Howland Street, adding Blenheim Street, and the following hospital schools: King's College; St George's; University. In addition, two others (apparently independent schools) are unfortunately illegible.

APPENDIX 2

DEFINITION OF 'CLAIMED'

CALCULATION OF FIGURES USED IN FIGURE 2

The *Report*'s Appendix 18 is a Table showing returns of the numbers of people dying in workhouses, or receiving parish funerals, in all London parishes and those of Middlesex and Surrey. It occupies three of the *Report*'s large pages, and is set in small type. Unfortunately it is too large to reproduce here. There are four major errors of calculation in the Table.

1 The first two columns on p.140 total 99 (not 89) and 92 (not 82).
2 Column III on p.142 totals 641 (not 541).
3 The *Report*'s text (p.19) says that 127 parishes appear in the Table, whereas there are in fact 131, showing 128 figure-entries.
4 The Note on *Report* p.142 says that 16 parishes made no return in Column V, and that these are marked by an asterisk. Only 14 are so marked in the Table.

So the figures themselves are slightly distorted from arithmetical inaccuracies. They also suffer distortion from the fact that entries in Column V (parish funerals unaccompanied by relations) do not take account of late 'claiming' as a result of poverty (see my text). In my calculations I have corrected for the former errors, but cannot do so for the latter as a result of lack of data.

Column IV (deaths in the community requiring parish burial) has been ignored in my calculations, as it has no relevance to the definition of 'claimed' and 'unclaimed' bodies in institutions. The 14 asterisked parishes offering no data for Column V have been deleted from my calculations. After these adjustments, the following revised figures are obtained:

I Total Workhouse Dead	II Number of total buried by parish	III Number of total buried by friends	V Number of Col. II not accompanied to parish burial by friends
2872	2351	521	821

These figures have been divided by 114 (the number of parishes submitting complete returns) and multiplied by 47 (14 parishes submitting no entry in Column V + 33 parishes with no entry at all in the Table) to give average figures adjusted for all the 161 parishes from whom returns were solicited by the Select Committee.

		REVISED TOTAL		÷ 114 × 47		ADJUSTED TOTAL
Column I	:	2872	+	1184	=	4056
Column II	:	2351	+	969	=	3320
Column III	:	521	+	215	=	736
Column V	:	821	+	338	=	1159

APPENDIX 3

CORPSES PER STUDENT, LONDON AREA: 40-YEAR TOTALS

Date	First Year Students	Bodies Dissected	Bodies per Student
[1826	?	592	?]
1843–4*	c.270	356	1.3
1883–4	593	553	0.9
1923–4	345	250	0.7
1963–4	1048	232	0.2
[1969–70†	1187	242	0.2]

* – first year for which full figures are available
† – last year for which full figures are available

This table is plotted below:

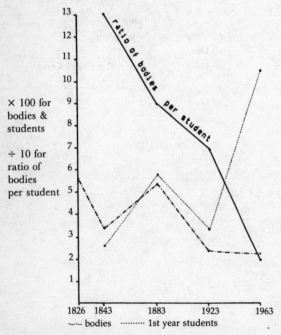

Sources: (1826 figure) *Report* Appx 14
(Remainder) MH74/16: Statistics of Subjects and Students.

Appendix 4

Parliamentary Chronology of Reform and Anatomy Bills

Reform Bill	Date	Anatomy Bill
	1831	
Bristol Reform riots	29/31 Oct.	
Reassembly of Parliament	22 Nov.	
New Reform Bill introduced in Commons: First Reading	12 Dec.	
	15 Dec.	Commons agree to new Anatomy Bill's introduction
	17 Dec.	First Reading
Second Reading	18 Dec.	
	20 Dec.	Second Reading deferred at c.4am.
	1832	
Cabinet minute sent to King asking for creation of peers	13 Jan.	
William IV agrees	15 Jan.	
	17 Jan.	Second Reading deferred again
First committee sitting	20 Jan.	Second reading
	23 Jan.	First committee sitting
	24 Jan.	Commons agree salaries for future Inspectors
22nd (last) committee sitting	10 Mar.	17 deferrals during this period
Commons Third Reading	22 Mar.	
Bill brought up to Lords	26 Mar.	
Lords Second Reading	14 Apr.	
	18 Apr.	Last committee sitting

Government defeated on crucial clause in Lords	7 May	
	8 May	Committee report and amendments read
King accepts Cabinet's resignations	9 May	
Commons motion in support of outgoing Ministers	10 May	
	11 May	Commons Third Reading
Wellington advises recall of Grey	15 May	Lords First Reading
William IV gives Grey authority to create new peers	18 May	deferred twice in this period
Lords Third Reading	4 Jun.	
Royal Assent for Reform Act	7 Jun.	
	19 Jun.	Lords Second Reading
	28 Jun.	Lords debate Cobbett's Petition against
	6 Jul.	Lords committee stage
Reform Act for Scotland receives Royal assent	17 Jul.	
	19 Jul.	Lords Third Reading
	21 Jul.	Commons agree Lords' amendments
	1 Aug.	Royal assent to Anatomy Act
Royal Assent to Reform Act for Ireland	7 Aug.	

Sources: *Commons Journal; Lords Journal; Hansard; Mirror of Parliament*; Brock, M., 1973.

BODIES TAKEN UNDER THE ANATOMY ACT: THE FIRST TEN YEARS' SOURCES

	1832–3	33–4	34–5	35–6	36–7	37–8	38–9	39–40	40–1	41–2
Parishes*	394	349	268	316	365	325	235	213	253	216
Hospitals	135	141	194	206	184	209	156	168	178	110
Hulks	8	58	73	31	39	39	27	58	82	47
Prisons	16	6	15	12	23	21	11	9	14	4
Asylums	5	2	7	9	13	4	6	6	4	1
Dwellings	51	23	25	9	6	4	4	3	0	0

* i.e.: parish workhouses
Source: MH74/16: Inspector's Return, 31.12.1842.

REFERENCES

NOTE

At various points in these references, I recognise that material is either lacking altogether, or, that if it exists I have missed it. Where I am sensible of gaps, I have referred back to this note. If any reader is willing to provide information to help fill these gaps, or to correct mistakes, I would be very grateful if they would contact me via my publishers.

ABBREVIATIONS

B.M.Add.Mss.	British Museum Additional Manuscripts (British Library).
BMJ	*British Medical Journal*
[Chadwick, E.]: 1843	Supplementary Report on Interment in Towns, which Edwin Chadwick produced to accompany the *Report* of the Select Committee on the Health of Towns in 1842.
CJ	*Commons' Journal*
Diary	The manuscript *Diary of a Resurrectionist* (attributed to Joshua Naples), RCS Library, London.
DNB	*Dictionary of National Biography*
Evidence	*Evidence* taken by the Select Committee on Anatomy, and published with its *Report*.
HofC: V&P	*Votes and Proceedings of the House of Commons.*
LJ	*Lords' Journal*
LMG	*London Medical Gazette*
NPU	National Political Union
OED	*Oxford English Dictionary*
RCP	Royal College of Physicians
RCS	Royal College of Surgeons
Report	*Report* of the Select Committee on Anatomy, 1828.
3730	*Address from One of the 3730 Electors of Preston*

HOME OFFICE and MINISTRY OF HEALTH PAPERS at the Public Records Office are listed as call numbers; e.g.: Ho83/1 or MH74/16 each followed by a date or page reference. I have endeavoured to make such references as full as possible, so as to be easily verifiable. Some few items in these files, however, are undated/loose sheets, and cannot be referred to more precisely.

I have simplified folio or column references in manuscripts and in *Cobbett's Weekly Political Register* and *Hansard* by substituting the simpler 'p.' or 'pp.'.

BOOKS are referred to by author and date;
ARTICLES by author and shortened title.
Full references are given in the bibliography.

EPIGRAPHS

Section I: 'The body is a source of great anxiety, derived above all from the fear of death,' *Kern, S.: 1975, p. ix.*

Section II: 'A necessity for doing something cannot be admitted to be identical with a necessity for doing mischief.' *Sadler, M.: 1842, p. 413.*

Section III: 'If you've got nothing, you can't do nothing about it.' *London Undertaker, quoted in Richardson, R.: 'Death in the Metropolis', unpublished 1978.*

INTRODUCTION

1 Dorson, R.M.: 1976, p. 145.
2 See Bishop Hall's aphorism in Southgate, H.: n.d., p. xxxix.
3 Mary Fissell, of the University of Pennsylvania, has produced some fine work on bodysnatching in the Bristol area, as yet unpublished.
4 See Cannadine's excellent 'War and Death, Grief and Mourning', 1981, p. 242.
5 My intellectual debts are many, and will become clear as you read. More personal debts are mentioned in my list of acknowledgments.
6 In their very different ways Thomas Wakley, Michel Foucault and F.B. Smith share the same commitment, and their work has fostered it in me.
7 See, for example: Morley, J.: 1971; Curl, 1972, 1980; Gorer, G.: 1965; Whaley, J.: 1981.
8 I have found short references in the work of Edward Thompson ('Eighteenth Century Society', 1978); Gwyn Williams (preface to Thompson, D.: 1971); R.J. Morris (1976, pp. 101–2), and Ursula Henriques (1979, p. 148).
   Only three papers have been found which address the Act and its social implications as topics worthy of independent historical inquiry: two excellent local studies, Alf Peacock's 'York & the Resurrection Men' and F.K. Donnelly's 'The Destruction of the Sheffield School of Anatomy'; and M.J. Durey's 'Bodysnatchers & Benthamites'. Why the rediscovery of the Anatomy Act should have occurred in the mid-1970s is unclear: Peacock and Donnelly both published in 1975, and myself and Durey in 1976. Each of us seems to have uncovered the story independently. Peacock's analysis is the nearest to my own, though I discovered his work too late to be influenced by it. I recognise his precedence with respect.
9 See chapter 5, note 65.
10 See chapter 5, note 67.
11 See for example, Crowther, M.A.: 1981, p.31. See also chapter 7, note 134.
12 See for example Newman, C.: 1957; Wolstenholme, G. & O'Connor, M: 1966. In a history of the English Health Service (1964, pp. 24–5), Harry Eckstein refers to widespread anxiety concerning death insurance and Poor Law health provision, but seems completely ignorant of the relationship between the two. A footnote summarises the reactions of many such historians: '. . . nothing seemed to hold greater terror for the working-class than the prospect of a "pauper's" burial'.
13 The questionable moral basis of certain bodies of knowledge concerning the human endurance and physique – notably material resulting from German and Japanese experiments on prisoners of war and the inmates of concentration camps – is generally held to cast doubt upon their legitimate uses in our own knowledge systems.

See Foucault, M.: 1979, p. 91: 'What has to be . . . calculated are the return effects of punishment on the punishing authority and the power that it claims to exercise.'

14 Compressed from Moorhouse, H.D.: 'History, Sociology and the Quiescence of the British Working Class', 1981.

15 Storch, R.D.: 1982, pp.10–14.

CHAPTER 1: THE CORPSE AND POPULAR CULTURE

1 Clodd, E. in Gurdon, E.C.: 1893, p. xii.

2 Lonsdale, H.: 1870, p. 108.

3 Law, S.I.: letter to *Northern Star*, vol. 1(5), November 1817, p. 352.

4 Curl, J.S.: 1972, p. 188.

5 See Puckle, B.S.: 1926;
Laqueur, T.: 'Bodies, Death', 1983.

6 Puckle, B.S.: 1926, still provides the best overall guide to the subject, despite his unscholarly approach. Gittings, C.: 1984, gives an idea of the early history.

7 See: Richardson, R. & Chamberlain, M.: 'Life and Death', 1983, and my own unpublished work in the bibliography, particularly 'Death in the Metropolis'.

8 Thomas, K.: 1978, pp. 42–4. My own work substantiates the latter view. See: Richardson, R. & Chamberlain, M.: 'Life and Death', 1983; and my own unpublished work listed in the bibliography.

9 Thompson, E.P.: 1979, p. 3.

10 The debate on the materiality of the mind is more fully dealt with in chapter 4. The *Lancet* advert also propounds interest in what F.B. Smith (1979, p. 337) would call 'rival magic' – the science of phrenology. In the adjacent column is a report of the hurried night burial near Bridgwater of a suicide, Richard Sparke.
See also: Chadwick, O.: 1960, pp. 85–7, concerning fear in 1847 in a Norfolk village that Queen Victoria had ordered the deaths of all children under five – a fear said to have been based on the fact that the Poor Law authorities had decreed 'that all the children in the poor house should be vaccinated'.

11 Burke, P.: 1978, pp. 3–23. See also: Dorson, R.M.: 1968; Morris, R.J.: 1976, pp. 189–90; Thompson, E.P.: 1979.

12 Perhaps because of their own family's upward social mobility, or from having absorbed such beliefs in childhood from household servants. Aubrey ([1686–7] 1881, p. 68) recognised the crucial importance of women and balladry in conserving old tales, beliefs, and past history. See also: Parson Woodforde's *Diary*: (1797) 1949, p. 7.

13 Pugin, A.: 1836–41.
One of Pugin's illustrations is reproduced here – see list of illustrations. See also Pennant's moral outrage at the disgusting state of pauper graves in London (1793, p. 180).

14 Dorson, R.M.: 1968, pp. 81–96.

15 Adams, C.P.: 1975, pp. 6–12; Bushaway, B.: 1982, pp. 1–33; Thompson, E.P.: 1979, p. 4.

16 Rowe, D.R.: 'Folk Life Materials', unpublished, 1979.

17 Burke, P.: 1979; Darnton, R.: 1985; Thomas, K.: 1978; Thompson, E.P.: 'Moral Economy', 1971; Thompson, E.P.: 'Rough Music', 1972.

18 Opie, I. & P.: 1951, pp. 8–9.

19 Lloyd, A.L.: 1969, p.18.

20 Jean & Wattie Quigley interviewed by Doc Rowe, August 1985 unpublished.
See also Ritchie, J.: 'An Account', 1912, p. 285; Bruford, A. & MacDonald, M.: 'Burkers', 1972.

21 Barrick, M.E.: 'Cumberland County', 1979.
The present-day decline of many of the Pennsylvania observances parallels a similar change here in Britain. The perception of a demise of folk culture has, however, long been a commonplace among collectors – see epigraph 3 to this chapter.

22 Clark, D.: 1982, p. 4.

23 Martin Werner (1957, p. 303) observes: 'By this process ecclesiastic Christianity could not truly conquer the paganism of the world in which it lived; rather it absorbed into itself and lapsed itself into it', and cites the veneration of saints and relics as instances of this development. The Venerable Bede records the orders of Pope Gregory to Augustine to take over existing customs, temples, sacrifices, and to christianise them. [I am grateful to Cris Genders for verification of this point.]
See also: Gomme, G.L.: 1908, p. 321; Puckle, B.S.: 1926, pp. 148–50; Thomas, K.: 1978, p. 54.

24 Addy, S.O.: 1895, p. 122; Moss, F.: 1898, p. 24; Pennant, T.: 1774, p. 254; Vulliamy, C.E.: 1926, pp. 51–3.

25 Gittings, C.: 1984, p. 49.

26 Rawnsley, S. & Reynolds, J.: 'Undercliffe Cemetery', 1977.
Barrick, M.E.: 'Cumberland County', 1979 confirms the same development in Pennsylvania.

27 Searches of the Libraries of the Folklore and Antiquarian Societies have so far yielded nothihg. More extensive work in this field, will, I feel sure, turn up such material. See also: Richardson, R. & Chamberlain, M.: 'Life and Death', 1983; and my own unpublished work listed in the bibliography. Please see my NOTE heading the References section.

28 [Chadwick, E.]: 1843.

29 I have referred to all available editions of Brand since 1777, but have found the edition of 1905 edited by Hazlitt the easiest to work with. Other folklore sources are referred to in individual notes, and in the bibliography.

30 Recent research on the subject has been undertaken in different ways and localities by: David Clark, Audrey Linkman, James Obelkevich, Elizabeth Roberts, and myself.
Please see my NOTE heading the References section.

31 Adams, C.P.: 1975, p. 31. For the dressing, viewing, and kissing of the dead during the 1832 cholera outbreak, see Morris, R.J.: 1976, p. 105.

32 For difficulties of interpretation, even of present-day materials, see McKelvie, D.: 'Oral Tradition', 1963.

33 Smith, F.B.: 1979, pp. 336–7.

34 Linebaugh, P.: 'Tyburn Riot', 1977, p. 102.

35   See the excellent discussion of just this point by David Clark (1982, introduction).

36   The transmission of folklore by non-verbal means ['action is a form of knowing'] is affirmed by C.R. Hallpike (1980).
The development and obsolescence of superstitions over time is evident in specific examples: e.g., the superstitions attaching to clocks and mirrors; and in particular, the belief that a missed drill during seed-planting forecast death amongst cattle as well as humans, a belief which – on the advent of the mechanical seed drill – transferred from broadcast sowing. *Choice Notes*: 1858(1), p. 128. A similar adaptation (R.D. Storch, 1982, p. 12, calls the process *mutation*) of a belief to new circumstances may be seen in the case in 1832 of Martha Wright, a Manchester washerwoman, who 'woke in a fright at 5 on a Sunday morning, [having] fancied she heard the rattling of the cholera van, and was instantly seized with diarrhoea.' Gaulter, H.: 1833, p. 193. See reference to the 'death cart', in note 72 below. See also, Dundes, A.: 1965, p. 218; Radford, E. & M.: 1961, p. 40; and Ernest Gellner's review of Hallpike: *TLS* 15.8.1980.

37   Clark, D.: 1982, introduction.
See also, Huntingdon, R. & Metcalf, P.: 1979, p. 87; Hick, J.: 1979, pp. 178–212; Obelkevich, J.: 1979. Death as a rite of passage in Britain is only just beginning to be seriously considered and documented. For a good analysis of the inadequacy of present published material on the subject, see Cannadine, D.: 'War and Death, Grief and Mourning', 1981, p. 242; Clark, D.: 1982, pp. vii–ix. I suspect that a great deal of material – like much of my own work – is on the verge of publication.

38   Gomme, G.L.: 1908, p. 321.

39   See note 37 above.

40   A prolonged discussion concerning the mental imagery of Hell may be found in Walker, D.P.: 1964. Direct prayers and masses for the dead were removed from church liturgy in 1552. (Frere, W.H.: 1901, pp. 630–8). Clare Gittings (1984) provides the best guide to death in the early modern period so far available.

41   For 'occasional conformity' see Smith, A.W.: 'Popular Religion', 1968; Williams, W.M.: 1956, p. 68. Support for my notion of a popular acceptance of spiritual insurance, even in the 'rationalist' Holyoake, see Budd, S.: 1977, p. 118.

42   Addy, S.O.: 1895, p. 124; Baker, M.: 1974, pp. 150–1; Blakeborough, R.: 1895, p. 117; Howlett, E.: 'Burial Customs', 1983, p. 174; Moss, F.: 1898, pp. 27–8; Moody, F.W.; 'Funeral Customs', 1959, p. 33.

43   Brand, J.: [1777] 1905, pp. 252, 614; Addy, S.O.: 1895, p. 124; Peacock, F.: 'Traditions', 1895, p. 331; Baker, M.: 1974, p. 117; Blakeborough, R.: 1895, pp. 150–1; Burne, C.S.: 1883, p. 305; Hole, C.: 1940, p. 51; Howlett, E.: 'Burial', 1893, p. 174; Moss, F.: 1898, pp. 27–8; Moody, F.W.: 'Funeral Customs', 1959, p. 33; *Choice Notes*: 1858(1), p. 121; Porter, E.: 1969, pp. 28, 34. The choice of willow is probably significant.
For material on funeral cakes see: Burne, C.S.: 1983, p. 309; Addy, S.O.: 1895, p. 124; Stevens, C.: 'Funeral Wake', 1976, p. 33.
Funeral cakes had traditional moulds and designs. In Yorkshire up to the end of the nineteenth century these moulds had at their centre the heart

motif, symbolic both of love and of the soul. See Peter Brears' excellent 'Heart Gravestones' paper, 1981.

44 Rowe, D.R.: 'Folk Life Materials', unpublished, 1979.
45 Gittings, C.: 1984, p. 41.
I.L. Sykes reported in 1748 an earlier conversation with Dr Samuel Clarke on 'the superstitious and dangerous mistaken notions in many poor ignorant persons of the Lord's Supper, who are ready to think that the bare receiving the sacrament with some external decency in a sober mood gives them a present title to heaven, just as common titles pass among men by formal conveyances in law; I then mentioning what strange purposes superstition could make this sacrament serve to, when even in St Austin's time we find a woman applying it to cure the blind eyes of her son, he said, it was so still with some among us, and that himself once had great contention with one, who pressed to have some of the remains of the sacramental wine to keep for some medicinal use, as she formerly had (as if the Eucharist were appointed to work bodily cures in a natural way like physic) but he refused . . .' Whiston, W.: 1748, pp. 23–4.
46 Addy, S.O.: 1895, p. 124.
47 Leather, E.M.: 1912, p. 121.
48 Porter, E.: 1969, pp. 26–7.
See also, Brand, J.: [1777] 1905, pp. 550–1; Baker, M.: 1974, pp. 151–2; Dyer, T.F.T.: 1881, p. 60; Hull, E.: 1928, pp. 224–5; Hole, C.: 1940, p. 51; Puckle, B.S.: 1926, p. 69; Radford, E. & M.: 1961, pp. 310–11. For an intermediary custom between sin-eating and doles, see Roberts, P.: 1815, p. 175.
49 For example, Burne, C.: 1883, p. 308 – calls it a 'debasing and repulsive' custom.
50 Brand, J.: [1777] 1905; pp. 550–1; Baker, M.: 1974, pp. 151–2; Dyer, T.F.T., 1881, p. 60; Hull, E.: 1928, p. 225; Hole, C.: 1940, p. 51; Porter, E.: 1969, p. 26; Radford, E. & M.: 1961, p. 311.
51 Jones, E.: 'Psychoanalysis and Folklore', [1928] 1974.
52 Gittings, C.: 1984, pp. 53, 87, 161–4.
53 Gittings, C.: 1984, p. 42.
54 Broadsheet, c.1830, St Bride Printing Institute.
55 Broadsheets, c.1830, St Bride Printing Institute, John Johnson Collection. For a twentieth-century version of this imagery see Stanley Spencer's 'Resurrection at Cookham'.
56 The British Library Department of Printed Books possesses a fine collection of *Ars Moriendi* housed at the British Museum, published mainly in Europe (in Latin, German, French, Catalan and Italian) between the 1460s and 1520s. Caxton's English version has since reprinted, but lacks plates: Holbein Society: [1490] Lond., 1881.
See also Comper, F.M.M.: 1917; O'Connor, M.C.: 1942.
Reproductions of the imagery of the *Ars Moriendi* may be found in Lehner, E. & J.: 1971, plates 125–6.
The visible soul of the *Ars Moriendi* also appears in folklore: Addy, S.O.: 1895, p. 123; Blakeborough, R.: 1895, p. 122; *Choice Notes* 1858: vol. 1, pp. 118–19.
57 The crucial issue is whether the body dissolves in the grave and the soul

acquires a new one at resurrection ('emancipation from the flesh') *or* whether the resurrection is a raising of the actual physical frame buried in the grave at the time of death ('restoration of what has perished': 'Not one hair of your head shall be lost'), Werner, M.: 1957, chapter 11 *passim*. See also Tristram, P.: 1976; James, L.: 1976; Gretton, T.: 1980.

58   Chadwick, O.: 1970–71.

59   F.B. Smith makes the important point (1979, pp. 336–7) that the spread of literacy in the nineteenth century may have conserved old beliefs as much as it propagated new ones, and cites cases of faith in witchcraft and magic from the 1830–60s. These sheets certainly support this view. Survival of these old images could occur simply by printers re-using old wood-blocks; though this one bears an early 19th century engraving style. For the traditional funerary elements in British ballads, see Wimberly, L.C.: 1927.

60   Gomme, G.L.: 1908, p. 276.

61   Smith, F.B.: 1979, p. 337, 'mentally existed in a world quite distinct from Christianity'. Theo Brown (1979, p.22) also observes the existence of two belief systems, and suggests that this post-dates the Reformation. My suspicion is that popular theology was hardly new then, and had probably existed in parallel with mediaeval Christianity, becoming more noticeable after the Reformation when superstition became frowned upon rather than fostered. See Thomas, K.: 1978, p. 75.
     See note 37 above.

62   Burrow, J.: 1985, p. 54.

63   Bourne, H.: 1725, pp. 15–16.

64   This is referred to in the text below, and in note 134 below.

65   Robert Redfield's ideas are discussed at some length by Burke, P.: 1978, p. 24. See also Storch R.D.: 1982, pp. 1–19.

66   Quoted as epigraph to Dave Harker's paper 'May Cecil Sharp be Praised?', 1982.

67   But, see material on the Lyke Wake Dirge which describes the posthumous journey of the soul: Brand, J.: [1777] 1905, reproduces one variant text, as does Walter Scott in his Border Minstrelsy. Several others are recorded at Cecil Sharp House. The singing of the Dirge seems to have been a northern custom, and most versions date from the eighteenth century. It is discussed by: Aubrey, J.: [1686–71] 1881, p. 221; Blakeborough, R.: 1895, p. 123; Hull, E.: 1928, p. 223; Hole, C.: 1940, p. 50; Porter, E.: 1969, p. 34.

68   See Brown, T.: 1979, p. 18.

69   The passage continues: '. . . To them pain and mishap present a far wider range of possibilities than gladness and enjoyment: their imagination is almost barren of images that feed desire and hope, but is all overgrown by recollections that are a perpetual pasture to fear.' George Eliot/Mary Ann Evans: *Silas Marner*, 1861, chapter 1. The novel is set between the 1790s and 1820s.

70   For example, the belief that rain at a funeral signified heaven's grief: Crombie Mss;
     Pennant, T.: 1774, vol. 3, p. 160;
     Folklife Index at Edinburgh School of Scottish Studies, refs: Eii8Ca, Eii8Be & Eii8Bj.

71   For death omens featuring coffin imagery see: Crombie Mss; Bloom, J.H:

1929, p. 44; Hole, C: 1940, p. 49; Peacock, F.: 'Traditions', 1895, pp. 334–5; Porter, E.: 1969, p. 24; Simpson, J.: 1973, p. 96.

For 'winding sheets' see *OED* and: Parson Woodforde's *Diary* (1797) 1949, p. 7; Bloom, J.: 1929, p. 44; Peacock, F.: 'Traditions', 1895, p. 334; Porter, E.: 1969, p. 24.

Sympathetic magic is explained in the text below – see note 105 below.

72 Death omens and their avoidance have a prodigiously large literature: see Brand, J.: [1777] 1905, p. 171; Baker, M.: 1974, pp. 148–9; Bloom, J.H.: 1929, p. 42; Crombie Mss; Dyer, T.F.T.: 1881, pp. 51, 54; Hole, C.: 1940, pp. 48,54; Peacock, F.: 'Traditions', 1895, p. 335; Porter, E.: 1969, p. 23; Radford, E. & M.: 1961, pp. 72,105,127,143; Simpson, J.: 1973, p.96.

See also the stories of 'corpse candles'; the 'death cart'; and the 'death rap', the last of which is used to dramatic effect in chapter 4 of George Eliot's *Adam Bede*.

See also Addy, S.O.: 1895, p. 124; Crombie Mss; Peacock, F.: 'Traditions', 1895, p. 334; Radford, E. & M.: 1961, p. 101.

73 For cures, see Grieve, M.: 1976, introduction, which mentions the herb skullcap (which bears an affinity to the shape of a skull) as a cure for headache. Cures were also believed available for other reasons from the bodies of hanged criminals: Linebaugh, P.: 'Tyburn Riot', 1977, p. 110; Lustig, I.S. & Pottle, F.A.: 1981, p. 39 [Boswell's *Journal*, 7.7.1785].

See also Bloch, M.: 1973; Aubrey, J.: [1686–7] 1881, p. 198.

– warnings: Dyer, T.F.T.: 1881, pp. 50–56.

– afterlife: Folklife Index at Edinburgh School of Scottish Studies, reference numbers Eii8Ca, Eii8Be & Eii8Bj.

– offerings: Crombie Mss.

– avoiding actions, e.g., never shutting a door upon a corpse: Hole, C.: 1953, p. 223; Radford, E. & M.: 1961, p. 128.

See also *Atheneum*, 17.10.1846, p. 1068;

– never shouldering a spade inside a house: Bloom, J.H.: 1929, p. 43;

– avoiding the sight of a dead person in a mirror: Radford, E. & M.: 1961, p. 127;

– never bringing lilac into the house: Simpson, J.: 1973, p. 96.

74 Brand, J.: [1777] 1905, pp. 172, 233; Addy, S.O.: 1895, p. 123; *Atheneum*, 17.10.1846, p. 1068; Baker, M.: 1974, p. 149; Blakeborough, R.: 1895, p. 119; Bloom, J.H.: 1929, p. 144; *Choice Notes*: 1858, vol. 1, pp. 117, 122; Hole, C.: 1940, p. 49; Hole, C.: 1953, p. 222; Radford, E. & M.: 1961, pp. 41, 126–7; Simpson, J.: 1973, p. 97.

75 McKelvie, D.: 'Oral Tradition', 1963, p. 92.

Many old death omens have become attenuated with time, to become indicators of bad luck. Keith Thomas (1978, p. 82) cites as an example the present-day warning of seven years' bad luck attached to the breakage of a mirror.

76 Dyer, T.F.T.: 1881, p. 53.

77 This idea is elaborated in the text below.

78 Details of the corpse's identity and the date and place of the ceremony were usually filled in by hand. Reproductions appear in Lewis, J.: 1962, pp. 149–50.

79 Huntingdon, R. & Metcalf, P.: 1979, p. 13.

80   Huntingdon, R. & Metcalf, P.: 1979, p. 13.
81   Glaister, J.: 1973, p. 116.
     See also Crombie Mss; Bloom, J.H.: 1929, p. 44; Peacock, F.: 'Traditions',
     1895, p. 333; Porter, E.: 1969, p. 23; Simpson, J.: 1973, p. 96.
82   Addy, S.O.: 1895, p. 123.
83   Brand, J.: [1777] 1905, p. 391.
84   Burne, C.S.: 1883, p. 298; Dyer, T.F.T.: 1881, p. 60; Hole, C.: 1940, pp. 51,
     57; Hole, C.: 1953, p. 224; Radford, E. & M.: 1961, pp. 344, 365; Stevens,
     C.: 'Funeral Wake', 1976, p. 40.
85   MacCulloch, J.A.: 1932, p. 90.
86   Glover, J.: 1977, pp. 43–5; Puckle, B.S.: 1926, pp. 23–4.
     The precise definition of death remains a difficulty: Jennett, B.:
     'Determination of Death', 1977; *Lancet* editorial, 1976(2), pp. 1069–70.
87   See note 81 above.
88   Walker, D.P., 1964; Hick, J.: 1979. Martin Werner (1957, chapter 11) says
     this confusion dates from the earliest days of Christianity.
89   Baker, M.: 1974, p. 150; Bloom, J.H.: 1929, p. 47; Hole, C.: 1940, p. 53;
     Hull, E.: 1928, p. 220; Puckle, B.S.: 1926, p. 52; Radford, E. & M.: 1961,
     pp. 75–6; Simpson, J.: 1973, p. 97.
90   For unknown, Newton St Loe churchyard, Somerset – Macmillan, A.S.:
     1924, p. 81.
91   For William Callow of Yarmouth, aged 77 – Cooper, J.F.: Ms. 1827–39.
92   For Samuel Roberts of Yarmouth, aged 48 – Cooper, J.F.: Ms. 1827–39.
93   For Sarah Ann Palmer, of Shalbourne, Wiltshire, aged 46. Extant interior
     church monument – recorded by myself, summer 1982.
94   For James (aged 1 year 10 months), George (aged 1 year), George Charles
     (aged 8 months) and Mary Ann (aged 2 years 8 months) – children of the
     Townsend family of Yarmouth – Cooper, J.F.: Ms, 1827–39.
95   Huntingdon, R. & Metcalf, P.: 1979, p. 81.
96   This paragraph owes a great deal to ibid. pp. 63–4, 78.
     For example, in the curative value of the corpse, see Aubrey, J.: [1686–7]
     1881, p. 198; Lustig, I.S. & Pottle, F.A.: 1981, p. 319 [Boswell's *Journal*,
     7.7.1785]; Linebaugh, P.: 'Tyburn Riot', 1977, p. 110; Smith, F.B.: 1979, p.
     336 – concerning the use of ground skull as an ingredient in folk medicine
     in the Bradford area in 1847.
     Anthropological material used in researching this chapter includes
     Bendann, E.: 1930; Douglas, M.: 1975; Geertz, C.: 1975; Goody, *et al.*:
     1976; Habenstein, R.W. & Lamers, W.M.: 1963; Hertz, R.: 1960;
     Huntingdon, R. & Metcalf, P.: 1979; Rosenblatt, P.C. *et al.*: 1976; Van
     Gennep, A.: 1960.
     See also Blauner, R.: 'Death and Social Structure', 1966.
97   Briggs, K.: 1971, vol. 1b, p. 563.
     See also Finucane, R.: 1982, pp. 148, 160.
98   Richardson, R.: unpublished, 1982.
99   Fletcher, R.: 1974.
100 Gittings, C.: 1984, pp. 62–3.
101 Richardson, R. & Chamberlain, M.: 'Life and Death', 1983.
102 See note 147 below.
103 Numbers 19: 19.

104 Huntingdon, R. & Metcalf, P.: 1979, p. 74; MacCulloch, J.: 1932, pp. 94–5.

105 Hill, C.: 1965, p. 149; Thomas, K.: 1978, p. 225.

106 Aveling, J.H.: [1872] 1967, pp. 6–7; Thomas, K.: 1978, pp. 63, 108.

107 See note 97 above.

108 Brown, T.: 1979, pp. 29, 66, 78.

109 Puckle, B.S.: 1926, p. 111.

110 R.R. interview with Mrs R.D.: Suffolk, 1980.

111 R.R. interviews with Mrs R.D.: Suffolk, 1980; and Mrs F.R.: London, 1980.
    See also: Reeves, M.P.: [1913] 1979, p. 52.

112 Hole, C.: 1953, p. 226.

113 Brand, J.: [1777] 1905, p. 569.
    The *OED* identifies the northern Middle English 'strek' (southern Middle English 'strech') and gives its meaning as 'to stretch'. None of the definitions given include the laying out of the dead, nor is the modern object known as a stretcher identified in any way with the streeking board.

114 Clark, D.: 1982, p. 128.

115 The former posture may have some connection with the childhood truth-telling oath 'cross my heart [and hope to die]' dated as nineteenth century by Eric Partridge (1961, p. 227), recorded by the Opies (1967, p. 121), and which was common currency in my own infant and junior schools, West London, 1950s.

116 Hole, C.: 1940, p. 53; Moss, F.: 1898, p. 19; Peacock, F.: 'Traditions', 1895, p. 333; Radford, E. & M.: 1961, p. 73.

117 See note 78 above.
    Certificates for burial in woollen often feature a similar image.

118 Gittings, C.: 1984, p. 115.

119 Brand, J.: [1777] 1905, p. 250; Puckle, B.S.: 1926, pp. 42–3; Gittings, C.: 1984, pp. 61, 115.
    A parish coffin, of uncertain age, survives at Easingwold, Yorks. It is housed at eye-level in the parish church, and seems to be of solid oak, very large – over six feet long – and extremely heavy. It has a hinged lid, so if it was used as a communal coffin – and its survival outside the grave suggests that this is likely – bodies would have been removed from it at the graveside, and lowered into the soil in their winding sheets. Regarded as an oddity in the 1820s, no local traditions or memories of its use survive. My own feeling, from the weight and style of construction, is that it could be Tudor or Jacobean. I am very grateful to Edith K. Warner, of Easingwold village, for information about the coffin.

120 Brand, J.: [1777] 1905, pp. 114, 251; Hole, C.: 1940, p. 53; Howlett, E.: 1893, p. 168; Radford, E. & M.: 1961, p. 74.

121 Clark, D.: 1982, p. 128; Hole, C.: 1953, p. 226.
    Morley, J.: 1971 reproduces a photograph of a traditional smocked shroud (plate 51). The parallel with sleep is again discernible.

122 For full references to these Acts, please see my bibliography.

123 See previous note, and Brand, J.: [1777] 1905, pp. 249, 664; Baker, M.: 1974, p. 150; Hole, C.: 1940, p. 53; Hole, C.: 1953, pp. 225–6; Porter, E.: 1969, pp. 30–1.

124 Addy, S.O.: 1895, p. 125; Radford, E. & M.: 1961, p. 74.

All four gospels refer to Christ's shroud as linen: Matthew 27: 59; Mark 16: 46; Luke 23: 53; John 19: 40.

125   Addy, S.O.: 1895, p. 124; Radford, E. & M.: 1961, p. 74.
See also Elizabeth Boile's threat to haunt a pawnbroker in Holborn, when he refused to return to her a smock in which to be buried after her execution at Tyburn in 1714: Linebaugh, P.: 'Tyburn Riot', 1977, p. 106.

126   Even today, elderly women in Suffolk have their traditional shrouds ready, with stockings and other articles. I have interviewed a woman who is often asked to help launder them: R.R. interview with Mrs R.D.: Suffolk, 1980.

127   Richardson, R. & Chamberlain, M.: 'Life and Death', 1983.

128   Radford, E. & M.: 1961, pp. 266–7.

129   Clark, D.: 1982, pp. 127–44; Richardson, R.: 'Death in the Metropolis', unpublished, 1978.

130   Rosemary is referred to in *Hamlet*. It seems likely that Shakespeare was referring to an established custom.

131   Addy, S.O.: 1895, p. 124; Bourne, H.: 1725, p. 19; Brand, J.: [1777] 1905, pp. 240, 424, 524–5, 614, 668; Hole, C.: 1940, pp. 56–7; Hole, C.: 1953, p. 224; Peacock, F.: 'Traditions', 1895, p. 331; Radford, E. & M.: 1961, p. 369.

132   For example:

'Sleep on, dear babe, and take thy rest,
God taketh those whom He loves best;
Thy youthful days were sweet to me,
Too soon I was deprived of thee.'

Memorial card to Robert Palmer, aged two months. Supplied by C. Lovegrove, Funeral Furnishing Undertaker, Friar Street, Reading: 1887. Reading Public Libraries.

133   Peacock, F.: 'Traditions', 1895, p. 331.

134   Brand, J.: [1777] 1905, pp. 240, 248–9; Hole, C.: 1953, p. 223; Radford; E. & M.: 1961, pp. 128–9.

135   Pepys' *Diary*, 6.7.1661.
See also Addy, S.O.: 1895, p. 125; Crombie Mss; Dyer, T.F.T.: 1881, p. 61; Hole, C.: 1940, p. 50; Porter, E.: 1969, pp. 26–7, 34.

136   *Evidence* of J. Glennon. Cases were known in which bodies were snatched even in the presence of mourners. See note 143 below.

137   See note 131 above.

138   Catrin Stevens' paper on the funeral wake in Wales [1976] gives a good guide to the history and changing nature of the Welsh Wake. Such research remains crucially necessary for England.

139   This emerges clearly in chapter 6, during discussion of the urban poor's death practices in Edinburgh at the time of Burke and Hare.

140   Dyer, T.F.T.: 1881, p. 60.
A description of a London wake of this type in the early years of the twentieth century from an interview gives a flavour of the event:

Cos there's high tea, there's cockles and there's the watercress, and the celery and all that. And after all the consolation of talks, little arguments start, and there's always a glass of beer to be had. And

there's no love without a song as the time gets on. In fact, as it started
out to be a wake, it ended up as a party . . . The atmosphere down
there was, the King is dead, long live the King.

Quoted in Richardson, R.: 'Traditional modes of coping with grief',
unpublished, 1982.

141   Adams, C.P.: 1975, p. 15; Dyer, T.F.T.: 1881, p. 60; Huntingdon, R. &
Metcalf, P.: 1979, p. 76; Thompson, E.P.: 1979, p. 15; Stevens, C.: 'Funeral
Wake', 1976, p. 30.

142   Stevens, C.: 'Funeral Wake', 1976, p. 30.

143   *The Times*, 29.12.1831. See chapter 5.

144   As far back as the fourteenth century a provincial synod issued a canon
against 'Disorders committed at people's watching a corpse before burial'
threatening excommunication to those who met for other purposes than
simply to offer prayers for the soul of the dead: 'this ancient and serviceable
usage was grown over with superstition and turned into a convenience for
theft and debauchery'. Brand, J.: [1777] 1905, p. 364.

145   Brand, J.: 1810, p. 28; Bourne, H. (1725) 1810, p. 23; Brand, J.: [1777]
1905, pp. 364–5.

146   Crombie Mss; Stevens, C.: 'Funeral Wake', 1976.

147   Gittings, C.: 1984, pp. 105–6.

148   Stevens, C.: 'Funeral Wake', 1976, p. 30.

149   Stevens, C.: 'Funeral Wake', 1976, p. 31.

150   Customs recorded by the folklorists seem almost deliberately to exacerbate
grief in the period immediately after a death: see Richardson, R.:
unpublished, 1982. Both Catrin Stevens (1976) and McCracken,
R.(unpublished, 1979) reach similar conclusions. It seems likely that full
exposure to the fact of death may have worked as a form of prophylaxis
against feelings of denial and disbelief which Lily Pincus (1978) and Colin
Murray Parkes (1975) agree can be a common problem in complications
afflicting those in grief today.
See also Rosenblatt *et al*: 1976, chapter 5; Douglas, M: 1975, p. 56.

151   Richardson R: 'Edwardian Post-Mortem Custom', unpublished, 1978.
See also Williams, W.M.: 1956, p. 228n; Clark, D.: 1982, pp. 128, 135.

152   Condensed from a passage in Enid Porter: 1969, p. 25.
See also, Baker, M.: 1974, p. 151; Hole, C.: 1953, p. 223; Moody, F.W.:
'Funeral Customs', 1959, p. 33; Peacock, F.: 'Traditions', 1895, p. 333;
Brand, J.: [1777] 1905, p. 248; Radford, E. & M.: 1961, p. 343; Stevens, C.:
'Funeral Wake', 1976, p. 40.

153   Willoughby, R.: 1936, pp. 30–31.

154   Peacock, F.: 'Traditions', 1895, p. 333.

155   Richardson, R: 'Death in the Metropolis', unpublished, 1978; Richardson,
R.: 'Edwardian Post-Mortem Custom', unpublished, 1978.

156   'The Unfortunate Fair; or, The Sad Disaster'. Broadsheet c.1800. British
Library. The significance of the captain's first utterance 'take this purse, let
her coffin be lead' goes beyond the expression of a simple desire for a good
funeral: lead coffins were the preserve of the financially fortunate.

157   The same pride has perhaps only been witnessed in our own time in the
cases of prominent figures – i.e.: at the lying-in-state of Churchill and
Mountbatten.

See also Obelkevich, J.: 1976, p. 88.

158   Addy, S.O.: 1895, p. 123; Blakeborough, R.: 1895, p. 121; Burne, C.S.:
       1883, pp. 297–8; Crombie Mss; Dyer, T.F.T.: 1881, p. 60; Hole, C.: 1940,
       p. 51; Hole, C.: 1953, p. 224; Peacock, F.: 'Traditions', 1895, p. 333;
       Radford, E. & M.: 1961, p. 343; Stevens, C.: 'Funeral Wake', 1976, pp. 30,
       40.

159   – dreams: Addy, S.O.: 1895, p. 123; Burne, C.S.: 1883, p. 298; Crombie
       Mss.
       – fear of death: Addy, S.O.: 1895, p. 123.
       – ill-luck: Peacock, F.: 'Traditions', 1895, p. 333; Hole, C.: 1940, p. 51;
       Stevens, C.: 'Funeral Wake', 1976, p. 40.
       – sympathy: Blakeborough, R.: 1895, p. 121.
       – no grudge: Dyer, T.F.T.: 1881, p. 60;
       – strength: Hole, C.: 1940, p. 51.

160   Hole, C.: 1940, p. 51; Radford, E. & M.: 1961, p. 343; Stevens, C: 'Funeral
       Wake', 1976, p. 40.

161   Gittings, C: 1984, p. 109.
       See also Burne, C.S.: 1883, p. 298; Dyer, T.F.T.: 1881, p. 60; Hole, C.:
       1940, p. 51; Hole, C.: 1953, p. 225; Radford, E. & M.: 1961, p. 343;
       Stevens, C.: 'Funeral Wake', 1976, p. 40.
       The idea also crops up in Gothic Novels – see Horace Walpole's *Castle of
       Otranto*, 1765.

162   Origins seem often to be of greater interest to antiquaries and folklorists
       than the reasons for a custom's contemporary survival, or demise. Trefor
       M. Owen rightly calls this a 'backward facing approach'. Folklore Society
       Fourth Katherine Briggs Lecture, 1984.

163   Richardson, R.: unpublished, 1982.
       Thomas Southwood Smith recognised the value of viewing in this respect;
       see his *Lecture over the Remains of Jeremy Bentham*, 1832, p. 66.

164   Jewitt, L.: 1870, p. 380; Radford, E. & M. 1961, p. 41; Thomas, K.: 1978,
       pp. 34, 56.

165   See Wood, W.: 1837, p. 45. The subject is discussed more fully in chapter
       10.

166   *Atheneum*, 17.10.1846, p. 1068; *Choice Notes*: 1858 (1), p. 117.
       See also Obelkevich, J.: 1976, p. 296.

167   Baker, M.: 1974, p. 149; Blakeborough, R: 1895, p. 122; *Choice Notes*:
       1858(1), p. 121; Hole, C.: 1940, p. 49; Radford, E. & M.: 1961, p. 128.

168   Crombie Mss.

169   Puckle, B.S.: 1926, p. 93.
       Mourning and status were, of course, intimately related in the Victorian
       period – see Morley, J: 1971.

170   These are instances of the development of superstitious beliefs and customs –
       possibly at an ascertainable historical period – which sadly were not
       addressed by antiquaries and folklorists. How they developed is not known,
       but their negativity is perhaps indicative of a contradictory or confused
       attitude towards novelty, or perhaps towards symbols of social status.
       See Grabes, H.: 1973, *passim*. I am indebted to Sarah Beckwith for discus-
       sions concerning meanings historically attached to mirrors. Professor J.D.
       Marshall, and the staff of the Victoria and Albert Museum provided

verification of the date/social distribution of clocks and mirrors.

I have in my own collection a seventeenth-century illustration which shows a churchman leading a woman, man and child to regard a mirror, which, rather than reflecting them, shows a skeleton. The illustration bears the caption: 'Watch & pray because you know not the houre' and cites the biblical text 'Facies Nativitatis suae James 1:23' – a text which reads '. . . For if anyone is a hearer of the word and not a doer, he is like a man who observes his natural face in a mirror . . .' The mirror transforms a straightforward reflection into a *memento mori*. See p. 28 above.

171 See chapter 4. For shared medical superstitions in the eighteenth century, see Le Fanu, W.R.: 'English Medicine', 1972, p. 342.
For the decline of ghostlore in the 'articulate' upper classes, and the gap between popular and educated culture in this respect during the same period, see Finucane, R.: 1982, pp. 164–9. But, see Lustig, I.S. & Pottle, F.A.: 1981, p. 325 [Boswell's *Journal*, 1781].

172 Report of Rex v. Cundick, 1822. *Report*, Appx. 22.

173 Puckle, B.S.: 1926, p. 15. Customs which may be seen in this way include the opening of windows and doors at death, the covering of mirrors, the burial of grave-goods and sin-eating.

174 Douglas, M.: 1975, p. 57.

175 *LMG*, 31.5.1828, pp. 792–4.

176 'The Resurrection', Wellcome Institute, London, c.1800.

177 Storch, R.D.: 1982, pp. 1–19.

178 Yeo, E.: 'Robert Owen', 1971, pp. 103–5.

CHAPTER 2: THE CORPSE AS AN ANATOMICAL OBJECT

1 Linebaugh, P.: 'Tyburn Riot', 1977, p. 69.

2 John Abernethy writing in *The Dissector*, Oct. 1827, pp. 25–6.

3 *Lancet* editorial 1829–30(1), pp. 42–5, 3.10.1829.

4 *Lancet* editorial 1832–3(2), pp. 183–5, 4.5.1833.

5 The phrase 'beyond the range of ordinary emotions' is from Youngson, A.J.: 1979, p. 30.
For William Hunter's introductory lecture to students, c.1780 – see St Thomas's Hospital Manuscript 55, p. 182 verso. I am indebted to Marion Bowman, of the Royal College of Surgeons Hunterian Museum, who kindly brought this manuscript to my attention.

6 Harvey, W.: 1961, p. 16.

7 Harvey, W.: 1961, p. 13. Harvey and Southwood Smith (see chapter 7) seem to be unusual in that they both dissected close relatives/friends. In general, the prevailing attitude among anatomists on this question was one of avoidance.

8 Greenhill, T.: 1705; Foucault, M.: 1976.
Cunningham, A.: 'The Kinds of Anatomy', 1975, p. 1 reproduces the first page of notes taken by Alexander Flint, a young medical student attending anatomy lectures in Edinburgh in 1672. The entire page is surmounted by an anatomically doubtful skeleton, whose head supports a winged hourglass, and the legend 'fugit hora'.

9 See e.g., the story concerning Benjamin Franklin, in Haagensen, C.D. and

Lloyd, W.E.B.: 1943, p. 55. For the modern currency of such tales see Smith, P.: 1984, p. 47.

10 My discussion of the history of anatomy owes a great deal to Russell, K.F.: 1963. Interestingly, Copernicus' *De Revolutionibus Orbium Coelestium* appeared in the same year as *De Fabrica*.

11 Harvey's entry in the *DNB*.

12 See note 14 below.

13 Linebaugh, P.: 'Tyburn Riot', 1977, and Plate 14 in the same volume. My discussion of this subject owes much to Michel Foucault's *Discipline and Punish* (1979), particularly to Part One: Torture.

14 The extract is from the Act of Parliament which enacted the union of the Company: Anno 32 Henrici Octavi c.42: An Act concernying Barbours and Chirurgeons to be of one Companie. See Beck, R.T.: 1974, pp. 187–8. See also Vicary, T; 1577, in which the author ('Sargeant Chirurgion to King Henry the Eyght') stresses Galen's emphasis upon 'anatomie': 'For (sayth he) it is as possible for a blindeman to carve and make an Image perfect, as a Chirurgion to worke without errour in mans body not knowing the Anatomie.'
See also Russell, K.F. & O'Malley, D.: 'Tudor Anatomy', 1961.

15 'Ecclesia abhorret a sanguine'. See Finch, E.: 'Medical Education', 1957.

16 Finch, E.: 'Medical Education', 1957.

17 See William Lawrence's discussion of the subject in a lecture printed in the *Lancet* 1829–30(1), pp. 35–6, 3.10.1829. Lawrence asserted that physic and surgery were 'one and indivisable' and attacked the existing division as irrational.

18 Versluysen, M.C.: 'Midwives', 1981; Jean Donnison: 1977.

19 *Report* of the Select Committee on Medical Education, 1834.

20 See Ivan Waddington's series of papers on this subject listed in the bibliography.

21 Gelfand, T.: 'Empiricism', 1970.

22 Gooch, B,: 1767–73. Introduction to volume 2.

23 Young, R.M.: *Animal Soul*. Ms, n.d.

24 This is clear from the text of the 1752 Act 25 Geo II c.37. See my discussion in the text, and Hartshorne, A.: 1891.

25 The history of the legislation is dealt with at some length by Guttmacher, A.F.: 'Bootlegging Bodies', 1935.

26 See Hay, D. et al.: 1977 and Thompson, E.P.: 1975 for discussions of the eighteenth-century criminal code. See also Hopkins, H.: 1985 passim.

27 Rodgers, P.: 'Smugglerius', 1985 dates the event from an artist's eye-witness report to 1775. See also Kemp, M.: 1975.

28 The observer was named Simmons, and the material quoted in Kemp, M.: 1975, is from information collected by Dr Helen Brock from Ms. notes in a copy of Simmons's Life, in Glasgow University Library. Simmons's account is corroborated by the artist John Deare's diary, quoted in Rodgers, P.: 'Smugglerius', 1985. See also Penny, N.: 'Smugglerius', 1986.

29 The process of flaying a corpse in sculpted form was known as 'ecorché' (from the French for 'peeled', 'flayed') and was well known in artistic and scientific circles in Europe during the eighteenth century. The technique was probably inspired by the drawings of Vesalius. The Dying Gladiator

pose was probably chosen as the head is lowered – concealing evidence of distortion to face and neck. See list of illustrations. Kemp reproduces a picture of another such figure, in which it is again worth noticing that the face appears distorted, suggesting that the body used was also that of a hanged criminal.

30 Kemp, M.: 1975, pp. 13–19, 40 and Finch, E.: 1957.
See also: Cross, S.J.: 'John Hunter', 1981; Dobson, J.: 1954, 1969; Hamilton, B.: 'Medical Professions', 1951, p. 157; and *DNB* entries for both brothers.
See also Porter, R.: 'William Hunter' in Bynum, W.F. and Porter, R. (eds): 1985, pp. 7–34.

31 Hamilton, B.: 'Medical Professions', 1951, p. 156, says Hunter was supported in the scheme by Lord Shelburne.

32 See note 30 above.

33 There is an immense literature on this important subject. Note 30 above provides an introduction to it. Marion Bowman, of the Hunterian Collection, Royal College of Surgeons, has given me valuable help on various aspects of the Hunters' careers, and of medical life in the eighteenth century.

34 Abernethy eulogised John Hunter as a man who 'cultivated Physiology, only as preparatory to the still more important science of Pathology'. John Abernethy: 1817, p. 6. For the history of pathological study in this period, see Newsholme, A.: 1927, pp. 49–56. For the European context at this period, see King, L.S.: 1958, pp. 265–82; and Shryock, R.H.: 1948.

35 Reference is made to the Hunters' work on aneurysm below.

36 For William Hunter's professional success see Porter, R.: 'William Hunter' in Bynum, W.F. & Porter, R. (eds): 1985, pp. 7–34. John Hunter was attached to St George's Hospital. With reference to the developing importance of teaching hospitals see Smith, B. Abel: 1964, pp. 16–18.

37 Only the Royal College of Physicians and Caius College Cambridge had similar dispensation. See Cheselden's *DNB* entry.

38 Peachey, G.: 1924, p.8.

39 Hamilton, B.: 1951. This was probably Samuel Sharpe, author of *A Treatise on the Operations of Surgery*, whose tenth edition was published in London in 1782. According to Cunningham, A.: 1975, the earliest recorded school of anatomy in London was that of a Dr Connors, in 1697.

40 Peachey, G.: 1924, pp. 30–40.

41 Hamilton, B.: 'Medical Professions', 1951.

42 See Rowley, W.: 1795. The most consistent and effective forum for such calls for reform was Thomas Wakley's *Lancet*, founded in 1823, which attracted vicious criticism and hostility among the medical and surgical elites. Dr Betty Bostetter has undertaken the immense task of writing a much-needed biography of Thomas Wakley, and has been a sincere friend and colleague to me in the writing of this history. No work of mine, or hers, however, can substitute for a reading of the *Lancet* itself to convey the flavour of the period, and the personality of its founder editor. Until Dr Bostetter's book is published the main sources for Wakley's life are: Wakley's *DNB* entry; Brook, C.: 1945, 1962; Sprigge, S.S.: 1897.

43 Margaret Pelling, in her *Cholera, Fever and English Medicine* (1978) says of

this era: 'The methods, content, and style of evaluation of English Medicine were inadequate, unsystematic, antiquated and corrupt . . .' p. 12. For the poor standard of English medical education see Smith, F.B.: 1979, p. 347; *LMG*, vol. 1, 1827–8, pp. 314–6; Rose, M.: 1981, pp. 38–40; Christison, R.: 1885–6, p. 193; Singer, C. & Holloway, E.A.: 1962, p. 17. It is important to note, however, that the impetus for reform came from within the profession. From at least the 1790s, the Company of Surgeons was unpopular among its membership. Hamilton, B.: 1951, p. 157.

See also Rowley, W.: 1795; Aesculapius: 1816. Recent historians' work in the field of medical reform include: Smith, F.B.: 1979; Singer, C. & Underwood, E.A.: 1962; Smith, B. Abel: 1964; Pelling, M.: 1978; Durey, M.: 1969; and Kennedy, A.E.C.: 'The London Hospitals', 1966.

Ivan Waddington's work listed in the bibliography provides useful material on the entire problem. He calls the conflict between the hospital consultant-orientated College and the general practitioners a 'structural tension within the profession'. Waddington, I.: 'General Practitioners', 1977, p. 182.

See also [Anon]: *An Address*, 1829, p. 14; Armstrong, J.: 1825.

44 Rowley, W.: 1795, p. 10 says that this eventually reached government consciousness only through the appalling levels of surgical mortality among British soldiers fighting in the American War of Independence. Even so, it was not until 1835 that a parliamentary Select Committee was established to investigate.

Oliver MacDonagh's remarkable book, *The Inspector General*, is a partial biography of the humanitarian Sir Jeremiah Fitzpatrick, whose problems with the Army Medical Board in the years 1795–1802 prefigure those of Florence Nightingale by fifty years. Medical ineptitude and negligence led to desperately high mortality among Anglo-Hanoverian soldiers. MacDonagh mentions the figure of a 30 per cent mortality, in one part of the war – 90 per cent of which was caused by illness unconnected with battle (1981, pp. 183–4).

The 'discovery' of surgical ineptitude provides an interesting parallel to that of widespread malnutrition amongst the poor during recruitment for the Boer War. See Anna Davin: 'Imperialism and Motherhood', 1978.

45 Gibson, J.: 1967, pp. 26–7. See also Smith, B. Abel: 1964, chapter 1, *passim*.

46 Bishop, W.J.: 1960, pp. 118–19.

47 Ellis, H: 1969.

48 Wells, L.A.: 'Aneurysm', 1970, pp. 411–24. William Hunter had encouraged his brother John to study under Cheselden in 1749.

49 Youngson, A.J.: 1979, pp. 22–41.
    For a comparison of death rates before and after the introduction of antisepsis, see Spencer, H.R.: 'Ovariotomy', 1957, pp. 188–99; Bishop, W.J.: 1960, p. 175.
    See also F.B. Smith's discussion of its impact (1979, pp. 272–4).

50 An early anatomy/operating theatre survives at St Thomas' Hospital, London, and is now a museum. For Darwin's description of the Edinburgh operations, see Darwin, F. (ed.): 1892, pp. 11–12.

51 South, J.F.: 1886, p. 129.

52   Surgical wards in public and charity hospitals were, according to
      Haagensen, C.D. & Lloyd, W.E.B.: 1943, p. 23: 'veritable forcing houses
      for sepsis'. They list the four diseases which together came to be known as
      'hospital diseases' from their comparative epidemic rarity elsewhere;
      erisypelas, pyaemia, septicaemia and gangrene. These diseases collectively
      caused countless working-class deaths in such institutions.

53   Liston, R.: 1837, introduction.
      See also Bishop, W.J.: 1959, pp. 42–3.

54   Liston, R.: 1837, p. 1.

55   See note 42 above.

56   J. Wardrop's evidence to the Select Committee on Medical Education,
      1834.

57   See note 42 above.

58   Brook, C.W.: 1945, pp. 43–4; 1962, p. 8; Macilwain, G.: 1853, vol. 2, p.
      254; Rose, M.: 1981, pp. 15–16, 58. Sir Astley Cooper's defence of his
      familial relationships at Guy's and St Thomas's may be found in his
      evidence before the Select Committee on Medical Education in 1834.
      Wakley's position was that: 'the system of nepotism that prevails in the
      distribution of patronage at our charitable institutions is foul and stinks to
      heaven. Human life is sacrificed to it; medical science is sacrificed to it; the
      character and respectability of the profession are sacrificed to it'. Brook,
      C.W.: 1962, p. 14.
      See also Brook, C.W.: 1945; 1962, p. 9 and Wakley's *DNB* entry.

59   Wakley had himself studied at the United Hospitals, and had been a near
      contemporary of Edward Grainger. Grainger had suffered severely as a
      result of the operation of the patronage system at the United Hospitals, and
      it is likely that the younger man had absorbed some of his distrust of the
      surgical hierarchy through his contact with one of its victims. Brook, C.W.:
      1945; 1962, and Wakley's *DNB* entry (as well as Sprigge) record that
      Wakley was taught by Grainger. Dr Bostetter believes this not to be the
      case. For Grainger, see Millard, A.: 1825.
         Sir Astley Cooper's deep resentment against Grainger stemmed from the
      personal history and social origins of the two men. Grainger did not
      originate from an affluent background, but was a very able anatomist. He
      was refused the job as Sir Astley's dresser (surgical registrar) not because
      he lacked ability, but because he did not possess sufficient funds to pay Sir
      Astley's customary courtesy fee. Perhaps in consolation, Sir Astley
      encouraged him to open an anatomy school in Birmingham. Instead, in
      1819 Grainger opened up just across the road from Guy's and was
      immediately popular among the students. Of course Grainger didn't have
      the advantage hospital anatomists possessed of obtaining bodies at a
      discount from their hospital mortuaries, so, to be sure of his own supply, he
      offered higher fees to the bodysnatchers, breaking the Anatomy Club's
      united front against them. For this, Astley Cooper never forgave him.
      Grainger died young, and his less controversial brother Richard
      subsequently took over the school.
         The best source for the social context of anatomy in the vicinity of Guy's
      at this time is Ann Millard. Her husband had been porter at St Thomas's,
      and took home stories from work. When he died in prison after having been

caught preparing for a bodysnatching expedition in the hospital graveyard, his wife – angry that he had not received Sir Astley's protection – spilled the beans. She is usually ignored or dismissed as a vulgar hysterical woman, but her account has a ring of truth about it – she incriminates her husband as well as Sir Astley Cooper. The detail is so precise, and conforms so closely to other observers' comments (where these are known) that I am inclined to believe her in preference to the rather weak dismissals of her allegations, which ring now not only of social but sexual condescension. Ann Millard shows the underside of Sir Astley Cooper's gentility, giving more than a glimpse into the corrupt world Wakley so ardently wished to reform.

60 Abernethy ordered the lights to be extinguished during one of his lectures so that Wakley would be denied his shorthand writer's notes. They were, in fact, being obtained from William Lawrence, another radical surgeon, employed at St Bartholomew's as Abernethy's assistant, with private access to his papers. Brook, C.W.: 1962, p. 7. Ignorant of Wakley's informant, and having failed to circumvent him, Abernethy attempted to curtail publication of lectures by recourse to law. In this he was supported by other hospital surgeons, who feared *Lancet* publication of their lectures would both diminish income from students who would read rather than pay to attend lectures, as well as expose their shortcomings to the public gaze. See Wakley's *DNB* entry.

61 *DNB*, and Brook, C.W.: 1962, pp. 7–8.
    Wakley had in fact completed publication of the lecture series, and made it clear that he had no intention of reprinting it: his pages had 'already been obscured with [Abernethy's] hypothetical nonsense during six tedious months', when he read the proofs of the final paragraph, he 'felt relieved of the most intolerable incubus'. Brook, C.W.: 1962, pp. 7–8.

62 Quoted in Poynter, F.N.L.: 1964, p. 148.
    It is worth noticing the distinction in meaning in this passage between the words 'people' and 'public'. Brian Abel Smith points to a similar distinction between 'patients' and 'public' (1979, p. 6). See also Williams, R.: 1976.

63 *Lancet*, 1829–30(2), p. 179, 1.5.1830.

64 Banks, A.: 1839.

65 Smith, B. Abel: 1964, pp. 18–19.
    See also Christison, R.: 1885–6, pp. 174–5, on undeserved knighthoods.

66 Figlio, K.M.: 'Sinister Medicine', 1979, p. 59.
    For persisting inequalities in health provision, see the *Report* of the DHSS Research Working Party on Inequalities in Health [The Black Report], 1980.

67 The poor standard of country doctors was commented upon by Warburton in Parliament, *Hansard*, 11.4.1832, p. 316. Later in the century, however, when Simon and others endeavoured to investigate differential mortality in surgical operations, they used country doctors as an epidemiological sample, and found that in terms of outcome they were much more successful than the metropolitan surgeons operating in hospitals.
    See Sir James Simpson's *Complete Works* (1871), vol. II: Hospitalism. Simpson uses figures calculated by Simon in 1867:

Of 2089 amputations in hospital practice, 855 died – 1 in 2.5.

Of 2089 amputations in country practice, 226 died – 1 in 9.

Relative skills may have been unimportant in the result: most of the deaths were caused by infection. Simpson commented: 'the man laid on an operating theatre in one of our surgical hospitals is exposed to more chances of death than the English soldier on the field of Waterloo' (p. 291). See also Lambert, R.: 1963.

68   Probably the most famous example is Princess Charlotte, who was heiress to the throne when she died in childbirth in 1818. Starved and bled to death, the poor woman probably died of exhaustion, although a complication of porphyria may have been responsible. See Macalpine, I. & Hunter, R: 1969, pp. 240–46. One of her accoucheurs later committed suicide. See *DNB*: Richard Croft.

69   Smith, F.B.: 1979, p. 274.
      Waddington, I.: 'The Role of the Hospital', 1973, pp. 218–19.
      For such operations upon the poor, see Gutteridge, T.: 1851, pp. 19–20.

70   Smith, F.B.: 1979, pp. 273–5.

71   Smith, F.B.: 1979, p. 274.

72   See cartoon: 'Essay on Modern Medical Education: Actual Practice' – etching by W. Heath, printed in the *Glasgow Looking Glass*, vol. 1(8), 17.9.1825, p. 3. [George, M.D: 1954, cat.no. 15069.]
      Roy Porter quotes Henry Fielding's observation that 'a physician can no more prescribe without a full wig, than without a fee'. ('William Hunter', 1985, p. 29) which may explain the practitioner's appearance in the cartoon. See also Paul Pry's 'A Few Illustrations for Mr Warberton's Bill', published May 1829. [George, M.D.: 1954, cat.no. 15777.] For reproductions of these cartoons, see pp. 96 and 220.

73   See Smith, B. Abel: 1964, title for chapter 2; Shryock, R.H.: 1948, p. 43; Poynter, F.N.L.: 1964, pp. 200–1; Gutteridge, T.: 1851, pp. 19–20.

74   Waddington, I.: 'Medical Ethics', 1975.

75   Smith, B. Abel: 1964, pp. 1, 23.
      See also note 52 above.

76   The sampler is reproduced in Brockbank, M.: 1952, p. 57.

77   See cartoon: 'Essay on Modern Medical Education: Practical Results: At Home' – etching by W. Heath, printed in the *Glasgow Looking Glass*, vol. 1(8), 17.9.1825, p. 3. [George, M.D.: 1954, cat. no. 15069.] For a reproduction of this cartoon, see p. 45.

78   Smith, B. Abel: 1964, p. 50.

79   The Cooper v. Wakley case generated a great deal of newspaper coverage. Both sides subsequently published their own versions of events, which effectively cover the basic points of each argument, and the events of the trial. See Cooper, B.B.: 1829; Wakley, T.: 1829.

80   Ellis, H.: 1969, p. 4; Gibson, J.: 1967.

81   Russell, K.F.: Introduction to Harvey, W.: 1961, p. 3.

82   Ellis, H.: 1969, pp. 68–9.

83   Original emphasis.

84   Rose, M.: 1981, p. 58, says that Thomas Hodgkin's *post-mortem* examination of Pollard's body cast doubt upon Lambert's report. Although appreciative of Hodgkin's probity, I am inclined to follow Wakley who felt that

Lambert's report explained Cooper's difficulties, which would otherwise
have remained inexplicable. Moreover, however 'objective' Hodgkin may
have wished to be, he was unwillingly placed at the crux of divided loyalty:
he worked for Sir Astley Cooper in Guy's Hospital Museum, and had been
all but nominated to the post by the baronet, one of his referees.
See Rose, M.: 1981, p. 50.

85   Brook, C.W.: 1945, p. 55.
86   Brook, C.W.: 1945, p. 58.
87   Wakley, T.: 1829, p. 2.
88   Versluysen, M.C.: 'Midwives', 1981, p. 33. See also Donnison, J.: 1977.
89   Golding, B.: 1819; Millard, A.: 1825.
     See also Smith, B. Abel: 1964, chapter 1, *passim*.
90   Versluysen, M.C.: 'Midwives', 1981; Donnison, J.: 1977.
     Both authors, and Roy Porter who also deals with the subject ('William
     Hunter', 1985, pp. 286–7) refer to the important work by Jewson, N.:
     'Medical Knowledge', 1974.
91   Versluysen, M.C.: 'Midwives', 1981, p. 33.
     See also Weiner, P.P.: 1973, vol. 2, p. 401: 'Down to the later nineteenth
     century, the hospital was predominantly a place for indigent patients, who
     were not under the personal care of a particular physician, but became
     'material' for observation and charitable treatment.' The passage goes on
     to mention the high mortality of Louis's experiments on poor pneumonia
     patients in Paris in the 1820s. See also Jewson, N.: 'Medical Knowledge',
     1974; Donnison, J.: 1977.
92   Wakley, T.: 1829, p. 128, mentions that 200 students watched the
     operation upon Pollard.
     South J.F.: 1886, p. 129, describes the inadequacy of the view in such
     places, and the jostling and fighting that went on among the students. See
     the *Lancet*, 1830–31(1) p. 286, 20.11.1830; pp. 317–18, 27.11.1830 for an
     exchange of letters on the propriety of students smoking in the operating
     theatres at St Bartholomew's.
93   Poynter, F.N.L.: 'Medical Education', 1968–70, p. 239.
94   'A public hospital or dispensary, is a theatre where the performer has to
     satisfy at once the general spectator, and the critics of the green room – the
     crowd to whom his display is addressed, and those behind the scenes, who
     are really conversant with his duty'. *LMG*, vol. 3, 1828–9, p. 293.
95   See passage by John Bell quoted in Wakley, T.: 1829, p. 2.
96   The *Glasgow Medical Journal*, vol. 2, 1829, pp. 335–6, reports such an
     operation done with great ease and excellent outcome on a man of 64, by
     Mr Lizars of Edinburgh. Two calculii were removed, one the size of a
     pigeon's egg at the time of the original incision, after which the patient was
     so tired it was decided to put him to bed. Three days later, when he had
     recovered his strength, a further stone the size of a chicken's egg was
     removed with a scoop.
     See also the *Appendix* to Wakley, T.: 1829.
97   Astley Cooper was a prime establishment figure – his status is more fully
     discussed in chapter 5.
98   Wakley, T.: 1829, p. 130. A modern reader, ignorant of the social relations
     of medicine in the early nineteenth century, would think unexceptionable

the 'Address' presented by the founders of the Middlesex Hospital Medical School to the Hospital's Board in 1835. Read with an informed eye, this document reveals precisely the motives Wakley vilified. It was reprinted apparently uncritically in the medical school's 150th anniversary commemorative pamphlet in 1985, and reads very differently over twenty-five years after the establishment of the National Health Service.

99 Liston, R.: 1831.
Liston also seems to have been one of the few authorities on surgery in this period to exhort readers to pay attention to a patient's state of mind/feeling as well as to the circulation and digestion. Most surgical writers at the time seem to have regarded the patient's psychological state as irrelevant to outcome. Liston's criticism of medical attitudes places him, with Wakley, at the forefront of the medical reform movement. His concern for his patients' experience of surgery caused him to be one of very first surgeons to use anaesthetics in Britain.

100 Throughout the medical literature I have read for this history, I have been struck by an apparent conflict in process throughout the late eighteenth and early nineteenth centuries, concerning whether medicine had the status of a science, an art, or a craft, or all three. Bentham calls it an 'art-and-science' (manuscript letter to Peel dated 27.3.1826), and a passage in Bransby Cooper's account of his case against Wakley (1829, p. vi) also seems to hold them jointly: 'by the improvement of art and cultivation of science'. On the other hand, Gooch refers to 'the Medical Art', (1767–73, vol. 3, p. xiii). I have no reason to believe that the debate ends in the 1830s. R.H. Shryock says of Hunter that he 'found surgery still a mechanical art, and left it an experimental science' (1948, p. 58). It certainly seems to me that 'art' is the older view, and that the desire to see medicine as a 'science' is associated with the desire for upward social mobility evident in the profession over the period on which I've been working. The debate and the repeated assertions of scientificity which emerge in the 1820s have something to do with public image as well as professional self-image. See Sadler, J.: 'Art & Science', 1978.

101 Versluysen, M.C.: 'Midwives', 1981; Donnison, J.: 1977.

102 Brock, R.C.: 1952, p. 13; Rose, M.: 1981, p. 17.

103 Gooch, B.: 1767, dedicatory epistle to vol. I. That this state of affairs continued well into the nineteenth century is evident from a Victorian reference to the post of town surgeon as 'surgeon to the Poor Law authority, . . . an ordeal all the medical men in town go through as a high road to better practice'. Quoted in Hennock, E.P.: 1973, p. 188.

104 Pollard's *post-mortem* report reproduced in Wakley, T.: 1829, p. 3.

105 Smith, F.B.: 1979, pp. 250–2.

106 Wakley made a point, during his summing up in court, of referring to the fact that 'not one word' had escaped opposing counsel or his witnesses on Pollard's sufferings. 'No, Gentlemen, they are, for the greater part, hospital surgeons themselves, and they know, too well, what the practices in our hospitals are, and the sufferings the wretched patients are in the habit of enduring at their hands, to feel for this man, or for any other . . . placed in a similar situation!' Wakley, T.: 1829, pp. 133–4.
The position was of course compounded for women undergoing

gynaecological treatment, by the power relations between the sexes. See Versluysen, M.C.: 'Midwives', 1981; Donnison, J.: 1977.

107   For the medical profession's eagerness to disassociate from Wakley and Lambert, see for example: *LMG*, vol. 3, 1828–9, pp. 102–3. Typical examples of Wakley's return fire may be found in the *Lancet* 1828–9(2), pp. 238–42, 23.5.1829 and pp. 306–9, 5.6.1829. Later hostile mention of Wakley appeared in *LMG*, vol. 8, 1831, pp. 605–9. According to Dr Bostetter, Lambert was persecuted 'literally to the grave' (personal communication).

108   Sir Astley Cooper's priorities are evident in his exhortations to 'young pupils' to study hard and succeed, because their 'friends have at great expense prepared them for an honourable and lucrative profession'. Cooper, A.: 1839, p. 6.
      For an indication of the variety and volume of surgical experience a major charitable foundation availed, see a report by the Senior Surgeon to the Glasgow Royal Infirmary, A.D. Anderson, of the cases treated in the surgical wards between November 1827 and May 1828. *Glasgow Med.J.*, vol. 1, 1828.

109   Whether or not dissection (as distinct from anatomy) was the basis of medical knowledge was disputed at the time. The debate is covered more fully in chapter 7.
      See also Geison, G.L.: 'English Physiology', 1972.

110   A side-effect of the increase in anatomical teaching, according to F.N.L. Poynter (1964, p. 199) was 'the exaggerated value attached to anatomy, as a result of its one-time importance, which afflicted medical education until quite recently'.
      See also Dooley, D.: 'A Dissection of Anatomy', 1973.

111   The philosophical implications of this depersonalisation/objectification are discussed with great clarity by the philosopher Martin Buber in his essay 'I and Thou', 1956.

112   For the innoculation experiments in 1721 see Le Fanu, W.R.: 'The Lost Half-century', 1972. Mary Wollstonecraft believed poor people in public hospitals were being used as medical guinea-pigs in her lifetime; see her novel *Maria*, 1798. For attitudes of medical men akin to that of Abernethy quoted as epigraph to this chapter, see Poynter, F.N.L.: 1966, pp. 64–5. See also chapter 5.

113   *Lancet*, 1829–30(1), p. 44, 3.10.1829.

CHAPTER 3:   THE CORPSE AS A COMMODITY

1   *Lancet* editorial 1828–9(2), p. 212, 15.5.1829.
2   Anon.: *An Address to the Public*, 1829, p. 7.
3   Linebaugh, P.: 'Tyburn Riot', 1977, p. 71.
4   Linebaugh, P.: 'Tyburn Riot', 1977, *passim.*
5   Linebaugh, P.: 'Tyburn Riot', 1977, pp. 109–10.
    Boswell's diary for 1785 mentions that at a public execution he witnessed '. . . four diseased persons . . . had themselves rubbed with the sweaty hands of malefactors in the agonies of death, and believed this would cure them.'
    [Lustig, I. & Pottle, F.A.: 1981, p. 319.]

6 Linebaugh, P: 'Tyburn Riot', 1977, p. 109.

7 Compare, for example *Evidence* of J.H. Green, Q280–3 with Guthrie, G.J.: 1829, p. 23.

8 Appendix 14 to the Select Committee's *Report*. Figures are also given for 1827, but as they are much less representative, they have not been used in this analysis. It is not known how these figures were reached, or how accurate they in fact were. The figure for 1810 comes from Guttmacher, A.F.: 'Bootlegging Bodies', 1935, p. 362.

9 I thank Mary White of the Shakespeare Birthplace Trust for kindly confirming the wording and spelling of this epitaph for me.

10 Guttmacher, A.F.: 'Bootlegging Bodies', 1935, pp. 358–9. From the tenor of the description of the interest aroused by the arrival of a skeleton from France to Flint's Edinburgh anatomy class in 1672 – six years before the gipsy's disappearance – it seems that at that period, first-hand access to a human skeleton was not a common occurrence. Cunningham, A.: 'The Kinds of Anatomy', 1975.

11 Guttmacher, A.F.: 'Bootlegging Bodies', 1935, p. 362.

12 *Evidence*, Q1280.

13 Millard, A.: 1825, p. 17; Christison, R.: 1885–6, p. 175; *BMJ*, 12.7.1947, p. 67.

14 Hamilton, D.: 1981, p. 152.

15 Linebaugh, P.: 'Tyburn Riot', 1977, p. 77.

16 Anon: *A View of London and Westminster*, 1728, p. 50.

17 Linebaugh, P.: 'Tyburn Riot', 1977, p. 72.
I have not yet located any eighteenth century sale catalogues for auctions of human specimens – but, for example, the sale of the Portland Museum was organised by Skinner & Co in 1786, and sold insect specimens and corals, and some mammal specimens. Manuscript margin notes in the copy at the RCS indicate that one of the Hunter brothers purchased several items.
I consider it very likely that similar auctions for human specimens were undertaken at an earlier date on a less formal basis, behind closed doors. Russell states that known sales of anatomical preparations date from the second half of the century (Russell, K.F.: 1963, p. 33) while Peachey mentions the sale of preparations at the death of John Douglas, of 3 Tun Court, London in 1752 (Peachey, G.: 1924, p. 24). The fact that this date is so early suggests to me that such sales may already have been taking place in the first half of the century. Russell & Peachey mention later eighteenth century sales.

18 Peachey refers to adverts and counter-adverts of extra tuition offered by competing anatomists in London in the 1740s. Peachey, G.: 1924, pp. 8–12. See an advert for the sale of skeletons in *The Dissector*, no. 9, 1.12.1827. 'Just arrived, four handsome skeletons'. Speaking of the resurrectionists who gave evidence to the Select Committee on Anatomy, Wakley observed that they had behaved as 'coolly as if they were regular dealers in hardware or calico'. Cited by Dr Betty Bostetter in her forthcoming biography of Wakley.

19 Linebaugh, T.: 'Tyburn Riot', 1977, p. 71.

20 Rowley, W.: 1795. Titlepage.

21 Personal communication with Stephen J. Cross (Cross, S.J.: 'John Hunter', 1981).
See also Day, W.M.H.: 'A Visit to the Tombs', 1948 – which indicates that in the Bristol area this mode of procurement was current, at least among

apprentices, virtually until the passage of the Act. Mary Fissell's work on bodysnatching [1986] in Bristol seems to confirm this.

See also Buchanan, G: 'On the Effects', 1855 – which suggests the same went for Glasgow.

22 Dopson, L.: 'St Thomas', 1949.
   A comparison of this gang's mode of work with Naples's entries (see for example, note 58 below) suggests that summer dissection in the private schools in London developed between 1795 and 1811.

23 See note 16 above.

24 Dopson, L.: 'St Thomas', 1949.

25 *Evidence*, Q93. A comparison of this description with the reference to Page below (concerning a theft from Newington parish dead-house) shows that Cooper had been accustomed to higher charges.

26 *Evidence*, Q949.

27 Lizars, A.J.: 1822–6 (Part 9, 1825); Christison, R.: 1885–6, p. 180; Cooper, B.B.: 1843, p. 373.

28 Astley Cooper discussed the use of bodies for this purpose in his evidence to the Select Committee, *Evidence*, Q12.

29 His precise height is the subject of debate, but his skeleton in the Hunterian Collection at the RCS is seven feet seven inches tall.

30 Guttmacher, A.F.: 'Bootlegging Bodies', 1935, p. 366.

31 *Catalogue* of the Hunterian Collection at the RCS London.
   The undertaker evidently got paid handsomely from both sides.

32 *Evidence*, Q776.

33 The bodysnatcher (who was identified only with the initials 'AB') was not asked to elaborate upon what other outlets there were for the corpses he supplied. See text below for discussion and Dopson, L.: 'St Thomas', 1949. I return to the subject in chapter 4.

34 For the gang see note 50 below. Cooper, B.B.: 1843, p. 413. Later in life, Bransby Cooper records that Naples 'destroyed his constitution' with drink. See Cooper, B.B.: 1843, p. 420.

35 Skegg, P.D.G.: 'Human Corpses', 1975, provides a good discussion of the history of the no-property rule.

36 *Cobbett's Weekly Political Register*, vol. 7(5), 28.1.1832, pp. 257–8. Original emphasis.

37 For the poaching wars see Thompson, E.P.: 1975, and Hopkins, H.: 1985.

38 In 1736, the grave-digger of St Dunstan's Stepney was whipped 'very severely' for selling bodies from the churchyard to a private anatomist. See Linebaugh, P.: 'Tyburn Riot', 1977, p. 71.

39 *The Times*, 22.3.1794.

40 Christison, R.: 1885–6, p. 175; Cooper, B.B.: 1843, p. 357; *BMJ*, 12.7.1947: letter signed 'WMHD'. See also Christison's entry in the *DNB*.

41 *The Times*, 30.3.1832.

42 *Evidence*, Q817.

43 Hill, A.W.: 1958. At about the same time, a leading surgical author declared that in London 'no opportunities are wanting to favour all [anatomical] pursuits'. See Gooch, B.: 1767, vol. 2, p. xv. Gooch's optimism seems to suggest that the second half of the eighteenth century was – as the Hunters attest – a very good time to be working in this field.

44 Harvey, P. (ed): 1969, p. 782.

45 Now just behind Centrepoint, near Tottenham Court Road Underground
    Station. St Giles was almost the scene of a bodysnatching riot in 1723 – see
    Linebaugh, P.: 'Tyburn Riot', 1977, p. 71.

46 Pennant, T.: 1793, p. 180.

47 Walker, G.A.: 1843, p. 24. While undertaking interviews for my MA thesis,
    'Death in the Metropolis', I interviewed an undertaker who assured me
    that in his own experience pauper graves could go 28 feet deep, depending
    on soil type, and the level of the water table.

48 This is discussed more fully in the next chapter.

49 Cooper, B.B.: 1843, p. 351.

50 I follow J.B. Bailey – who published the *Diary* in 1896, with commentary –
    in attributing to Naples the authorship of the *Diary*. The *Diary* is a
    manuscript (never intended for publication), housed in the Library of the
    Royal College of Surgeons, London. Its provenance is unknown, but its
    authenticity is unquestioned. It seems likely that it came into Bransby
    Cooper's possession when he was investigating bodysnatching for his
    biography of his uncle. Where it has been possible to compare Bailey's
    work with other sources, it has usually proved reliable. The diary is
    referred to as the *Diary* is these notes.

51 My knowledge of the lives of the bodysnatchers is largely derived from J.B.
    Bailey's notes on the *Diary*, Bransby Cooper's biography of his uncle, and
    some manuscript notes by Sir Richard Owen, transcribed by Jessie Dobson
    in the 1960s, and housed in the Library of the Royal College of Surgeons,
    London. Bransby Cooper uses much of Owen's material verbatim, and
    where differences have arisen between them, I have generally preferred
    Owen's testimony, as the primary source. Information on the London
    graveyards is mostly obtained or confirmed by Isabella Holmes'
    manuscript *Notes* on the *Diary*, and from her book *The London Burial Grounds*,
    1896.

52 See Appendix 1: Anatomy Schools in London.

53 See Appendix 1: Anatomy Schools in London.

54 *Diary*: entry for 17.1.1812.

55 This was probably a common arrangement – see Cooper, B.B.: 1843, p.
    374. The ground was referred to as 'Harp's', according to Isabella Holmes,
    probably Harpur's Fields, another name for the ground belonging to St
    George's Hanover Square, from which Sterne was supposed to have been
    snatched. Two streets near Theobald's Road bear the name 'Harpur'.

56 According to Isabella Holmes' Ms. *Notes* on the *Diary*, probably at
    Horsleydown.

57 This is said to have been practised among the less scrupulous
    bodysnatchers. Bailey, J.B.: 1896 – note to 7.8.1812 entry.

58 Bailey, J.B.: 1896 – note to 24.8.1812 entry.

59 Anon.: *Address to the Public*, 1829, p. 7. It is customary for Jews to bury their
    dead within twenty-four hours of death.

60 Cooper, B.B.: 1843, p. 351.

61 Cooper, B.B.: 1843, p. 352.

62 Cooper, B.B.: 1843, p. 351.

63 *Evidence*, Q50.

64 *Evidence*, Q51.
65 *Lancet*, 1829–30(2), pp. 50–52, 10.4.1830. See below for discussion on the social origins of dissected bodies.
66 There seems to have been some question as to how long the patient had in fact survived the operation: compare Cooper, B.B.: 1843, p. 403 with a letter from T. Madden Stone in the *Medical Times*, 24.3.1883, p. 343.
67 *Medical Times*, 24.3.1883, p. 343. Letter from T. Madden Stone.
68 *Medical Times*, 24.3.1883, p. 343. Letter from T. Madden Stone.
69 Cooper, B.B.: 1843, pp. 385–7; Medicus: 1829, p. 13.
70 *Voice of the People*, 5.2.1831.
71 *Medical Times*, 24.3.1883, p. 343. Letter from T. Madden Stone.
72 Cooper, B.B.: 1843, p. 389.
73 Cooper, B.B.: 1843, p. 382; see also note 59 above.
     Mary Fissell's work on bodysnatching in Bristol has revealed a case where this expedient was successfully used over a long period at a workhouse infirmary. Fissell, M., unpublished, 1986.
74 Cooper, B.B.: 1843, p. 390.
75 See note 17 above.
76 This is discussed more fully below.
77 Cooper, B.B.: 1843, p. 406.
78 See Brookes' own account which appears as Appendix 19 to the Select Committee's *Report*.
79 Cooper, B.B.: 1843, p. 406.
80 *Evidence*, Q30.
81 Porter, R.: 'William Hunter' in Bynum, B.F. & Porter, R. (eds): 1985.
82 I owe this observation to an unpublished term-paper by Hilary Fine, 1980.
83 See note 60 above.
84 Sir R. Owen manuscripts.
85 The words are those of the London burker Bishop, according to the confession attributed to him in the *York Chronicle*, 8.12.1831. Naples's *Diary* refers to several occasions on which an exhumed body was found to be in too late a stage of putrefaction for sale to the anatomists; in such cases, only the 'canines' (bodysnatchers' slang for sets of teeth) were removed. Five guineas seems to have been a typical fee. See entries for 8.8.1812, 28.8.1812 and 28.11.1812. Teeth extracted from the bodies of the dead also probably formed a valuable part of the regular 'perquisites' of para-medical attendants in public institutions, such as hospitals and prisons. In the mid-1820s a case came to light in which it was alleged that, when they collected her body for burial, the family of a young woman who had died in the Middlesex Hospital had found all her teeth extracted. See Millard, A.: 1825, p. 57.
86 Cooper, B.B.: 1843, pp. 399–400.
87 That is, £1.50 sterling. For the wages of the urban and rural poor, see Burnett, J.: 1979.
88 *Diary*, entry for 10.10.1812.
89 The Lambeth bodysnatchers were paying five shillings per corpse as hush-money to gravediggers in the 1790s. See Dopson, L.: 'St Thomas', 1949.
90 Cooper, B.B.: 1843, p. 435. Cooper goes on to mention that in the process

of researching his uncle's *Life*, he interviewed a bodysnatcher who told him that 'nearly one of his first acts in the business brought him into possession of £38, when he belived he had never before had £5 in his hands'.

91 *Report*, p. 8.

92 Sources of information contained in the table and in my discussion are given in note 51 above.

93 Brodie, B.C.: 'Observations', 1832. Certainly Brodie's analysis seems to have been correct for the life of Crouch. According to Bransby Cooper, his hotel at Margate failed because the means by which he had acquired his capital became known. After this failure, Crouch returned to London and was noted by Owen to have been 'deeply connected with thieves', after frequenting the public house he had formerly used as a resurrectionist. Cooper describes a similar failure in Millard's unsuccessful attempt to run a restaurant in the Borough. Cooper, B.B.: 1843, pp. 440–6.

94 Millard, A.: 1825, pp. 28, 56.

95 It is difficult to place Sir Astley's precise status in a social matrix which included the younger sons of the aristocracy, and self-made nabobs. The social complexion of the Committee and the manner in which Astley Cooper emphasised his own gentility is discussed in chapter 5.

96 With reference to eighteenth-century loss of deferential attitudes, especially in those operating outside the law, see Hay, D. *et al.*: 1977, p. 132.

97 Sir R. Owen Manuscripts. This information was overlooked by Cooper, B.B.: 1843, p. 413.

98 All these treatments, which corpses have undergone in the cause of anatomy, appear in items to which reference is made in these notes or in the bibliography. See for example: *LMG*, vol. 1 (1827–8), pp. 794–5; Lonsdale, H.: 1870, pp. 60–61; Cooper, B.B.: 1843, p. 356; Dopson, L.: 'St Thomas' 1949; Latona case: Bickerton Papers.

99 The bodies of each of the people named here were found to have been stolen from the churchyard of St Nicholas, Yarmouth, in December 1827. Cooper, J.F.: Ms, 1827–1839. I discuss this episode at some length in chapter 5.

CHAPTER 4: THE SANCTITY OF THE GRAVE ASSERTED

1 *Lancet*, editorial, 1829–30(2), p. 50, 10.4.1830.

2 *LMG*, 1827–8(1), p. 672.

3 Cooper, D.D.: 1974, pp. 6, 21; Linebaugh, P.: 'Tyburn Riot', 1977, p. 67. This movement from public to private realm is dealt with by Michel Foucault in *Discipline and Punish*, 1979.

4 Lonsdale, H.: 1870, p. 50n.

5 Linebaugh, P.: 'Tyburn Riot', 1977, pp. 102–5.

6 Linebaugh, P.: 'Tyburn Riot', 1977, pp. 102–5.

7 Linebaugh, P.: 'Tyburn Riot', 1977, pp. 102–5; Cooper, D.D.: 1974, p. 6; Lonsdale, H.: 1870, pp. 49–51.

8 But, see Linebaugh, P.: 'Tyburn Riot', 1977, p. 104 – case of John Hayes.

9 *OED*.

10 *Sheffield Iris*, 10.2.1835, p. 4. See also Medicus: 1829, p.10.

11 *Lancet*, 1827–28(2), pp. 659–63, 23.8.1828.

12 *Lancet*, 1827–28(2), pp. 659–63, 23.8.1828.

13 Whether repugnance to the dissection of the dead was 'natural', arose from its association with punishment, or from the 'disgusting offence' of bodysnatching (*Lancet*, 1827–28(2), pp. 659–63, 23.8.1828.) was a subject on which the Select Committee heard conflicting views. See chapters 7 and 8.

14 Raphael, B.: 1984; Parkes, C.M.: 1978; Gorer, G.: 1965; Hinton, J.M.: 1967; Pincus, L.: 1978; Ross, E.K.: 1975, 1982; Richardson, R.: unpublished, 1982. See particularly Parkes, C.M.: 1978, pp. 70–71.

15 Parkes, C.M.: 1978, p. 70.

16 See notes 101–14 below.

17 Beverley Raphael, Professor of Psychiatry at the University of New South Wales, and author of *The Anatomy of Bereavement* (1984) endorses my view that normal grief processes would have been (possibly severely) disrupted in cases of bodysnatching (personal communication).
    There would seem to have been several levels of reaction operating:
    – on a religious/superstitious level, the fear that grave-robbery threatened the future resurrection of the soul,
    – that it nullified all the customs/observances which the bereaved had observed prior to burial,
    – that it denied the bereaved any hope of 'togetherness' in grieving at the graveside,
    – that it denied the bereaved the future possibility of themselves, at death, lying in the grave beside the newly dead.
    Such mourners would therefore have been trebly bereaved – bereaved in life, in death, and in the future life.

18 *The Times*, 2.2.1832, p. 6.

19 Quoted in Dopson, L.: 'St Thomas's', 1949.

20 *CJ.*, 1746–47, vol. 25, pp. 274–5.

21 Kensal Green and Highgate cemeteries in London, and the Necropolises of Liverpool and Glasgow were early examples of this process. Morley, J.: 1971. See my forthcoming 'Why was Death so Big in Victorian Britain?'.

22 George Parker: 1781, vol. 2, pp. 144–6.

23 Bailey, J.B.: 1896, pp. 58, 64–5, 165; *Lancet*, 1829–30(2), p. 50, 10.4.1830; Cooper B.B.: 1843, p. 374; *Report*, Q36, Q791–793, Q809, Q810.

24 See Walker, G.A. 1843. When the large new cemeteries were opened in the suburbs, clergy from central London parishes demanded financial recompense for loss of income from their own graveyards. Curl, J.S.: 1980, p. 214. But, see Chadwick, O.: 1970, pp. 326–8 – who says that the compensation given to churchmen in the Acts of incorporation of the new cemeteries were 'unobtainable'.

25 *3730*, 31.12.1832.

26 [Chadwick, E.] Select Committee on the Improvement of Health in Towns, *Supplementary Report on Interments in Towns*, 1843. The Duke of Wellington had *four* coffins when he was buried in 1852. Morley, J.: 1971, p.81.

27 Puckle, B.S.: 1926, pp. 273–5.

28 *Funeral Books of W. Garstin and Sons*, St Marylebone Public Library.

29 *Funeral Books of W. Garstin and Sons*, St Marylebone Public Library.

30   *Lancet*, 1828–9(1), p. 563, 31.1.1829. I am indebted to Dr Betty Bosetter for
     this reference. Wakley seems to have been in agreement with Prof. G.J.
     Guthrie concerning the number of bodies necessary to adequate tuition of
     anatomy. See chapter 3.

31   *Patent No. 1307*: Thomas Wright; for Making and Preserving Metal Coffins,
     1781. Patent Office Library.

32   A ballad was composed about it by Charles Dibden, which sold as a
     broadsheet in the London streets – a copy of which may be found in the St
     Bride's Institute Collection. Another such song is reproduced in Raven, J.:
     1978, p. 180. See p. 82.

33   *Patent No. 4250*: Edward L. Bridgman: Coffins, 1818. Patent Office Library.
     An example of a surviving patent coffin discovered in excavations to clear
     the crypt of St Bride's Church, Strand, was on view there at the time of
     writing.
     See also *LMG*, 1827–8(1), p. 672.

34   *Patent No. 4843*: John Hughes: Securing Bodies in Coffins, 1823. Patent
     Office Library.

35   *Patent No. 5239*: James Butler: Coffins, 1825. Patent Office Library.

36   See *Scottish National Dictionary*.

37   Struthers, J.: 1867, pp. 21–2.
     These mortsafes were still *in situ* in 1985. Greyfriars churchyard was a
     known resort of bodysnatchers in 1714. See Peachey, G.: 1924, p. 12.

38   The philosopher David Hume had a watch set on his grave in 1776; see
     Cohen, R. (ed.): 1965, p. 1. I am indebted to Professor Marcus Cunliffe for
     this reference.
     See also *LMG*, 1827–8, p. 794, 31.5.1828; and chapter 7.

39   See for example, a report in the *Weekly True Sun*, no. 20, 12.1.1834, p. 155, of
     the case of two resurrectionists shot by watchmen set to guard the grave of
     a 'lady' at Rathfarnam. It is worth noticing that this case occurred after
     1832, illustrating that bodysnatching did *not* cease immediately upon the
     Anatomy Act's passage. See also evidence of 'AB' to the Select Committee;
     and note 42 below.

40   Cooper, B.B.: 1843, pp. 379–80.

41   Moss, F.: 1898, pp. 21–2.

42   Watchers' houses survive in some parish churchyards – see, for example,
     the two huts in the churchyard at Warblington, near Havant, Hants, which
     are now listed buildings. The *Aberdeen Evening Express* of 22.7.1967 carried a
     report of one extant at Nigg, Aberdeenshire, and another is recorded at
     Aberlour, Banff, in the *Folklife Studies Index* at the Edinburgh School of
     Scottish Studies. The *Vestry Minutes* of St Pancras Parish churchyard, of
     10.4.1787 show that such huts were sometimes inhabited at parish expense:
     'It was resolved to appoint a proper watch for the churchyard, consisting of
     one man straight through the year, and an additional one in the winter.
     The watchman should have a blunderbuss, a bayonet fixt, with a supply of
     powder and balls, a greatcoat, lanthern and rattle.' I am indebted to John
     Richardson for this extract.

43   A letter from J. Bennet in *Country Life*, 6.10.1977, refers to an extant lamp at
     Mallusk, Co. Antrim. Many churchyards today possess lamps which seem
     invariably to remain unused. It seems likely that at least some of them date

from this era, and that they were erected against the bodysnatchers.

44 See *Scottish National Dictionary*. See James Ritchie's two papers 'Watch-houses', 1912; 'Relics', 1921. Scotland seems to have been particularly rich in this respect, but churchyards in the rest of the British Isles often possess less spectacular examples, and as far as I have been able to discover, England and Wales have so far lacked a Ritchie.

45 Allardyce, J.: 1913, p. 15.

46 Allardyce, J.: 1913, pp. 16–17; Ritchie, J.: 'Relics', 1921, pp. 227–8.

47 Somerville, A.: 1951, p. 24.

48 *Cobbett's Weekly Political Register*, 31.12.1831. According to Hamilton, D.: 1981, p. 152, these vigils were a working-class expedient. See also Taylor, F.: 1916, pp. 40–43.

49 Cooper, J.F.: Ms, 1827–1839.

50 Dopson, L.: 'St Thomas', 1949.

51 Cooper, J.F.: Ms, 1827–1839.
    Other epitaphs commenting upon bodysnatching are reproduced in *Proc.R.Soc. Med.*, vol. 7, p. 212 – but no dates or provenance are offered.

52 *True Sun*, 29.5.1832.

53 In his evidence to the Select Committee (*Evidence* pp. 106–12) James Macartney referred to beatings, attempted drownings, and deaths of bodysnatchers at the hands of enraged Dublin crowds in the 1820s. See also Cameron, C.: 1886, p. 181 and note 70 below.

54 *Evidence*, Q949.

55 Christison, R.: 1885–6, p. 177; *Evidence*, Q1253; *Lancet*, 1829–30(1), p. 704, 20.2.1830.

56 The ease with which a policeman might lose his post may be ascertained from a report in the *Ballot*, 13.3.1831, p. 3.

57 See notes 49 above, and 119 below.

58 Cooper, B.B.: 1843, p. 396.

59 *Evidence*, Q36, Q340–341.
    See also *Medical Times*, 24.3.1883, p. 343.

60 Much of the time, these notions of mutual responsibility provided the basis of a workable system. But if either side showed signs of withdrawing from the arrangement, the reaction of the other could be one of alarm, simply by virtue of the degree of mutual dependence and the hazardous nature of the enterprise. See, for example, Crouch's cutting of corpses (*Report*, Appx 19; *Evidence*, Q957) – an isolated event referred to so many times in the annals of bodysnatching, that it seems to have assumed almost mythical proportions. Compare this with Ann Millard's account of Astley Cooper's treatment of her husband – according to her, because he was suspected of supplying corpses to Grainger, whom Cooper hated. J.F. South's *Memorials* substantiate several elements of her account.

61 *The Times*, 10.1.1832.

62 *The Times*, 19.4.1832.

63 Most gravestones are erected about a year after burial has taken place, to allow for settlement of the earth to take place, so this need not be taken as too fine a measure of relative solvency.

64 This is a chapter title from Rude, G.: 1964.

65 Census returns from 1831 record a local population of 24,553. I am

indebted to the staff of Greenwich Public Libraries for this information.

66 *The Times*, 19.4.1832.

67 Thompson, E.P.: '18th century English Society', 1978; 'The Moral Economy', 1971; 'Patrician Society', 1974; 'Rough Music', 1972; Rude, G.: 1969; Morris, R.J.: 1976; Genovese, E.: 'Moral Economy', 1973; Wells, R.: 'Counting Riots', 1978.

68 See Hopkins, H.: 1985, *passim*.

69 Thompson, E.P.: '18th century English Society', 1978; 'The Moral Economy', 1971; 'Patrician Society', 1974; 'Rough Music', 1972.

70 Darwin, F. (ed.): 1892, p. 22.

71 See note 67 above.

72 *Westminster Review*, 1828–29(10), p. 128.

73 See note 32 above.

74 See Cobbett's comment on the 'free trade' in corpses given as epigraph to my next chapter.

75 The most comprehensive report, from the *Aberdeen Journal*, was reprinted in *Cobbett's Weekly Political Register*, 14.1.1832, pp. 184–7.

76 *Halifax and Huddersfield Express*, 5.5.1832.

77 See the riots already mentioned in this chapter, at Lambeth, Yarmouth, Greenwich, Inveresk; as well as those at Paisley and Manchester discussed in chapter 9.

78 My discussion of elements in the riot, such as the long-standing warning, informed crowd nucleus, popular consensus and nascent demands for redress has been suggested by Thompson, E.P.: '18th century English Society', 1978; 'English Trade Unionism', 1968; 'The Moral Economy', 1971; 'Patrician Society', 1974; 'Rough Music', 1972. See also note 67 above.

79 In the case of food riots, prices were sometimes dropped. See note 67 above.

80 Compare this description with that of the Swan Street rioters carrying a headless corpse through the town, an exposure to public view of the enormity that had been perpetrated. See chapter 9.

81 Thompson, E.P.: 'The Moral Economy', 1971.

82 Genovese, E.: 1973. In this case it is evident that prudence consisted in permitting what they were powerless to prevent, while nevertheless endeavouring to maintain credibility.
See Thompson, E.P.: 'The Moral Economy', 1971, p. 88; Wells, R.: 'Counting Riots', 1978; Dopson, L.: 'St Thomas', 1949.

83 Thompson, E.P.: 'English Trade Unionism', 1968; 'The Moral Economy', 1971; 'Rough Music', 1972; Thompson, E.P. *et al.*: 'Eighteenth century Crime', 1972.

84 Rowley, W.: 1795, titlepage.

85 A rare instance is to be found in *Cobbett's Weekly Political Register*, 7.7.1832, p. 39.

86 A good example is provided in *LMG*, vol. 1, 1827–8, p. 793.
See also note 11 above.

87 Young, R.M.: 'Animal Soul', unpublished, n.d.

88 Oxonian: 1820. The subject generated a pamphlet literature. See for example: Lawrence, W.: 1832; Rennell, T.: 1819; Philostratus: 1823. Natural theologians, arguing after Paley for hierarchy in the animal

kingdom and in heaven naturally also accepted and promulgated the view
that hierarchies as rigid were justified in human societies. Abernethy
(1819) understood the political as well as the religious implications of the
debate, and spoke in violent opposition to Lawrence. Wakley, on the other
hand, championed him. Dr Betty Bostetter will be dealing with the debate
in her forthcoming biography of Wakley.

O. Temkin provides a good discussion of the Lawrence controversy in
'Basic Science', 1963. See also Stinson, D.: 1969.

89 Lawrence was quite aware on what grounds he was under attack, and
    replied in kind. See note 98 below.

90 Rev. M.D..s, *Lancet*, 1828–9(1) p.6, 12.12.1828. Dermott's lecture had
    appeared in the *Lancet* on 11.10.1828. See also Dermott, G.D.: 1830. A Dr
    Ryan in the *Lond. Med & Surg. Jnl.*, July 1829, asserted that mind and soul
    were one and the same. For a historical discussion of the problem, see Hall,
    T.S.: 1969; Peacock, A.: 'Soul and Brain', 1982, pp. 83–98.

    For the eighteenth-century attempt to locate the soul in the 'sensorium
    commune', see Wright, P. & Treacher, A. (eds): 1982, p. 77.

91 The *Lion*, vol. 3, March 1829, pp. 426–7. The comment is doubly ironical,
    in that Taylor *was* himself a priest. An odd figure – trained surgeon and full
    priest in the Church of England – Taylor had been indicted for atheism in
    1827, and attended his trial in full canonicals. He had served a year's
    sentence. See his *DNB* entry.

    See also Weiner, J.: 1983, p. 139, 36n.

92 Oxonian: 1820; Rennell, T.: 1819. Nicholls, the eighteenth-century
    surgeon/anatomist was a 'militant agnostic'. Peachey, G.: 1924, p. 60. See
    also previous note.

93 Aesculapius: 1816, pp. 55–65 offered a rather confused notion of precisely
    which God was responsible. For a less problematic statement of the
    argument that dissection revealed the Creator's handiwork and thus served
    as a refutation of atheism, see *LMG*, vol. 1, 1827–8, p. 793; *LMG*, vol. 9,
    1832, p. 790; Lizars, A.J.: 1822–6, preface to part 9.

94 Stinson, D.: 1969, p. 27.

95 Philostratus: 1823, pp. 113–14. The promulgation of silence – even of an
    embargo on thought – on the subject, is explicit in Richard Todd's warning
    to his students in the opening lecture at a London anatomy school, of the
    'danger of forming any speculations upon the intimate nature or essence of
    life, or as to its source or origin'. Todd, R.B.: 1832.

96 Most medical defences of dissection were not involved in its legitimation
    other than by self-reference.

97 Similar observations could be made concerning the modern equivalents of
    these manuals.

98 William Lawrence, quoted in *The Dissector*, no.8, November 1827, p. 252.
    Lawrence's actual words concerned the absurdity of 'the very idea of
    resorting to this low and dirty source for a proof of so exalted and refined a
    truth' as the soul. In his opinion, 'an immaterial and spiritual being could
    not have been discovered amid the blood and filth of the dissecting room'.
    Lawrence argued: 'the theological doctrine of the soul, and its separate
    existence, has nothing to do with . . . physiological questions'. 'These
    sublime dogmas could never have been brought to light by the labours of

the anatomist'. Lawrence, W.: 1822, p. 7.

99 Guthrie, G.J.: 1832, pp. 3–6.

100 Thompson, E.P.: '18th Century English Society', 1971, p. 115, says that rumours were 'often based in a shallow soil of fact', an observation which is confirmed in all the cases of riot discussed in this chapter.

101 Original emphasis. Millard, A.: 1825, p. 14. Oblique substantiation is offered for the words in upper case. See also *Punch*, 1841, vol. 1, p. 184 for the irreverence of medical students.

102 Peachey, G.: 1924, p. 30. The model, called the 'New Figure of Anatomy' was created by Mr Chouet, surgeon, and was exhibited at the premises of Mr Lamark, surgeon, in Orange Street, Leicester Fields, London, in 1733.

103 Lonsdale, H.: 1870, p. 101. See also chapter 6 for Burke's confession; 'Echo of Surgeons' Square: 1829, p. 8. Dr Betty Bostetter informs me that an undated fragment of a letter survives from Robert Liston to Wakley which adds an interesting dimension to this story. According to Liston, he saw Mary Paterson's body in Knox's rooms and immediately suspected foul play. He knocked Knox down after an altercation in front of his students – Liston assumed that some students had slept with her when she was alive, and that they should dissect her body offended his sense of decency. He removed the body for burial. Liston was certainly an outspoken man, and such an act would not have been out of character. Wakley received the letter in London, shortly after the Select Committee's last hearing. According to fairly reliable chronology, Mary Paterson was murdered on 9 April 1828. The Select Committee's last hearing was on 23 May 1828. It is unlikely that a letter would have taken quite so long to arrive from Edinburgh, if it had been a fresh body which Liston interred. So Liston's story and Burke's confessions may be complimentary, rather than contradictory, as they at first might appear. The letter is important, as it contains evidence of Liston's suspicions of Knox long before Burke and Hare were exposed, and of Knox's awareness of others' doubts concerning his sources. It seems tragic that neither Liston nor Wakley blew the whistle on Knox's complicity in murder, before burking was finally discovered six months – and eleven further murders – later.

104 See Millard, A.: 1825, p. 14.
Pisanus Fraxi: 1877, p. 415, gives an eye-witness account of a case of corpse-profanation at St Bartholomew's Hospital, London, c. 1830.

105 'The Resurrection, or an internal view of the Museum in Windmill Street, on the Last Day'. Wellcome Institute, London.

106 *York Chronicle*, 17.11.1831.

107 Letter dated 2.12.1818 from Dr John Cheyne to Sir Edward Percival, reprinted *BMJ*, 16.1.1943, p. 74. See also Malcolm, J.P.: 1802–7, vol. 4, p. 358, who reprinted an entry dated 28.2.1615 from the register of St Martin's Ludgate: 'Buried an anatomy from the Co[mpany] of Physicians'. Malcolm commented: 'this entry may serve as an useful hint to some surgical or medical reader, who may learn from it that their predecessors disposed of the remains of a fellow creature in a decent and proper way'. Malcolm seems to have been inferring that burying dissected remains was being neglected by his own contemporaries. It seems worthy of notice that

the seventeenth-century anatomists did not give the body they so kindly buried an identity.

108 Cooper, B.B.: 1843, p. 593.
109 Medicus: 1829, p. 9.
110 Quoted in the *True Sun*, 20.4.1832. According to Medicus (1829), human remains from dissection rooms were 'cast away as mere filth, or given as food to animals'. See also *Political Anecdotists*, no. 3, 2.7.1831: 'The Anatomical Department of King's College will be situate nearest the Thames, for the greater facility, it is supposed, of "feeding the fish" '. One wonders whether John Hunter's arrangement to receive for dissection all the wild animals dying in the Tower Menagerie (Dobson, J.: 1967) was thus reciprocated.
111 Dopson, L.: 'St Thomas', 1949. For the belief that dissected human remains were treated as manure, see Roberts, S.: 1845, p. 13; Crowther, M.A.: 1981, p. 31.
112 Lonsdale, H.: 1870, p. 83. Quite what would have occurred in a badly-conducted dissecting-room, was left to his readers' imagination.
113 Peachey, G.: 1924, p. 42 quotes William Hunter's imprecations to his students of the need for silence out of doors.
114 Christison, R.: 1885–6, pp. 192–3. I have found no other such reservations expressed by members of the medical profession during the era of the Anatomy Act's inception. Christison's work did not appear in print until both he and Cullen were dead.
115 As far as I have been able to discover, none of the major medical figures – from Abernethy and Astley Cooper to Wakley – left their own bodies for dissection. Millard, A.: 1825, p. 15; Guthrie, G.S.: 1832; *Lancet*, 1831–2(1), pp. 664–6, 4.2.1832.
   But, see also chapter 7 for cases in which members of the medical profession did show willing.
116 *CJ*, vol. 77, p. 237, 22.4.1823.
117 Letter from 'Erinensis', *Lancet*, 1828–9(1), p. 777, 21.3.1829.
118 *Lancet*, 1829–30(2), p. 50, 10.4.1830.
   See also *Report*, Appx 19, p. 143.
119 Sentences handed down to the Aberdeen rioters compare very favourably with, for example, those of convicted Swing rioters. Anatomy riot cases were also reported more leniently in the press. See Harry Hopkins's *Long Affray* (1985, *passim*) for the vicious punishments meted out to poachers.

CHAPTER 5:   FOREGONE CONCLUSIONS

1 Henry Hunt: *3730*, 31.12.1832.
2 William Horsley: Open letter to Henry Warburton dated December 1828. Reprinted in *Cobbett's Weekly Political Register*, 28.1.1832, pp. 270–4.
3 *Cobbett's Weekly Political Register*, 28.1.1832, pp. 267–9.
4 *CJ*, 22.4.1828, p. 260. See note 71 below.
5 Cooper, B.B.: 1843, pp. 407–8.
   The medical historian Charles Newman, for example, dates the Burke and Hare murders to 1827 and says that 'the addition of murder to the public nuisance and the professional scandal was at last enough to rouse the

authorities. A Parliamentary Committee was set up in 1828 to investigate the teaching of anatomy and the provision of material, under the Chairmanship of Henry Warburton . . .' See Newman, C.: 1932, p. 39.

6   Smith, T.S.: 1832, p. 33.
    The two papers written by James Ritchie in 1912 and 1921 cover only the physical remains of this public vigilance surviving in one district (Aberdeenshire) nearly a hundred years later. His catalogue is evidence of an active and general public desire to thwart the bodysnatchers.

7   *Evidence*, pp. 113–14.

8   Cooper, B.B.: 1843.

9   For substantiation of Wakley's view, see the evidence of J. Carpue, Select Committee on Medical Education, 1834: *Evidence*, p. 202.

10 Cooper, B.B.: 1843, p. 368 protests that this was not the case, but see *Evidence*, Q951; Millard, A.: 1825, p. 12. A letter from 'Erinensis' which appeared in the *Lancet*, 1828–9(1), p. 775, 21.3.1829, contains the following passage: 'The proprietors of the schools . . . are well known to purchase dead bodies, and to retail them to their pupils at a considerable profit'. For an idea of the fees actually involved, see *Lancet*, 1829–30(1), p. 455.

11 Smith, T.S.: 1832, p. 49; *Evidence*, Q248; *Report*, Appx 19, p. 143.

12 Lizars, J.: 1822–6, preface to Part IX, p. x.

13 Lizars, J.: 1822–6, Part II, p. 11.

14 A touchstone of the social sympathies of those who came to power after 1789.

15 *Report*, p. 4.

16 Cooper, B.B.: 1843, p. 368.

17 Macartney gave evidence that in 1828 at least one man made a living in Dublin by exporting bodies. *Evidence*, Q1279. Violence against bodysnatchers is discussed in the previous chapter.

18 'Robbery of Dead Bodies': Broadsheet, c. 1831/2.

19 *The Times*, 29.12.1831. A similar case was reported in the *Voice of the People*, 3.2.1831.

20 Cooper, B.B.: 1843, pp. 370–2.

21 The anatomist J.F. South more generously likened a resurrectionist gang to a joint stock company: Feltoe, C.L. (ed.): 1884, pp. 98–9. See also Cooper, B.B.: 1843, pp. 369–70.

22 Cooper, B.B.: 1843, pp. 18–20. The claim is repeated many times in the secondary literature.

23 *Evidence*, Q271.

24 Thompson, E.P.: 1963, pp. 174, 217. The Combination Acts had been repealed in 1824.

25 Feltoe, C.L. (ed.): 1884, p. 110.
    A list of members of the 'Anatomical Society' in c. 1810 appears in the *Evidence* Q172, and is reproduced here:

Chair: William Blizard
Members:

John Abernethy,	Charles Bell,
T.J. Armiger,	B.C. Brodie,
Matthew Baillie,	Henry Cline,

Members *(continued)*

Edward Coleman,	Everard Home,
Astley Cooper,	Christopher Pegge,
H.J. Frampton,	John Shaw,
Joseph Henry Green,	Edward Stanley,
John Haviland,	H.L. Thomas,
R.C. Headington,	James Wilson.

Dobson, J.: 1954, p. 37 refers to this organisation as the 'Anatomy Society'. It had been this 'combination' that Grainger's school had broken, much to the chagrin of its members. See n. 59, p. 311.

26 See chapter 4.

27 Cross, S.J.: 'John Hunter', 1981, p. 8; Porter, R.: 'William Hunter', 1985. See also *DNB* entries for Cooper, Abernethy, Brodie, Lawrence *et al.*

28 *LMG*, vol. 1, 1827–8, pp. 672–3; Cooper, B.B.: 1843, p. 408.

29 Cooper, B.B.: 1843, pp. 360, 369.

30 It was probably Naples's deferential attitude which ensured him a job after the Act was passed. See chapter 4.

31 Riots mentioned here which occurred in the spring of 1832 include those at Hereford, Inveresk, Greenwich, Aberdeen, and Paisley.

32 *Cobbett's Weekly Political Register*, 14.1.1832, p. 182, printed a lone voice. See also *Lancet*, 1828–9(1), p. 819, 28.3.1829.

33 Rose, M.: 1981, pp. 72–3.
   See also *Cobbett's Weekly Political Register*, 14.1.1832, p. 182.

34 Feltoe, C.L. (ed.): 1884, p. 103; *Evidence*, Q951, Q,1355–7; *LMG*, vol. 9, 1832–3, p. 268.

35 *Evidence*, Q89–91; Select Committee on Medical Education, 1834, *Evidence*, p. 205.

36 *Evidence*, Q952–5.

37 *Evidence* Q952–5; Millard, A.: 1825, pp. 6–7.

38 See Peel's letter given in the text.

39 Millard, A.: 1825, pp. 24–8; Feltoe, C.L. (ed.): 1884, p. 96.

40 Golding, B.: 1819, p. 225.

41 Feltoe, C.L. (ed.): 1884, p. 96; Millard, A.: 1825, pp. 9,27.

42 Golding, B.: 1819, pp. 225, 244; Feltoe, C.L. (ed.): 1884, pp. 124–5.

43 Millard, A.: 1825, p. 9.

44 Millard, A.: 1825, pp. 8–9.
   This is corroborated by Guthrie, G.J.: 1829, p. 33.

45 Millard, A.: 1825, pp. 6–9. The fate of the sureties paid by these people to the hospital is unknown: Ann Millard says they went towards the building of the hospital anatomical theatres.

46 Millard, A.: 1825, pp. 24–6; Feltoe, C.L. (ed.): 1884, p. 96. Why the London Hospital should have been alone among the metropolitan hospitals in this ability, was pondered at the time. According to Ann Millard, the hospital's higher mortality may have been a contributory factor (1825, pp. 24–6), and in addition, the hospital had a relatively small number of students in attendance

(see *Report*, Appx 14). Brian Abel Smith suggests a more basic cause: the hospital charged no entry fees/securities, it took in the poorest patients – with a higher level of mortality, and a higher proportion of pauper funerals. Smith, B. Abel: 1964, p. 12.

47 *Evidence*, Q1352.

48 Cooper, B.B.: 1843, *passim*; *Evidence*, pp. 14–28.

49 Cooper, B.B.: 1843, pp. 359, 404, 407–8; *Evidence*, Q451, Q115.

50 *Evidence*, Q45, Q73; *Report* Appx 19, p. 144. For Wellington's social disgust of his own soldiers, see also Dinwiddy, J.R.: 'The Campaign against Flogging', 1982.

51 Cited in Cole, H.: 1963, p. 83. Professor Macartney's rebuke came in a letter to a Dublin newspaper which I have been unable to verify independently. See also Crosse, V.M.: 1968, p. 63.

Cooper, B.B.: 1843, pp. 399–402 said that every dentist in London was supplied with teeth from graveyard corpses, and that many of the wealthier classes possessed teeth from the slain in the Peninsular War. An advert on the front page of the *Sheffield Iris*, 3.2.1835 offered natural replacement teeth for the 'Nobility and Gentry'.

52 Field, J.: 'Social Control', 1978, pp. 46–9.

53 Rex v. Davies *et al.* (1828): Lancaster Assizes, 14.3.1828. *Report*, Appx 23; Bailey, J.B.: 1896, pp. 95–8.

54 *Report*, Appx 23.

55 Three cases generally referred to as having been crucial in developing the law on the subject are: Rex v. Young (unreported).

                      Rex v. Lynn (1788).

                      Rex v. Cundick (1822)

See *Report*, p. 6; *Evidence*, Q1154; Burn, R.: 1825, vol, 1, pp. 380–82. For discussion of the legal situation see Bailey, J.B.: 1896, pp. 90–95; Smith, T.S.: 1832, pp. 33–41.

56 *Report*, p. 6.

Rex v. Gill (1828), Liverpool Quarter Sessions, 8.2.1828. See Bickerton, T.H.: 1936, pp. 84–6.

57 *LMG*, vol. 1, 1827–8, p. 638 reported the launch of a subscription fund to help pay the costs of the case. The list of subscribers was headed by Sir Astley Cooper and Sir Henry Halford. See also *LMG*, vol. 1, 1827–8, p. 744.

58 The Committee was elected on 22 April 1828.

The Times reported sentencing on 19 May. Only one day's evidence was taken after this date – see the calendar on p. 13 of the *Report*.

59 See Mill's 'Essay on Bentham' in Leavis, F.R. (ed.): 1971, pp. 47,58. Bentham's *Constitutional Code* which recommended the expedient of dissecting the poor was written at some time between 1820 and his death in 1832. See Bowring, J. (ed.): 1843, vol.2, pp. 628–9. See also Richardson, R. & Hurwitz, B.: 'Bentham's Self Image'. Forthcoming 1987, and Richardson, R: 'Bentham & Bodies for Dissection', 1986.

60 Twenty-two other Select Committees of 1828 have been analysed, with the following results:

[Mean values]	Other 1828 committees	Anatomy Committee
number of witnesses	15.2	40
length of report (pages)	8.2	10
(with evidence & appendices)	132.3	293
days' evidence	6.6	8

61 Burns, J.H.: 1962, p. 3. James Mill was said to have been Warburton's 'chief political instructor'. See Hamburger, J.: 1965, p. 14.

62 *Place Papers*: BM Add. Mss. 27828. Confirmed independently by Dr Betty Bostetter, from other sources.

63 Dr Brian Mawhinney, quoted in a report in the *Guardian* newspaper 20.7.1984 by Julia Langdon, concerning the Select Committee on the Environment.

64 Webb, S. & B.: 1929, p. 72.

65 Brown, L.: 1958; Finer, S.E.: 'Transmission of Benthamite Ideas', 1972. Finer seems to have overlooked the Anatomy Act as being a Benthamite measure.
    See also Aydelotte, W.O.: 'Conservative and Radical Interpretations of Early English Social Legislation', 1967; Cromwell, V.: 'Interpretations of Nineteenth Century Administration', 1966; Hart, J.: '19th century Social Reform', 1965; MacDonagh, O.: 'The 19th century Revolution in Government, 1958; MacDonagh, O.: 1961, 1977, 1981; Parris, H.J.: 'The 19th century Revolution in Government: a Reappraisal Reappraised', 1960; Parris, H.J.: 1969; Roberts, D.F.: 1960.
    A wise discussion of the entire debate is to be found in the final chapter of Oliver MacDonagh's *The Inspector General*, 1981.

66 The phrase is from the title of MacDonagh's 1958 paper.

67 The Anatomy Inspectorate was established when the Act became law on 1st August 1832. See *2 & 3 Gul IV c.75*.
    Djang, T.K.: 1940 – whose focus is the Factory Inspectorate excusably doesn't mention anatomy inspection. J.S. Harris's *British Government Inspection* makes no mention of the Anatomy Inspectorate. and dates the inception of government inspection to 1833, with the Factory Act. (Harris, J.S.: 1955, pp. 7–8). David Roberts (1960, pp. 92–5) perpetuates the misunderstanding by erroneously dating the Anatomy Inspectorate to 1839. Aydelotte follows Roberts ('Interpretations', 1967, p. 226.) Peter Bartrip is unique in dating the 1832 Inspectorate correctly. Bartrip, P.: 'British Government Inspection 1832–1875', *Hist. J.*, 25(3), 1985.

68 Abernethy, J.: 1819. I do not ascribe the idea as original to Abernethy himself. Not only was he an unlikely innovator of ideas, but it seems unlikely that the expedient was not already being discussed in medical circles at the time. His *Oration*, however, is the earliest published work I have so far found which recommends it, apart from two eighteenth-century references in Peachey, G.: 1924, pp. 42, 94–6. The first is from an 'Essay Towards the Improvement of Physic', by the Quaker John Bellers, dating

from 1714; and the second, a letter signed 'Publicus' which appeared in the *Westminster Journal*, 20.12.1746. Both recommended that the bodies of hospital patients be taken for dissection.

69 For the Cooper correspondence, see *Peel Papers*: BM. Add. Mss 40371. Wakley's specific influence on the Anatomy Act is dealt with in Dr Betty Bostetter's forthcoming biography. For the available alternatives to dissecting paupers, see chapter 7.

70 Finer, S.E.: 'Transmission of Benthamite Ideas', 1972.

71 A list of those appointed to the Select Committee appears in the *CJ*, 22.4.1828, p. 260: '. . . a Committee was appointed of Mr Warburton, Mr Secretary Peel, Mr George Dawson, Mr Stuart Wortley, Mr Ronald Ferguson, Mr Spring Rice, Mr Hume, Mr Alderman Wood, Sir James Graham, Sir John Wrottesley, Sir Thomas Baring, Mr Littleton, Lord Nugent, Mr Home Drummond, Mr John Smith, Sir Robert Wilson, Mr Bransby Cooper, Mr Paulet Thompson, Mr Leycester, Mr Protheroe, Mr Hobhouse: And they are to meet To-morrow, in the Speaker's Chamber'. See notes 72 and 104 below. See also Dod, C.R.: 1833; Brown, L.: 1958, p. 13; Dinwiddy, J.R.: 'The Campaign against Flogging', 1982, particularly p. 371.
Thompson, E.P.: 1963, p. 564 discusses the packing and grooming of witnesses (by Place and Hume) of the more laudable Select Committee on the Combination Acts.

72 Judd, S.P.: 1972, entry 1262.

73 Finer, S.E.: 'Transmission of Benthamite Ideas', 1972, p. 21.

74 Visitors to University College will be familiar with Bentham's effigy in its showcase. A forthcoming paper by myself & Dr B.S. Hurwitz deals with this subject in some detail.

75 If I have missed published discussion of these manuscripts, I would be very grateful to hear of it.

76 *Bentham* Mss 11b, 180–3. (Draft transcription by Philip Schofield of the University College Bentham Project.)

77 *Bentham* Mss 11b, 184. (My own transcription.)

78 Personal communication with Dr Alun Howkins.

79 Personal communication with Philip Schofield.

80 *Bentham* Mss 11b, 189–92. (Draft transcription by Philip Schofield.)

81 *Bentham* Mss 11b, 193–5. (Draft transcription by Philip Schofield.)

82 *Bentham* Mss 11b, 220–224. (Draft transcription by Philip Schofield and myself.)

83 Dod, C.R.: 1833.

84 *Hansard*, 22.4.1828.

85 See note 61 above. See also Grote, H.: 1866, 1878.

86 Dr Bostetter's forthcoming biography will discuss Wakley's key role in the struggle against this clause.

87 Had provisions suggested in the first bill for the Act's administration been adopted, the Act would have been a far more efficient piece of legislation that it subsequently emerged. See Section III.

88 Finer refers to the process as 'preselection': see note 125 below. According to Ivan Waddington ('General Practitioners', 1977, p. 167) in 1834 of 6000 members of the RCS, only 200 were purely surgeons – i.e., without any

'general practice' input, not practising physic and/or acting as apothecaries. The seventeen who appeared before the Committee therefore represent a significant proportion of this rather exclusive group. It goes without saying that no woman was asked for her views.

89 This was James Macartney, Professor of Anatomy & Surgery at Trinity College, Dublin. He had come forward to state his belief that the growth of private/independent schools of anatomy was the root cause of the difficulty in procuring bodies. He had worked in London in the 1790s when things had been very different.

90 The resurrectionists were referred to as 'AB', 'CD', and 'FG'. The one who referrred to his own written evidence was 'CD'.

91 Dr Betty Bostetter has·found that Wakley assisted Warburton in framing questions put to witnesses, that when Wakley himself appeared as a witness he was interrogated by Hume, and that Benjamin Harrison was questioned by Warburton himself.

92 *Evidence*, Q143.

93 *Evidence*, Q326.

94 *Evidence*, Q194.

95 *Evidence*, Q779.

96 This suggests that Somerville was instrumental in procuring the witness, 'AB'. Somerville had given his own evidence on the previous day.

97 Although we have no means of knowing whether the seating arrangements enhanced the official atmosphere of the committee chamber, it can hardly be doubted that a working-class man would feel intimidated, as much by the process as the interrogation methods to which he was subjected.

98 See for example *Evidence*, Q812,821.

99 Because magistrates and police had been directed to permit – or at least not to hinder – the supply of subjects for anatomy. See *Evidence*, Q436–7, 1253. See also: Christison, R.: 1885–6, p. 177; *Lancet*, 1828–30(1), p. 704.

100 *Evidence*, Q40.

101 His sarcophagus may be found in Guy's Hospital chapel.

102 Judd, G.P.: 1972, pp. 34–5.

103 Judd, G.P.: 1972, pp. 34–5.

104 These were Sir Thomas Baring, Mr George Dawson and Lord Nugent.

105 Dod, C.R.: 1833; Stenton, M. (ed.): 1976; Burke's *Peerage and Baronetage*, 1980; Burke's *History of the Landed Gentry*, 1965; *DNB*.

106 Judd, G.P.: 1972, pp. 52–3.

107 Judd, G.P.: 1972, p. 48.

108 *Evidence*, Q115.

109 Brock, R.C.: 1952, p. 41.

110 See Warburton's *DNB* entry.

111 Select Committee on Medical Education, 1834. The material generated by this Committee includes an impressive amount of evidence supportive of Wakley's views.

112 Brock, R.C.: 1952, *passim*.

113 *Peel Papers*: BM.Add.Ms. 40390, p. 221.

114 *Evidence*, Q44–6.

115 *Evidence*, Q115–119.

116 *Evidence*, Q443–452.

117   Cooper, B.B.: 1843, p. 407.

118   Cooper, B.B.: 1843, p. 408; *Evidence*, Q444.

119   It is likely that as Chairman of the Select Committee, Warburton would have initiated proceedings.

120   *Evidence*, Q49.

121   Sir Astley was the Committee's first witness.

122   Except Cobbett's – see for example: *Cobbett's Weekly Political Register*, 31.1.1829, pp. 146–51.

123   The stultifying historical influence, especially upon physiology, of the excessive stress upon dissection is shown in Ben-David, J.: 1971, pp. 188–90, Tables 1–3.
      See also Geison, G.: 1978, pp. 18–47.

124   Wakley ridiculed the myth that schools of anatomy aided in discovering the aetiology of disease, *Lancet*, 1831–2(1), p. 481, 31.12.1831. Thomas Hodgkin's *Morbid Anatomy of Serious and Mucous Membranes*, published 1836–40 was based on work done in the 1820s. His biographer M. Rose (1981) considers it to be 'the first attempt to treat morbid anatomy as a separate discipline in the English Medical Curriculum'. Wakley's views on the lamentably low priority given to morbid anatomy are substantiated by Rose, M.: 1981, p. 125. During Hodgkin's absence from Guy's 1836–42, no post-mortems were undertaken. Dr Betty Bostetter attributes this failure to Benjamin Harrison, the powerful Secretary of the hospital, villain of Rose's book. His position is perhaps explained in some oblique way by Mary Fissell's work on the struggles between surgeons and hospital management in Bristol in the later eighteenth century. See Fissell, M.E.: 'Bodysnatching', unpublished, 1986.

125   Finer, S.E.: 'Transmission of Benthamite Ideas', 1972, p. 22: 'What was done for Select Committees could be done, and was done, even more effectively for Royal Commissions. It was equally easy, perhaps easier, to pre-select the witness[es]; even more important was the facility with which the authors of the *Report* could pick and choose among the evidence supplied by them, giving prominence to the views they wished to recommend and suppressing views which contradicted them.'

126   See chapters 8 and 9.

127   See Williams, R.: 1976.

128   *Report*, pp. 9–10.

129   A further instance of leading questioning and apparent grooming of witnesses: *Evidence*, Q61–74.

130   Compare, for example the following: *Evidence*, Q392, 455, 828, 846, 855, 910–916, 1068.

131   See chapters 8 and 9.

132   *Evidence*, Q392.

133   *Evidence*, Q828.

134   *Evidence*, Q910–916.

135   *Report*, Appendices 16, 17, 18 & 24.

136   See the Polly Chapman case in chapter 9.

137   Wade, J.: 1820, 1823, 1831, 1832, 1835. Wade listed all known recipients of State pensions, gratuities, sinecures, etc. His book was widely read and extracts found a wide readership in newspapers and broadsheets during the Reform era.

138   The tables from the *Report*'s Appx 18, and a discussion of the analysis given
      here may be found in my Appendix 2.
139   The 1827 returns are incomplete: compare the *Report*'s Appx 14 with
      Evidence, Q21–22.
140   Somerville, J.: 1832, pp. 11–12.
141   *Lancet*, 1828–9(1), p. 787, 21.3.1829.
142   Godwin, W.: 1809, p. 4 says, with regard to the burial place, 'to the dead
      man (as a dead man) it is indeed a matter of indifference what becomes of
      his body. But to the dead man, if we take into account his nature while
      living, as a creature "looking before and after" and capable of imaging out
      and dwelling upon the things that shall be, it may not be indifferent'.
      Brandon, S.G.F.: 1967, p. 1 says that historically human beings have been
      regarded as different from other species of animal as a result of the
      capability to foresee and contemplate personal demise.
143   *25 Geo II c 37.*
144   Moreover, the murderer would suffer the apprehension only between crime
      – or capture – and punishment; whereas the poor might suffer it for the
      duration not only of their stay in the workhouse, but for their entire lives.
      For the reaction of workhouse inmates, see chapter 9.
145   Guthrie, G.J.: 1829, p. 5. Emphasis added.
146   *Evidence*, Q75.
147   *Evidence*, Q652, 844, 860, 1264–1266.
148   *Evidence*, Q983–4, 1264–66.
149   *Evidence*, Q78.
150   *Evidence*, Q74.
151   *Evidence*, Q60.
152   See discussion above concerning Bentham's correspondence with Peel, and
      draft bill.
153   *LMG*, vol.5, 1829–30, p. 762.
154   The accusation of affectation and disguise concerning the text of the 1st bill
      appeared in the *Petition* from the Worcester Political Union, 7.3.1832.
      Benthamite doubletalk was pilloried by Parson Bull when he translated the
      linguistic meaning of the Poor Law (Amendment) Act thus: 'A Guardian',
      he said, was 'a delegate of the three despots', 'relief' meant 'grief and
      deprivation' and 'relieving officers' were 'men appointed to screw down the
      poor to the last point of endurance'. Bull, Rev. G.S.: 1837.

CHAPTER 6: 'TRADING ASSASSINS'

1   The words 'trading assassins' in my chapter title come from Wakley in the
    Lancet, 1828–9(2), pp. 465–6, 10.1.1829. For their context see chapter 7,
    note 23.
2   *Lancet* editorial, 1828–9(1), pp. 818–21, 28.3.1829.
3   *Ballad on William Burke*, c.1829. Quoted in Macgregor, G.: 1884, p. 291.
4   *Lancet* editorial, 1832–3(1), pp. 243–5, 17.11.1832.
5   Wakley apparently had reasons for a strong suspicion that murder was
    occurring prior to the discovery of Burke and Hare, and that by mid-1828

Robert Liston had shared with Wakely his suspicions of Knox. See p. 327.

6   The chronology of events is as follows:

1828

22 April	Select Committee appointed
23 May	Last evidence taken
22 July	Select Committee on Anatomy Report published
28 July	Parliament goes into recess
1 November	Burke and Hare Murders first discovered
24–25 December	Trial – Hare turns King's evidence

1829

28 January	Burke is publicly hanged, and publicly dissected the following day
5 February	New session of Parliament begins. Hare freed after legal wrangle
11 February	Self-appointment of Edinburgh lay committee of enquiry
12 February	Edinburgh skimmington
12 March	Warburton gains leave to bring in the first bill
21 March	Report of the lay committee investigating Knox's role, and Knox's only public utterance, published together

The chronology of the murders committed by Burke and Hare is problematic, but a comparison of the two confessions (see text) and other sources would suggest the following:

Identity (where known)	Date murdered	Price paid
	1827	
– Joseph (lodger)	mid/late Dec.	£10
	1828	
– Abigail Simpson (salt seller)	12 Feb.	£10
– Englishman (match seller)	?	£10
– Old woman (lodger)	?	£10
– Mary (or Margaret) Paterson (prostitute)	9 Apr.	£8
– Effie (cinder gatherer)	?	£10
– Drunk woman (from police custody)	?	£10
– Old woman and her grandson (deaf mute)	early June	£16
– Woman (killed by Hare alone)	midsummer	£8
– Mrs Ostler (washerwoman)	?	£8
– Ann MacDougal (distant relative of Burke's)	?	£10
– Mary Haldane	?	£8
– Peggy Haldane (Mary's daughter)	?	£8
– 'Daft' Jamie Wilson (local street character/ beggar)	early Oct.	£10
– Mary Docherty (beggar)	31 Oct.	£5

In compiling this chronology, I find I coincide with Douglas, H.: 1974, pp. 133–6. My account of the Burke and Hare murders and their aftermath is

the result of a wide trawl of contemporary(1) and secondary(2) material, in particular, contemporary newspapers, the *Caledonian Mercury, Edinburgh Evening Courant, The Edinburgh Observer, The Scotsman, Blackwood's Edinburgh Magazine*. Also(1): Christison, R.: 1885–6; 'Echo of Surgeons' Square' [pseud.]: 1829; Leighton, A.: 1861; Stone, T.: 1829; [Anon]: *The Story of Daft Jamie*. 1829.
(2): Bolitho, W.: 1926; Bruford, A. & MacDonald, M.: 'Burkers and Resurrectionists', 1972; Cole, H.: 1964; Douglas, H.: 1974; Hamilton, D.: 1981; Lonsdale, H.: 1870; MacGregor, G.; 1884; Rae, I.: 1964; Roughead, W.: 1921; St Clair, R.E.W.: 'Murder for Anatomy', 1961; Tait, H.P.: 'Some Edinburgh Medical Men', 1948; Turner, C.H.: 1932.
I refer occasionally to Burke's 'official' confession and his 'Courant' confession. I explain the distinction in the text. Both were published in the *Edinburgh Evening Courant*, 7.2.1829.

7   *Evidence*, Q903. Astley Cooper implied something similar in his reply to Q40. For Bentham's letter to Peel see chapter 5. Halford was voicing an opinion which had obviously had currency for a considerable length of time in medical circles. Brookes had said as much in writing in 1823 (see *Report*, Appx 19) and Guthrie had warned that dissection might be being used to dispose of murdered bodies in a published open letter to the Home Secretary in 1829 (1829, pp. 25–6). However, Halford put his finger upon the fact that the high prices anatomists offered for corpses might act as a premium for murder.

8   Both men denied any involvement in the resurrection trade. See Burke's *Courant* confession, and Douglas, H.: 1974, p. 89.

9   One of the students was Wharton Jones, who later became Professor of Ophthalmology at University College, London. See Merrington, W.R.: 1976, p. 213.

10   Burke's *Courant* confession. Note Burke's adoption of medical terminology here – using a phrase signifying clinical detachment to distance himself from his victims.

11   Roughead, W.: 1921, p. 65.

12   Royal College of Surgeons Letter to the Home Secretary, reprinted in *Cobbett's Weekly Political Register*, 14.1.1832, p. 188.

13   Medicus: 1829, p. 5.

14   Laying out would have been discernible by the plugging of orifices. Moreover, had the bodies been buried, traditional burial care notwithstanding, they would have been a lot less fresh than these murdered bodies in fact were.

15   All the previous bodies had been destroyed. Burke and Hare had been careful in general to murder itinerants and street folk whose deaths would not be noticed quickly, if at all. Mary (or Margaret) Paterson and Daft Jamie were exceptions, and both were accepted by Knox. See next note.

16   Possession of the body did not aid the prosecution, as the manner of death was not detectably violent. Sir R. Christison was one of the anatomists involved in the autopsy report, see Christison, R.: 1885–6.

17   A verdict available to Scottish juries.

18   Both texts appeared in the *Edinburgh Evening Courant*, 7.2.1829.

19   See note 5 above.

20 The phrase 'asked no questions' appears several times in Burke's confessions. He and Hare seem to have gained temerity from the lack of indications of suspicion on the part of Knox and his staff. The body was that of 'a woman from Gilmerton', a stranger to Edinburgh.

21 'Echo of Surgeons' Square' [pseud.]: 1829.

22 'Echo of Surgeons' Square' [pseud.]: 1829, p. 34.

23 'Echo of Surgeons' Square' [pseud.]: 1829, p. 32.

24 The precise date of the publication of the Echo's pamphlet is unknown. It was advertised for sale in the *Courant* on 29 January 1829, the day Burke was dissected. However, the only accessible copy (in Edinburgh Public Library) mentions Burke's *Courant* confession (on p. 10). This may mean that the author of the pamphlet had access to the confessions prior to their publication on 7 February, that the pamphlet's text was amended after their publication, or that the surviving copy is a revised edition. It is not clear from internal evidence which is the case.

25 'Echo of Surgeons' Square' [pseud.]: 1829, pp. 13–14.

26 'Echo of Surgeons' Square' [pseud.]: 1829, pp. 17–18, 29.

27 'Echo of Surgeons' Square' [pseud.]: 1829, titlepage; and advert in the *Edinburgh Evening Courant*, 29.1.1829, p. 3.

28 Douglas, H.: 1974, p. 138.

29 *Lancet*, 1828–9(1), p. 786, 21.3.1829.

30 *Lancet*, 1828–9(1), p. 787, 21.3.1829.

31 My description of the events of 12 February is the result of a wide reading of available contemporary newspapers, in particular *The Caledonian Mercury, The Edinburgh Evening Courant, The Edinburgh Observer*, and the *Scotsman*.

32 *Edinburgh Evening Courant* account, 14.2.1829, p. 3. Plainly Burke had paid his penalty.

33 The *Scotsman*, 14.2.1829, p. 102: 'The mob halted at the gentleman's door, and a number of lads deliberately proceeded to 'Burke' the effigy, amid loud huzzas. Having squeezed and throttled the figure for some time, they tied a rope about its neck, and suspended it . . .'

34 *Edinburgh Evening Courant*, 14.2.1829, p. 3.

35 Alford, V.: 'Rough Music', 1959; Thompson, E.P.: 'Rough Music', 1972.

36 Alford, V.: 'Rough Music', 1959.

37 *Caledonian Mercury*, 12.2.1829, p. 3 called Hare a 'bloody monster'. This choice of language is indicative of the violent revulsion the murders caused in circles other than that of the street crowd.

38 *Edinburgh Evening Courant*, 14.2.1828, p. 3.

39 They were described as 'lads and boys'. The most active participants were said by the *Courant* to have been bakers. The *Caledonian Mercury* 14.2.1829 called them 'trades lads'.

40 *Caledonian Mercury*, 16.2.1829, p. 3.

41 Douglas, H.: 1974, p. 139. I have been unable to confirm this independently.

42 *Caledonian Mercury*, 14.2.1829, p. 3. It was not suggested at the time that Knox himself may have footed the bill – though this is of course possible.

43 Hamilton, D.: 1981, p. 153, believes Knox's silence dignified. My personal view coincides with Christison's: possibly innocent, but culpably negligent.

44 See note 31 above. Even when not overtly sympathetic to the crowd, the newspapers were certainly hostile to Knox, though mindful of libel.

45 Douglas, H.: 1974, p. 139. Douglas says the passage is from the *Edinburgh Weekly Chronicle*, though I have been unable to verify this.

46 Rae, I.: 1964, charts the anticlimax of Knox's once promising career.

47 This was Mary (or Margaret) Paterson – see Burke's *Courant* confession.

48 Christison, R.: 1885–6, p. 311.

49 The equation of the poor with bestiality is discussed below.

50 Foucault, M.: 1979, pp. 44–7.

51 Several broadsheet and newspaper accounts of Burke's execution record the use of the word. See e.g.: *Edinburgh Evening Courant*, 29.1.1829; *The Times*, 2.2.1829; *Blackwood's Magazine*, March 1829, p. 386. The sympathy with the crowd expressed in such reports is noteworthy.

52 Burke's skeleton may be seen today in the Edinburgh University Museum. Prior to articulation, Burke's body was preserved in salt, and with 'peculiar propriety' (according to Roughead, W.: 1921, p. 66) was 'stored in barrels for later lectures'. His skin was tanned. The contradiction in Burke's sentence is in the fact that the preservation of his skeleton kept it whole, though unburied.

53 Christison, R.: 1885–6, pp. 71–2.

54 Estimates vary – compare Roughead, W.: 1921, p. 66 with Christison, R.: 1885–6, p. 72. A description, probably by an eyewitness, may be found in Leighton, A.: 1861.

55 Wakefield, E.G.: 1832, pp. 207–8.

56 *Lancet*, 1829–30(1), pp. 921–3, 27.3.1830. Wakley recommended repeal on the grounds that although it would not necessarily allay prejudice, it would be disgraceful for the poor to be equated in law with murderers.

57 *Lancet*, 1831–2(1), pp. 664–6, 4.2.1832.

58 Original emphasis.

59 Guthrie, G.J.: 1832, p. 3.

60 It seems most likely that Guthrie was overlooked because his opinions would not have been welcome.

61 See previous chapter.

62 *Hansard*, 12.3.1829, pp. 998–1005. M.J. Durey's assertion that the introduction of the Bill coincided with Burke's execution ('Bodysnatchers and Benthamites', 1976, p. 204) is erroneous.

63 Leycester's speech resembles the argument found in Bentham's draft bill of 1826, headed 'the considerations here brought to view might be eliminated out of the Bill: and not otherwise be employed than as reasons in the mouths of supporters'. *Bentham Mss* 11b, 220.

64 I coincide in this view with the Dickens scholar Prof. Kathleen Tillotson. (Personal communication.)

65 Oastler, R.: 1837, p. 15. Cobbett used the word 'revolutionary' to describe the New Poor Law – see his Letters to the Earl of Radnor, 1834, pp. 1,3.

66 *Petition of the Poor Women of the Hampnett Union [workhouse] to His Grace the Duke of Richmond*, printed by Williams and Pullinger, Chichester, 1837. Stephen Burke Collection. The women appealed to the scriptures, protested at being separated from husbands and children, complained of the meagre diet and prison regime, and pleaded that his

grace should pull down the workhouse and erect almshouses instead.

67 Pugin, A.: 1836/41, 'Contrasted Residences for the Poor'. See my list of illustrations. For this kind of use of mediaevalism in this period, see also William Cobbett: 1824.

68 Dickens placed the story just prior to the enactment of the New Poor Law, but the architectural presence of the workhouse very much conveys the atmosphere of the new workhouse described by Fanny Trollope in her *Jessie Phillips* (1844): 'that bare-faced monster of a union poorhouse which seems to glare upon us from a hundred eyes from what used to be the prettiest meadow in the Parish!' p. 85.

69 *Oliver Twist*, 1839, chapter 8.

70 Young, A.: 1771, vol. 4, p. 361.

71 Colquhoun, P.: 1806, p. 73.

72 Malthus, T.R.: [1798] 1970, p. 101.

73 Malthus, T.R.: [1798] 1970, p. 103.

74 *Hansard*, 19.2.1807.

75 Thompson, E.P.: 1963, p. 850. For Bentham's Panopticon see Bowring, J. (ed.): 1843, vol. 4, *passim*. Pugin's 'Modern Poor House' (see p. 269) is built on the panopticon principle.

76 Burton, J.H.: 1843, p. 351.

77 Huzel, J.P.: 'Malthus, the Poor Law, and Population', 1969, p. 451.

78 Baugh, D.A.: 'The Cost of Poor Relief', 1975, p. 57.

79 Head, F.: 1835, p. 77. The curious syntax is original.

80 Burn, J.D.: n.d. (c.1830).

81 Pritchard, J.C.: 1843.

82 Gaskell, P.: 1836.

83 Rude, G.: 1981, p. 205 refers [seriously or tongue in cheek?] to them as 'the common herd'.

84 *Hansard*, 12.3.1829, pp. 998–1005.

85 For a fine instance of eulogy of science/medicine in this period, see the following reference.

86 *Hansard*, 22.4.1828, p. 16. The speech would appear to have been unprepared. Emphasis added.

87 The best coverage of these lectures appears in *The New London Mechanics' Register*, vol.2, 1827. See also *Place Papers*, BM.Add.Mss,27828, p. 123.

88 Warburton asserted in Parliament that the body had been disinterred (*Hansard*, 12.3.1829, pp. 998–1005) but Place recorded in his memoirs on the subject that Warburton was in error. He said it had been obtained from Whitechapel workhouse, and that it was the body of a resurrectionist: *Place Papers*, BM.Add.Mss. 27828, facing p. 271.

89 *Lancet*, 1828–9(1), p. 820, 28.3.1829.

90 *New London Mechanics' Register*, vol. 2, 1827, p. 1.

91 Thompson, E.P.: 1963, chapter 16, *passim*, particularly p. 798; and Harrison, J.F.C.: 1961. See also note 93 below.

92 Thompson, E.P.: 1963, p. 402.

93 Cooter, R.: 'The Power of the Body', 1979. See also: Williams, G.: 'The Infidel Working Class', 1974; Harrison, J.F.C.: 'The Owenite contribution to freethought', 1974; Shipley, S.: 'Science and atheism in mid-Victorian London', 1974.

94 The physiological similarity of rich and poor had long been symbolised in popular mythology and iconography in the role of Death, who 'levelled' all ranks. Many examples survive of this imagery persisting to the 1830s. See my discussion of the Leeds banner of 1832, in chapter 9.

95 Wakley concurred with Cobbett in the view that the insecure economic status of the lower middle and 'comfortable' working classes could mean they had relatively little to buffer themselves against the chance that illness, sickness, accident or old age might return them to the Poor Law's tender mercies. For early concepts of the poverty cycle, see *Cobbett's Weekly Political Register*, vol. 75(5), 28.1.1832, pp. 262–6; Stratton, J.Y.: 'Farm Labourers', 1870. For a case of comparative wealth fallen on hard times, see chapter 7 notes. See also Thomas Murphy's speech at the NPU mentioned in the text below.

96 Thompson, E.P.: 1963, p. 508.

97 See Edward Thompson's qualifying remarks about Place's estimate of his own importance – Thompson, E.P.: 1963, pp. 505–14. For Place, Hume and the Combination Acts, see Thompson, E.P.: 1963, p. 564.

98 Thompson, E.P.: 1963, p. 846.

99 Stenton, M.: 1976.

100 One has only to delve into Place's Mss papers (see below) to appreciate Edward Thompson's grasp of him. Thompson, E.P.: 1963, *passim*. For Place's recognition of his own unpopularity on the anatomy question: BM.Add.Mss. 27828, pp. 285–6. The British Library possesses a prodigious collection of Place's papers, many of which he wrote up long after the events they describe. The crucial volume for the anatomy question is numbered Add.Mss. 27828, and was written up in 1836 (see p. 330). The *Proceedings* of the NPU were also written up by Place, and the published proceedings of the NPU anatomy debate are composed almost solely of Place's own address: see note 113 below. See also Linebaugh, P.: 'Eighteenth Century Crime', 1972, pp. 14–15; Finer, S.E.: 'Transmission of Benthamite Ideas', 1972, pp. 18–19.

101 The *Radical*, 12.11.1831, p. 50.
    National Political Union: 1832, pp. 2–3.
    Place also reported on the question in: National Political Union: 1833, p. 18.

102 Maccoby, S.: 1935, p. 63.

103 The letter-writers are not identified in the published *Proceedings*. The description of Bowyer and the text of his letter is taken from there. Place says that Bowyer's reply was solicited by a 'gentleman' on the Council, by which august term he meant himself.

104 National Political Union: 1832.

105 The Chairman was giving the NPU rules on the subject. Doubtless it was the power to silence opposition during these meetings which commended them to Place. See BM.Add.Mss. 27828, pp. 286–7. Place says that the discussion on 29.2.1832 was well-attended; that the audience included several 'well-dressed women', and that the proceedings were conducted more like a general meeting.

106 For Place's disparaging comments upon Murphy's personal appearance, see BM.Add.Mss. 27828, p. 310, and his speech see p. 304. There may also

have been an element of anti-Irish feeling here. The London Irish were renowned for their superstitious attachment to the corpse.

107 We have no way of knowing what Murphy was about to say. Parliament had in fact agreed to some minor amendments to the proposed Bill in the early hours of the 28 February 1829 – the eve of the NPU meeting. Place may indeed have assumed that Murphy was going to mention something which had been altered. The interruption also, however, served both to draw attention to the ignorance of the opposition, and to take the wind from Murphy's sails. It was a clever tactic.

108 Wakeley's speech is covered in BM.Add. Mss. 27828, pp. 304–5. Neither his speech, nor Murphy's, appeared in the printed *Proceedings*, but Place instead included an extract from Wakley's evidence to the Select Committee, and a direct quotation from the *Report*: once again using the Benthamite tactic of denying the validity of opposition by leaving it in silence.

109 Added emphasis.

110 Apart from brief newspaper reports, I have been unable to trace any other record of the NPU meeting.

111 The speaker was a surgeon, Mr Cartwright-Thomas. BM.Add.Mss. 27828, pp. 305.

112 BM.Add.Mss. 27828, p. 306. Speech of Mr Fox.

113 For details of the subscription to and distribution of this pamphlet see BM.Add.Mss. 27828, pp. 307–8. Copies were sent to every (Political) Union in London, and a great many in the Country, to 'every association and reading room where working men were admitted, to many coffee shops' and to members of both Houses of Parliament. The adjourned discussion was delayed by other business, and, Place says, 'this time was gained for the distribution of a large number of copies'. Place made no mention of how production and distribution were funded. During this period the Worcester Political Union submitted a petition to Parliament against the Bill, which may have been an unlooked-for result of Place's propaganda.

114 BM.Add.Mss. 27828, p. 310. Speech of Mr Churchill.

115 It is interesting to notice that the charge of opponents' emotionalism and ignorance, (as against supporters' rationality, judgement and scientificity) bears similarities to the manner in which women are traditionally intellectually dismissed by some men.

116 BM.Add.Mss. 27828, p. 312.

117 See the reports of Place's triumph in the *Albion and Evening Star*, 29.3.1832.

118 *Petition* of the National Political Union, members of. *CJ*, vol. 87, p. 300, 8.5.1832.

119 Thompson, E.P.: 1963, p. 564.

120 Thompson, E.P.: 1963, pp. 564–9.

121 Hume was on the Select Committee, and his name appears repeatedly in the *Hansard* reports of parliamentary proceedings. He had himself trained in surgery, returning from service in India with a fortune.

122 *Lancet*, 1828–9(2), p. 319, 5.6.1829. Letter signed 'R. Gibson'.

123 *Hansard*, 5.6.1829, pp. 1746–50.

124 *Hansard*, 5.6.1829, p. 1748: Harewood.

125 *Hansard*, 5.6.1829, p. 1748.

126 *Hansard*, 5.6.1829, p. 1747, Malmesbury.
127 *Hansard*, 5.6.1829, p. 1749, Tenterden.
128 *Hansard*, 5.6.1829, p. 1748, Wellington.
129 Leave to bring in a new bill on the subject was given in the House of Commons on 15.12.1831.

CHAPTER 7: ALTERNATIVE NECROLOGY

1 Lord Calthorpe, speaking in the House of Lords, 5.6.1829. *LMG*, vol. 4, 1829, p. 58. The first Bill was thrown out of the Lords on the same day. *Hansard* does not print this extract.
2 Original spelling of 'eminate', line 6.
3 *The Christian's Appeal against the Poor Law Amendment Act*, reprinted by H. Talbot, Cambridge, c. 1834. St Bride Printing Institute.
4 The 1832 edition of Southwood Smith's *Uses of the Dead to the Living* was printed on the *Lancet* presses. Personal communication with Dr Betty Bostetter.
5 An invitation dated 8.6.1832 may be found in BM.Add.Mss. 34661, p. 32. Bentham was dissected the following day.
6 Marmoy, C.F.A.: 'The Auto Icon', 1958.
7 Eighteenth-century educated opinion may be indicated by the philosopher David Hume who had a watch set on his own grave in 1776 – see chapter 4 notes. But, David Harley has kindly referred me to a case recorded in Nottinghamshire County Record Office in which Robert Green, MA, a Fellow of Clare Hall, Cambridge, bequeathed his body for dissection in 1721, also bequeathing monies for the publication of the results.
8 Despite Bentham's expressed ideal that 'every man' could thus be his own statue, even he recognised that not all dead bodies could reasonably be preserved in this way. He recommended burial in quicklime for them. See Bentham, J.: [c.1842] For a full discussion of Bentham's auto-icon, see Richardson, R. & Hurwitz, B.: forthcoming (1987).
9 *Westminster Review*, 1829 (10), pp. 128–48.
10 Smith, T.S.: [*Lecture*] 1832.
11 Smith, T.S.:[*Lecture*] 1832, pp. 71–2.
12 The confiscation use of the 'unclaimed', and the means by which they were specified in law as dissection material, does not arise as a subject of discussion in any of the medical histories consulted.
13 Massachusetts adopted the recommendations of the Select Committee *Report* in 1830. Other US States followed. Haagensen, C.D. & Lloyd, W.E.B.: 1943, p. 55. Wakley was a key figure in transatlantic medical reform in this era. See Dr Bostetter's forthcoming biography.
14 Anatomical Society Memorial, BM.Add.Mss. 40371, pp. 337–8; letters from Carpue, Shaw and Stanley, BM.Add.Mss. 40371, pp. 323–4, 315–18. Letters originally sent to Astley Cooper dated 1823, probably passed on to Peel c.1824.
15 BM.Add.Mss27828, p. 263. Place seems to have been completely ignorant of Bentham's role, perceiving his own personal conviction as causal, rather than symptomatic, of a more general change. I therefore assume the immediate influence upon him to have been not Bentham but Hume.

16   BM.Add.Mss40371, pp. 311–38.

17   The letter was dated 10.12.1831 and appeared in *Cobbett's Weekly Political Register* and other newspapers. The text used here is from *LMG*, vol. 9, 1831–2, pp. 487–8.

18   It interesting that Cooper should have wanted to circumnavigate the resurrectionists at this particular time. The letters coincide with two possibly interesting developments: the RCS regulations limiting qualifications to those who had trained in London hospital anatomy schools during the winter season, dated from 1823 & 1824; and the fact that Grainger had set up his Webb Street School in 1819 – its success would probably have been apparent by this period.

19   Original spelling of 'horor'.

20   See also Pappworth, M.: 1969.

21   Bishop and Williams were discovered to have murdered an Italian boy on 5 November 1831, and later confessed to other murders. They were tried on 2 December, hanged on 5 December, and afterwards dissected. The RCS letter to the Home Secretary was dated 10 December 1831. Warburton gained permission to introduce his new Bill into Parliament on 15 December 1831.

22   In respect of the lack of pity, the letter is worthy of comparison with the RCP statement published at the time of Burke and Hare. *LMG*, vol. 3, 1828–9, pp. 231–2.
     For Wakley's comment, see *Lancet*, 1831–2(1), p. 510, 7.1.1832.

23   The closure of dissection rooms was suggested by Wakley in 1829, in the aftermath of the Burke and Hare murders: 'Nothing but the immediate closure of the dissecting rooms of the Metropolis, can effectually protect the public against atrocities similar to those which have just been detected at Edinburgh. If the commerce between anatomists and resurrectionists be suffered to continue, and if murder be perpetuated by trading assassins in this metropolis, will not an awful responsibility attach to those who had it in their power to prevent the crime by seasonable interposition?' *Lancet*, 1828–9(2), pp. 465–6, 10.1.1829. Wakley drew attention to the class issues involved in the Anatomy Bill, and advocated greater equity. His wish to prevent further murders, it seems to me, was genuinely humanitarian. Those who took up his cry, however, failed also to accept his point about social equity, and lacked his humanity.

24   Guthrie, G.J.: 1832, p.3.

25   *Quarterly Review*, vol. 42(83), 1830, pp. 1–17.
     See also Somerville, J.C.: 1832; *LMG*, vol. 9, 1831, pp. 270–5; *LMG*, vol. 9, 1831, pp. 363–7.

26   Petition from the Inhabitants of Blackburn: *HofC : V&P* Appx, 15.2.1832.

27   This may refer to the Benthamite Joseph Hume – who had trained as a surgeon in earlier life – or to Thomas Wakley: towards both of whom College people would have held dislike.

28   By 'committees' Guthrie meant both the Select Committee and the Committees of the two Houses of Parliament which considered the Bill in its committee stage. Guthrie, G.J.: 1832, pp. 6–7.
     Guthrie was ridiculed and criticised by Wakley: *Lancet*, 1828–9(2), pp. 465–6, 10.1.1829.

29   *LMG*, vol. 1, 1827–8, pp. 637–8; *LMG*, vol. 9, 1831–2, pp. 270–5.

30   Please see my NOTE heading the References section.

31   *LMG*, vol. 1, 1827–8, pp. 668–9, 764; *LMG*, vol. 8, 1831, pp. 122–4.
See also *Evidence*, Q1307.

32   The great majority of petitions to Parliament in favour of Warburton's Bill
were from surgeons and surgery students. See, for example, *CJ*, vol. 87, pp.
73, 143, 157, 215, 229.

33   Letter dated 7.2.1832 from B. Travers, *LMG*, vol. 9, 1831–2, pp. 714–17.

34   Maccoby says of the NUWC procession: 'Never had infidelity raised its
head in England so openly before or so combatively'. Maccoby, S: 1935, p.
43. The *Morning Chronicle* estimated the procession to have had 100,000
participants.

35   Morris, R.J.: 1976; Durey, M.J.: 1979.

36   Hobhouse, J.C.: 1909–11, vol. 4, pp. 83–4. Palmerston courageously
refused a national fast for the 1853 cholera epidemic, on the grounds that a
nation inactive in sanitary reform would be fruitful in death, in spite of its
supplications. See Wohl, A.: 1983, p. 122.

37   The *Lion*, vol. 3, 1829, pp. 393–400.

38   The author refers to himself as male in the first paragraph: *Lion*, vol. 3,
1829, p. 393. The Charlotte Baume case discussed in chapter 9 reveals that
the 'scholar' was Peter (or Pierre) Baume. See his *DNB* entry.

39   It is not ascertainable from the text whether this refers to what is now
University College, or to another of the author's schemes. He refers to 'the
contemplated philosophical university, or any other institution for the
improvement of the happiness of the whole human species'. *Lion*, vol. 3,
1829, p. 511. His phraseology indicates the pervasion of Benthamite
language/ideas through the radical 'left' at this period.

40   *Lion*, vol. 3, 1829, p. 511.

41   *Lion*, vol. 3, 1829, pp. 358–9.

42   See the epigraph to this chapter taken from *The Christian's Appeal against the
Poor Law Amendment Act*.

43   Penny, N.: 1981. p. 10.

44   George, M.D.: 1954, vol. 11, p. 270. Caption to item no. 16050.

45   *Lion*, vol. 3, 1829, pp. 353–9. Carlile's dissection was reported in the *Lancet*,
1842–3(1), p. 774, 18.2.1843. The oration was given by Robert Grainger,
who used it as an occasion to mention the failures of the Anatomy Act.
Carlile's family refused to have his skeleton kept as a medical specimen at
St Thomas' Hospital, and buried him instead at Kensal Green where a
scene was caused by a minister's insistence that the burial service be read
to a crowd of atheist mourners – who left or remained to jeer. See Brook,
C.W.: 1943, pp. 52–4. For the 'French Scholar's' sister, see note 38 above.

46   This is characteristic; see Thompson, E.P.: 1963, p. 839.

47   Please see my NOTE heading the References section.

48   Lonsdale, H.: 1870, p. 100. Peachey, G.: 1924, pp. 42–3 quotes a very
similar letter [perhaps the same one?]. See also Wadd, W.: 1824, p. 80. See
also bequest letter to Sir Astley Cooper in Cooper, B.: 1843, pp. 398–9.

49   A feature of many bequests commented upon in *LMG*, vol. 1, 1829, p. 637.

50   Dr Sims: *LMG*, vol. 1, 1828, pp. 247–9; Dr Courtney: *Lancet*, 1831–2, vol. 1.
p. 667; Lyster: *The Times*, 10.2.1832. For the radical newsvendors, see the

Cosmopolite, 9.6.1832. For Major Cartwright, see *Radical Reformer*, 12.1.1832.

51 Please see my NOTE heading the References section.

52 *LMG*, vol. 1, 1828, pp. 249–50. One fears that the opposition resulted from potential loss of perquisites.

53 *LMG*, vol. 1, 1828, pp. 764–5.

54 *Figaro's Monthly Newspaper*, 1.1.1835, p. 8.

55 [Anon]: *An Address*, 1829, p. 30. This belief seems to have been an old one – Aubrey mentioned the fact that 'Mariners will not endure . . . a dead corps' on ship for fear that 'a storme will seize on them'. Aubrey, J.: [1686–7] 1881, p. 200.

56 *Evidence*, Q101.

57 Macartney's *Evidence*, Q1279.

58 *LMG*, vol. 1, 1828, pp. 510–11.
    Medicus [pseud.]: 1829, p. 10.

59 Thomas Hood: 1826.

60 See stanza 35.

61 Hood's poem contains 43 stanzas, of which only 38–41 are quoted here. He evidently despised both resurrectionists and anatomists.

62 *Evidence*, Q66.

63 Astley Cooper Papers, Library of the Royal College of Surgeons, London. Note Sir Astley's stress upon feeling.

64 Medicus [pseud.]: 1829, p. 10.

65 See, for example *Lancet*, 1831–2(1) pp. 451–6, 24.12.1831, and pp. 707–8, 11.2.1832.

66 Letter signed 'A Lover of Justice': *Lancet*, 1831–2(1), pp. 521–2, 7.1.1832.

67 See for example, petitions against the bills from: (a) The Inhabitants of Tenterden, Kent. *HofC : V&P* Appx, 12.5.1829, no.3023. (b) Mechanics of the Parish of Lambeth. *HofC : V&P* Appx, 24.1.1832, no.68.

68 See for example, Lord Wynford's speech against the 2nd Bill: *Hansard*, 19.6.1832.

69 Guthrie, G.J.: 1832, pp. 5–6. See also the recent view of Lord Atkin, quoted in the *Observer*, 22.10.1981: 'Convenience and Justice are often not on speaking terms'.

70 See the petitions from: (a) Mechanics of the Parish of Lambeth: *HofC : V&P* Appx, 24.1.1832, no.68; (b) Blackburn Inhabitants: *HofC : V&P* Appx, 15.2.1832.

71 Petition of several poor persons now living in the Workhouse of St Ann, Blackfriars, in the City of London: Abridged text: *CJ*, vol. 84, p. 178, 27.3.1829.

72 *Quarterly Review*, vol. 42(83), 1830, pp. 1–17.

73 See for example: Medicus [pseud.]: 1829, p. 13.

74 Quoted in Guthrie, G.J.: 1832, p. 5.

75 Guthrie, G.J.: 1832, p. 5.

76 Horsley's letter appeared in *Cobbett's Weekly Political Register*, 28.1.1832, pp. 270–4.

77 *Cobbett's Weekly Political Register*, 28.1.1832, pp. 270–4.

78 Letter dated 25 May 1829 from a Worcestershire Workhouse: *Lancet*, 1828–9(2), p. 320, 5.6.1829.

79   Report in *Lion*, vol. 3, 1829–30, pp. 648–51.
80   Petition of several poor persons now living in the Workhouse of St Ann, Blackfriars, in the City of London: Abridged text: *CJ*, vol. 84, p.178, 27.3.1829.
81   Petition from the Inhabitants of Tenterden, Kent. *HofC : V&P* Appx, 12.5.1829, no.3023.
82   Petition of Mechanics of the Parish of Lambeth. *HofC : V&P* Appx, 24.1.1832, no.68.
83   Wakefield, E.G: 1832, Appx, pp. 208–9.
84   Smith, T.: 1859 for example, lists 21 operations and 25 amputations which could be accomplished on a single corpse. The first chapter opens with the statement: 'It rarely happens that the student of operative surgery in this country has a choice of bodies for his purpose . . .' No comparable material has been found for the period before the Anatomy Act's passage. See Section III for a discussion of shortages after the Act.
85   Some medical schools, in the last fifteen years or so, have moved dissection from its hitherto introductory/primary position in the curriculum. Personal communication with Dr B.S. Hurwitz.
     See Dooley, D.: 'A Dissection of Anatomy', 1973.
86   See particularly my discussion on the use of the phrase 'anatomical examination' in the 2nd Anatomy Bill in chapter 8.
87   Poynter, F.N.L.: 1966, p. 199.
88   See, for example, Alexipharmacus [pseud.]: 1829; Letter from Horsley, W.: *Cobbett's Weekly Political Register*, 28.1.1832.
89   [Anon]: *An Address*, 1829, pp. 20–21.
90   Letter from Horsley, W.: *Cobbett's Weekly Poltical Register*, 28.1.1832.
91   See Gooch's discussion in his *Quarterly Review* article, vol. 42(83), 1830, pp. 2, 7–8.
92   Letter from Horsley, W.: *Cobbett's Weekly Political Register*, 28.1.1832; [Anon]: *An Address*, 1829; Alexipharmacus [pseud.]: 1829; Letter from H. Payne in *Cobbett's Weekly Political Register*, 14.1.1832.
93   [Anon] *An Address*, 1829. Is this an argument in favour of anaesthesia?.
94   Letter from Horsley, W.: *Cobbett's Weekly Political Register*, 28.1.1832.
95   (Anon]: *An Address*, 1829; Letter from Payne, H.: *Cobbett's Weekly Political Register*, 14.1.1832; Letter from Horsley, W.: *Cobbett's Weekly Political Register*, 28.1.1832.
96   [Anon]: *An Address*, 1829; Letter from Payne, H.: *Cobbett's Weekly Political Register*, 14.1.1832; Letter from Horsley, W.: *Cobbett's Political Register*, 28.1.1832.
97   Letter from Horsley, W.: *Cobbett's Weekly Political Register*, 28.1.1832.
98   *Lancet*, 1829–30(1), pp. 42–5, 3.10.1829.
99   *Lancet*, 1829–30(1), pp. 42–5, 3.10.1829.
100 *Lancet*, 1831–2(1), pp. 521–2, 7.1.1832.
101 *Lancet*, 1831–2(1), pp. 454–6, 24.12.1831. Wakley's attack was aimed partly at Benjamin Harrison, Treasurer at Guy's, who refused post-mortem examinations in the hospital. Personal communication with Dr Bostetter.
102 The speaker was a Mr Mickle, and he was attending a meeting at the Ebenezer Chapel, Blackburn, on the evening of Monday 6 February 1832, reported in the *Bolton Chronicle*, Saturday 11 February 1832. At the same

meeting a Mr Leycock said: 'I perfectly coincide with those who are in favour of dissection; it is against the poor and friendless only being selected as subjects for the doctors that I object to'. A Mr Hammond said he thought that as a result of the bill 'the destitute and friendless shall be racked in their minds, upon a bed of painful sickness'.

103 Petition from the Worcestershire Political Union. *HofC : V&P* Appx, 7.3.1832, no.356.

104 See, for example, *LMG*, vol. 7, 1831, p. 693.

105 Petition from the Paisley Reform Society: *HofC: V&P* Appx, 3.2.1832, no.114.

106 *Lancet*, 1828–9(2), pp. 553–4, 1.8.1829.

107 *Lion*, vol. 3, 1829, pp. 358–9. See also the epigraph to this chapter taken from *The Christian's Appeal*.

108 A report concerning the Leadenhall Butchers' and Salesmen's petition, as well as the intended text appeared in Carlile's *Lion*, vol. 3, 1829–30, pp. 648–51. The report says that the mayor's 'gravity' was shaken, but it is unclear whether this meant he was shocked or amused; from the immediate context, it would appear the former.

109 Guthrie, G.J.: 1832, p. 3.

110 See, for example, Dermott, G.W.: *Lancet*, 1828–9(2), pp. 553–4, 1.8.1829; Petition of the Paisley Reform Society: *HofC : V&P* Appx, 3.2.1832, no.114; Petition of Mechanics of the Parish of Lambeth. *HofC: V&P* Appx, 24.1.1832, no.68.

111 *LMG*, vol. 7, 1831, p. 693.

112 Note that those considered to suffer grief at a doctor's demise include friends.

113 [Anon]: *An Address*, 1829, p. 23.

114 This is, of course, not the whole story. For the political reasons behind support for the bills, see the end of this chapter, and discussion in Section III.

115 This became a key phrase during the campaign against Old Corruption. See, for example, *True Sun*, 23.10.1832, and a speech by Cobbett reported in the *Manchester Guardian*, 8.9.1832. The contradistinction made in this argument between the extremes of society finds a close parallel to that which emerged in a critique of two insults which were commonly used against the poor at this time: 'scum and dregs'. 'Scum', the readers of the *Radical* newspaper of 3.9.1831 were reminded, 'floats to the top'.

116 Petition from the Inhabitants of Blackburn: *HofC : V&P* Appx, 15.2.1832.

117 *Lion*, vol. 3, 1829–30, pp. 648–51.

118 Petition of Mechanics of the Parish of Lambeth. *HofC : V&P* Appx, 24.1.1832, no.68.

119 *LMG*, vol. 7, 1831, p. 693.

120 The *Liverpool Mercury* of 14.2.1811 quoted a passage from a correspondent in Finland: 'The school of anatomy is not in need of subjects for dissection, as there is a law in the city of Abo, in Finland, that all persons holding offices or pensions from the Crown are bound to leave their bodies to be dissected.' The *Liverpool Mercury* commented: 'what a number of fine anatomical preparations we should have if this law was passed in England! As we cannot have the pleasure of cutting up our pensioners and sinecurists

when dead, or making any other use of them, we may content ourselves by cutting them up whilst living by that sharp machine, the press'.

121 Wakefield, E.G.: 1832; Appx, p. 211.

122 Petition from the Worcestershire Political Union. *HofC : V&P* Appx, 7.3.1832, no.356.

123 Petition from the Inhabitants of Blackburn: *HofC : V&P* Appx, 15.2.1832.

124 It remains unclear upon what constitutional basis this assumption rests.

125 Petition from the Worcestershire Political Union. *HofC : V&P* Appx, 7.3.1832, no.356.

126 Petition of the Paisley Reform Society: *HofC : V&P* Appx, 3.2.1832, no.114.

127 *Lancet*, 1828–9, vol. 2, pp. 553–4, 1.8.1829.

128 Please see my NOTE heading the References section.

129 *True Sun*, 4.12.1832.

130 *LMG*, vol. 9, 1831–2, pp. 604–9.
    Please see my NOTE heading the References section.

131 Wakefield, E.G.: 1832.

132 Wakefield, E.G.: 1832, pp. 211–3. Compare Wakefield's ideas with note 120 above.

133 Claims for the yield of corpses from the sequestration of the 'unclaimed' certainly proved exaggerated. See Section III below.

134 Blaug, M.: 'The Myth of the Old Poor Law', 1963; Brundage, A.: 1978; Checkland, G.G. & E.O.A. (eds): 1964; Crowther, M.A.: 1981; Digby, A.: 1978; Edsall, N.: 1971; Fraser, D. (ed.): 1976; Henriques, U.: 'How Cruel was the Victorian Poor Law?', 1968; Ignatieff, M.: 'Total Institutions', 1983; Kaijage, F.J.: 'Poor Law Catechism', 1981; Longmate, N.: 1974; Marshall, J.D.: 1968; Poynter, J.R.: 1969; Roberts, D.: 'How Cruel was the Victorian Poor Law?', 1963; Rose, M.E.: 1971, 1972; 'The Anti-Poor Law Agitation', 1970; 'The Anti-Poor Law Movement', 1966; Thompson, E.P.: 1963, p. 294; Webb, S. & B.J.: 1910, 1929. See also *Report* and *Evidence of the Select Committee on the Poor Laws, 1834*; 4 & 5 Gul IV c.76: Poor Law (Amendment) Act, 1834.

135 Thompson, E.P.: 1963, p. 295.

CHAPTER 8: BRINGING 'SCIENCE TO THE POOR MAN'S DOOR'

1 Henry Warburton, reported in *Hansard*, 11.4.1832, p. 312.

2 Charles Dickens: *Martin Chuzzlewit*, 1843–4, chapter 8.

3 *Cobbett's Weekly Political Register*, 7.7.1832, pp. 41–2.

4 George Eliot: *Middlemarch*, 1871, chapter 10.

5 *Evidence*, Q1280.

6 For example, tales of children kidnapped to work on the American plantations, and of child-stealing by gipsies. The *OED* dates 'kidnap' to 1682.

7 *Evidence*, Q1280.

8 *Evidence*, Q1280.

9 Southwood Smith referred to an 'intense and fearful anxiety' of burking among the public. *Westminster Review*, 1829(10), p. 116. See also my list of

illustrations for the Seymour cartoon entitled 'Burkiphoby', (see note 11 below). 'Attempted murder of a boy', *York Chronicle*, 1.12.1831; 'Atrocious Outrages', *Edinburgh Weekly Journal*, 18.2.1829.
See also Andrews, W.M.: 1895, p. 169.

10 *Scotsman*, 18.2.1829, p. 10.

11 Caption to a cartoon by R. Seymour, in the *Looking Glass*, no.24, Dec. 1831, p. 2. See George, M.D.: 1954, cat.no.16914. Reproduced in the text – see p. 196.

12 *York Chronicle*, 24.11.1831.

13 *York Chronicle*, 1.12.1831.

14 *York Chronicle*, 1.12.1831; *Scotsman*, 18.2.1829.

15 *York Chronicle*, 1.12.1831.

16 *Edinburgh Weekly Journal*, 18.2.1829, p. 52.

17 *Scotsman*, 18.12.1829. More seriously, a case of attempted murder in emulation of the burkers by two boys upon another was reported in the *York Chronicle*, 22.12.1831, p. 4.

18 This description is a composite picture gleaned from contemporary newspaper reports in such papers as the *York Courant, York Chronicle, Leeds Intelligencer, Halifax and Huddersfield Express, Yorkshire Herald.*

19 The chronology of the case was as follows:
   30.10.1831: Hudson found hanged.
   31.10.1831: Investigation mounted.
   1.11.1831: Inquest, suicide verdict, and burial.
   Night of 2/3.11.1831: Body stolen and packaged up. Bodysnatchers failed
         to get it on the coach to Edinburgh.
   7.11.1831: Package opened, and the gang apprehended.

20 Newspapers carried details of the gang's oaths of allegiance and secrecy, tools, techniques, reconnaissance methods, and the logistics of the packaging and transportation of corpses. The informer had joined the gang in the previous September, unable to obtain other employment.

21 Open Letter to Peel from J.C. Badeley, MD, dated 12.2.1827: *LMG*, vol. 2, 1828, pp. 524–6: '. . . were it not for the hardihood of a desperate few, whose only mode of sustenance consists in the contraband traffic of this commerce, medical science must inevitably stagnate'.

22 'The law in this country was determined by the Anatomy Act, which in turn had resulted from the nefarious activities of Burke and Hare, the Bodysnatchers or Resurrection Men. These men raided fresh graves to provide bodies for dissection in the anatomy Schools, but when demand exceeded supply they took to murdering living victims: this led to Burke's execution and to stringent reform in the medical use of dead bodies.'
   Ryecroft, P.V.: 'Corneal Transplantation', 1966, p. 46.

23 Bishop had worked for an illicit glassmaker before supplying the anatomy schools: Bailey, J.B.: 1896, pp. 112–3. At the end of the trial, Williams threatened prosecution witnesses with revenge, and that the threat was not idle is shown by the complaint of a witness of a violent attack on his life. See *York Chronicle*, 29.12.1831.

24 *York Chronicle*, 8.12.1831: Bishop's confession.

25 This description is a composite picture gleaned from contemporary newspaper reports. The *York Chronicle* published a comprehensive account

of the trial, confessions and execution of the two men 8.12.1831.

26   *York Chronicle* 8.12.1831: 'Report of the capture of the Burkers'.
     One suspects there was an element of blame in this observation.
     After the murderers' execution, a dentist in the Borough was said to have
     exposed 'in his window, a set of finely polished teeth, with this label
     attached to them: "The teeth of Carlo Ferrier, the murdered Italian Boy" ':
     York Chronicle, 20.12.1831. The boy's teeth had been sold for 12 shillings
     and 6 pence: *York Chronicle*, 24.11.1831.

27   *Bishop's House of Murder*, printed and sold by J. Sands, Ebenezer Street,
     Leeds. Broadsheet in the John Johnson Collection. Reference to a fuller
     confession was also made in the newspapers e.g.: *York Chronicle*, 8.12.1831;
     Letter from J. Sewell, a London police magistrate: *Cobbett's Weekly Political
     Register*, 28.1.1832, pp. 258–9.

28   Several people were hurt (some said two were killed) in the crush at the
     execution.

29   *York Chronicle*, 24.1.1831.

30   The chronology of the case was as follows:
     5.11.1831: murder discovered.
     5.12.1831: Bishop and Williams hanged.
     May was condemned alongside them at the trial, but was respited after
     both condemned men denied his involvement.

31   See the Seymour cartoon mentioned in note 11 above. George, M.D.: 1954,
     cat.no.16914. Reproduced on p. 196. See also *Place Papers*, BM.Add.Mss.
     27828, p. 279. For the correct medicinal use of pitch plasters, see
     Longmate, N.: 1966, p. 69.

32   *Place Papers*, BM.Add.Mss. 27828, pp. 274–5, 278; Andrews, W.: 1895, p.
     169; (Anon]: *An Address*: 1829, p. 31.
     See also reports of the Eliza Ross case in which burking was suspected, *York
     Chronicle*, 3.11.1831, 10.11.1831, 24.11.1831.

33   Somerville, J.: 1832, p. 13. If Wakley and Somerville were correct, it
     suggests that some of the urban legends mentioned at the beginning of this
     chapter were rooted in fact rather than fear.

34   The *Ballot*, 13.11.1831: editorial. See also Dr Betty Bostetter's forthcoming
     biography of Wakley.

35   *Hansard*, 11.5.1832, p. 902: Robinson.

36   *Hansard*, 11.4.1832, p. 319: Warburton.

37   *Hansard*,
       24.1.1832, p. 828: Lord Chancellor.
       11.4.1832, p. 319: Warburton.
       28.6.1832, p. 1086: Lord Minto.
       19.7.1832, p. 534: Lord Minto.

38   *Cobbett's Weekly Political Register*, 28.1.1832, p. 265.

39   *Hansard*, 17.1.1832, p. 578.

40   *Bentham* Mss., Box 11a. 'JB for H Br. Suggestions for *Modus Prociendi* in Law
     Reform Motion'. Brougham was Lord Chancellor during the second bill's
     passage, and spoke in support at crucial junctures – see note 37 above. He
     was also instrumental in the passage of the New Poor Law.

41   *Hansard*, 17.1.1832, pp. 584–5.

42   The two colleagues were J. Hume and M. O'Donnell – see *Hansard*,

15.2.1832, pp. 377–9.

43 The clause is quoted in full later in this chapter – see note 83. Lacking records, it is not known if Warburton was in the house during the debate on the Blackburn petition. He nevertheless failed to seize the opportunity to rectify his colleagues' error less than a fortnight later, in the Bill's committee stage.

44 Warburton was forced to defend his reputation against criticism of late debates and thin houses: *Hansard*, 17.1.1832, p. 584. This took place at circa 4am, when only 32 members were present: see *CJ*, vol. 87, p. 35. For the comments of Lord William Lennox, *Hansard*, 11.5.1832, p. 896. For Henry Hunt, see Thompson, E.P.: 1963, p. 682, and John Belchem's biography: *Orator Hunt*, 1986.

45 *3730*, 25.2.1832. I am extremely grateful to John Belchem (see previous note) for bringing the Preston paper to my attention.

46 See *CJ*, vol. 87, pp. 161, 165, 168, 171, 175, 180, 182, 185, 194, 198, 201, 209, 218, 225, 229, 232, 237, 279, 305.

47 *Hansard*,
    17.1.1832, p. 580: Hume.
    20.1.1832, p. 702: Warburton.
    24.1.1832, p. 827: Calvert.
    24.1.1832, p. 828: Warburton.
    27.2.1832, p. 838: Warburton.
    11.5.1832, p. 903: Warburton.
    6.7.1832, p. 150: Lord Holland.

48 *Hansard*, 6.7.1832, pp. 150–1.

49 *Hansard*, 24.1.1832, pp. 825–9.

50 *Hansard*, 11.4.1832, pp. 316–17; 18.4.1832, pp. 667–8.

51 *Hansard*,
    24.1.1832, p. 827: Briscoe, Sibthorp.
    27.1.1832, p. 832: Hunt.
    11.4.1832, p. 315: Sibthorp.
    11.4.1832, p. 319: Briscoe.
    11.4.1832, p. 319: Wason.
    11.4.1832, p. 321: Courtenay.
    11.4.1832, p. 321: Dawson.
    6.7.1832, p. 150: Kenyon.

52 *Hansard*, 11.4.1832, p. 322.

53 Unlike any other opponent of the Bill, Hunt spoke in every single Commons debate.

54 See for example the Commons 3rd reading, *Hansard*, 11.5.1832.

55 *3730*, 25.2.1832: Letter dated 16.2.1832.

56 Although Finer, S.E.: 'Transmission of Benthamite Ideas', 1972, would probably not classify Macaulay as a 'first degree' Benthamite, he certainly behaved as one during the Bill's passage through Parliament, and was regarded by his constituents as crucially identified with it – see my discussion of the 1832 General Election at Leeds, in chapter 9.

57 *Hansard*, 28.6.1832, p. 1086.

58 *Hansard*, 19.6.1832, p. 828.
Fife was addressing the Lords during the Bill's 2nd reading.

Richard Oastler's analysis of the support for the New Poor Law also applied to the Anatomy Bill: 'It was supported by the Tory Wellington, the Whig, Brougham, and the Radical Hume. Let us have no more, then, about it being a Whig measure . . . It is an Act passed by the union of every faction, in the hope of their being able to crush the rights of the people – the working people'. Oastler, R.: 1837. Samuel Roberts attributed the New Poor Law's passage less to malice than apathy: 'I do most firmly believe, that there are hundreds of our legislators, who, were there . . . a clause in the [Poor Law] Act to shoot half the paupers, would pass it from inattention, from their eagerness to be upon the High Moors . . '. Roberts, S.: 1834, p. 28.

59 Thompson, E.P.: 1963, p. 564.
60 *Hansard*, 27.2.1832, pp. 834–5: Inglis and Wason.
61 Workhouse and hospital personnel were under popular suspicion of profiting from the deaths of inmates. The cartoon by Paul Pry entitled 'A Few Illustrations for Mr Warberton's Bill' (1829: George, M.D.: 1954, cat.no.15777) shows dismembered human carcases hung up outside a shop, like butchers' meat. Reproduced on p. 220.
62 The final vote in the Commons registered only four votes against the Bill. They were probably those of Hunt and some ultra-Tories.
63 Hunt's threat: *Hansard*, 11.4.1832, p. 319; 18.4.1832, p. 666. Sibthorp publicly refused support: 11.5.1832, p. 895.
64 *Hansard*, 27.2.1832, p. 837.
65 *Hansard*, 11.5.1832, p. 900.
66 *Hansard*,
     11.5.1832, pp. 895–6: Fane.
     11.5.1832, p. 896: Lennox.
     11.5.1832, p. 898: Inglis.
     18.5.1832, pp. 665–6: Robinson.
67 *Hansard*, 11.5.1832, p. 901: Sadler.
68 *CJ*, vol. 87, pp. 287–8. The votes were taken on the night of 18/19 April 1832 on clauses concerning:
     (a) the death certification of workhouse inmates,
     (b) the punishment of capital crimes.
69 *3730*, 28.1.1832, p. 6.
70 *Hansard*, 11.5.1832, p. 900: Sadler.
71 *Hansard*,
     27.2.1832, p. 843: Macaulay.
     11.4.1832, p. 321: Attorney General.
72 See Finer, S.E.: 'Transmission of Benthamite Ideas', 1972, p. 21. Margaret Pelling, speaking of Chadwick, says he was 'no more than typical of the Benthamites, and of middle class reformers in general, in having limited popular sympathies and no egalitarianism'. Pelling, M.: 1978, p. 10.
73 *Hansard*,
     24.1.1832, p. 827.
     11.4.1832, pp. 321–2.
74 *LMG*, vol. 4, 1829, pp. 331, 692–3.

Hansard,
> 27.2.1832, pp. 842–3.
> 11.4.1832, p. 321.

75 *Hansard,*
patrons of science and medicine, e.g.:
> 17.1.1832, p. 585.
> 11.4.1832, p. 311.

enlightened victims of prejudice and ignorance, e.g.:
> 27.2.1832, pp. 843–4.
> 11.4.1832, p. 321.

champions of social equity, e.g.:
> 15.12.1831, p. 307.
> 15.2.1832, pp. 377–8.
> 11.4.1832, p. 320.
> 11.4.1832, p. 321.
> 18.4.1832, p. 664.

protectors of the dead and the living, e.g.:
> 27.2.1832, p. 842.
> 11.4.1832, p. 311.
> 11.4.1832, p. 319.

benefactors of the poor, e.g.:
> 17.1.1832, p. 585.
> 2.2.1832, p. 1150.
> 15.2.1832, p. 377.
> 27.2.1832, p. 842.
> 11.4.1832, p. 312.
> 11.4.1832, p. 319.
> 11.5.1832, p. 899.

76 Bowring, J. (ed.): 1843, vol. 7, p. 280.

77 Burton, J.H.: 1843, p. 351.

78 *3730*, 25.2.1832. See the letters from Warburton, Hume, and John Wood.

79 *Execution of Thomas Brown*, for murder and rape (1820); *Execution of John Williamson*, for the murder of his wife (c.1817) – both broadsheets in the John Johnson Collection.

80 For example, the radical newspapers the *Poor Man's Guardian* and the *Sheffield Iris* (10.11.1832 & 3.2.1835 respectively) called the measure the 'Dissecting Act' and the 'Dissecting Bill'. The latter reference suggests that in radical circles the name stuck. Cobbett, of course, called it the 'Dead Body Bill'.

81 *Hansard*, 11.5.1832, p. 899: Attorney General.
Hansard references to alternatives suggested in Parliament:
control of demand (i.e. need overestimated), e.g.:
> 27.2.1832, p. 838: Wayland.
> 11.5.1832, p. 899: Sadler.

all unclaimed except workhouse dead, e.g.:
> 27.2.1832, p. 836: Trench.

voluntary or exemplary bequest, e.g.:
> 11.4.1832, p. 316: Hunt.
> 11.5.1832, p. 895: Fane.

11.5.1832, p. 901: Sadler.

28.6.1832, p. 1086: Wynford.

importation, e.g.:

15.12.1831, p. 303: Sadler.

sale while alive, e.g.:

15.12.1831, p. 302: Hunt.

15.12.1831, p. 303: Sadler.

27.2.1832, p. 833: Inglis.

27.2.1832, p. 836: Trench.

criminals, e.g.:

24.1.1832, p. 826: Wynford.

27.2.1832, p. 837: Sibthorp.

82   Abernethy, J.: 1819.

83   2&3 Gul.c.75: *An Act for Regulating Schools of Anatomy*, Clause VII.

84   Benjamin Brodie's *Evidence*, p. 25.

85   Abernethy, J.: 1819, pp. 35–6; its effects are discussed in Section III.

86   See the *Hansard* coverage of the Commons committee stage.

87   *Hansard*, 17.1.1832, p. 580.

88   *Hansard*, 2.2.1832, p. 1151.

89   Hunt, speaking of George Robinson (MP for Worcester) in *3730*, 25.2.1832.

90   *Hansard*, 18.4.1832, p. 665.

91   *Hansard*,

27.2.1832, p. 842: Hunt.

11.4.1832, p. 320: Hunt.

18.4.1832, p. 667: Hunt.

92   Petition of the Worcester Political Union. *HofC : V&P* Appx, 7.3.1832, no.356.

93   Wakley's campaign against the murderers' clause will be discussed more fully in Dr Bostetter's biography of Wakley.

94   Smith, A.T.H.: 'Stealing the Body', 1976.

95   Roberts, W.: 1843, discusses this topic.

96   Wakley accused anatomists of being accessories to the fact of murder: *Lancet*, 1831–2(1), pp. 373–6, 10.12.1831.

97   Most *Lancet* and *Ballot* editorials on anatomy make this point, e.g.: *Ballot*, 13.11.1831.

98   *LMG*, vol. 19, 1831–2, pp. 714–5: Letter dated 7.2.1832.

99   Somerville, J.: 1832, p. 9.

100 *Lancet*, 1831–2(1), pp. 373–6, 10.12.1831.

101 See Baylen, J.O. & Gossman, N.J.: 1979; Stenton, M. (ed.): 1976. Warburton himself was a member of the Free Trade Club. *Dod's Parliamentary Companion* of 1833 gave this description of Warburton's views: 'A radical Reformer; an advocate of perfect freedom of trade, desirous of following up principles as far as they will go'.

102 Thompson, E.P.: 'Moral Economy', 1971, pp. 89–93, 99.

103 The preamble to the Act reluctantly recognised the evil effects of unfettered free trade.

104 *Hansard*, 22.5.1846. See also a passage quoted by David Roberts [1979, p. 207] from John Allen, speaking of his experience as a Victorian school inspector: 'The let alone doctrines of the political economist are wrong

when applied to material doctors (including hospitals) and spiritual doctors (schoolteachers, clergy, etc.) . . .'

105 Taylor, A.J.: 1972, p. 57.
106 Thompson, E.P.: 1963, p. 90.
107 Taylor, A.J.: 1972, p. 64.
108 Figlio, K.M.: 'Sinister Medicine', 1979, p. 59.
109 *Hansard*, 11.4.1832, p. 312: Warburton.
110 *3730*, 25.2.1832.
111 *Northern Star*, 16.12.1837: Report of a Great Anti-Poor Law meeting at Dewsbury.
112 This passage is inspired by Carson, W.G.: 'Early Factory Legislation', 1974, p. 132.
113 Anatomy Inspectors were funded by central government, and no further provision was made for local administrative costs. Tutors were responsible only for burial costs, which were much lower than the charges made by the resurrectionists – a pauper funeral was estimated to cost £1 in 1828 (*Evidence*, Q929). No evidence has yet been found to suggest that the costs of tuition fell accordingly. Please see my NOTE heading the References section.
114 Poynter, F.N.L.: 1966, pp. 199–200.
115 See Roberts, W.: 1855, p. 14. Private country schools, away from the expansionist aspirations of the large teaching hospitals, seem to have survived longer. See also Singer, C. & Holloway, S.W.F.: 'Early Medical Education', 1960, p. 8. Charles Webster has pointed out that the disappearance of the small anatomy schools was part of a larger process of restructuring in medicine in this period, in which the teaching hospital emerged as the focus for medical teaching [Personal communication]. I take the point entirely.
116 Warburton was not ignorant – he had already attempted to reform the corrupt RCS (see his *DNB* entry), and was a key proponent of the Select Committee on Medical Reform, in 1834.
117 That is, apart from old wives, bonesetters and other unofficial and 'unrecognised' practitioners.
118 2&3 Gul.c.75: *An Act for Regulating Schools of Anatomy*, Clause 1. See also *HO83/1*, 12.11.1832.
119 *Hansard*, 11.4.1832, p. 313: Hunt had been pressing for more inspectors than the second Bill allowed.
120 Hodgkinson, R.: 1967, pp. 74–8.
121 Rogers, J.: 1889, p. 10.
122 Hodgkinson, R.: 1967, p. 110.
123 Hodgkinson, R.: 1967, pp. 79–91.
124 Smith, F.B.: 1979, pp. 385–7.
125 See Rogers, J.: 1889.
126 Smith, F.B.: 1979, p. 390.
127 See *Lancet Sanitary Commission*, 1866, *passim*.
128 There were no qualifications available at this period. Nursing was low status work, usually done by patients or ex-patients. See Smith, B. Abel: 1979, passim.
129 Smith, F.B.: 1979, pp. 387–9.

130 *Lancet Sanitary Commission*, 1866, *passim*.

131 *Lancet Sanitary Commission*, 1866, *passim*.

132 Rogers, J.: 1889.

133 *Lancet Sanitary Commission*, 1866, and Smith, B. Abel: 1964, pp. 37–9 discuss the numbers excluded from them.

134 *Lancet Sanitary Commission*, 1866, pp. iv–v. The *Lancet* Commission was established by his sons after Wakley's death, as a direct result of his concern for the inadequacies of workhouse medical care. Its findings resulted in an outcry, prompting the establishment of the Royal Sanitary Commission, 1868–71, which instituted changes – particularly in the London area.

135 *Lancet Sanitary Commission*, 1866, pp. iv–v. Compare this view with that discussed by Smith, F.B.: 1979, pp. 382–9, concerning the 1890s.

136 Singer, C.J. & Holloway, S.W.F.: 'Early Medical Education', 1960, p. 9; Waddington, I.: 'General Practitioners', 1977, p. 169. For the advent of medical clubs, see Hodgkinson, R.: 1967, pp. 215–39, showing how difficult it was to draw such a line in time of sickness. In the 1870s, Jean Brand (1965, p. 86) says 'medical care for the poor was still marked by a chilling and pervasive atmosphere of deterrence'.

137 Waddington, I.: 1979, pp. 309–10.

138 Tudor Hart summarises the theory thus: 'The availability of good medical care tends to vary inversely with the need for it in the population served. This inverse care law operates more completely where medical care is most exposed to market forces, and less so where such exposure is reduced'. Hart, J. Tudor: 'The Inverse Care Law', 1971.

CHAPTER 9:   THE ACT 'IS UNINJURIOUS IF UNKNOWN'

1 John Abernethy: *The Dissector*, October 1827, p. 27.

2 Richard Carlile, quoted in Weiner, J.: 1983, pp. 20–1.

3 *Leeds Intelligencer*, 1.11.1832.

4 *Lancet* editorial, 1831–2(1), p. 480, 31.12.1831.

5 A great deal more work remains to be done in workhouse records concerning the Act. The records I used in the course of my research were utterly defective for the purpose – most records were missing, destroyed, lost or whereabouts unknown. An ex-workhouse master whom I interviewed in 1980, and who wished to remain anonymous, told me that before the workhouse in which he had worked was turned over to the NHS on the appointed day in 1948, all records were deliberately burnt.

6 Please see my NOTE preceding the References section.

7 *Morning Herald*, 20.3.1829. Sockett's letter continued: 'It is said that only the paupers who are unclaimed by their relatives are to undergo this punishment – not for their crimes, but for their misfortunes. . . . Why should they be supposed to be destitute of the feelings possessed by their more fortunate fellow-creatures?'

8 The events at Swansea are remarkable in that in 1817 there had been no parliamentary discussion of the subject, and neither Abernethy, Bentham, nor Southwood Smith had yet articulated their recommendations for legislation.

Mary Fissell's recent work on bodysnatching in Bristol shows that there may well have been a real basis for the rumours. Fissell, M.: 1986, unpublished.

9 Petition of Several Poor Persons now living in the Workhouse of St Ann, Blackfriars, in the City of London, *CJ*, vol. 84, p. 178, 27.3.1829. For the letter from a Worcestershire Workhouse, see chapter 7, note 78.
Morning Chronicle, 30.5.1829.
The report the man read out probably concerned the Lords' first reading on 20 May.

10 Such incidents elsewhere may be buried in parish and workhouse records anywhere in the country. Please see my NOTE preceding the References section.

11 Paul Pry's cartoon, 'A Few Illustrations for Mr Warberton's Bill', (1829: George, M.D.: 1954, no.15777) is reproduced on p. 220.

12 See Petition of the Worcester Political Union. *HofC:V&P* Appx, 7.3.1832, no.356; and see Hunt in *Hansard*, 27.2.1832, p. 842; 11.4.1832, p. 320; 18.5.1832, p. 667. In a *Lancet* editorial of 28.7.1832, Wakley warned that such transactions would be the result of the Act, and that supporters of the Bill also knew this, but thought that 'exposures would not be of frequent occurrence, as the sales would always be managed in the workhouses'. He believed, correctly, that time would prove him right. (*Lancet*, 1831–2(2), pp. 537–8.)

13 Ashton, J.: 1888, pp. 351–2. Prof. Kathleen Tillotson tells me that the ballad was probably circulating in the 1830s or early 1840s. [Personal communication]. M.A. Crowther (1981, p. 31) mentions a Poor Law Inspector's record that in 1839 in Kent there was a rumour in circulation that 'children in the workhouses were killed to make pies with'.

14 The key works on cholera used here have been: Morris, R.J.: 1976; Pelling, M.: 1978; Longmate, N.: 1966, and Durey, M.: 1979. Other sources used are given in individual notes.

15 Morris, R.J.: 1976 has an excellent chapter on the relationship between class, power and cholera, and mentions (p. 99) a popular belief that the 1831 census had been 'a government enquiry into surplus population'.

16 Nor was choleraphobia confined to the poor: Trevelyan, G.O.: 1959, pp. 186–7 discusses choleraphobia and cholera rumours among the London social elite in June/July 1832.

17 Memorial dated 30.3.1832, published in the *Paisley Advertiser* the following day. Materials used here on the cholera at Paisley, are due to the kind assistance of Ken Hinshallwood, Local History Librarian at Paisley.

18 This case is discussed in chapter 4.

19 Morris, R.J.: 1976, pp. 108–9; *The Visitor*, p. 107.

20 Morris, R.J.: 1976, p. 109.

21 *True Sun*, 20.3.1832.

22 *CJ*, vol. 87, 3.2.1832.

23 Brown, R.: 1886, pp. 276, 280.

24 *Paisley Court Book and Corporation Minute Book*, 2.3.1832.

25 Consecration is mentioned in none of the available sources.

26 A watch was set on the cholera ground only after the riot: Brown, R.: 1886, p. 285.

27 *Paisley Advertiser*, 31.3.1832. The people involved in the riot pulled up the 'stobs' or stakes of which the fence was composed, and carried them into town.

28 *Paisley Advertiser*, 31.3.1832.

29 *Paisley Advertiser*, 31.3.1832; Brown, R.: 1886, p. 280.

30 Fowler's *Directory of Renfrewshire*, 1832, p. 129. The Society was formed in 1829, and Hugh Kerr of Blacklaw Lane (also referred to as 'Lone') is listed in the 1832/1834 directories as 'officer' of the Society.

31 *The Visitor*, p. 91.

32 *The Visitor*, p. 106.

33 *The Visitor*, p. 98.

34 *Paisley Advertiser*, 31.3.1832. See particularly the report of a meeting chaired by John Taylor.

35 *Paisley Advertiser*, 31.3.1832.

36 *The Visitor*, p. 107.

37 *The Visitor*, p. 98.

38 *The Visitor*, p. 107.

39 *Paisley Advertiser*, 31.3.1832.

40 *Paisley Court Book and Corporation Minute Book*, 3.7.1832.
    The *Visitor*, p. 106 estimated the damage at about £130.

41 Morris, R.J.: 1976, pp. 108–14; Durey, M.: 1979, pp. 177–82; Longmate, N.: 1966.

42 A cartoon appeared in *The Times*, 14.2.1832, expressing the belief that choleraphobia was a self-delusion designed to profit the medical profession. The *True Sun*, 22.3.1832 reported local opposition to the construction of a cholera hospital in St Mary's parish, Newington: 'The majority of the parishioners present were opposed to the formation of a cholera hospital, on the ground that no disease except that produced by poverty, prevailed in the parish'. The report mentioned that two doctors at the meeting declared 'their utter disbelief in the existence of Asiatic cholera in this country'. The same paper carried similar stories on 5.3.1832 and 9.3.1832.

43 Morris, R.J.: 1976, p. 109; *The Visitor*, p. 91.

44 Copies of the texts of street notices issued by the Oxford Board of Health appear in an appendix to Thomas, V.: 1835. See also Morris, R.J.: 'Religion and Medicine', 1975.

45 Such moral warnings were, however, common. See for example a religious tract entitled: *Why are you afraid of the cholera?* 1832, which includes the statement 'The greater part of those who have died have been bad, dirty, drunken, and idle people!'

46 Thomas, V.: 1835, pp. 13–22.

47 The words in inverted commas are those of J. Branston of the Doncaster Medical Board of Health, reporting in the *Cholera Gazette*, Lond., 1832, p. 21. My description of the symptoms and progress of the disease is based upon cases reported in the contemporary medical press, the *Cholera Gazette*, and *Price's Textbook of Medicine*.

48 Andrews, W.: 1895, pp. 186–8.
    See also *True Sun*, 28.8.1832; *Devonshire Chronicle*, 29.7.1832.

49 J. Burton MD. report in the *Cholera Gazette*, Lond., 1832, p. 22.

50 Morris, R.J.: 1976, pp. 105–7; *True Sun*, 25.8.1832.

51 Morris, R.J.: 1976, p. 105; Shapter, T.: 1849, p. 173.

52 Barnett, M.: 'The 1832 Cholera Epidemic in York', 1972, pp. 32, 36; Morris, R.J.: 1976, pp. 105–7.

53 Barnett, M.: 'The 1832 Cholera Epidemic in York', 1972, pp. 32, 36; Morris, R.J.: 1976, pp. 105–7.

54 *True Sun*, 2.4.1832; 26.7.1832; Head, G.: 1837, pp. 26–31; Morris, R.J.: 1976, pp. 104, 112–13, 116–17; Barnett, M.: 'The 1832 Cholera Epidemic in York', 1972, p. 31; Durey, M.: 1979, p. 178.

55 Brown, R.: 1886, p. 281; *Paisley Advertiser*, 31.3.1832.

56 Fires of aromatic wood were used as a fumigant against plague in Thucydides' time. See Lord Amulree: 'Hygienic Conditions in Ancient Rome and Modern London', 1973, pp. 244–55.

57 A wide reading of contemporary medical literature on cholera commonly yields similarly mistaken treatments for cholera victims, like emetics – which could actually have encourged the process of dehydration, and opium, which can be contra-indicated. See Morris, R.J.: 1976, pp. 162–6; *Price's Textbook of Medicine*. The discovery during the epidemic, by Thomas Latta of Leith, of the modern treatment by saline infusion was, on the other hand, largely ignored by the medical establishment as it was unorthodox, uneven in success (probably as a result of ignorance of antisepsis), and its champion was a nobody. Morris, R.J.: 1976 provides good commentary on the subject.

58 *Manchester Guardian*, 8.9.1832; *True Sun*, 7.9.1832; *Poor Man's Advocate*, 15.9.1832; *Poor Man's Guardian*, 8.9.1832.
   See also Morris, R.J.: 1976, pp. 110–11; and next note.

59 It is more than likely that the word 'burked' was being used.

60 *Republican and Radical Reformer*, 15.9.1832. The story's headline was: 'Cheap Knowledge versus Cheap Gin.'

61 *Poor Man's Advocate*, 15.9.1832. The story's headline was: 'The Cholera Riot No Proof of the People's Ignorance'.

62 Thompson, E.P.: 1963, pp. 899–908.

63 The description is Somerville's: MH74/12, 29.10.1832.

64 *Leeds Patriot*, 17.10.1832.

65 *Leeds Patriot*, 17.10.1832; *Leeds Intelligencer*, 1.11.1832; *Cobbett's Weekly Political Register*, 10.11.1832; *True Sun*, 6.11.1832; 8.11.1832.

66 MH74/12, 29.10.1832.

67 *Leeds Intelligencer*, 8.11.1832.

68 *Leeds Intelligencer*, 8.11.1832, speech of Mr Foster.

69 Fraser, D.: 'Politics and Society', 1980; Fraser, D.: 'The Leeds Churchwardens', 1971; Fraser, D.: 'Poor Law Politics in Leeds', 1971.

70 See Thompson, E.P.: 1963, pp. 899–908 for justification of this view.

71 *Leeds Intelligencer*, 13.12.1832. The graphic reconstruction of the scene reproduced in the text is by Doc Rowe, and is subject to copyright. See p. 231.

72 Baines's newspaper the *Leeds Mercury* called the banners 'inflammatory and atrocious flags': *Leeds Mercury Extraordinary*, 11.12.1832.

73 *Leeds Mercury Extraordinary*, 11.12.1832; Thompson, E.P.: 1963, pp. 907–8.

74 *LMG*, vol. 11, 5.1.1833, p. 455.

75 MH74/12, 18.12.1832; 31.12.1832.

76 *LMG*, vol. 11, 9.2.1833, p.640.

77 MH74/12, 2.1.1833.

78 *Leeds Intelligencer*, 8.11.1832.

79 MH74/12, 16.1.1833.

80 Fraser, D.: 1980, pp. 278–9.

81 *True Sun*, 24.9.1832.

82 *True Sun*, 4.12.1832.

83 *True Sun*, 4.12.1832.

84 *The Times*, 27.12.1832; 28.12.1832; *Figaro's Monthly Newspaper*, 1.1.1833.

85 HO64/16, bundle 3, re 'Baume'. I am indebted to John Noyce for directing me to this material. Baume is described by Joel Weiner as a 'working-class activist': 'the French-born "Reforming Optimist" ' of Carlile's antichristian School of Free Discussion, 'who subsequently opened several [atheist] "chapels", and became a publisher of cheap political literature'. Weiner, J.: 1983, pp. 148–9. I thank Joel Weiner for showing me his notes on Baume.

86 According to the accoucheur, Charlotte Baume died of 'inflammation of the peritoneum' (MH74/12, 27.12.1832), and her child of erysipelas. I have discussed this diagnosis with Dr Brian Hurwitz MRCP, who has confirmed my own suspicions that this probably meant she died either:

   – from rupture of the uterus, possibly through the unskillful use of forceps,

   – from caesarian section, which at this period had an appallingly high mortality,

   – of puerperal fever, the stigma of which the surgeon did not wish to admit.

Caesarian section was a desperately dangerous procedure in Britain at this time. Even twenty years later mortality in the Bristol area was nearly 75 per cent. Continental results were lower – 41 per cent – but if Charlotte had to undergo such an operation, her chances of survival were very slim. See Wangensteen, P.H. & Wangensteen, S.: 1978, p. 207. The fact that the child died of erysipelas would support the last interpretation, as the two diseases are caused by the same organism. If this was the case, her body would have been dangerous to dissect. Oliver Wendell Holmes was drawn to make the connection between puerperal fever and sepsis as the result of the death of an anatomist friend after sustaining a wound in such a dissection. See also Loudon, I: 'Obstetric Care, Social Class', 1986, which shows that Victorian maternal mortality tended to be higher when a doctor was in attendance.

87 *The Times*, 27.12.1832; MH74/12, 27.12.1832.

88 MH74/12, 28.12.1832; 31.12.1832.

89 From the point of view of the Home Office, Baume was a highly suspect individual, from his association with Carlile – so no apology was likely to have been given. If such an apology was ever made, I would be delighted to hear of it.

90 Roberts, W.: 1843, p. 16.

91 A report of Carlile's dissection and Grainger's oration appears in the *Lancet* 1842–3(1), 18.2.1843, p. 774. See also Weiner, J.: 1983, pp. 259–60; Brook, C.: 1943; *DNB* Detrosier, Julian Hibbert.

CHAPTER 10: THE BUREAUCRAT'S BAD DREAM

1 *Lancet*, 1832–3(2), p. 708, 24.8.1833. Letter from John Birtwhistle, Surgeon.
2 *Lancet*, editorial 1841–2(1), pp. 235–8, 13.11.1841.
3 HO83/1, 29.11.1836; 30.12.1836.
4 Roberts, W.: 1855, p. 13 thought the arrangement gave facility for 'the operation of partisanship'.
5 HO83/1, 8.9.1842.
6 HO83/2, 1.10.1842. After 1844, London and the provinces were again administered by one Inspector, so this division of tasks may have been little more than cosmetic. See note 49 below.
7 See discussion of parliamentary agreement for funding the office in my previous chapter.
8 HO83/1, 22.2.1842.
9 HO83/1, 22.2.1842.
10 MH74/12, 11.1.1834.
11 *Poor Man's Guardian*, 10.11.1832.
12 MH74/12, 11.1.1834.
13 See for example MH74/12, p. 76, where Somerville suggests to a Sheffield anatomist that he should let the Inspector know the political affiliations of recalcitrant overseers, and if 'any influential figure of that persuasion is in London with whom [Somerville] might communicate'.
14 HO83/1, 18.1.1834.
15 MH74/12, 1.10.1833. It is worth noticing the way in which Somerville's phraseology carefully encouraged compliance, a technique he used on other occasions with greater success. He offered to come and explain personally to Gregory why Spitalfields should adopt the plan in use in 'other Parishes'.
16 MH74/12, n.d., p. 140.
17 MH74/12, 11.1.1834. According to Dr Betty Bostetter, the idea was Wakley's.
18 *Lancet*, 1836–7(1), p. 645, 28.1.1837.
19 MH74/12, 11.1.1834.
20 HO83/1, 22.4.1842. The protestation is implicit in Phillipps's reply.
21 MH74/12, 4.4.1834; 15.4.1834.
22 MH74/12, 4.4.1834; 15.5.1834.
23 HO83/1, 5.11.1833.
24 MH74/12, 15.1.1835.
25 MH74/12, 11.1.1834.
26 See, for example, MH74/12, 4.4.1834; 15.4.1834.
27 MH74/12, 9.10.1834.
28 Carson, W.G.: 'Early Factory Legislation', 1974, p. 120 – quoting Marx.
29 HO83/1, 13.6.1834.
30 MH74/13, Quarterly Report, January 1836.
31 As directed by Clause IV of the Act. The system included an early form of death certification, as civil registration was not enacted until 1836.
32 See, for example: MH74/12, 19.3.1834; 28.8.1834. See also: MH74/13, 12.10.1841. HO83/1, 18.12.1838; 28.12.1839.

33 A case in point is a letter to the London anatomist, Lane, written in April 1834 [MH74/12, 2.4.1834]. Somerville stated the charge with the utmost gravity:

> I am compelled in the discharge of my duty . . . to enclose for your consideration a letter from Mr Hamilton Teacher of Anatomy in the London Hospital by which it appears that the Coffin from your School containing the remains of a body for interment, if opened, as sometimes happens, by the Parish Authorities would have led to exposures and to results the occurrence of which it is not possible to contemplate without serious alarm.

He then appealed to the anatomist's best intentions, by seeking his appreciation of: '. . . the strong reliance which I am at all times disposed to place upon the honour of every Teacher in the fulfillment of this duty to the Government and the Public' . . . and asked him in future rigidly to adhere to the Act's burial clause. Somerville then proceeded politely to state his conviction that the misdeed was due to a servant, and encouraged Lane to feel indebted to him by intimating that although 'in duty bound' to report upon such a matter (presumably to the Home Secretary), he had refrained from doing so in the belief that Lane's directions would in future be more strictly obeyed. This is a 'gentlemen's agreement' in process; and its technique – turning a blind eye to misbehaviour on the assumption of an undertaking that it won't happen again – is the basis upon which Somerville largely depended to keep the Act in operation. He was not simply 'disposed' to place reliance upon anatomists' honour – the Act was defective to such a degree that he was *obliged* to do so. There may have been an element of public hospital v. private school rivalry going on in Mr Hamilton's disclosure of misdeeds to the Inspector, and some lack of tact in the Inspector's decision to forward the letter – which also means that no copy survives in Anatomy Office records. Somerville may have known Lane personally.

34 MH74/12, 2.4.1834.

35 MH74/12, 15.1.1835. The supply was resumed again in 1834–6, and then stopped again, see MH74/16, p. 89.

36 MH74/16, pp. 89, 91.

37 HO83/1, 30.11.1837.

38 MH74/12, 1.10.1833.

39 HO83/1, 21.1.1835.

40 MH74/12, 5.11.1832.

41 MH74/12, 28.9.1832.

42 MH74/12, 2.7.1833. It will be shown below that such observances were not kept up.

43 HO83/1, 22.9.1837; 29.11.1841.

44 I discussed the Swan Street riot in my previous chapter. Another case of an illicit beheading – this time of a smallpox victim – took place at St Giles's Workhouse, London, in 1840: MH74/13, 22.1.1841. Obviously the Act's failure to legislate on parts of bodies left a door wide open to nefarious deals. See next note. See also note 99 below.

45 MH74/12, 12.10.1832. In 1846, a workhouse medical officer was discovered dismembering corpses. Each body was being divided into six

parts, probably in accordance with the mode in which students purchased them: head and neck/truck/four limbs. *Lancet*, 1846(2), p. 675, 19.12.1846.

46   MH74/12, 15.1.1835.

47   MH74/16.

48   MH74/16.

49   Sheppard, F.: 1971, p. xix, for reservations about the use of the terms 'provinces' and 'provincial'. The Inspectorate and its central administrative records are divided on these lines – Metropolitan, Provincial, Scotland.

50   See, for example, MH74/12, 18.10.1832; 17.11.1832; 13.12.1833; 28.1.1834; 27.11.1835.

51   MH74/16.

52   *Report*, p. 138 – the only approximately reliable figures available for the period prior to the Act.

53   I have been unable to find evidence of an English version of the memorandum of praise for the Act which was issued by Dublin anatomists, and published in the *Lancet*, 1836–7(1), 18.2.1837, p. 767. Scotland produced one, but much later: see Buchanan, G.: 'On the effects of Mr Warburton's Anatomy Bill', 1855. For complaints of maldistribution/shortage later in the century, see for example: HO83/2, 2.2.1858; 17.3.1868.

54   See for example, *Lancet*, 1832–3(2), pp. 84–5, 13.4.1833; 1836–7(1), p. 477, 24.12.1836; 1841–2(1), pp. 235–8, 13.11.1841. See also: HO83/1, 13.3.1834; 11.12.1837. MH74/14 – a mass of correspondence between 20.10.1841 – 1.9.1842 shows that Somerville was assailed on all sides by accusations, non-cooperation and shortages. He seems to have allowed (or lost control of) arrears of burial certificates in all quarters, despite the circular of 18.12.1838 (in HO83/1).

55   I have found only one other historian to have examined the reasons for Somerville's demise. See Durey, M.: 'Bodysnatchers and Benthamites', 1976.

56   HO83/1, 23.2.1842.

57   HO83/1, 22.2.1842.

58   See note 55 above, 65 below, and Roberts, W.: 1843; 1855.

59   Roberts, W.: 1843, 1855.

60   There is evidence on both sides as to whether Roberts's 'process' was effective – most of which leans in his favour. Many eminent surgeons and anatomists, including Astley Cooper, Benjamin Brodie, Joseph Henry Green, Grainger, Birkbeck, Skey, Stanley and other important figures signed memoranda in 1836 to approve Roberts's application for a government gratuity (Roberts, W.: 1855, pp. 39–43). Even Somerville wrote testimony of its efficacy at that time (Roberts, W.: 1855, p. 39). Later, in c.1841, Somerville found a comparatively unknown anatomist – Edward Cock, lecturer on anatomy at Guy's – to contradict these more weighty views, possibly – as Roberts believed – for mercenary motives (Roberts, W.: 1855, p. 30; MH74/13, pp. 415–18). He reported then that the process altered the texture of the corpse from that to which anatomists were accustomed in fresh bodies, that the viscera were generally satisfactory, but that the brain 'flowed out in a liquid mass of putridity causing a dreadful stench'.

61   HO83/1, 23.11.1838. See also Roberts's pamphlets (1843, 1855), and the

account of his activities in MH74/13: 3.10.1837; Somerville's Quarterly Report, 11.1.1839; an undated letter to Sir James Graham, pp. 407–10 (c.30.9.1841); 13.12.1841; 12.10.1843; 10.1.1844.
See also Durey, M.: 'Bodysnatchers and Benthamites', 1976, pp. 212–17.

62   MH74/13, Quarterly Report, January 1839. Popular intolerance of the Act may have worked as a more effective regulator upon workhouse personnel than the Inspectorate.

63   Durey, M.: 'Bodysnatchers and Benthamites', 1976, pp. 213–14.

64   HO83/1, 23.11.1838; MH74/13, Quarterly Report, January 1841.

65   Durey echoes this hostility. I feel sure, however, that if he had seen Roberts's pamphlets, which he evidently did not, his view may have been different.

66   Roberts was supported by local politicians in St Marylebone, particularly Jonas Pope, see MH74/14, 29.11.1841, by the anatomists Dermott, Tatum and Foster, and by several MPs, including Duncombe, Fitzstephens, French, Hardy and Maclean. His popular appeal is evident in the impact of his campaign.

67   Maccoby, S.: 1935, pp. 66–7.
       Durey, M.: 'Bodysnatchers and Benthamites', 1976, p. 212.

68   *True Sun*, 17.10.1832.

69   MH74/16, Return No.1.

70   Roberts, W.: 1843, p. 8.

71   Roberts, W.: 1843, p. 8.

72   Roberts, W.: 1843, pp. 15–16.

73   Roberts, W.: 1843, pp. 15–16.

74   Roberts, W.: 1843, p.10.

75   Compare Roberts's view with that of the anonymous author of *An Address*, 1829: 'The assertion is unsupported that after dissection the body is interred [unless] a substance minced and thrown into a lime-hole can be called a funeral decently performed', (p. 24).

76   Roberts, W.: 1855, p. 43.

77   MH74/14, 13.12.1841.

78   Roberts, W.: 1855, p. 21. Even if 42 shillings (£2.10p) was the price paid for the burial of remains (which is unlikely, see *Evidence*, Q929), there would still have been a profit of over £5 to be made on each corpse. Dr Betty Bostetter will be publishing material on the profitability of the hospital schools in her forthcoming biography of Wakley.

79   Roberts, W.: 1855, pp. 10,14.

80   Jones, N.H.: 'Medical Education', 1984; Merrington, W.R.: 1976, p. 6; Durey, M.: 'Bodysnatchers and Benthamites', 1976, p. 215.

81   Roberts, W.: 1855, p. 14.

82   Tactics seem to have involved attempts to provoke anatomy riots in central London. Durey, M.: 'Bodysnatchers and Benthamites', 1976.

83   MH74/13, 3.10.1837.

84   MH74/14, 13.12.1841.

85   Roberts, W.: 1855, p. 23.

86   Roberts, W.: 1855, p. 34.

87   HO83/1, 14.2.1841; Durey, M.: 'Bodysnatchers and Benthamites', 1976, p. 217.

88   Roberts, W.: 1855, p. 12.

89   Hamburger, J.: 1965, pp. 69n, 266.

90   See HO83/1. Warburton's 'commissioners' consisted of himself, Charles A.
     Gore, Frederick Byng, and Benjamin Hawes jun., 23.1.1840. References to
     their failure to report are recorded on 5.3.1841; 4.5.1841; 9.9.1841. A change
     of regime brought Sir James Graham into the Home Office, who on
     20.9.1841 demanded to see Warburton's report, evidently without success,
     as the demand was repeated on 27.11.1841, and again on 15.2.1842 – by
     which time another course of action had evidently been decided upon – see
     next note. See also Roberts, W.: 1855, p. 24.

91   HO83/1, 8.12.1841; 16.12.1841; 14.2.1842. Sir James Graham appointed (at
     a fee of 25 guineas each) a Mr Rogers QC, of Inner Temple, and Mr J.H.
     Green of Hadley, Barnet, Herts (the St Thomas's surgeon) to investigate
     allegations against Somerville by Mr John Foster of 49 Welbeck Street and
     Mr Jonas Pope, of 3 Manchester Square. Somerville was permitted to
     employ counsel in his own defence: HO83/1, 18.12.1841. The allegations
     were found to be 'not established by proof', but Somerville was admonished
     by Sir James Graham to ensure the observance of the burial clause. See also
     Durey, M.: 'Bodysnatchers and Benthamites', 1976, p. 217.

92   Correspondence with Foster, Green and Rogers continued through to the
     following September, when Somerville was informed that the Home
     Secretary required a new inspector. The RCS was given the task of
     appointing a committee to investigate shortages of corpses in May 1842, to
     which body the Home Secretary permitted access to Somerville's records:
     HO83/1, 28.5.1842. Receipt of the report was acknowledged by the Home
     Office: 31.8.1842, and Somerville received notice almost immediately, see
     next note.

93   HO83/1, 8.9.1842. The new Inspectors, Dr A. Wood, Rutherford Alcock
     and Mr Bacot were appointed within the month. HO83/2, 1.10.1842.

94   See Somerville's *Letter to the Lord Chancellor*, which he published while the
     second Anatomy Bill was in its final parliamentary stages. By 1840,
     Somerville's Home Office superiors were reprimanding him for unexplained
     absences from the Anatomy Office. See HO83/1, 22.9.1840.

95   MacDonagh, O.: 1981.

96   The timing of his *Letter* (see note 94 above) coincided closely with decisions
     concerning the appointment of Inspectors under the new Act.

97   See Weiner, J.: 1983, p. 158.

98   A report of the entire proceedings appeared in the *Lancet*, 1844–5(1),
     15.6.1844, pp. 391–2.
     See also Hay, D.: 'Property, Authority and the Criminal Law', 1977, p. 51.
     For the text of a contemporary petition against the Anatomy Act see
     Baxter, G.R.W.: 1841, p. 593.

99   MH74/13, 22.1.1841. Somerville expressed profound relief that due to the
     'prudence' of the parochial authorities of St Giles's, the decapitation of a
     workhouse inmate's body (see also note 44 above) had not become public
     knowledge.

100 Warburton's vilification of Roberts was accepted by Parliament after he
     read aloud some of Roberts's publicity to show the extent of his infringement
     of 'decency' in ignoring officially created silence. He had disrupted the
     process of sequestration by informing workhouse inhabitants of their legal

right to object, and moreover publicised details of the wholesale wastage and destruction of paupers' corpses.

101 Wade, J.: 1829 had recommended this mode of proceeding.

102 MH74/36, 30.1.1882. Birkett's view was justified in the circumstances: the following November, students at the Sheffield school sent a plea for assistance, as the city supply had entirely ceased: MH74/36, 12.11.1883.

103 For example, reports concerning Somerville were not laid on the Commons table, despite requests. Roberts, W.: 1855, pp. 24–5. See also note 90 above.

104 HO83/1, 29.11.1839; 23.12.1839; 27.2.1840; and an undated entry in March 1840. See also MH74/13, 3.12.1839.

105 Now Lexington Street, London W1.

106 In 1858 it was officially – but not publicly – recognised that 'bodies which were not unclaimed had been improperly sent for dissection' and that teachers made applications to workhouses without the knowledge of the Inspectors. Discrepancies between workhouse records and those kept by the Inspectors sometimes turned up – but since the Inspectors' reports and returns were never published, and were closed to public scrutiny, such differences must have gone unnoticed in many cases. See HO83/2, 17.2.1858, and the allegations of Jonas Pope – see notes 66 and 91 above.

107 My coverage of Alcock is based mainly upon O'Rahilly, R.: 1948. See also: Dobson, J.: 1946, p. 17.

108 See for example the Gillard case discussed above, the Sophia Quin case at Newcastle in 1841 (MH74/13, 1.2.1841; 16.3.1841) and the Craven case in 1834, which concerned allegations of bodysnatching in a petition from the inhabitants of Hull. On the Home Secretary's orders, Somerville visited the school of Messrs Craven and Wallis, which had been daubed with graffiti, including 'many opprobrious epithets designating the Teachers as Burkers and the School as a Burking Shop'. Both anatomists gave the Inspector a solemn assurance of their integrity, ascribing the rumours in the town to 'the ignorance and prejudice of the lowest orders aided by certain malicious individuals'. Somerville then made an inspection of the premises, and discovered – apparently to everyone's surprise – several parts of bodies entirely unaccounted for in the returns submitted to him. He reported back to his superiors that the school had been involved in illegal transactions: HO83/1, 23.5.1834; 5.6.1834; MH74/12, 3.6.1834.

See also the Hesbrook case, in which the body of a woman registered as having been buried at St Martins in the Fields on 18.12.1839 was discovered in process of dissection at Charing Cross Hospital School the following day: HO83/1, 28.12.1839. Nothing was done in either of these cases, despite clear contraventions of the law.

109 34 & 35 Vict. c.16: *An Act to Amend the Act for Regulating Schools of Anatomy*, 1871.

110 MH74/14, 13.12.1841.

111 MH74/6–9; MH74/16; MH74/36.

112 MH74/16: London Returns provide the following figures:

	W'house	Hosp.	Prison	Hulks	Asylums
[1832	445	135	15	8	4]
[1882	557	27	–	–	–]
1907	329	5	–	–	22
1908	234	9	–	–	97
1913	147	23	–	–	125
1914	151	7	–	–	120

[Figures for 1832 and 1882 are offered for comparison only.]
The table illustrates particularly well the process by which in the early twentieth century, the mentally handicapped/ill began to substitute for the workhouse poor on the slab. It shows, moreover, the small number of bodies available before the Great War in London, relative to the Act's first fifty years. More research is required before the decline of workhouse bodies can be ascribed to the advent of Old Age pensions, but the figures are suggestive. Aschrott gives figures of a census of Poor Law inmates in 1899: 90 per cent were old, sick, children, or mentally ill/handicapped. By far the greatest proportion were the elderly. See Aschrott, P.F.: 1902, p. 247.
See Neate, A.R.: 1967: 'During 1911 the number of inmates at the St Marylebone Workhouse fell by over 200 to 1,689, and by the end of 1914 it had dropped further to 1,443'. In 1918 the figure was 658, and in 1930, 577.

113 MH74/30, 30.9.1920.
114 See above table.
115 MH74/30, 30.9.1920.
116 MH74/30, Alexander Macphail: 1st Quarterly Report, 1920.
117 *Surrey Comet*, 25.10.1924.
118 MH74/16 Anatomy Registers.
119 *Surrey Comet*, 25.10.1924.
120 MH74/30, 30.9.1920.
121 *West London Observer*, 7.9.1923, 21.9.1923.
122 *West London Observer*, 7.9.1923, 21.9.1923.
123 MH74/30, letter from H.E. Granger dated 27.9.1923, in Macphail's autumn Quarterly Report for 1923.
124 In decimal currency 12.5 pence.
125 *Essex Times*, 15.10.1921; *Romford Times*, 19.10.1921.
126 MH74/30.
127 As far as I can discern, no material on early nineteenth century opposition to the Act had been collected until my work and that of other scholars in the 1970s. See n.8, p. 295.
128 See MH74/16, *Return* of Bodies given to Medical Schools in London 1913–1944, on which there is a handwritten note, signed 'W.O'Sullivan' and dated 31.8.1938: 'Dr Alex Macphail Inspector of Anatomy retired on pension in July 1938 (after long illness) died on 28th August 1938 – body sent to Oxford for dissection at his own request and with the consent of his relatives on 30th August 1938'.
129 MH74/16. These *Returns* may not be wholly accurate, and since the parallel *Registers* are missing, we may never know the number of bequests between 1832 and 1918, particularly as the bequests known to have taken place (e.g.: Baume, Carlile) are not recorded separately in the *Returns*. The

Returns seem to have been compiled 'from the Office records' in about 1918, and then added to and amended by various hands. A category 'Dwelling Houses' has been added at a late date to what may originally have been Somerville's original source-categories – 'Unions' (workhouses), Hospitals, Prisons, Hulks, Asylums; and numbers have been inserted for the years 1832–57. Most entries in this column after 1843 are a simple dash signifying that no corpses were obtained from this source. Unfortunately, although there are 135 corpses registered under this category between 1832 and 1857, and 99 of these appear in Somerville's first three years of office, there is no way of identifying them. Some of them may have been bequests, but most are likely to have been the bodies of poor people dying in lodgings in need of parish burial – like John Crosby. One suspects that the impossibility of keeping the collection and dissection of such bodies secret, and the risks of opposition, led to their rapid diminution in numbers; or that alternatively, insurances and other working-class expedients (collections, friendly leads, etc.) speedily prevented the Inspector from obtaining bodies in this way. In Edinburgh and Aberdeen public mortuaries were established as apparently 'neutral' depots in cases of unidentified or unclaimed dead. A primary function was the apparently innocuous acquisition of corpses for the anatomists. (Edinburgh: HO83/1, 6.10.1834; 31.7.1839; 24.12.1839. Aberdeen: HO83/1, 12.11.1833). It is possible that a similar arrangement was increasingly used in the metropolis – that workhouse mortuaries were used as staging posts for 'unclaimed' dead poor dying in the community.

130 MH74/16. See Figures 4 & 5 (p. 259).

Data for figure 4 is given below:

	total	bequests	%
1934–5	371	11	3
35–6	343	17	5
36–7	407	17	4
37–8	312	14	4
38–9	295	22	7
39–40	287	16	6
40–1	253	14	6
41–2	255	9	4
GAP IN DATA			
1958–9	244	177	72
59–60	236	155	65
60–1	260	211	81
61–2	249	223	89
62–3	241	224	93
63–4	232	213	92
64–5	277	247	89
65–6	306	281	92
66–7	207	207	100
67–8	277	270	97
68–9	216	213	99
69–70	242	238	98

Data for figure 5 is given below:

	GB deaths (approx)	GB cremations (approx)	% of total
1900	670,000	440	.07
1910	555,500	840	.15
1920	534,300	1,800	.34
1930	519,700	4,530	.87
1940	654,300	25,200	3.8
1950	574,300	89,550	15.5
1960	588,000	204,020	34.7
1970	638,800	353,980	55.4

131 I am myself about to undertake such a study.

132 I am grateful to the Cremation Society of Great Britain for providing the information which has enabled me to draw up the table concerning cremation given in the text.

133 The impact of the Great War cannot be overestimated – see Cannadine, D.: 'Death and Grief in Modern Britain', 1981; Richardson, R.: 'Old People's Attitudes to Death', 1984.

134 Preliminary work on this area seems to indicate that the real changes did not take place until after the establishment of the National Health Service.

135 I am myself about to undertake such a study.

136 This view is based upon my own interviews.

CHAPTER 11: THE UNPARDONABLE OFFENCE

1 Beaumont, G.: [The Warriors' Looking Glass. Sheffield, 1808] quoted in Thompson, E.P.: 1963, p. 512.

2 *Twopenny Dispatch*, 10.9.1836.

3 James Somerville to Benjamin Harrison, Secretary/Treasurer of Guy's Hospital. MH74/12, 14.12.1833.

4 Cobbett, W.: 1834.

5 Bailey, J.B.: 1896, p. 118.

6 Thompson, E.P.: 1963, pp. 899–900. See note 31 below.

7 Thompson, E.P.: 1963, p. 903: 'demarcate and exclude' is E.P. Thompson's phrase.

8 See *Appendices*.

9 See list of illustrations, and note 23 below.

10 Thompson, E.P.: 1963, p. 899.

11 Thomas, W.: 1979, p. 427.

12 *Sheffield Independent*, 31.1.1835; 11.4.1835; *Sheffield Iris*, 27.1.1835, 3.2.1835; *Weekly True Sun*, 1.2.1835; HO83/1, 19.2.1835; Donnelly, F.K.: 'The Destruction of the Sheffield School of Anatomy', 1975.

13 Baxter, J.: 'Samuel Holberry', 1978, p. 9.

14 *Cambridge Chronicle*, 6.12.1833; *Derby Mercury*, 11.12.1833; *The Times*, 7.12.1833; *Weekly True Sun*, 8.12.1833.

15 In HO83/1, 9.12.1833. Somerville calls the overseers 'most culpably imprudent' to have called the meeting. See also MH74/12, 4.12.1833: 'we are

in sad want [of corpses] . . . in consequence of the . . . fine unseasonable weather'.

16 MH74/13, 28.2.1836 – marked '*Secret and Confidential*'.

17 See chapter 10, note 108.

18 MH74/13, Inspector's Quarterly Report for spring 1842.

19 Early 1832 was a key period for anatomy riots, among which have been discussed: Aberdeen, Hereford, Greenwich, Inveresk, and Swan Street Manchester. See also coverage of the Bolton cholera riots in the *Morning Chronicle*, 29.9.1832.

20 Other cases than Gillard's are already known:

    Hull 1834: See chapter 10, note 108.

    Spalding, 1835: *The Times*, 11.3.1836; MH74/13, 30.11.1835.

    Newcastle, 1841: Sophia Quin/Rosanna Rox case, 1841: MH74/13, 1.2.1841; HO83/1, 12.2.1841; 1.3.1841; 4.3.1841; 24.3.1841; *Lancet*; 1840–1(1), pp. 867–9, 13.3.1841.

    Newington, London, 1858: Trial of Feist (a workhouse master accused of fraudulently recording funerals for the bodies of the poor whom he was actually selling to anatomists), *The Times*, 25.2.1858; Regina v. Feist, 1858. Feist was convicted, but cleared on appeal.

    Sheffield, 1862: A sexton's house was demolished after a bodysnatching scandal – Furness, J.M.: 1893, p. 21.

    Sheffield, 1882: Wrong corpse sent for dissection, *The Times*, 26.1.1882, 27.1.1882.

Communications between the Anatomy Office and regional schools seem to have been extremely poor. The Newcastle press reported the Quin/Rox case over a month before the Inspector came to hear of it. It is likely that many less spectacular cases occurred without the Inspectors's knowledge, and that a large proportion never found space in local newspapers. It is more than likely that further work will bring more such cases to light. Please see my NOTE heading the References section.

21 See previous note.

22 *The Christian's Appeal against the Poor Law Amendment Act*. Broadsheet, c.1834.

23 M.D. George's *Catalogue* (1954) of political cartoons provides a good guide to the prevailing concerns of the press in 1832. Although there are a number which picture the Reform Bill being 'Burked' and dissected/dismembered, almost none refer to the Anatomy Bill itself. In 1829 this had not been the case. See Richardson, R.: 'Burking the Bill' (in preparation). See back of jacket.

24 Figlio, K.M.: 'Chlorosis', 1978, p. 596.

25 See for example, Jones, M.W.: 1978, p. 56.

26 Inspiration for this insight is owed to Karl Figlio ('Chlorosis', 1978, p. 596).

27 See the account of the NPU debate in chapter 6.

28 Thompson, E.P.: 1963, pp. 902, 904, 910; Baxter, J.: 'Samuel Holberry', 1978, pp. 1–9.

29 See Kaijage, F.J.: 'Poor Law Catechism', 1981, p. 27.

30 Please see my NOTE heading the References section.

31 This passage owes its inspiration to Carson, W.G.: 'Early Factory Legislation', 1974.

32 Thompson, E.P.: 1963, p. 902.

33 Gwyn A. Williams – preface to Thompson, D.: 1971.

34 See notes 6 and 7 above.

35 The words in inverted commas are those of Mr Mott, a Poor Law Commissioner in the 1830s, cited in Driver, C.: 1946, p. 332.

36 Thompson, E.P.: 1963, pp. 853–7; Morris, R.J.: 1976, p. 99.

37 See for example, Baxter, G.R.W.: 1841.The phrase 'deterrent workhouse' is, I think, M.A. Crowther's (1981, p. 37).

38 Digby, A.: 1978, p. 126. See also Baxter, G.R.W.: 1841 – in which an entire chapter is entitled 'Union Bastiles are Prisons'. One of the old paternalists, Earl Stanhope, is cited as saying in 1838: 'He had been told in the House of Lords, that he was wrong in giving the new Workhouses the name of prisons, and that the proper description was asylums; as if Newgate was an asylum for criminals, and the Fleet an asylum for debtors!' (p. 188).

39 Marcus (pseud.): *On the Possibility of Limiting Populousness*, (Lond., 1838) reprinted Lond., 1839, p. 9. The passage quoted summarizes Marcus' 'Theory of Painless Extinction'.

40 The authorship is attributed to 'One of the Three', i.e.: the three Poor Law Commissioners. See titlepage. The Tory radical Joseph Rayner Stephens attributed the authorship to Brougham. See Wythen Baxter, G.R.: 1841, p. 77. The anger in this accusation goes a long way towards explaining working-class hostility to birth control in this period.

41 Marcus (pseud.): *On the Possibility of Limiting Populousness* (Lond., 1838) reprinted Lond., 1839, p. 9.

42 Roberts, S.: 1839.

43 *Blackwood's Edinburgh Magazine*, April 1838; Godwin, G.: 1859, p. 30.

44 Pakenham, T.: 1979, p. 300, pp. 490–520.
    Bettelheim, B.: 1960, pp. 109–12. This passage owes a great deal to discussion with Paul Weindling, and to my own interviews.
    A photograph showing numbered paupers' graves is reproduced in Melanie Phillips: 'A Pauper's Grave', 1976.
    See also Ignatieff, M.: 'Total Institutions', 1983.

45 Bray, J.F.: 1939, p. 93.

46 The phrase is from Harrison, F.: 1977, p. 157.

47 Ignatieff, M.: 'Total Institutions', 1983.

48 See chapter 7, note 134.

49 See Humphreys, N.A.: 1885, p. 418.

50 Thomas Wakley, writing in the *Lancet*, 1840–1(2), 1.5.1841, p. 194. Original emphasis.

51 See G.R.W. Baxter's *Book of the Bastiles* (1841). Even if 50 per cent of Baxter's material is exaggerated, as David Roberts seems to claim ('How Cruel?', 1963) there's an old saying about there not being smoke without fire. The Poor Law historian Michael Rose has agreed with me in this view (personal communication). Hollingshead's piece 'A New Chamber of Horrors', 1861, shows that mortality inside workhouses is not the only form of measurement that modern historians should be seeking.
    See also Henriques, U.: 'How Cruel?', 1968.

52 A mass meeting in Sheffield in 1835 called for the repeal of the Anatomy Act: Baxter, J.: 'Samuel Holberry' 1978, p. 9; Oastler petitioned Parlia-

ment for its repeal in 1841: Baxter, G.R.W.: 1841, p. 593; and William Roberts's activities (see chapter 10) were clearly having an effect among the north London poor until at least mid-century. See chapter 10 for mention of the number of workhouse inmates signing declarations, and the drop in the number of corpses available from St Marylebone and other north London parishes in the 1840s and 1850s. A similar sort of obstruction was used in Anti-Poor Law strongholds in the north of England. See also note 111 below. Please see my NOTE heading the References section.

53   *3730*, 22.9.1832, p. 1 – 'Workhouses and Whigs'.

54   See also epigraph to chapter 7.

55   See for example: Oastler, R.: 1837, p. 12; Feargus O'Connor's speech at Bradford in 1837 reported in Baxter, G.R.W. 1841, p. 126; Roberts, S.: 1834, p. 4.

56   See note 12 above, and Samuel Roberts's entries in the Bibliography.

57   Maccoby, S.: 1935, pp. 66–7.

58   See Baxter, J.: 'Samuel Holberry', 1978, p. 9; Kaijage, F.J.: 'Poor Law Catechism', 1981, p. 28; Richardson, R.: 'Language and Imagery of Class', unpublished, 1978, pp. 5–6, which quotes a fine example of the transformation process: In Oldham in 1838, a Mr Quarmby was reported to have addressed a large Anti-Poor Law meeting thus: 'He concluded by imploring the people, if they prized their own interests . . . to struggle . . . for universal suffrage and the five radical principles connected with it, and then they could soon obtain the repeal of the diabolical Poor Law Amendment Act, and all other laws by which they were oppressed and degraded'.

59   *Northern Star*, 6.2.1841, p. 1.

60   Smith, F.B.: 1979, p. 361.

61   Select Committee on Medical Education, 1834: *Evidence*, pp. 207–8.

62   The figure of half a percent is a high estimate. See *Returns* and *Registers* of Bodies at the Public Record Office.

63   See chapter 10, notes 37 and 64.

64   Field, J.: 'Social Control', 1978, p. 46.

65   For a good example of the meaning and use of the word 'respectable' in a funerary context, see Chadwick's *Supplementary Report on Interment in Towns*: pp. 49–50. Tom Laqueur's excellent 'Bodies, Death and Pauper Funerals' (1983) is the finest historical discussion of the British pauper funeral I have seen. I read it at a time when I had been thinking and writing round this subject-area for several years, and this chapter was already in draft form. His work confirmed many of my own thoughts, and gave shape to others. Our work agrees upon the funerary gradation of respectability and the fact that the pauper funeral served up its antithesis (Laqueur, pp. 114–17). We also agree on the extent to which the latter was an administrative construct. We diverge, however, in our estimate of the importance of graverobbery in the early promotion of undertaking, and upon the power of dissection as the ultimate indignity. Although we did not really thrash these problems out on our delightful jaunts to Woking and Kensal Green cemeteries, I hope Tom may be at least partly persuaded by what I have written.

66   Puckle, B.S.: 1926; Gittings, C.: 1984.

67   This is my own view. Other commentators on the Victorian funeral seem

not to subscribe to any better theory (or even to suggest one at all) for the reasons behind the nineteenth-century emphasis upon death – and not another rite-of-passage. I expand on this idea in my 'Why was Death so Big in Victorian Britain?', 1987. See Puckle, B.S.: 1926; Gorer, G.: 1965; Morley, J.: 1971; Curl, J.S.: 1972.

68   See chapter 4 notes.

69   [Chadwick]: 1843, p. 49; Gittings, C.: 1984, particularly chapter 8.

70   Aries, P.: 1981, p. 359.

71   BM Add. Mss. 27828, p. 337. Wellington's coffins are discussed in Morley, J.: 1971, p. 81.

72   Rawnsley, S. & Reynolds, J.: 'Undercliffe Cemetery', 1977; and other volumes mentioned in note 67 above.

73   'Mediculus', in *LMG*, vol. 9, 1832, p. 790.

74   Church of England: 1962, p. 209. See also Badham, P.: 1978.

75   Laqueur, T.: 'Bodies', 1983.

76   Laqueur, T.: 'Bodies', 1983; Roberts, S.: 1834; Gorman, J.: 1973. 'The unskilled had no spokesmen and no organisations (apart from friendly societies)'. Thompson, E.P.: 1963, p. 896.

77   For a poetic description of an early New Poor Law pauper's funeral, see 'The Pauper's Grave' a poem by William Wood: 1837, pp. 41–9. For a better-known later Victorian version, see T. Noel's poem, 'The Pauper's Drive', which has the well-known refrain:
         'Rattle his bones over the stones,
             It's only a pauper whom nobody owns',
reproduced in Mulgan, J.: 1938, p. 100. Of course, 'owns' is another word for 'claim' in this context.

78   For further descriptions of the small-minded cost-cutting in Poor Law funerals, and the contempt in which it was popularly held, see Baxter, G.R.W.: 1841, pp. 65, 116, 126–7, 130–1, 182–3, 188–9, 592–3, 609. See also Wood, W.: 1837, pp. 41–9.

79   Twining, L.: 1880, p. 82; unpublished interview between ex-workhouse inmate and R. Richardson, Bradford, 1980; Laqueur, T.: 'Bodies', 1983. Charlotte Burne (Shropshire Folklore, 1883, p. 310) mentions a woman begging round the parish for money to pay for bells to be rung at her husband's parish funeral, in the 1880s; and the Shropshire custom of purchasing a coffin in advance of death to avoid death on the parish, p. 200. See also previous note, and note 44 above.

80   The phrase 'religion of parsimony' is David Cannadine's. See his paper on ritual in Hobsbawn, E. & Ranger, T. (eds): 1983, p. 113.

81   Spufford, M.: 1981 – shows that from at least the late seventeenth century, chapbooks glorified non-aristocratic hero-figures, capitalistic ethics, and the upward mobility of the poor.

82   See Richardson, R.: 'Language and Imagery of Class', unpublished, 1978.

83   Oastler, R.: 1837, p. 16.

84   Foote, G.W. & McLaren, A.D.: 1933.

85   See for example the description of the enormous procession at Cobbett's funeral: [Anon]: *The Life of William Cobbett*, 1835, pp. 294–6. The description includes the fact that Cobbett had a lead coffin, that he was buried in 'a brick vault securely formed' and that 'three large stone flags

were placed over the coffin with a view to greater security'. Cobbett died in 1835, three years after the Act was passed.

86   Laqueur, T.: 'Bodies', 1983. See also the imagery on trades union banners reproduced in Gorman, J.: 1973.

87   Richardson, R.: 'Death in the Metropolis', unpublished, 1978. See especially chapter 8. Wilson, A. & Levy, H.J.: 1938. Compare the amounts mentioned here in 1938 with those to which I referred in chapter 4, and with [Chadwick]: 1843.

88   Gosden, P.H.J.H.: 1961, p. 29. Gosden does not mention the Anatomy Act as a stimulus to this meteoric growth – he suggests that the Poor Law may have been responsible. The relatively slow implementation of the New Poor Law, however, suggests to me that the fear of dissection may have been an important factor that has been overlooked. Gosden points out that the increase was *not* due to any rise in affluence in the 1830s.

89   Gosden, P.H.J.H.: 1961, p. 29; [Chadwick]: 1843, p. 70.

90   Gosden, P.H.J.H.: 1961, pp. 205–10. The Benefit Society Act was passed in 1829, the same year the first Anatomy Bill failed.

91   Gosden, P.H.J.H.: 1961, p. 205.

92   [Chadwick]: 1843, p. 54.

93   Gosden, P.H.J.H.: 1961; Richardson, R.: 'Death in the Metropolis', unpublished, 1978.

94   [Chadwick]: 1843, pp. 58–9.

95   Baernreither, J.M.: 1889, pp. 188–99.

96   Reeves, M.P. (ed.): [1913] reprinted 1979, pp. 69–70.

97   Wilson, A. & Levy, H.J.: 1938; *Report* and *Evidence* of the Royal Commission on Friendly Societies and Burial Societies, 1871–4.

98   [Chadwick]: 1843, p. 56.

99   Sims, G.R.: 1904–6, pp. 78–99; Binder, P.: 1975, pp. 38–45.

100 A similar arrangement was being observed in collections raised for needy cases in a large West London factory in the 1980s (personal communication). See chapter 8 of my 'Death in the Metropolis', unpublished, 1978 – which is devoted to such collections.

101 Binder, P.: 1975, p. 42. People also went into debt – see Beames, T.: 1852, pp. 193–6; Morrah, D.: 1955.

102 'Broken Up!' sung by Walter Munro. *Ta-ra-ra Boom-de-e Songster* [c.1890].

103 Raven, J.: 1978. See also 'In Memoriam. Sad Accident at Fieldhouse Mills: "He Laid down his life for his friend" '. Commemorative sheet 'price one penny' dated 1906, Manchester Studies Unit Archive.

104 Richardson, R.: 'Death in the Metropolis', unpublished, 1978. See also [Anon]: *The Story Teller*. Chapbook, n.d.

105 See previous chapter.

106 Richardson, R.: 'Death in the Metropolis', unpublished, 1978.

107 Ritchie, J.: 'Account', 1912; 'Relics', 1921.

108 [Chadwick]: 1843, pp. 31–45; Marshall, A.C.: 1968, pp. 22–3. See also Ladies Sanitary Association: 1866.

109 George Godwin, in *The Builder*, 1853, p. 257. Godwin sketched the scene, but found it 'so painfully repulsive' that he forbore to print it.

110 Marshall, A.C.: 1968, pp. 22–3.

111 *Free Lance*, 13.3.1869, p. 87. See also Dr B. Bostetter's forthcoming biography of Wakley.

112   *Free Lance*, 13.3.1869, p. 87.

113   *Poor Man's Guardian*, vol. 1, p. 84; Marshall, A.C.: 1968, pp. 27–8.
      See also Hollingshead: 'A New Chamber of Horrors', 1861.

114   Bray, J.F.: [1850], 1957, p. 20. See also *The Poor Charlies Lamentation*,
      broadsheet, c.1839[?].

115   Langbridge, F.: 1887 – 'Jeannie's Martyrdom'.

116   James, L.: 1976, p. 131.

117   See note 114 above.

118   [Chadwick]: 1843, p. 48.

119   *Pall Mall Gazette*, 25.3.1898.

120   The latter phrase is from Harrison, F.: 1977, p. 169.

121   Roberts, S.: 1834, p. 4.

122   Reeves, M.P.: [1913] 1979, pp. 69, 82–7.

123   Wilson, A. & Levy, H.J.: 1938, p. 61.

124   Richardson, R.: 'Death in the Metropolis', unpublished, 1978.

125   Steiner, G.: 1969 – essay entitled 'Language and Silence'.

126   Richardson, R.: 'Death in the Metropolis', unpublished, 1978.

127   Richardson, R.: 'Death in the Metropolis', unpublished, 1978.

128   Local respondent recorded in the 1970s and quoted in an article by Audrey
      Linkman: *Salford City Reporter*, 20.1.1978. I am very grateful to Audrey
      Linkman for bringing this article to my attention, and for sharing other
      work with me.

      Available evidence is contradictory on when the silence surrounding the
      dissection of paupers developed – on the one hand, the reports in the *Free
      Lance* (13.3.1869; 11.12.1869) – refer to the legislation as if in only-just-
      informed knowledge: 'It appears that there is an Act of Parliament. . .'.
      A report signed 'CLC' in the *Charity Organisation Reporter* (2.8.1884)
      describes how the 'worn out frames' of workhouse inmates 'come under the
      dissecting knife, and the mutilated fragments are gathered up and interred
      with Christian ceremony by the parish undertaker', as though this was
      common knowledge, at least among social investigators.
      In 1912, E.M. Leather, a folklore collector seeking origins for the fear of the
      pauper funeral was obviously ignorant of the Act when she suggested: 'it is
      possible that the origin of this anxiety may be found in the fact that at one
      time, the bodies of those who died in debt were actually left unburied. Or it
      may go farther back to the widespread belief in the necessity for proper
      burial, since without it, the soul, when separated from the body, could find
      no repose'. (Leather, E.M.: 1912, p. 121).
      The indignation expressed in the opposition to Macphail at Romford and
      elsewhere in the 1920s seems to me to have a freshness about it – as though
      the Act's provisions were not common currency then.

BIBLIOGRAPHY

NOTES

The bibliography is divided as follows:

CONTEMPORARY (PRIMARY) SOURCES

Manuscripts
Official papers and publications
Published Parliamentary papers, Unpublished Parliamentary papers,
Parliamentary Acts and Bills, Reports, Petitions, Patents.
Printed materials
Books and pamphlets, Newspapers and periodicals, Articles/papers from books
and periodicals.
Broadsheets

SECONDARY SOURCES

Printed materials
Books and pamphlets, Articles/papers from books and periodicals.
Unpublished material

ANONYMOUS ITEMS

Are listed as they would appear in the British Museum Catalogue.

CONTEMPORARY SOURCES

Manuscripts

Bentham Papers. University College, London.
Bentham Papers: Autographs of Jeremy Bentham. British Museum Add.Mss,
   34661.
Bickerton Papers. Public Library Archives, Liverpool.
Cooper, J.F.: *Transcribed inscriptions from Headstones in Yarmouth (compiled c.1827–*

1839) with added manuscript notes entitled *Bodies stealing from Great Yarmouth 1827*. British Museum Add. Mss. 23738.

Clift, W.: *Manuscript diaries*. Royal College of Surgeons of England, London.

Crombie, J.E.: *Death Customs in Aberdeenshire. Manuscript Notes and Observations*. Folklore Society Archives.

Garstin, W. & Sons: *Funeral Books*. St Marylebone Public Libraries.

Holmes, I.: *Manuscript Notes on the Diary of a Resurrectionist*. Royal College of Surgeons of England, London.

Liverpool Literary and Scientific Society: *Minutes*. Public Library Archives, Liverpool.

London Mechanics' Institution: *Minutes 1823–45*. Birkbeck College, University of London.

[Naples, J.]: *Manuscript diary (The 'Diary of a Resurrectionist')*. Royal College of Surgeons of England, London.

Owen, R.: *Manuscript notes transcribed by Jessie Dobson*. Royal College of Surgeons of England, London.

Paisley: *Court Book and Corporation Minute Book*. Renfrew District Libraries.

Paisley: *Police Commissioners' Minutes*. Renfrew District Libraries.

Place Papers: British Museum Add. Mss, 27828, 27835.

Peel Papers: British Museum Add. Mss, 40371, 40390.

St Thomas' Hospital, Mss. 55.

Workhouse of St Ann, Blackfriars: *Records*. Guildhall Library, London.

Workhouse of Clayton, W.Yorks: *Records*. Central Library, Leeds.

Stow Union Workhouse, Suffolk: *Records*. Suffolk Record Office, Ipswich.

Official papers and publications

Parliamentary papers at the House of Lords Records Office and the British Library Official Publications Library:
Appendices to Votes and Proceedings
Commons Journal
Lords Journal
Hansard
Votes and Proceedings

Acts

32 Henrici VIII c.42: An Act concernyng Barbours and Chirurgeons to be of one Companie. 1540.

25 Geo. II c.37: An Act for Better Preventing the Horrid Crime of Murder, 1752.

2&3 Gul. IV c.75: An Act for Regulating Schools of Anatomy, 1832.

2&3 Gul. IV c.45: Representation of the People. 1832.

4&5 Gul. IV c.76: Poor Law (Amendment) Act. 1834.

34&35 Vict. c.16: An Act to Amend the Act for Regulating Schools of Anatomy. 1871.

Bills

A Bill for Preventing the Unlawful Disinterment of Human Bodies. 1829.

Reports

Report and Evidence of the Select Committee on Anatomy. 1828.

Report and Evidence of the Select Committee on Medical Education. 1834.

Report and Evidence of the Select Committee on the Poor Laws. 1834.

Report and Evidence of the Select Committee on Education. 1835.

Report and Evidence of the Select Committee on the Improvement of Health in Towns. 1842.

Select Committee on the Improvement of Health in towns: Supplementary Report on Interment in Towns. [by Edwin Chadwick]. 1843.

Report and Evidence of the Select Committee on the Andover Union. 1846.

Report and Evidence of the Royal Commission on Friendly Societies and Burial Societies. 1871-4.

Report and Evidence of the Parmoor Committee on Industrial Assurance. 1920.

Report and Evidence of the Cohen Committee on Industrial Assurance. 1933.

Report of the DHSS Working Party in Inequalities on Health [The Black Report]. 1980.

Petitions

Petition from the Inhabitants of Tenterden, Kent. H of C: V&P Appx., 12.5.1829, no.3023.

Petition of Mechanics of the Parish of Lambeth. H of C: V&P Appx, 24.1.1832, no.68.

Petition of Several Poor Persons now living in the Workhouse of St Ann, Blackfriars, in the City of London. CJ, vol 84, p. 178, 27.3.1829.

Petition from the Inhabitants of Blackburn. H of C: V&P Appx, 15.2.1832, no.186.

Petition from the Worcestershire Political Union. H of C: V&P Appx, 7.3.1832, no.356.

Petition from the Paisley Reform Society. H of C: V&P Appx, 3.2.1832, no.114.

Petition of Members of the National Political Union. CJ., vol. 87, p. 300, 8.5.1832.

Unpublished government papers at the Public Record Office, Kew.

HO83/1-3.

HO44/27, 31.

HO64/16, 18.

MH58/2-3.

MH74/1-3, 6-9, 10-16, 18-19, 24, 30-35, 36, 42-43, 47, 54, 62, 83, 89.

Patents at the Patent Office Library, British Library Science Reference Library.

No.1307: Thomas Wright: For Making and Preserving Metal Coffins, 1781.

No.4250: Edward L. Bridgman: Coffins, 1818.

No.4843: John Hughes: Securing Bodies in Coffins, 1823.

No.5239: James Butler: Coffins, 1825.

Printed materials

Books and pamphlets

ABERNETHY, J.: *Hunterian Oration.* Lond., 1819.

ABERNETHY, J.:   *Physiological Lectures.* Lond., 1817.

ACLAND, H.W.:   *Memoir on the Cholera at Oxford in the year 1854.* Lond., 1856.

ADAMS, J.:   *Memoirs of the Life and Doctrines of the Late John Hunter.* Lond., 1817.

ADDISON, W.:   *A Letter to William Lawrence on the Nature and Causes of Intellectual Life and the Mind.* Lond., 1830.

An ADDRESS *to the Public, drawn from Nature and Religion, against the unlimited Dissection of Human Bodies.* Lond., 1829.

AESCULAPIUS (pseud.) (i.e.: Potts, L.H.):   *Oracular Communications Addressed to Students of the Medical Profession.* Lond., 1816.

AINSWORTH, W.F.:   *Observations on Pestilential Cholera at Sunderland.* Lond., 1832.

ALEXIPHARMACUS (pseud.):   *A General Exposition of the Present State of the Medical Profession . . . Embracing the Question Relative to the Removal of the Existing Obstructions to the Study of Human Anatomy.* Lond., 1829.

ARBUTHNOT, Mrs: *The Journal of Mrs Arbuthnot.* (Bamford, F., ed.) Lond., 1950.

ARMSTRONG, J.:   *An Address to the Members of the Royal College of Surgeons on the Injurious Conduct and Defective State of that Corporation.* Lond., 1825.

AUBREY, J.:   *Remaines of Gentilisme and Judaisme.* [1686–7] Lond., 1881.

BAILEY, J.B.:   *The Diary of a Resurrectionist.* Lond., 1896.

BAILLIE, M.:   *Morbid Anatomy.* Lond., 1793.

BAKER, T.E.:   *An Appeal to the Common Sense of the People of England in favour of Anatomy.* Lond., 1832.

BANKS, A.:   *Medical Etiquette.* Lond., 1839.

BARROW, J.H.:   *Mirror of Parliament.* Lond., 1829–32.

BAXTER, G.R.W.:   *The Book of the Bastiles.* Lond., 1841.

BEAMES, T.:   *The Rookeries of London.* Lond., 1852.

BECHER, J.T.:   *The Anti Pauper System.* Lond., 1834.

BENTHAM, J.:   *Auto Icon, or, Further Uses of the Dead to the Living, A Fragment.* Lond., [c.1842].

BENTHAM, J.:   *Collected Works.* (Burns, J.H., ed.) Lond., 1968.

BONET, T.:   *Prodromus Anatomiae Practicae.* Geneva, 1675.

BONET, T.:   *Sepulchretum.* Geneva, 1700.

BOURNE, H.:   *Antiquitates Vulgares.* Newcastle, 1725.

BOWRING, J.(ed.):   *The Works of Jeremy Bentham.* Lond., 1843.

BRAND, J.:   *Observations on Popular Antiquities.* Lond., 1777, 1813, 1841–2, 1870, 1905.

BRAY, J.F.:   *Labour's Wrongs and Labour's Remedy.* [1839] Lond., 1931.

BRAY, J.F.:   *A Voyage From Utopia.* [1850] Lond., 1957.

BRODIE, B.C.:   *Hunterian Oration.* Lond., 1837.

BRODIE, B.C.:   *Papers Relative to the Question of Providing Adequate Means for the Study of Anatomy.* Lond., 1832.

BULL, G.S.:   *The Horrors of the Whig Poor Laws.* 1837.

BURKE, W.:   *A Popular Compendium of Anatomy.* Lond., 1813.

BURN, J.D.:   *A Glimpse at the Social Condition of the Working Classes.* (c.1830).

BURN, R.:   *The Justice of the Peace and Parish Officer.* Lond., 1755, 1793, 1814, 1825.

BURTON, J.H.:   *Benthamiana.* Lond., 1843.

'C':   *Thought, not the Function of the Brain.* Lond., 1827.

CASTLE, T.:   *A Manual of Modern Surgery, founded on the principles of Sir Astley Cooper Bart., FRS., Surgeon to the King, and J.H. Green Esq., FRS., Professor of Anatomy to the Royal Academy, Surgeon to and Lecturer on Surgery, St Thomas's Hospital.* Lond., 1828.

CHADWICK, E.:   *An Essay on the Means of Insurance.* Lond., 1836.

CHRISTISON, R.:   *The Life of Sir Robert Christison.* (Edited by his sons). Edin., 1885–6.

COBBETT, W.:   *The Last Confession and Dying Speech of Peter Porcupine, with an account of his dissection.* N.Y., 1797.

COBBETT, W.:   *Cobbett's History of the Protestant Reformation in England and Ireland; showing how that event has impoverished and degraded the main body of the People in those Countries.* Lond., 1824.

COBBETT, W.:   *Rural Rides.* [1830] Harmondsworth, 1967.

COBBETT, W.:   *Cobbett's Manchester Lectures.* Lond., 1832.

COBBETT, W.:   *Letters to the Earl of Radnor . . . on the Poor Law Scheme.* Lond., 1834.

COBBETT, W.:   *Surplus Population and The Poor Law Bill, A Comedy in Three Acts.* Lond., 1834.

COCKBURN, H.:   *Memorials of his Time.* (Gray, W.F., ed.) [1856] Edin., 1909.

COLQUHOUN, P.:   *A Treatise on Indigence.* Lond., 1806.

CONNOLLY, J.:   *The Physicians: The Cholera.* Lond., 1832.

COOPER, A.:   *Lectures.* Lond., 1824–7, 1830, 1835, 1836–43.

COOPER, A. & TRAVERS, B.:   *Surgical Essays.* Lond., 1818–19.

COOPER, B.B.:   *Report of the Trial Cooper versus Wakley for Libel.* Lond., 1829.

COOPER, B.B.:   *The Life of Sir Astley Cooper.* Lond., 1843.

CRAIK, G.L: *The Pursuit of Knowledge under Difficulties.* Lond., 1830–31.

DARWIN, F.(ed.):   *Charles Darwin; His Life Told in an Autobiographical Chapter, and in a Selected Series of his Published Letters.* Lond., 1892.

DERMOTT, G.D.:   *A Discussion of the Organic Materiality of the Mind.* Lond., 1830.

DICKENS, C.:   *Oliver Twist.* Lond., 1839.

DICKENS, C.:   *Martin Chuzzlewit.* Lond., 1844.

DICKENS, C.:   *Our Mutual Friend.* Lond., 1865.

DICTIONARY of the Vulgar Tongue. Lond., 1811.

DIRECTIONS For Plain People as a Guide for their Conduct in the Cholera. Lond., 1831.

DOD, C.R.:   *Dod's Parliamentary Companion.* Lond., 1833, 1835.

DOD, C.R.:   *Electoral Facts 1832–52.* [1853] Brighton, 1972.

DOUCE, F.:   *Illustrations of Shakespeare.* Lond., 1807.

DUNCOMBE, T.H.:   *The Life and Correspondence of T.H. Duncombe.* Lond., 1868.

ECHO of Surgeons' Square (pseud.):   *A Letter to the Lord Advocate.* Edin., 1829.

EDGUARDUS, D.:   *De Indiciis et Precognitionibus.* [1532] Lond., 1961. (cf: RUSSELL, K.F. & O'MALLEY, C.D.).

ELIOT, G.:   *Middlemarch.* Lond., 1871.

FARRE, J.R.:   *An Apology for British Anatomy,* Lond., 1827.

FOOT, J.:   *The Life of John Hunter.* Lond., 1794.

FOOT, J.:   *A Letter on the Necessity of a Public Enquiry into the Cause of Death of Her Royal Highness the Princess Charlotte and her Infant.* Lond., 1817.

FORSTER, T.:   see PHILOSTRATUS [pseud.].

FOWLER'S Commercial Directory of Renfrewshire. Paisley, 1832, 1834, 1851.

FROST, T.:   *Forty Years' Recollections.* Lond., 1880.

GASKELL, P.:   *Artisans and Machinery.* Lond., 1836.

GAULTER, H.:   *The Origins and Progress of the Cholera in Manchester.* Lond., 1833.

A GENTLEMAN of the Faculty: *Anatomical Dialogues.* Lond., 1796.

GODWIN, G.:   *London Shadows.* Lond., 1854.

GODWIN, G.:   *Town Swamps & Social Bridges.* Lond., 1859.

GODWIN, W.:   *An Essay on Sepulchres*. Lond., 1809.

GOLDING, B.:   *An Historical Account of St Thomas's Hospital Southwark*. Lond., 1819.

GOOCH, B.:   *A Practical Treatise on Wounds and other Chirurgical Subjects*. Norwich, 1767–73.

GOUGH, R.:   *Sepulchral Monuments*. Lond., 1786, 1796.

GRAVES, R.:   *An Address Delivered at a Meeting of the Dublin Medico-Chirurgical Society*. Dublin, 1836.

GREEN, J.H.:   *A Letter to Sir Astley Cooper*. Lond., 1825.

GREENHILL, T.:   *The Art of Embalming*. Lond., 1705.

GREVILLE, C.C.F.:   *The Greville Memoirs*. (Reeve, H., ed.) Lond., 1875.

GUTHRIE, G.J.:   *A Letter to the Right Hon. the Secretary of State for the Home Department, containing Remarks on the Report of the Select Committee of the House of Commons, on Anatomy*. Lond., 1829.

GUTHRIE, G.J.:   *Remarks on the Anatomy Bill now before Parliament*. Lond., 1832.

GUTTERIDGE, T.:   *The General Hospital, Birmingham*. Lond., 1844.

GUTTERIDGE, T.:   *General Hospital, Birmingham: The Crisis*. Edgbaston, 1851.

HARVEY, W.:   *Lectures on the Whole of Anatomy*. [annotated trans. Russell, K.F.]. Lond., 1961.

HEAD, F.:   *English Charity*. Lond., 1835.

HEAD, G.:   *A Home Tour through the Manufacturing Districts of England in the Summer of 1835*. Lond., 1836.

HEAD, G.:   *A Home Tour through various parts of the United Kingdom*. Lond., 1837.

The HISTORY of the London Burkers. Lond., 1832.

HOBHOUSE, J.C.:   *Recollections of a Long Life*. Lond., 1909–11.

HODGKIN, T.:   *A Catalogue of the Preparations in the Anatomical Museum of Guy's Hospital*. Lond., 1829.

HODGKIN, T.:   *Morbid Anatomy of Serous and Mucous Membranes*. Lond., 1836–40.

HOLLINGSHEAD, J.:   *Ragged London in 1861*. Lond., 1861.

HOOD, T.:   *Whims and Oddities*. Lond., 1826.

THE HOSPITAL SHIP, GRAMPUS. Lond., c.1827.

HUMANUS (pseud.):   *A letter to John Abernethy*. Lond., 1823.

HUNT, H.:   *The Preston Cock's Reply to the Kensington Dunghill: A twopenny exposure of Cobbett's fourteen-pennyworth of falsehoods*. Lond., 1841.

A JUNIOR PRACTITIONER: *A Letter addressed to Henry Warburton*. Lond., 1834.

LADIES SANITARY ASSOCIATION: *Healthfullness of Homes and Workshops*. [Lond.?], 1866.

LANCET: *Lancet Sanitary Commission for Investigating the State of the Infirmaries of Workhouses*. Lond., 1866.

LANGBRIDGE, F.:   *Poor Folks' Lives*. Lond., 1887.

LAWRENCE, W.:   *An Introduction to Comparative Anatomy*. Lond., 1816.

LAWRENCE, W.:   *Lectures on Physiology*. Lond., 1819–1822.

LAWRENCE, W.:   *Fact versus Fiction!* Lond., 1832.

LE DRAN, H.F.:   *Observations in Surgery*. (trans. Sparrow, J.) Lond., 1758.

LEIGH, W.:   *An authentic Account of the Melancholy Occurrences at Bilston . . . during the . . . visitation . . . by cholera in 1832*. Wolverhampton, 1833.

LEIGHTON, A.:   *Court of Cacus*. Lond., 1861.

LE MARCHANT, D.:   *The Reform Ministry and the Reformed Parliament*. Lond., 1833.

LE MARCHANT, D.:   *Memoir of Lord Althorp*. Lond., 1876.

LIETAUD, J.:   *Historia Anatomico-Medica*. Paris, 1767.

The LIFE of William Cobbett. Lond., 1835.

LISTON, R.:   *Elements of Surgery.* Lond., 1831–2, 1840.

LISTON, R.:   *Practical Surgery.* Lond., 1837, 1846.

LIZARS, A.J.:   *A System of Anatomical Plates of the Human Body.* Edin., 1822–1826.

LIZARS, A.J.:   *Elements of Anatomy.* Edin., 1844.

LOANE, M.E.:   *The Queen's Poor: life as they find it.* Lond., 1905.

LOANE, M.E.:   *Neighbours and Friends.* Lond., 1910.

LOVETT, W.:   *Life and Struggles.* Lond., 1876.

MALCOLM, J.P.:   *Londinium Redivivum.* Lond., 1802–7.

MALKIN, B.H.:   *Account of a New Tour in Wales.* Lond., 1804.

MALKIN, B.H.:   *The Scenery, Antiquities and Biography of Wales.* Lond., 1804.

MALMESBURY, Lord: *Memoirs of an Ex-Minister.* Lond., 1885.

MALTHUS, T.R.:   *A Treatise on Population.* [1798] Harmondsworth, 1971.

MARCUS (pseud.):   *An Essay on Populousness.* Printed for private circulation, 1838.

MARCUS (pseud.):   *On the Possibility of Limiting Populousness.* Lond., 1838.

MARCUS (pseud.):   *The Book of Murder! A Vade Mecum for the Commissioners and Guardians of the New Poor Law throughout Great Britain . . . Being an exact reprint of the Infamous Essay. . . by Marcus, One of the Three.* Lond., 1839.

MAUNDER, C.F.:   *Operative Surgery adapted to the Living and the Dead Subject.* Lond., 1860–1.

MAYHALL, J.:   *Annals of Yorkshire.* Leeds, 1866.

MEDICUS (pseud.):   *An Exposure of the Present System of Obtaining Bodies for Dissection.* Lond., 1829.

MILLARD, A.:   *An Account of the Circumstances attending to the Imprisonment and Death of the late William Millard.* Lond., 1825.

MISSON, H.:   *Memoires and Observations.* (trans. Ozell, T.) Lond., 1719.

The MOURNER'S Solace. Lond., 1836.

NATIONAL POLITICAL UNION: *Proceedings . . . respecting legislative interference in the Study of Anatomy.* Lond., 1832.

NATIONAL POLITICAL UNION: *Proceedings at the Second Annual meeting of the NPU.* Lond., 1833.

NATIONAL POLITICAL UNION: *Report of the Council.* Lond., 1832.

NOEL, T.:   *Rymes and Roundelayes.* Lond., 1841.

OASTLER, R.:   *Damnation! Eternal Damnation to the Fiend-Begotten 'Coarser Food' New Poor Law. A Speech.* Lond., 1837.

OASTLER, R.:   *The Fleet Papers, being Letters . . . from Richard Oastler.* Lond., 1841–2.

ONE OF THE PEOPLE CALLED CHRISTIANS: *Cursory Observations on the Lectures on Physiology By W.L.* [i.e.: William Lawrence] Lond., 1819.

OXONIAN: *The Radical Triumvirate, or, Infidel Paine, Lord Byron, Surgeon Lawrence.* Lond., 1820.

PALEY, W.:   *Natural Theology.* Lond., 1844.

PARKER, G.:   *A View of Society and Manners in High and Low Life.* Lond., 1781.

PEEL, R.:   *Memoirs,* Lond., 1857.

PENNANT, T.:   *A Tour in Wales.* Lond., 1778–81.

PENNANT, T.:   *Some Account of London.* Lond., 1793.

PERCIVAL, T.:   *Medical Ethics.* Manc., 1803.

PETTIGREW, T.I.:   *Medical Portrait Gallery.* Lond., 1839.

PHILOSTRATUS (pseud.) [i.e.: FORSTER, T.]:   *Somatopsychonoologia.* Lond., 1823.

PORTER, W.O.:   *Medical Science and Ethicks.* Bristol, 1837.

POTTS, L.H.: see AESCULAPIUS (pseud.).

PRITCHARD, J.C.: *The Natural History of Man*. Lond., 1843.

The Medical PROFESSION in England. Lond., 1834.

PRY, PAUL: *The Blunders of Big Wig [i.e.: Lord Brougham] or, Paul Pry's Peeps into the Sixpenny Sciences*. Lond., 1827.

PRY, PAUL: *The Second Visit of Paul Pry to Mary-le-Bone, with an Exposure of the Annual Accounts*. Lond., 1827.

PUGIN, A.: *Contrasts*. Lond., 1836/41.

REEVES, M.P.: *Round About a Pound A Week*. [1913] Lond., 1979.

RENNELL, T.: *Remarks on Scepticism*. Lond., 1819.

ROBERTS, P.: *Cambrian Popular Antiquities*. Lond., 1815.

ROBERTS, S.: *England's Passing Bell, or the Obsequies of National Holiness, Liberty and Honour*. Lond., 1834.

ROBERTS, S.: *The Lecturers Lectured*. Sheffield, 1834.

ROBERTS, S.: *Mary Wilden, A Victim of the New Poor Law, or, The Malthusian and Marcusian System Exposed*. Lond., 1839.

ROBERTS, S.: *The Wickedness of the New Poor Law*. Sheffield, 1839.

ROBERTS, S.: *Truth, or, The Fall of Babylon the Great*. Sheffield, 1845.

ROBERTS, S.: *Autobiography and Select Remains*. Lond., 1849.

ROBERTS, W.: *Mr Warburton's Anatomy Bill*. Lond., 1843.

ROBERTS, W.: *An Address on the Necessity for Investigating the Operation of the Anatomy Act*. Lond., 1855.

ROGERS, J.: *Reminiscences*. Lond., 1889.

ROWLEY, W.: *On the Absolute Necessity of Encouraging instead of Preventing or Embarrassing the Study of Anatomy; with a Plan to Prevent Violating the Dormitories of the Defunct*. Lond., 1795.

ROYAL COLLEGE OF SURGEONS OF ENGLAND: *Catalogue of the Hunterian Collection*. Lond., 1830–1.

SADLER, M.J.: *Memoirs*. Lond., 1842.

SANDERS, L.C.: *Lord Melbourne's Papers*. Lond., 1889.

SCROPE, G.P.: *Memoir of the Life of the Right Hon. Charles Lord Sydenham*. Lond., 1843.

SEARLE, C.: *Cholera: Its Nature, Cause and Treatment*. Lond., 1831.

Honourable SEPULTURE the Christian's Due. Lond., [c.1852].

SHAPTER, T.: *The History of the Cholera in Exeter in 1832*. Lond., 1849.

SHARP, S.: *A Critical Enquiry into the Present State of Surgery*. Lond., 1750.

SHARP, S.: *A Treatise on the Operations of Surgery*. Lond., 1782.

SHUTTLEWORTH, J.P.K.: *Autobiography*. (Bloomfield, B.C., ed.). Lond., 1964.

SIMPSON, J.Y.: *Complete Works*. Edin., 1871.

SMITH, T.: *A Manual of Operative Surgery on the Dead Body*. Lond., 1859.

SMITH, T.S.: *A Lecture delivered over the Remains of J. Bentham*. Lond., 1832.

SMITH, T.S.: *The Use of the Dead to the Living*. Lond., 1832.

SOMERS, P.: *Pages from a Country Diary*. Lond., 1904.

SOMERVILLE, A.: *Autobiography of a Working Man*. [1848] Lond., 1951.

SOMERVILLE, J.C.: *A Letter Addressed to the Lord Chancellor, on the Study of Anatomy*. Lond., 1832.

SOUTH, J.F.: *The Dissector's Manual*. Lond., 1825.

SOUTH, J.F.: *St Thomas's Hospital Reports*. Lond., 1836.

SOUTH, J.F.: *Memorials of the Craft of Surgery*. Lond., 1886.

STEWART, L.:   *Remarks on the Present State of the Medical Profession*. Lond., 1826.

STEWART, L.:   *Modern Medicine Influenced by Morbid Anatomy*. Lond., 1830.

STONE, T.:   *Observations on the Phrenological Development of Burke, Hare, and Other Atrocious Murderers*. Edin., 1829.

The STORY of Daft Jamie, one of the Victims of Burke and Hare. Edin., 1829.

The STORY TELLER. Glasgow, n.d.

TA-RA-RA BOOM-DE-E Songster. Lond., c.1890.

THOMAS, H.P.:   *The Work and Play of a Government Inspector*. Lond., 1909.

THOMAS, V.:   *Memorials of the Malignant Cholera at Oxford*. Oxf., 1835.

THOMPSON, A.T.:   *The Authentic Medical Statement of the Case of HRH the late Princess Charlotte of Wales*. Lond. [c.1818].

THOMPSON, C.:   *A Letter to the Public on the Necessity of Anatomical Pursuits*. Lond., 1830.

TODD, R.B.:   *A Lecture Introductory to the Course of Anatomy*. Lond., 1832.

TRAILL, T.S.:   *Suggestions for the Medico-Legal Examination of Dead Bodies*. Edin., 1839.

TREVELYAN, G.O.:   *The Life and Letters of Lord Macaulay*. Lond., 1959.

TROLLOPE, F.:   *Jessie Phillips*. Lond., 1844.

TWINING, L.:   *Workhouses and Women's Work*. Lond., 1858.

TWINING, L.:   *A Letter to the President of the Poor Law Board on Workhouse Infirmaries*. Lond., 1866.

TWINING, L.:   *Recollections of Workhouse Visiting*. Lond., 1880.

VICARY, T.:   *A Profitable Treatise of the Anatomie of Man's Body*. Lond., 1577.

A VIEW of London and Westminster. Lond., 1728.

WADD, W.:   *Mems, Maxims and Memoirs*. Lond., 1827.

WADE, J.:   *The Black Book; or, Corruption Unmasked!* Lond., 1820, 1823.

WADE, J.:   *A Treatise on the Police and Crimes of the Metropolis*. Lond., 1829.

WADE, J.:   *The Extraordinary Black Book*. Lond., 1831, 1832, 1835.

WADE, J.:   *Glances at the Times, and Reform Government*. Lond., 1840.

WAKEFIELD, E.G.:   *Householders in Danger from The Populace*. Lond., [c.1831].

WAKEFIELD, E.G.:   *Facts Relating to the Punishment of Death in the Metropolis*. Lond., 1832.

WAKLEY, T.:   *A Report of the Trial of Cooper v. Wakley for an Alleged Libel*. Lond., 1829.

WALKER, G.A.:   *Gatherings from Graveyards*. Lond., 1839.

WALKER, G.A.:   *Interment and Disinterment*. Lond., 1843.

WARREN, S.:   *Passages from the Diary of a Late Physician*. [1838] Edin., 1864.

WHISTON, W.:   *Historical Memoirs of the Life and Writings of Dr Samuel Clarke*. Lond., 1748.

WOLLSTONECRAFT, M.:   *Maria, or the Wrongs of Woman*. Paris, 1798.

WOOD, W.:   *The Genius of the Peak*. Lond., 1837.

WOODFORDE, J.:   *Diary of a Country Parson*. (Beresford, J., ed.) Oxf., 1949.

YOUNG, A.:   *A Tour through the East of England*. Lond., 1771.

Newspapers and periodicals

PLACE Collection of Newspaper Cuttings

Aberdeen Evening Express

Aberdeen Journal

Address from one of the 3730 Electors of Preston ['3730']

Albion and Evening Star

All the Year Round

Atheneum

Ballot

Blackwood's Edinburgh Magazine

Bolton Chronicle
Bradford Observer
Builder
Caledonian Mercury
Cambridge Chronicle
Carpenter's Monthly Political Magazine
Chambers' Edinburgh Journal
Charity Organisation Reporter
Cholera Gazette
Cobbett's Twopenny Trash
Cobbett's Weekly Political Register
Cosmopolite
Crisis
Derby Mercury
Devonshire Chronicle and Exeter News
Dissector
Edinburgh Evening Courant
Edinburgh Medical and Surgical Journal
Edinburgh Medical Journal
Edinburgh Observer
Edinburgh Weekly Journal
Essex Times
Examiner
Exeter Times
Figaro in London
Figaro's Monthly Newspaper
Free Lance
Glasgow Herald
Glasgow Looking Glass
Glasgow Medical Journal
Good Words
Halifax and Huddersfield Express
Household Words
Journal of Morbid Anatomy
Journal of the Royal Agricultural Society
Journal of the Royal Statistical Society
Lancet
Leeds Intelligencer
Leeds Mercury
Leeds Patriot
Lion
Literary Gazette
Liverpool Mercury
London Magazine
London Medical Gazette

London Medical and Surgical Journal
Manchester Chronicle
Manchester Courier
Manchester Guardian
Medical Museum
Medical Student
Medical Times
Midland Medical and Surgical Reporter
Midlands Representative
Morning Chronicle
Morning Herald
New London Mechanics' Register
New Monthly Magazine
Northern Star
Oxford University, City and County Herald
Paisley Advertiser
Pall Mall Gazette
Parliamentary Review
Porcupine
Poor Man's Advocate
Poor Man's Guardian
Punch
Punch in London
Quarterly Review
Radical
Republican and Radical Reformer
Romford Times
Scotsman
Sheffield Independent
Sheffield Iris
Surrey Comet
The Times
Transactions of the Provincial Medical and
    Surgical Association
True Sun
Twopenny Dispatch
The Visitor: Cholera Lists
Voice of the People
Weekly True Sun
West London Observer
Westminster Review
Workman's Compositor
York Chronicle
York Courant
Yorkshire Herald

Articles from books and periodicals

ANDERSON, A.D.: 'Report of cases treated in the Surgical Wards of the Glasgow

Royal Infirmary, 1827–1828', *Glas.Med.J.*, vol. 1, 1828.

BRODIE, B.C.: 'Observations on the Anatomy Question'. In Brodie, B.C.: 1832.

BUCHANAN, G.: 'On the Effects of Mr Warburton's Anatomy Bill . . . in Glasgow.'
Glas.Med.J., 3rd Ser., vol. 2, 1855.

'CLC': 'Among the Poor'. *Charity Organisation Reporter*, vol. 543, 1884.

[GOOCH, B.]: 'A Bill for Preventing the Unlawful Disinterment of Human Bodies
and for Regulating Schools of Anatomy'. *Quarterly Review*, vol. 42, 1830.

GUY, W.A.: 'On the Mortality of London Hospitals and incidentally on the Deaths
in the Prisons and Public Institutions of the Metropolis'. *J.R. Stat. Soc.*, vol. 30,
1867.

HOLLINGSHEAD, J.: 'A New Chamber of Horrors'. *All the Year Round*, vol. 4, 1861.

LEADENHALL BUTCHERS and salesmans petition. *The Lion*, vol. 3, 1829–30.

LITTLE H.J.: 'The Agricultural Labourer: Provident and other Societies'. *J.R.
Agric. Soc.*, 2nd Ser., vol. 14, 1878.

SMITH, T.S.: 'The Use of the Dead to the Living'. *Westminster Review*, vol. 1, 1824.

SMITH, T.S. & BENTHAM, J.: 'Anatomy'. *Westminster Review*, vol. 10, 1829.

STRATTON, J.Y.: 'Farm Labourers, their Friendly Societies and the New Poor
Law'. *J.R.Agric.Soc.*, 2nd Ser., vol. 6, 1870.

SYKES, I.L.: 'Eulogium'. In Whiston, W.: 1748.

Broadsheets

BISHOP'S HOUSE OF MURDER. Broadsheet, 1831. John Johnson Collection.

THE CHRISTIAN'S APPEAL AGAINST THE POOR LAW AMENDMENT ACT. Broadsheet, c.1834.
St Bride Printing Institute. (Reproduced on the front cover of *Studies in
Labour History*, no.4, 1979/80.)

DIBDEN, C.: *The Patent Coffin*. Broadsheet, c.1818. St Bride Printing Institute.

EXECUTION OF THOMAS BROWN, FOR MURDER AND RAPE. Broadsheet, c.1820. John
Johnson Collection.

EXECUTION OF JOHN WILLIAMSON, FOR THE MURDER OF HIS WIFE. Broadsheet, c.1817.
John Johnson Collection.

EXECUTION. A Full and Particular account of the Execution of W. Burke. Broadsheet,
1829. Royal College of Surgeons of England, London.

EXTRAORDINARY OCCURRENCE AND SUPPOSED MURDER. Broadsheet, 1828. Royal
College of Surgeons of England, London.

MORE DEAD BODIES DISCOVERED!! Broadsheet, 1824. Royal College of Surgeons of
England, London.

NEW BURYING GROUND. Broadsheet, 1832. Renfrew District Libraries.

*PETITION FOR PARLIAMENTARY REFORM . . . from the Inhabitants of Paisley and its
Neighbourhood*. Broadsheet, c.1831. Renfrew District Libraries.

*PETITION OF THE POOR WOMEN OF THE HAMPNETT UNION [workhouse] to His Grace the
Duke of Richmond*. Broadsheet, 1837. Collection S.Burke.

THE POOR CHARLIES LAMENTATION. Broadsheet, c.1830[?]. John Johnson Collection.

*REPORT TO THE MAGISTRACY AND THE BOARD OF HEALTH, concerning the Investigation of
the New Burying Ground at the Moss Lands*. Broadsheet, 1832. Renfrew District
Libraries.

*REPORT TO THE MAGISTRATES concerning the supposed Abstraction of Bodies from the New
Burying Ground at the Moss Lands of Paisley*. Broadsheet, 1832. Renfrew District
Libraries.

THE RESURRECTIONISTS. Broadsheet, c.1830. St Bride Printing Institute.

ROBBERY OF DEAD BODIES. Broadsheet, c.1831/2. St Bride Printing Institute.

THE STAGES OF LIFE. Broadsheet, c.1830. St Bride Printing Institute.

THE STAGES OF MAN'S LIFE. Broadsheet, c.1830. St Bride Printing Institute.

TRIAL AND EXECUTION OF THE BURKERS, for Murdering a Poor Italian Boy. Broadsheet, 1831. St Bride Printing Institute.

TRIAL, EXECUTION AND CONFESSION OF THE BURKERS. Broadsheet, 1831. John Johnson Collection.

THE UNFORTUNATE FAIR; OR, THE SAD DISASTER. Broadsheet, c.1800. British Library.

SECONDARY SOURCES:

Printed materials

Books and pamphlets

ACKERKNECHT, E.H.: *A Short History of Medicine*. NY., 1982.

ACKERKNECHT, E.H.: *Medicine at the Paris Hospital, 1794–1848*. Baltimore, 1967.

ADAMS, C.P.: *Local History and Folklore*. Lond., 1975.

ADDY, S.O.: *Household Tales*. Sheffield, 1895.

ALDWINCKLE, R.: *Death in the Secular City*. Lond., 1972.

ALLARDYCE, J.: *Bygone Days in Aberdeenshire*. Aberdeen, 1913.

ANDREWS, W.: *The Doctor in Literature, History and Folklore*. Hull, 1895.

ANNING, S.T.: *The General Infirmary at Leeds*. Lond., 1963.

ARCHBOLD, J.F.: *The Poor Law*. Lond., 1930.

ARIES, P.: *Western Attitudes to Death*. Lond., 1974.

ARIES, P.: *The Hour of Our Death*. Lond., 1981.

ARMSTRONG, D.: *Political Anatomy of the Body*. Camb., 1983.

ARNOLD, T.W.: *The Folklore of Capitalism*. New Haven, Conn., 1959.

ARNOLD, T.W.: *The Symbols of Government*. N.Y., 1962.

ASCHROTT, P.F.: *The English Poor Law System*. (Thomas, H.P., trans.) Lond., 1902.

ASHTON, J.: *Modern Street Ballads*. Lond., 1888.

ASPINALL, A.: *Lord Brougham and the Whig Party*. Manc., 1927.

ATKINSON, C.M.: *Jeremy Bentham*. Lond., 1905.

AVELING, J.H.: *English Midwives*. [1872] Lond., 1967.

AYERS, G.M.: *England's First State Hospitals 1867–1930*. Lond., 1971.

BADHAM, P.: *Christian Beliefs about Life after Death*. Lond., 1978.

BAERNREITHER, J.M.: *English Associations of Working Men*. Lond., 1889.

BAILEY, P.: *Leisure and Class in Victorian England*. Lond., 1978.

BAINES, E.: *The Life of Edward Baines*. Lond., 1851.

BAKER, M.: *Folklore and Customs of Rural England*. Newton Abbot, 1974.

BAKER, T.: *The Laws Relating to Burial*. Lond., 1855.

BALL, J.M.: *The Sack 'Em Up Men*. Edin., 1928.

BARNES, B.: *Scientific Knowledge and Sociological Theory*. Lond., 1974.

BARNES, B. & SHAPIN, S. (eds): *Natural Order*. Lond., 1979.

BARTON, R.M.: *Life in Cornwall in the 19th Century*. Truro, 1970–2.

BASEVI, W.H.F.: *The Burial of the Dead*. NY., 1920.

BASTOLM, E.: *The History of Muscle Physiology*. Copenhagen, 1950.

BATTER, T.: *Funeral Cakes and Ale*. Camb., 1951.

BAYLEN, J.O. & GOSSMAN, N.J.: *A Biographical Dictionary of Modern British Radicals*. Hassocks, 1979.

BECK, R.T.: *The Cutting Edge: The Early History of the Surgeons of London.* Lond., 1974.

BELCHEM, J.: *Orator Hunt.* Oxf., 1986.

BELLAMY, J.M. & SAVILLE, J.: *Dictionary of Labour Biography.* Lond., 1972–82.

BELLOT, H.H.: *University College London.* Lond., 1929.

BENDANN, E.: *Death Customs.* Lond., 1930.

BEN-DAVID, J.: *The Scientist's Role in Society.* Englewood Cliffs, 1971.

BENSON, L.: *The Book of Remarkable Trials and Notorious Characters.* Lond., 1871.

BENTHALL, J.: *The Body Electric.* Lond., 1976.

BERLANT, J.L.: *Profession and Monopoly.* Berkeley, 1975.

BERNARD, C.: *An Introduction to the Study of Experimental Medicine.* [1865] NY., 1967.

BETTELHEIM, B.: *The Informed Heart.* NY., 1960.

BICKERTON, T.H.: *A Medical History of Liverpool.* (BICKERTON, H.R. & MACKENNA, R.M.B., eds). Lond., 1936.

BINDER, P.: *The Pearlies.* Lond., 1975.

BISHOP, W.J.: *A History of Surgical Dressings.* Chesterfield, 1959.

BISHOP, W.J.: *The Early History of Surgery.* Lond., 1960.

BLACK, C.S.: *The Story of Paisley.* Paisley, c.1957.

BLAKEBOROUGH, R.: *Wit, Character, Folklore and Customs in the North Riding of York.* Lond., 1895.

BLOCH, M.: *The Royal Touch.* Lond., 1973.

BLOCH, M.E.F.: *Placing the Dead.* Lond., 1971.

BLOOM, J.H.: *Folklore, Old Customs and Superstitions in Shakespeare Land.* Lond., 1929.

BOCOCK, R.: *Ritual in Industrial Society.* Lond., 1974.

BOLITHO, W.: *Murder for Profit.* Lond., 1926.

BOND, M.F.: *A Guide to the Records of Parliament.* Lond., 1971.

BOOTH, C.: *Life and Labour.* Lond., 1889, 1902, 1903.

BOOTH, C.: *The Aged Poor in England and Wales.* Lond., 1894.

BRAND, J.: *Doctors and the State.* Baltimore, 1965.

BRANDON, S.G.F.: *The Personification of Death.* Manc., 1961.

BRANDON, S.G.F.: *The Judgment of the Dead.* Lond., 1967.

BRATTON, J.S.: *The Victorian Popular Ballad.* Lond., 1975.

BRIGGS, A.: *William Cobbett.* Lond., 1967.

BRIGGS, K.: *Dictionary of British Folktales.* Lond., 1970–77.

BRIMELOW, W.: *Political and Parliamentary History of Bolton.* Bolton, 1882.

BROCK, M.: *The Great Reform Act.* Lond., 1973.

BROCK, R.C.: *The Life and Work of Sir Astley Cooper.* Lond., 1952.

BROCKBANK, E.M.: *The Foundation of Provincial Medical Education in England.* Manc., 1936.

BROCKBANK, W.: *Portrait of a Hospital.* Lond., 1952.

BROOK, C.W.: *Carlile and the Surgeons.* Glasgow, 1943.

BROOK, C.W.: *Battling Surgeon.* Glasgow, 1945.

BROOK, C.W.: *Thomas Wakley.* Lond., 1962.

BROWN, J.B.: *First Principles of Ecclesiastical Truth.* Lond., 1860.

BROWN, L.: *The Board of Trade and the Free Trade Movement 1830–1842* Oxf., 1958.

BROWN, R.: *History of Paisley.* Paisley, 1886.

BROWN, T.: *The Fate of the Soul.* Ipswich, 1979.

BRUNDAGE, A.: *The Making of the New Poor Law*. Lond., 1978.
BUBER, M.: *The Writings of Martin Buber*. (Herberg, W., ed.) NY., 1956.
BUDD, S.: *Varieties of Unbelief*. Lond., 1977.
BURKE, P.: *Popular Culture in Early Modern Europe*. Lond., 1979.
BURKE, P.: *Sociology and History*. Lond., 1980.
BURKE's *Genealogical and Heraldic History of the Landed Gentry*. (Townend, P., ed.) Lond., 1965.
BURKE's *Peerage and Baronetage*. (Samuels, W.S., ed.) Lond., 1980.
BURNE, C.S.: *Shropshire Folklore*. Lond., 1883.
BURNE, C.S.: *A Handbook of Folklore*. Lond., 1914.
BURNETT, J.: *A History of the Cost of Living*. Harmondsworth, 1969.
BURNETT, J.: *Useful Toil*. Harmondsworth, 1974.
BURNETT, J.: *Plenty and Want*. Lond., 1979.
BURNS, J.H.: *Jeremy Bentham and University College*. Lond., 1962.
BURROW, J.W.: *Gibbon*. Oxf., 1985.
BURTON, J.H. (ed.): *Benthamiana*, Lond., 1843.
BUSHAWAY, R.: *By Rite*. Lond., 1982.
BUTCHER, E.E. (ed.): *Bristol Corporation of the Poor*. Bristol, 1932.
BUTLER, J.R.M.: *The Passing of the Great Reform Bill*. Lond., 1914.
BYNUM, B. & PORTER, R. (eds): *William Hunter and the 18th Century Medical World*. Camb., 1985.
CAMERON, C.: *History of the Royal College of Surgeons of Ireland*. Lond., 1886.
CAMERON, H.C.: *Mr Guy's Hospital*. Lond., 1954.
CARTWRIGHT, F.F.: *A Social History of Medicine*. Lond., 1977.
CHADWICK, O.: *Victorian Miniature*, Lond., 1960.
CHADWICK, O.: *The Victorian Church*. Lond., 1966, 1970–72.
CHAMBERLAIN, M.: *Old Wives' Tales*. Lond., 1981.
CHAPMAN, R. *et al.*: *The Archeology of Death*. Camb., 1981.
CHECKLAND, S.G. & E.D.A. (eds): *The Poor Law Report of 1834*. Harmondsworth, 1974.
CHESNEY, K.: *The Victorian Underworld*. Harmondsworth, 1972.
CHESTER, N.: *The English Administrative System*. Oxf., 1981.
CHURCH OF ENGLAND: *Archbishop of Canterbury's Commission on Doctrine*. Lond., 1962.
CLARK, D.: *Between Pulpit and Pew*. Camb., 1982.
CLARK, G.S.R.K.: *An Expanding Society*. Camb., 1967.
CLIFFORD, F.: *A History of Private Bill Legislation*. Lond., 1885–7.
CLOKIE, H.A. & ROBERTSON, J.W.M.: *Royal Commissions of Enquiry*. Stanford, Calif., 1937.
COHEN, E.M.: *The Growth of the British Civil Service 1789–1939*. Lond., 1931.
COHEN, R. (ed.): *The Essential Works of David Hume*. Lond., 1965.
COHN, N.: *The Pursuit of the Millennium*. Lond., 1970.
COLE, F.J.: *A History of Comparative Anatomy*. Lond., 1944.
COLE, H.: *Things for the Surgeon*. Lond., 1964.
COLLISON, R.: *The Story of Street Literature*. Lond., 1973.
COMPER, F.M.M.: *The Book of the Craft of Dying*. Lond., 1971.
COOK, C. & KEITH, B.: *British Historical Facts, 1830–1900*. Lond., 1975.
COOKE, T.: *Dissection Guides*, Lond., 1892.
COOPER, D.D.: *The Lesson of the Scaffold*. Athens, Ohio, 1974.

COPE, G.F.:   *Dying, Death, and Disposal.* Lond., 1970.

COPE, Z.:   *Sidelights on the History of Medicine.* Lond., 1957.

COPE, Z.:   *The History of the Royal College of Surgeons.* Lond., 1960.

CREIGHTON, C.:   *A History of Epidemics in Great Britain.* [1894] Lond., 1965.

CROFT, W.R.:   *The History of the Factory Movement; or, Oastler and his Times.*
Huddersfield, 1888.

CROSSE, V.M.:   *A Surgeon in the early 19th Century.* Edin., 1968.

CROWTHER, M.A.:   *The Workhouse System.* Lond., 1981.

CULLEN, M.J.:   *The Statistical Movement in Early Victorian Britain.* Hassocks, 1975.

CURL, J.S.:   *The Victorian Celebration of Death.* Newton Abbot, 1972.

CURL, J.S.:   *A Celebration of Death.* Lond., 1980.

DARNTON, R.: *The Great Cat Massacre.* Harmondsworth, 1985.

DAVID, J.B.:   *The Scientist's Role in Society.* Englewood Cliffs, 1971.

DAVIES, M.R.R.:   *The Law of Burial and Cremation.* Lond., 1982.

DEARSLY, H.R. & BELL, T.:   *Crown Cases Reserved.* Lond., 1858.

DEBRETT'S *Peerage and Baronetage* (Smith, P.M., ed.) Lond., 1980.

DICEY, A.V.:   *Lectures on the Relation between Law and Public Opinion in England during
the Nineteenth Century.* [1905] Lond., 1924.

DIGBY, A.:   *Pauper Palaces.* Lond., 1978.

DIGBY, A.:   *The Poor Law in 19th century England and Wales.* Lond., 1982.

DJANG, T.K.:   *Factory Inspection in Great Britain.* Lond., 1940.

DOBSON, J.:   *Anatomical Eponyms.* Lond., 1946.

DOBSON, J.:   *William Clift.* Lond., 1954.

DOBSON, J.:   *John Hunter,* Edin., 1969.

DONAJGRODSKI, A.P. (ed.):   *Social Control in Nineteenth Century Britain.* Lond., 1977.

DONNISON, J.:   *Midwives and Medical Men.* Lond., 1976.

DORSON, R.M.:   *Folklore and Fakelore.* Lond., 1976.

DORSON, R.M.:   *The British Folklorists.* Lond., 1968.

DOUBLEDAY, F.:   *The Political Life of Sir Robert Peel.* Lond., 1856.

DOUGLAS, H.:   *Burke and Hare.* Lond., 1974.

DOUGLAS, M.:   *Implicit Meanings.* Lond., 1975.

DOUGLAS, M.:   *Purity and Danger.* Lond., 1966.

DRIVER, C.: *Tory Radical: The Life of Richard Oastler.* NY., 1946.

DUNCAN, A.S. *et al.*:   *Dictionary of Medical Ethics.* Lond., 1977.

DUNDES, A.:   *The Study of Folklore.* Englewood Cliffs, 1965.

DUREY, M.:   *The Return of the Plague.* Dublin, 1979.

DYER, T.F.T.:   *Domestic Folklore.* Lond., 1881.

DYER, T.F.T.:   *Old English Social Life.* Lond., 1898.

ECKSTEIN, H.H. :   *The English Health Service.* Camb., Mass., 1959.

EDSALL, N.C.:   *The Anti Poor Law Movement.* Manc., 1971.

ELLIS, H.:   *The History of Bladder Stone.* Oxf., 1969.

ENRIGHT, D.J.:   *The Oxford Book of Death.* Oxf., 1983.

ESDAILE, K.A.:   *English Monumental Sculpture since the Renaissance.* Lond., 1927.

ESQUIROS, A.:   *The English at Home.* Lond., 1861–3.

ESQUIROS, A.:   *Religious Life in England.* Lond., 1867.

EVANS, E.J.:   *Social Policy 1830–1914.* Lond., 1978.

EVERETT, C.W.:   *Jeremy Bentham.* Lond., 1966.

EYLER, J.M.:   *Victorian Social Medicine: the Ideas and Methods of William Farr.*
Baltimore, 1979.

FEILING, K.: *The Second Tory Party*. Lond., 1938.

FELTOE, C.L. (ed.): *Memorials of JF South*. Lond., 1884.

FINER, S.E.: *The Life and Times of Sir Edwin Chadwick*. Lond., 1970.

FINUCANE, R.: *Appearances of the Dead*. Lond., 1982.

FLETCHER, R.: *The Akenham Burial Case*. Lond., 1974.

FLEW, A.: *Body, Mind and Death*. Lond., 1964.

FLINN, M.W.: *Public Health Reform in Britain*. Lond., 1968.

FOOTE, G.W. & MACLAREN, A.D.: *Infidel Death Beds*. Lond., 1933.

FORD, P. & G.: *A Guide to Parliamentary Papers*. Shannon, 1972.

FOUCAULT, M.: *The Order of Things*. Lond., 1970.

FOUCAULT, M.: *The Birth of the Clinic: An Archeology of Medical Perception*. Lond., 1973.

FOUCAULT, M.: *Discipline and Punish: the Birth of the Prison*. Harmondsworth, 1979.

FRASER, D.: *The Evolution of the British Welfare State*. Lond., 1973.

FRASER, D. (ed.): *The New Poor Law in the Nineteenth Century*. Lond., 1976.

FRASER, D.: *Urban Politics in Victorian England*. Leics., 1976.

FRASER, D.: *Power and Authority in the Victorian City*. Oxf., 1979.

FRASER, D.: *A History of Modern Leeds*. Manc., 1980.

FRASER, D. (ed.): *Municipal Reform and the Industrial City*. Leics., 1982.

PISANUS FRAXI (pseud.) [i.e. Ashbee, H.S.]: *Index Librorum Prohibitorum*. Lond., 1877.

FRAZER, W.: *The History of English Public Health 1834–1939*. Lond., 1950.

FREIDSON, E.: *Professional Dominance: The Social Structure of Medical Care*. NY., 1970.

FREIDSON, E.: *Profession of Medicine. A Study of the Sociology of Applied Knowledge*. NY., 1970.

FREIDSON, E.: *Doctoring Together*. NY., 1975.

FRENCH, R.K.: *Robert Whytt, The Soul and Medicine*. Lond., 1969.

FRERE, W.H.: *A New History of the Book of Common Prayer*. Lond., 1901.

FURNESS, J.M.: *Record of Municipal Affairs 1843–93*. Sheffield, 1893.

GASH, N.: *Politics in the Age of Peel*. Lond., 1953.

GASH, N.: *Mr Secretary Peel: The Life of Sir Robert Peel to 1830*. Lond., 1961.

GASH, N.: *Reaction and Reconstruction in English Politics 1832–52*. Oxf., 1965.

GASH, N.: *Sir Robert Peel: The Life . . . after 1830*. Lond., 1972.

GEERTZ C.: *The Interpretation of Cultures*. Lond., 1975.

GEISON, G.L.: *Michael Foster and the Cambridge School of Physiology*. Princeton, 1978.

GELFAND, T.: *Professionalising Modern Medicine*. Lond., 1981.

GEORGE, M.D.: *Catalogue of Political and Personal Satires in the Prints and Drawings Department of the British Museum*. Lond., 1954.

GIBSON, J.: *The Development of Surgery*. Lond., 1967.

GILBERT, B.B.: *The Evolution of National Insurance in Great Britain*. Lond., 1966.

GITTINGS, C.: *Death, Burial and the Individual*. Lond., 1984.

GLAISTER, J.: *Medical Jurisprudence*. (Rentoul, E. & Smith, H., eds) Lond., 1973.

GLOVER, J.: *Causing Death and Saving Lives*. Harmondsworth, 1977.

GOMME, G.L.: *Folklore as an Historical Science*. Lond., 1904.

GOODY, J.: *Death, Property and the Ancestors*. Lond., 1962.

GOODY, J. et al.: *Family and Inheritance*. Camb., 1976.

GORER, G.: *Death, Grief and Mourning in Contemporary Britain*. Lond., 1965.

GORMAN, J.: *Banner Bright*. Lond., 1973.

GOSDEN, P.H.J.H.:   *The Friendly Societies in England.* Manc., 1961.

GRABES, H.:   *Speculum, Mirror & Looking Glass.* Tubingen, 1973.

GREENWOOD, M.:   *Medical Statistics: Graunt to Farr.* Camb., 1948.

GREGORY, R.:   *Mind in Science.* Lond., 1984.

GRETTON, T.:   *Murders and Moralities.* Lond., 1980.

GRIEVE, M.:   *A Modern Herbal.* Harmondsworth, 1976.

GRINDON, L.H.:   *Cremation considered in reference to the Resurrection.* Lond., 1874.

GROTE, H.:   *The Philosophical Radicals of 1832.* Lond., 1866.

GROTE, H.:   *A Brief Retrospect of the Political Events of 1831–2.* Lond., 1878.

GURDON, E.C.:   *Country Folklore; Suffolk.* Lond., 1893.

HAAGENSEN, C.D. & LLOYD, W.E.B.:   *A Hundred Years of Medicine.* [1936] NY., 1943.

HABENSTEIN, R.W. & LAMERS, W.M.:   *Funeral Customs the World Over.* Milwaukee, 1963.

HACKMAN, H.:   *London Churchyards.* Lond., 1981.

HALEVY, E.:   *The Growth of Philosophic Radicalism.* [1928] Lond., 1972.

HALL, T.S.:   *A History of General Physiology 600BC – 1900AD.* Lond., 1969.

HALLPIKE, C.R.:   *The Foundations of Primitive Thought.* Oxf., 1980.

HAMBURGER, J.:   *Intellectuals in Politics.* Lond., 1965.

HAMBURGER, J.:   *J.S. Mill and the Art of Revolution.* Lond., 1963.

HAMBURGER, J.:   *J.S. Mill and the Philosophic Radicals.* Lond., 1965.

HAMILTON, D.: *The Healers.* Edin., 1981.

HARRIS, J.S.:   *British Government Inspection.* Lond., 1955.

HARRISON, B.:   *Drink and the Victorians.* Lond., 1971.

HARRISON, F.:   *The Dark Angel: Aspects of Victorian Sexuality.* Lond., 1977.

HARRISON, J.F.C.:   *Social Reform in Victorian Leeds.* Leeds, 1954.

HARRISON, J.F.C.:   *Learning and Living.* Lond., 1961.

HARRISON, J.F.C.:   *Robert Owen and the Owenites in Britain and America.* Lond., 1969.

HARRISON, J.F.C. & THOMPSON, D.:   *A Bibliography of the Chartist Movement.* Hassocks, 1978.

HARTSHORNE, A.:   *Hanging in Chains.* Lond., 1891.

HARVEY, P. (ed.):   *The Oxford Companion to English Literature.* Oxf., 1969.

HAY, D. *et al.*:   *Albion's Fatal Tree.* Harmondsworth, 1977.

HENNOCK, E.P.:   *Fit and Proper Persons.* Lond., 1973.

HENRIQUES, U.:   *Before the Welfare State.* Lond., 1979.

HERTZ, R.:   *Death and the Right Hand.* Lond., 1960.

HICK, J.:   *Death and Eternal Life.* Lond., 1979.

HILL, A.W.:   *John Wesley among the Physicians.* Lond., 1958.

HILL, C.:   *The World Turned Upside Down.* Oxf., 1965.

HINTON, J.M.:   *Dying.* Harmondsworth, 1967.

HOBSBAWM, E. & RANGER, T. (eds):   *The Invention of Tradition.* Camb., 1983.

HOBSBAWM, E. & RUDE, G.:   *Captain Swing.* Lond., 1969.

HODGKINSON, R.:   *The Origins of The National Health Service.* Lond., 1967.

HOLBEIN SOCIETY: *Caxton's 'Iytill treatise short and abridged spekynge of the arte and craft to know well how to dye'.* [*Ars Moriendi, that is to saye that craft for to dye for the health of man's sowle*]. [1490] (Bullen, G.: Introduction) Lond., 1881.

HOLBERRY SOCIETY: *Samuel Holberry 1814–1842.* Sheffield, 1978.

HOLE, C.:   *English Folklore.* Lond., 1940.

HOLE, C.:   *English Customs and Usage.* Lond., 1950

HOLE, C.:   *The English Housewife.* Lond., 1953.

HOLLIS, P. (ed.):   *The Poor Man's Guardian 1831–5*. Lond., 1969.

HOLLIS, P.:   *The Pauper Press*. Oxf., 1970.

HOLLIS, P.:   *Class and Conflict in Nineteenth Century England*. Lond., 1973.

HOLLIS, P.:   *Pressure from Without*. Lond., 1974.

HOLMES, I.:   *The London Burial Grounds*. Lond., 1896.

HOLMES, R.C.:   *The Melancholy of Anatomy*. Leeds, 1967.

HONE, A.:   *For the Cause of Truth: Radicalism in London 1796–1821*. Oxf., 1982.

HOOD, R.G.:   *Crime, Criminology and Public Policy*. Lond., 1974.

HOPKINS, H.:   *The Long Affray*. Lond., 1985.

HORTON, R. & FINNEGAN, R.:   *Modes of Thought*. Lond., 1973.

HOVEL, M.:   *The Chartist Movement*. Manc., 1925.

HUCH, R.K.:   *The Radical Lord Radnor*. Minneapolis. 1977.

HULL, E.:   *Folklore of the British Isles*. Lond., 1928.

HUMPHREYS, N.A. (ed.):   *Vital Statistics: A Memorial Volume of Selections from the Writings of William Farr*. Lond., 1885.

HUNT, J.C.C.:   *Natural History Auctions 1700–1972*. Lond., 1976.

HUNTINGDON, R. & METCALF, P.:   *Celebrations of Death: The Anthropology of Mortuary Ritual*. Camb., 1979.

HUSBAND, H.A.:   *The Student's Handbook of Forensic Medicine*. Edin., 1889.

IGNATIEFF, M.:   *A Just Measure of Pain*. Lond., 1978.

JAMES, L.:   *Print and the People*. Lond., 1976.

JEWITT, L.:   *Church Bells*. Lond., 1870.

JEWITT, L.:   *English Antiquities*. Lond., 1879.

JONES, E.:   *Psycho Myth, Psycho History*. NY., 1974.

JONES, G.S.:   *Outcast London*. Harmondsworth, 1971.

JONES, M.W.:   *George Cruikshank*. Lond., 1978.

JUDD, G.P.:   *Members of Parliament 1734–1832*. Vale, 1972.

KANTOROWICZ, E.:   *The King's Two Bodies*. Oxf., 1957.

KAY, A.W.:   *The Evolution of Scientific Surgery*. Sheffield, 1960.

KEATING, P.:   *Into Unknown England*. Lond., 1976.

KELLY, T.:   *George Birkbeck*. Liverpool, 1957.

KEMP, M. (ed.):   *Dr William Hunter at the Royal Academy of Arts*. Glasgow, 1975.

KERN, S.:   *Anatomy and Destiny*. Indianapolis, 1975.

KEYNES, G.L.:   *The Life and Works of Sir Astley Cooper*. Lond., 1922.

KING, L.S.:   *The Medical World of the Eighteenth Century*. Chicago, 1958.

KING, L.S.:   *The Growth of Medical Thought*. Lond., 1963.

KING, L.S.:   *The Road to Medical Enlightenment*. Lond., 1970.

KIRBY, R.C. & MUSSON, A.E.:   *The Voice of the People. John Doherty*. Manc., 1975.

KROHN, W. *et al.*:   *The Dynamics of Science and Technology*. Dordrecht, 1978.

LAMBERT, R.:   *Sir John Simon 1818–1904 and English Social Administration*. Lond., 1963.

LASSEK, A.M.:   *Human Dissection*. Springfield, Illinois, 1958.

LEATHER, E.M.:   *The Folklore of Herefordshire*. Lond., 1912.

LEAVIS, F.R. (ed.):   *Mill on Bentham & Coleridge*. Lond., 1971.

LEHNER, E. & J.:   *Devils, Demons, Death and Damnation*. NY., 1971.

LEVER, T.J.P.:   *The Life and Times of Sir Robert Peel*. Lond., 1942.

LEWIS, G.:   *Dr Southwood Smith: a Retrospect*. Lond., 1898.

LEWIS, J.:   *Printed Ephemera*. Ipswich, 1962.

The LIFE of William Cobbett. Lond., 1835.

LLOYD, A.L.: *Folk Song in England.* Lond., 1969.

LONGMATE, N.: *King Cholera.* Lond., 1966.

LONGMATE, N.: *The Workhouse.* Lond., 1974.

LONSDALE, H.: *A Sketch of the Life and Writings of Robert Knox.* Lond., 1870.

LOVETT, W.: *Life and Struggles.* [1876] Lond., 1920.

LUSTIG, I.S. & POTTLE, F.A.: *The Applause of the Jury.* Lond., 1981.

MACALPINE, I. & HUNTER, R.: *George III and the Mad-Business.* Lond., 1969.

MACCOBY, S.: *English Radicalism 1832–52.* Lond., 1935.

MACCOBY, S: *English Radicalism 1786–1832.* Lond., 1955.

MACCOBY, S.: *The English Radical Tradition.* Lond., 1966.

MACCULLOCH, J.A.: *Mediaeval Faith and Fable.* Lond., 1932.

MACDONAGH, O.: *Early Victorian Government.* Lond., 1977.

MACDONAGH, O.: *The Inspector General.* Lond., 1981.

MACFARLANE, A.: *The Origins of English Individualism.* Oxf., 1978.

MACFARLANE, A.: *The Justice and the Mare's Ale.* Oxf., 1981.

MACGREGOR, G.: *The History of Burke and Hare.* Glasgow, 1884.

MACILWAIN, G.: *Memoirs of John Abernethy.* Lond., 1853.

MACK, M.P.: *Jeremy Bentham.* Lond., 1962.

MACLAREN, A.: *Social Class in Scotland: Past and Present.* Edin., 1976.

MCMANNERS, J.: *Death and the Enlightenment.* Oxf., 1981.

MACMILLAN, A.S.: *Somerset Epitaphs.* Lond., 1924.

MAEHL, W.H.: *The Reform Bill of 1832.* NY., 1967.

MALVERY, O.: *The Soul Market.* Lond., 1906.

MARSHALL, A.C.: *Prepare to Shed Them Now.* Lond., 1968.

MARSHALL, J.D.: *The Old Poor Law.* Lond., 1968.

MATHER, F.C.: *Public Order in the Age of the Chartists.* Manc., 1966.

MATHER, F.C.: *Chartism.* Lond., 1968.

MATHIAS, P.: *Science and Society.* Camb., 1972.

MAUD, J. & FINER, S.: *Local Government in England and Wales.* Lond., 1953.

MEIKLEJOHN, A.: *The Life, Work and Times of C.T. Thackrah, Surgeon.* Edin., 1957.

MELLER, H.: *London Cemeteries.* Amersham, 1981.

MERCHANT, C.: *The Death of Nature.* Lond., 1979.

MERRINGTON, R.: *University College and its Medical School.* Lond., 1976.

MIDDLETON, J.: *Lug Bara Religion.* Lond., 1960.

MILLER, H.: *The Dissector.* Lond., 1976.

MINEKA, F.E. (ed.): *The Earlier Letters of J.S. Mill.* Toronto, 1963.

MORLEY, J.: *Death, Heaven and the Victorians.* Lond., 1971.

MORRAH, D.: *A History of Industrial Life Assurance.* Lond., 1955.

MORRIS, R.J.: *Cholera 1832.* Lond., 1976.

MOSS, F.: *Folklore.* Didsbury, 1898.

MOUATT, F.J.: *Hospital Construction and Management.* Lond., 1883.

MULGAN, J.: *Poems of Freedom.* Lond., 1938.

MUNK, W.: *The Gold-Headed Cane.* Lond., 1884.

MUNK, W.: *The Life of Sir Henry Halford.* Lond., 1895.

MUNK, W. *et al.*: *The Roll of the Royal College of Physicians of London, 1518–1965.* Lond., 1878, 1955, 1968.

MYERS, E.: *Lord Althorp.* Lond., 1980.

NEATE, A.R.: *The St Marylebone Workhouse and Institution, 1730–1965.* Lond., 1967.

NEWMAN, C.: *The Evolution of Medical Education in the Nineteenth Century.* [1932] Lond., 1957.

NEWSHOLME, A.:   *The Evolution of Preventive Medicine*. Lond., 1927.
NEWTON, S.M.:   *Health, Art and Reason*. Lond., 1974.
NISBET, R.:   *The Sociological Tradition*. Lond., 1967.
NISBET, R.:   *History of the Idea of Progress*. Lond., 1980.
Choice Notes from Notes and Queries. Lond., 1858.
OBELKEVICH, J.:   *Religion and Rural Society*. Oxf., 1976.
OBELKEVICH, J.:   *Religion and the People*. Chapel Hill, Carolina. 1979.
O'CONNOR, M.C.:   *The Art of Dying Well*. NY., 1942.
OPIE, I. & P.:   *The Lore and Language of Schoolchildren*. [1959] Oxf., 1967.
OPIE, I. & P.:   *Children's Games in Street and Playground*. Oxf., 1969.
OPIE, I. & P.:   *The Oxford Dictionary of Nursery Rhymes*. Oxf., 1977.
O'RAHILLY, R.:   *Benjamin Alcock*. Oxf., 1948.
[OWEN, R.]:   *The Life of Sir Richard Owen*. Lond., 1894.
PAKENHAM, T.:   *The Boer War*. Lond., 1979.
PALMER, R.:   *A Ballad History of England*. Lond., 1979.
PAPPWORTH, M.:   *Human Guinea Pigs*. Harmondsworth, 1969.
PAREKH, B.C. (ed.):   *Jeremy Bentham*. Lond., 1974.
PARKER, C.S.:   *Sir Robert Peel from his Private Papers*. Lond., 1899.
PARKES, C.M.:   *Bereavement*. Harmondsworth, 1978.
PARKIN, D.:   *Palms, Wine and Witnesses*. Lond., 1972.
PARKIN, F.(ed.):   *The Social Analysis of Class Structure*. Lond., 1974.
PARRIS, H.:   *Constitutional Bureaucracy*. Lond., 1969.
PARRY, N. & J.:   *The Rise of the Medical Profession*. Lond., 1976.
PARSONS, F.:   *The History of St Thomas's Hospital*. Lond., 1932–6.
PARTRIDGE, E.:   *A Dictionary of Historical Slang*. Lond., 1961.
PEACHEY, G.:   *A Memoir of William & John Hunter*. Plymouth, 1924.
PELLING, M.:   *Cholera, Fever, and English Medicine, 1825–65*. Oxf., 1978.
PENNY, N.:   *Mourning*. Lond., 1981.
PETERSON, M.J.:   *The Medical Profession in mid-Victorian London*. Calif., 1978.
PETTIGREW, T.J.:   *Medical Portrait Gallery*. Lond., 1839.
PINCUS, L.:   *Life and Death; coming to terms with Death in the Family*. Lond., 1978.
POLLARD, S. & SALT, J.:   *Robert Owen, Prophet of the Poor*. Lond., 1971.
PORRITT, E. & A.G.:   *The Unreformed House of Commons*. Camb., 1903.
PORTER, E.:   *Cambridgeshire Customs and Folklore*. Lond., 1969.
PORTER, R. (ed.):   *Patients & Practitioners*. Camb., 1985.
PORTER, W.S.:   *The Medical School in Sheffield, 1828–1928*. Sheffield, 1928.
POWICKE, F.M. & FRYDE, E.B.:   *Handbook of British Chronology*. Lond., 1961.
POYNTER, F.N.L. (ed.):   *The History and Philosophy of Knowledge of the Brain and its Functions*. Oxf., 1958.
POYNTER, F.N.L. (ed.):   *The Evolution of Hospitals in Britain*. Lond., 1964.
POYNTER, F.N.L. (ed.):   *The Evolution of Medical Education in Britain*. Lond., 1966.
POYNTER, J.R.:   *Society and Pauperism*. Lond., 1969.
PRICE'S *Textbook of Medicine*. (SCOTT, R.B., ed.) Oxf., 1978
PRITCHARD, E.E.:   *Social Anthropology*. Lond., 1951.
PUCKLE, B.S.:   *Funeral Customs: Their Origin and Development*. Lond., 1926.
RADFORD, E. & M.:   *Encyclopaedia of Superstitions*. Lond., 1961.
RAE, I.:   *Knox the Anatomist*. Edin., 1964.
RAPHAEL, B.:   *The Anatomy of Bereavement*. Lond., 1984.
RAVEN, J.:   *Victoria's Inferno*. Wolverhampton, 1978.
REED, J.:   *Victorian Conventions*. Athens, Ohio, 1976.

REISER, T.J.:   *Medicine and the Reign of Technology.* Camb., 1978.

RICHARDSON, J.:   *The Local Historian's Encyclopaedia.* Barnet, 1974.

RICHARDSON, S.I.:   *Edmonton Poor Law Union 1837–54.* Lond., n.d.

ROBERTS, D.:   *Victorian Origins of the British Welfare State.* New Haven, 1960.

ROBERTS, D.:   *Paternalism in Early Victorian England.* Lond., 1979.

ROBERTS, H.:   *Women, Health & Reproduction.* Lond., 1981.

ROSE, F.C. & BYNUM, N.F. (eds):   *Historical Aspects of the Neurosciences.* NY., 1982.

ROSE, M.:   *Curator of the Dead: Thomas Hodgkin 1798–1866.* Lond., 1981.

ROSE, M.E.:   *The English Poor Law 1780–1930.* Newton Abbot, 1971.

ROSE, M.E.:   *The Relief of Poverty 1834–1914.* Lond., 1972.

ROSENBERG, C.E. (ed.):   *Healing and History.* Folkestone, 1979.

ROSENBLATT, P.C. *et al.*:   *Grief and Mourning in Cross-Cultural Perspective.*
    [?Minnesota], 1976.

ROSS, E.K.:   *Living with Death and Dying.* Lond., 1982.

ROSS, E.K.:   *Death: The Final Stage of Growth.* Lond., 1975.

ROUGHEAD, W. (ed.):   *Famous Trial Series; Burke and Hare.* Lond., 1921.

ROME, D.J.:   *London Radicalism 1840–43.* Lond., 1970.

ROYLE, E.:   *Radicals, Secularists and Republicans: Popular Freethought in Britain.*
    Manc., 1980.

RUDE, G.:   *The Crowd in History.* Lond., 1964.

RUDE, G.:   *Paris and London in the Eighteenth Century: Studies in Popular Protest.*
    Lond., 1970.

RUSSELL, K.F.:   *British Anatomy 1525–1800: A Bibliography.* Melbourne, 1963.

SAINTY, J.C.:   *Home Office Officials.* Lond., 1975.

SAMUEL, R.:   *People's History and Socialist Theory.* Lond., 1981.

SANDERS, A.:   *Charles Dickens, Resurrectionist.* Lond., 1982.

SCASE, R. (ed.):   *Industrial Society.* Lond., 1977.

SCOTT, R.:   *The Body as Property.* Lond., 1981.

SHEPARD, L.:   *John Pitts, Ballad Printer of Seven Dials.* Lond., 1969.

SHEPARD, L.:   *The History of Street Literature.* Newton Abbot, 1973.

SHEPHERD, J.A.:   *Spencer Wells: The Life and Work of a Victorian Surgeon, 1818–1897.*
    Lond., 1965.

SHEPPARD, F.:   *Local Government in St Marylebone 1688–1835.* Lond., 1958.

SHEPPARD, F.:   *London 1808–1870; The Infernal Wen.* Lond., 1971.

SHRYOCK, R.H.:   *The Development of Modern Medicine.* Lond., 1948.

SIMS, G.R.:   *How the Poor Live.* Lond., 1883.

SIMS, G.R.:   *Living London.* Lond., 1904–6.

SIMPSON, J.:   *Folklore of Sussex.* Lond., 1973.

SINCLAIR, H.M. & SMITH, A.H.T.R.:   *A Short History of Anatomy Teaching in Oxford.*
    Oxf., 1950.

SINGER, C.:   *The Evolution of Anatomy.* Lond., 1925.

SINGER, C.:   *A Short History of Scientific Ideas.* Oxf., 1959.

SINGER, C. & UNDERWOOD, E.A.:   *A Short History of Medicine.* Oxf., 1962.

SLACK, P.:   *Plague in Tudor & Stuart England.* Lond., 1985.

SMITH, B. ABEL: *The Hospitals.* Lond., 1964.

SMITH, B. ABEL: *A History of the Nursing Profession.* Lond., 1979.

SMITH, F.B.:   *The People's Health 1830–1910.* Lond., 1979.

SMITH, H.S.:   *The Parliaments of England.* Chichester, 1973.

SMITH, P.:   *The Book of Nasty Legends.* Lond., 1984.

SMOUT, T.C. (ed.): *The Search for Wealth and Stability.* Lond., 1979.

SOUTHGATE, H.: *Many Thoughts of Many Minds.* Lond., n.d.

SPATER, G.: *William Cobbett.* Camb., 1982.

SPRIGGE, S.S.: *The Life and Times of Thomas Wakley.* Lond., 1897.

SPRIGGE, S.S.: *Medicine and the Public.* Lond., 1905.

SPRIGGE, S.S.: *Some Considerations of Medical Education.* Lond., 1910.

SPUFFORD, M.: *Small Books and Pleasant Histories.* Lond., 1981.

STANNARD, D.E.: *The Puritan Way of Death.* NY., 1977.

STEINER, G.: *Language and Silence: Essays 1958–66.* Harmondsworth, 1969.

STEINTRAGER, J.: *Bentham.* Lond., 1977.

STENTON, M. (ed.): *Who's Who of British Members of Parliament.* Hassocks, 1976.

STINSON, D.T.: *The Role of Sir William Lawrence in Nineteenth Century English Surgery.* Zurich, 1969.

STORCH, R.D. (ed.): *Popular Culture and Custom in Nineteenth Century England.* Lond., 1982.

STRUTHERS, J.: *A Historical Sketch of Edinburgh Anatomy School.* Edin., 1867.

SUDNOW, D.: *Passing On: The Social Organisation of Dying.* Englewood Cliffs, 1967.

SUPPLE, B.E.: *The Royal Exchange Assurance.* Lond., 1970.

SUPPLE, B.E.: *Essays in British Business History.* Oxf., 1977.

SUTHERLAND, G.: *Studies in the Growth of Nineteenth Century Government.* Lond., 1972.

TAWNEY, R.: *Religion and the Rise of Capitalism.* [1962] Harmondsworth, 1980.

TAYLOR, A.J.: *Laissez Faire and State Intervention in Nineteenth Century Britain.* Lond., 1972.

TAYLOR, F.: *Johnstone and Cooperation.* Johnstone, 1916.

TAYLOR, L.: *Mourning Dress.* Lond., 1983.

TEGG, W.: *The Last Act.* Lond., 1876.

TEMKIN, O.: *Double Face of Janus.* Baltimore, 1977.

TEMKIN, O.: *Respect for Life in Medicine, Philosophy and the Law.* Baltimore, 1977.

THANE, P.: *The Origins of British Social Policy.* Lond., 1978.

THANE, P.: *Foundations of the Welfare State.* Lond., 1982.

THERNSTROM, A.S. & SENNETT, R.: *Nineteenth Century Cities.* Yale, 1969.

THOMAS, J.: *Matters of Life and Death.* Toronto, 1978.

THOMAS, K.: *Religion and the Decline of Magic.* Harmondsworth, 1978.

THOMAS, K.: *Man in the Natural World.* Lond., 1983.

THOMAS, L.V.: *Anthropologie de la Mort.* Paris, 1980.

THOMAS, W.: *The Philosophical Radicals.* Oxf., 1979.

THOMPSON, D.: *The Early Chartists.* Lond., 1971.

THOMPSON, E.P.: *The Making of the English Working Class.* Harmondsworth, 1963.

THOMPSON, E.P.: *Whigs and Hunters.* Harmondsworth, 1975.

THOMPSON, E.P.: *Folklore, Anthropology and Social History.* Brighton, 1979.

TILLOTSON, K.: *Novels of the Eighteen-Forties.* Oxf., 1983.

TIMBS, J.: *Romance of London.* Lond., 1865.

TITMUSS, R.: *The Gift Relationship.* Lond., 1979.

TREVELYAN, G.O.: *Life and Letters of Lord Macaulay.* Lond., 1959.

TRISTRAM, P.: *Figures of Life and Death.* Lond., 1976.

TURNER, C.H.: *The Inhumanists.* Lond., 1932.

TURNER, C.J.R.: *A History of Vagrants and Vagrancy.* Lond., 1887.

TURNER, J.: *Reckoning with the Beast.* Baltimore, 1980.

TURNER, V.:   *The Ritual Process.* Lond., 1969.

TYACK, G.S.:   *Lore and Legend of the English Church.* Lond., 1899.

UNIVERSITY of California School of Medicine: *The History of Medicine.* Los Angeles, 1968–70.

VAN GENNEP, A.:   *The Rites of Passage.* Chicago, [1909] Lond., 1960.

VANSINA, J.:   *Oral Tradition.* Lond., 1965.

VAUX, J.E.:   *Church Folklore.* Lond., 1902.

VEBLEN, T.:   *The Theory of the Leisure Class.* Lond., 1970.

VINCENT, D.:   *Bread, Knowledge and Freedom.* Lond., 1981.

VULLIAMY, C.E.:   *Immortal Man.* Lond., 1926.

WALKER, D.P.:   *The Decline of Hell.* Lond., 1964.

WALLAS, G.:   *The Life of Francis Place.* [1898] Lond., 1918.

WANGENSTEEN, O.H. & WANGENSTEEN, S.:   *The Rise of Surgery.* Minneapolis, 1978.

WARD, J.T.:   *The Factory Movement 1830–1855.* Lond., 1962.

WARD, J.T.:   *Sir James Graham.* Lond., 1967.

WARD, J.T.:   *Popular Movements.* Lond., 1970.

WARD, J.T.:   *Chartism.* Lond., 1973.

WARNE, A.:   *Church and Society in Eighteenth Century Devon.* Newton Abbot, 1969.

WEBB, B. & S.J.:   *English Poor Law History.* Lond., 1910.

WEBB, B. & S.J.:   *The State and the Doctor.* Lond., 1910.

WEBB, B. & S.J.:   *English Local Government: English Poor Law History.* Lond., 1929.

WEBSTER, C. (ed.):   *Health, Medicine and Mortality in the Sixteenth Century.* Camb., 1979.

WEINDLING, P. (ed.):   *Information Sources in the History of Science and Medicine.* Lond., 1983.

WEINER, J.:   *The War of the Unstamped.* Lond., 1969.

WEINER, J.:   *A Descriptive Finding List of Unstamped British Periodicals.* Lond., 1970.

WEINER, J.:   *Radicalism and Freethought in Nineteenth Century Britain: The Life of Richard Carlile.* Lond., 1983.

WEINER, P.P. (ed.):   *Dictionary of the History of Ideas.* NY., 1973.

WERNER, M.:   *The Formation of Christian Dogma.* Lond., 1957.

WESTERMARK, E.A.:   *The Origin and Development of Moral Ideas.* Lond., 1906.

WHALEY, J.:   *Mirrors of Mortality.* Lond., 1981.

WILKINSON, R.:   *Governing Elites.* NY., 1969.

WILKS, S.:   *A Memoir.* Lond., 1911.

WILKS, S. & BETTANY, G.T.:   *A Biographical History of Guy's Hospital.* Lond., 1892.

WILLIAMS, R.:   *Keywords.* Lond., 1976.

WILLIAMS, W.M.:   *The Sociology of an English Village.* Lond., 1956.

WILLOUGHBY, R.:   *Funeral Formalities and Obligations.* Lond., 1936.

WILSON, A. & LEVY, H.J.:   *Industrial Assurance.* Lond., 1937.

WILSON, A. & LEVY, H.J.:   *Burial Reform and Funeral Costs.* Lond., 1938.

WILSON, G.:   *Memoir of Edward Forbes.* Edin., 1861.

WIMBERLY, L.C.:   *Death and Burial Lore.* Nebraska, 1927.

WOHL, A.:   *Endangered Lives.* Lond., 1983.

WOLSTENHOLME, G. & O'CONNOR, M.:   *Ethics in Medical Progress.* Lond., 1966.

WOODFORDE, J.:   *Diary of a Country Parson.* (Beresford, J., ed.) Oxf., 1949.

WOODWARD, J. & RICHARDS, D. (eds):   *Health Care and Popular Medicine in Nineteenth Century England.* Lond., 1977.

WOODWARD, J.:   *To do the Sick No Harm.* Lond., 1978.

WRIGHT, P. & TREACHER, A. (eds): *The Problem of Medical Knowledge*. Edin., 1982.
YOUNG, K. & GARSIDE, P.: *Metropolitan London : Politics and Urban Change, 1837–1981*. Lond., 1982.
YOUNGSON, A.J.: *The Scientific Revolution in Victorian Medicine*. Lond., 1979.

Articles from books and periodicals

AGNEW, L.R.C.: 'Sir Astley Cooper and William Millard: a Vindication'. *J.Hist.Med.*, vol. 18, 1963.
ALFORD, V.: 'Rough Music'. *Folklore*, vol. 70, 1959.
AMULREE, LORD: 'Hygienic Conditions in Ancient Rome and Modern London'. *Med.Hist.*, vol. 17(3), 1973.
ANDERSON, J.: 'Medical Education and Social Change'. In POYNTER, F.N.L. (ed.): 1966.
ANNING, S.T.: 'Provincial Medical Schools in the Nineteenth Century'. In poynter, f.n.l. (ed.): 1966.
AYDELOTTE, W.D.: 'Conservative and Radical Interpretations of Early Victorian Social Legislation'. *Victorian Studies*, vol. 9(2), 1967.
BAILEY, V.: 'Crime, Criminal Justice and Authority in England'. *Bull.Soc.Study Lab.Hist.*, vol. 40, 1980.
BARNET, M.: 'The 1832 Cholera Epidemic in York'. *Med.Hist.*, vol. 16(1), 1972.
BARRICK, M.E.: 'Cumberland County Death Lore'. *Pennsylvania Folklife*, vol. 38(4), 1979.
BAUGH, D.A.: 'The Cost of Poor Relief in SE England 1790–1834'. *Econ.Hist.Rev.* (2nd Ser.), vol. 28, 1975.
BAXTER, J.: 'The Life and Struggle of Samuel Holberry, Sheffield's Revolutionary Democrat'. In HOLBERRY SOCIETY: 1978.
BLAUG, M.: 'The Myth of the Old Poor Law, and the Making of the New'. *J. Econ. Hist.*, vol. 23(2), 1963.
BLAUNER, R.: 'Death and Social Structure'. *Psychiatry*, vol. 29, 1966.
BRAND, J.L.: 'The Parish Doctor: England's Poor Law Medical Officers and Medical Reform'. *Bull.Hist.Med.*, vol. 35, 1961.
BREARS, P.: 'Heart Gravestones of the Calder Valley'. *Folk Life*, vol. 19, 1981.
BRIGGS, A.: 'The Background of the Parliamentary Reform Movement in Three English Cities 1831–2'. *Camb.Hist.J.*, vol. 10, 1952.
BROWN, T.: 'From Mechanism to Vitalism'. *J.Hist.Biol.*, vol. 7, 1974.
BRUFORD, A. & MACDONALD, M.: 'Burkers and Resurrectionists'. *Tocher Journal*, vol. 5, 1972.
BUBER, M.: 'I and Thou'. In BUBER, M.: 1956.
BUCHANAN, G.: 'On the effects of Mr Warburton's Anatomy Bill, and the Study of Practical Anatomy in Glasgow'. *Glasgow Med.J.*, ser.III, vol. 2, 1855.
BYNUM, B.: 'Anatomical Method, Natural Theology and the Functions of the Brain'. *Isis*, vol. 64, 1973.
CANNADINE, D.: 'War and Death, Grief and Mourning in Modern Britain'. In WHALEY, J.: 1981.
CANNADINE, D.: 'The Context, Performance and Meaning of Ritual'. In HOBSBAWM, E. & RANGER, T.: 1983.
CAPENER, N.: 'John Sheldon and the Exeter Medical School'. *Proc.R.Soc.Med.*, vol. 52, 1959.

CARSON, W.G.: 'Symbolic and Instrumental Dimensions of Early Factory Legislation'. In HOOD, R.G.: 1974.

CARTER, L.: 'The Scottish Peasantry'. In SAMUEL, R.: 1981.

CLANCHY, M.T.: 'Remembering the Past and the Good Old Law'. *History*, vol. 55(84), 1970.

COOTER, R.: 'The Power of the Body'. In BARNES, B. & SHAPIN, S. (eds): Lond., 1979.

CROMWELL, V.: 'Interpretations of 19th Century Administration: an Analysis'. *Victorian Studies*, vol. 9, 1966.

CROSS, S.J.: 'John Hunter, the Animal Oeconomy, and Late Eighteenth Century Physiological Discourse'. *Studies in the History of Biology*, vol. 5, 1981.

CUNNINGHAM, A.: 'The Kinds of Anatomy'. *Med.Hist.*, vol. 19, 1975.

DAVIN, A.: 'Imperialism & Motherhood'. *History Workshop J.*, vol. 5, 1978.

DAY, W.H.M.: 'A Visit to the Tombs'. *Brit.Med.J.*, vol. 2, 1948.

DINWIDDY, J.R.: 'The early 19th century Campaign against Flogging in the Army'. *Eng.Hist.Rev.*, vol. 97, 1982.

DONNELLY, F.K.: 'The Destruction of the Sheffield School of Anatomy in 1835: A Popular Response to Class Legislation'. *Trans.Hunter Archeol.Soc.*, vol. 10(3), 1975.

DOOLEY, D.: 'A Dissection of Anatomy'. *Ann.RCS.Eng.*, vol. 53, 1973.

DOPSON, L.: 'St Thomas's Parish Vestry Records and a Body-snatching Incident'. *Brit.Med.J.*, vol. 2, 1949.

DUREY, M.: 'Bodysnatchers and Benthamites'. *London J.*, vol. 2, 1976.

EDWARDS, L.F.: 'Resurrection Riots during the Heroic Age of Anatomy in America'. *Bull.Hist.Med.*, vol. 25, 1951.

EGAN, R.W.: 'What Price a Corpse?'. *Sphincter*, vol. 20, 1958.

FIELD, J.: 'Social Control'. *Bull.Soc.Study Lab.Hist.*, vol. 36, 1978.

FIGLIO, K.M.: 'Chlorosis and Chronic Disease in Nineteenth Century Britain: The Social Constitution of Somatic Illness'. *Int.J.Health Services*, vol. 8(4), 1978.

FIGLIO, K.M.: 'Sinister Medicine'. *Radical Science J.*, vol. 9, 1979.

FIGLIO, K.M.: 'The Metaphor of Organisation'. *History of Science*, vol. 14, 1976.

FINCH, E.: 'The Influence of the Hunters on Medical Education'. *Ann.RCS.Eng.*, vol. 20, 1957.

FINER, S.E.: 'The Transmission of Benthamite Ideas 1820–50'. In SUTHERLAND, G. (ed.): 1972.

FLEETWOOD, J.F.: 'The Irish Resurrectionists'. *Irish J. Med.Sci.*, 1959.

FLETCHER, T.B.: 'The Association between Famous Artists and Anatomists'. *Johns Hopkins Hosp. Bull.*, 1906.

FLINN, M.W.: 'Poor Law Medical Services'. In FRASER, D. (ed.): [The New Poor Law] 1976.

FRASER, D.: 'The Leeds Churchwardens 1828–50'. *Thoresby Miscellany*, vol. 53, 1971.

FRASER, D.: 'Poor Law Politics in Leeds 1833–55'. *Thoresby Miscellany*, vol. 53, 1971.

FRASER, D.: 'Edward Baines'. In HOLLIS, P.: 1974.

FRASER, D.: 'Politics and Society in the 19th century'. In FRASER, D.: 1980.

GATTRELL, V.A.C.: 'Incorporation and the Pursuit of Liberal Hegemony in Manchester, 1790–1839'. In FRASER, D. (ed.): 1982.

GEISON, G.L.: 'Social and Institutional Factors in the Stagnancy of English

Physiology, 1840–1870'. *Bull.Hist.Med.*, vol. 46(1), 1972.

GELFAND, T.: 'Empiricism & 18th Cent French Surgery'. *Bull.Hist.Med.*, vol. 44, 1970.

GELFAND, T.: 'The Paris Manner of Dissection: Student Anatomical Dissection in early 18th century Paris'. *Bull.Hist.Med.*, vol. 46(2), 1972.

GENOVESE, E.: 'The Many Faces of Moral Economy: contribution to a debate'. *Past & Present*, vol. 58, 1973.

GUTHRIE, D.: 'The Patient: A Neglected Factor in the History of Medicine'. In COPE, Z.: 1957.

GUTTMACHER, A.F.: 'Bootlegging Bodies'. *Bull.Soc.Med.Hist.*, Chicago, vol. 4(4), 1935.

HAMILTON, B.: 'The Medical Professions in the 18th century'. *Econ.Hist.Rev.*, (2nd Ser.), vol. 4, 1951.

HARKER, D.: 'May Cecil Sharp be Praised?' *Hist.Workshop J.*, vol. 14, 1982.

HARRISON, J.F.C.: 'The Owenite Contribution to.Freethought in the nineteenth century'. *Bull.of Soc.for Study Lab.Hist.*, vol. 29, 1974.

HART, J. Tudor: 'The Inverse Care Law.' *Lancet*, 1971(1), 27.2.1971.

HAY, D.: 'Eighteenth Century Crime'. *Bull.Soc.Study Lab.Hist.*, vol. 25, 1972.

HAY, D.: 'Property, Authority and the Criminal Law.' In HAY, D. *et al.*: 1977.

HENRIQUES, U.: 'How Cruel was the Victorian New Poor Law?'. *Hist.J.*, vol. 9(2), 1968.

HEWER, R.L.: 'The Sack 'Em Up Men'. *St Bartholomew's Hosp.J.*, vol. 58, 1954.

HOLLOWAY, S.W.F.: 'Medical Education in England, 1830–1858'. *History*, vol. 49, 1964.

HOWELL, W.B.: 'Some Humble Workers in the Cause of Anatomy'. *Ann.Med.Hist.*, vol. 8. 1926.

HOWLETT, E.: 'Burial Customs'. *Westminster Review*, August 1893.

HUZEL, J.P.: 'Malthus, the Poor Law, and Population in Early Nineteenth Century England'. *Econ.Hist.Rev.* (2nd Ser.), vol. 22, 1969.

IGNATIEFF, M.: 'Total Institutions and Working Classes'. *Hist.Workshop J.*, vol. 15, 1983.

JENNETT, B.J.: 'Determination of death'. In DUNCAN, A.S. *et al.*: 1977.

JONES, E.: 'The Symbolic Significance of Salt'. [1912]. In JONES, E.: 1974.

JONES, E.: 'Psychoanalysis and History'. [1928]. In JONES, E.: 1974.

JONES, G.S.: 'Some Problems in reconstructing the Culture and Attitudes of the Poor in mid and late Victorian London'. *Bull.Soc.Study Lab.Hist.*, vol. 27, 1973.

JONES, N.H.: 'Medical Education & Practice in Britain 150 years ago'. *Brit.Med.J.*, vol. 288, 1984.

KAIJAGE, F.J.: 'Poor Law Catechism'. *Bull.Soc.Study Lab.Hist.*, vol. 42, 1981.

KASS, E.H. *et al.*: 'Thomas Hodgkin and Benjamin Harrison: Crisis in Promotion in Academia'. *Med.Hist.*, vol. 24, 1980.

KENNEDY, A.E.C.: 'The London Hospitals and the Rise of the University'. In POYNTER, F.N.L. (ed.): 1966.

LAQUEUR, T.: 'Bodies, Death and Pauper Funerals'. *Representations*, vol. 1(1), 1983.

LE FANU, W.R.: 'The Lost Half-century in English Medicine'. *Bull.Hist.Med.*, vol. 46, 1972.

LINEBAUGH, P.: 'Eighteenth Century Crime.' *Bull.Soc.Study Lab.Hist.*, vol. 25, 1972.

LINEBAUGH, P.: 'Eighteenth Century Disorders'. *Bull.Soc.Study Lab.Hist.*, vol. 28, 1974.

LINEBAUGH, P.: 'The Tyburn Riot Against the Surgeons'. In HAY, D. *et al.*: 1977.

LOUDON, I.: 'Obstetric Care, Social Class, and Maternal Mortality'. *B.M.J.* vol. 293, 1986.

MACDONAGH, O.: 'The Nineteenth Century Revolution in Government: A Reappraisal'. *Hist.J.*, vol. 1, 1958.

MCENEMEY, W.H.: 'Education and the Medical Reform Movement'. In POYNTER, F.N.L. (ed.): 1966.

MCKELVIE, D.: 'Aspects of Oral Tradition and Belief in an Industrial Region'. *Folk Life*, vol. 1, 1963.

MCQUEEN, W.: 'Scotch Funerals'. *Macmillan's Magazine*, vol. 46, 1882.

MARMOY, C.F.A.: 'The Auto Icon of Jeremy Bentham at University College, London'. *Med.Hist.*, vol. 11(2), 1958.

MOODY, F.W.: 'Funeral Customs at Addingham'. *Trans.York.Dialect Soc.*, vol. 10(56), 1959.

MOORHOUSE, H.D.: 'History, Sociology, and the Quiescence of the British Working Class'. *Social History*, vol. 4, 1981.

MORRIS, R.J.: 'Religion and Medicine: the Cholera Pamphlets of Oxford 1832, 1849 & 1854'. *Med.Hist.*, vol. 10, 1975.

NEUBERGER, M.: 'British Medicine and the Gottingen Medical School in the Eighteenth Century'. *Bull.Hist.Med.*, vol. 14, 1943.

NEWMAN, C.: 'The Hospital as a Teaching Centre'. In POYNTER, F.N.L. (ed.): 1964.

PARRY, N. & J.: 'Social Closure and Collective Social Mobility'. In SCASE, R.(ed.): 1977.

PEACOCK, A.: 'The Relationship between the Soul and the Brain'. In ROSE, F.C. & BYNUM, W.F. (eds.): 1982.

PEACOCK, A.J.: 'York and the Resurrection Men'. *York Hist.*, vol. 1, n.d.

PEACOCK, F.: 'Traditional and Customs relating to Death and Burial in Lincolnshire'. *The Antiquary*, Nov. 1895.

PENNY, N.: 'Smugglerius'. Royal Academy *Catalogue* to the Reynolds Exhibition, 1986.

PHILLIPS, M.: 'A Pauper's Grave'. *New Society*, 28.10.1976.

PORTER, R.: 'Laymen, doctors and Medical Knowledge in the 18th century'. In PORTER, R. (ed.): 1985.

PORTER, R.: 'William Hunter: a surgeon and a Gentleman'. In BYNUM, B. & PORTER, R. (eds): 1985.

POWER, D.: 'The Rise and Fall of the Private Medical Schools of London' *Brit.Med.J.*, vol. 2, 1895.

POYNTER, F.N.L.: 'Medical Education in England since 1600'. In University of California School of Medicine: 1968–70.

RAWNSLEY, S. & REYNOLDS, J.: 'Undercliffe Cemetery, Bradford'. *Hist.Workshop J.*, vol. 4, 1977.

RICHARDSON, R.: 'A Dissection of Anatomy'. *Studies in Labour History*, 1976.

RICHARDSON, R.: 'Further Thoughts on the Anatomy Act'. *Studies in Labour History*, 1980.

RICHARDSON, R.: 'Old People's Attitudes to Death'. *Soc.for the Social Hist.of Med.Bull.*, vol. 34, 1984.

RICHARDSON, R.: 'Bentham & Bodies for Dissection'. *Bentham Newsletter*, Summer 1986.

RICHARDSON, R. & CHAMBERLAIN, M.: 'Life and Death'. *Oral Hist.J.*, 1983.

RICHARDSON, R. & HURWITZ, B.S.: 'Bentham's Self-image: an Exemplary Bequest for Dissection'. *Br.Med.J.* vol. 295, 1987.

RITCHIE, J.: 'An Account of the Watch-houses, Mortsafes, and Public Vaults in Aberdeenshire Churchyards'. *Proc.Soc.of Antiquaries, Scotland*, vol. 46, 1912.

RITCHIE, J.: 'Relics of the Bodysnatchers'. *Proc.Soc.of Antiquaries, Scotland*, vol. 55, 1921.

ROBERTS, D.: 'Jeremy Bentham and the Victorian Administrative State'. *Victorian Studies*, vol. 2, 1959.

ROBERTS, D.: 'How Cruel was the Victorian Poor Law?' *Hist.J.*, vol. 6, 1963.

RODGERS, P.: 'Smugglerius'. *Royal Academy Magazine*, 1985.

ROLLESTON, H.: 'Provincial Medical Schools a Hundred Years Ago'. *Camb.Univ.Med.Mag.*, vol. 10, 1923.

ROLLESTON, H.: 'The Early History of the Teaching of I: Human Anatomy in London, II: Morbid Anatomy and Pathology in Great Britain'. *Ann.Med.Hist.*, 3rd Ser., vol. 1, 1939.

ROSE, M.E.: 'The Anti-Poor Law Movement in the North of England'. *Northern History*, vol. 1, 1966.

ROSE, M.E.: 'The Anti-Poor Law Agitation'. In WARD, J.T.: 1970.

ROSENBERG, C.E.: 'The Therapeutic Revolution'. *Perspectives in Biology and Medicine*, vol. 20, 1977.

ROSS, I & C.U.: 'Bodysnatching in Nineteenth Century Britain: From Exhumation to Murder'. *Brit.J.Law & Soc.*, vol. 6(1), 1979.

RUDE, G.: 'English Rural and Urban Disturbances on the Eve of the First Reform Bill 1830–1'. *Past & Present*, vol. 36. 1967.

RUSSELL, K.F. & O'MALLEY, D.: 'Tudor Anatomy'. In EDGUARDUS, D.: [1532] 1961.

RYECROFT, P.V.: 'A recently established procedure: Corneal Transplantation'. In WOLSTENHOLME, G. & O'CONNOR, M.: 1966.

SADLER, J.: 'Ideologies of "Art" and "Science" in medicine'. In KROHN, W. *et al.*: 1978.

ST CLAIR, R.E.W.: 'Murder for Anatomy'. *NZ Med.J.*, vol. 60, 1961.

SHIPLEY, S.: 'Science and Atheism in mid-Victorian London'. *Bull.Soc.Study Lab.Hist.*, vol. 29, 1974.

SHORE, L.R.: 'The Anatomist's Vade Mecum'. *St Bartholomew's Hosp.J.*, vol. 34(8), 1927.

SINGER, C.J. & HOLLOWAY, S.W.F.: 'Early Medical Education in England'. *Med.Hist.*, vol. 4, 1960.

SKEGG, P.D.G.: 'Human Corpses, Medical Specimens, and the Law of Property'. *Anglo-Am.Law Review.* vol. 4(4), 1975.

SMITH, A.T.H.: 'Stealing the Body and its Parts'. *Crim.Law. Rev.*, vol. 10, 1976.

SMITH, A.W.: 'Popular Religion'. *Past & Present*, vol. 40, 1968.

SMITH, G.: 'Literary Sources and Folklore Studies in the Nineteenth Century: a reassessment of armchair scholarship'. *Lore and Language*, vol. 2(9), 1978.

SPENCER, H.R.: 'The History of Ovariotomy'. In COPE, Z.: 1957.

STEVENS, C.: 'The Funeral Wake in Wales'. *Folk Life*, vol. 14, 1976.

TAIT, H.P.: 'Some Edinburgh Medical Men at the Time of the Resurrectionists'. *Edin.Med.J.*, vol. 55, 1948.

TEMKIN, O.: 'The Role of Surgery in the Rise of Modern Medical Thought'. *Bull.Hist.Med.*, vol. 25, 1951.

TEMKIN, O.: 'Basic Science, Medicine and the Romantic Era'. *Bull.Hist.Med.*, vol. 37, 1963.

THOMAS, W.: 'The Philosophic Radicals'. In HOLLIS, P.: 1974.

THOMPSON, E.P.: 'English Trade Unionism and other Labour Movements before 1790'. *Bull.Soc.Study Lab.Hist.*, vol. 16, 1968.

THOMPSON, E.P.: 'The Moral Economy of the English Crowd in the Eighteenth Century'. *Past & Present*, vol. 50, 1971.

THOMPSON, E.P.: ' "Rough Music": le Charivari anglais'. *Annales*, 1972.

THOMPSON, E.P.: 'Patrician Society, Plebeian Culture'. *J.Soc.Hist.*, 1974.

THOMPSON, E.P.: 'The Crime of Anonymity'. In HAY, D. *et al*.: 1975.

THOMPSON, E.P.: '18th Century English Society: class struggle without class?' *Social History*, vol. 3(2), 1978.

THOMPSON, E.P. *et al*.: '18th century Crime'. *Bull.Soc.Study Lab.Hist.*, vol. 25, 1972.

VERSLUYSEN, M.: 'Midwives, Medical Men and "poor women labouring of child" '. In ROBERTS, H.: 1981.

VINCENT, D.: 'Love and Death and the Nineteenth Century Working Class'. *Social History*, vol. 5(2), 1980.

WADDINGTON, I.: 'The Role of the Hospital in the Development of Modern Medicine'. *Sociology*, vol. 7(2), 1973.

WADDINGTON, I.: 'The Struggle to Reform the Royal College of Physicians, 1761–71'. *Med.Hist.*, vol. 17(2), 1973.

WADDINGTON, I.: 'The Development of Medical Ethics'. *Med.Hist.*, vol. 19(1), 1975.

WADDINGTON, I.: 'General Practitioners and Consultants in Early Nineteenth Century England'. In WOODWARD, J. & RICHARDS, D. (eds): 1977.

WADDINGTON, I: 'Competition and Monopoly in a Profession: The Campaign for Medical Registration in Britain'. *Amsterdams Sociologisch Tijdschrift*, vol. 6(2), 1979.

WAKLEY, C.: 'John Hunter and Experimental Surgery'. *Ann.RCS. Eng.*, vol. 16(2), 1955.

WEINER, J.: 'The Working Class Press'. *Bull.Soc.Study Lab.Hist.*, vol. 25, 1972.

WELLS, L.A.: 'Aneurysm and Physiological Surgery'. *Bull.Hist.Med.*, vol. 44, 1970.

WELLS, R.: 'Counting Riots in Eighteenth Century England'. *Bull.Soc.Study Lab.Hist.*, vol. 37, 1978.

WILLIAMS, G.A.: 'The Infidel Working Class 1790–1830'. *Bull.Soc.Study of Lab.Hist.*, vol. 29, 1974.

WRIGHT, D.G. 'A Radical Borough'. *Northern History.*, vol. 4, 1969.

YEO, E.: 'Robert Owen and Radical Culture'. In POLLARD, S. & SALT, J., 1971.

Unpublished material

BARROW, L.: 'Democratic Epistemology: mid-19th century Plebeian Medicine'.

BOSTETTER, B.: *Draft chapters* of forthcoming biography of Thomas Wakley.

ECCLES, A.: 'Some Problems in the Calculation of Maternal Mortality'. *Draft*, 1980.

FINE, H.: 'Whose body was it anyway?'. *Term paper*: University College London, 1980.

FISSELL, M.E.: 'Bodysnatching in 18th Century Bristol'. *Draft*. University of Pennsylvania, 1986.

FOLKLIFE STUDIES INDEX. Edinburgh School of Scottish Studies.

MCNEIL, M.: 'From Leviathan to Frankenstein: changing images of the Body in the 18th century'. *Discussion paper*, c.1980.

MARSHALL, J.D.: 'Social Structure and Wealth in Pre-Industrial England'. *Draft*, c.1980.

RICHARDSON, R.: 'Death in the Metropolis'. *MA thesis*: University of Sussex, 1978.

RICHARDSON, R.: 'Edwardian Post-Mortem Custom'. *MA dissertation*: University of Sussex, 1978.

RICHARDSON, R.: 'The Language and Imagery of Class During the Peak of Anti-Poor Law Activity 1836–9'. *MA dissertation*: University of Sussex, 1978.

RICHARDSON, R.: 'Traditional Modes of Coping with Grief'. *Folklore Society Annual Conference Lecture*, 1982.

RICHARDSON, R.: 'Dr Knox and the Doctrine of Signatures'. *Folklore Society Guest Lecture*, 1985.

RICHARDSON, R.: 'Why was Death so Big in Victorian Britain'. Social History Society Annual Conference Lecture, 1987.

ROWE, D.R.: 'Folk Life Materials: a Proposal'. *Draft*, 1979.

SHARPE, J.A.: 'Domestic Homicide in Early Modern England'. University of Sussex *Lecture*, 1980.

YOUNG, R.M.: 'Animal Soul'. *Draft*, n.d. A version appeared in EDWARDS, P. (ed.): *Encyclopaedia of Philosophy*. N.Y., 1967.

INDEX

PLEASE NOTE: Apart from ANATOMY & ANATOMISTS, all medical and paramedical disciplines & professions are placed together under MEDICAL DISCIPLINES/PROFESSIONS.

'AB' [bodysnatcher]: 60, 115
Aberdeen, Grampian: 83, 91–2, 202;
  destruction of anatomy school 90–3, 372
Aberdeen Journal: 91
Aberdeen, Lord Provost of: 91
Aberdeenshire: 23, 83, 329
Aberlour, Grampian: 323
Abernethy, John: 30, 38. 42, 100,108, 115,
  119, 156, 205–6. 312, 329
Act for Regulating Schools of Anatomy *see*
  Anatomy Act
Acts for Burial in Woollen *see* Popular culture
  of death
Adams, Charles Phythian: 6
Addy, S.O.: 8
Afterlife *see* Eschatology; Dissection; Popular
  culture of death
Alcock, Benjamin: 254–5
Alcock, Rutherford [Inspector of Anatomy]:
  254
Alford, Violet: 138
Allan, Alexander: 91
Alternatives to requisition *see* Corpses for
  dissection; Consent; Poor
Althorp, Lord: 200
America *see* United States
'anatomical examination' *see* Semantics
'Anatomical Society': 163; members listed
  329–30; *see also* Anatomists
Anatomical specimens: collections/museums
  55, 57, 64, 172; procurement 64–5; sale/
  auctions 55, 317; no provision for in
  Anatomy Act 208; *see also* Anatomy
  schools; Bentham, J.; Corpse; Corpses for
  Dissection; Dissection; Dissected remains;
  Skeletons; next entries
Anatomists: 244; accessories to murder 133,
  368; alternatives to employment of
  bodysnatchers 104; clinical detachment
  31; collaboration: with bodysnatchers 55,
  57, 86–7, 104, 318, 325, with executioner
  76, 176, with bench 86, with students 102;
  destruction of evidence against 133, 136,
  338; entrepreneurs 55, 242–3; hostility

towards/revenge upon 3, 53, 76; illicit
  corpse supplies 106, 208–9; professional
  silence 94–8, 326; prosecution 107; ruses
  for hoodwinking parish authorities 244;
  schools demolished 90–3, 263, 372;
  suggestions on sources for corpses 163;
  unease towards dissection 185–6; views of
  Anatomy Act 242, 368; *see also*
  Bodysnatchers; Corpses for dissection;
  Crowd activity: anatomy riots; Dissection;
  Medical professions; named individuals;
  previous & following entries
Anatomy, comparative: 35
Anatomy, distinct from dissection: 180
Anatomy, corpses for *see* Corpses; Dissection
Anatomy, history: 30–51, 93–4
Anatomy, in medical education: costs of
  tuition 357; necessity not disputed 349;
  public lectures 151; stultifying influence
  335; *see also* Anatomy schools
Anatomy, morbid: 335
Anatomy, Royal patronage: 32–6
Anatomy, Select Committee on [1828]: 100–
  130 passim., 50, 54, 57–8, 60, 63, 65, 71,
  101, 103–4, 109, 145, 157, 179, 188, 191,
  198; Benthamite influence/bias 108–16,
  119, 121–9, 150, 166, 203, 205; demand for
  new committee 167; establishment after
  case law change [1828] 107, 113, 151;
  ignorant of Burke & Hare 101, 131, 337;
  London bias 114; members 109, 113, 117–
  8, 146, 149, 152, listed 333; witnesses 86,
  109, 114–21; Evidence 22, 106, 108, 116,
  114–21, 132; Report xv, 101, 106, 108, 116,
  119, 121–3, 130, 145, 150, 162, 166, 186,
  204, 245, written by Warburton 128–9, key
  recommendation/analysis 121–9, 130,
  eclipses alternatives 162, foregone
  conclusion 100–130 passim., 119–21, view
  of poor 128, 130; *see also* Anatomists;
  Bentham, J.; Bodysnatchers; Corpses for
  dissection; Semantics; Warburton, H.;
  previous & following entries
Anatomy Act [2 & 3 Gul.c.75 An Act for

Regulating Schools of Anatomy, 1832]: xiv–xvii, 3, 32, 41, 51, 61–2, 75, 77, 79, 93, 99, 102, 108, 147–8, 162, 188, 190, 192, 228, 232, 234–5, 240, 244, 262, 265, 266–8, 271, 274; alternatives *see* 160–192 passim, 184, suppressed 109, 119, 162, 176–7, 191, 204; *see also* Petitions; Corpses for dissection; amended [34 & 35 Vict.c16 An Act to Amend the Act for Regulating Schools of Anatomy 1871] 255; apothecaries denied right to dissect 213; basis of modern law xv; Benthamite 108–114; bequests unexpected 237; burial clause 208, 240, 243, 250; burking, institutionalised, fear of 220–2; class issues 146, 150, 155, 169, 177–9, 186, 193, 201, 205–6, 211, 219, 247; coercion/consent: legality questioned 185, 188, 206–7; designs on administration by RCS 119, 166, 242, 245, 250–2; direction of benefit 159, 211–5; dishonour to profession 177; identified with New Poor Law 192, 240, 244, 246, 261, 264–7, 271; ignorance of xiv–xv, 295, 328–9, 332, 376–7; fostered by Inspectorate 252–5, 280; medical education 100, 177, 210, 212, 356; murderers' clause 113–4, repealed 207; next-of-kin rule 110, 113, 124, 207, 234–5, 238; semantics/meaning 203–7; opposition to Act, parliamentary 198–203, 211–2, popular 202–3, 211–2, fear of 157–8, 190

Anatomy Act, implementation: 219–281 passim.; contraventions ignored 368, 372; corruption 239–60 passim.; debated again in Parliament [1842] 251–2; drafting inadequate 240, 243, 245–6, 250–1; government growth 210, 239–60 passim.; difficulties 239–60, 252; illicit corpse-deals continue 233–4, 237, 249, 253; maldistribution 235–8, 241–6, 249; scandals hushed up 237, 243–4, 252–5, 263–4; Somerville attempts to circumvent opposition 240–4; opposition to Act 154–5, 169, 219–223, 230–5, 239–40, 243–52, 241, 246–52, 254–5, 263, 366, 374, absorbed into Anti Poor Law Movement/Chartism 270–1; petitions against 175–9, 183, 187, 199, 202, 204, 221, 224, 292, 343, 347, 367, 373; shortcomings/loopholes 114, 206–8, 211–5, 234, 244–5, 249, 368, 372; workhouses, terror of dissection in 128, 177–9, 221–2; *see also* Anatomists; Bodysnatchers; Corpses for dissection; Crowd activity: anatomy riots; previous & following entries

Anatomy Act & New Poor Law: 192, 240, 244, 246, 261, 264–7, 271

Anatomy Act & Reform Bill: 100, 104, 188, 194

Anatomy Bills: 179, 192, 198, 222; Parliamentary progress, chronology 113, 291–2, style 'taisez-vous' 198–201; 1st Bill 146, 157, 161, 166–7, 169, 221, drafted by Bentham 112–3, Commons Passage 109, 146, fails in Lords 157–8, 166, 181, 194; 2nd Bill 154, 156, 165–6, 183, 188, 194, 198–202, 215, 223–4, 263, assisted by discovery of London burkers 165, 197, chronology 291–2, Commons Passage 202, Lords Passage 292, becomes law 215; political importance 191–2; supporters 100, 192, 198–203, 211–2, 230–2, criticised 181; petitions in favour 154–7, 162, 346; riots against 87, 90–3, 104, 202, 223–6, 228, 264, 325, 372; view of poor 114, 128, 207; *see also* Anatomists; Corpses for dissection; Crowd Activity: anatomy riots; previous & following entries

Anatomy Inspectorate: xv, 230, 256, 258; established [1832] 332; predates Factory Inspectorate xv, 332; political importance 108, 191–2; not proposed by Bentham 114; administrative character 239, 240; communication problems 372; intervention in free market 210; limited powers 207; need to use patronage/influence 233, 240–1; paperwork 243; relations with Home Office/Ministry of Health 231, 252, 256; salaries agreed in advance of Act 200; scandals/outrages 239–60 passim.; secrecy 252–6, 359; staff 239–40, 252, 254, 256, 258–9, 367, 369; turns a blind eye to contraventions 368, 372; unprepared for bequests 236–7; *see also* Home Office; Somerville, James; previous & following entries

Anatomy museums: 29, 37, 39, 55, 57, 64, 172, 317

Anatomy riots *see* Crowd activity

Anatomy schools: 37, 287; advertising 55, 317; & bodysnatchers 58, 62, 52–72 passim.; & burkers 197; commercial basis 101; competition 39, 55, inimical to operation of Anatomy Act 237; daubed with graffiti 263; costs of tuition 357; demolition of schools 90–93, 263, 372; history 39; indecency towards corpses 96; hospital schools: 96, 287, advantages 104–6, benefit from Anatomy Act 241–2, 245–6, 248–9; private schools: 37, 39–40, 55, 57, 86, 96, 212, 242, 287, 334, 357; disadvantages 104–6, disadvantaged by Anatomy Act 241–2, 245–6, 248–9; professional silence 94–8, 326; profitability

248, 329; proposed closure 345; provincial 182 [see also geographical entries]; public prohibited from 244; riots 87, 90–3, 104, 202, 223–6, 228, 264, 325, 372; seasonal teaching 40, 57, 318; teaching methods: alternatives to human dissection 104, 165, anatomical preparations 104, influence 316, ratio of bodies to students 290, rote learning 40, 'Parisian method' 37, waste of post-mortem facilities 182; *see also* Anatomical specimens; Anatomists; Bodysnatchers; Corpses; Dissection; Physiology; geographical entries

Anatomy students: 40, 181–2, 236, 314; costs of tuition 357; discontent 102; going abroad 101–2; bodysnatching 54, 107; registration inadequate 242; *see also* previous entry

Aneurysm, treatment *see* Anatomical specimens, procurement; Medical professions: surgery

Angelo, Henry: 80

Animals *see* Anatomy, comparative; Physiology; Soul; Zoos

Anti-Poor Law Movement: 270–1, 275, 340, 357, 374

Antiquaries *see* Popular culture

Antisepsis: 310–11; *see also* Hospitals; Infection

Apothecaries *see* Medical professions

Aries, Philippe xiv

Armiger, T.J. 329

Army Medical Board 310

Ars Moriendi 10–11, 299; *see also* Popular literature

Art of Dying Well *see Ars Moriendi*

Artists & anatomy: 38, 58, 135

Artists, Incorporated Society of: 38

Arts, Royal Academy of: 38

Asiatic Cholera *see* Cholera; Crowd activity: cholera riots

Atheism 341, 346; and dissection 94, 168–71, 326; and disposal 72, 168–9, 171, 173, 236–7, 346, 362; and medical professions 194; upsurge during Reform era 168; *see also* 'General Farce'; Materiality of mind

Atkins, Charlotte 72

Australia, Van Dieman's Land 194

'Auto-Icon' *see* Bentham, J.

Autopsy *see* Post-mortem

Bacot, Mr [Inspector]: 367

Bailey, James B.: 62, 261

Baillie, Matthew: 329

Baines, Edward: 233, 262

Baker, Mr [Coroner]: 234

Ballads *see* Popular literature

Ballot: 208

Banners, election: 231–2

Barbers & Surgeons, Company of: 32, 34; *see also* Medical professions; Edinburgh

Baring, Sir Thomas: 109

Bartrip, P.: 339

Bath, Avon: 172

Baume, Charlotte: 72, 171, 173, 236–7, 362

Baume, Peter [the 'French Scholar']: 168–9, 171, 236, 237, 362

Beaumont, G.: 261

Beccles, Suffolk: 64–5

Beck, Elizabeth & George: 84, 88

Bell, Charles: 61, 329

Bells, funeral: begging for 375

Bennett, W.H. [Inspector of Anatomy]: 256

Bentham, Jeremy: 197, 153, 159, 191, 199, 250; advice on law reform 204; Auto-Icon 159–61, 169, 333; correspondence with Peel 109–12, 132; drafts Anatomy Bill 112–14; dissection 108, 129, 159–61, 169, 171–2, 183; influence 109–114; & medical reform 111; oration 161; Panopticon 149, 269, 341; semantics 204; Parliamentary tactics 199; *see also* next entry

Benthamites/Benthamite influence: 108, 147, 162, 191–2, 203, 211, 215, 231, 249–50, 266, 271, 354; hypocrisy attacked 161; & free trade 149, 210, 356; government growth xv, 210, 243, 332; view of poverty 149; parliamentary tactics 198–202; *see also* Anatomy, Select Committee; Macaulay; Warburton; previous entry

Bequests for dissection *see* Corpses for dissection

Bettelheim, Bruno: 373

Birmingham, W. Midlands: 83; distressed button makers 171

Birkbeck, George: 151–3

Birkett, Mr: [Inspector of Anatomy] 253

Birth control: 373

Birtwhistle, John: 239

Bishop & Williams: 72, 143, 165, 193–7, 222; discovery & 2nd Bill 165; executed 197; experienced bodysnatchers 196; *see also* Burking; Ferrier, C.

Black Book see Wade, J.: Civil List

Black Death: 228

Blackburn, Lancs: petition against Anatomy Act 182, 186, 188, 199, 204, 211, 348

Blackwood's Edinburgh Magazine: 286

Bladder stone *see* Medical disciplines: Surgery, lithotomy

Blizard, W.: 329

Body, human *see* Corpse; Dissected remains

Bodysnatchers: anatomists as bodysnatchers 54, 57, 106; professional bodysnatchers

102–3; students as bodysnatchers 54, 107; antipathy towards 3, 85, 87–90, 174, 194, 324; dissection & fear of 69, 341; earnings/ fees 57, 64, 102; entrepreneurs 55, 317, 329; evidence to Select Committee 58, 60, 115; historical importance xiii, xv, 66, 351; Jewish 62; life histories/social profile 58–72, 116; official connivance of 106, 119; prosecution 59, 86, 106; relations with anatomists 57–72, 86–7, 104, 324, with gravediggers & sextons 62, 80, 89, with other bodysnatchers 58, 62, with undertakers 80; rendered redundant by Anatomy Act 237; reputed criminality 68–71; risks 61–2, 68, 102; suspected of murder 195; *see also* Anatomy schools; Corpses; Hood, Thomas; Law; Punishment; next entry

Bodysnatching 52–99 passim., 554–72; from graveyards 57, 58, 60; before inquest 65; before burial 65; all social classes vulnerable 63–4, 80–1, 98–9, 247; assumed association with crime 116; assumed development to murder 165, 195, 209; cover for other crimes 116; discovery rare 87; fear of lynch law 86; geographical distribution 83; history 57, 272–5; law 58–9, 85–6, 106–7, 331; not a crime 68; not outlawed by Anatomy Act 207; official indulgence 57; opposition/hostility 27, 75, 85–6, 160–1, 323, 329; parallels with poaching 58–9; persists after Anatomy Act 237, 245, 263, 323; prevention 27, 75–99 passim.; profitability 67–9; punishment of 59, 70, 86; spoof broadsheet 56; techniques/tools & equipment 59, 61–3, 224, 351; violence against 84–5, 87–90, 324; widespread antipathy towards 3, 27, 85, 87–90, 174, 194, 324; *see also* Burial; Corpses for dissection; Crowd activity; Grief; Law; Naples; Punishment; Geographical entries; previous entry

Bolton, Gtr Manchester: cholera riot/ disturbance 372
Bourne, Henry: 12, 22–3
Bowyer, Thomas: 154–5
Bradford, W. Yorks: Undercliffe cemetery 297
Brain & soul *see* Soul; Materiality of mind
Brand, J.: 6, 20, 22–3
Bray, James: 270, 279
Bridgman, Edward L.: 81–2, 273
Bridport, Dorset: 101, 108, 205, 250
Brightman, Eliza: 72
Bristol, Avon: 83; bodysnatching in 318; infirmary 172; Reform riots 192–3
Britain, death customs *see* Popular culture

British Forum: 168
British Legion: 69
Broadsheets & ballads *see* Popular literature
Broadstairs, Kent: 172
Brodie, Sir Benjamin: 106, 115, 118–19, 205–6, 246, 329
Brookes, Joshua: 57, 61, 70, 97, 163, 338
Brougham, Henry: 46, 161, 199, 249, 268, 354, 373
Brown, Lucy: 109
Bull, Parson: 336
Bunyan, John: *Pilgrim's Progress* 147
Burdell, Jane: 72
Burdett, Francis: 154
Burial: bodysnatching investigations 78, 84, 88, 224; burial ground 'management' 61; ownership by an anatomist 81; burial grounds, types: cemeteries 6, 79, 273, 322, cholera 76–7, 223–5, churchyards 195, hospital 71, Jewish 62, Non-conformist 107, urban, overcrowded/vulnerable 60–1, 79, 273, workhouse 233–7, 319; burial out of town 80; burial reform 61, 79; denial of burial to murderers 36–7; premature, fear of 227; in quicklime 227; grave security, social profile 63, 75–99 passim.; 273–5; graves, defence of 75–99 passim.; 81, 83–4, 89, 224, 273–5, 324, 329, orientation 89, pauper graves 60, 274, 319, 373, sextons 89, 318, vaults 67; *see also* Bodysnatching; Coffins; Dissected remains; Epitaphs; Eschatology; Funerals; Popular culture of death; geographical entries
Burial care, traditional *see* Popular culture of Death
Burial societies *see* Insurance
Burke and Hare: 72, 95, 97, 101, 131, 133–8, 140–7, 165, 193–7, 222; confessions 133, 135–7; murders 96, 131; discovery 133, 337; not bodysnatchers 132; popular revulsion against 338; victims 132, 337
Burke, Nelly: 133
Burke, William: ballad on 131; confessions 135–7; execution & dissection 133, 135, 142–3
Burking [murder for dissection] 72, 131–2, 131–58 passim., 193–7, 252, 338; apotheosis of Free Trade in corpses 195, 209; assumed development from bodysnatching 132, 165, 195, 209; confirmed, Edinburgh 132, 337; confirmed, London 193; copycat crimes 194, 197; detection 133, 165, 197; foreseen 132; government responsibility 131; iconography 262; institutionalised, fear of 220–2, 359; punishment 133, 143, 197; revulsion not confined to poor 339;

suspected 327, 336, in bequest case 236–7, in bodysnatching case 195; techniques 132, 196, fear of pitch plasters 194, 196; undetected cases 133; urban legends 194; *see also* Burke & Hare; Bishop & Williams; Ross, E.; previous & next entries

Burkophobia: 193–8, 202, 222–3, 247, 352; strategic value to Anatomy Act lobby 194, 252

Burn, James Dawson: 150

Burwell, James: 72

Butler [bodysnatcher]: 66, 69

Byron, Lord: 93

Caledonian Mercury: 140

Callaway, Mr: 46

Calthorpe, Lord: 159

Cambridge, Cambs: 60, 83, 89, 159, 263–4, 309

Cannadine, David: xiv, 370, 375

Cannibalism: fear of in workhouses 220–2, 359

Canterbury, Archbishop of: 59, 157, 274

Capital Punishment *see* Punishment

Carlile, Richard: 168, 171, 183, 219; dissection/funeral 171, 346, 362; *The Lion* 94, 168–9

Carlisle, Cumbria: 75–6

Carlisle, Sir Anthony: 47, 163–4

Carpue, J.: 61, 163

Carrington, Lord: 112

Carrol: 102

Cartwright, Major: 172

Cartoons *see* Iconography

Casts *see* Anatomical specimens; Ecorche

Catnach, James: 10–11

'CD' [bodysnatcher, probably Naples]: 115

Censuses: 359

Chadwick, Edwin: 6, 203, 273, 276–8, 354

Chadwick, Owen: 11, 251

Chaplin, Mr [of Rochester]: 234

Chapman, Israel [bodysnatcher]: 62

Chapman, Mary Ann 'Handsome Poll': 124, 234–5, 238, 278

Charles II: 36

Charlotte, Princess: 171, 313

Chartism: 29, 271, 279, 374

Cheap Repository Tracts: 13

Cheselden, William: 39–41, 44

Childbirth, mortality in: xiii, 34, 88, 236, 252, 313, 362

Children: child-stealing 350; corpses sold by the inch 57, 98; corpses decapitated 230

Chillingham, Northumberland: castle 94

Cholera: 168, 194, 222–30; description of disease 227; disbelief in 223, 226–7; dissection riots 223–9; ignorance of at all

levels 228; moral retribution 227; prevention, mistaken measures 361, town fumigations 228, treatments 227, 361; regulations 264; victims, burial 76–7, 223–5; *see also* Burial grounds; Crowd activity; next entry

Choleraphobia: 202, 359–60

Christianity: 297; & popular culture 3–29 passim., 6–7; *see also* Dissection; Eschatology; Funerals; Popular culture

Christian's Appeal against the Poor Law Amendment Act *see* Poor Law

Christison, Sir Robert: 59, 98, 141, 338

Civil List, qualification for dissection: in Finland 349; advocated in Britain [rich paupers argument] 100, 125, 184, 186–8, 190, 202, 349–50

'Claimed/Unclaimed' *see* Semantics

Clark, David: 7, 20

Cline, Henry: 38, 61, 329

'Clinical detachment': 30–51 passim., 75

Clodd, E.: 3

Cobbett, William: 58, 83, 100, 147, 177, 230; funeral 375; *Political Register* 100; petition against Anatomy Act 291–2; *Surplus Population* 261

Coble, Peter: 84

Cock, Edward: 365

Coercion *see* Consent

Coffins: burial without 20, 303; communal parish coffins 303; double, triple, quadruple 80, 273, 322; for dissected remains, description 258; lead 80, 275, 306; reinforced 81, 273; social gradient 63–80, 258, 273; patent coffins 81–2, 273; pauper coffins 258, 274–5; strength & status 80, 273; *see also* Burial; Funerals

Cole, Dr [of Charlotte St]: 236

Coleman, Edward: 330

Colville, Lady Elizabeth: 80

Colquhoun, Patrick: 148

Combination Acts, repeal [1824]: 154, 157, 201, 333

Commons Journal: 200

Concentration camps: 268–70

'Concentration System': 268–70

Company of Barbers & Surgeons *see* Barbers

Connolly, Patrick: 69

Consent, to dissection: 206, 241, 246, 258, 260; denied to workhouse inmates 207, 222; *see also* Corpses for dissection: bequests; Poor

Cooper, Sir Astley: 38, 42–3, 46–50, 57, 63–6, 69, 71, 86, 100, 106, 109, 113–4, 117–20, 123, 129, 153, 155–6, 163–4, 174, 246, 273, 312, 330–1; character 65–6; disgust of

bodysnatchers 117; fear of dissection 117;
clientele 118; social status 117–18;
influence on Select Committee
129–30
Cooper, Bransby [Sir A. Cooper's nephew]:
44–8, 62–8, 70–1, 97, 101, 104, 119, 129,
180
Cooper v. Wakley case: 45–50
Cooper, Bransby [Sir A. Cooper's brother]:
109; *see also* Anatomy, Select Committee
Cooper, J.F.: 84
Cooter, Roger: 152–3
Copycat crimes *see* Bodysnatching; Burking
Cork, Eire: Queen's College 254
Cornwall: 25
Coroners *see* Inquests
Corpse, human – cultural, clinical and
commercial attitudes:
1: cultural: 3–72 passim., 30–1, 57, 260,
society-wide 28; defence of 75–99 passim.,
89; curative value 53; fear of on board ship
173; importance of integral burial 276–8;
identity 29, 327–8; pollution 26, 95;
popular tolerance/solicitude 3–29 passim.;
sentience, belief in 15; spiritual status 7,
15–17; traditional care of 3–29 passim., 72;
lacking on burked bodies 133, suicides 195;
20th century changes in attitude 260;
2: clinical: clinical detachment from 30–51
passim., 31, 50–1, 75; scientific value
Chapter 2 passim.; utilitarian views of
159–61, 168–9;
3: commercial value of 51, 52–72 passim,
54–5, 57, 100, 272, 317, 329, 366; persists
after Act's passage 237; property status: in
law 58–9, in commerce 237, prices paid/
financial value 1, 64, 67, 75, 132, 135, 141,
165; premium for murder 165; not
prohibited by Anatomy Act 208;
decommodification urged 208–9; *see also*
Burial; Dissected remains; Dissection
rooms; Popular culture; previous &
following entries
Corpse, human – physical processes/
treatments: cannibalism 359;
decomposition 15; embalming 171;
flaying/ecorche 36–7, 164, 308, 264;
gallows corpses, revivification 54, 76, hope
of, denied 76; curative value 301–2; human
artefacts: soap, candles, spermacetti, chair
covering etc. 97, 160, 169; kept for long
periods 262, 278–9; maltreatment 78, 102–
3, 324, decapitation 228, 230, 264, 325,
364–5, destruction of identifying features
136, dismemberment 72, 354, not
outlawed by Anatomy Act 208, 244–5, 249,
immersion in boiling water 264, judicial

destruction 32, 36–7, profanation 95–6,
327, violence towards 96–7; packaging &
transportation 60, 72, 87, 96; preservation
methods 104, 365, pickling 340, Roberts'
process 246, tanning 340; protection/
defence 63, 75–99 passim.; *rigor mortis* 15,
19, 37, 196; corpse as a sanitary problem
15, 262, 278–9; *see also* Bentham, J.; Burial;
Dissected remains; previous & following
entries
Corpses for dissection: sources:
1: before Anatomy Act: licit: gallows
corpses 32, 35, 36–7, 39, 52–4, 301, 309,
316; inadequate supply 39, 52; illicit: xv;
authorised stealth 70, 106, 111, 118–19,
162–3; criminals 163, 248; family members
31; Jewish corpses 62; hospital corpses
106, 248; hulks corpses 263, preferred 248;
importation 102, 118–20, 163, 173, 329;
theft 65, 86, 102; workhouses bodies 78,
163, 320, 341; bogus claims 64, 102; *see also*
Bodysnatching
2: after Anatomy Act: 293; licit sources
263, 369–70; institutions housing poor
121–5, 271, 369; lunatic asylums 256, 369;
paupers' consent solicited/denied 241,
246; sale not prohibited 249; workhouse
corpses 222, 369–70 (mainly the elderly)
248; value of mortuaries 370; illicit:
bodysnatching persists 262; sales continue
222, 233–4, 237–8, 253, 255; numbers
needed 53–4, 179; overestimated 179–82,
335; numbers supplied by bodysnatching
54; gluts and slovenly dissection 164;
shortages before Anatomy Act 100–6;
optimistic forecasts of new yield from
Anatomy Act 125–6; numbers actually
supplied under Anatomy Act 245;
shortages after Act 230, 235–8, 243–6,
[1920s] 256, 260, 263, 276, 279; drop after
190B/1911 256; *see also* Anatomy
Inspectorate, consent; Dissected remains;
Poor; Popular culture; Punishment;
Somerville, J.; previous & following
entries
Corpses for dissection: suggestions for
alternative sources: 109, 119, 162–3, 189–
91, 204, 341, 355–6; medical views 163,
328;
1: bequests for dissection 259; associated
with unbelief 168–71; demand for, after
Anatomy Act 236–7; exemplary bequests
108, 158, 171–3, 183, 185, 236–7;
individual cases 167–73, 236–7, 344, 362;
Inspectorate unprepared for 237; long-
term influence of Anatomy Act 258–9;
mechanisms for promotion 189, 224;

Dublin mass pledge 167–8, 171; Royal College of Surgeons mortuary fund; not seen as a feasible alternative to coercion 168; numbers available 369–70; sharp rise in 20th century 258–60; *see also* Baume, C.; Baume, P.; Bentham, J.; Carlile, R.J. 2: other sources: anatomists/surgeons should constitute own supply 155, 162–4; 187; Members of Parliament 187; authorised stealth 162–3; Civil List 100, 125, 184, 186–8, 190, 202, 349–50; coercion & its opponents 160–92 passim., 189–91; conservation/wastage debate 179, 182, 248, 348; criminals 163, 175, 187, 356; duellists 187; honest poor, opposition to use of 175–9, 189–91; horse-stealers 202; purchase while alive 52, 174–5, 189–91; purchase from relatives 140–1, 174–5; royal corpses 100, 159, 171; suicides 163, 187; *see also* Bodysnatching; Burking; Corpse: physical processes

Corpses, illustrious and curious: interest in 57–9, 64, 248; *see also* Anatomical specimens; O'Brien

Corpses, royal: bequests suggested 100, 159, 171

Corruption *see* Medical professions

Cosmopolite: 172

Courtney, Dr: 172

Craigie, M. [Inspector of Anatomy]: 240, 242

Crail, Fife: 83–4

Craven [anatomist, Hull]: 263, 368

Cremation: 236, 259

Crime and criminals *see* Bodysnatching; Burking; Corpses for dissection; Poor; Prisons

Crimean War: 213

Crombie Mss: 23

Cromwell, Oliver: 159

Crosby, John: 258

Crouch, Ben [bodysnatcher]: 66–7, 69–71, 324

Crouch, Jem [bodysnatcher]: 69

Crowd activity: anatomy riots: prior to Anatomy Act 87, 90–3, 104, 202, 223–6, 325, 372; after Anatomy Act 226, 228, 263; bodysnatchers, violence against 84–5, 87–90, 324, reasons for 90; burial grounds, mass investigation 78, 84, 88, 224; cholera riots 223–6, 228; exacerbated by fears of the Anatomy Act 223–6, 228, 264, 372; effigy-burning 138–42, 232; elections/ politics 231; processions 231; banners 231; executions 133–4, 197; food riots 79; funeral demonstrations 229, 258; gallows riots 53, 75; graffiti 263; opposition to

street sale of anatomy pamphlet 169; reform riots 372; skimmingtons 138–42; Swing activities 193–4, 328; systematic damage to medical practitioners' premises 224; provenance 59, 224, 229, 327; responses: press coverage 328, 340; 'respectable' outrage 226; by authorities 91–2, 193, 328; crowd participants 88–91, 226, 229, 231, 339; notions of justice 85–6; damage 226; demolition of anatomy schools 263; *see also* Burke, execution

Cullen: 98

Curl, James Stevens: 3

'Daft Jamie' *see* Wilson, James

Daily Mail: 257

Darwin, Charles: 41, 89

Davis, Mrs: 102

Dawson, George: 109; *see also* Anatomy, Select Committee

Dead Houses *see* Bodysnatching, prevention

Death, definition of: 15, 302, 227; certification/registration 189, 363

Death, cultural history: xiv–xvii, 3–29 passim., 232; cultural gap 262, 267, 278; Victorian celebration of xiv, 4, 262, 272–5; 20th century 260; *see also* Funerals; Iconography; Insurance; Popular culture; Undertaking

Death duties, plan to waive for bequests: 190

Death grant: 260

Death insurance *see* Insurance

Death omens *see* Popular culture

Death on the parish *see* Pauper funerals

Decomposition *see* Corpse

Demonstrations *see* Crowd Activity

Dermott, G.W.: 93–4, 183, 189–91, 236, 249

Detrosier: 362

Dickens, Charles: 148, 150; *Oliver Twist*, politically contentious 147; *Martin Chuzzlewit* 193; *Pickwick* 147

Dibden, Charles: 82

Digby, Ann: 268

Disposal *see* Burial; Cremation; Funerals; Punishment; next entry

Dissected remains: disposal; after Anatomy Act 243; mock funerals 250; undignified 257–8, 364; cause of riot 91–2; animal food 33, 97, 328; burial 327; as detritus 97, 248; soap and candles 97, 160, 169; spermaceti 97, 160, 169; fear of, in workhouse food 221–2; manure 328; modern parallels 97; in quicklime 169, 344, 366; *see also* next entries

Dissection:
1: attitudes towards: a 'Mark of Infamy' 37; associated with punishment, promoted

by law 143, 322; breach of taboo 28–9; clinical detachment 30–1; denial of burial 36; fate worse than death 32; fear emotional, not rational 156, 343; gross indignity 144; honour/dishonour 144; natural theology/revealing deity 94; trade rather than science 182;
2: popular repugnance: spanned class barriers 27, 52–3, 75–77, 150–2, 183, 194, 219–222, 247; believed 'prejudice' 151, 156, 160; natural 322; confined to 'vulgar' & 'ignorant' 151, 163; effect of education on prejudice 151–2; losing force in 20th century 260, 173;
3: medical considerations: alternatives inadequate 104; danger from sepsis 362; destruction of identity 29, 76, 327–8; direction of benefit 161; dissection/post mortem 110, 129, deliberate conflation 204; dissection rooms: 'dirty source of knowledge' 95, malpractice in 94–8, management 328, seasonality 40, 57, professional silence concerning 94–8, 326, slovenly dissections 164; eschatological implications 29, 76–7, 93–4, 171, 273–5, 326–7; exemplary dissections 171, 185; fear of premature dissection 227, justified 98; medical unease 94–98, 129, 145, 185–6; public dissection of criminals 33–4, 39, 143–4; lectures for non-medical audiences 152–3; premature dissection 98; private dissections 39; rationalist approach 183, 209; *see also* Anatomy Schools; Burking; Corpses; Dissected remains; Poor; Post-mortem; Punishment; previous entry

'Distress' *see* Semantics
Disturbances *see* Crowd activity
Doctors *see* Medical professions
Dobson, Jessie: 319
Docherty, Mary: 133, 136, 337
Doles: 9
Donegal, Eire: 133
Dorset: 267
Dorson, Richard M.: xiii
Drummond, Home: 333; *see also* Anatomy, Select Committee
Dublin, Eire: 83, 96, 119, 167–8, 194, 324, 329; Hospital Fields 106; Humane Society of St John 106; Trinity College 106
Dublin mass pledge: 171, 185, 189
Dumfries: 56
Dunbar, Lothian: 83
Duncombe, Thomas: 252

Easingwold, N. Yorks: parish coffin 303
East Anglia: 9, 19, 296; *see also* individual placenames

East Ardsley, W. Yorks: 195
East India Company: 97
Echo of Surgeons' Square see Paterson, D.
Ecorche figures [flayed corpses]: 37–8
Edinburgh: 31, 41, 46, 54, 68, 83, 85, 101–2, 133, 136–7, 142–3, 195; anatomy schools 131–2, 242; cholera riot/disturbance 223; districts: Bow Lane 102; College St 103; Cowgate 139–141; Grassmarket 141; Greyfriars' churchyard 81; High St 139; Jamaica St 102; Newington 138; Princes St 139; Surgeons' Square 132–3, 139; West Port 134, 139, 141; Knox skimmington 138–42, 146; Procurator Fiscal 135; Sherriff 135; *see also* Burke & Hare
Edinburgh Evening Courant: 135; *see also* Burke & Hare
Edinburgh College of Surgeons: 54, 103, 139
Edinburgh Guild of Surgeons and Barbers: 32
Eire *see* Ireland and individual placenames
Eldon, Earl of: 206
Elections: 230–3, 250
Eliot, George [Mary Ann Evans]: *Middlemarch* 13, 193
Embalming *see* Corpse
Epitaphs: 16, 54, 85
Eschatology: 4, 15–17, 21, 27, 75–7, 273–5, 300, 327; *see also* Christianity; Dissection; Popular culture of death
Essex Times: 258
Ethics, medical *see* Medical etiquette
Etiquette, medical *see* Medical etiquette
Euphemism *see* Semantics
Examiner: 77
Executions *see* Punishment
Exeter, Devon: 83
Exhumation *see* Bodysnatching
Experimental surgery *see* Medical disciplines: surgery: experimental; Vivisection

Fabian Women's Group: *Round About a Pound a Week* 280
Factory Inquiry [1833]: 108
Factory Inspectorate: 108, 322
Fairclough, Jane: 197
Farr, William: 270
Feist case: 372
Fenland: 9; *see also* East Anglia and individual placenames
Ferguson, Ronald: 333; *see also* Anatomy, Select Committee
Ferrier, Carlo ['the Italian Boy']: 196; teeth displayed 352; *see also* Bishop & Williams
Fife, Scotland: 84
Fife, Lord: 201

Figlio, Karl: 210
Finer, S.E.: 109
Finland, dissection of sinecurists: 349
Fistulae, anal *see* Medical disciplines: surgery
Fitzpatrick, Jeremiah: 251, 310
Flaying *see* Corpse; Ecorche
Flint, Alexander: 31
Food *see* Funerals
Folklore *see* Popular culture
Foster, John: 249, 367
Foucault, Michel: 141, 295
Frampton, H.J.: 61, 330
France: 35, 67, 102, 141, 194; Academie Royale de Chirurgerie 35; status of surgery 35; *see also* individual placenames
Frankenstein see Shelley, Mary
Fraser, Derek: 230
Freaks *see* Corpses, illustrious & curious
Free Lance: 279
Free trade: in medicine 30; in corpses 100; apotheosis in burking 131–2, 165; conflict with public safety xvii, 209–10, 356–7; government intervention 210; inimical to operation of Anatomy Act 237, 240–6; 'Inverse Care Law' 214–5
Free Trade Club: 356
'French Scholar' *see* Baume, Peter
Friendly & burial societies *see* Insurance
Funerals: funeral food & drink 8–9, 22–3; history 272–5; decent 17, 235, 277; impressive 29, 375; military 71, 258; mock funerals 105, 249–51; pauper funerals 27, 272–6, 280–1, 295, 357, 374–5, avoidance strategies 276–80, costs 357, demonstrations 229, 258, fear of death on the parish 275–80, 295, persists 280–1; public expenditure cut 274; shrouds, description 274; 'respectable' funerals 4, 272–5, 374–5; social gradient 80, 272–5; working class 262, 272–81; *see also* Atheism; Corpse; Dissected remains; Insurance; Popular culture; Undertaking

Galen: 32
Gallows *see* Corpses for dissection; Crowd activity; Punishment
'General Distribution' *see* Anatomy Inspectorate
General Election [1832]: 230
'General Farce'/General Fast: 168
General Practitioners *see* Medical professions
George III: 37, 171
Gibbetting *see* Punishment
Gidney, Mary: 85
Gillard case: 253–4, 264
Gilmerton, Lothian: 339

Gipsies: 54, 317; child stealing 350
Gittings, Clare: 25
Glasgow, Strathclyde: cholera disturbances 223; 'Glasgow Spinners' 267; Gorbals cholera disturbance 223; Royal Infirmary 316; University Museum 17, 83
Glennon, James: 86
Godwin, George: 268, 278, 376
Godwin, William: xiii, 150; *Essay on Sepulchres* xiii
Gomme, G.L.: 7
Gooch, Benjamin: *Practical Treatise on Wounds* 35, 49
Gooch, Robert: 166, 176; advocates Anatomy Act 185; ensures his own safe burial 185
Government growth *see* Anatomy Inspectorate; Factory Inspectorate; next entry
Government inspection: 322
Graham, Sir James: 109, 246, 252, 367; *see also* Anatomy, Select Committee
Grainger, Edward: 311, 330, 345
Grainger, Richard: 159, 311, 362
Granger, H.E. [of Hammersmith]: 257–8
Grave-clothes *see* Popular culture of death
Gravediggers: 61, 318, 320; *see also* Bodysnatchers
Grave-robbers *see* Bodysnatchers
Graves *see* Burial grounds
Great War: 256, 259, 280–1
Great Yarmouth, Norfolk: 83, 85–9
Green, Joseph Henry: 115, 330, 367
Green, Robert: 163, 344
Gregory, Rev [of Spitalfields]: 241
Grief: 23, 26, 77–9, 305, 322; customs 23–7; exacerbated by Anatomy Act 234–5, 238, 253, 280; by bodysnatching 77, 322; manifestation on mass scale 78, 84
Grose, Francis: 97
Grote: 161
Guyton, Jacob: 89
Guthrie, G.J.: 94–5, 128, 130, 144, 150, 163–4, 166–7, 175–6, 185; admits poor patients used for experimental surgery 164; *Letter to the Secretary of State* 145; *Remarks on the Anatomy Bill* 95; verdict on Select Committee 130, 167

Haldane, Mary and Peggy: 337
Halford, Sir Henry: 34, 132, 331, 338
Hamilton, Mr [London Hospital]: 364
Hamilton, Mr [of Paisley]: 226
Hamilton, Martha: 226
Handywomen *see* Popular culture
Hanging *see* Punishment
Hampshire: 83

Hardinge, Sir Henry: 172
Hardman, William: 87
Hardy, Thomas: 13; *Mayor of Casterbridge* 138
Hare: turns King's evidence 133; *see also* Burke & Hare
Hare, Mrs: 132
Harewood, Lord: 157
Harley, Martha: 80
Harnett, Bill: 66, 69, 71
Harnett, Jack: 66–7, 69
Harrison, Benjamin: 261
Hart, Julian Tudor: 214
Harvey, William: 31–2, 44, 52; *De Moto Cordis et Sanguinis* 31; dissects own relatives 31
Haviland, John: 330
Hawkins, Charles [Inspector of Anatomy]: 256
Hay, Douglas: 252
Hazlitt, William: 23
Head, Sir Francis: 149
Headington, R.C.: 330
Health care, inequalities in: 43–4, 212–15, 312, 315, 358
Health, Central Board of: 222, 225, 229
Health, Ministry of: 252, 256
Health of Towns Commission [1834–5]: 108
Heath, W. [cartoonist]: 44–5, 96
Hell, jaws of *see* Iconography
Henry VIII: 32, 36
Hereford & Worcester: 9, 372; *see also* individual placenames
Hereford, H. & W.: 87, 202
Hertford, Herts: 25
Hesbrook case: 368
Hibbert, Julian: 362
Highley [medical publisher]: 162
Hobhouse, J.C.: 109, 154; *see also* Anatomy, Select Committee
Hodgkin, Thomas: 313, 335
Hogarth, William: *Reward of Cruelty* 33, 97; *The Harlot's Progress* 26
Holiday, Mr: 234
Hollis, Bill: 64–6, 69
Holmes, Isabella: 319
Holmes, Oliver Wendell: 362
Home Office: 236; anatomy scandals hushed up 237, 243–4, 252–5, 263–4; limits damage to Act by sacking Somerville 250–1; personnel 240; persuading parishes 240–1; protection of trade in corpses 119; & Anatomy Inspectorate 231, 252, 256
Home, Everard: 330
Hood, Thomas: *Jack Hall* 174
Horsley, William: 100, 129, 177
Hospitals: appropriation of patients' bodies 104–6, 253–4; charitable foundations 43; and experiments on patients 44, 164, 193,

316; cholera hospital anatomy riots 228; hospital diseases 41, 44, 311; lying-in hospitals 253–4; military and naval hospitals, supply of corpses from 106; mortality 49; popular perceptions of 44; questionable motives 43; teaching 30, 309; workhouse infirmaries 214, 319, 358; *see also* Anatomy schools; Burial grounds; geographical entries; Medical professions
Houses of Correction *see* Punishment
Huddersfield, W. Yorks: 275
Hudson, Robert: 195
Hulks [prison ships]: corpses from 248, 263
Hull *see* Kingston-upon-Hull
Hullock, Baron: 107, 113
Human experimentation *see* Medical disciplines: surgery: experimental; Vivisection
Humane Society of St John [Dublin]: 106
Hume, David: 323, 344
Hume, Joseph: 109, 149, 153–4, 157, 200–1, 206, 211, 249, 343, 354; see also Anatomy, Select Committee
Hunt, Henry ['Orator Hunt']: 100, 187, 199–202, 211–14, 353; main parliamentary opponent of Anatomy Act 199–202; views borne out by events 214
Hunter, John: 37, 39, 41, 57–8, 64, 66; influence 37–9; museum 37, 64
Hunter, William: 30, 37, 39, 57, 66, 272; influence 39; museum 37

Iconography: anatomical 31; burking 262, back jacket; cartoons 192, 220, 372; death 10, 20, 31, 299; *Ars Moriendi* 10–11; dance of death 232; leveller 342; memento mori 28, 31, 307; personification of death 31, 231–2, 307, 342; hell 10–11; graffiti 263; last judgment 11; political imagery/banners 29, 231–2; rites of passage 10–11; *see also* Popular literature
Indian Mutiny: 258
Infection: 41, 44, 311, 362; danger from corpses 362; *see also* Hospitals; Medical disciplines
Infidelity *see* Atheism
Innerwick, Lothian: 83
Inquests: 64–5, 351; thefts of corpses before 64–5; and Anatomy Act 234–5, 279
Insurance: death insurance promoted by Anatomy Act 262, 275–7; Royal Commission on 277; notion of in burial customs 274; health insurance less important than death insurance 276
Inveresk, Lothian: 85, 87, 202, 372
'Inverse Care Law': 214–15, 358
Ipswich, Suffolk: Board of Guardians 256

Ireland: 22, 254, 255; Anatomy Act 255; Dublin mass corpse bequest 167–8; Irish wakes 22, 277–8; Lord Lieutenant 255; source of corpses for mainland Britain 120, 136, 173; violence against bodysnatchers 324; *see also* individual placenames
'Irish Giant' *see* O'Brien
'Italian Boy' *see* Ferrier, Carlo
Italy, Padua: 32

Jacobs, Joseph: 13
Jackson, W.A.: 232–3
James IV of Scotland: 32
Jenner: 38
Jews' cemeteries *see* Burial grounds; Corpses, sought after *see* Bodysnatching
Jones, Ernest: 9
Jones, Wharton: 338
Judd, G.P.: 117
Judicial dissection *see* Dissection

Kent: 83; West Kent Gang, apprehension of 89
Kern, Stephen: 1, 294
Keywords *see* Semantics
Kingston-upon-Hull, Humberside: 263, 368, 372
Kingston-upon-Thames, Surrey: Board of Guardians 257
Knox, Robert: 96–8, 132–43, 146; anatomy school 137; Edinburgh skimmington 138–42; punishment, symbolic 138, 141–3; suspicions against 95, 133, 135, 137, 327; *see also* Burke & Hare

'L' [bodysnatcher]: 69
Labour Party, on Boards of Guardians [1920s] 256–8
Lake District: 17
Laissez-faire *see* Free trade
Lambert, Mr [Romford, Essex]: 258, 313, 316
Lambert, James [*Lancet* reporter]: 46
Lancaster, Lancs: 107
The Lancet: 5, 30, 42, 45–7, 49–50, 52, 75, 77, 93, 109, 137, 144, 155–7, 178, 181, 185, 189, 208, 219, 221, 239, 249, 309; *see also* Lambert, James; Wakley, Thomas
Lancet Sanitary Commission: 214, 319, 358
Lane [anatomist]: 364
Language *see* Semantics
Lansdowne, Marquis of: 119
Laqueur, Tom: 374
'Last Look' *see* Popular culture: viewing the dead
Latta, Thomas: 361
Laurie, Sir Peter: 78

Law, on bodysnatching and dissection: 86, 106–7; *see also* Anatomists; Bodysnatching; Punishment
Law, SI: 3
Lawrence, William: 93–5, 168, 312; *see also* Materiality of mind
Laying out the dead *see* Popular culture
Leeds, W. Yorks: 195, 230, 232, 262, 266–7, 353; anatomists 230, 232–3; election banner [1832] 230–3, 353; workhouse, Anatomy Act furore 230
Leeds Intelligencer: 219, 231
Leeds Mercury: 233
Lennox, Lord William: 353
Lewes, Sussex: 44
Leycester, Ralph: 146; *see also* Anatomy, Select Committee
Life after death *see* Eschatology
Life cycle, iconography *see* Iconography
Ligatures *see* Medical disciplines: surgery
?Light, Tom [bodysnatcher]: 69
Lincolnshire: 22; *see also* individual placenames
Linebaugh, Peter: 30, 53
Liston, Robert: 41–2, 49, 315, 327; *Practical Surgery* 49
Lithotomy *see* Medical Disciplines: surgery
Littleton, Mr: 109, 333; *see also* Anatomy, Select Committee
Liverpool, Lord: 119
Liverpool, Merseyside: 83; Anatomy school 107
Lizars, A.J.: *System of Anatomical Plates*, 1825 102, 314
'London burkers' *see* Bishop & Williams
London College of Medicine: 172, 181, 244
London Mechanics' Institution: public lectures in anatomy 151
London Medical Gazette: 29, 75, 172–3, 185, 208, 232, 273
London Phrenological Society: 168
London University: 169; *see also* London, University College
London and Westminster, A View of: 55
London: 22, 29, 58, 67–8, 80, 125, 223; cholera disturbances 223; environs 79, 101, 181, 244; executions 30, 37, 53–4, 75; funeral wakes, 20th century 304; Metropolitan Police 194; Thames Police 119 – old districts/burial grounds: Aldgate High St 185; Battle Bridge xiii; Belgravia, Lower Grosvenor St 80; Bethnal Green workhouse 178; Bloomsbury, University College 160, 199, 236, 245, 248–9; Borough 159, 345; Camberwell 87; Charing Cross 62; City, Guildhall 78; Covent Garden 39, Albion Public House, Gt Russell St 235,

237; Cripplegate, burial ground 233, workhouse 78, 204, 237; Deptford 87–9, 202; East End 280; Fleet Prison 373; Fleet River xiii; Globe Fields 250; Golden Square 253; Gray's Inn Lane 278; Greenwich 87, 89, 202, 372; Hammersmith, Board of Guardians 257; Hatton Garden, police office 236; Harpur's Fields 319; Holborn 304, workhouse 249; Horsleydown 319; King's Cross xiii; Lambeth 84, 87, 179, 280, burial ground 57, 78, mechanics' petition 179, 187, 202; Leadenhall, butchers' petition 184, 187; London Dock 234; Newgate prison 52, 75; Notting Hill xvi, 280; Old Bailey 197; Peckham 87; River Thames, police 119; Romford, Board of Guardians 258; St Andrew, Holborn 79; St Ann, Blackfriars, workhouse inmates' petition 176, 178, 221; St Botolph, Aldgate 60; St Dunstan's, Stepney 318; St George, Hanover Sq 60; St Giles-in-the-Fields 55, 60, workhouse 247, 263; St James, Piccadilly 114, 124; St John's 62; St Martin-in-the-Fields 368; St Martin, Ludgate 327; St Mary, Newington 360; St Marylebone 80, 271, 369, non-cooperation with Anatomy Act 247; St Pancras xiii, 55, 62, 174, 247, 323; St Paul, Shadwell 221; St Saviour's 55; Shadwell, workhouse 221–2, 342; Shoreditch, corruption 243; Southwark 86 [see also Borough above]; Spa Fields 199; Spitalfields 178, paupers' anatomy register 241, weavers 66; Strand Union workhouse 214; Tyburn 30, 37, 53–4, 75; Westminster, elections 154, Parliament, fire 108; Whitechapel 178, corruption 243, non-cooperation with Anatomy Act 240; Woolwich 87, hulks 248, 263

London, hospitals/anatomy schools: 287; history 42, 61, 102, 104, 125, 196, 245; locations: Blenheim St 57; Charing Cross Hospital Medical School 368; Charlotte St 236; Cline 61; Dermott 93–4, 183, 189–91, 236, 249; Frampton 61; Grainger 159, 345; Gt Windmill St 37; Guy's 44, 46–50, 69–71, 105, 181, 242, 261; King's College 196, 236; Little Windmill St 253; London Hospital 105–6, 234, 243, 330–1, illicit appropriation of corpses 106; Middlesex Hospital Medical School 315, 320; Queen Adelaide's Lying-in Hospital 253; St Bartholomew's Hospital 62, 98, 105, 182, 233, 236, 242; St George's Hospital 106; St Thomas's Hospital/anatomy school 42, 47, 61, 69, 104–5, 115, 172, 208; Tatum &

Foster's anatomy school 366; United Hospitals (St Thomas's and Guy's) 42, 106; University College 160, 199, 236, 245, 248–9; Webb St, Southwark 159, 345; Westminster Hospital 47

London, Lord Mayor of: 184–5, 187
London, Sheriff of: 53–4
Long, Sir John: 254
Lonsdale, H. 3
Lord Advocate *see* Scotland
Lord Mayor *see* London
Louis XIV [France]: 35
Louis XV [France]: 35
Louis Philippe: 194
'Lover of Justice' [pseud.]: 182
Lying-in Hospitals *see* Hospitals
Lyke Wake Dirge *see* Popular culture of death
Lynch, Dr: 228
Lyster, St George: 172

Macartney, James: 96, 106, 167
Macaulay, Thomas Babington: 200, 203, 210, 231, 232, 249, 353; recognises danger to society of laissez-faire 210; unpopularity 231
Maccoby, S.: 154
MacDonagh, Oliver: xi, 310, 332
MacDougal, Ann: 337
McKelvie, Donald: 14
Mackenzie [anatomist]: 242
Macphail, Alexander [Inspector of Anatomy]: 256, 259; bequeaths his own body for dissection 258, 369
Malkin: 22
Mallusk, Co. Antrim: 323
Malmesbury, Lord: 157
Malthus, Thomas: 149, 267; influence 192, 274
Manchester, Gtr Manchester: 82, 231; Gaythorn Tavern 65; Infirmary 44; Piccadilly 228; Swan St cholera riot 228–9, 244, 372
Manchester Guardian: 228
Manchester Unity of Oddfellows 275
Manning, Mr [*Daily Mail*]: 257
'March of Intellect': 7, 29, 152
'Marcus' [pseud.]: 268; *Theory of Painless Extinction* 373
Margate, Kent: 69
Marshall, Chapman: 233
Marshall [Leeds]: 230–2
Materiality of Mind debate: 5, 93–4, 168, 326; *see also* Lawrence, W.
Maternal Mortality *see* Childbirth
May [associate of Bishop & Williams]: 196–7
Mayo: 94, 163
'Mechanics': 151, 179; *see also* London

Mechanics' Institution

Medical disciplines, anaesthesia: 41, 315

Medical disciplines, dentistry: 106, 320; teeth: removal from corpses 67, 106, 196, 320, 331; battlefield 66, 331; displayed in shop windows 352; financial value 67, 331

Medical disciplines, midwifery/obstetrics: xiii, 19, 34, 88, 236, 252, 313, 362

Medical disciplines, nursing: 357

Medical disciplines, physic: critique of overemphasis on dissection 180

Medical disciplines, surgery: 30–51 passim., 41; caesarian section, mortality 362; experiments, on poor patients 164, 193, popular fears of 223, premature dissection 98; incompetent surgery 40, 42–8; mortality 40, 49, 312–3; patients 42–7, 49; private practice 48; sepsis 41, 44; social relations 43–50; social status 34–5, 165–6; students 41, 48; surgical instruments 41; surgical operations 45–50, fistulae, anal 35, ligatures 40, lithotomy 40–1, 44–5, 180, a deux temps 48, 314; teaching 41, 45, 47, 48; wounds & dressings 41; *see also*: Anatomy; Childbirth; Corpses for dissection; Dissection; Medical headings

Medical education: harrowing experience 41; stultifying influence of anatomy 335; *see also* Anatomy

Medical Education, Select Committee on [1834]: 34, 42, 271, 334

Medical ethics *see* Medical etiquette

Medical etiquette: xvii, 43

Medical practitioners: damage to premises 90–93, 224, 263, 372; dissection of suggested 155, 162–4, 187; popular distrust 219; medical protest against Paisley anatomy riot 226; participation in elections 232–3; urge professional reform 40, 42, 118, 163–6, 181–2, 236

Medical professions, apothecaries: 242; denied right to dissect 213; widely used by 19th century poor 214

Medical professions, general practitioners: 333–4

Medical professions, physicians: [Royal] College 34, 213, 309, 313, 327; attitudes towards surgery and midwifery 34; social status 34; perception of over-emphasis on dissection 180

Medical professions, surgeons: bodysnatching 57; incompetence 41–3, 45–6; dissection of surgeon/anatomists suggested 155, 162–4, 187; professional silence 50, 280; social status/aspirations 66, 117–18; *see also* Anatomists; Poor Law; Liston; Wakley; next entry – Company/

Royal College 33, 35, 37, 39, 40, 50, 53–4, 58, 61, 64, 95, 97, 104, 113–14, 117, 128, 144–5, 166, 172, 175, 182, 213, 245, 250–2; Anatomy Act, designs on administration 113, 119, 166, 242, 245, 250–1, murderers' clause 114; intellectually stagnant 40, 181; corrupt 40, 118–19, 181–2, 242; examinations 38–40; Hunterian Museum 39; incompetence 42, 45; judicial role 32–5, 53; membership 333–4; mortuary fund scheme 189–91; nepotism 39, 42, 46, 48, 311; Open Letter to the Home Secretary 164–5; pressure for reform 40, 42, 118, 163–6, 181–2, 236; regulations 101, 180, 345; *see also* Barbers; Edinburgh; Dublin

Medical reform: 40, 42, 118, 163–6, 181–2, 236; Bentham 111; *see also* Liston; Wakley

Medical students *see* Anatomy students

Medicine, history: xiv–v; free trade and entrepreneurial medicine 30, 51; physic/surgery split 34–5; science/art viii, 110–1, 146, 203, 211, 315; science/trade 30, 182; social relations 43–50

Melbourne, Lord: 223, 237, 240

Memento mori *see* Iconography

Meritocracy *see* Medical reform

Methodist Revival: 11

Midwifery *see* Childbirth; Medical disciplines, midwifery/obstetrics

Mill, James: 332

Mill, John Stuart: 108, 113, 161, 250

Millard, Ann: 71, 105, 311–12, 324

Millard, William: 69

Mind *see* Materiality; Soul

Minto, Lord: 200

Moir, Mr: 91

Modern parallels: 97, 160, 169, 268–70

Moorhouse, H.D.: xvi

Monro [Edinburgh]: 132, 242

Morgan, William: 172–3

Morning Chronicle: 222

Morning Herald: 4, 221

Mortuaries: 64–5, 370

Mourning *see* Grief

Municipal Corporations, Commission on [1834–5]: 108

Murder, Act for Better Preventing the Horrid Crime of [1752]: 35

Murder for dissection *see* Burking

Murphy [bodysnatcher]: 67–9

Murphy, Thomas: 155–6

Murray, Alex: 91

Murray, J.: 172

Naples, Joshua: 61–2, 66, 69, 105, 318; *Diary* 61–2, 66–7, 71, 115

Napoleonic Wars: 173

National Health Service: xvi, 260, 358
National Political Union: 154–7, 266
National Union of the Working Classes: 154, 168
Natural theology: 94, 325
Nazi practices *see* Modern parallels
Nepotism *see* Medical professions: surgeons
New London Mechanics' Register: 151
New Poor Law *see* Poor Law
Newcastle-upon-Tyne, Tyne and Wear: 372; Surgeons' Hall 264
Newgate Prison *see* London
Newspaper Proprietors' Association: 257
Next-of-kin rule *see* Anatomy Act; Poor
Nicholls, Dr: 39
Nigg, Grampian: 323
Nightingale, Florence: 213, 310
Noddy, Lord Tom: 258
Non-Conformity: 17
Norfolk: 296; *see also* East Anglia and individual placenames
North Shields, Tyne & Wear: 177
Norwich, Norfolk: 77, 84
Nottingham, Notts: riots 192, 194
Nugent, Lord: 333; *see also* Anatomy, Select Committee
Nursing: 357

Oastler, Richard: 147, 233, 275, 354, 373
O'Brien ['Irish Giant']: 57–8, 272
O'Brien, Bronterre: 261
Obstetrics *see* Childbirth; Medical disciplines
O'Connor, Feargus: 212
O'Connor, Prof: 254
Oddfellows, Manchester Unity of: 275
Oldham, Gtr Manchester: Anti-Poor Law meeting 374
Omens of death *see* Popular culture
Opie, Iona and Peter: 5
Oral Traditions *see* Popular culture: transmission
Orientation *see* Burial; Popular culture
Ostler, Mrs: 337
Owen, Sir Richard: 66, 68, 70
Oxford, Oxon: 83, 227

Page [bodysnatcher]: 65
Paine, Tom: 93
Paisley, Strathclyde: 25, 226; anatomy riot 59, 223–7; Board of Health 224–5; cholera 224–6, 228; cholera burial ground 225, investigation, personnel 225; Fumigating Committee 228; Police Commissioners 223; poverty 223, 226; Reform Society, petition 183, 189, 224; Society for Protecting the Dead 224

Paisley Advertiser: 226
Paley, William: 325
Paris, France: St Louis Hospital 110; Treaty of [1815] 102
Parkes, Colin Murray: 78
Patents: coffins 81; coffin reinforcement devices 81
Paterson, David [*Echo of Surgeons' Square*]: 135–7
Paterson, Mary/Margaret: 96, 135–6, 327, 337
Patrick —: 172–3
Pauper funerals *see* Funerals
Paupers *see* Poor
Peacock, Florence: 24
Peebles, Borders: 56
Peel, Robert: 109, 113–4, 118–9, 127, 146, 149, 151–2, 162–4; correspondence with Bentham 110–12, 132; favours stealth 111, 162; own fear of dissection 151; ridicules benefits of working class education 151; *see also* Anatomy, Select Committee
Pegge, Christopher: 330
Peninsular War: 67
Pennant, Thomas: 6, 23, 60
Pepys, Samuel: 44
Peterloo: 199
Petitions *see* Anatomy Act
Phillipps, S.M. [Home Office]: 240, 246
Phrenology: 168
Physical freaks *see* Corpses
Place, Francis: 153–7, 162, 266
Poaching: 88; and bodysnatching 58–9; punishment 59, 86
Police/policing: 86–8, 91, 119, 138–9, 194, 228, 232–3, 236; Metropolitan Police 194; Thames Police 119
Pollard, Stephen: 44–50, 62
Poor: avoid workhouse after Act 276, 279; corpses kept in Victorian slums 278–9; definition of 'poor' xvi; poverty cycle 342; promotion of prudential habits 275–7; medical experimentation upon 164, 317; workhouse poor/paupers 369; mainly elderly 248, 268; reactions to prospect of dissection 121–5, 128, 176–9, 221–2, 247, 252, 281, 342, 358; 'claimed'/'unclaimed', definition *see* Semantics; next of kin 110, 113, 124, 207; registering wish to avoid dissection 207, 247, 252, 374; *see also* Civil List; Consent; Funerals: pauper funerals; Health care; next entries
Poor, attitudes towards: 130, 147–150, 179, 232, 262–3, 265–70 [20th century] 260, 268–70; bestiality 147–150, 179, 268–70; imputed criminality 147, 175–8, 183, 192
Poor Law: and Anatomy Act 148, 240, 244,

246, 261, 264–7, 271; 'concentration system' 268; cruelty 373; cutting public expenditure on pauper funerals 274; health provision 213, 315, 358, 373; new brutality towards poor 262–3; Old Poor Law 178; Poor Law (Amendment) Act, 1834 (New Poor Law) xv, 147, 149, 159, 170, 192, 200, 203, 263, 266–8, 269–71, 296, 350, 354; Christian's Appeal against 158, 170, 264–5; Poor Law Commissioners 244, 266, 268, 275; Report 1834 108; 'revolutionary' 340; – workhouses 219, 340, 358, 373; 'bastiles' 267–8, 270; deterrent 358; fear of death in xvi, 264–5, 279; inmates *see* Poor; masters/guardians executors under Anatomy Act 206; mortality 113, 125, 213–4, 270, 279; illicit appropriation of corpses after Act 233–4, 237–8; terror deliberately created 267–270; *see also* Anti-Poor Law Movement; Funerals: pauper funerals

Poor Law Medical Officers' Association: 214
Poor Man's Advocate: 229
'Poor Workhouse Boy', ballad: 222
Pope, Jonas: 367
Popular culture: folklore & customs 3–29 passim.; accuracy 5–6; animism 7; antiquaries/folklorists 3, 5–6, 12, 306; antiquity 5–6; continuity 5–6, 298, 300; decency 92; definition xvii; fatalism 7; folktales, anatomy 31, gallows rescues 76; meaning/lessness 19, 22; notions of justice 36, 85–90, 141; 'old' popular culture 29; provenance 59, 224, 229, 327, 352; rumour 98, 194, 197, 327, 352; robustness/survival 5–6; symbolism 13, 18–19; theology 7–11; transmission xvi–xvii, 10–11, 300; urban legend 194; *see also* Christianity; Crowd Activity; next entries
Popular culture of death: xiv, 3–29 passim., 261–281 passim.; *Ars Moriendi* 11; afterlife 4, 15–16, 26–8, 77; bells 375; consecrated ground 235; corpse, central role 7, 14–15; defence of traditional observances 227, 229, 235, 277; doles 9; incomprehension of 9, 24, 262, 267, 278; continuity 6, 298, 300; evil spirits 11; fear of death on the parish 274–80; food and drink 8–9, 22–3; ghostlore & incomplete remains 17; grave clothes 20–1, importance of 304; insurance, spiritual 274; laying out the dead 19, 20–21; Lyke Wake Dirge 300; memento mori 28, 306–7; mirrors and clocks 27, 306–7; omens 6, 13–14; orientation 27; provenance 98, 306–7, 326, 350, 352, 359; relationship with Christianity 6–10, 12–31; no distinct

belief-system 12; prayers for the dead 9; respect for the dead in all social classes 99; role of women/handywomen 17, 19, 300; rosemary 18, 21; secular funerary rituals 8–9, 12, 17–23, 195; significance of display 275; sin-eating 9; solicitude 17; touching the corpse 25; traditional care lacking in suicides 195; and burked victims 197, 338; viewing/'last look' 18, 23–4, 141; washing the corpse 18–19, 26; watching & waking 12, 22–3, 102–3, 141, 304; workhouse, death in, popular fear of xvi, 261–281 passim.; *see also* Crowd activity; Funerals; Grief; Poor; previous & next entries
Popular literature: broadsheets & ballads 10–11, 24, 25, 82, 134, 158, 169–170, 225, 246, 264–5, 335, 359; chapbooks 375; gallows literature 142; pamphlets 169, 246; unstamped press 172; vendors 169, 172
Popular medicine: 53, 302, 316
Population: birth control, hostility to 373; census, fear of 359; Cobbett *Surplus Population & the New Poor Law Bill* 261; fear of institutionalised burking 220–2, 359; Malthus 149, 192, 267, 274; Marcus *Theory of Painless Extinction* 268, 373
Portland Museum: 317
Post-Mortem/Autopsy: 110, 121, 129, 182, 335, 248
Postan, Mr: 233
Poverty *see* Poor; Poor Law
Poynter, F.N.L.: 47
Preservatives *see* Anatomical specimens; Corpse
Preston, Lancs: 80, 299, 211; *see also* Hunt, H.; '3730'
Prince, J.: 172
Prisons: corpses from 106; criminals suggested as alternative to dissection of poor 163, 175, 187, 202; prisoners, condemned: selling own corpses 52–3; *see also* Corpses for dissection: criminals; Hulks; individual placenames
Procurator Fiscal *see* Scotland
Prodigies *see* Corpses, illustrious
Prostitution: 234, 337
Protheroe, Mr: 333; *see also* Anatomy, Select Committee
Pry, Paul: *A Few Illustrations for Mr Warberton's Bill* 220, 222
Puerperal fever *see* Childbirth; Infection
Pugin, Augustus Welby: 149; *Contrasts* 5, 147, 268, titlepage
Punishment: 99, 328; dissection after execution: xv, 28–30, 32, 35–6, 59, 75, 133, 143, 177–9, 318; encourages burking 143; meaning 76; symbolic 138, 141–3;

transferred from murder to poverty xv, 113, 176–9, 183, 207, 235; unease concerning 144–5, 176–9 – executions, publis 142; exemplary disposal 235; gibbeting/hanging in chains 35–6; imprisonment: for anatomy rioters 91; for bodysnatching 86; for other crimes 175; for workhouse anatomy disturbance 221–2; transportation: for theft of grave clothes [bodysnatching] 70; for corpse-rescue 37; for other crimes 175; for poaching 59, 86; for gallows rescues 37; *see also* Bodysnatchers; Corpse

Quarterly Review: 166, 176, 185
Quin, Sophia: 264

Radical community: 247; divided on Anatomy question 152; *see also* 'General Farce'; March of intellect
Radnor, Lord: 273
Rationalism, and Anatomy question: 151–7; *see also* Atheism
Reformation: 6–7, 300
Reform Act ('Great Reform Bill') [1832]: 117, 188, 194, 202, 223, 230, 262, 265–7; chronology 291–2; demarcation of voteless/powerless 230–3, 262, 371; reform agitation/riots 165, 192; Reform Crisis 158, 221, 266; Anatomy Bill reintroduced during 188, 194; and anatomy riots 104; attitudes to poverty harden 262–3, 265–70; disillusion during aftermath 266–70
Renfrewshire *see* Paisley
Republican and Radical Reformer: 229
Requisition of corpses *see* Corpses; Consent; Poor
Resurrection *see* Dissection: eschatological implications; Epitaphs; Eschatology; Iconography
Resurrectionism *see* Bodysnatchers; Bodysnatching
Rice, Spring: 109, 118, 200; *see also* Anatomy, Select Committee
Richmond, Duke of: 147
Riddell, Lord: 257
Rigor Mortis *see* Corpse
Riots *see* Crowd activity
Rites of Passage *see* Iconography; Popular culture
Rivett, Mark: 72
Roberts, Samuel: 271
Roberts, William: 246–52, 255, 271, 365–8; effective 247; 'process' 246–7, 365; pamphlets 247; supporters 246–7, 365–6; and Somerville 246–7, 250, 251
Rochester, Kent: 234

Rogers, Joseph: 214
Rogers, Mr QC [Inner Temple]: 367
Romford, Essex *see* London
Romford Times: 258
Rose, Thomas: 124
Ross, Rliza: 352
Rough Music *see* Crowd activity
Rowlandson, Thomas: *Death in the Dissection Room*; *see also* endpapers
Rox, Rosanna: 264
Royal Academy of Arts: 37
Royal African Company: 97
Royal Colleges, *see* Medical professions
[Royal] Humane Society: 76
Russell, Lord John: 194, 252

Sadler, Michael: 73, 147, 202, 231–3
St Germans, Earl of: 255
Salisbury, Wilts: 171, 244
Sampson, George [Salisbury]: 244
Scales, Michael: 185
Scarlett, Sir James: 46–7
'Science': attitudes towards xvii, 110–11, 146, 203, 211, 315; divides radical community 152–7
Scotland: 9, 22–3, 32, 54, 81, 83, 278, 324; Lord Advocate 137, 146, 150; Royal patronage of anatomy 32; *see also* individuals and placenames
Scott, Sir Walter: 133, 137
Searchers: 236
Secular death rites *see* Atheism; Popular culture of death
Select Committees *see* Anatomy; Medical education
Semantics: 129, 204, 221, 257–8, 336; 'anatomical examination' 110, 128–9, 204, 355; 'burke', new verb 143, 223, 339; 'claimed'/'unclaimed' 121–9, 186–9, 228–9, 234–5, 264, 271; corpse: 'subject'/'thing' 72, 135, 338; 'distress'/'feelings' 121–9, 146–7, 159, 186–9, 224, 234, 358; 'respectable' 272, 275, 374
Sepsis *see* Infection
Seven Years' War: 37
Sextons *see* Bodysnatchers; Burial grounds
Seymour, cartoonist: 196
Shakespeare, William: epitaph, 54
Sharp, Cecil: 5
Sharp, George: 91
Sharpe [anatomist]: 39
Shaw, John: 163, 330
Sheffield, S. Yorks: 76, 252, 372–4; anatomy school 253; destruction of 263
Shelley, Mary [nee Wollstonecraft-Godwin]: xiii, xvii *Frankenstein* xiii, xvii
Shelley, Percy Bysshe: xiii

Shillibeer's omnibuses: 194

Shropshire: 375

Shrouds *see* Popular culture of death

Sibthorp, Colonel: 202

Simpson, Abigail: 337

Sims, Dr: 172

Sin-eating *see* Popular culture of death

Skeletons: 33, 347; Anatomy Act overlooks 208; articulation 159; importation 317; sale 317; *see also* Iconography

Skimmingtons *see* Crowd activity

Skinner & Co [auctioneers]: 317

Skinner, Mr [anatomist, Sheffield]: 253

Smallpox: 62, 67, 264; innoculation experiments 316; vaccination, fear of 296

Smith, John: 109, 112–4, 149, 249; *see also* Anatomy, Select Committee

Smith, Thomas Southwood: 160–2; on hypocrisy of Benthamites 161; oration over Bentham's body 159, 161; perceives political implications of Anatomy Act 161; *Use of the Dead to the Living* 110, 159, 161

'Smugglerius': 37

Sockett, H.: 221

Somerville, Alexander: 83

Somerville, James [Inspector of Anatomy]: 197, 209, 232–3, 237, 240, 246, 257, 261, 263; admission concerning 'unclaimed' 271; assailed on all sides 245–6, 249–50; attempts to wield influence 116, 241–2, 252, 363; blamed for corpse shortages 173; burial clause corruption, Globe Fields 250–1; character 251; corruption alleged 238, 247–51; evidence to Select Committee 119; duties 239, 243–4, 251; importance 115, 118–19, 250–1; *Letter to the Home Secretary* 127, 367; role in early corpse importation scheme 119; ruses suggested to anatomists 244; sacked 237, 250, 254, 367; self-promotion 241, 256; secrecy 241–2; *see also* Anatomy Inspectorate; Roberts; Wakley; Warburton

Soul: animal 35; human 8, 28, 93–4; conflated with mind 326; location 94; *see also* Eschatology; Popular culture; Materiality of mind

South, James Flint: *Memorials* 324

Spain: 67

Spalding, Lincs: 372

Specimens, medical *see* Anatomical specimens; Skeletons

Staithes, N. Yorks: 20

Stanhope, Lord: 372

Stanley, Edward: 163, 240–3, 330

Steiner, George: *Language & Silence* 280

Stephen, Mr [RCS 'mortuary fund']: 190

Stephens, Joseph Rayner: 373

Sterne, Laurence: 60

Stevens, Catrin: 22

Storch, R.D.: xvi

Street Literature *see* Popular literature

Suffolk: 19; *see also* East Anglia

Suicides: denied traditional burial care 195, 234; suggested dissection 163, 187

Sunderland, Tyne & Wear: cholera 194

'Superstition': 4, 7, 14, 21, 27, 152, 156, 169, 299–300

Surgeons *see* Medical professions

Surgery *see* Medical disciplines

Surrey: 83; *see also* individual placenames

Surrey Comet: 257

Sussex: 83; *see also* individual placenames

Swansea, W. Glam: anatomy disturbance in House of Industry 221, 358

Swift, Dean: 64, 268

'Swing' riots *see* Crowd activity

Talbot, H. [Cambridge]: 170, 264

Tatum [anatomist]: 249

Taylor, Robert: 94, 326

Taxes on Knowledge: 229

Teale, Mr [anatomist]: 232

Teeth *see* Medical disciplines: dentistry

Ten Hours Movement: 231

Tenterden, Kent: 178

Tenterden, Lord: 157

Thanatory reform: xiv, 295

Thucydides: 361

Thomas, H.L.: 330

Thompson, Edward: 149, 152, 192, 262

Thompson, Paulet [or Poulett]: 109, 333; *see also* Anatomy, Select Committee

'3730' [Preston newspaper]: 211, 270

Tillett, Joseph: 80

Times: 59, 78, 87, 102, 172, 236–7

'Tolpuddle Martyrs': 267

Tory-radical alliance: 147, 187, 200, 231, 233

Tours, Council of: 34

Tovey, Henry: 233, 237

Transportation *see* Punishment

Transportation and packaging of corpses *see* Corpses

Travers, Benjamin: 168, 208–9

Trollope, Fanny: *Jessie Phillips* 341

Trotter, G.: 172

True Sun: 234, 236

'Two Nations', inception: 267

Tyburn *see* London

'Unclaimed', One of the [Worcestershire workhouse inmate]: 178, 22, 235; *see also* Semantics

Undertakers and undertaking: 4, 21, 80, 217, 272–5; and bodysnatching 58, 62; and

burial insurance 276–7; suspicion of 62, 65
United Brothers' and Sisters' Burial Society: 277
United Hospitals *see* London, Guy's & St Thomas's Hospitals
United States of America: Massachusetts 344; Pennsylvania 6
Universal suffrage: 229
University College *see* London
Utilitarianism: 107, 149, 168; *see also* Baume, P.; Bentham, J.; Benthamites

Vaccination *see* Smallpox
Valentine, Rev: 105
Vaughan [bodysnatcher]: 64–5, 69, 84, 86, 89
Vesalius, Andreas: *De Humani Corporis Fabrica* 32
Victims *see* Bodysnatching; Burking; Grief; Vivisection
Victoria, Queen: 40, 142, 255, 281, 296
Victorian celebration of death *see* Death
Viewing the dead *see* Popular culture
Villiers, Hyde: 109, 146, 333; *see also* Anatomy, Select Committee
Vinci, Leonardo da: 32
Vivisection: experiments on human beings 164, 193, 316; incompetent surgery on poor patients 40, 42–8; popular fear of becoming guinea pigs 223, 296; premature dissection 98

Waddington, Ivan: 319, 333–4
Wade, John: *Black Book* 125
Wakefield, Edward Gibbon: 143–4, 179, 190–1
Waking and watching the dead *see* Popular culture
Wakley, Thomas: campaign for medical reform 42–4, 46–8, 101, 166, 175, 180–2, 197, 241, 309, 344–5; character 42; on dissection and eschatology 77; evidence to Select Committee on Anatomy 101, 119–20, 334; founds *Lancet* 42; and *Ballot* 208; on grave robbery 80, 98, 127; on high workhouse mortality 270, 279; idea for general corpse distribution 363; and murderers' clause 114, 144, 356; sons appoint Lancet Sanitary Commission 214; speaks against Anatomy Bill 155; suspicions of Knox 137, 327; urges corpse decommodification 175, 207–9, 212, 249; views borne out by events 212; wished to promote modern system of bequest 209; *see also* Cooper v. Wakley case; *Lancet*
Wales: 9; Welsh wakes 22–3; *see also* individual placenames

Walker, G.A.: 61
Warblington, Hants: 323
Warburton, Henry: author of Select Committee *Report* 127–8; Benthamite politics 108–9, 149, 191, 356; chairs Select Committee on Anatomy 101, 108, 113, 120, 127; chairs Select Committee on Medical education 271, 351; character 203, 248, 250; direction of benefit debate 211; fails to decommodify corpses 208–9; Free Trade Club member 356; implicated in corruption 250; limited popular sympathy 151–4; medical reform 118, 146–7, 165–6, 171, 175, 177, 186–7, 194, 197, 213, 223; murderers' clause 113–14, 178–9; Warburton's opponents 113–14, 183, 203, 208, 220–1, 246–7; out of Parliament 248–9; parliamentary tactics 104, 157–8, 167, 185, 198–201, 203–5, 251, 252, 353, misinformation 214–5; shareholder in anatomy school 248–9; & Somerville 250; supporters 168, 203, 255, self-image 203, 355; uninterested in alternatives to coercion 173, 191–2; unpopular 203, 223; Utilitarianism 149; *see also* Anatomy, Select Committee
Wardrop, James: 42
Warrington, Cheshire: bodysnatching case 107
Webb, Beatrice and Sidney: 108
Webster, John: 124
Welfare State: xvi, 280; *see also* National Health Service
Wellington, Duke of: 29, 118, 157, 273, 322, 331, 354
West Hampnett, Sussex: 147
West Kent Gang of bodysnatchers: 89
Westminster Medical Society: 144, 150
Westminster Review: 110, 160
Wetherell, Samuel: 149
William IV 'The Sailor King': 194
Williams [burker] *see* Bishop & Williams; Burking; Ferrier
Williams, Gwynn: 267
Williams, Raymond: xvii
Williamson, Mary: 44
Willis, T. & J.: 172
Wilson, Mr [overseer]: 234
Wilson, James: 330
Wilson, James ['Daft Jamie']: 136
Wilson, Sir Robert: 333; *see also* Anatomy, Select Committee
Woolstonecraft, Mary: xiii, xvii; *Maria* 316
Wood, A. [Inspector]: 367
Wood, Alderman: 333; *see also* Anatomy, Select Committee
Wood, John: 211

Worcester, H. & W.: 178, 221; Political Union petition 188. 343: workhouse inmate's letter 178, 221, 235
Wordsworth, Dorothy: 17
Workhouse inmates *see* Poor; *see also* Funerals: pauper; Hospitals; Poor Law; Semantics: 'unclaimed'
Workhouses *see* Poor Law; geographical entries
Wortley, Stuart: 333; *see also* Anatomy, Select Committee
Wounds *see* Medical disciplines: surgery
Wrottesley, Sir John: 333; *see also* Anatomy, Select Committee

Wynford, Lord: 355–6

Yarmouth, Norfolk: 83, 85–9
York, N. Yorks: 195, 295, 361
York Chronicle: 96
Yorkshire: 8; East Riding 15; *see also* individual placenames
Young, Arthur: 148
Young, R.M.: 35

Zoos and menageries: 97, 169, 328